Re-Thinking Autism

of related interest

Can the World Afford Autistic Spectrum Disorder?
Nonverbal Communication, Asperger Syndrome and the Interbrain
Digby Tantam
ISBN 978 1 84310 694 4
eISBN 978 1 84642 936 1

Re-Thinking Autism

Diagnosis, Identity and Equality

Edited by
Katherine Runswick-Cole,
Rebecca Mallett
and **Sami Timimi**

Jessica Kingsley *Publishers*
London and Philadelphia

First published in 2016
by Jessica Kingsley Publishers
73 Collier Street
London N1 9BE, UK
and
400 Market Street, Suite 400
Philadelphia, PA 19106, USA

www.jkp.com

Library of Congress Cataloging in Publication Data
Names: Runswick-Cole, Katherine, editor. | Mallett, Rebecca, editor. | Timimi, Sami, editor.
Title: Re-thinking autism / edited by Katherine Runswick-Cole, Rebecca Mallett, and Sami Timimi.
Description: London ; Philadelphia : Jessica Kingsley Publishers, 2016. | Includes bibliographical references and index.
Identifiers: LCCN 2016000932 | ISBN 9781849055819 (alk. paper)
Subjects: LCSH: Autism.
Classification: LCC RC553.A88 R483 2016 | DDC 616.85/882--dc23 LC record available at http://lccn.loc.gov/2016000932

British Library Cataloguing in Publication Data
A CIP catalogue record for this book is available from the British Library

ISBN 978 1 84905 581 9
eISBN 978 1 78450 027 6

MIX
Paper from responsible sources
FSC® C013604

CONTENTS

Introduction 7
Katherine Runswick-Cole, Rebecca Mallett and Sami Timimi

PART I WHAT IS AUTISM?

1. Understanding This *Thing* Called Autism. 19
Katherine Runswick-Cole

2. What Have We Learned from the Science of Autism?. 30
Sami Timimi and Brian McCabe

3. Does Everybody with an Autism Diagnosis Have the Same Underlying Condition?. 49
Richard Hassall

4. The Biopolitics of Autism in Brazil. 67
Francisco Ortega, Rafaela Zorzanelli and Clarice Rios

PART II DECONSTRUCTING AUTISM

5. Life Without Autism: A Cultural Logic of Violence 93
Anne McGuire

6. The Commodification of Autism: What's at Stake? 110
Rebecca Mallett and Katherine Runswick-Cole

7. How Rude? Autism as a Study in Ability 132
Kim Davies

8. Autism and the Human. 146
Dan Goodley

9. Autism Screening and Diagnostic Tools 159
Sami Timimi and Brian McCabe

PART III CHANGING PRACTICE

10. Schools without Labels. 185
Nick Hodge

11. Does a Diagnosis of ASD Help Us to Help a Person with Intellectual Disabilities? 204
Graham Collins

12. Critical Systemic Therapy: Autism Stories and Disabled People with Learning Difficulties 221
Mark Haydon-Laurelut

13. Critical Autism and Critical Neuroscience: Towards a Science of Research and Practice 239
Tom Billington

14. Early Diagnosis of Autism: Is Earlier Always Better? 252
Ginny Russell

15. Thinking Systems: 'Mind' as Relational Activity 269
Gail Simon

16. The Ethics and Consequences of Making Autism Spectrum Disorder Diagnoses. 288
Saqib Latif

17. Examining Language and Communication in Autism Spectrum Disorder – In Context 300
Tom Muskett

Conclusion: Future Directions 317
Katherine Runswick-Cole, Rebecca Mallett and Sami Timimi

The Contributors 320

Subject Index 325

Author Index 332

INTRODUCTION

Katherine Runswick-Cole, Rebecca Mallett and Sami Timimi

This book is the first edited collection that is firmly located within the previously non-existent field of critical autism studies. For us, critical autism studies are concerned with two distinct but interrelated questions:

1. Is the diagnosis of autism scientifically valid?
2. Is a diagnosis of autism useful in the lives of people so labelled, their families and allies?

In contemporary (global North) cultures, autism is usually understood as a biomedical disorder. A biomedical model of autism first emerged in the 1940s and is premised on the view that autism is a cognitive disorder/disability ('deficit model') (Baron-Cohen 2002, 2004; Frith 2003; Kanner 1943). More recently, a different model of understanding autism has emerged; this is the view that autism is a 'different' way of being ('difference model') as the result of 'differently wired brains' (Jaarsma and Wellin 2012; Kapp *et al.* 2012; Kras 2010). The deficit model advocates for research into the biological basis and treatment of 'the disorder', whereas a difference model suggests that people who identify with the label of autism are a minority group who organise around their biological citizenship (Hughes 2009) and, as such, should have equality of rights similar to those of other marginalised groups (such as by race, class and gender).

We see critical autism studies as a cross-disciplinary endeavour bringing together ideas from a variety of perspectives such as critical psychiatry, critical and community psychology, social sciences, disability studies, education, cultural studies, and 'experts by experience'. The different disciplinary locations of the authors within this book means different discourses are encountered. However, all the authors share a commitment to challenging non-critical approaches to autism that limit, and sometimes damage, people who attract and receive the label.

The broad aim of this book is to unsettle any of the current accepted understandings that view autism as a biologically based biomedical disorder or

brain difference. The authors in this text seek to examine the pseudo-scientific claims upon which autism as biological disorder and difference are premised as well as to explore how autism is produced, consumed and commodified, and for what purposes, in the twenty-first century, while being mindful of the impact of these debates in the lives of people labelled with autism. The book is radical in calling for a move away from diagnosing autism as the starting point for improving service provision for those who experience the type of difficulties that could lead to such a diagnosis.

The book has four specific aims:

1. To challenge the evidence base for biomedical models of autism.
2. To explore the impact of the diagnosis on the lived experience of people so labelled.
3. To offer a conceptual critique of the production, consumption and commodification of autism in the twenty-first century in a global context.
4. To explore ideas for service provision and practice that move beyond a focus on the diagnosis.

The book also seeks to develop critical autism studies as a distinct conceptual domain. Many of the authors are members of a network of critical autism studies academics based in the United Kingdom. The impetus for the book came from this network. However, the book has a global reach and includes authors from outside the UK including North America, South America and Australia.

The book is intended for people labelled with autism and their families and allies and those practitioners working with them in health, education and social care. It will also be of interest to undergraduate and postgraduate students, researchers and academics in psychology, psychiatry, disability studies, cultural studies, childhood studies, social work, health, social care and education. By engaging with critical autism approaches and understandings, we aim to inspire people to think about and work differently with people labelled with autism and to respond in enabling ways to perceived difference and diversity.

We know that many will find much of the content of this book deeply challenging of their views and understanding of autism. As Dan Goodley reminds us in Chapter 8, 'Any debate, analytical intervention or rhetorical interrogation of the many faces of autism has the potential to upset somebody.' We know that getting involved with the critical autism studies perspective is a complex and sensitive endeavour, but we hope that readers will engage with this text in the spirit in which it is written: one of openness, inquiry, and the desire to help improve people's lives. Despite the dangers inherent in challenging the existence of any orthodoxy, it is through our personal and professional relationships with

people labelled with autism that we have become convinced that now is the time to challenge conceptions of autism that can both limit and damage lives.

What most of the current so-called 'experts' in the field of 'autism' have been reluctant to acknowledge to both academics and the general public is that no matter what area of their research one chooses, whether it is genetics, neuroimaging, screening, interventions, outcomes and so on, the more studies are published the further away we seem to be from the goal of finding a biological marker or some other 'handle' on what autism 'is'. To account for an increasing list of disparate results, their answer has been to develop ever more complicated theories and attempts to appeal to the logic that we are not finding clear answers because it's 'complicated' and therefore we need more money to do more research. These recurrent failures of any visible progress in academic attempts at discovering what autism 'is' serve to obscure a simpler and more likely possibility – that the reason science is not uncovering what autism is, is because it doesn't exist at the biological level. If, as seems likely, this is the case, then autism can only be understood through examining 'it' as a socially/culturally produced phenomenon.

This book thus functions as a tiny antidote to the one-sided mainstream literature on autism, where autism is uncritically accepted as a biological fact, and where socially constructed elements are only examined through the lens of the assumed existence of such a biological fact. It is high time we got a robust critique of autism that does not shy away from challenging the central conviction of autism being a fact of 'nature', rather than a fact of 'human nature'. We are in desperate need of opening up spaces where carefully considered critiques such as those in this book can be heard and engaged with. We believe this book brings something new and of great importance for the autism literature. We have managed to bring together a variety of perspectives, who comment on various aspects of the international 'scene' in autism in what we believe is a unique text, the first of its kind, to specifically target the critical autism studies field in all its wonderful variety.

As Ramilow (2006, cited in Runswick-Cole 2014, p.8) has noted, neoliberal politics is consumed by a concern to maintain the boundaries between 'us' and 'them'. In the United Kingdom in contemporary times, this approach is exemplified by the current preoccupation with sorting the 'scroungers' from the 'strivers' – the feckless and work-shy from the responsible and hard-working. Only the 'worthy poor' (an ever-shrinking category) will benefit from the redistributive policies of the welfare state (Runswick-Cole 2014). In the United Kingdom, as in many other countries, diagnostic labels, like autism, do crucial boundary work: first, to maintain the categories of 'us' and 'them', the 'ab/normal' and the 'dis/ordered'; but also to maintain the distinction between the 'un/worthy' poor, the 'scrounger' and the 'striver'. A diagnosis can seem

to offer to smooth the path to access to services and support – although as the authors reveal in this text, this is often far from the case.

Our stated aim is to challenge the pseudo-scientific claims upon which autism as biological disorder and difference are premised as well as exploring how autism is produced, consumed and commodified, and for what purposes, in the twenty-first century. At the same time we are mindful of the impact of these debates in the lives of people labelled with autism and their families and other allies. In a time of austerity, we are acutely aware of the risk that our work could be misappropriated and taken up by those who might want to exclude people from the services and support that they need. However, our aim is that, by moving away from diagnosing autism, this might instead act as the starting point for improving service provision for those who experience the type of difficulties that could lead to such a diagnosis and, indeed, those who experience difficulties but do not meet the criteria for diagnosis.

Challenging any orthodoxy is a risky business, made even more so when one challenges an orthodoxy in which people are so heavily invested, emotionally, politically and financially. We would like to thank the contributors to this edited book, and our publishers, for taking that risk and hope that this book will be received in the spirit that it was written – one of openness and inquiry.

The book consists of eighteen chapters divided into three parts, as outlined below. The structure of the book is designed to give the text coherence from start to finish but it is also possible for readers to 'dip into' individual chapters, depending upon their particular interests.

PART I: WHAT IS AUTISM?

In this section, the authors map out the many and varied ways in which autism is understood in historical and contemporary cultural contexts. The chapters cover a range of issues from questioning the lack of conceptual clarity in describing what autism is, to considering the pros and cons of continuing to construct the diagnosis of autism as a coherent category in health and social care, education and day-to-day life.

In *Chapter 1*, Katherine Runswick-Cole tracks her relationship with what she describes as 'this thing called autism'. Katherine locates herself as both an academic writing from the field of disability studies and as the mother of a child labelled with autism. She offers a personal account in which she describes how her understanding of autism has changed over time. She concludes by describing autism as only one of a host of possible stories to tell about her child, but one that dominates in ways that she now believes are unhelpful and disabling.

In *Chapter 2*, Sami Timimi and Brian McCabe tackle the science of autism. They describe the contemporary crisis in diagnosis triggered by the publication

of the fifth edition of the *Diagnostic and Statistical Manual of Mental Disorders* (DSM-5) and note the exclusion of autism from debates about the utility and validity of psychiatric categories. They offer a brief history of the development of autism as a diagnosis, before critiquing the claims of genetic, brain imaging, diagnostic, treatment, and outcome studies focused on autism. They also describe the problem of heterogeneity that contributes to the lack of conceptual clarity about what autism is. Sami and Brian describe the shifting cultural contexts in which contemporary understandings of autism are situated before calling for a serious debate that engages patients, the public and professionals on the pros and cons of continuing to use the diagnosis of autism.

In *Chapter 3*, Richard Hassall takes up the question of heterogeneity by asking whether everybody with an autism diagnosis has the same condition. Richard argues that there are strong grounds for answering this question with a 'No!' Drawing on his clinical experience, Hassall reflects on how different people diagnosed with autism are from one another. He suggests that if the diagnosis of autism has little explanatory or predictive power then it has little use as a scientific concept. He draws attention to the stigmatising effects of the label and concludes by asking: When someone receives this diagnosis, what in actuality have they been diagnosed with?

In *Chapter 4*, Francisco Ortega, Rafaela Zorzanelli and Clarice Rios discuss the central role of identity politics. They report on an ongoing ethnographic, qualitative inquiry that focuses on public negotiations of the category of autism in Brazil. The chapter focuses on three arenas where autism is being debated: the first is in what they refer to as the 'autism wars' that followed the enactment of a 2012 law creating policies for 'protecting the rights of the person with an autistic spectrum disorder'; the second is the representations of autism in the print media in Brazil; and the third is in online social networks. The authors argue that what emerges from their studies in each site is that autism is socially constructed within public spheres and our beliefs about autism are no longer determined only, or even primarily, by the authority of medicine.

PART II: DECONSTRUCTING AUTISM

The contributors to this section of the book turn their attention to critiquing cultural representations of autism and the impact of these on labelled people. In doing so they contribute to deconstructing the category. This section includes accounts of the 'logic' of violence against people labelled with autism, a sustained critique of the cultural commodification of autism, and a discussion of the relationship between the category of 'autism' and the category of the 'human'. Finally, in this section, the focus shifts to the deconstruction of the diagnosis of autism through a critique of a number of contemporary screening and diagnostic tools.

In *Chapter 5*, Anne McGuire considers the 'normative violence' inflicted on people labelled with autism alongside the cultural production of autism advocacy. Anne details several accounts of violence against 'autistic' individuals in the global North, including the murders of 'autistic' children by their parents. She describes the complex cultural processes through which autism is conceptualised as a 'thing' that renders some lives more vulnerable to violence than others. Anne concludes that such understandings and orientations create the necessary conditions for normalising some of the violence experienced by 'autistic' people.

In *Chapter 6*, Rebecca Mallett and Katherine Runswick-Cole turn their attention to the cultural production of autism. Rebecca and Katherine reflect on how 'impairment labels' function in culturally specific ways. They explore the ways in which autism is 'constructed, produced and consumed through varied social, cultural, political and economic contingencies'. Rebecca and Katherine consider autism as a commodity in diverse markets, including film, theatre, book, education, therapies and interventions, in a search for information that will render difference 'normal'. They conclude by asking readers to be suspicious of the 'certainty' promised by the offer of impairment labels, to be 'conscious' of the implications of the commodification of impairment, and to show a commitment to respecting difference 'in its full glory'.

In *Chapter 7*, Kim Davies draws upon the work of Fiona Kumari Campbell to 'stalk ableism by stalking autism'. Davies describes the ways in which 'autistic people' are marginalised on the boundary of 'human being-ness' as they are positioned as lacking the very qualities of 'the human'. The chapter deconstructs the Theory of Mind account of autism before calling for the disruption of normative identity politics that requires the identification of 'ability' in some at the expense of 'disability' in others.

In *Chapter 8*, Dan Goodley also takes up the theme of autism and the human. Drawing on postcolonial theory, Dan explores the relationship between autism and the human and reflects on the complex issues of positionality and politics in the field of critical autism studies. By reflecting on autism as a 'social and cultural concern' and, thus, a 'public issue', Dan is able to explore what 'the category of autism' gives to and what it takes away from our 'shared humanness'.

In *Chapter 9*, Sami Timimi and Brian McCabe pick up on the role of the autism industry in the construction of the category of autism as they reflect on the industry's methodology for identifying 'cases'. They dissect a number of diagnostic screening tools and illustrate how little they have to offer in understanding the person to whom they are applied. Sami and Brian trace the broadening of the criteria for a diagnosis of autism since the 1950s with a host of revisions to the *Diagnostic and Statistical Manual of Mental Disorders* (DSM). They also cast a critical eye on the development of diagnostic practice, diagnostic tools and approaches to screening for autism and conclude that use of diagnostic

tools and screening for autism and ASD is not recommended and should not be undertaken.

PART III: CHANGING PRACTICE

In the first two sections of this book, the aim was to question the dominant biomedical model of autism, drawing on scientific and cultural critiques of the diagnosis. In this section, chapter authors also offer a critique of the biomedical model and begin to apply their different understandings to the world of practice, including diagnostic, therapeutic, and educational approaches to people labelled with autism.

In *Chapter 10,* Nick Hodge offers a critical analysis of the practices of diagnosis and labelling drawing on his experience as a practitioner in English schools. Reflecting on labelling practices as 'agents of disablism', Nick links his insights to his study of families whose children were being assessed for a diagnosis of autism. He considers how 'schools without labels' could work in practice and explores how teachers, parents/carers and/or disabled people might use (or reject) labels in ways that help diminish their disabling effects.

In *Chapter 11,* Graham Collins turns his attention to the question of how a diagnosis of autism impacts on the life of a person with an intellectual disability. Reflecting on his practice as a clinical psychologist in England, Graham argues that each of the so-called 'distinctive' features of autism may also be shown by people given the label of 'intellectual disability'. In the context of practice, Graham questions what the diagnosis of autism adds to attempts to understand a person. Furthermore, his analysis of 'special treatments' for people with autism reveals that such treatments might work equally well for people without the label of autism. Graham suggests that spending time assessing and diagnosing a person often delays support being put in place with an attending risk that people thus diagnosed end up at risk of receiving 'block treatments' rather than responses to them as individuals. He also discusses the dangers inherent in creating a two-tier system in intellectual disability services in which people diagnosed with autism access support and services from which others would benefit, but are excluded.

In *Chapter 12,* Mark Haydon-Laurelut discusses autism, learning difficulties and critical systemic therapy. Mark outlines a critical systemic therapeutic approach to working with people and explains how a critical systemic therapy lens suggests that each member of a system will tell a different story about a person or behaviour. Giving examples from his own practice, Mark urges therapists to engage with autism not as something pre-discursive but as a 'social reality' made in communication with others.

In *Chapter 13,* Tom Billington reflects on his work as an educational and child psychologist in England working in education and in the family courts.

Tom describes how he began to question the lexicon for exploring what we have been thinking of as autism and its place in the world as, through his work with children and young people, the current approach was revealed as incomplete and unsatisfactory. Tom seeks to challenge the authority of medicalised discourses in order to engage with young people's experiences both in practice and in academic research. Tom also draws on phenomenology to offer a critique of the expansion of contemporary neuroscience and its claims to inform notions of what it is to be human. Tom cautions against a neuroscientific turn and for practice that is not driven by diagnostic and technicist approaches but by the principles of inquisitive inquiry.

In *Chapter 14*, Ginny Russell questions contemporary calls for an investment in early diagnosis and intervention. In the autism literature, the assumption is made that early diagnosis and intervention is desirable and always better than later intervention or no intervention at all. Ginny challenges these claims: first, by questioning the effectiveness of the interventions on offer; second, by demonstrating that it is difficult to determine who may or may not benefit from any effects of intervention; and third, by describing the inadvertent (negative) effects that labelling very young children can have.

In *Chapter 15*, Gail Simon sets out to foreground dialogue over diagnosis. She argues for a shift of focus away from the 'mind' of a person diagnosed with Asperger Syndrome to a dialogue with the person and those around them. She argues that 'human beings are relational beings' and as such she calls for a focus on human systems, rather than individual minds. Such an approach, she argues, would allow practitioners to avoid diagnostic determinism, which limits the lives of labelled people. Using case material, she explores alternatives to seeing a person's special interest as a symptom of disorder, demonstrating how a relational approach creates new opportunities for meaning-making and relationship-building between people. Gail concludes that diagnosis is often a monological activity by one person about another, whereas dialogue can lead to improved communication with people and to better coordination with them.

In *Chapter 16*, Saqib Latif describes the ethics and consequences of making a diagnosis of ASD. Saqib describes the neoliberally driven changes in the nature of ASD definitions, including changes in thresholds for diagnosis, the fluidity of the boundaries of classification of psychiatric disorders, and the strengthening of a medical model of mental health through classification. Saqib discusses the ethics of labelling a person with a diagnosis that increases stigma, is associated with lack of hope and an expectation of poor outcomes, and which makes the person dependent on the expert, potentially denying them personal responsibility or agency in their lives. He calls instead for a 'values-based practice' that builds on the individual diversity and accepts that there is no 'right outcome', only a 'good process' for balanced decision-making in partnership with service users.

In *Chapter 17*, Tom Muskett draws on Conversation Analysis (CA) to examine language and communication of people labelled with autism in practice. Tom challenges psychiatric diagnostic frameworks that mark specific language and communication behaviours as signs of mental disorders. Drawing on CA to explore two interactions with diagnosed children, Tom argues that language and communication, often framed as signs of mental disorder, can be repositioned as contextually meaningful communication.

REFERENCES

Baron-Cohen, S. (2002) 'The extreme male brain theory of autism.' *Trends in Cognitive Science 6*, 6, 248–254.

Baron-Cohen, S. (2004) 'Theory of Mind.' In J. Neisworth and P. Wolfe (eds) *The Autism Encyclopaedia.* Baltimore: Brookes Brothers.

Frith, U. (2003) *Autism: Understanding the Enigma.* Oxford: Blackwell.

Hughes, B. (2009) 'Disability activism: social model stalwarts and biological citizens.' *Disability and Society 24*, 6, 677–688.

Jaarsma, P., and Wellin, S. (2012) 'Autism as a natural human variation: reflections on the claims of the Neurodiversity movement.' *Health Care Analysis 20*, 1, 20–30.

Kanner, L. (1943) 'Autistic disturbances of affective contact.' *Nervous Child 2*, 2, 217–230.

Kapp, S.K., Gillespie-Lynch, K., Sherman, L.E., and Hutman, T. (2012) 'Deficit, difference, or both? Autism and Neurodiversity.' *Developmental Psychology 49*, 1, 59–71.

Kras, J. (2010) 'The "Ransome notes" affair: when the Neurodiversity movement came of age.' *Disability Studies Quarterly 30.* Available at www.dsq-sds.org/article/view/1065/1254, accessed on 4 November 2015.

Runswick-Cole, K. (2014) '"Us" and "them"? The limits and possibilities of a politics of neurodiversity in neoliberal times.' *Disability and Society 29*, 7, 1117–1129.

PART I

WHAT IS AUTISM?

Chapter 1

UNDERSTANDING THIS *THING* CALLED AUTISM

Katherine Runswick-Cole

INTRODUCTION

It seems popular these days to 'go on a journey'. In the UK, television schedules are awash with reality shows where competitors take to the dance floor, or to the ice rink, or even to the jungle, to construct a 'journey narrative' in their efforts to win the show. Here, I want to sketch out a different kind of journey – with no prize to win, apart from, perhaps, a shift in understanding. I'm going to talk about my journey with autism. This is, I suppose, a theoretical journey, a journey that begins with assumptions of autism's pathology, tragedy, deficit and lack but then moves through a rejection of medicalised and tragic discourses of impairment, to a continuing love affair with the social model of disability (Goodley 2011) through a brief flirtation with the neurodiversity movement (Ortega 2009) and finally, and controversially perhaps, to my current view that autism is a contemporary cultural phenomenon so that labelling people with it is no longer helpful (Goodley and Runswick-Cole 2012; Mallett and Runswick-Cole 2012; Timimi, Gardner and McCabe 2010).

THEORETICAL JOURNEY

Theoretical journeys are sometimes seen as controversial in my academic disciplinary home (disability studies), particularly in a context of economic austerity where there is a strong contemporary urge by some within academia to get back to either the material 'basics' of disablism (Barnes 2003) or to recognise the 'devastating reality' of impairment (Shakespeare 2006). And yet, it is my personal and professional relationship with what I describe as this *thing* called 'autism' (Mallett and Runswick-Cole 2012) that drives the writing of this theoretical journey, not simply a love of theory for theory's sake, but a desire to harness theory for its disruptive and transformative potential in people's lives (Goodley and Runswick-Cole 2014). My relationship with autism is framed by

my position both as a mother of a child labelled with autism and as a university researcher in the field of critical disability studies in the UK.

ETHICS

I begin my journey, however, with a dilemma. As I describe below, my journey with autism pre-dates the birth of my son, but the fact that he has been labelled 'autistic' is certainly the reason that I'm writing about autism here. I have written elsewhere (Ryan and Runswick-Cole 2008) about the struggles some mothers of disabled children face as non-disabled mother-researchers, occupying a liminal space, neither disabled researchers nor 'proper' mothers. Mothers of disabled children find themselves in a troubling space; they have often been vilified by the disabled people's movement as oppressors of their disabled children while simultaneously being pathologised by the professions as 'grief stricken' or 'in denial' in 'coming to terms with' having a child who is marked as deviant or disordered (Ryan and Runswick-Cole 2008). As mother-researcher, I face a dilemma: how much should I reveal about either my status as a mother or about the (private) life of my child? I know that being the mother of a disabled child has influenced the way I carry out research, not least the way in which I make relationships with other parents of disabled children and, indeed, with disabled children and young people. Yet, I've been cautious in talking and, even more so, writing about my status as mother-researcher. This is partly for fear that my research won't be taken 'seriously' in (often male-dominated) academia or that, even in the context of qualitative research that pays attention to the 'positionality' of the researcher, my work will be dismissed as 'biased' and 'partisan'.

As a mother writing about a child labelled with autism, I follow in numerous others' footsteps. Well-known examples include Jacqui Jackson (2004) and Charlotte Moore (2004) who have both published popular memoirs documenting the lives of children labelled with autism. More recently there has been an explosion of 'mommy blogs' (Morrison 2011). Mommy bloggers document their domestic lives in detail, including information about their children, and share this online. In the United States, popular bloggers make money by placing products in their blogs and receiving payment from sponsors. In the United Kingdom, there are a number of 'mommy blogs' where parents of disabled children talk about their lives. Recently, the ethics of blogging about family life have also been the focus of some academic interest. Yet, Archer and Pettigrew's (2011) study, based in Australia, found that about 70 per cent of the 'mommy bloggers' thought there were 'no ethical issues' in blogging about family life (as long as they were not paid by sponsors to write the blog).

In contrast to the response of the Australian 'mommy bloggers', it seems to me that there are several ethical issues for mothers in talking about their children

in the public domain. First, there is the question of consent. Is it possible for a mother to gain consent from their own child given the power imbalances implicit in the relationship? How can mothers maintain their children's anonymity while at the same time claiming authorship of the blog, book or chapter? How can I protect my child's confidentiality, while at the same time talking about autism?

At first, I thought it might be possible to resolve this dilemma by arguing that my son, although labelled with autism, is not this *thing* called autism. Yet, it has proved impossible for me to talk about autism without reference, at times, to what people have said to or about my son or indeed what he has said himself. So I approach writing this chapter carefully and cautiously with the belief that the ethical risks to my son and to other people labelled with autism are greater if I stay silent. I acknowledge that others may not agree with this decision.

You may have noticed that in the discussion above I referred only to mothers of children labelled with autism. Fathers are often the absent presence in accounts of family life and, indeed, as the story-tellers, and so it is in my own account. This absence is not, perhaps, surprising given that it is the mother–child dyad that is the focus of attention in global North psychology and psychiatry. As Nadesan (2005) reveals in her account of the social construction of autism, the history of autism is inextricably entangled with a history of mothering. Nadesan's exploration of the conditions in which it became possible for autism to be produced is as much an exploration of the socio-cultural production of mothering as it is of autism. Even in the twenty-first century, the ghost of Bettelheim's (1972) 'refrigerator mothers' continues to haunt the lives of mothers of children labelled with autism.

THE JOURNEY BEGINS

Like most people in the UK in the late twentieth century, I imagine, I had a vague knowledge of what autism was before I became a mother, three weeks earlier than expected, on a cold winter day in the late nineties. I'd seen the film *Rain Man* (1988). Autism was tragic, frightening, to be avoided, someone else's world, someone else's problem. In the 1990s, I was an early years teacher in the south of England and a child came into the reception (entry) class at the school where I worked who was 'autistic'. This was the first time that this had happened at a school I had worked in. The child's parents were very keen for him to be included in mainstream school; the head teacher was too, the staff was less welcoming. As I was pregnant, a colleague suggested I should stay away from the child at playtime: 'He is volatile... He might kick you... He might hurt the baby.' I took her advice. Shortly afterwards, we had our baby son – perfect, ten tiny fingers, ten tiny toes...and soon to be labelled autistic.

In the first few months and years of his life, autism remained someone else's concern and someone else's problem – although the labels 'bottom shuffler', 'very late walker', then 'developmental delay' and 'dyspraxia' should have sounded the alarm that all was not 'as it should be'. But I had yet to be enculturated into the world of autism; I didn't know the 'signs'. I didn't know that I should have been looking for the 'red flags' of the disorder (McGuire 2011). I hadn't picked up on the subtle, and not so subtle, hints from professionals anxious about hitting me with the 'autism' word. So it fell to an educational psychologist to ask, when my son started school: 'Have you heard the word "autism" before?' Of course I had: I'd seen *Rain Man*, I'd seen (from a safe distance) the autistic child in the playground and I was in the middle of a psychology degree, I'd read the chapter on autism. How could autism be in any way relevant to my world?

It wasn't until a year later that the diagnosis was confirmed. A clinical psychologist visited me at home (while my husband was at work) to tell me that my son did, indeed, have 'Asperger Syndrome' (interestingly that diagnosis changed over time and he has since been labelled with autism). I remember asking, urgently, 'Will he live independently?' The clinical psychologist replied that four out of five children diagnosed at this age [five] would not. I don't remember any help being offered; I remember nothing more than a gloomy prognosis. I was sure it couldn't be right. Grief-stricken and in denial, as psychologists would have doubtless have described me (Lazarus and Folkman 1994), I wasn't yet prepared to give up my son to the diagnosis of autism.

BECOMING AN AUTISM EXPERT

But the word was there now, troubling me, and I was curious. So, like many other parents of children given a diagnosis of autism, I read and I read. Tony Attwood (2007), an expert in Asperger Syndrome, was, I discovered, essential reading. Claire Sainsbury (2009) and Luke Jackson (2002), two people who identify as autistic, gave the 'insider' perspective. Jacqui Jackson (2004) and Charlotte Moore (2004) gave the mother's point of view. Carol Stock Kranowitz (2005) taught me about sensory integration difficulties. And, slowly but surely, I learned about autism and its cultures.

Eventually, I was referred to a support group for parents of 'autistic children', which I was keen to attend. But I remember being asked by another mother, in the waiting room before the first meeting, 'How bad is he?' I hesitated, I didn't know how to answer the question, and so she clarified, 'Does he speak?' 'Is he toilet-trained?' 'Is he violent?' 'Are your other children autistic?'

Despite my initial reticence, through my reading and my interactions with other mothers, I was seduced by the autism culture. I began to speak the language of autism too and to recognise behaviours such as 'stimming' and 'meltdowns'

that I had previously thought (naively?) were arm-flapping and being cross. I learnt the stories of the culture, I knew about the triad of impairments (impaired social and emotional relationships, impaired language and communication skills, and restricted imagination), lack of Theory of Mind, weak central coherence and the details of the Sally–Anne test (Baron-Cohen, Leslie and Frith 1985; McGuire and Michalko 2009). I began to look for autistic pathology in family members to spot it in my husband and in myself. I learnt about the great figures in history and contemporary culture who were 'autistic' – Einstein, Bill Gates, Sherlock Holmes (Frith 2003). And yet, I could never quite absorb the autism canon completely; I didn't take the speech therapist's advice to make him 'look at me'.

AUTISM IS *NOT* THE PROBLEM

And then, through a friend, who also had a disabled daughter, I heard about the social model of disability and a love affair began! The social model sees disability as something imposed upon people with impairments; it is the result of social arrangements that oppress people with impairments (Oliver 1990). Social oppression theories of disability recognise disability not as an individual, medical problem but as the product of a disabling society that 'is geared to, built for and by, and controlled by non-disabled people' (Swain, French and Cameron 2003, p.2). The social model of disability has been hugely influential in the fight for equality for disabled people; it is a powerful 'heuristic' device or thinking tool (Oliver 1990) that has enabled disabled people and their allies to expose and challenge the discrimination they sadly continue to face. So I learned that what I had understood was wrong. Autism was not the problem; it was the systems, attitudes, and environments that disable people with autism that should be the focus of my concern. The social model gave me a tool, a hammer, with which to rain down blows against the disabling practices we as a family continue to be subjected to. A social model discourse underpins much of the current advocacy work I do for my son; I hold that hammer very tightly.

DIFFERENCE, NOT DISORDER?

A little while later, another mother of a disabled child suggested I visit a website and there I discovered the neurodiversity movement. The neurodiversity movement fights for the rights of 'autistics' arguing that autism is a naturally occurring brain difference, not a disorder (Runswick-Cole 2014). The Institute for the Study of Neurotypicals (ISNT) (non-autistic people) playfully reverses the pathology to construct 'neurotypical' people as having deficits and being in

lack *because of their neurotypicality*, as the offer of an 'Online Screening Test' for neurotypicality illustrates.[1]

This approach attracted me because it celebrates autistic difference. I could affirm my son's identity as autistic, rather than deny it or try to correct it. My flirtation with the neurodiversity movement was brief. Neurodiversity is seductive – it offers affirmation and a political identity that allows people to celebrate their sense of self (Runswick-Cole 2014). But it, and indeed the social model of disability, does little to trouble this *thing* called autism. Neurodiversity relies on the discourses of medical pathology. Neurodiverse advocacy is premised on a claim that people with autism have differently wired brains and that this difference, while not disordered, is real and biologically based (Runswick-Cole 2014). The stories of the medical world remain pervasive and powerful, they are the dominant meta-narratives in our contemporary culture, but they are just that – stories. Both social model theory and the neurodiversity movement fail to trouble the construction of autism as a coherent, biomedical category, a diagnosable condition, a reality, or brute fact. And that for me is where their limitations lie.

BUT AUTISM STOLE MY CHILD…

Autism as 'brute fact' is widely viewed as a 'bad thing'. McGuire (2011) has powerfully critiqued the war that groups like Autism Speaks in the United States have launched on autism. Mothers talk about wrestling their child back from autism's pervasive grip and of saving their child and making him (it usually is him) normal. Celebrity mothers (note mothers, not fathers), such as Jenny McCarthy in the United States, or Sally Bercow in the UK, lead the charge. It is the mothers' duty to free their sons from the autism that is holding them hostage – the biological deficit, the disorder that must be exposed, treated and vanquished.

So, given that I am arguing that the category of autism is of limited use to those diagnosed with it, you may be surprised to hear that, like other 'autism moms', I also believe autism stole my child. But my son has not been taken by the autism, the biological disorder; I do not believe that he is locked within an autistic world, out of reach and alone. Rather I argue the *thing* called autism that has stolen my child is a contemporary cultural construct, a story. This autism story tells of an all-encompassing label, a narrative lens that accounts for every aspect of my son's behaviour and personality, so much so that there is nothing left of him that cannot be accounted for without reference to the autism story. It is *this* autism that has stolen my child.

Autism is, we are told:

---

1 See http://isnt.autistics.org/ntscreening.html.

- the reason why our son liked *Thomas the Tank Engine*
- why he now likes *Star Wars*
- why he made up words as a young child
- why he likes to play chess.

When I rang up to view a post-sixteen education provision for him, I was asked:

- What is his diagnosis?
- Does he have challenging behaviour?

Not one question about what he likes/what he doesn't, what interests him, what I admire about him, nor even how he communicates – because autism has, I believe, stolen away the spaces for those questions to be asked.

Just for a moment, let's consider the following:

- He likes *Thomas the Tank Engine* because I do – Percy was always my favourite engine. I read those books and I passed them onto him.
- He likes *Star Wars* because his sister does – they watch it together.
- He just likes making up new words; young children do.
- He likes playing chess because his dad does too.

But even in my attempt to rescue my son from autism's grip, it may be that for some readers I simply confirm the ripples of autism in the family – my partner, daughter and I clearly have autistic traits too, as evidenced by our love of *Thomas the Tank Engine*, *Star Wars* and chess.

This *thing* called autism has such a grip on my child and my family that attempts to steal him back simply become evidence of my pathology.

COMMODIFYING AUTISM

This *thing* called autism is everywhere; it is embedded in contemporary culture – popular magazines, newspapers, books, films, academic journal articles, and conferences that both describe and produce autism (Mallett and Runswick-Cole 2012; see also Chapter 6). The processes of neoliberal marketisation have spread the story from global North to South (Hyun Uk 2012). The number of children labelled with autism across the globe continues to rise as debates rage about whether better diagnosis or an increase in prevalence is to blame. Autism has, excuse the inappropriateness of the phrase, gone 'viral'. For example, recently on Facebook, there was a trend for friends to fill in an online test for autism

(the Autism Quotient) and then post their scores on the newsfeed – diagnosing autism is the new app.

Clearly, there is money to be made in autism through therapies, treatments, specialist programmes, research into cause and amelioration, training courses for professionals and parents and people labelled with autism (see also Chapter 6). In speaking, and writing about autism I contribute to that industry and I have been criticised for doing so from a position of privilege as a white, middle-class, 'non-autistic' university-employed mother of a disabled child.

While I accept that I occupy a position of privilege, I also recognise that it is not possible to comment on the autism industry without contributing to it. Nor does a position of privilege mean that I can easily dismantle the autism industry; I cannot wish it away. Any attempts to do so face a tidal wave of resistance from powerful vested interests in the form of big business, large charities, people who have invested in a label that they believe brings resources, understanding and relief from stigma and blame. I understand and accept that many people, including people labelled with autism and family members, have a great sense of community and indeed relief as the result of diagnosis.

So let me try to achieve something a little smaller than total abolition of the category. Let me try to reframe autism as *one* of the stories people tell about my son and other people labelled with autism, not the only, or crucially, the most important story (Goodley and Runswick-Cole 2012).

WHAT DOES THIS MEAN FOR PEOPLE LABELLED WITH AUTISM?

I am arguing that the contemporary cultural autism story told about people with the label drowns out all the other stories that could be told about them. Crucially, despite the (often broken) promise of access to services the autism label seems to offer, having the label of autism is a risky business. There are numerous examples of 'therapeutic violence' (Timimi *et al.* 2010) against people labelled with autism – a school in the United States is still using electric shock-based behavioural therapy. Sometimes, having the label of autism or not is literally a matter of life or death: for example, through my work as a researcher within disability studies, I met a child whose paediatrician refused to take seriously the health implications of his very restricted diet because this was a result of his 'autism' and so nothing could be done. Recently, I met another family whose son was refused surgery that would have given him back his mobility because the child's autism meant he 'wouldn't understand what was going on'.

WHEN AUTISM IS NOT *THE* STORY

So, for me, autism is a story but it is not *the* story. Now it is the story I might have to trot out for medical assessments. I sometimes secretly play a game with professionals when they first meet our family – it is called 'See how far you can get without mentioning the "A" word.' And the answer is that you can get a long way. At a recent transition assessment with a Learning Disability nurse, I answered all her questions without reference to a diagnosis. We got to the end of the conversation and the nurse looked at her notes and said, 'Ah, yes, I've got the diagnosis here: autism.' After a detailed and lengthy discussion about my son, I wonder what that word added to the conversation.

Following my encounter with the Learning Disability nurse, I wonder, is it possible to imagine services differently? How about a service that labels people, but only with their names (see also Chapter 10); where practitioners ask questions of and about a person, not a disorder; and where they offer solutions based on the person's hopes, dreams and aspirations, rather than intervening to 'correct' perceived symptoms and deficits.

BUT WHAT DOES *MY SON* THINK?

I wrote at the beginning about the ethical complexities of speaking about the label that my son has been given while being mindful of protecting his right to privacy and confidentiality. I have often been asked when I've spoken publicly in this way about autism: 'This is all very well, what *you've* told us, but what are *your son's* feelings about the label?' I take this question seriously but I answer it cautiously in quoting my son directly:

> Henry[2] was out with his PA, Andrew, in Morrison's Café [a supermarket] having a cola and his favourite chocolate lumpy bumpy cake. Andrew's friend Graham arrived. Graham identifies with the label of Asperger Syndrome. After chatting for a while, Graham asked Andrew, 'Is Henry autistic?' Andrew (rightly) replied that he couldn't give that kind of information about Henry to a stranger, but suggested that Graham could ask Henry himself. So Graham asked Henry, 'Are you autistic?' Henry replied, 'What's that?' 'Well,' said Graham, 'Do you find it difficult to communicate with people?' Henry: 'No.' 'Do you find things difficult to understand?' Henry: 'No.' 'Do you find it difficult to imagine things?' Henry: 'No.'

2 All names have been changed.

CONCLUSION

I end this chapter with another story from my own experience:

> I came back from the bar at the Burns' night ceilidh [Scottish country dancing to celebrate the Scottish poet Rabbie Burns], glass in hand and in high spirits after 'Stripping the Willow' [a dance] with my husband and son. A woman approached me and, with no preamble, said, 'Is your son autistic?' I felt my face tighten and I stumbled a little as I said, 'Henry's just Henry.' She looked uncomfortable and countered, 'I'm not being offensive, it's just my son's child minder has a son who is autistic, and your son sounds just like him.' I muttered, half-heartedly, 'My son doesn't need a label to define him,' and wandered off, spirits dampened, back to my son and husband.

What can we make of this encounter? The woman in the story was keen to demonstrate that she knew the signs of autism; perhaps she had heard a monotone in Henry's voice? Perhaps she had detected some evidence of 'stimming' in his dancing? And yet, in some way, I felt that she was reaching out to me, telling me that she too knew this *thing* called autism; she imagined, perhaps, that we had a shared understanding? Perhaps she was offering me pity for being the mother of a 'disordered' child. I have since wondered how she expected me to reply, what was the answer she waiting for? 'Yes, he is autistic,' followed by more information about the signs of the disorder, perhaps, a description of how 'bad' he is, and how 'hard' my life is, but also how we, as a family, 'overcome'. It is also worth noting that she approached me and not Henry's father – it is me, never his father, who must account for our son's being. And, crucially, she did not approach my son, but perhaps this was because she didn't really *see* him. She saw symptoms and signs, deficit and disorder, where I saw a joyful young man, dancing with his parents and friends. My son is invisible to her, hidden by this *thing* called autism. By buying into the autism story, she is missing so much of him; perhaps *I* should pity *her*?

We are all caught up in this *thing* called autism – a powerful story but a story that can and must be challenged.

ACKNOWLEDGEMENTS

With thanks to my family for giving me permission to share the stories of our family life.

REFERENCES

Archer, C., and Pettigrew, S. (2011) 'A tale of power, passion and persuasion: bloggers, public relations and ethics.' *Asia Pacific Public Relations Journal 15*, 1, 37–54.

Attwood, T. (2007) *The Complete Guide to Asperger's Syndrome.* London: Jessica Kingsley Publishers.

Barnes, C. (2003) 'What a difference a decade makes: reflections on doing emancipatory disability research.' *Disability and Society 18*, 1, 3–17.

Baron-Cohen, S., Leslie, A.M., and Frith, U. (1985) 'Does the autistic child have "Theory of Mind"?' *Cognition 21*,1, 37–46.

Bettelheim, B. (1972) *The Empty Fortress: Infantile Autism and the Birth of the Self.* New York: Free Press.

Frith, U. (2003) *Autism: Understanding the Enigma.* Oxford: Blackwell.

Goodley, D. (2011) *Disability Studies: An Interdisciplinary Introduction.* London: Sage.

Goodley, D., and Runswick-Cole, K. (2012) 'Reading Rosie: the postmodern dis/abled child.' *Educational and Child Psychology 29*, 2, 53–66.

Goodley, D., and Runswick-Cole, K. (2014) 'Becoming dis/human: thinking about the human through disability.' *Discourse.* Published online on 26 June 2014 at http://dx.doi.org/10.1080/01596306.2014.930021.

Hyun Uk, K. (2012) 'Autism across cultures: rethinking autism.' *Disability and Society 27*, 4, 535–545.

Jackson, J. (2004) *Multicoloured Mayhem: Parenting the Many Shades of Adolescents and Children with Autism, Asperger Syndrome and AD/HD.* London: Jessica Kingsley Publishers.

Jackson, L. (2002) *Freaks, Geeks and Asperger Syndrome: A User Guide to Adolescence.* London: Jessica Kingsley Publishers.

Lazarus, R., and Folkman, S. (1994) *Stress, Appraisal and Coping.* New York: Springer.

Levinson, B. (dir.) (1988) *Rain Man.* United Artists.

Mallett, R., and Runswick-Cole, K. (2012) 'Commodifying Autism: The Cultural Contexts of "Disability" in the Academy.' In D. Goodley, B. Hughes and L.J. Davis (eds) *Disability and Social Theory.* Basingstoke: Palgrave MacMillan.

McGuire, A. (2011) 'Representing Autism: A Critical Examination of Autism Advocacy in the Neoliberal West.' Unpublished PhD thesis, University of Toronto.

McGuire, A., and Michalko, R. (2009) 'Minds between us: autism, mindblindness and the uncertainty of communication.' *Educational Philosophy and Theory 43*, 2, 162–177.

Moore, C. (2004) *George and Sam.* London: Penguin Books.

Morrison, A. (2011) '"Suffused by feeling and affect": the intimate public of personal mommy blogging.' *Biography 34*, 1, 37–55.

Nadesan, M.H. (2005) *Constructing Autism: Unravelling the 'Truth' and Constructing the Social.* Abingdon: Routledge.

Oliver, M. (1990) *The Politics of Disablement.* London: Macmillan.

Ortega, F. (2009) 'The cerebral subject and the challenge of neurodiversity.' *BioSocieties 4*, 425–445.

Runswick-Cole, K. (2014) '"Us" and "them"? The limits and possibilities of a politics of neurodiversity in neoliberal times.' *Disability and Society 29*, 7, 1117–1129.

Ryan, S., and Runswick-Cole, K. (2008) 'Repositioning mothers: mothers, disabled children and disability studies.' *Disability and Society 23*, 3, 199–210.

Sainsbury, C. (2009) *Martian in the Playground: Understanding the Schoolchild with Asperger's Syndrome.* London: Sage.

Shakespeare, T. (2006) *Disability Rights and Wrongs.* Abingdon: Routledge.

Stock Kranowitz, C. (2005) *The Out-of-Sync Child: Recognizing and Coping with Sensory Processing Disorder.* New York: Berkley.

Swain, J., French, S., and Cameron, C. (2003) *Controversial Issues in a Disabling Society.* Buckingham: OU Press.

Timimi, S., Gardner, N., and McCabe, B. (2010) *The Myth of Autism.* Basingstoke: Palgrave MacMillan.

CHAPTER 2

WHAT HAVE WE LEARNED FROM THE SCIENCE OF AUTISM?

Sami Timimi and Brian McCabe

INTRODUCTION

Autism is currently thought of as a lifelong neurodevelopmental disorder (a problem with the development of the nervous system). The percentage of people thought to have this neurodevelopmental problem has increased from about 4 in 10,000 in the 1960s to approaching 1 in 50 now, a 50-fold rise in just four decades. In this chapter we outline how this change in thinking about the nature of autism came about through largely ideological changes and then present the key findings from genetic, brain imaging, diagnostic, treatment and outcome studies. Highlighting the lack of evidence supporting such a radical change in conceptualisation and practice, we ask the reader to consider the political context that may have contributed to the rise in popularity of the diagnosis and to reflect on the social, personal and ethical consequences of making a diagnosis.

A CRISIS IN DIAGNOSIS

The status of diagnosis in psychiatry is in trouble. Marcia Angell, former editor of the *New England Journal of Medicine*, launched a blistering attack on the orientation and practice of modern psychiatry in a series of book reviews (Angell 2011a, 2011b). The development of the *Diagnostic and Statistical Manual* fifth edition (DSM-5; American Psychiatric Association 2013) has been severely criticised by the chair of the fourth edition taskforce (DSM-IV, American Psychiatric Association 1994) as being over-inclusive and lacking a proper scientific basis, citing 'autistic disorder' as one of three 'false epidemics' created by DSM-IV (Frances 2010); arguing that DSM-IV criteria caused an 'epidemic' by massive over-diagnosis of autism. For many years there has been a campaign to abolish use of the diagnosis of schizophrenia (Hilpern 2007). The status and relevance of diagnosis to modern mental health care is thus being actively debated (Timimi 2013). If schizophrenia is the 'sacred cow' of diagnosis for adult psychiatry, then

autism is child psychiatry's equivalent – one that, until recently, was assumed to be unquestionably valid.

With regard to Autistic Spectrum Disorder (ASD), UK guidelines (from the National Institute for Health and Care Excellence – NICE) encourage earlier recognition, which is likely to lead to more people with this diagnosis (Baird, Douglas and Murphy 2011), whilst new DSM-5 criteria propose to simplify the diagnostic construct and eliminate some subcategories that are under the autistic spectrum rubric such as 'Asperger's' (Szatmari 2011), leading to a lively debate about the validity and utility of such changes (Volkmar and Happé 2012). However, neither DSM-5 nor NICE guidelines consider the possibility that, like schizophrenia and other formal psychiatric categories, the diagnosis of autism and its spectrum is neither scientifically meaningful nor clinically useful. If the construct of autism does not correspond with naturally occurring boundaries in some meaningful manner (e.g. biologically or cognitively), then it is unlikely to be useful for building scientific knowledge or for constructing rational clinical interventions. We argue that we have been researching autism for long enough and with little enough return for us to conclude that autism may not be a useful construct and future debates should not be limited to arguments about where its boundaries lie.

A BRIEF HISTORY

In 1911, psychiatrist Eugene Bleuler first used the term 'autistic' to denote the state of mind of psychotic individuals who were socially withdrawn (Bleuler 1911). 'Autism' and 'autistic' stem from the Greek word 'autos', meaning self. Thus the term autism originally referred to a basic disturbance found in schizophrenia (another term introduced by Bleuler) characterised by an extreme withdrawal of oneself from the fabric of social life, and so autism first entered medical terminology as a description for a particular mental state rather than an enduring set of personality traits.

Autism as a diagnostic construct was proposed by Leo Kanner in 1943 to describe a group of 11 children who were emotionally and intellectually impaired and showing an extreme 'aloneness' from early life (Kanner 1943). By 1955 Kanner had reported a total of 120 cases of what he described as 'infantile autism'. He differentiated this condition from childhood schizophrenia as he felt autism was evident almost from birth. Kanner, writing with Eisenberg (1956), hypothesised about aetiology, and concluded that it was unhelpful to try and tie aetiology to solely biological or environmental causes, stating:

> There is little likelihood that a single etiologic is solely responsible for the pathology of the behavior. Arguments that counter pose 'hereditary' versus

> 'environmental' as antithetical terms are fundamentally in error. Operationally, they are interpenetrating concepts. The effects of chromosomal aberrations can be mimicked in the phenotype by environmental pathogens, and genetic factors require for their complete manifestation suitable environmental conditions. (Kanner and Eisenberg 1956, p.563)

By the 1960s, Kanner's diagnosis of 'infantile autism' had become a recognised diagnosis for what was considered as a rare disorder primarily found in children with moderate to severe intellectual impairments. The first epidemiological study was published in 1966 and arrived at a prevalence figure for autism of 4.5 per 10,000 (Lotter 1966).

The year after Kanner first proposed 'autism' as a diagnosis, Hans Asperger published a paper, largely ignored at the time, in which he described children with no easily recognisable intellectual impairment, but with social communication problems (Asperger 1944). In the 1970s, psychiatrist Lorna Wing saw a similarity in some people she was seeing and those described by Asperger. Dr Wing's ideas intersected with another psychiatrist, Michael Rutter, and formed the basis for the expansion of the concept of autism into Autistic Spectrum Disorders.

Revisiting the seminal papers by Wing and Rutter reveals the extent to which this expansion of the concept of autism was not the result of any new scientific discoveries, but rather new ideologies. For example, in her paper proposing the 'Asperger Syndrome' diagnosis, Wing (1981) describes six case histories with little in common with Asperger's classic four cases beyond sharing a lack of social reciprocity. Four of Wing's cases were adults, whereas all of Asperger's were children; two had some degree of learning disability, whereas none of Asperger's did; most of Wing's cases spoke late whereas most of Asperger's spoke early; most of Wing's cases were described as having little capacity for analytical thought whereas Asperger's cases were described as highly analytical; and none of Wing's cases were described as manipulative, mendacious, cheeky, confrontational or vindictive (terms Asperger used about his cases). Furthermore, it is not clear why a lack of social reciprocity should warrant a diagnosis, or if it did, why it might not include most who have some degree of general intellectual disability or mental health problems.

In addition to supporting the hypothesis that autism is genetic and that these genes act on an 'autism spectrum', Sir Michael Rutter also provided early support for Wing and Gould's (1979) proposal that autism is characterised by a 'triad' of symptoms. Rutter (1978) reinforced the now familiar 'triad' by defining autism as being: (1) impaired social development which has a number of special characteristics out of keeping with the child's intellectual level; (2) delayed and deviant language development that is also out of keeping with the child's

intellectual level; and (3) 'insistence on sameness' as shown by stereotyped play patterns, abnormal preoccupations or resistance to change.

Since then, Rutter has consistently argued that autism and its spectrum is, beyond reasonable doubt, genetic in origin. Referring to autism spectrum disorders he states:

> The estimate of heritability is something of the order of 90 percent. Because the twin and family studies provide the same conclusions, there can be considerable confidence that the heritability is very high with genetic factors accounting for the majority of the population variance in liability to develop the disorder. (Rutter 2006, p.68)

This quite deterministic approach to autism contrasts with Kanner and Eisenberg's (above) and with other more general statements that Rutter makes about the accuracy and utility of estimating genetic contributions:

> It is of little value to attempt to quantify the relative influence of the two [genes and environment] in any precise way, because it will vary by population and over time. Moreover, the precise estimates for the strength of genetic and of environmental influences have few policy or practice implications. (Rutter 2006, p.221)

By the 1980s much research was underway to try to find the biological cause of autism. This necessitated that psychiatrists and psychologists develop new theoretical concepts to give researchers a practical way forward for their investigations. Thus it was proposed that a lack of Theory of Mind (ToM) was the central deficit found in autism. ToM refers to the ability to understand that other people have their own plans, thoughts, beliefs, attitudes and emotions. It was suggested that there was an underlying cognitive structure responsible for ToM, which was viewed as an innate 'module' that is activated at around three years of age. The ToM Module (ToMM) was seen as dedicated, specific, fast, automatic, at least partly encapsulated, and its functioning as being largely independent of the general intellectual capacities of the individual (Baron-Cohen 1995). Autistic children were found to have a significantly lower performance on certain tasks said to measure ToM compared with other cognitive tasks for testing intelligence and language capacities, leading to the hypothesis that autism was the consequence of a specific (biological) deficit in the ToMM.

However, by the late 1990s, interest in ToM was waning. As the diagnosis of autism was increasing, no genes responsible for the ToMM had been found, inconsistencies in ToM findings were apparent, the diagnosis was being made mainly in males, and interest in behavioural and biological continuums was increasing (Timimi, Gardner and McCabe 2010).

Moving away from the idea that autism is caused by a discrete pathology, Professor Simon Baron-Cohen put forward the 'extreme male brain' theory of autism. His new theory was the first to properly recognise that a theory of causation must be able to explain the gender disparity (with the majority receiving a diagnosis being male) and so he concluded that people with autism simply match an extreme of the male profile, with a particularly intense drive to systemise and a low drive to empathise. In other words, autistic traits are biologically male, normally distributed, found as a continuum in the population, and autism is simply the extreme end of this (male) continuum (Baron-Cohen 2003).

A deficit in ToMM and the extreme male brain are two high-profile theories put forward in recent years in an attempt to explain the assumed biological basis of ASD. However, they are just two of multiple theories with plenty of others such as dysfunctional immune systems, abnormalities in certain brain structures, problems in neurological connectivity, problems in early neuronal cell migration, effects of vaccines, and so on, to choose from. The presence of multiple, as yet unconfirmed, theories reflects the lack of progress in identifying the biological basis of autism.

Despite this, the concept of ASD has proved highly popular and it seems the more attention it has received the wider its boundaries have become as it has now expanded into a condition said to potentially affect 160 per 10,000 (1.6%) of the population (Baron-Cohen *et al.* 2009), an over 3500 per cent increase in prevalence in just four decades. Failure to find any specific treatment, growing concern about an autism 'epidemic', and media coverage of the alleged link with vaccines have all contributed to the high public profile of the diagnosis.

THE SCIENCE

Evidence to support the claim that autism is a 'neurodevelopmental disorder' comes mainly from genetic and neuroimaging studies.

Genetic studies

The argument that autism is a strongly genetic condition rests primarily upon twin and family studies (see below). Most of these studies focus on what might be called 'core' autism rather than broader ASD diagnoses such as Asperger Syndrome (Freitag 2007). In addition, there are no adoption studies (studies comparing the biological families with the adopted families of adoptees adopted early in life and who are subsequently diagnosed with autism), with the one study that included subjects who had been adopted (Szatmari *et al.* 2000) being a familial aggregate study comparing what the authors called the 'lesser variant' of

Pervasive Developmental Disorders (PDD) (i.e. traits that do not amount to a full diagnosis) amongst the relatives of adopted children with a diagnosis of a PDD compared with the relatives of non-adopted children with a PDD diagnosis, and thus it is not a true adoption study.

Methodological problems are numerous in the twin studies, including: selection bias; establishing zygosity; generalising results from twins to non-twins; the sex ratio in autism twin studies (of similar numbers of female and male twins); and, most importantly, heritability estimates relying on an assumption that the environments Mono-Zygotic (MZ/identical) and Di-Zygotic (DZ/non-identical) twins experience are the same (Joseph 2006). To conclude that a concordance rate difference between sets of MZ and DZ twins (with MZ twins who share all their genes having higher rates of both getting the diagnosis than DZ twins who share on average half their genes) is the result of genetics only, one must first assume that both sets of twins experience similar psychosocial environments – the equal environment assumption (EEA). If MZ twins are treated more similarly than DZ twins then any, or all, of the difference in concordance rates could also be explained by non-genetic factors.

It is well established that MZ twins are treated more similarly and experience more similar environments than do DZ twins or singletons (Joseph 2006). In addition, being an identical twin produces its own psychological dynamic with identity confusion and swapping roles occurring more commonly. Therefore the assumption that the higher incidences of ASDs found in MZ twins can only be attributable to genetics is not sustained.

Some researchers have reacted by trying to stand the criticism on its head, through suggesting that genetic factors lead twins to 'choose' their more identical environments. With such an argument (that genes are responsible for disrupting the EEA, therefore the difference in rates between MZ and DZ twins is still genetic) it is difficult to see how evidence could settle this without clear pathways being identified from specific genes to specific behaviours.

Notwithstanding these methodological issues, the findings from twin studies do not appear to provide particularly strong evidence that, after taking intellectual disability into account, much heritability for autism on its own is left. For example, in their classic study Folstein and Rutter (1977) studied 21 same-sexed twin pairs (11 MZ and 10 DZ) in which at least one twin was diagnosed with autism. There was a 36 per cent concordance rate for autism in MZ twins (i.e. 4 out of the 11 twin pairs) compared with 0 per cent in DZ twins. In addition, 9 out of the 11 MZ twin pairs (including all the autism diagnosed pairs) were concordant for 'cognitive deficits', whereas only one of the DZ twins were. In other words 'cognitive deficits' was much more likely to be found as a concordant factor in MZ twins than autism – and separating generalised intellectual disability from autism *per se* continues to bedevil the autism research literature.

In family studies it is even more difficult to separate environmental from genetic influences as children 'inherit' their family's environment as well as genes. Despite this, it remains rare in the studies to come across the presence of a relative who has enough symptoms to warrant a diagnosis of an ASD (Timimi *et al.* 2010). In addition, confounds such as learning difficulties and cognitive impairments are often found to be just as strongly associated in families of those with an ASD diagnosis (Starr *et al.* 2001).

The lack of clear evidence that autism is genetic is reflected in the lack of any genes for autism being discovered in molecular genetic studies. Thus various candidate genes, linkage studies, genome scans, and chromosome studies have failed to produce and reliably replicate any particular genes for autism. The more failures that pile up, the more 'complex' autism genetics must be according to advocates, whilst the most likely explanation for this finding – that there is no such thing as genes that 'cause' autism – remains unmentionable. The continuing failure to identify specifics seems to have resulted in the majority of the human chromosome being identified as potentially harbouring autism genes (Tsai 2004). Others have come to the more honest (and predictable) conclusion that:

> Though numerous linkages and associations have been identified, they tend to diminish upon closer examination or attempted replication. (Wassink *et al.* 2004, p.272)

> No major genome scan has produced significant and reproducible results... no candidate gene from a genome scan has shown a reproducible and statistically significant association with autism...no candidate gene that has inspired multiple studies has shown a robust and reproducible connection to autism. (Blaxill 2005, cited in Joseph 2006, pp.251–252)

More recent studies have focused on the number and density of Copy Number Variants (CNVs – these are bits of genetic code that are either missing where they should be or replicated where they shouldn't be). These studies have come to similar conclusions, with CNV patterns being predictive of intellectual impairments but not ASD specifically (Crespi and Croft 2012; Gallagher and Merikangas 2012). Reviews of the genetic research published in *Nature* in articles written by some of the leading academics in this area concluded:

> Many research teams have searched for genes that may be involved. They haven't turned up any prime candidates yet, only dozens, maybe hundreds of bit players. (Hughes 2012, p.S2)

> Genome wide association studies have failed to turn up any parts of the genome with statistical significance. (Williams 2012, p.S5)

Now that we have faster and cheaper technology for whole-genome scanning, the fact that despite thousands of these scans being completed we cannot find evidence beyond a tiny non-significant proportion of the assumed total genetic risk and with these small genetic associations being heterogeneous, crossing psychiatric diagnostic boundaries and more strongly related to learning difficulties than a diagnosis of ASD *per se*, should lead researchers to be less optimistic about finding ASD-specific genes. Researchers ought to be concluding that until proven otherwise we must assume there are no autism genes, rather than the current state of affairs where the assumption is that there are but we just can't find them yet.

The high ratio of males to females in ASD diagnoses also poses a problem. Genetic mechanisms need to account for this, such as autism being transmitted through the X chromosome, and thus far molecular genetic studies have failed to find an X- or Y-link. Some researchers have suggested that for disorders such as autism a 'bottom-up' rather than 'top-down' approach to molecular genetics is needed, where small contributions are additive. This approach seems to also cast doubt on the validity of a unitary concept of autism, recognising that these small genetic associations are heterogeneous and cross psychiatric diagnostic boundaries rather than being specific to any one (Verhoeven, Tuinier and Van Der Burgt 2008).

A variety of studies also find higher rates of autism symptoms amongst psychologically or socially vulnerable groups, such as severely neglected children in some Romanian orphanages who have been described as having 'quasi-autism' (Rutter *et al.* 1999). However, as they meet the descriptive criteria for a diagnosis, there is no 'quasi' about it.

Neuroimaging

An important consideration to take into account in any analysis of neuroimaging profiles is that of 'neuroplasticity'. This refers to the remarkable ability of the nervous system (particularly in children) to grow and change in response to environmental stimuli. The remarkable plasticity of the human brain makes it difficult to determine precise cause and effect when individuals with differential life experiences subsequently show what appear to be differences in neurological structure or functioning.

For example, Sadato and colleagues (1996) reported activation of the primary visual cortex by Braille reading, when studying participants who became blind early in life. Using positron emission tomography to assess activation in blind and sighted participants during tactile discrimination tasks, they discovered that blind subjects showed activation of primary and secondary visual cortex areas during these tasks, while sighted controls showed deactivation.

What these and other similar studies suggest is a profound ability of the brain to remap its own contours, based on differential life experience. While these findings have opened new avenues of investigation for neuroscience, they make efforts to link neurological differences with behavioural disorders more difficult. When a group of individuals with what is categorised as aberrant behaviour are found to have statistically significant different patterns of brain functioning from normal controls, we must ask ourselves if the neurological discrepancies are a cause or an effect of the behavioural differences. This inconvenience makes it difficult for researchers to 'pin down' behavioural aberrations into neurologically valid and clinically meaningful categories. Thus, neuroanatomical and functional differences could be the result of environmental factors affecting brain development (like psychological trauma), differential maturation rates and variations resulting from heterogeneity in the sample (for example the effects of confounds such as intellectual ability).

The biggest problem for autism studies, however, comes from the lack of consistently replicated findings. For example, studies focusing on the cerebellum have documented an increase in cerebellar volume among children diagnosed with an ASD, while others have found smaller than average cerebellar volumes; yet others have reported no significant differences (Timimi *et al.* 2010). Similarly, studies on the amygdala have found wide inconsistencies, including some studies that found significant differences in volume and others that found no differences (Anagnostou and Taylor 2011; Dziobek *et al.* 2006). Similar inconsistencies have been found in cortical thickness with differences often becoming insignificant once intellectual ability level was controlled for (Hardan *et al.* 2006, 2009). In reviewing these discrepancies, sample heterogeneity (such differences reflecting differences in cognitive ability rather than ASD) is regularly cited as a problem (Nadesan 2005).

Every now and then a new 'brain scan' study on autism announcing a breakthrough hits the headlines. In each case the claim has proven to be misplaced, but keeps the illusion that 'we are close to understanding the biological basis of autism' going. For example, in 2011 a study (Lai *et al.* 2011) that claimed it correctly predicted an autism diagnosis in 36 out of 39 children based on their functional magnetic resonance imaging proved to be over-optimistic. Critical review of this study concluded that all the authors had done was use technology to identify an area related to language problems and not something that can be used for differential diagnosis (Lange 2012).

Thus, from whatever angle you come at autism, we are no further forward to discovering the biological basis of autism than when Kanner first articulated the concept. It is likely that this is because autism and ASD do not describe a coherent biological construct.

TREATMENTS, PROGNOSIS AND THE PROBLEM OF HETEROGENEITY

Consistent with other major reviews (National Autistic Society 2003) we could find no evidence of methodologically sound and replicated research that demonstrates that particular interventions (whether educational, psychological, social or physical) *specifically and differentially* help those who have any form of autism (Timimi *et al.* 2010). Until specific treatments for ASD (as opposed to treatment approaches that work equally well with other individuals of similar ability levels) are adequately demonstrated through replicated controlled trials, we cannot and should not assume that the diagnosis has clinical value.

With regard to prognosis, the same behaviourally defined syndrome (ASD) is applied to residents of institutions with little hope of living independently and has been suggested for men who have achieved greatness, such as Mozart, Van Gogh, Edison, Darwin – all of whom, along with many others, have been retrospectively diagnosed as having an ASD (Fitzgerald 2004, 2005). From an 'impairment' perspective, this is virtually the entire human spectrum, suggesting that ASD, as it is currently defined, is too heterogeneous to have prognostic value. Not surprisingly therefore, more recent prospective studies have shown remarkably diverse outcomes, with many who have been diagnosed with an ASD in childhood reportedly having few or no symptoms by adulthood (Szatmari 2011) and many of those diagnosed in adulthood having high levels of psychosocial functioning (Hofvander *et al.* 2009).

This heterogeneity in what is now considered as 'autism' or 'autistic' is particularly problematic. Not only do the 'core' features such as difficulties in social communication have a large cross-over with people who would not consider themselves as having a 'disorder', but autism as a mental state (referring back to Bleuler's original use of the term autism to denote a state of social withdrawal) and elements of autism symptoms as traits are common in a variety of mental health diagnoses from ADHD to depression and anxiety to psychosis (see Table 2.1). No wonder it is difficult to design a specifically 'autistic' intervention for the diagnosis.

Heterogeneity is widely accepted as an issue in 'mainstream' publications about autism. However, far from seeing this as a major problem with regard the validity of the concept, it is explained away as a reflection of the 'complexity' of autism. Rutter and Schopler (1987) had argued in favour of the validity of autism, suggesting that it can be differentiated from the 'ordinary run' of emotional and behavioural disorders of childhood by its:

> strong association with mental retardation and with organic brain dysfunction, as well as in its worse prognosis, and its persisting differences in symptomatology. (Rutter and Schopler 1987, p.162)

At this stage Rutter and Schopler are pinning their hopes on the identification of a 'brain deficit' that 'defines' autism. The lack of identification of any characteristic brain deficit doesn't seem to have dampened the conviction that autism must be the result of some specific neurodevelopmental dysfunction despite the massive expansion of its boundaries. Unfortunately, since then the issue of the reliability and validity of autism and its spectrum has not been given the attention it merits. Subsequent publications (including those of Rutter) have come to simply accept the validity of this construct and no longer feel the need to ask serious questions about it.

However, wherever you look, heterogeneity and a lack of conceptual clarity about what autism is, is evident. This confusion is apparent when examining diagnostic criteria for other diagnoses. For example, under-socialised conduct disorders are characterised by the inability to form bonds with peers and egocentrism, which is shown by a readiness to manipulate others for favours without any effort to reciprocate together with a general lack of feelings for others. This description bears (arguably) a closer resemblance to the descriptions of the cases Hans Asperger wrote about than Lorna Wing's cases (discussed above). One of the core features of the autistic spectrum is meant to be a lack of empathy, a lack that is meant to cause enduring difficulties in social interactions. How is this type of 'lack of empathy' to be differentiated from the lack of empathy found in conduct disorder or, indeed, the 'personality disordered' criminal.

Other disorders, such as 'attachment disorder', also describe children who lack empathy and have dysfunctional patterns of social interaction. Attachment disorder is described as often associated with some form of neglect, abuse or trauma; however, in the absence of robust evidence on aetiology in autism, the distinction between social dysfunction in the context of conduct disorder, attachment disorder or ASD becomes little more than a matter of the semantics carried by the subjective opinion of the diagnoser. This confusion of symptom cross-over is not limited to conduct disorder and attachment disorder but spans potentially the entire spectrum of psychiatric diagnoses (see Table 2.1).

TABLE 2.1 SYMPTOM HETEROGENEITY IN ASD

Trait	Overlapping psyychiatric and other presentations
Lack of eye contact	Depression, anxiety, social anxiety disorder, shyness, low self-esteem and a lack of self-confidence. The same person may exhibit widely different degrees of reciprocal eye-contact in different social situations. Many cultures have practices that prohibit or limit eye contact (for example, in hierarchies such as between children and adults).

Poor 'reading' of non-verbal communication	Language disorders, ADHD, anxiety, depression, personality disorder, attachment disorders, bipolar affective disorder, psychosis, intellectual disability. As with most behavioural traits its importance is always relative to what you're comparing it to. Other overlaps include side-effect of medications, disinterest, a sense of alienation, and normal variation. Apparent poor reading of non-verbal communication could also be the result of deliberate provocation, boredom, a strong desire for attention, love and so on.
Stereotyped and restricted patterns of interest (restricted imagination)	OCD, obsessional personality disorder, schizoid personality disorder, ADHD (such as with computer games), depression (morbid preoccupation with negative aspects), eating disorders (fixation with food and/or weight). Most men (e.g. with football!). Sportsmen and women. Humanity: obsessive interest in a restricted sphere is characteristic not only of a depressed state of mind, but also of a phase of discovery and exploration. If someone had not fixated long enough on the tendency of logs to roll down slopes, the wheel may never have been invented! Most high achievers/perfectionists 'fixate' on their area of interest/expertise.
Failure to develop peer relationships appropriate to developmental level	ADHD, language disorders, intellectual disability, attachment disorder, personality disorders, conduct disorders, social anxiety and other anxiety disorders. This is an important reason why many parents, teachers or social workers may seek to have children under their care diagnosed in the first place – a failure to fit in. Failure to fit in can have many more ordinary associations such as clumsiness (particularly in boys), different interests to peers, unhappy home circumstances, and other traumas that preoccupy the young person.
A lack of empathy	Depression, conduct disorder, psychosis, ADHD, personality disorders, attachment disorder. A lack of self-confidence in social situations and a preoccupation with one's own problems tends to reduce interest in other people's lives and interests. The extent to which one can feign interest in all subjects or empathise with all predicaments is limited. As expectations for social empathy (e.g. in school and in the workplace) increase, so more may appear to lack this capacity. For isolated immigrants, a lack of familiarity with cultural expectations may also be a factor. Poor achievement or a sense of inferiority in a competitive culture may also lead people to turn away from a range of common interests.
Hyper-sensitivities and/or hypo-sensitivities	Depression, anxiety disorders, ADHD, personality disorders, attachment disorder. There is a range of 'sensitivities' amongst the population. Some hate loud noises; others crave them. These change from situation to situation, with cultural etiquette, familiarity, age and so on.

POLITICS

Given the lack of evidence to support the contention that autistic disorders arose out of new scientific knowledge or that it has any clinical utility, it seems to us reasonable to speculate about socio-cultural factors that may have contributed to the rapid change in ideology and practice around ASD.

As ASD diagnoses are disproportionately applied to males (as are some other psychiatric diagnoses such as ADHD and conduct disorders), an understanding of current social gender dynamics may be helpful. Whilst girls and women also have to face specific cultural gender dynamics that lead them to be more vulnerable to developing other problems such as self-harming and eating disorders, understanding why boys are more likely to present with behavioural problems such as aggression and social withdrawal can be helped by an examination of dominant cultural beliefs and practices around gender.

Masculinity and the cultural space of 'boyhood'

Three models of viewing and understanding the nature of the challenges facing boys, and how we respond to these, in Western societies have emerged. The first model, the 'boys will be boys' perspective (Gilbert and Gilbert 1998), starts from an assumption that boys and girls are biologically different, with boys 'programmed' to be more physical, aggressive, risk-seeking, controlling, independent, and so on. The second model, the 'boy code' model, emphasises the dominant cultural beliefs about what it means to be a 'man' and how this affects growing boys' socialisation by pushing them towards cultures of self-reliance and where the only acceptable emotional displays are those of anger and aggression (Connell 1995). The third model posits a more complex interaction between culturally constructed models of masculinity. In this 'multiple masculinities' model, it is argued that an increasing number of culturally constructed models of 'what it means to be a man' are available; however, they exist relative to the dominant model, articulated above in the 'boy code'. Thus, while boys and men may depart from the dominant model of masculinity and express other identities (such as 'bookish', 'geek', 'gay'), such a contravention carries risks as they can become targets for bullying, teasing and exclusion by their male peers (Kimmel 2004). The dominant models not only support a construct of maleness that encourages independence and a lack of empathy, but exclusion from peer relationships is more likely to occur if you struggle to uphold certain valued traits for 'masculinity' such as physical prowess, being non-academic, and being good at sports.

For some boys these dynamics leave them in a lonely place, where they feel unwelcome, unvalued and caught in cycles of progressive alienation, negative attention-seeking behaviour, jealousy, and low self-esteem as they fail to live

up to the dominant masculine ideal and sometimes with few male role models to turn to for help to find a healthy and positive way out of their situation (Timimi 2005).

Feminisation of education

There is a body of literature that supports the notion that educational methods currently used in Western schools (such as continuous assessment and socially orientated work sheets) are favoured more by girls than boys (Burman 2005). This is mirrored in national exam results where girls are consistently achieving higher grades than boys, even in some traditionally 'male' subjects such as mathematics and science. Boys also dominate special needs provision in schools. With schools under market economy political pressure to compete in national league tables, boys have come to be the 'failed' gender for schools. As it is boys who are increasingly unable to fulfil the cultural expectations of an essentially non-gendered set of school expectations, medicalisation of the behaviours that lie outside the increasingly narrow norm has become a culturally acceptable pathway to attempting to solve this set of problems (Timimi 2005).

Working environments

The feminisation of certain aspects of the most developed form of masculine culture (neoliberal market-economy-based cultures) also has an impact on working environments. Ideas such as cultivating 'emotional intelligence' to develop 'better' ways to motivate the workforce and manipulate the consumer have become popular (Gordo-Lopez and Burman 2004). Thus, modern Western culture demands more convoluted and complicated forms of 'instant' socialising (in an image-obsessed age) than in the past or many other cultures.

Economic changes have resulted in a decline of the manufacturing sectors and growth in the service industries. Communities of men who worked and socialised together (such as the miners) have largely disappeared. The new economic order demands a workforce with strong 'people skills' leading to greater political and personal demand for men to have enhanced social/emotional competence that they didn't previously need (Dunlop and Mletzko 2011).

Closer surveillance of boy culture

Many forms of surveillance, followed by attempts to intervene to correct and 'discipline' nonconformist children are apparent, from education to health to legal. Children (often boys) who refuse to accommodate to certain expectations of stressed teachers are deemed to require corrective interventions from 'experts'

(as opposed to more ordinary strategies such as altering teaching methods, classroom structures or support for teachers). These 'experts', through diagnoses such as 'autism', provide the rationale for 'extra' measures (pharmacology, transfer to special schools, and so on) to be taken. Individuals often internalise these psychosocial 'disciplinary' discourses and the labels then become part of their identity, thus helping embed the labels as representing something 'real' in the child (Timimi 2010).

The problem of essentialism

One of the difficulties inherent in highlighting gender issues pertaining to boys and men is that we can forget that, in terms of social justice and equality, men undoubtedly remain the dominant gender. Focusing on and discussing how our gender constructions may affect certain groups of boys and men can lead to a wave of sympathy about loss of social power and a nostalgia toward the 'good old days' when men could be men (and presumably tell 'their' women what to do). This essentialisation of gender (boys and girls are *essentially* different) and the idea that the good old days were better, misses the point. We have changing challenges and discourses around gender. Whilst we may have overlooked some of challenges that boys face because of a more visible discourse around women's oppression, ultimately feminist discourse involves challenges that requires both genders to consider their socio-cultural beliefs and practices.

All of us (men and women) are materially and psychologically impacted by the nature of the political/societal beliefs and structures we live within. For those of us living in neoliberal societies, we are arguably all subjugated by the winner/loser rather macho nature of the way the world gets organised in those societies. Viewed from this lens, the gender problem for men is still largely created by other men, and what the alienated boy could do with is a society that has more nurturing qualities, where it is easier to feel unconditionally accepted, rather than being forced to 'perform' in certain ways in order to feel that you have value and are not thrown into a 'loser' pile.

CONCLUSION

A belief that 'autism' is a diagnosis that is applied to a group who have a real biologically based condition is probably related to the origins of the label as one identifying a group of children who presented with strong evidence that they are neurocompromised through them having moderate or severe learning difficulties and/or high rates of epilepsy. However, the boundaries associated with the label have expanded rapidly without any accompanying evidence that this expansion is tied to new biological knowledge on the condition. Instead the change to

the current definition of an 'autism spectrum' has been the result of ideological changes rather than through new scientific knowledge, that is, as a result of a change in how the construct of 'autism' is conceptualised.

As one of the authors (BM) has experienced, the ASD label is no less stigmatising than other psychiatric labels (Timimi *et al.* 2010). There will always be people we cannot easily understand because we experience them as 'different'. Dealing with difference is a task for all humans to engage in. History teaches us that trying to avoid facing the uncertainty and anxiety we experience when we encounter difference by defining and categorising people into simplistic reified categories leads to untold violence and subjection of people. Categorising is all too often about control of 'otherness' (Scheff 1966). Therefore we believe that to genuinely open up a constructive approach to the group who attract the 'autism' label, we may have to reconsider the helpfulness of labelling them.

The challenge created by either discontinuing the use of the label or limiting its use to the more severely neurodisabled is considerable. A significant 'culture change' for clinicians and patients to depart from what has become 'conventional wisdom' is not easy. Those who present for a potential diagnosis, and those already diagnosed, are experiencing difficulties and are looking for services to help them. Our concern is that a diagnosis of autism does not shed any new or specific light on what might be contributing to their difficulties or how they might move forward. By 'shoe horning' a group with heterogeneous presentations, and therefore needs and wants, into narrow pathways of care may not only lead to unnecessary and at times irrelevant forms of intervention, but may, through the process of 'labelling', lead to an acceptance of long-term disability in a way that reduces the chances of those labelled being accepted and noted for their strengths and qualities.

Our position is broadly consistent with that of a 'disability studies' perspective. This challenges a view of disability as an individual deficit or defect that can be remedied solely through medical intervention or rehabilitation by 'experts' and instead explores models and theories that examine social, political, cultural and economic factors that define disability and help determine personal and collective responses to difference (Siebers 2008). From intellectual disability to physical disability, the problem resides not so much in the individual, but in the relationship to society. The challenge then becomes not just that of assessing and supporting the unique constellation of difficulties facing a person (as opposed to a uniform diagnostic specific pathway), but in addition a human rights perspective that focuses on political and social reform to eradicate discrimination and improve social inclusion across the board.

We believe that we must now have a serious debate, of the type that has yet to occur, that engages patients, the public, and professionals on the pros and cons of continuing to use the diagnosis of autism. If not, we risk sleep-walking

into labelling ever-larger numbers of people with all manner of unforeseen consequences for their and our society's futures.

REFERENCES

American Psychiatric Association (1994) *Diagnostic and Statistical Manual of Mental Disorders, Fourth Edition (DSM-IV).* Washington, DC: APA.

American Psychiatric Association (2013) *Diagnostic and Statistical Manual of Mental Disorders, Fifth Edition (DSM-5).* Washington, DC: APA.

Anagnostou, E., and Taylor, M.J. (2011) 'Review of neuroimaging in autism spectrum disorders: what have we learned and where we go from here.' *Molecular Autism 2,* 4.

Angell, M. (2011a) 'The epidemic of mental illness: why?' *The New York Review,* 23 June 2011. Available at www.nybooks.com/articles/archives/2011/jun/23/epidemic-mental-illness-why, accessed on 4 November 2015.

Angell, M. (2011b) 'The illusions of psychiatry.' *The New York Review,* 14 July 2011. Available at www.nybooks.com/articles/archives/2011/jul/14/illusions-of-psychiatry/?pagination=false, accessed on 4 November 2015.

Asperger, H. (1944) 'Autistic Psychopathy in Childhood' (translated and annotated by U. Frith). In U. Frith (ed.) (1991) *Autism and Asperger Syndrome.* Cambridge: Cambridge University Press.

Baird, G., Douglas, H.R., and Murphy, S. (2011) 'Recognising and diagnosing autism in children and young people with autism; summary of the NICE guidelines: the matrix of assessment and treatment of autism spectrum disorders.' *British Medical Journal 343,* d6360.

Baron-Cohen, S. (1995) *Mindblindness: An Essay on Autism and Theory of Mind.* Cambridge, MA: MIT Press.

Baron-Cohen, S. (2003) *The Essential Difference: The Truth About the Male and Female Brain.* New York: Basic Books.

Baron-Cohen, S., Scott, F.J., Allison, C., Williams, J., Bolton, P., and Matthews, F.E. (2009) 'Prevalence of autism-spectrum conditions: UK school-based population study.' *British Journal of Psychiatry 194,* 500–509.

Bleuler, E. (1911) 'Dementia Praecox oder gruppe der schizophrenien.' In G. Aschaffenburg (ed.) *Handbuch der Psychiatrie.* Leipzig: Deuticke.

Burman, E. (2005) 'Childhood, neo-liberalism and the feminization of education.' *Gender and Education 17,* 351–367.

Connell, R.W. (1995) *Masculinities.* Cambridge: Polity Press.

Crespi, B., and Croft, H. (2012) 'Association testing of copy number variants in schizophrenia and autism spectrum disorders.' *Journal of Neurodevelopmental Disorders 4,* 15.

Dunlop, B., and Mletzko, T. (2011) 'Will current socioeconomic trends produce a depressing future for men?' *British Journal of Psychiatry 198,* 167–168.

Dziobek, I., Fleck, S., Rogers, K., Wolf, O.T., and Convit, A. (2006) 'The "amygdala theory of autism" revisited: linking structure to behavior.' *Neuropsychologia 44,* 1891–1899.

Fitzgerald, M. (2004) *Autism and Creativity: Is There a Link Between Autism in Men and Exceptional Ability?* London: Brunner-Routledge.

Fitzgerald, M. (2005) *The Genesis of Artistic Creativity: Asperger's Syndrome and the Arts.* London: Jessica Kingsley Publishers.

Folstein, S., and Rutter, M. (1977) 'Infantile autism: a genetic study of 21 twin pairs.' *Journal of Child Psychology and Psychiatry 18,* 297–321.

Frances, A. (2010) 'The first draft of DSM-5: if accepted, will fan the flames of false positive diagnoses.' *British Medical Journal 340*, c1168.

Freitag, C.M. (2007) 'The genetics of autistic disorders and its clinical relevance: a review of the literature.' *Molecular Psychiatry 12*, 2–12.

Gallagher, L., and Merikangas, A. (2012) 'Relating Copy Number Variation to Phenotype – Bridging Phenotype Gaps.' Presentation at the International Society for Autism Research Conference, Sheraton Centre, Toronto, 18 May 2012. Available at https://imfar.confex.com/imfar/2012/webprogram/Paper11285.html, accessed on 4 November 2015.

Gilbert, R., and Gilbert, P. (1998) *Masculinity Goes to School.* St. Leonards: Allen & Unwin.

Gordo-Lopez, A., and Burman, E. (2004) 'Emotional capital and information technologies in the changing rhetoric around children and childhoods.' *New Directions in Child Development 105*, 63–80.

Hardan, A.Y., Muddasani, S., Vemulapalli, M., Keshavan, M.S., and Minshew, N.J. (2006) 'An MRI study of increased cortical thickness in autism.' *American Journal of Psychiatry 163*, 1290–1292.

Hardan, A.Y., Libove, R.A., Keshavan, M.S., Melhem, N.M., and Minshew, N.J. (2009) 'A preliminary longitudinal magnetic resonance imaging study of brain volume and cortical thickness in autism.' *Biological Psychiatry 66*, 320–326.

Hilpern, K. (2007) 'Muddy thinking.' *The Guardian*, Tuesday 9 October 2007.

Hofvander, B., Delorme, R., Chaste, P., Nydén, A., Wentz, E., Ståhlberg, O., *et al.* (2009) 'Psychiatric and psychosocial problems in adults with normal-intelligence autism spectrum disorders.' *BMC Psychiatry 9*, 35.

Hughes, V. (2012) 'Epidemiology: complex disorder.' *Nature 491*, S2–S3.

Joseph, J. (2006) *The Missing Gene: Psychiatry, Hereditary, and the Fruitless Search for Genes.* New York: Algora.

Kanner, L. (1943) 'Autistic disturbances of affective contact.' *Nervous Child 2*, 217–250.

Kanner, L., and Eisenberg, L. (1956) 'Early infantile autism 1943–1955.' *American Journal of Orthopsychiatry 26*, 556–566.

Kimmel, M. (2004) *The Gendered Society.* Oxford: Oxford University Press.

Lai, G., Schneider, H., Schwarzenberger, J., and Hirsch, J. (2011) 'Speech stimulation during functional MR imaging as a potential indicator of autism.' *Radiology 260*, 521–530.

Lange, N. (2012) 'Imaging autism.' *Nature 491*, S17.

Lotter, V. (1966) 'Epidemiology of autistic conditions in young children: I. prevalence.' *Social Psychiatry 1*, 124–137.

Nadesan, M. (2005) *Constructing Autism: Unravelling the 'Truth' and Understanding the Social.* London: Routledge.

National Autistic Society (2003) *National Autism Plan for Children.* London: National Autistic Society.

Rutter, M. (1978) 'Diagnosis and definition of childhood autism.' *Journal of Autism and Developmental Disorders 8*, 139–161.

Rutter, M. (2006) *Genes and Behaviour: Nature–Nurture Interplay Explained.* Oxford: Blackwell.

Rutter, M., and Schopler, E. (1987) 'Autism and pervasive developmental disorders: concepts and diagnostic issues.' *Journal of Autism and Developmental Disorders 17*, 159–186.

Rutter, M., Anderson-Wood, L., Beckett, C., Bredenkamp, D., Castle J., and Groothues, C. (1999) 'Quasi-autistic patterns following severe early global privation.' *Journal of Child Psychology and Psychiatry 40*, 537–549.

Sadato, N., Pascual-Leone, A., Grafman, J., Ibanez, V., Deiber, M.P., and Dold, G. (1996) 'Activation of the primary visual cortex by Braille reading in blind subjects.' *Nature 380*, 526–528.

Scheff, T. (1966) *Being Mentally Ill: A Sociological Theory.* Chicago: Aldine.

Siebers, T. (2008) *Disability Theory.* Michigan: University of Michigan Press.

Starr, E., Berument, S.K., Pickles, A., Tomlins, M., Bailey, A., and Papanikolaou, K. (2001) 'A family genetic study of autism associated with profound mental retardation.' *Journal of Autism and Developmental Disorders 31,* 89–96.

Szatmari, P. (2011) 'New recommendations on autism spectrum disorder.' *British Medical Journal 342,* d2456.

Szatmari, P., MacLean, J., Jones, M.B., Bryson, S., Zwaigenbaum, L., and Bartolucci, G. (2000) 'The familial aggregation of the lesser variant in biological and nonbiological relatives of PDD probands: a family history study.' *Journal of Child Psychology and Psychiatry 41,* 579–586.

Timimi, S. (2005) *Naughty Boys: Anti-Social Behaviour, ADHD, and the Role of Culture.* Basingstoke: Palgrave Macmillan.

Timimi, S. (2010) 'The McDonaldization of childhood: children's mental health in neo-liberal market cultures.' *Transcultural Psychiatry 47,* 686–706.

Timimi, S. (2013) 'No more psychiatric labels: campaign to abolish psychiatric diagnostic systems such as ICD and DSM (CAPSID).' *Self and Society 40,* 4, 6–4.

Timimi, S., McCabe, B., and Gardner, N. (2010) *The Myth of Autism: Medicalising Boys' and Men's Social and Emotional Competence.* Basingstoke: Palgrave MacMillan.

Tsai, L. (2004) 'Autistic Disorder.' In J. Weiner and M. Dulcan (eds) *Textbook of Child and Adolescent Psychiatry* (Third edition). Washington, DC: American Psychiatric Association Press.

Verhoeven, W.M., Tuinier, S., and Van Der Burgt, I. (2008) 'Top-down or bottom-up: contrasting perspectives on psychiatric diagnoses.' *Biologics 2,* 409–417.

Volkmar, F., and Happe, F. (2012) 'Where next for autism?' *New Scientist 213,* 30–31.

Wassink, T.H., Brzustowicz, L.M., Bartlett, C.W., and Szatmari, P. (2004) 'The search for autism genes.' *Mental Retardation and Developmental Disabilities Research Reviews 10,* 272–283.

Williams, S.C. (2012) 'Searching for answers.' *Nature 491,* S4–S6.

Wing, L. (1981) 'Asperger's Syndrome: a clinical account.' *Psychological Medicine 11,* 115–129.

Wing, L., and Gould, J. (1979) 'Severe impairments of social interaction and associated abnormalities in children: epidemiology and classification.' *Journal of Autism and Childhood Schizophrenia 9,* 11–29.

CHAPTER 3

DOES EVERYBODY WITH AN AUTISM DIAGNOSIS HAVE THE SAME UNDERLYING CONDITION?

Richard Hassall

INTRODUCTION

Does everybody with an autism diagnosis have the same underlying condition? This might seem like an odd question to ask. Surely, people who have been assessed as autistic by skilled professionals using standard diagnostic criteria must have something in common which defines them as autistic. So the answer to this question offered by most people is likely to be 'Yes'. In this chapter, however, I argue that there are strong grounds for thinking that the answer is in fact 'No' – that is, that there is no single underlying condition which can be regarded as the defining characteristic of autism and which accounts for all the varied symptoms displayed by those individuals who have received the diagnosis. In other words, there appears to be no *single* distinctive psychological or neurodevelopmental disorder represented by the concept of 'autism'. This may seem like suggesting that there is really no such 'thing' as autism. However, this way of stating the position is apt to imply, wrongly, that people who have been diagnosed with autism do not experience any real disability. On the contrary, those with the diagnosis generally do display significant disabilities of one sort or another, although there is wide variation in the nature and severity of these.[1]

1 I am aware that there are differing views about whether people with an autism diagnosis have 'disabilities' or whether they display characteristics that are just *different* from those of the non-autistic population. Because so much of the current discussion about autism is influenced by the terminology of the psychiatric diagnostic manuals, which involve the language of 'disorder', it is simplest for my purposes to talk about the presumed disabilities associated with autism, in order to address the question of whether or not autism is a distinct form of disorder or disability. I am also making no assumption about whether the presumed 'disability' is something internal to the individual or is better understood as a function of the individual's relationship to the social environment in which they live.

Much debate about the nature of autism hinges on this last point. My own experience, working as a clinical psychologist in various parts of the United Kingdom, has led me to be struck, not by how similar people with autism are to each other, but by how *different* they are. It is very difficult to see what there is in common, in terms of a shared disability, between one person with severe and multiple intellectual disabilities who requires full-time care for life and another diagnosed with Asperger Syndrome who is able to live independently and form a fulfilling personal relationship with somebody else. This is sometimes referred to as the issue of 'heterogeneity' (e.g. Happé and Ronald 2008; Rutter 2013). In addition, it can be very difficult, or even meaningless, to try to disentangle the relative effects of autism and severe intellectual disability in the former type of case.

In order to show how autism is typically understood, I begin by discussing the most recently published diagnostic criteria for autism in the fifth (and latest) edition of the American Psychiatric Association's *Diagnostic and Statistical Manual* (DSM-5) (APA 2013). These are contrasted with those listed in previous editions of the manual (DSM-III and DSM-IV)[2] noting significant changes in the conceptualisation of autistic disorders since these earlier classifications were published, including the disappearance of Asperger Syndrome as a distinct category. Autism as currently understood appears to be significantly different from the condition first formally described by Leo Kanner in the 1940s (Kanner 1943). According to Kanner, autistic children are characterised principally by 'autistic aloneness' and 'obsessive desire for sameness' (Kanner 1943). Our current view of autism seems to colour our understanding of the nature of the syndrome that Kanner originally described, such that we tend to think of autism as some kind of stable entity, which has existed in fundamentally the same form since Kanner's first publications. All that has changed, we think, is that we have steadily refined our conception in a continuous and incremental fashion thanks to accumulating scientific knowledge. However, the changes in conception that have taken place over this time appear in important respects to be discontinuous, even confusing, such that we can reasonably doubt whether there is really any stable entity describable as 'autism' (Verhoeff 2013).

Various psychological theories have been proposed to account for the characteristic grouping of symptoms of autism, none of which has succeeded in explaining the occurrence of all these symptoms. I give a brief overview of some of these to indicate some of the explanatory difficulties they face. Furthermore, no genetic or neurological basis for autism has so far been reliably established, despite extensive research studies conducted over a long period throughout the world. These considerations raise the question of what exactly is the condition

---

2 Earlier editions of the DSM (e.g. DSM-IV) used Roman numerals. This changed to Arabic numerals with DSM-5, although in some earlier papers it is referred to as DSM-V.

or disorder which supposedly occurs in all those who have been diagnosed with autism and not in those who are not autistic.

If the concept of autism really does represent a distinct entity, one would expect it to carry significant implications about the aetiology of the disorder and its expected course. One would also expect it to provide some indication of appropriate treatments. However, autism, as a diagnostic category, fails in these respects. Although it is generally agreed that there is no single treatment applicable for autism, very many interventions can be offered, none of which are exclusively appropriate only for autism. In other words, most disease and disability diagnoses have significant implications for aetiology or treatment (or both), but 'autism' as a diagnosis has neither of these.

If the diagnosis of 'autism' explains little and predicts little, it can claim little value as a *scientific* concept. If it were to have such value, we could reasonably expect it to resemble other disease or disability concepts. A diagnosis such as malaria implies a specific causal process that leads to the condition and supports predictions about the prognosis and suitable treatment (if any). I discuss how such disease concepts can be regarded as examples of what philosophers of science call 'natural kinds'. Examples of natural kinds in other sciences include the chemical elements and biological species, the identification of which has led to the successful development of chemistry and biology. I argue that many types of medical diagnosis can be seen as natural kinds for similar reasons, but this does not work for the concept of 'autism'. In this respect, autism is similar to most psychiatric diagnostic categories, which have little explanatory or predictive value (e.g. Haslam 2014; Zachar 2014).

I conclude therefore that there is no reason to believe, on the basis of current evidence, that there is one single identifiable medical or psychological disorder that uniquely characterises autism. Rather, the available evidence points to a diverse range of characteristics and symptoms covered by the notion of autism as a rather loose umbrella concept. Whilst something close to this conclusion appears now to be acknowledged by several autism experts, much of their discussion is still dominated by thinking of it as a distinct category with the corresponding need to 'solve the enigma' or 'find the explanation' of autism, as if they still believe that there is *one* solution or explanation waiting to be found. This manner of thinking has had a profound impact on everyday thinking about autism, such that the idea that autism represents a distinct type of disability has penetrated deeply into popular consciousness. Its persistence in popular belief systems may well increase the risk of stigmatising those with the diagnosis.

CHANGES IN THE CONCEPTUALISATION OF AUTISM

The manner in which the criteria for diagnosis have been specified in the diagnostic manuals and the changes made to these criteria over the years have substantially influenced the way in which autism has been conceived in both professional and popular discourse. Various writers have described how the classification has changed over time (e.g. Baron-Cohen 2008; Frith 2003). Typically these accounts present the history of the changing conception of autism as one of a steady development and refinement of a distinct disease entity, first identified by Kanner (1943) and assumed to be the same essential entity which has undergone subsequent refinements in successive diagnostic manuals. It is naturally tempting to view the classification of autism in the most up-to-date psychiatric manuals as being the definitive statement of the condition, and it tends to appear this way until the following edition of the manual is published with newly revised criteria. It also tends to influence the manner in which the history of the disorder is interpreted, such that earlier descriptions of the condition are viewed as being essentially similar to, if less well developed than, the disorder as currently understood, and thus overlooks significant *discontinuities* in how the supposedly unique condition has been characterised (Verhoeff 2013). Looking at its most recent conceptualisation and contrasting this with earlier definitions can demonstrate some of these discontinuities.

The most recently published criteria for diagnosis are those appearing in DSM-5 (APA 2013) which supersedes the previous edition (DSM-IV). There is now a single diagnostic category of 'Autism Spectrum Disorder', without any subdivisions. To meet the criteria for a diagnosis the individual concerned needs to display two defining types of impairment: (1) persistent deficits in social communication and interaction; and (2) restricted or repetitive behaviours and interests (RRBIs). This in effect amounts to the current definition of autism, albeit in brief form. Some symptoms need to be present (but not necessarily evident) during the child's early development and, at the time of diagnosis, the symptoms must cause clinically significant impairment in the individual's functioning.

The new category of Autism Spectrum Disorder contrasts with the previous categorisation in DSM-IV, which listed five subcategories of what was then termed 'Pervasive Developmental Disorders' (PDD) – these were: autism, Asperger Syndrome, Rett Syndrome, childhood disintegrative disorder (CDD), and pervasive developmental disorder (not otherwise specified) (PDD-NOS). Whilst 'autism' has now been omitted as a formal category, it nevertheless remains in regular use as shorthand for the new category, with which it appears virtually synonymous. There were various reasons for excluding the other subcategories from DSM-5. Rett Syndrome is a rare genetic disorder predominantly affecting

girls and can be classified as a distinct medical disorder. CDD is also a very rare condition, and there is significant uncertainty as to whether it actually constitutes a distinct disorder. PDD-NOS refers to cases where the individual displays some autistic traits which are typically mild and do not contain all the symptoms necessary to make a definitive diagnosis. Some of these are now covered in DSM-5 by the separate category of 'Social Communication Disorder'.

The most notable exclusion from DSM-5 is Asperger Syndrome. The criteria in DSM-IV failed to distinguish it clearly from autistic disorder, and particularly from high-functioning autism, and there has been wide variation in how it has been applied in practice (Happé 2011). Specifically, the application of the diagnoses of Asperger Syndrome, autism and PDD-NOS has often been a function of the particular knowledge base and inclinations of the clinician making the diagnosis (Lord and Jones 2012). Consequently the problems of unreliability in the application of the diagnosis of Asperger Syndrome, particularly the difficulty in distinguishing between it and autism, have led to its disappearance from DSM-5. This raises two puzzling questions. Are autism diagnostic teams now able to continue applying this diagnosis to children or adults who present for assessment? And should those who already have the diagnosis now have it replaced by a diagnosis of 'Autism Spectrum Disorder' or the alternative diagnosis of 'Social Communication Disorder', which is not classed as an autistic disorder at all – or can they still legitimately describe themselves as having Asperger Syndrome?[3] It is far from clear how these questions should be answered.

The picture is further confused because Asperger Syndrome continues to be listed in the tenth edition of the World Health Organisation's *International Classification of Diseases* (ICD-10) (WHO 1992), which has diagnostic criteria similar to those of DSM-IV. Furthermore, some autism experts continue to argue that the previously listed subdivisions of ASD *can* be meaningfully distinguished from each other and that therefore it would be reasonable to retain the category of Asperger Syndrome (e.g. Tsai and Ghaziuddin 2014). Many services continue to base their assessment and diagnostic procedures on the criteria in ICD-10, which would seem to imply that Asperger Syndrome is still a legitimate diagnosis. However, at the time of writing, a new edition of the ICD (ICD-11) is scheduled to appear around 2016 or 2017, which is also expected to incorporate a single overall category similar to that of Autism Spectrum Disorder in DSM-5 (Rutter 2013). If this turns out to be the case, Asperger Syndrome will no longer be listed as a diagnosable disorder in either of the two major taxonomies of mental disorders.

---

3 Those who have already received a diagnosis of Asperger Syndrome are apparently being assured that they can still keep it, despite its formal elimination. The logic of this position is not immediately obvious.

Asperger Syndrome was first introduced as a formal diagnostic category in DSM-IV in 1994, after only coming to the attention of the English-speaking world in the 1980s. It was first described by the Austrian paediatrician Hans Asperger, in a paper published in German in 1944. Asperger illustrated the syndrome by providing four case histories of affected children. It finally became widely known in the English-speaking world following a paper published by the British psychiatrist, Lorna Wing (1981a). Asperger himself viewed the syndrome he had identified as something quite different from the condition of 'early infantile autism' described by Kanner (van Krevelen 1971). However, from the 1980s onwards the view that Asperger Syndrome and autism are essentially similar was promoted strongly by Lorna Wing and others. In her paper (1981a), Wing described six case histories of affected individuals, of whom four were adults at the time of assessment and for whom it would have been difficult to obtain reliable childhood histories. It has been pointed out that there are many *differences* between Asperger's cases and Wing's, such that it is not evident that they are actually comparable (Timimi, Gardner and McCabe 2010). Wing's choice of case histories seems to have made it more likely that Asperger Syndrome would appear similar in important respects to classical autism, as described by Kanner.

The notion of the 'autistic spectrum' emerged during this period, with Asperger Syndrome being assimilated into it. The word 'spectrum' suggests a metaphor, inviting an analogy with the optical spectrum, in which the visible colours appear in a linear fashion with each one shading, without clear boundaries, into the next. All the colours and the invisible parts of the spectrum are essentially the same kind of thing – that is, electromagnetic radiation. The idea became accepted, virtually without question, that all the conditions characterised by the 'autistic spectrum' must be fundamentally similar, differing principally in their level of severity. Asperger Syndrome was positioned at the less severe end of the spectrum. Although Asperger Syndrome has been excluded from DSM-5, the notion of a generalised Autistic Spectrum Disorder remains and constitutes the basis of the current diagnostic category.

Another important change introduced in DSM-5 is the reduction in the defining impairments from three to two. Autism was first formalised as a diagnostic category in 1980 in the third edition of the DSM (APA 1980), when it was defined by the 'triad of impairments'. In DSM-III, these can be roughly described as: (1) impairment in social relationships; (2) deficits in language and communication; and (3) repetitive and restricted behaviours and interests (RRBIs). The description of these features was changed in significant respects in a revised version (DSM-IIIR) published in 1987 (APA 1987) – for example, 'pervasive lack of responsiveness to other people' became 'qualitative impairment in reciprocal social interaction' in the revised version – and the

triad was retained in DSM-IV (APA 1994).[4] The reduction in DSM-5 to two defining impairments – social communication and RRBIs – is a consequence of the difficulty in distinguishing between social impairments and communication deficits (Baron-Cohen 2008; Lord and Jones 2012).

The conceptualisation of an autistic triad was strongly driven by an epidemiological study carried out in London by Wing and Gould (1979) aimed at establishing the prevalence of these three abnormalities and the extent to which they occur together. They studied a group of 132 children who had been identified with learning disabilities or one or more of the autistic impairments. They found that all the children in a subgroup with social impairments also had language impairments along with RRBIs. They took this as strong support for the hypothesis that these three characteristics are likely to occur together. However, this conclusion has been criticised on the basis that the methodology and the nature of the sample studied did not exclude the possibility that the co-occurrence of these impairments may have arisen by chance and there have been few other systematic attempts to study whether these impairments co-occur at above chance levels (Mandy and Skuse 2008).

Even if the triad of impairments do occur together at above chance levels, it is now generally recognised that there is a substantial degree of separability between them (Happé and Ronald 2008). This is characterised by Happé and Ronald as the 'fractionable autism triad'. According to their and others' research, each of these impairments frequently occurs by itself – that is, they are 'fractionable'. Furthermore, they argue that the separate aspects of the triad seem to have largely independent causes at the genetic, neural and cognitive levels. This seems to amount to an admission that the concept of autism does not represent any unique form of disease or disability. However, Happé and Ronald recoil from reaching this conclusion. Instead they assert:

> The suggestion that the different aspects of the ASD triad have fractionable causes...is sometimes taken as an attack on the validity of the diagnosis of autism... However, it is quite compatible to assert that the resulting mix has a special quality, distinct prognosis and response to intervention, and is therefore worthy of a distinct diagnostic label. (Happé and Ronald 2008, p.299)

However, whether or not autism has a 'special quality' is precisely what is at issue here. If it does have such a quality, it seems extraordinarily difficult to explain what exactly this is, as the changing diagnostic criteria over many years demonstrate. Moreover, autism does not actually appear to have a prognosis and response to intervention that is *distinct* in the sense of distinguishing it from other conditions.

---

4 See Verhoeff (2013) for a more detailed discussion of how such changes have affected the diagnosis of autism.

Happé and Ronald go on to argue that their position is likely to have implications for the issue of diagnosis. If so, one would expect, on the basis of autism being seen as a combination of impairments in three relatively independent areas of functioning, that the diagnostic criteria would specify these three areas separately as fundamental elements in a diagnosis, as in DSM-III and DSM-IV. However, in DSM-5 the two elements of social interaction and communication have been collapsed into a single element – understood as 'social communication' – and when impairments in 'social communication' are combined with RRBI a diagnosis of Autism Spectrum Disorder can be made. Given that Francesca Happé was a member of the DSM-5 workgroup that drew up the revised diagnostic criteria, one might have expected that DSM-5 would have retained the triad of impairments given the evidence of their 'fractionation', but this has not happened. In describing how the workgroup arrived at these criteria, Happé (2011) explains their thinking on Asperger Syndrome, but makes no mention of the change from the triad to a 'duo' of impairments.

Another puzzling issue concerns the third element in the triad (or second element of the duo in DSM-5), namely that of repetitive and restricted behaviours and interests (RRBIs). As noted, the triad itself, and the inclusion of RRBIs in it, was largely based upon the work of Wing and Gould (1979). Subsequently, however, Wing (1981b) characterised this third element as an impairment of 'social imagination'. Presumably, an impairment of social imagination could be manifested in repetitive behaviours or restricted interests – this may just be a matter of interpretation. However, Wing and Gould more recently state clearly that impairment of social imagination is something quite *different* – they say:

> This is the decreased capacity to think about and predict the consequences of one's own actions for oneself and for other people... We believe that it should not have been ignored by the designers of the DSM-IV or the DSM-V (and ICD-10). *The DSM instead introduced repetitive behaviour patterns, not the impaired social imagination, as the last leg of the triad.* (Wing, Gould and Gillberg 2011, p.769; emphasis added)

This difference cannot be explained as a matter of interpretation. Yet it was largely due to the work of Wing and Gould that the triad of impairments, *including* RRBIs, formed the basis of the diagnostic criteria in the DSM, for which they have explicitly claimed the credit whilst simultaneously *repudiating* the RRBIs element of it (Wing *et al.* 2011). Furthermore, there is some evidence for the existence of distinct subtypes of RRBIs with differential associations with other impairments (Lam, Bodfish and Piven 2008), which suggests that the RRBIs element may itself be fractionable to some extent. So it is difficult to decide how one should conceptualise this element in the triad (or the duo in DSM-5) and its place in the diagnostic criteria.

To summarise, autism has been with us in one form or other for over 70 years. It began with Kanner's description of extreme self-isolation and obsessional need for sameness as its primary symptoms. Following the changes introduced by the DSM, its conceptualisation has undergone several metamorphoses, through a variously defined triad of impairments (which in any case has not achieved a consensus, given the confusion about the nature of the third element), and in its latest incarnation emerging as a duo of impairment categories. These two categories are now much wider in their scope than those originally described by Kanner. To date, there seems no reason to suppose we have yet reached any kind of stable conceptualisation, something that would seem an essential prerequisite if people with an autism diagnosis are believed to have any significant condition in common with each other.

PSYCHOLOGICAL THEORIES OF AUTISM

Various theories about underlying psychological deficits have been proposed to account for the symptoms of autism. The principal motivation for advancing such theories is that a successful theory could reveal autism as a disorder with an underlying unitary character. The hope would be that such a unifying psychological deficit could be associated with an identifiable neurological abnormality, which would explain the nature of the disorder. However, no theory so far advanced has been able to do this and several autism researchers are now asking whether any such explanation is even possible (e.g. Happé, Ronald and Plomin 2006).

Typically, the psychological theories put forward have tended to focus on hypothesised cognitive deficiencies in people with an autism diagnosis. These supposed deficiencies include mindblindness (an impaired ability to mind-read or understand the mental states of others), weak central coherence (difficulty in integrating detailed information into larger meaningful wholes), and executive dysfunction (an inability to plan and coordinate actions to achieve intended goals). Of these, the concept that has generated the most amount of research interest is that of mind-reading. This can be tested experimentally by means of 'false-belief' tasks. These test whether children are able to infer the behaviour of an actor who has a false belief about a given situation. To answer correctly, the child has to recognise that the actor's behaviour will be governed by the *belief* she has about the situation, rather than what the reality may be.[5] Children of around

5 The classic experiment is the 'Sally–Anne' test. The child watches a short action sequence involving two dolls enacted by the experimenter. One of the dolls (Sally) places a marble in a covered basket and then leaves the room. The other doll (Anne) transfers the marble to a box and covers this. When Sally returns, the child is asked where he thinks she will look for the marble. To answer correctly he needs to understand that Sally has a false belief about the present location of the marble.

four years of age will generally answer these tests correctly, whereas similar aged children with a diagnosis of autism often fail to do so. This, along with similar findings, is frequently taken as important evidence that mindblindness is the key impairment underlying autism.

However, some children with autism diagnoses do actually pass these tests, indicating that autism cannot be specifically characterised by a mind-reading impairment. Moreover, these tests are only applicable to children with normally developing cognitive and language abilities, and they therefore say nothing about the nature of autism in children with more severe intellectual disabilities. Although other experiments aimed at testing for false beliefs have been devised for pre-linguistic infants, the results are more difficult to interpret and do not necessarily predict later autism diagnoses. In addition, the theory of a mind-reading impairment cannot clearly explain the various restricted and repetitive behaviours and interests (RRBIs) associated with autism, a problem shared by the other theories mentioned above.

Simon Baron-Cohen (2002) proposes a more complex theory, arguing that autism is characterised by a deficit in 'empathising' skills combined with strong 'systemising' abilities. This pattern of abilities is said to correspond to the 'extreme male brain', reflecting a brain structure presumed to be characteristic of males rather than females. The notion of 'empathising' employed is a complex one, which combines the idea of 'mind-reading' with that of emotional empathy as ordinarily understood. However these two components of Baron-Cohen's notion of 'empathy' seem relatively independent of each other and it is not clear that this combination represents any distinct kind of psychological capacity. His notion of 'systemising' is intended to refer generally to the ability to analyse mechanisms and construct systems. As such, it supposedly accounts for the RRBIs in autism, including the restricted and obsessive interests associated with high-functioning autism and the stereotyped behaviours and repetitive sensory stimulation characteristic of more severe cases. However, even if restricted interests can be understood as expressions of systemising abilities, it is not clear how repetitive and stereotyped behaviours can be seen in this way. Hence, it is hard to see how all such behaviours can be understood as expressions of a single systemising ability. Therefore the theory provides no clear specification of any *unifying* psychological deficit. Moreover, the supposition that autism reflects characteristics of the 'extreme male brain' is controversial and has been subject to criticism from various sources (e.g. Levy 2004).

Another recent theory proposes that autism is characterised by a deficit in social motivation (Chevallier *et al.* 2012), differing from other theories by focusing less on cognitive deficits. As such, this characterisation is reminiscent of Kanner's original notion of 'autistic aloneness'. However, it is not clear whether a social motivation deficit can account adequately for all subtypes of autism,

including those individuals who do seek some social contact. Also, it does not obviously discriminate autism from other conditions (e.g. schizophrenia) that involve social deficits. Moreover, this theory, like previous ones, does not suggest any clear explanation of RRBIs.

So far, no psychological theory that has been proposed has been able to account for all the symptoms of autism. The failure of such theories should probably generate little surprise, in view of the regular changes made to the diagnostic criteria for autism over the years and particularly the widening of classical autism into the autistic spectrum from the 1980s onwards. Any successful theory would have a great deal of explanatory work to do.

One might ask why there should be a need to construct a psychological theory, if we already had a clear neurological or genetic explanation of autism. If, for example, we had already identified a specific neurological abnormality in most of those people with autism and absent from most of those without it, we could conclude that this was a primary cause of the autistic features, without needing in addition some fundamental psychological explanation. However, despite a massive amount of international research over many years, no consistent neurological pattern underlying all (or even most) cases of autism, nor any specific genetic defect to account for the condition, has been found. There may of course be a scientific breakthrough in the future, but there is now increasing belief amongst autism experts that the prospects for a single neurological or genetic explanation of autism are slim, as are the prospects for a clear and unifying psychological account (e.g. Lord and Jones 2012; Rutter 2013).

AUTISM AS A 'NATURAL KIND'?

The foregoing discussion has examined the most recent and prominent attempts to say what kind of 'thing' autism is. The history of its changing definition and diagnostic criteria must lead one to ask whether any stable and enduring definition of autism is possible. This doubt is reinforced by the inability of the psychological theories so far proposed to provide a unifying and parsimonious account of the supposed underlying deficit in autism. Furthermore, the lack of any neurological or genetic explanation raises the question of whether the concept of 'autism' names any distinct kind of disease or disability entity at all. In other words, when somebody receives a diagnosis of autism, what exactly is it that he or she has actually got? Is there a 'natural kind' of disorder, a specific disease entity, which everyone with the diagnosis clearly shares?

Natural kinds in science

Progress in many areas of science depends upon the identification of categories, or kinds, of things that are presumed to exist in nature. The successful identification of such kinds enables the relevant phenomena to be organised into meaningful schemes of classification. Natural kinds can provide the basis for explanations of salient phenomena and support reliable predictions about future phenomena in which the kinds may feature. These kinds are classes of objects, individuals or entities, which share some important common essence or underlying structure which can account for their explanatory power. The paradigmatic examples of natural kinds are the chemical elements, such as sodium and chlorine. Many of the chemical properties of the individual elements are explicable in terms of their atomic number and structure. Biological species are also frequently cited as examples of natural kinds.

Many physical diseases can be regarded as natural kinds (Dragulinescu 2010). One example is malaria, which is defined by the presence in the patient's body of the malaria parasite. Knowing that the patient is suffering from this implies a clear explanation for the infection – that is, that a certain type of mosquito bit the patient. The likely course of the disease can also be predicted and a specific treatment prescribed. More complex diseases can similarly be regarded as natural kinds. For example, Graves disease is a complex autoimmune disease with various characteristic symptoms, not all of which will necessarily be displayed by the individual patient. These include enlargement of the thyroid gland (goitre), protruded eyes (exophthalmia), weight loss and tiredness. The diagnosis depends on identifying specific signs such as the presence of thyroid receptor antibodies in the blood and raised levels of thyroxine. These hormonal changes produce various biochemical effects that generate the symptoms of the disease, although the manifestation of particular symptoms also depends on external variables (e.g. a history of smoking) and internal variables (e.g. genetic predispositions). Hence the identification of biochemical signs is crucial for the ability to support important predictions about the course and effects of the disease.

Even complex diseases such as Graves disease can be compared to chemical kinds regarding their capacity to generate predictions about causal processes and co-occurrence of properties in their respective scientific domains, these being key criteria for attributing natural kind status. Graves disease and sodium are both natural kinds due to their capacity to reflect relevant causal structures in the world (Dragulinescu 2010). Hence, in the field of general medicine, it is entirely reasonable to regard malaria and Graves disease as distinct disease entities, since these kinds fulfil our explanatory requirements very well. However, if a putative kind of disorder fails to contribute much to our scientific understanding, there can be little reason to treat it as representing any substantive disease entity.

Mental disorders as natural kinds

There is much debate over whether mental disorders can constitute natural kinds. Some writers argue that some mental disorders may be natural kinds, although few examples of disorders are suggested which might actually fit this conception. The most usual examples offered are Alzheimer's disease and Huntington's disease. Both of these have clear and identifiable biological underpinnings – general neurological deterioration in the first case and a genetic abnormality in the second. Hence it can be argued that they are natural kinds in the same way as physical diseases generally. However, most mental disorders have no such identifiable biological signs and diagnoses are based entirely upon descriptions of symptoms given by the patients and their relatives and close associates. There is thus no independent check on the validity of the diagnoses given.

Much of the debate in this area revolves around the particular conception of natural kind, which is assumed to be applicable. There is general agreement that mental disorders, other than those with identifiable biological causes, are not natural kinds in the sense of being characterised by a defining common essence as in the case of the chemical elements, or many physical diseases (e.g. Cooper 2007; Haslam 2014; Zachar 2014). Those who do argue that they may be natural kinds (e.g. Cooper 2007) base their arguments on a more liberal understanding of natural kinds, such that members of a kind may simply cluster together on the basis of loose resemblances rather than any shared essential property. Others (e.g. Haslam 2014) argue that such a liberal conception is too loose to constitute a meaningful natural kind – that is, that it cannot adequately function either as an explanatory concept or as one able to support reliable predictions. In order to function in these ways, any cluster of varied properties would need to be generated by some kind of shared underlying causal mechanism, such as a genetic mutation or a specific brain abnormality. This does seem to be the case for many physical diseases, but there is little evidence that most mental disorders can be understood as manifestations of any distinct underlying essence. Whilst it is frequently asserted that mental disorders are really brain diseases (e.g. Andreasen 1997), this is no more than an assumption or an aspiration with currently limited empirical support. Unless and until substantial empirical evidence is provided to the contrary, this seems also the case for autism.

The status of autism

The philosopher Ian Hacking (1995) has argued that mental disorders are better viewed as 'human kinds' rather than natural kinds, due to what he calls a 'looping effect'. This effect, he argues, is operative when someone is diagnosed with a psychiatric disorder, such that the individual's awareness of the diagnosis alters their behaviour in diverse ways – for example, behaving in ways that further

reinforce the diagnosis. This can also operate at the socio-cultural level, where the creation of the diagnostic category has important implications for some social groups, who then work in various ways to modify and shape the category in ways that may seem socially desirable. Although there is some debate about whether human kinds are fundamentally distinct from natural kinds, it does seem likely that the looping effect is a significant phenomenon, which does not apply to other natural kinds. This is evident in the case of autism. Thus Hacking describes autism as:

> ...an amazing story of the making and molding of a new classification hand-in-hand with the making and molding of the people who fall under the classification. There is an extraordinary back-and-forth looping effect between the category of autism and autistic people. (Hacking 2015, p.329)

Hacking further describes how activists and advocacy organisations have had a major influence in shaping the category compared with the relatively lesser role played by science, despite the massive amount of research conducted over the past forty years into the nature of autism. What this suggests is that autism as a concept has been in continual flux. People with autism, and especially their parents, have sought to construct and shape a condition that gives them a distinctive way of being a person and determining their identity. This does not fit easily with the usual conception of natural kinds as located firmly within a particular scientific framework.

Nevertheless, to the extent that there has been a dominant underlying assumption behind autism research, it is that the condition is a natural kind of some sort, the essence of which remains to be elucidated. Associated with this is the belief that autism is biological in origin, despite the absence of any consistent biological markers for the condition. The psychiatrist and philosopher Berend Verhoeff describes this research as follows:

> It is guided and regulated by the depiction of autism as a bona fide scientific and physical object that can be discovered and identified with systematic biomedical and neuroscientific investigation. Autism is imagined to exist as an objective entity independent of its embodiment in particular individuals. (Verhoeff 2012, p.411)

He goes on to criticise this natural kind approach to autism research in respect of two issues: first, the pervasive heterogeneity of the condition; and second, the socio-historical background against which autism has been defined as a disease entity. Regarding the latter, Verhoeff argues that the concept of autism is inseparable from prevailing norms of the kinds of behaviour regarded as acceptable or unacceptable within contemporary society. Whilst it is beyond the

scope of this chapter to discuss this in more detail, it is undoubtedly a relevant and generally neglected issue.

I have focused here on the first issue, the heterogeneity of autism. This heterogeneity is evident in the very large diversity of characteristics that can count as autistic traits and correspondingly in the large range of individuals who receive the diagnosis. It is further reinforced by the vagueness of the boundary around the concept of autism and the periodically shifting diagnostic criteria. Moreover, the lack of any broadly agreed theory about a common underlying deficit, coupled with the failure to find any neurological or genetic explanation for the condition, must raise doubts about whether the term 'autism' actually refers to any stable and unique entity at all. The history of changes in the conception of autism shows that it has not yet achieved the level of stability in its application necessary to ground clear explanations for the presumed autistic traits in those diagnosed, and there is little reason to suppose that this will change following the publication of DSM-5. Given this lack of stability, along with the limited explanatory and predictive power of the concept, it is difficult to conceive of autism as a meaningful natural kind, in the way that one can readily do for many physical diseases. There is no reason to believe that everyone with an autism diagnosis suffers from one unique and identifiable disease or disability.

CONCLUSION

The view that there is no one single abnormality underlying autism is not new – indeed it now *appears* to be widely accepted. This was apparently recognised more than forty years ago by Lorna and John Wing (1971) and has been increasingly acknowledged by a range of academics more recently (e.g. Happé and Ronald 2008; Lord and Jones 2012; Rutter 2013). Nevertheless, despite this now customary acknowledgement, the custom seems to be, in Hamlet's words, 'more honour'd in the breach than the observance'. So the search for a unifying theory of autism, what Verhoeff (2012) calls 'the tenacious search for autism's essence', has continued to the present day. Yet if the idea of the fractionable autism triad is to be taken seriously, it is difficult to see how autism can hold together as a clear and coherent category.

Autism is still frequently conceived as a natural kind with a distinct essence, something for which specialist assessment teams and support services are needed. Thus Francesca Happé, talking about the elements of the triad, says: 'When you get the particular mix that is autism all together, you get something that qualitatively looks different so that that really is autism' (Happé 2014, p.764). It is scarcely surprising if this is reflected in the common view of autism, a view that professionals generally do much to encourage. Indeed, one of the most striking experiences for any professional in an autism diagnostic service, at least

for those who choose to reflect on it, is the enormous *power* one exercises over the individual being assessed. In the short term, the assessment team has the power to determine whether a child or young person can receive support services, in schools or the community, for those given the autism label by a recognised diagnostic service. More generally, the professionals concerned have the power to affect how individuals are perceived in the long term, both by others and by themselves.

There has been little systematic investigation into the personal consequences of the diagnosis on those concerned – we have very little understanding of the extent of any associated stigma. However, personal accounts of the effects of an ASD diagnosis are described in the book *The Myth of Autism* (Timimi *et al.* 2011) by two of its co-authors, which go some way to countering any facile claim that there is no stigmatising effect. The natural kind approach to conceptualising mental disorders as fundamentally biological deficiencies is likely to reinforce the perception of those afflicted as being *essentially* different and abnormal, and hence to encourage stigma (Haslam 2014). There is no obvious reason why autism should be any different in this respect.

To the question of whether everyone with an autism diagnosis has the same underlying disorder, the answer surely is that there is no good reason to think so. 'Autism' does not represent a meaningful natural kind. At best, it is an umbrella term covering a wide range of socio-cognitive impairments, abnormalities or differences, some of which appear as 'disorders' only when set against a socio-cultural background which extols certain personal qualities over others (Timimi *et al.* 2011; Verhoeff 2012). When someone is diagnosed as 'autistic' it is difficult to attach any precise meaning to this. Sometimes it seems to mean little more than that the individual concerned is socially awkward. So the question remains: when someone receives this diagnosis, *what* in actuality have they been diagnosed *with*?

REFERENCES

American Psychiatric Association (APA) (1980) *Diagnostic and Statistical Manual of Mental Disorders, Third Edition (DSM-III).* Washington, DC: APA.

American Psychiatric Association (APA) (1987) *Diagnostic and Statistical Manual of Mental Disorders, Third Edition Revised (DSM-IIIR).* Washington, DC: APA.

American Psychiatric Association (APA) (1994) *Diagnostic and Statistical Manual of Mental Disorders, Fourth Edition (DSM-IV).* Washington, DC: APA.

American Psychiatric Association (APA) (2013) *Diagnostic and Statistical Manual of Mental Disorders, Fifth Edition (DSM-5).* Washington, DC: APA.

Andreasen, N.C. (1997) 'Linking mind and brain in the study of mental illnesses: a project for a scientific psychopathology.' *Science 275*, 5306, 1586–1593.

Baron-Cohen, S. (2002) 'The extreme male brain theory of autism.' *Trends in Cognitive Sciences 6*, 6, 248–254.

Baron-Cohen, S. (2008) *Autism and Asperger Syndrome: The Facts.* Oxford: Oxford University Press.

Chevallier, C., Kohls, G., Troiani, V., Brodkin, E.S., and Schultz, R.T. (2012) 'The social motivation theory of autism.' *Trends in Cognitive Sciences 16*, 4, 231–239.

Cooper, R. (2007) *Psychiatry and Philosophy of Science.* Durham: Acumen Publishing.

Dragulinescu, S. (2010) 'Diseases as natural kinds.' *Theoretical Medicine and Bioethics 31*, 5, 347–369.

Frith, U. (2003) *Autism: Explaining the Enigma* (Second edition). Oxford: Blackwell.

Hacking, I. (1995) 'The Looping Effects of Human Kinds.' In D. Sperber, D. Premack and A.J. Premack (eds) *Causal Cognition.* Oxford: Oxford University Press.

Hacking, I. (2015) 'On the Ratio of Science to Activism in the Shaping of Autism.' In K.S. Kendler and J. Parnas (eds) *Philosophical Issues in Psychiatry III: The Nature and Sources of Historical Change.* Oxford: Oxford University Press.

Happé, F. (2011) 'Criteria, categories, and continua: autism and related disorders in DSM-5.' *Journal of the American Academy of Child and Adolescent Psychiatry 50*, 6, 540–542.

Happé, F. (2014) 'Interview: A creative, interpersonal, social scientist. (Interviewed by J. Sutton.)' *The Psychologist 27*, 10, 762–765.

Happé, F., and Ronald, A. (2008) 'The "fractionable autism triad": a review of evidence from behavioural, genetic, cognitive and neural research.' *Neuropsychology Review 18*, 4, 287–304.

Happé, F., Ronald, A., and Plomin, R. (2006) 'Time to give up on a single explanation of autism.' *Nature Neuroscience 9*, 10, 1218–1220.

Haslam, N. (2014) 'Natural Kinds in Psychiatry: Conceptually Implausible, Empirically Questionable, and Stigmatizing.' In H. Kincaid and J.A. Sullivan (eds) *Classifying Psychopathology: Mental Kinds and Natural Kinds.* Cambridge, MA: MIT Press.

Kanner, L. (1943) 'Autistic disturbances of affective contact.' *Nervous Child 2*, 217–250.

Lam, K.S.L., Bodfish, J.W., and Piven, J. (2008) 'Evidence for three sub-types of repetitive behaviour in autism that differ in familiality and association with other symptoms.' *Journal of Child Psychology and Psychiatry 49*, 11, 1193–1200.

Levy, N. (2004) 'Book review: Understanding blindness.' *Phenomenology and the Cognitive Sciences 3*, 315–324.

Lord, C., and Jones, R.M. (2012) 'Re-thinking the classification of autism spectrum disorders.' *Journal of Child Psychology and Psychiatry 53*, 5, 490–509.

Mandy, W.P.L., and Skuse, D.H. (2008) 'Research review: What is the association between the social-communication element of autism and repetitive interests, behaviours and activities.' *Journal of Child Psychology and Psychiatry 49*, 8, 795–808.

Rutter, M. (2013) 'Changing concepts and findings on autism.' *Journal of Autism and Developmental Disorders 43*, 8, 1749–1757.

Timimi, S., Gardner, N., and McCabe, B. (2010) *The Myth of Autism.* Basingstoke: Palgrave Macmillan.

Tsai, L.Y., and Ghaziuddin, M. (2014) 'DSM-5 ASD moves forward into the past.' *Journal of Autism and Developmental Disorders 44*, 2, 321–330.

van Krevelen, D.A. (1971) 'Early infantile autism and autistic psychopathy.' *Journal of Autism and Childhood Schizophrenia 1*, 1, 82–86.

Verhoeff, B. (2012) 'What is this thing called autism? A critical analysis of the tenacious search for autism's essence.' *BioSocieties 7*, 4, 410–432.

Verhoeff, B. (2013) 'Autism in flux: a history of the concept from Leo Kanner to DSM-5.' *History of Psychiatry 24*, 4, 442–458.

Wing, L. (1981a) 'Asperger's syndrome: a clinical account.' *Psychological Medicine 11*, 1, 115–129.

Wing, L. (1981b) 'Language, social, and cognitive impairments in autism and severe mental retardation.' *Journal of Autism and Developmental Disorders 11*, 1, 31–44.

Wing, L., and Gould, J. (1979) 'Severe impairments of social interaction and associated abnormalities in children: epidemiology and classification.' *Journal of Autism and Developmental Disorders 9*, 1, 11–29.

Wing, L., and Wing, J. (1971) Multiple impairments in early childhood autism. *Journal of Autism and Childhood Schizophrenia 1*, 3, 256–266.

Wing, L., Gould, J., and Gillberg, C. (2011) 'Autism spectrum disorders in the DSM-V: better or worse than the DSM-IV?' *Research in Developmental Disabilities 32*, 2, 768–773.

World Health Organisation (1992) *The ICD-10 Classification of Mental and Behavioural Disorders. Clinical Descriptions and Diagnostic Guidelines.* Geneva: WHO.

Zachar, P. (2014) 'Beyond Natural Kinds: Towards a "Relevant" "Scientific" Taxonomy in Psychiatry.' In H. Kincaid and J.A. Sullivan (eds) *Classifying Psychopathology: Mental Kinds and Natural Kinds.* Cambridge, MA: MIT Press.

CHAPTER 4

THE BIOPOLITICS OF AUTISM IN BRAZIL

Francisco Ortega, Rafaela Zorzanelli and Clarice Rios

INTRODUCTION

This chapter sketches preliminary results from ongoing ethnographic and qualitative research around the biopolitics of autism in Brazil. Autism constitutes a psychiatric category exposed to public negotiation by medical and non-medical actors. The ontological status of autism – a 'problematic category' (Rosenberg 2006) – is being disputed.

The chapter will focus on three different instances of public negotiation of the category of autism in Brazil. First, we will examine the 'autism wars' that transpired within mental health policies and services after the enactment of the 'Law creating policies for protecting the rights of the person with an autistic spectrum disorder' in December 2012. Recent controversies around the nosological status of autism – whether autism is a mental disorder or an intellectual disability – and the mental health policies for treating individuals diagnosed with autism have polarised the Brazilian mental health community. Psychiatrists and psychologists working in public mental health services, the Psychosocial Care Centres (CAPS), oppose the idea of special centres for the treatment of autism and their emphasis on behavioural therapies. Second, we will explore representations of autism in a sample taken from printed media in Brazil between 2000 and 2012. Our analysis focuses on how media narratives construct certain perceptions about autism in Brazil. The analysed narratives reflect culturally constructed beliefs not just about the autistic person and their family, but also about expectations regarding the role of the state, science, and education. Finally, we will present the results of qualitative research with Brazilian online social networks examining the public construction of the diagnosis of autism. The main issues addressed are: causes of autism, treatments, forms of health and political activism, and inclusion in education.

THE AUTISM WARS IN BRAZIL

Background: The Brazilian Psychiatric Reform

The Brazilian health care system was organised after the 1988 Constitution was enacted. The Constitution states that health is a social right and that the state has a duty to provide health services. Since the creation of the National Health System (SUS) in 1990, there have been steady and continuous efforts towards universal health coverage and care. The SUS system is organised regionally, with a decentralised network of health services formed by a complex set of public, private and philanthropic providers, under coordinated management at each level of government and with strong community participation (Lobato and Burlandy 2000; Souza 2002).

In spite of the advances in the last two decades, there are several challenges to consolidating SUS as a universal public system that can provide quality services to the entire Brazilian population. These difficulties include: attaining universal coverage and proliferation of private health care plans among middle and upper classes; insufficiency and inadequacy of health care financing; challenges pertaining to the health care model, which was designed for acute diseases and neglects chronic conditions; an inadequacy of human resources, as well as the challenge of social participation (Biehl 2005; CONASS 2006). SUS mental health policies have been shaped by the Brazilian psychiatric movement 'Reform', which in turn was inspired by the Italian democratic-psychiatry movement led by Franco Basaglia in Trieste and the Lacanian-inspired institutional psychotherapy program of La Borde in France (Barros 1994; Passos 2009). In Brazil, a faction of mental health professionals and relatives of patients with mental illnesses started this movement in the early 1970s. Brazilian mental health workers, together with trade unions and left-wing politicians, advanced the so-called 'anti-asylum struggle' (*luta anti-manicomial*) and criticised the psychiatry establishment's collaboration with the dictatorship. This movement developed within the context of the country's redemocratisation and the social political mobilisation of that time (Amarante 1995; Delgado 1992: Tenório 2002).

Following guidelines set up by the Caracas Declaration (1990), in recent decades psychiatric care in Brazil has moved from a hospital-oriented system to primary health care, promoting alternative community-centred treatment models. In 2001, the Psychiatric Reform Law (Federal Law 10.216) was approved, which guards the protection and rights of those with mental disorders and redirects the model of care in mental health (Csillag 2001). The Brazilian Mental Health Policy originates from this law. It encourages the programmed reduction of admission to psychiatric wards for extended periods of time, promoting the idea that psychiatric admission, when necessary, should take place in general hospitals and should last for only short periods of time. Apart from that, it promotes the

de-institutionalisation of patients who have been admitted for long periods of time in psychiatric wards and actions that advance psychosocial insertion through work, culture and leisure (Ministério da Saúde 2004).

The Psychosocial Care Centres (*Centros de Atenção Psicossocial* – CAPS) are specialised mental health services that provide outpatient care or partial hospitalisation as day or night treatment. The CAPS system has become the basis of the Brazilian Psychiatric Reform and mental health care should be centralised at CAPS level. CAPS are responsible for treating severe mental disorders and if possible averting in-patient admissions (psychiatric hospitals or psychiatric wards in general hospitals) as well as for articulating the link with primary care units to coordinate psychiatric care in a defined catchment area (Mateus *et al.* 2008; WHO-AIMS 2007).

The CAPS system opposes framing mental health policies according to specific diseases and organising specialised services for different diagnoses. Therefore, the notion of a 'citizen burdened by mental suffering' should replace different psychiatric labels, regardless of whether the individuals are labelled schizophrenic, autistic, or alcoholic. At CAPS, writes anthropologist Joao Biehl, 'questions concerning the true nature of psychosis and the best medical way to treat it were displaced by the problem of how the individual was culturally recognised as psychotic' (Biehl 2005, pp.134–135). The therapeutic action should follow the 'primacy of the ethical' and promote the patient's unique experiences and his position as a moral subject (Biehl 2005; Goldberg 1994).

Autism at CAPS

Autism is one among other forms of 'mental suffering' that the multidisciplinary team professionals at these Centres (CAPS) seek to assist. Before the Psychiatric Reform and the creation of the CAPS network, the destiny of many children with autism was institutionalisation in psychiatric wards. Nowadays, institutionalisation should only be used in extreme cases. On the other hand, long before the creation of the Psychosocial Care Centres for children and adolescents (CAPSi) (Ministério da Saúde 2002) there were also organisations formed by civil society that sought to provide services and information to parents about autism and intellectual disabilities in general. These organisations range from philanthropic institutions to parent advocacy and support groups. They offer a scope of services, from information and support for parents to medical and educational services (Block and Cavalcante 2014; Cavalcante 2003).

The CAPSi are strategic elements of mental public health attention for children and adolescents suffering from persistent and severe mental disorders. They are organised in a network that extends beyond the health field and interacts with community resources in order to promote the social inclusion of

children and adolescents. The interdisciplinary team at CAPSi may also count on the partnership of families, society, schools, and other sectors. Diagnoses in CAPSi are based on the principle of the 'amplified clinic' (*clinica ampliada*), which conceives them as an ongoing process. Diagnoses should be made and re-evaluated throughout the evaluation and treatment process and the diverse elements of the care strategy (psychotherapy, rehabilitation, medication) should always focus on the singularity of the child, their history, family, relationships and everyday life (Couto 2004, 2012; Couto, Duarte and Delgado 2008).

However, several parent associations disagree with the CAPSi principle of not framing services according to specific diagnoses. They demand specific services for autistic children involving multidisciplinary teams. Parents also want their opinions to be considered not just as objects of therapeutic interventions but in terms of their role as political actors. Parents' associations have been traditionally neglected in CAPSi (Nunes 2014). Additionally, parents stress the need to acknowledge the clinical-theoretical diversity in autism treatments. Despite claims of multidisciplinarity, several CAPSi – particularly in the State of Rio de Janeiro, where our fieldwork was conducted – have a psychoanalytic orientation and promote a discourse of self-sufficiency and exclusivity of psychoanalytic treatment for autistic children, especially with Lacanian psychoanalysis. Describing the work conducted at a CAPSi in Rio de Janeiro, Pinto self-confidently writes:

> Given its ethical, theoretical and methodological commitments, psychoanalysis represents the clinic we believe is the best to work with such severe patients at CAPSi. To believe that impasses should be approached from the clinic already constitutes a step forward and to believe that the clinic is the psychoanalytic clinic seems to be a key step in CAPSi. (Pinto 2005, p.22)

Autism as disability

In Brazil, autism has historically been classified as a mental disorder and just recently has been included in the category of 'disability'. In recent years a movement of families and self-advocates, with the support and collaboration of specialists, has sought to expand policy definitions of disability to provide autistics with the civil rights and protections available to 'disability' groups (Block and Cavalcante 2014). Several parent advocacy organisations were formed in the 1980s. The 'Friends of Autistics Association' (*Associação dos Amigos do Autista* – AMA) was the first to be established in Sao Paulo. The end of the Military Regime took place alongside the process of de-institutionalising psychiatric patients. The lack of effective community-based services to accommodate those patients provoked the criticism of several parents, and AMA's mission was to make up for this lack of community-based services for autistic children. By the turn of the millennium

several organisations had emerged, including 'Brazilian Autism Association' (*Associação Brasileira de Autismo* – ABRA), 'Brazilian Association for Action for the Rights of People with Autism' (*Associação Brasileira para Ação por Direitos das Pessoas com Autismo* – ABRAÇA), 'Autism and Reality' (*Autismo & Realidade*), 'Association in Defence of Autism' (*Associação em Defesa de Autismo* – ADEFA), 'Association of Parents of Autistics and the Mentally-Disabled' (*Associação de Pais de Autistas e Deficientes Mentais* – APADEM), and 'Blue World' (*Mundo Azul*), to address the lack of appropriate services for autistic children and adults and to press the government to establish effective policies for that neglected population (Block and Cavalcante 2014; Cavalcante 2003; Mello, Dias and Andrade 2013; Nunes 2014).

The pressure exerted by parent associations led to the enactment of the law creating policies for protecting the rights of the person with an autism spectrum disorder in December 2012 (Law 12.764, 27 December 2012 – 'Autism Law'). Before that, in 2008, Brazil had ratified the United Nations Convention on the Rights of Persons with Disabilities. The second article of the law determines that 'the person with an autism spectrum disorder is considered as a person with disability for all legal purposes'. The law granted full assistance for the health needs of persons diagnosed with autism spectrum disorders, including early diagnosis, multi-professional assistance, and access to pharmaceuticals and nutrients. According to the law, the main rights of persons with autism spectrum disorders are the rights to a dignified life, physical and moral integrity, free development of personality, security and leisure, protection against any form of abuse and oppression, education, housing, work and social inclusion.

Alongside these developments leading to the transformation of autism into a disability category, there have been several critiques of psychoanalytic treatment of autism in Brazilian public services. In September 2012, the São Paulo State's health department opened a public bidding for institutions working with autism. The bidding required psychologists to be working exclusively with behavioural therapies. A few weeks later, the same health department ended its long-term collaboration with/funding of the psychoanalytically-oriented 'Reference Centre for Childhood and Adolescence' (*Centro de Referência da Infância e Adolescência* – CRIA), which was associated with the Federal University of Sao Paulo. The rationale was that 'psychoanalysis-based services do not possess proved efficacy'.

After huge protest the centre was reopened. As a reaction to what they called 'a series of actions aiming to disqualify psychoanalytic approaches to treat persons with autism' more than 300 members from 95 psychoanalytic associations, NGOs and universities created the 'Psychoanalysis, Autism and Public Health Movement'.[1] The movement's goal is to 'promote and affirm the place of psychoanalytic practices and their ethical position against the current

1 See http://psicanaliseautismoesaudepublica.wordpress.com.

landscape of public policies aimed at the treatment of people with autism and their families'. Luciano Elia, a Lacanian psychoanalyst and professor of psychology at the State University of Rio de Janeiro, believes that 'attacks against psychoanalysis are exclusive and frontal, because so far only psychoanalysis has proved to be effective, in the clinical-institutional practice, in making important developments in autism care and research'. He labels behavioural psychologists as 'pseudoscientists', who have success not only with the families of autistic individuals but with the 'managers of the technocratic right wing and of compulsory institutionalisation', and with the middle classes that 'crave for a hygienist and fascistoid social order' (Elia 2013).

Following the enactment of the Autism Law in December 2012, the Ministry of Health's mental health department prepared a document for public consultation titled 'Guidelines for treatment of persons with autistic spectrum disorders and their families in the psychosocial care network of the National Health System' (*Linha de Cuidado para a atencão a pessoas com transtorno do espectro do autismo e suas famílias na rede de atencão psicossocial do Sistema Único de Saúde*) (Ministério da Saúde 2013a) to be launched on 2 April 2013 (Autism Awareness Day). The guidelines acknowledge all epistemological and etiological conceptions, from psychoanalytic to cognitive and neurological. They assume that the diagnostic process will be undertaken by a multidisciplinary team committed to achieving a 'unique therapeutic project' (*projeto terapêutico singular*) considering specificities and needs of each case according to their difficulties and potentialities. Further, the document presents several 'technologies of care' (*tecnologias de cuidado*), from psychoanalytic-based clinical treatment and Applied Behavioural Analysis (ABA) to medication, since, as they remark, 'there is no single approach to be privileged in the treatment of persons with ASD. It is recommended that the choice among the different existing approaches be made according to the singularity of each case' (Ministério da Saúde 2013a).

On the same day, the Health Ministry also launched the 'Care Guidelines for the Rehabilitation of the Person with Autism Spectrum Disorder' (*Diretrizes de Atençao à Reabilitação da Pessoa com Transtornos do Espectro do Autismo*), formulated by the Ministry's 'Department for Persons with Disabilities' (*Secretaria da Pessoa com deficiencia*) (Ministério da Saúde 2013b). In this document autism is defined as a neuropsychiatric disorder. The focus lies on early diagnosis and though the idea of an individualised therapeutic project is explicitly mentioned, there is no reference to any form of treatment/therapeutics. Critics say that the latter document focuses exclusively on rehabilitation and therefore promotes only behavioural therapies and rejects psychoanalysis. As a consequence the singularity and subjectivity of persons with autism are disregarded. Moreover, it concentrates treatment of individuals with autism in specialised rehabilitation centres with limited connection to other sectors (especially educational). It therefore goes

against the SUS principle of intersectorality (involving partnerships with social assistance and education programs). Additionally, the document was not submitted for public consultation.

Both guidelines were expected to be presented on 2 April 2013 (Autism Awareness Day). However, only the document elaborated by the department for persons with disabilities was released on that date. This provoked an enormous uproar among psychoanalysts and other professionals working in CAPS. Cristina Ventura, Psychoanalyst and Adviser at the Ministry of Health, writes on an email discussion group:[2]

> The manoeuvre of replacing a document...that was available for public consultation for more than one month with another which nobody knows how it was made and that wasn't made available to public consultation, is antidemocratic and authoritarian... More than a historic setback – the reduction of mental problems in children and adolescents to the category of disability characterised the creation of the Brazilian republic, and set the tone during eight decades of the 20th century. We all very well know the harmful consequences of this reduction.

Following these developments, the above-mentioned Psychoanalysis, Autism and Public Health Movement launched a Manifesto at the first National Conference of CAPSi held at the Institute for Social Medicine of the State University of Rio de Janeiro in April 2013. The first sentence of the Manifesto states:

> Faced with the recent attempts to exclude psychoanalytical practices from the public policies to treat persons with autism, Mental health professionals associated with the Psychoanalysis, Autism and Public Health Movement come public to assert their action principles and their ethical position in the assistance of persons with autism and their families. (Manifest 2013)

The Manifesto's goals include disseminating and asserting the place of psychoanalytical practices and their ethical position in the treatment of persons with ASD and their families; supporting plurality, diversity, and scientific and methodological debate about different approaches to treat autism and the different diagnostic criteria; accompanying and accommodating families of autistic individuals considered to be fundamental partners in the treatment; fully including children with autism in regular schools with the support of an interdisciplinary and intersectoral network; and opposing the current exaggerated medicalisation of childhood and adolescence.

2 Email discussion group *Escola de Saúde Mental do Rio de Janeiro* (ESAM): ESAM_Rio_Forum@yahoogrupos.com.br.

The last chapter of this ongoing struggle was settled in April 2014 when the 'National Council for the Rights of Persons with Disabilities' (*Conselho Nacional dos Direitos da Pessoa com Deficiência* – CONADE) presented the regulatory decree for the Law 12.764 – the 'Autism Law', which foresaw in its third article the 'Qualification and Strengthening of the Psychosocial Care Network for the Treatment of Persons with Autism Spectrum Disorder'.[3] The possibility that autistic individuals had to be treated in CAPS was seen as a betrayal by several parent associations (in fact, the issue divided the parent associations). A petition against that decree claims that to treat autism in CAPS represents 'the worst that could be offered to our children', because CAPS 'is not the place for our autistics'. CAPS were instituted to 'treat people with severe mental disorders such as schizophrenia, and crack, alcohol, licit and illicit drugs addicts'. And to treat autistic individuals in CAPS would represent a '50-year setback' in the rights of individuals with ASD. The petition highlights that those who signed it don't 'have prejudices', nor are they 'segregating', since they 'are segregated everyday'.[4]

Autism activists such as Berenice Piana, who is the mother of an autistic and gives Law 12.764 its name, states that CAPS are unable to meet the specific needs of autistic individuals. According to her, the disorder is defined as a multiple and complex disability, and the treatment of autism, due to the complexity of its spectrum, requires specific therapies and skilled professionals and therefore could not take place in the same space as assistance to drug addicts and the mentally ill. 'It is not that the autistic is better or worse than the mentally ill, but they are different cases, with different needs', observes Claudia Moraes, coordinator of the Autistic Pride Brazil Movement (MOAB) in Rio de Janeiro (cited in Franco 2014).

This is an ongoing struggle that unfortunately is far from being settled in the immediate future. Psychiatrists and psychologists working in public mental health services are certainly right when they oppose the idea of special centres for the treatment of autism focusing almost exclusively on behavioural therapies. One should keep in mind that while, according to international literature, the current diagnostic criteria for ASD reflect consensus on clinical features of autism, there is still no consensus on an explanatory framework that integrates aetiology, neural structures, cognitive processes, and behaviours (Volkmar *et al.* 2004). In view of this heterogeneous field of research, it has been proposed that autism is best understood as a 'multi-system disorder' (Charman 2006). In other words, and despite many years of research, we still lack a convincing, well-replicated brain-based autism biomarker (Walsh *et al.* 2011). Nor is there consensus about the methodology to be used in clinical interventions (Feinberg and Vacca 2000). Given the lack of consensus regarding autism aetiology and

3 See www.pessoacomdeficiencia.gov.br/app/node/888.

4 See www.peticaopublica.com.br/pview.aspx?pi=BR72114.

clinical interventions, the therapeutic syncretism and plurality proposed by the 'Guidelines for treatment of persons with autistic spectrum disorders and their families in the psychosocial care network of the National Health System', the instruction that no single approach be privileged in the treatment of individuals with ASD, and that the singularity of each case should inform the treatment choice, makes sense. That being said, one should also be aware that, in some regions of Brazil, such as Rio de Janeiro, for many years several CAPS almost exclusively offered (and still offer) psychoanalytical treatment. The adoption of a multidisciplinarity and therapeutic plurality is relatively recent, and although salutary, it follows from the mentioned changes in public policies for mental health and not from a conviction that plurality is best.

On the other hand, the Brazilian psychoanalytic movement's critiques of the reconceptualisation of autism in Brazil as a disability category identify the latter with the 'medical model of disability', and disqualify disability policies as strategies to repair, rehabilitate, and hence to normalise the autistic subject. Still, as we can attest when attending conferences and interviewing its main actors, the Brazilian psychoanalytic movement is largely unaware of the 'social model of disability', which *de facto* underlies Brazilian disability policies. The social model of disability has several convergences with the ideology of the Brazilian psychiatric reform, such as the constitution of the autistic individual as a subject endowed with social, civic and citizenship rights or the emphasis on the social, economic, political and cultural determinants of mental suffering, which in the case of the social model correspond to the disabling barriers experienced by autistic individuals.

So we see how the nosological category of autism is being negotiated within Brazilian mental health polices and services and the subsequent recent emergence of autism wars. Beyond the mental health community and mental health policies, we now turn to other forms of negotiation of the autism label in public media and online social networks.

REPRESENTATIONS OF AUTISM IN BRAZILIAN PRINTED MEDIA

As part of our research on the biopolitics of autism spectrum disorders in Brazil, we examined material published in printed media from 2000 to 2012. The data was collected through a digital search for the terms 'autistic' and 'autism' on the archives of three major newspapers (*Folha de São Paulo, Estado de São Paulo, O Globo*) and one nationwide magazine (*Veja*), resulting in a database of 476 articles. The main goal of this specific part of the research was to understand how autism

was mapped into media narratives, making it visible for a large and lay audience in culturally specific ways. Among other things, we sought to identify the main social arenas in which narratives unfolded, as well as the social actors and the plots that were part of these narratives. By mapping the circumstances and ways in which autism and people with autism participated in media narratives, we sought to identify culturally constructed beliefs, not only about the person with autism and his family, but also about the role of the government and science in dealing with autism.

In the perspective taken here, narratives are not simply representations of reality, but serve to structure human experience and to organise our actions in the cultural contexts in which they take place. As such, media narratives not only shape the controversies that surround autism in Brazil, but also actively contribute to such debates, to the extent that they affect the meaning-making activity on the part of the reader.

Although part of the research involved measuring the frequency with which certain themes, social actors, and other narrative elements showed up in the database, we also sought to establish a criterion of relevance for the different journalistic texts based on some basic features of a narrative. Inspired by the classic article by Ochs and Taylor (1995) on family dinnertime narratives, we paid special attention to 'problem-centred narratives'. These were also the narratives that presented controversies and evoked other related narratives, either in the form of related articles or in the readers' response section of the newspaper. We refer to them as 'trigger-narratives', given the controversial nature of the themes they discuss. Together these articles formed larger narratives that simultaneously shape and express the current challenges and dilemmas of the biopolitics of autism spectrum disorders in Brazil.

An epidemic of increased visibility

As the idea of an autism epidemic has captured the public imagination, the most agreed-upon explanations for this phenomenon relate to social and historical changes rather than biological causations. Vaccine and neurotoxins exposure scares notwithstanding, the most popular explanations for the so-called epidemic relate to changes in the diagnostic criteria and a greater awareness among the public and experts (Eyal *et al.* 2010; Silverman 2012). The news media has certainly been playing an important role in giving visibility to autism, but how exactly is that happening in Brazilian media? According to our findings, autism became an object of increased attention in the printed media in two different and yet interrelated ways. The first, identified through quantitative measurement of some narrative elements, concerns the increased number of published articles that revolve around scientific research on autism, with a special focus on its

neurobiological nature. The second, identified through a qualitative analysis of the above-mentioned 'trigger-narratives', comprises a larger narrative with a culturally specific plot that involves the state, the health and education systems, and the activism of parents of children with autism in Brazil.

The growing visibility of autism in print media can be observed in Figure 4.1, which shows the number of articles published over the 12-year period. And as we can see in Figure 4.2, an increasing number of these articles revolve around the scientific research on autism.

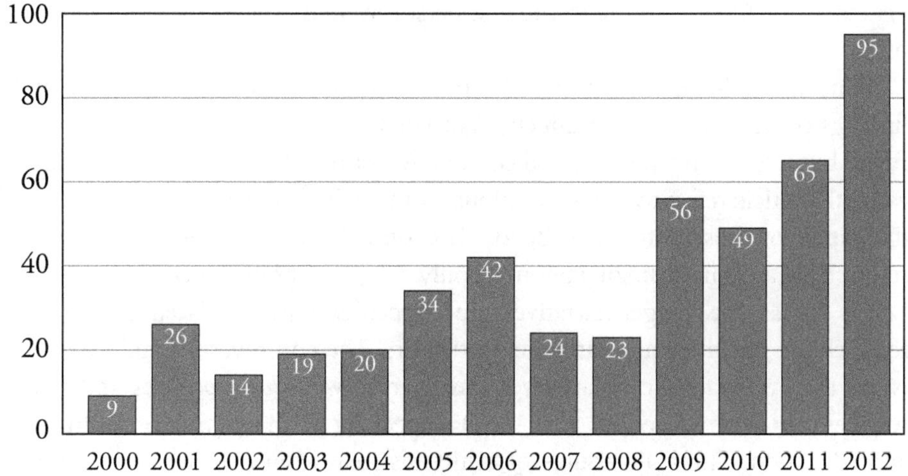

Figure 4.1 Number of articles on autism published in the print media, 2000–2012

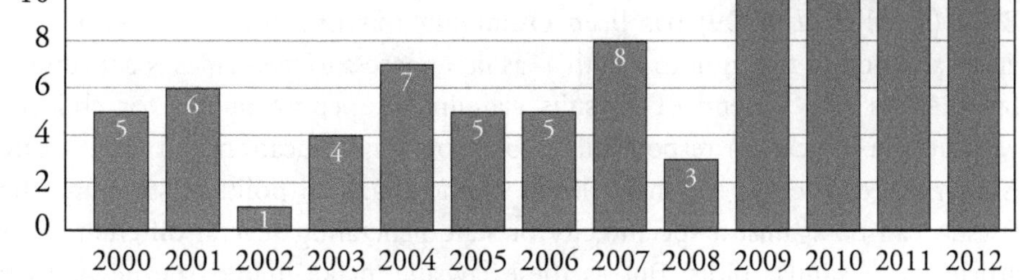

Figure 4.2 Number of articles in the print media with scientific research on autism as the main theme, 2000–2012

Overall, the scientific research referred to in these articles originates from the field of neurosciences. In such cases, autism is depicted as a genetic disorder that affects the brain, but whose aetiology has still not been discovered by science. References to epidemiological data related to autism, diagnosis and treatment usually complement the background information provided. In terms of the social actors who show up in these articles, scientists also lead in terms of frequency – they are present in 41 per cent of the articles in which autism is the main theme or there is some discussion about it, parents and caretakers in 35 per cent, and persons with ASD in 30.1 per cent (although referred to in the third person). Persons with ASD speaking in the first person were present only in 6.1 per cent of the articles.

One interesting finding is that 75.5 per cent of the articles that report scientific findings on autism are either directly translated from foreign media or written in Brazil but refer to the international context. As for the rest, in 18.6 per cent of the cases, the article refers to the international context, but there is some discussion of the impact of those findings in Brazil. The journalistic narratives about scientific research on autism in Brazil amount to only 5.9 per cent of the cases.

As far as the trigger-narratives are concerned, issues related to scientific research are not the main narrative-motivators. The controversies and polemical issues that motivate these narratives usually revolve around policies and public services directed to people with ASD, especially with regard to health care and education. The main source of criticisms stem from the fact that although Brazilian legislation guarantees universal health care and promotes inclusion for children with ASD in regular schools, there is a widely shared perception among parents of children with ASD that these laws are not properly applied. A typical media narrative regarding health care, for example, starts with a story of some lawsuit moved by parents of children with ASD against the state for not delivering the treatments that their children are entitled to.

With the adoption of Brazil's democratic Constitution in 1988, health care became a public right and a duty of the state. Yet the existing health care system has not been able to meet the huge demands in this area, which led a growing number of patients to sue the government for access to proper health care. João Biehl (Biehl *et al.* 2009) has been examining this phenomenon – known as 'judicialisation of the right to health' – as far as access to medicines is concerned, but there is also a trend of lawsuits claiming proper treatments for children with autism. Since the responsibility for providing education and health care is distributed through the many levels of the Brazilian political structure, the lawsuit can be against a specific city or state generating several different news articles with similar plots. But as these lawsuits make it into the news, they become the starting point for a longer narrative that mixes complaints about the insufficiency of health care services in general and the inadequacy of the services

already offered for children with ASD. More precisely, the lawsuits discussed in these articles reinforce the perception that there are no services whatsoever for people with ASD in the public health system. The narrative of insufficiency becomes so dominant in these trigger-narratives that any discussion about the already existing services offered by the government is overshadowed.

Such is the case with a famous series of articles, published on 2006 in *O Globo*. The first article presents the story of a woman who made her living as a maid and did not have a place to leave her autistic son in order to work. With the help of some free legal advice service she finally won a lawsuit against the government of São Paulo, which was then obliged to pay for the boy's treatment at a specialised institution. The legal decision was based on the fact that there was no specialised treatment available for her son in the public health sector. But even after the legal decision, the state was still not paying for the treatment. The article also brought dramatic stories collected through interviews with 30 other autistic people 'with no treatment, whose families were scared and forgotten by the government' (Carvalho 2006). The series of articles that followed brought additional information and opinion from legal experts and representatives from the government. According to a Ministry of Health representative, the treatment offered by the public health sector for autistic people was still insufficient at the time, but not totally non-existent, as the previous articles suggested. He explained, for example, that the treatment of people with autism was a complex issue, and that the government had been trying to deal with that in partnership with the existing non-governmental organisations in this field. A congressman also stressed that the public sector was still trying to find ways to deal with the question. The professionals at the public sector were not totally trained to deal with autism, and that was the reason these organisations were playing this role. On the other hand, explained the congressman, these organisations draw heavily on foreign methodologies and there were still controversies about their use in Brazil. Yet, the main message in this series of articles is clear and stated in the headline of the first article: 'With no treatment, and not covered by the state, young people are held captive at home under the improvised care of their mothers' (Carvalho 2006). No further details on the existing services are provided.

The other major area of controversies generating trigger-narratives is education. The 1988 Constitution also affirmed the universal right to education, guaranteeing in one of its articles specialised educational services for disabled people, preferably in the regular school system. Since then, the legislation and public policies have progressively moved towards including all students with disabilities in the regular school system. In the case of autism specifically, that means that children with autism have the right to be enrolled in regular schools, regardless of the severity of their symptoms. The controversies that make it into the printed media regarding this refer to the obstacles in implementing this

policy. Schools, especially those in the private sector, do not always accept an autistic child's enrolment. In this case, what initially catch the media's attention are the lawsuits moved by parents against these schools. Another major source of media narratives is the lack of a specialised educational support for these students once they are enrolled, especially in public schools. Both controversies are part of a larger debate on the limits of inclusive education and the role of specialised schools in the current scenario. The state is implicated in these narratives either for not enforcing the laws, as in the case of private schools, or not creating the proper structure for making inclusive education a viable option, as in the case of public schools.

These trigger-narratives and the increasing number of articles related to scientific research on autism do not only make autism more visible in the printed media. They also intersect in interesting ways with the larger discussion on health and education strategies for autism in Brazil. They form a narrative of abundance of resources and knowledge located abroad, while aggravating the perception of scarcity of services and expertise in the Brazilian context. They also help to understand how certain perceptions on autism become privileged at the expense of others. For example, we did not find in our database any discussion about the social and cultural elements that affect the experience of people with autism in Brazil, aside from the general argument of social deprivation and lack of assistance. The emphasis on the neurobiological aspects of autism and on foreign research and treatment strategies helps to reinforce the perception that there is already a well-established 'specialised' and scientific way to deal with autism with the majority of Brazilians lacking the resources to access it. In other words, depicted solely as a neurobiological disorder, autism becomes a monolithic entity in media representations, frequently followed by critical discussions around public policies for autism in Brazil. Variation in its manifestation, on the other hand, is strongly associated with social inequality and lack of access to services and information.

THE CONSTRUCTION OF AUTISM DIAGNOSIS IN A BRAZILIAN VIRTUAL COMMUNITY

At this point, we have already provided an overview of the political disputes surrounding autism's ontological status and how it should be addressed in Brazilian public health care facilities, as well as having presented our broad research of printed media stories on the theme. We must now turn to a third point in order to complete this overview of autism in Brazil, namely, its presence in virtual social networks. The internet has become a salient space for personality development for persons with autism (Blume 1997; Kenway 2009) and an important number of empirical studies have been done on the subject in cyberspace (Cascio 2014; Clarke and van Amerom 2007; Davidson 2008; Ortega *et al.* 2013).

Broadly speaking, there are several qualitative researches and sources through which information on the subject has been obtained, such as autistics' autobiographies and accounts by parents, family members and health care professionals (Ariel and Naseef 2006; Chamak, Bonniau and Jaunay 2008; Davidson 2008; Hacking 2009; Osteen 2008). Other ethnographic studies examine autistic individuals' identity construction (Bagatell 2007; Bertilsdotter Rosqvist, Brownlow and O'Dell 2013; Ochs and Solomon 2010). The set of subjects addressed in these investigations encompasses subjects such as parents' and patients' understanding of the autistic condition; perceptual *differences* and their implications for the autistic individual; emotion expression and management, particularities of sexuality and romantic relationships between autistic persons; and the role played by the internet and new communication technologies in the interaction between autistics.

The research in virtual communities is part of this effort to study the construction of the autism diagnosis through the opinions of a Brazilian virtual social network, taking into account information which enabled us to evaluate how the autism diagnosis was understood, evaluated, managed and debated (Baker 2011; Eyal *et al.* 2010; Ortega 2009).

Method

The research targeted users of virtual social networks, specifically Orkut, which at the time of data collection was the most popular social network in Brazil. Created in 2004, Orkut was terminated in 2014 due to its obsolescence in the face of newer networks, such as Facebook, Twitter and Tumblr. Nonetheless, during the data collection period, Orkut was the most used social network in Brazil. Until December 2011, it had over 30 million users worldwide, most of whom lived in Brazil. In Orkut, groups called 'communities' were formed based on affinities. In communities, users created 'topics' (discussion forums) centred on themes they themselves posted.

The study's method involved collecting topics and posts in Orkut communities connected to autism. We searched for 'autism' in the system's interface and selected eight of the first 20 occurrences. We used instruments in order to collect specific data about the communities, for example community 'moderator', community description and number of members. We cut and pasted posts within topics that were previously selected as pertinent to our sample from within each pre-selected community. Only topics that fell completely outside the theme (such as sales of weight loss products or advertisements for erotic products) were excluded from the total. We collected a total of 530 posts from 190 topics in eight communities.

The eight communities were selected from among the first 20 results for a search for 'autism'. Selection was based on number of users: the communities

with the largest numbers were included. Information was collected between September 2009 and December 2010 and involved communities whose data were public. This means we did not include communities that had been closed by the moderators. At a later time, we used content analysis in order to tabulate the main themes present in the posts. This analysis was carried out on the 530 posts, which were representative of all selected communities.

Results

We cannot say that our community sample reflects the general dynamics of discussions on autism in Orkut, but we can point to trends in the results, based on the most frequent themes present in the selected communities.

The most frequent thematic categories included: stigma; explanations for autism (genetics, brain, heavy metals, vaccines, and nutrition among others); diverse therapies such as Applied Behaviour Analysis (ABA), Treatment and Education of Autistic and Related Communication Handicapped Children (TEACCH), Picture Exchange Communication System (PECS); Son-Rise; special education; parents' evaluations of services offered by inclusive schools; calls to fight for autistics' rights.

One of the topics' main functions was the search for contact with others, both for information about the condition and for mutual support (emotional, professional and institutional). Information exchange involved requesting contact with other participants in order to obtain information about the diagnosis, ways of dealing with an autistic person and recommendations of experts.

Parent testimonies were also frequently present. In these testimonies, parents recounted the tortuous path to a diagnosis and shared their demands for health benefits, especially in terms of treatments. The most frequent posters were parents, caregivers or relatives (siblings, aunts or uncles), who shared medical information, research and treatment protocols with which they had had positive or negative experiences.

In the posts, there were references to different types of media where information on autism could be found: printed stories in magazines; films; other Orkut communities; stories broadcast on television; websites and blogs; and YouTube videos (usually videos of participants' autistic children or relatives in everyday situations or performing activities or tasks). In the communities we researched, information is not only divulged, but is itself treated as a product to be sold – courses, manuals, didactic videos and other materials were offered and commercialised.

With regard to health rights, we found calls to fight for health benefits and offers of help in filing lawsuits against government agencies with the goal of acquiring benefits, as well as mobilisation for participating in movements such

as Autistic Pride. Bills for protecting autistic persons were also proposed. This trend is consistent with the international literature, which describes patients' mobilisation for their rights through virtual means, establishing a new type of health activism (Chamak 2008; Epstein 2008; Gillet 2003).

As for therapies, several methods were mentioned, such as TEACCH, Son-Rise, PECS, ABA, and sensory integration. There was also mention of therapies traditionally associated with psychological disorders, such as psychoanalysis and cognitive-behavioural therapy, though they were less present. Users displayed a pragmatic attitude toward therapies: the most endorsed therapies were those with the most immediate results and most geared toward ensuring gains in autonomy (even if minor) for the autistic person. A 'therapy that works', in this context, broadens an autistic person's capacities and enables them to achieve some degree of autonomy (picking up a spoon and feeding themselves, making small sounds to indicate needs, being able to sit in a chair without constantly moving, being cooperative with everyday activities such as baths or meals).

There are two notable lines of problematisation in terms of explanations for the illness. The first is whether or not autism is curable/treatable. The second is the discussion of possible causing agents, such as immunity, ingestion of heavy metals and, above all, vaccines, echoing an international controversy on the subject (Deer 2011; Wakefield *et al.* 1998). Within these discussions, parents' access to information originating in scientific research is worth noting. The social network thus became a means for diffusing medical findings through the rapid sharing of academic articles.

Analytical considerations of the social network findings

The possibility of anonymous and virtual interactions between users alters patients' and/or caregivers' experiences of the illness. Outside the virtual world, that experience is typically private, discussed only with physicians and family members, with no communication, contact or exchange of experiences with others in the same situation. The possibilities brought about by virtual contacts turned patients into co-participants in their diagnoses, prognoses and treatments. Thus, 'virtual communities' that form around autism have become active participants both in disseminating research findings and in directing financial support to some of these studies, often influencing policy formulation and the struggle for rights (Chamak 2008; Orsini and Smith 2010; Ortega 2009; Silverman 2012).

Sources such as blogs, personal pages in social networks and virtual support groups therefore produce knowledge based on each patient's lived experience. This knowledge is managed, exchanged, shared and multiplied through diverse forms of virtual contact, transforming these patients into what Collins and Evans (2002) define as experience-based experts, that is, experts whose knowledge is

based on their everyday experiences, the limitations imposed by these experiences, and the particular ways each of them finds to overcome their difficulties.

The communities are predominantly made up of laypeople, among whom a clear hierarchy is established between, on the one hand, the oldest members, the most active members (those who post most often) and those with greatest experience on the subject, and on the other hand, newcomers or those with the least experience in dealing with an autistic relative. Experience rules, so that participants with the most experiences (with treatments, physicians, solutions for everyday difficulties) to recount and share, are the ones whose opinions are most respected, gaining trust and serving as references for neophyte parents/relatives in the community.

Medical science plays a paradoxical role: while it is the site of hope that the likely cause of autism will be found, it is not the exclusive locus where autism is 'understood and unveiled', allowing for legitimacy of patients' and caregivers' experience-based knowledge constructed on parents' and caregivers' daily actions toward a specific person for whom they care. That experience and shared knowledge becomes a source for theories they develop themselves about the illness and the most adequate treatments. These theories and treatments lie beyond what medical science says about autism and involve any practices that fulfil daily needs, experiences and worldviews of those dealing directly with the illness.

Our data show that patients' online interactions reduce physicians' authority and exclusivity as purveyors of information on autism. A new information economy arises regarding ways of dealing with autism and divergences with the opinions of physicians responsible for the patients often occur. Network users are in search of contact with others who share the experience of being a parent or caregiver of a person with autism. What they largely seek is not medical information, but access to other sources that offer a different type of information: that which only those who share the experience of having an autistic relative can have and understand.

These are only trends to which the data point, in what is still an incipient field of investigation in Brazil. This reveals the need for more research that contributes to understanding the role of virtual social networks in shaping public opinion about autism. This research can also shed light on the nature of the ongoing autism movements and on the new types of relationships developing between patients and/or caregivers and health care professionals.

CONCLUSION

This overview of autism in Brazil does not provide us with any definitive answers about the state of the art of the theme, but it does enable us to indicate trends that

arise from the articulation of the three lines of this broader research. In the first line, we see the emergence of a recent dispute surrounding the ontological status of autism (mental disorder or disability) and the theories/practices that follow from these conceptions. These disputes have ramifications in legal debates, in parents' and guardians' search for benefits and in the demand for more adequate types of care to be made available by the National Health System.

The second line, based on the analysis of stories published by the Brazilian press between 2000 and 2012, shows not only an increased presence of autism in the media, but also that certain perceptions of autism are privileged: stories emphasised medical research and treatments that sell the hope for a well-established scientific treatment for autism and its associated problems. This focus neglects socio-cultural elements that affect not only the experiences of people with autism in Brazil, but also the extent to which a context of privation or lack of assistance defines or limits their capacity to effectively obtain care for their condition.

In the third line of analysis, community posts in the largest virtual network in Brazil showed, above all, a paradoxical situation in terms of the role medicine plays: a clear demand by users (above all, parents and caregivers) for the most recent research on the subject (divulging recent findings from medical science) and an ascension of the layperson as an authority. Here physicians and health care professionals are no longer omnipotent in dealing with persons with autism, with those responsible for caring for these persons having a salient role in diffusing information.

Broadly speaking, what is noticeable in the three lines of analysis is that autism is no longer decided exclusively within the domain of medical science. The debate surrounding the condition is extended to other public spheres, involving activists (parents and caregivers of autistic children), lawyers and virtual social networks. This is the case with *contested illnesses*, that is, clinical conditions that involve physical symptoms and mental suffering for which no demonstrable abnormalities in the organism's tissues and structure are found. Their status and treatment remains, therefore, an open field of debate and dispute. These clinical conditions are immersed within the debate about their legitimacy and medical, social, epistemic and ontological status (Brown, Morello-Frosch and Zavestoski 2011). They generate legal debates, administrative categorisations and legislative manoeuvres; they are therapeutically different and it is difficult to find a solution that isn't case by case; they are interconnected through common co-morbidities and symptoms; they are marked by a search for objectivity and legitimacy through complementary exams and biotechnological instruments. Faced with this context, those who bear these illnesses or their caregivers become activists, mobilising facts in favour of the condition's legitimacy and forming groups through which they share their experiences and fight for rights.

In the absence of lesions or of a biological root and in the face of uncertainty regarding aetiology and the best form of care, how can one fight for social benefits, such as medical leave and disability retirement, when the patient is unable to work or must rely on others for care? All these questions, despite involving medicine, are negotiated outside of the medical arena. For that reason, the means of communication shape social perceptions and systems of belief within which these diagnoses are included and disseminated. The interaction between popular beliefs and media and other forms of disseminating information may influence the public's acceptance of technological innovations, overstate incipient findings from the medical field, highlight benefits and minimise risks. The transition of information from medical science to the media and the degree to which public understanding is retroactive has still not been extensively evaluated within the field of autism. What is observed, at least in this case, is that socially shared information and conceptions decisively contribute to forming ideas about diagnoses and treatments considered to be adequate.

REFERENCES

Amarante, P. (ed.) (1995) *Loucos pela vida: a trajetória da reforma psiquiátrica no Brasil.* Rio de Janeiro: SDE/ENSP.

Ariel, C.N., and Naseef, R.A. (eds) (2006) *Voices from the Spectrum: Parents, Grandparents, Siblings, People with Autism, and Professionals Share their Wisdom.* London: Jessica Kingsley Publishers.

Bagatell, N. (2007) 'Orchestrating voices: autism, identity and the power of discourse.' *Disability and Society 22*, 4, 413–426.

Baker, D.L. (2011) *The Politics of Neurodiversity: Why Public Policy Matters.* Boulder, CO: Lynne Rienner Publishers.

Barros, D. (1994) *Jardins de Abel: Desconstrução do Manicômio de Trieste.* Sao Paulo: Editora da Universidade de São Paulo.

Bertilsdotter Rosqvist, H., Brownlow, C., and O'Dell, L. (2013) 'Mapping the social geographies of autism – online and off-line narratives of neuro-shared and separate spaces.' *Disability and Society 28*, 3, 367–379.

Biehl, J. (2005) *Vita: Life in a Zone of Social Abandonment.* Berkeley, CA: University of California Press.

Biehl, J., Petryna, A., Gertner, A., Amon, J., and Picon, P. (2009) 'Judicialisation of the right to health in Brazil.' *The Lancet 373*, 2182–2184.

Block, P., and Cavalcante, F. (2014) 'Historical Perceptions of Autism in Brazil: Professional Treatment, Family Advocacy, and Autistic Pride, 1943–2010.' In S. Burch and M. Rembis (eds) *Disability Histories.* Champaign, IL: University of Illinois Press.

Blume, H. (1997) *'Autism and the Internet' or 'It's the Wiring, Stupid'.* Available at www.web.mit.edu/comm-forum/papers/blume.html, accessed on 6 November 2015.

Brown, P., Morello-Frosch, R., and Zavestoski, S. (eds) (2011) *Contested Illnesses. Citizens, Science, and Health Social Movements.* Berkeley, CA: University of California Press.

Carvalho, S. (2006) 'Os meninos do porão.' *O Globo.* Primeiro Caderno,18.

Cascio, A (2014) 'New directions in the social study of the autism spectrum: a review essay.' *Culture, Medicine, and Psychiatry 38*, 2, 306–311.

Cavalcante, F. (2003) *Pessoas Muito Especiais: a construção social do portador de deficiência e a reinvenção da família.* Rio de Janeiro: Fiocruz.

Chamak, B. (2008) 'Autism and social movements: French parents' associations and international autistic individuals' organizations.' *Sociology of Health and Illness 30,* 1, 76–96.

Chamak, B., Bonniau, B., and Jaunay, E. (2008) 'What can we learn about autism from autistic persons?' *Psychotherapy and Psychosomatics 77,* 5, 271–279.

Charman, T. (2006) 'Autism at the crossroads: determining the phenotype matters for neuroscience.' *Nature Neuroscience 9,* 10, 1197.

Clarke, J., and van Amerom, G. (2007) '"Surplus suffering": differences between organizational understandings of Asperger's syndrome and those people who claim the "disorder".' *Disability and Society 22,* 7, 761–776.

Collins, H.M., and Evans, R. (2002) 'The third wave of science studies: studies of expertise and experience.' *Social Studies of Science 32,* 2, 235–296.

Conselho Nacional de Secretários de Saúde (2006) *SUS: avanços e desafios.* Brasilia: CONASS.

Couto, M. (2004) 'Por uma Política Pública de Saúde Mental para crianças e Adolescentes.' In T. Ferreira (ed.) *A criança e a saúde mental: enlaces entre a clínica e a política.* Belo Horizonte: Autêntica.

Couto, M. (2012) 'Política de Saúde Mental para crianças e adolescentes: especificidades e desafios da experiência brasileira (2001–2010).' PhD Dissertation, Institute of Psychiatry, Federal University of Rio de Janeiro.

Couto, M., Duarte, C., and Delgado, P. (2008) 'A saúde Mental Infantil na Saúde Pública Brasileira: situação atual e desafios.' *Revista Brasileira de Psiquiatria 30,* 4, 390–398.

Csillag, C. (2001) 'Psychiatric reform law comes into effect in Brazil.' *The Lancet 357,* 1346.

Davidson, J. (2008) 'Autistic culture online: virtual communication and cultural expression on the spectrum.' *Social and Cultural Geography 9,* 7, 791–806.

Deer, B. (2011). 'Wakefield's article linking MMR vaccine and autism was fraudulent.' *British Medical Journal 342,* c7452.

Delgado, P. (1992) *As razões da tutela: psiquiatria, justiça e cidadania do louco na Brasil.* Rio de Janeiro: Te-Corá.

Elia, L. (2013) 'Psicanalise, ciencia e universidade.' In *Psicanalise, autismo e saúde pública.* Available at www.psicanaliseautismoesaudepublica.wordpress.com/2013/04/14/psicanalise-ciencia-e-universidade, accessed on 6 November 2015.

Epstein, S. (2008) 'Patient Groups and Health Movements.' In E.L. Hacket, O. Amsterdamska, M.E. Lynch and J. Wajcman, J. (eds) *The Handbook of Science and Technology Studies.* Cambridge, MA: MIT Press.

Eyal, G., Hart, B., Onculer, E., Oren, N., and Rossi, N. (2010) *The Autism Matrix: The Social Origins of the Autism Epidemics.* Cambridge and Malden: Polity.

Feinberg, E., and Vacca, J. (2000) 'The drama and trauma of creating policies on autism: critical issues to consider in the new millennium.' *Focus on Autism and other Developmental Disabilities 15,* 3, 130–137.

Franco, S. (2014) 'Familiares criticam regulamentação da lei de proteção ao autista.' *Jornal do Senado Federal.* Available at www12.senado.gov.br/jornal/edicoes/2014/04/03/autistas-familias-criticam-tratamento-nos-caps, accessed on 6 November 2015.

Gillet, J. (2003) 'Media activism and internet use by people with HIV/Aids.' *Sociology of Health and Illness 5,* 6, 608–642.

Goldberg, J. (1994) *Clínica da psicose: um projeto na rede pública.* Rio de Janeiro: Te-Corá/Instituto Franco Basaglia.

Hacking, I. (2009) 'Autistic autobiography.' *Philosophical Transactions Royal Society B 364,* 1521, 1467–1473.

Kenway, I.M. (2009) 'Blessing or curse? Autism and the rise of the internet.' *Journal of Religtion, Disability and Health 13*, 2, 94–103.

Lobato, L., and Burlandy, L. (2000) 'The Context and Process of Health Care Reform in Brazil.' In S. Fleury, S. Belmartino and E. Baris (eds) *Reshaping Health Care in Latin America. A Comparative Analysis of Health Care Reform in Argentina, Brazil, and Mexico.* Ottawa: IDRC Books.

Manifest (2013) *Manifesto do Movimento Psicanálise, Autismo e Saúde Pública.* Available at www.sedes.org.br/site/sites/default/files/manifesto_movimento_psicanalise_autismo_saudepublica.pdf, accessed on 6 November 2015.

Mateus, D., Jair, J., Mari, J.J., Delgado, P.G.G., *et al.* (2008) 'The mental health system in Brazil: policies and future challenges.' *International Journal of Mental Health Systems 2*, 12.

Mello, A.M., Dias, I., and Andrade, M. (2013) *Retratos do autismo no Brasil.* São Paulo: Secretaria de Direitos Humanos.

Ministério da Saúde (2002) *Portaria 336, de 19 de fevereiro de 2002. Dispõe sobre as normas e diretrizes para organização dos CAPS.* Brasília: Diário Oficial da União.

Ministério da Saúde (2004) *Legislação em Saúde Mental – 1990–2004* (5a edição ampliada). Brasília: Editora do Ministério da Saúde.

Ministério da Saúde (2013a) *Linha de Cuidado para a Atenção às Pessoas com Transtornos do Espectro do Autismo e suas Famílias na Rede de Atenção Psicossocial do Sistema Único de Saúde.* Brasília: Editora do Ministério da Saúde.

Ministério da Saúde (2013b) *Diretrizes de Atenção à Reabilitação da Pessoa com Transtornos do Espectro do Autista (TEA).* Brasília: Editora do Ministério da Saúde.

Nunes, F. (2014) 'Atuação política de grupos de pais de autistas no Rio de Janeiro: perspectivas para o campo da saúde.' MS Dissertation, Institute for Social Medicine, State University of Rio de Janeiro.

Ochs, E., and Solomon, O. (2010). 'Autistic sociality.' *Ethos 38*, 1, 69–92.

Ochs, E., and Taylor C. (1995) 'The Father Knows Best. Dynamic in Family Dinner Narratives.' In K. Hall and M. Bucholtz (eds) *Gender Articulated: Language and the Socially Constructed Self.* New York and London: Routledge.

Orsini, M., and Smith, M. (2010) 'Social movements, knowledge and public policy: the case of autism activism in Canada and the US.' *Critical Policy Studies 4*, 1, 38–57.

Ortega, F. (2009) 'The cerebral subject and the challenge of neurodiversity.' *Biosocieties 4*, 4, 425–45.

Ortega, F., Zorzanelli, R., Kozslowski Meierhoffer, L., Almeida Rosário, C., *et al.*(2013) 'A construção do diagnóstico do autismo em uma rede social virtual brasileira.' *Interface-Comunicação, Saúde, Educação 17*, 44, 119–132.

Osteen, M. (2008) *Autism and Representation.* New York: Routledge.

Passos, I. (2009) *Reforma psiquiátrica: As experiências francesa e italiana.* Rio de Janeiro: Fiocruz.

Pinto, R. (2005) 'CAPSI para crianças adolescentes autistas e psicóticas. A contribuição da psicanálise na construção do dispositivo clínico.' MS Dissertation, Institute of Psychology, State University of Rio de Janeiro.

Rosenberg, C.E. (2006) 'Contested boundaries: psychiatry, disease, and diagnosis.' *Perspectives in Biology and Medicine 49*, 407–424.

Silverman, C. (2012) *Understanding Autism: Parents, Doctors, and the History of a Disorder.* Princeton: Princeton University Press.

Souza, R. (2002) *O Sistema Público de Saúde Brasileiro.* Brasília: Editora do Ministério da Saúde.

Tenório, F. (2002) 'A reforma psiquiátrica brasileira, da década de 1980 aos dias atuais: história e conceito.' *História, Ciências, Saúde – Manguinhos 9*, 1, 25–59.

Volkmar, F.R., Lord, C., Bailey, A., Schulz, R.T., and Klin, A. (2004) 'Autism and pervasive developmental disorders.' *Journal of Child Psychology and Psychiatry 45*, 1, 135–170.

Wakefield, A., Murch, S.H., Anthony, A., Linnell, J., *et al.* (1998) 'Ileal-lymphoid-nodular hyperplasia, non-specific colitis, and pervasive developmental disorder in children.' *Lancet 351*, 9103, 637–641.

Walsh, P., Elsabbagh, M., Bolton, P., and Singh, I. (2011) 'In search of biomarkers for autism: scientific, social and ethical challenges.' *Nature Reviews Neuroscience 12*, 10, 603–612.

WHO-AIMS (2007) *Report on Mental Health System in Brazil.* Brasilia: WHO and Ministry of Health Brazil.

PART II

DECONSTRUCTING AUTISM

CHAPTER 5

LIFE WITHOUT AUTISM
A CULTURAL LOGIC OF VIOLENCE

Anne McGuire

INTRODUCTION

The West has a long and violent history of targeting autistic people in particular and disabled people in general (Brown 2014; Smith 2006; Snyder and Mitchell 2006). In contemporary times, such acts of violence are occurring with an aching frequency; we are continually and even routinely encountering resonant stories of violence against autistic people as these stories circulate through our news sources, through our culture and through our lives. Such acts of violence seldom go unnoticed by disability advocates and activists. Autistic self-advocates and their allies, for example, have long been watching the headlines, marking and mourning the surging numbers of autistic victims of violence and demanding political action (ASAN 2012a, 2012b; Çevik 2012; Chew 2006; Smith 2006).

As with other forms of ableist violence (see Chapter 7), instances of autism violence are seldom understood by mainstream society as pointing to a troubling social phenomenon or as symptomatic of deeply entrenched ableist systems of exclusion. To the contrary, instances of violence against autistic people are most often framed by news media and mainstream advocacy organisations alike as 'unthinkable' and 'senseless': unpredictable random individual tragedies.

Throughout this chapter, I argue that the persistent social move to locate autism violence outside the bounds of reason dangerously obscures the mundane and deadly ways in which autism violence is being rendered absolutely thinkable, reasonable and even normal. Attending to the normative and normalising nature of such stories of autism violence enables us to ask difficult and important questions about the culture in which we live. Critically attending to such stories allows us, for example, to ask the following: how do dominant versions of autism that characterise it as a condition of human life instead of a lived human condition – a some 'thing' and not a someone – allow for and even catalyse a collective cultural failure to recognise violence against autistic people as a significant and pressing socio-cultural problem? How are dominant cultural understandings of autism as some 'thing' pathological and so, as some 'thing' to be 'against', creating the conditions of possibility that render some lives more vulnerable to murder and other forms of (normative) violence?

ON 'LIVING WITH' AUTISM

In contemporary times and in Western/ised spaces, there seems to be a collective, cultural fixation on – or, perhaps even, obsession with – 'life with' autism (Broderick and Ne'eman 2008; Mallett and Runswick-Cole 2012). These words – 'living' and 'with' – are so commonly strung together in relation to autism in everyday life that they appear everywhere from newspaper articles to government reports, from scientific studies to celebrity appeals, from fundraising initiatives to self-help books. Consider but a few of a vast number of recent examples:

- A *Vancouver Sun* headline: '*Living with* Autism' (McMartin 2007)
- A BBC headline: '*Living with* Autism in the UK' (Guerry 2008)
- An article published in *Redbook* Magazine: '*Living with* Autism: Losing My Little Boy' (Rones 2009)
- A common phrase: '1 out of every 110 children is *living with* autism'
- A parent resource: '*Living with* Autism: Practical Strategies for Supporting People with Autism Spectrum Disorders' (Autism Association of Western Australia 2007)
- An *Evening Herald* headline: 'Breakthrough brings fresh hope for families *living with* autism' (Connor 2010)
- Kathleen Dillon's (1995) book: '*Living with* Autism: The Parents' Stories
- An oft-repeated 'fact' that '1 to 1.5 million Americans *live with* Autism Spectrum Disorder'
- A 2008 Easter Seals Study '*Living with* Autism'
- A *Daily Press* article: '*Living with* autism disconnects kids from the world' (Freehling 2001)
- An edited collection of stories: 'That's *Life with* Autism: Tales and tips for families with autism' (Ross and Jolly 2006)
- The common biomedical observation: 'Many persons *living with* autism have significant communication challenges'
- Elizabeth Attfield and Hugh Morgan's (2006) book: '*Living with* Autistic Spectrum Disorders: Guidance for Parents, Carers and Siblings'
- A talk show episode '*Living with* Autism' (Winfrey 2007).

The proliferation of this 'living with autism' phraseology demonstrates many things, but one thing is certain: in contemporary times and in Western/ising spaces, the category of autism is involved in the re/production of notions of 'life'.

Perhaps the most literal way of reading the meaning of the phrase 'living with autism' is as an instance of 'person first' language – a dominantly used and widely accepted system of naming disability that places the 'person' before the 'disability' (e.g. 'person with a disability' or 'people with autism'). When confronted with the phraseology 'living with autism', we might reasonably and literally understand it as referencing an individual life 'with' autism, as referencing, in other words, a person with autism. Indeed, there are many instances where the 'living with' phraseology is evoked precisely in this way. To draw on a few examples from the list above: '1 to 1.5 million people in the USA *live with* an Autism Spectrum Disorder' or 'many persons *living with* autism have significant communication challenges' or '*living with* autism disconnects kids from the world'. Each of these statements suggests that the condition of 'living with autism' is a condition of an individual 'with' it.

As a great many disability studies scholars and activists have argued, far from being merely a politically correct system of naming, the 'person-first' lexicon also functions to organise disability meanings in particular ways (Linton 1998; Michalko 1999; Overboe 1999; Sinclair 1999; Titchkosky 2001). In her critique of person-first language, Titchkosky (2001, p.126) observes: 'Wherever and however this ["person-first"] lexicon appears, it always recommends that disability should be spoken of as something that comes along "with" people.' Indeed, if one out of every 110 children is a child *with* autism, it follows that autism – at least in some sense – can only be located 'with' that one child. It is, in other words, discursively forbidden from being 'with' the other 109 children. Statements such as 'many persons *living with* autism have significant communication challenges' suggest that communication challenges do not, in any essential way, belong to all of us – to the realm of social interaction, for example – but, rather, belong to persons afflicted 'with' a biomedical condition: persons with autism (McGuire and Michalko 2011). Far from being merely a politically correct system of words or names, the 'person first' lexicon functions to systematically organise disabled people as 'just people' – regular, ordinary people who happen to have a disability (Brown 2011; Michalko 1999; Overboe 1999; Titchkosky 2001). In organising disability (and so autism) in this way, the 'person first' lexicon functions to localise disability squarely in the individual, thereby forbidding any conceptualisation of its existence outside of the individual: in the socio-cultural environment, for example, or in inter-subjective relations.

The solidification of disability's status as an individual condition is not, however, the only interpretive move made by person-first language. Person-first language does, as Brown (2011) suggests, possess a kind of 'attitudinal nuance'.

In problematising the specificity of the phrase 'person with autism', Sinclair (1999) offers us three critiques. First, he argues, the phrase 'person with autism' suggests that the person and autism are somehow separate entities:

> I can be separated from things that are not part of me, and I am still the same person. I am usually a 'person with a purple shirt,' but I could also be a 'person with a blue shirt' one day, and a 'person with a yellow shirt' the next day, and I would still be the same person, because my clothing is not part of me. But autism is part of me. (Sinclair 1999)

What Sinclair reminds us, in other words, is that the phrase 'person with autism' suggests that autism is not essential to personhood. He continues:

> Characteristics that are recognised as central to a person's identity are appropriately stated as adjectives, and may even be used as nouns to describe people: We talk about 'male' and 'female' people, and even about 'men' and 'women' and 'boys' and 'girls,' not about 'people with maleness' and 'people with femaleness'. (Sinclair 1999)

Finally, Sinclair suggests that the 'person-first' nomenclature presumes a state of bad-ness or wrongness. In his words, '[i]t is only when someone has decided that the characteristic being referred to is negative that suddenly people want to separate it from the person' (Sinclair 1999).

Further examining the phraseology 'person with autism', the preposition 'with' – wedged between person and autism – functions, discursively, to separate the ideological category of 'person' from a biomedical condition of 'autism'. It creates an artificial disconnect between the (good) individual person and the (bad) autism that comes to be associated 'with' it as an add-on to this person. To be 'with' autism (and not, for example, to be of it, or in it) is to locate autism 'with' the individual while asserting its essential separation from it (Michalko 1999). The 'with', thus, performs a paradoxical act of separation *and* association. As a 'person-first' lexicon organises autism into some 'thing' located squarely in the individual, it also, and simultaneously, forbids it from being understood as entwined with or integral to a person's personhood (Brown 2011; Linton 1998; Michalko 1999; Overboe 1999; Sinclair 1999, 2012; Titchkosky 2001).

As we analyse the social significance of the 'living with' phraseology in terms of a 'person-first' lexicon, we must account for the meaningful slippage between the expression 'person *with* autism' and its vital permutation: 'person *living with* autism'. While these two expressions are certainly related linguistic technologies that seem to be used interchangeably in everyday talk, they are not equivalent formulations and, as such, the interpretive work they perform is not identical. While, in the former phraseology, the word 'with', alone, is wedged between the person and the autism, in the latter, two words – 'living with' – are wedged

between, and this difference is significant. While the 'with' posits autism as some kind of a personal possession or appendage that has become associated with or tied to an individual person, the 'living with' underscores autism as an appendage that has become attached to *the life* of the person. Where the phrase 'person with autism' renders autism as some (undesirable, pathological) 'thing' some people happen to 'have', the phrase 'person living with autism' renders autism as some (undesirable, pathological) 'thing' some people have to 'live with'.

Most interestingly, let us note how the vital permutation of 'person-first' language has opened up the condition of being 'with' the individualised pathology of autism to not only include 'persons living with autism' as this is conceived of in the strictest sense, but also to include people who, quite literally, have autism in their lives. Indeed, we are, for example, seemingly, constantly confronted in the media, in advocacy initiatives as well as in everyday conversation with parent narratives that characterise their relationship with their autistic child in terms of a 'life with autism'. Families, as well as communities, nations and, indeed, (the) United Nations, are all commonly understood to be 'living with autism'. While each of the examples of cultural artefacts appearing in the long list above succeeds in confirming autism's taken-for-granted status as an individual condition, very few of them articulate living with autism as a condition of the individual alone.

For example, Dillon's (1995) book *Living with Autism* does not recount stories of individuals living with autism, as its title would seem to suggest. Rather, the book tells the stories of individuals (parents, in this case) living with individuals living with autism. Oprah Winfrey's (2007) 'Living with Autism' episode focused on the narratives and perspectives of relationally non-disabled parents, siblings, advocates and physicians; people who, in some way, had autism in their lives. Likewise, the Easter Seals study 'Living with Autism' surveyed over 1600 parents of autistic people about their 'life with autism' (Easter Seals 2008). With these examples, it becomes evident: another way the phrase 'living with autism' comes to be employed and understood in contemporary times is as a way to describe a collective condition of 'life with' the individualised condition of autism.

This vitalised 'people-first' system of meaning produces autism (as is, invariably, embodied by an individual autistic person or a group or subpopulation of individual autistic people) as a condition afflicting the social whole, as some pathological element that is separate from this whole, and that has, as a matter of misfortune, become attached to collective life. Indeed, in mainstream Western culture, autism is almost exclusively depicted as an undesirable pathological 'condition' of the (social *and* individual) body, a 'condition' that is rendered conditional to particular individuals (marked as unfortunate) and their (equally 'unfortunate') families, communities and nations. And so while autism *is* framed as 'a part' of human life...as 'something' that 'we' as humans do from time to

time, in various ways, come to 'live with'...it is not, we are told, the 'stuff' of human life, it is not essential to or continuous with human vitality.

This ideological abjection from the category of human life has a long history rooted in the rise of liberalism and the resultant proliferation of diagnostic categories under this regime. Autism is not a way of living, says modern medicine and the biological sciences in chorus, it is a series of pathological 'tendencies'; a characteristic 'trait', declared Bleuler back in 1911 (Feinstein 2010); a collection of 'symptoms', calculated Kanner in 1943, it is 'echolalia', 'stereotypy', 'literalness'. Autism is not life, promised Bettelheim (1972); it is a prison. It is, he said, a 'withdrawal' from humanity – a chilling effect of a cold mother. Autism is not life, said Lovaas (1987), it is an exhibition of 'inappropriate behaviours'. It is a mind blind to intentionality, according to Baron-Cohen (1997). It is inhumane: a 'lack of empathy' (for an analysis of how notions of mindblindness dehumanise autistic people, see Yergeau 2013).

Such a history of pathologisation is continuous with the present moment. Autism-as-pathology is some 'thing' other than human life, says contemporary biomedicine. It is 'misfiring' neurons, 'too slow' development and an erroneous set of genes.

And now sliding outside of biomedicine proper, autism is not a life, say dominant mainstream advocacy organisations, it is that which threatens life. It is a disease of epidemic proportions, spreading faster, to borrow a commonly evoked advocacy phrase, than 'AIDS, diabetes, and cancer combined'. Autism is not a life, say governments and the UN, for it gets in the way of the good life of neoliberal development (or at least so the myth goes...) (McGuire 2012). Autism, we are told, prevents otherwise respectable citizens from the 'full' enjoyment of humanity and its ostensibly guaranteed rights and freedoms. Autism forbids individuals, communities and nations from 'fully' living. And so this idea is repeated over and over again by a great many people and in myriad different ways; to 'live with' autism – whether it be collectively or individually or both – is to bear a condition (i.e. pathology) of life.

What sensibility of life do such contemporary representations of autism permit us to think, or better, what do they inaugurate? As the category of living person, living human, or perhaps 'life' more broadly, is, under a liberal rule of life, discursively, made to come before and so to exist as separate from 'autism', and as 'autism' is transformed into some pathological 'thing' that is not of life but has, as a matter of misfortune, come to be affixed to it, we can observe how the vital category of the living human – the vital category of life itself – is emptied, in some essential way, of any possibility of being autistic. Life, in other words, is being made a condition of non-autism. And while life is always life, the condition of 'life with' autism comes to be immediately understood as *lives that bear the origin of their own undoing*.

This overwhelmingly prominent cultural logic is both dangerous and deadly. Autism violence is being managed through a powerful cultural understanding that the only vital way to 'live with' autism is to long for, and indeed work toward, 'life without it'. Within this framework, the living autistic body – the body that does not, cannot or chooses not to move toward a convincing performance of non-autism – is cast as an ideological and material site of resistance and so a threat to (collective) normative, liberal life. As a way to both address and assess this danger, I move to trace out the danger of rationalising autism in this way by attending to a series of newspaper articles reporting on two recent autism murders – the murders of Jason Dawes and Katie McCarron – where autism was articulated as the target of, and the underlying reason for, violence. Both of these instances of violence tell the story of an autistic person (i.e. an 'individual living with autism') who was murdered by a non-autistic individual 'living with' this 'individual living with autism'.

LIFE WITHOUT AUTISM: THE MURDERS OF JASON DAWES AND KATIE MCCARRON

On 4 August 2003, ten-year-old Jason Dawes was murdered in New South Wales, Australia (Lamont 2004b, para. 2). His mother, Daniela Dawes, admitted to suffocating Jason before attempting to kill herself (she was discovered and revived). Dawes was arrested and charged, initially, with murder, a charge that was soon reduced to manslaughter when the Crown accepted that the defendant was experiencing depression at the time of the killing. To this charge of manslaughter due to diminished responsibility, Dawes pleaded guilty. On 2 June 2004, the Parramatta District Court ruled that Dawes be immediately released on a five-year good behaviour bond. From a by-line in the Sydney Morning Herald: 'Her son died at her own hand but a judge ruled yesterday that Daniela Dawes had been through too much to be sent to jail' (Lamont 2004b, para. 1). After this unusual non-custodial sentence was handed down, Justice Roy Ellis addressed Daniela Dawes directly: 'I wish you all the best', he said (Lamont 2004b, para. 2).

Three years later, on 13 May 2006, three-year-old Katie McCarron was suffocated in her grandmother's home in Morton, Illinois (Sampier 2008a). Katie's mother, Dr Karen McCarron, confessed to the murder. McCarron also attempted suicide and she too survived. McCarron was arrested and charged with murder in the first degree, to which she pleaded not guilty by reason of insanity. On 17 January 2008, Dr McCarron was convicted of the murder of her daughter in the first degree and was given a life sentence of 36 years in prison.

I have chosen to focus on these two stories of violence not because they are particularly unusual or rare. They are neither. In the past decade, dozens upon dozens of reports of autism-related murders have circulated through the

popular Western/ised news media. Joel Smith's website *This Way of Life* (archived since 2006) was foundational in documenting these reports, providing a space to acknowledge and connect instances of autism violence and track their judicial outcomes. Smith's website also made it possible for the autistic community and their allies to, collectively, mourn the victims of autism violence. The task of bearing witness has, in many ways, become central to the work of autistic self-advocacy.[1]

While Smith's site is now archived, other community members have continued this difficult work of monitoring the headlines and mourning the victims of ableist violence (see, for example, the work of Kerima Çevik and her website *The Autism Wars*). In 2012, the Autistic Self Advocacy Network (ASAN) (in collaboration with other disability organisations such as Not Dead Yet and the National Council of Independent Living) held a Day of Mourning, remembering disabled people who were killed by a parent or caregiver. In a statement on the ASAN website, Zoe Gross writes: 'On March 30th, 2012, we held vigils in 18 cities to remember those we have lost, and to remind the world that their lives had value. On March 31st, 2012, a 4-year-old autistic boy named Daniel Corby was drowned in a bathtub by his mother' (ASAN 2012b). As Gross's statement makes clear, this work is ongoing. While the phenomenon of autism violence is well known, documented and felt in autistic communities (e.g. the day of mourning is now marked annually with vigils held around the world), in mainstream culture the names of victims of autism violence are seldom linked together, an act of forgetting that is also an act of violence. Even less often are these names linked to a culture that so often produces autism as somehow separate from the category of life.

I should note that my interest in the re/telling of these stories of violence, is not, at least strictly speaking, a search for quick or easy origins. I do not, in other words, attempt to empirically decipher who or what is responsible for the violence enacted against these children. My critique – an interpretive one – resists the (persistent, seductive, collective) desire for moral clarity in favour of an analysis of the ways violence is functioning in our culture – how this violence is made possible and even how it is framed as necessary. Rather than attempting to isolate an underlying cause, these instances of violence against autistic people must be read as an immediate cause for concern, an observation that demands that we – all of us 'living with autism' and so all of us who belong to and participate in the making of this culture – look again to the cultural meanings we are, collectively, making of autism and non-autism and the relationship between the two. I suggested, earlier, that the conceptualisation of autism as some

1 Recall, of course, that, as articulated by Baggs (2012), Durbin-Westby (2012) and others, autistic notions of 'self-advocacy' non-normatively presupposed an understanding of 'self' that is both individual and collective.

pathological 'thing' that is not 'lived' but 'lived with' – where this 'living with' is understood, implicitly, as something done by *both* individuals and collectives – is animating dominant enactments of autism advocacy in this contemporary moment. I suggested, too, that this *animus* is generating dangerous and deadly ideological and material consequences. Let us examine this further and in relation to the stories of violence detailed above.

MAKING SENSE OF MURDER

In the media coverage of the Dawes and McCarron trials, autism was never represented to be continuous with life. Reflecting dominant cultural understandings of autism, autism was narrated – in the newspaper headlines and in the articles that followed them, from the defence strategies to those of the prosecution, from the perpetrators' confessions to witness testimonials to the judges' final pronouncements – as nothing more than life's unfortunate and undesirable condition; a condition, moreover, that served the purpose of rendering thinkable the seemingly unthinkable: the act of murdering one's own child. Put differently, Jason and Katie's murders were transformed into one more unfortunate and undesirable outcome of the unfortunate and undesirable condition of 'living with autism'.

Severity

In both court cases and the media coverage that surrounded them, the biomedical status of the victim (and their subsequent 'potential') became a, or perhaps even *the*, salient detail that was evoked, substantiated, contested and debated over. The murders were qualified with questions of autism's 'severity' and of the subsequent potential of (all) life living 'with' it (i.e. not just the autistic children's potential but the potential of the parents and families 'living with' the child living with autism). While Katie McCarron's autism was repeatedly characterised as 'not severe', as 'mild' even, Jason Dawes was described as having had 'severe autism'. His mother, Daniela Dawes, in the words of the judge presiding over her sentencing hearing, 'was required to educate, feed, toilet, bathe, entertain and love' him (Lamont 2004b, para. 10). There is a straightforward biopolitical logic of violence that underpins this cultural preoccupation with 'severity': if autism is not continuous with human life but is – as per the dominant refrain of our culture – that which must be 'lived with'...if autism is not, in other words, conceived of as (integral to) a living person, but is, instead, understood as a pathology that has become attached to this person, it follows that a person 'living with' autism is a person whose relative 'amount' or 'quality' of life is, and can be, determined through a calculus of autism's severity.

The implicit, and surely violent, logic goes something like this: if a 'mild' autism (as pathology) becomes attached to a presumed otherwise normative life, this life is mostly un-afflicted and unaffected. In other words, normative life – unquestionably naturalised as inherently healthy and apolitically understood as at once good and desirable – is (at least mostly) unencumbered, permitted to thrive. However, as the 'severity' of autism's pathology increases, and as it increases its hold on life, normative life is understood to be ever more compromised: weakened, siphoned, lessened. The act of characterising Katie's autism as 'mild' evoked a simultaneous understanding of a mostly normative life, one that minimally affected the normative lives of those around her. Jason's autism, by contrast, became understood as a condition that was inhibiting the very human possibility of life itself. Jason's status as severely autistic was framed as preventing him (and his parents, who 'lived with' him and his autism) from fitting in to the normative order of human life: a vital and vitalising order where parents ought not *be required to* bathe and toilet (and love!) their ten-year-olds and where children ought to be endowed with the (presumed) human promise of growing up to become 'fully' independent adults. In other words, Jason's autism was framed and so understood as inhibiting and even draining an otherwise normative life and the otherwise normative lives of his parents, family and community.

The violence inflicted on the bodies of these two children, to borrow from Michalko's haunting analysis of the murder of Tracy Latimer in Canada in 1993, was 'governed and evaluated by a rationality of opposites' (Michalko 2002). The relationship between disability and non-disability, autism and non-autism, is split here into a simple binary. In both the McCarron and the Dawes murder cases, non-autism was made synonymous with the hope of human possibility, while autism came to be understood as hopelessness and limiting. Where non-autism was conceived of as life, autism was made a life-draining pathology, a kind of biopolitical death. With this in mind, non-autistic life 'living with' autism is reframed not only as a life tied to death, as we all invariably are, but as a life that has become affixed to and with a pathological non-life.

Spectrum

Yet, just as we are given with this bleak image of autism wasting away (normative) life, we are simultaneously confronted with the spectral quality of the DSM-IV and most especially the DSM-5 versions of autism. Indeed, the newly minted fifth edition *Diagnostic and Statistical Manual* does away with the various categories of autism diagnoses (Asperger Syndrome, Rett Syndrome and so on) in favour of a single wide-reaching diagnosis of 'Autism Spectrum Disorder'. The DSM-5 represents a move away from *categorical* diagnosis (i.e. so you either meet the diagnostic criteria of this thing called autism or you don't), favouring instead a

dimensional diagnosis (i.e. to what degree do you meet diagnostic criteria) (American Psychiatric Association 2013). This notion of autism not as a static pathology but as a graded range or 'spectrum' of pathologies represents a biopolitical rationality insofar as it functions to manage the normative category of life. The notion of spectrum offers a hopeful (which, from the vantage point of capitalism, most often means lucrative) narrative of the possibility for an incremental recovery of normative life. Indeed, the moral hierarchy of the 'autism spectrum' functions dangerously to condition the emergence of a popular and violently normative understanding that 'life with autism' always can and ought to be actively moving along the pathological gradations of autistic difference toward the most vital pole of 'life without it'.

The spectral quality of the autism spectrum as a conceptual device for thinking about a range of autism 'severities' gives birth to a whole range of vital possibilities (ways of getting better) and non-vital limits (ways of wasting) within the category of autism itself: it organises many small and incremental ways of 'living' and, also and necessarily, many and incremental ways of 'dying'. In this way, the 'spectrum' makes possible an array of new kinds of living people: people who 'live with' a pathological or 'life-threatening' autism; and 'not yet living' people who – depending on the 'severity' of their (non-vital) signs of autism and the degree to which they have the capacity to approximate the (vital) signs of non-autism or normalcy – become conceptually understood as 'almost living' or 'mostly dead'.

A rational calculus of life and death

I return now to the two murder cases in order to give an account of the danger of this spectral logic. Even as Jason Dawes was narrated as 'severely autistic', his life was not understood to be, by virtue of the 'severity' of his autism, *ipso facto* without potential (Lamont 2004a). Rather, the narrative of his life and death told in the courts and by the media was the story of a life that had, gradually, *lost its vital potential*. In the newspaper reports of the murder and subsequent trial Daniela Dawes was called a 'crusader for her son', having 'battled doggedly for years to get the educational, behavioural and medical support her son needed', moving the family around to secure the best treatments and services – treatments and services they 'didn't get' (Lamont 2004a, paras. 8–9). Jason was narrated as entering puberty at the time he was killed and, at this time, time was understood to have run out. According to the *Herald*: 'When Jason was diagnosed with autism at 18 months, doctors had recommended he get 20 hours of early intervention help a week. All his parents could secure for him was three hours a week' (Lamont 2004a, para. 16). Due to lack of access to biomedical 'early intervention' therapies (an issue that had much to do with the family's

class and rural location), at ten years old, Jason, we were told, had outgrown the crucial 'window' of opportunity where his 'severe autism' might have been lessened by a normative rehabilitation. And so, the child was, in the word of defence lawyer, Roland Bonnici, 'doomed' (Lamont 2004a). Interpreted as being fixed to and with autism (i.e. as living 'with' severe autism in a permanent way), Jason's life was conceptually organised as life marked with, and therefore for, death: 'doomed'.

The logic of violence extends beyond the particularities of Jason's individual life, however. His mother, too, was framed as having to 'live with' the fixity of this ostensibly non-vital human state. Said Judge Roy Ellis: '[Daniela Dawes] constantly lived with the fact that her son had lost his best chance of acquiring greater life skills because of the failure of authorities to provide appropriate intervention during his early formative years' (Lamont 2004b, para. 10). And so Daniela Dawes, whose life and the life of her son came to be understood as being 'with autism' in a permanent way, was subsequently interpreted as having been 'driven' to commit a 'tragic' but, nonetheless, understandable act of murder; an act that was framed as acting in the name of life (her own, her family's, the community, the nation) and was thus, under a liberal rule of life, coded as both reasonable and, even, as necessary (Lamont 2004a).

The story of the life and death of Katie McCarron, however, presents us with still another permutation of the dangerous story of what happens when autism and non-autism are understood be fixed 'with' one another. Unlike the Dawes case, the murder of Katie McCarron was *not* represented as a condition of how severe or demanding or trying (her) autism was; Katie's autism was understood to be 'mild', her behaviours were described as 'good', palatable, approximating the norm. At the trial, Katie's father told the court that his daughter 'wasn't prone to kicking, screaming, biting or behavior sometimes associated with more severe autism cases' (Sampier 2008a, p.A1). 'Katie was always a well-behaved little girl', he said, adding that she was developmentally behind for her age but [had] 'learned the alphabet, knew shapes and colors, and recognised various animals' (Sampier 2008a, p.A1). Neither was Katie's murder made to be a condition of the accessibility or availability of resources. Her family was, in many ways, privileged; they were white, wealthy, educated, they had help in the home and were otherwise well positioned to secure for Katie the latest in rehabilitation treatments. Indeed, the court heard of how as a two-year-old (unlike Jason, still 'form-able') Katie was sent to a top-notch out-of-state school where she received intensive therapeutic 'interventions'. By all accounts, Katie was catching up to her milestones, moving her way along the spectrum toward normalcy.

Yet, despite Katie's purported proximity to the markers and milestones of normativity, the court transcripts describe a mother who saw an otherwise normative or non-autistic child that was 'unfixable' insofar as she was 'fixed' with

and to her autism. 'I loved Katie very much, but I hated the autism so, so much', said McCarron in a taped confession that was played at the trial. '…I hated what it was doing to her… I just wanted autism out of my life' (Sampier 2008b, p.A1). Indeed, in a cross-examination McCarron told defence lawyer Marc Wolfe that she did not intend to kill her daughter. Said Wolfe: 'Who did you think you were killing?' 'Autism,' replied McCarron.

It was this portrait of a three-year-old child with 'mild' autism who was rapidly moving in the right and vital direction of good, human life without it that led many to conclude that – unlike the violent act of Daniela Dawes that was understood to be necessitated by autism's presence – McCarron's act of killing her daughter had little to do with autism at all (Luciano 2006, p.A1). In a statement to reporters, Katie's grandfather, Michael McCarron said:

> I am positively revolted when I read quotes that would imply any degree of understanding or hint at condoning the taking of my granddaughter's life. […] [This is] a very straight-forward murder case. This was not about autism. […] We're not dealing with desperation here. We're not dealing with 'we have to end this child's pain. (Luciano 2006, p.A1)

Vis-à-vis Karen McCarron's confession where she repeatedly and explicitly describes her hate of autism, as well as her explicit intent to rid her daughter of autism by killing 'it', this murder most certainly had everything to do with autism. Michael McCarron's attempt to recuperate his granddaughter's humanness both exposes and reconfirms the taken-for-granted logic that a murder motivated by autism (Jason's murder, for example) is a murder that, at least in some sense, is understandable, condonable, necessary, even.

Michael McCarron's rationalisation was echoed in the courts and in the papers: Karen McCarron's act of violence was recognised as unjustifiably taking life. The lethal violence inflicted on Katie was (popularly and legally) judged to be a non-vital or 'murderous' violence: violence that was enacted in the name of death and not life.

While Dawes was framed and so understood as justifiably performing the vital act of releasing herself and an 'almost-dead' child from autism's morbid grip, McCarron was framed and so understood as unjustifiably taking the life of an 'almost-living' child. Daniela Dawes was granted a non-custodial murder sentence; Karen McCarron was sentenced to life in prison. While I do not want to make the claim that more imprisonment is the necessary 'good' here, the glaring differences in the sentencing, however, demonstrate the very salient detail that when bodies are marked as outside of the vital limits of the human, they move, simultaneously, outside the bounds of the law.

What the murder trials and the media responses that surrounded them demonstrate – and what the case of Katie McCarron makes very explicit – is

the material danger of a global and globalising culture of puzzling threats, red flags and global epidemics. A culture that understands itself to be living with autism and that wishes to – and works to – live without it. The dominant ways that we are, as a culture, orienting to autism by fighting it, battling it, hating it, waging a war against it, and by working to eliminate it, require us to think of autism, not as itself a way of living, but as that which must be 'lived with'. In this culture, individual people and, indeed, whole populations are being split cleanly in two – part 'living' people and part 'life draining' pathology. A part to cultivate and a part to eliminate. Such a parsing up of life and non-life, people and pathologies, promises that there, in fact, *can* be life without autism, that if autism is eliminated or cured, someone without autism remains.

Of course, such a promise is both a false one and a dangerous one. And, while I'm in no way suggesting that cultural understandings and orientations forced McCarron's or Dawes' hand in killing their children, such understandings and orientations certainly provide the necessary conditions that continue to make this kind of violence possible and even – for those of us monitoring the headlines – normal. Born of our culture, the violence enacted against Katie and Jason (and the great many other disabled people subjected to individual and systemic acts of violence) is a cultural problem. In the words of Michalko, disability violence is therefore 'a problem for all of us' (Michalko 2002, p.111).

CONCLUSION

Discourse is material. The everyday ways we collectively talk and think about autism are involved in the making of the meaning of people. Dominant assumptions and articulations about the quality and character of autistic lives teach us about what autism is and can be and govern the terms of our collective and individual responses to autism. We are currently living in the context of a (Western/ising, neoliberal) culture that is increasingly engaged in the process of organising various non-normative thoughts, behaviours, responses, movements and affects into graded pathological spectrums anchored by oppositional poles of life and death.

In this context, autism is discursively framed as some 'thing' separate from the fully living human/person: some 'thing' to be 'fought', 'battled', 'hated', waged war on (McGuire 2015). Autism, our culture tells us, must be eliminated in the hopes of recuperating the presumed goodness/rightness of normative life. Such a parsing up of life and non-life, people and pathologies, promises that if autism is eliminated, someone without autism will remain. As is painfully evident throughout this chapter, such a promise is as false as it is dangerous. Autism, here, is not some *a priori* thing-in-the-world but is, rather, an interpretive device used to make sense of the bodies of actual people. As discourse inevitably marks the

body and gives it shape and possibility, 'person' and 'autism' cannot be separated in any easy or straightforward way (Sinclair 1999). Katie and Jason were not 'people living with autism' but *living autistic people* – fighting their autism meant fighting them; hating their autism was hating them; killing their autism, killed them. In attending to some of the dominant discourses of autism that circulate in and through our culture and our lives, and by exposing the underlying logics that give these stories shape and coherence, it is my hope that this chapter has offered a means for further understanding – and further contesting – the ways autism violence is being normalised as reasonable and even as necessary.

Excerpt from *War on Autism: On the Cultural Logic of Normative Violence*, forthcoming in May 2016.

REFERENCES

American Psychiatric Association (APA) (2013) *Diagnostic and Statistical Manual of Mental Disorders, Fifth Edition (DSM-5)*. Washington, DC: APA.

ASAN (2012a) *And Straight on until Morning: Essays on Autism Acceptance*. Washington, DC: The Autistic Press.

ASAN (2012b) *Take Action: Help Us Mourn Murders of Disabled People*. Available at www.autisticadvocacy.org/2012/03/take-action-help-us-mourn-murders-of-disabled-people, accessed on 6 November 2015.

Attfield, E., and Morgan, S.H. (2006) *Living with Autistic Spectrum Disorders: Guidance for Parents, Carers, and Siblings* (Illustrated edition). London: Paul Chapman.

Autism Association of Western Australia (2007) *Living with Autism: Practical Strategies For Supporting People with Autism Spectrum Disorders*. Subiaco, W.A.: Autism Association of Western Australia.

Baggs, A. (2012) 'The Meaning of Self-Advocacy.' In A. Bascom (ed.) *Loud Hands: Autistic People Speaking*. Washington, DC: ASAN.

Baron-Cohen, S. (1997) *Mindblindness: An Essay on Autism and Theory of Mind*. Cambridge, MA: MIT Press.

Bettelheim, B. (1972) *The Empty Fortress: Infantile Autism and the Birth of the Self*. New York: Free Press.

Broderick, A., and Ne'eman, A. (2008) 'Autism as metaphor: narrative and counter-narrative.' *International Journal of Inclusive Education 12*, 5–6, 459–476.

Brown, L. (2011) 'The significance of semantics: person-first language, why it matters.' *Autistic Hoya*. Available at www.autistichoya.com/2011/08/significance-of-semantics-person-first.html, accessed on 6 November 2015.

Brown, L. (2014) 'It's illegal to torture prisoners and animals but not disabled people.' *Washington Post*, 22 July. Available at www.washingtonpost.com/posteverything/wp/2014/07/22/its-illegal-to-torture-prisoners-and-animals-but-not-disabled-people, accessed on 6 November 2015.

Çevik, K. (2012) *The Autism Wars*. Available at www.theautismwars.blogspot.ca, accessed on 6 November 2015.

Chew, K. (2006) 'Let's not blame the victim: a call for restraint and responsibility.' *Autism Vox*. Available at www.blisstree.com/2006/06/22/mental-health-wellbeing/lets-not-blame-the-victim-a-call-for-restraint-and-responsibility, accessed on 6 November 2015.

Connor, S. (2010) 'Breakthrough brings fresh hope for families living with autism.' *Dublin Herald*, 10 June. Available at www.herald.ie/lifestyle/health-beauty/breakthrough-brings-fresh-hope-for-families-living-with-autism-2215041.html, accessed on 6 November 2015.

Dillon, K.M. (1995) *Living with Autism: The Parents' Stories* (Illustrated edition). Boone, NC: Parkway Publishers.

Durbin-Westby, P. (2012) 'I am not a self-advocate.' [Blog.] Available at www.paulacdurbinwestbyautisticblog.blogspot.ca/2012/11/i-am-not-self-advocate.html, accessed on 6 November 2015.

Easter Seals (2008) 'Easter seals study sheds new light on parents' life-long fears, anxieties and critical supports needed to raise a child with autism.' [Press release.] Available at www.easterseals.com/site/PageServer?pagename=ntl_pr_autism_study, accessed on 6 November 2015.

Feinstein, A. (2010) *A History of Autism: Conversations with the Pioneers* (Illustrated edition). Malden, MA: Wiley.

Freehling, A. (2001) 'Living with autism: disorder disconnects kids from world.' *Daily Press*, 18 February. Available at http://articles.dailypress.com/2001-02-18/news/0102150192_1_raleigh-s-mother-secretin-gel, accessed on 6 November 2015.

Guerry, Y. (2008) 'Living with autism in the UK.' *BBC News*, 2 April. Available at http://news.bbc.co.uk/2/hi/uk_news/7326323.stm, accessed on 6 November 2015.

Kanner, L. (1943) 'Autistic disturbances of affective contact.' *Nervous Child 2*, 2, 217–230.

Lamont, L. (2004a) 'When love is not enough.' *Sydney Morning Herald*, 1 June. Available at www.smh.com.au/articles/2004/05/31/1085855494917.html, accessed on 6 November 2015.

Lamont, L. (2004b) 'Dawes "has suffered too much".' *Sydney Morning Herald*, 3 June. Available at www.smh.com.au/articles/2004/06/02/1086058923624.html, accessed on 6 November 2015.

Linton, S. (1998) *Claiming Disability: Knowledge and Identity*. New York: New York University Press.

Lovaas, O. I. (1987) 'Behavioral treatment and normal educational and intellectual functioning in autistic children.' *Journal of Consulting and Clinical Psychology 55*, 1, 3–9.

Luciano, P. (2006) 'This was not about autism.' *Peoria Journal Star*, 26 May, p.A1.

Mallett, R., and Runswick-Cole, K. (2012) 'Commodifying Autism: The Cultural Contexts of "Disability" in the Academy.' In D. Goodley, B. Hughes and L.J. Davis (eds) *Disability and Social Theory*. Basingstoke: Palgrave MacMillan.

McGuire, A. (2012) 'Buying time: the s/pace of advocacy and the cultural production of autism.' *Canadian Journal of Disability Studies 2*, 3, 98–124.

McGuire, A. (2015) '"Life Worth Defending": An Analysis of the "War on Autism" in Times of Terror.' In S. Tremain (ed.) *Foucault and the Government of Disability* (Second edition). Ann Arbor, MI: University of Michigan Press.

McGuire, A.E., and Michalko, R. (2011) 'Minds between us: autism, mindblindness and the uncertainty of communication.' *Educational Philosophy and Theory 43*, 2, 162–177.

McMartin, P. (2007) 'Living with autism.' *Vancouver Sun*, April 21. Available at www.bowdiges.org/documents/files/Vancouver_sun_article.pdf, accessed on 21 January 2016.

Michalko, R. (1999) *The Two-In-One: Walking with Smokie, Walking with Blindness*. Philadelphia, PA: Temple University Press.

Michalko, R. (2002) *The Difference that Disability Makes*. Philadelphia, PA: Temple University Press.

Overboe, J. (1999) 'Difference in itself: validating disabled people's lived experience.' *Body and Society 5*, 4, 17–30.

Rones, N. (2009) 'Living with Autism: "Losing My Little Boy".' *Redbook Magazine*, July 19. Available at www.redbookmag.com/kids-family/advice/living-with-autism-0208, accessed on 6 November 2015.

Ross, D.S., and Jolly, K.A. (2006) *That's Life with Autism: Tales and Tips for Families with Autism.* Philadelphia, PA: Jessica Kingsley Publishers.

Sampier, K. (2008a) '"She wanted the autism gone": Prosecution lays out case in McCarron trial; girl's father says condition wasn't severe.' *Peoria Journal Star*, 8 January, p.A1.

Sampier, K. (2008b) '"I hated the autism so, so much": Jury in McCarron trial hears confession tape; defense begins presenting its case.' *Peoria Journal Star*, 11 January, p.A1.

Sinclair, J. (1999) 'Why I dislike "person first" language.' Available at www.jimsinclair.org/person_first.htm, accessed on 21 January 2016.

Sinclair, J. (2012) 'Don't mourn for us.' *Autonomy: The Critical Journal of Interdisciplinary Autism Studies 1*, 1. (Original work published in 1993.)

Smith, J. (2006) 'Murder of autistics.' *This Way of Life.* Available at www.geocities.ws/growingjoel/murder.html, accessed on 6 November 2015.

Snyder, S.L., and Mitchell, D.T. (2006) *Cultural Locations of Disability.* Chicago, IL: University of Chicago Press.

Titchkosky, T. (2001) 'Disability: a rose by any other name? People-first language in Canadian society.' *Canadian Review of Sociology/Revue Canadienne De Sociologie 38*, 2, 125–140.

Winfrey, O. (2007) 'Living with autism.' *The Oprah Winfrey Show* [Television Programme]. Available at www.oprah.com/world/Living-with-Autism, accessed on 6 November 2015.

Yergeau, M. (2013) 'Clinically significant disturbance: on theorists who theorize Theory of Mind.' *Disability Studies Quarterly 33*, 4.

CHAPTER 6

THE COMMODIFICATION OF AUTISM
WHAT'S AT STAKE?

Rebecca Mallett and Katherine Runswick-Cole

INTRODUCTION

We (the authors of this chapter) are both disability studies 'academics' but we also both have personal experience of disablement (by that we mean the oppression caused by disabling barriers and ideas) so, for us, 'disability' is always theoretical, political *and* personal. This chapter explores the intersections of theory, politics and personal experience to put forward the suggestion that, in the contemporary socio-economic context, autism has become a commodity; it is produced, exchanged, traded and consumed. From here we ask what is at stake for those labelled with the now commodified category of 'autism' and further suggest that liberation will only be achieved through recognising the processes of commodification at the moments they occur. These suggestions have been long in the making and represent many, many conversations over coffee, reflections during country walks and emotional reactions at academic conferences. We appreciate that people will disagree with our conclusions and will perhaps question our right to speak. We offer our thoughts here in the hope of contributing to continuing debates about the use and viability of labelling people, the dominance and power of medicine and the possibility of an inclusive response to human difference. We begin our chapter where all this began, with sharing two tales from our own lives.

> *Tale One*: Waiting at the airport, my son became upset. I approached the woman at the check-in and said, 'I'm really sorry I don't speak Italian, my son is autistic, he finds waiting difficult, please could you let us through?' She replied enthusiastically 'autistico handicappi!' – she cleared our way past the line and waved us through. I wondered whether 'autism' was now a code word, universally understood. (Author's personal encounter, 2007)

> *Tale Two*: In a lift, I was asked that question, prefaced as it always is, with a caveat – 'I hope you don't mind me asking but...what's wrong with you?' I

> replied, 'Nothing.' I took less than a second but it took some thinking about. Knowing I was to leave the lift at the next floor and therefore only had time to state a label, and knowing that mine is a diagnosis without a media profile, I also knew that the label on its own would not answer the question. (Author's personal encounter, 2003, cited in Mallett and Runswick-Cole 2014, p.125)

In both tales above, difference is, as Titchkosky (2008, p.133) comments, 'demarcated and encoded as some "thing" found wrong in individuals', as some 'thing' needing explanation. Furthermore, in both tales difference as a 'thing' is (or is expected to be) encapsulated and labelled by a named category of impairment. However, all is not equal. The two impairment categories in these tales function in very distinctive and, we argue, specifically *cultural* ways. In Tale One, at the airport, the impairment category appears to have a high, even international, status and performs a crucial function in communicating a shared understanding and shortens the queuing time. In Tale Two, in the lift, the impairment category is unfamiliar, is considered to lack a profile and is then denied the ability to communicate a shared knowledge of its meaning. Both label a state of 'impairment' but those labels function in very different ways – and that troubled us.

At first we thought it was because there was a lack of vocabulary to help us frame the 'trouble' we were feeling. It may be true, as Linton (1998, p.530) has commented, that, 'we are deficient in language to describe [impairment] any other way than as a "problem"'. And, make no mistake, we were in trouble, in already troubled waters. Goodley and Roets (2008, p.239) have told us that 'impairment is a tricky issue' and later, before offering an overview of the place of impairment in disability studies, Goodley (2011, p.28) reiterated, 'impairment talk creates conflict'. Given this fraught and fractious area within UK disability studies (for reasons we explore shortly) we proceeded with care. It wasn't long before we realised that our troubles would not be solved by replacing the allusion to 'handicap' with more a positive description, and neither would they be ameliorated by more awareness of the lesser-known impairment category.

In part because there has been an exponential growth in the number of impairment labels in recent decades (Goodley 2014), it seemed to us that trying to raise 'awareness' of each individual impairment label is, ultimately, a fruitless and self-defeating task. Crucially, we thought there was a more deep-rooted inequality at work and improving labels or increasing awareness would not change the terms of engagement. As we thought more closely about where the inequality was, we realised that it was not in how these impairment categories were used, but in their *capacity* to be used and this put us on a path to thinking about this issue in terms of social and cultural relations.

We first told these tales to each other over seven years ago and since then we have been busy interrogating the socio-cultural production and consumption of impairment categories; exploring their relationship to ideas of 'normal', examining the mundane cultural work they take on and investigating their limits and possibilities within both academia and political activism (Mallett and Runswick-Cole 2010, 2012, 2014, 2016; Runswick-Cole 2014). In this chapter we build on these previously presented and published areas of our work to further explore the category in our tales which seems to have achieved 'culturally useful' status, that of autism.

We want to suggest that a way of explaining the processes by which an impairment category, such as autism, gains and maintains its *capacity* to be used, is to argue that far from being neutral or 'natural', impairment is, and impairments are, constructed, produced and consumed through varied social, cultural, political and economic contingencies. Therefore it is crucial that when trying to account for inequalities in how impairment categories function, and thereby how they are experienced and responded to, we must pay attention to the prevailing socio-economic contexts and use theoretical approaches that enable us to do so. We do this by exploring the part played by contemporary capitalist consumer culture in the making and sustaining of autism as a commodity (Mallett and Runswick-Cole 2012). We will show how work which considers 'culturally useful objects' (Miller 2003) – particularly, the commodification of 'natural objects' – can be very useful in understanding the logics of contemporary capitalist consumer culture, and thereby in understanding how all is not equal when it comes to the formation and use of impairment categories.

For us, acknowledging and understanding the commodification of impairment categories is crucial in ensuring that we – as academics, practitioners, friends, family members, indeed as ourselves – do not perpetuate a disservice to disabled people.[1] For this reason, the remainder of the chapter considers the implications of the commodification of autism. We focus on autism because this is an impairment label with which we have been personally and professionally associated, but also, as we describe in later sections, because autism has become a particular focus of attention in academia and in wider social and cultural contexts (Mallett and Runswick-Cole 2012). However, we want to underline that our arguments could be applied to many other impairment categories; we are using autism as an exemplar. At a time when many impairment categories are jostling

1 In line with our position on the distinction between impairment and disability, we use the collective term 'disabled people' in order to underline 'the view that disability is something done to a person, not something a person individually has' (Mallett and Runswick-Cole 2014, p.4). In doing so, we acknowledge this as a theoretical, personal and political choice.

for position in the public consciousness (a perfect example of which was the 2014 'Ice Bucket Challenge' to raise awareness of, and funds for, Motor Neurone Disease) we want to start a conversation about capitalism's increasing role in 'impairment', with a view to highlighting the dangers therein.

OUR STARTING POINTS: DEFINING IMPAIRMENT(S)

Previously we have discussed the mechanisms by which autism has become a commodity within the world of academia (Mallett and Runswick-Cole 2012). In order to do so, we are already coming from two significant starting points: (a) that impairment can be (theoretically) considered as different from disability; and (b) that impairment categories should not be considered to be 'objective concepts' but are instead constructed through social relations. Before discussing autism as a commodity, we explain these starting points in a little more detail.

(a) Impairment can be considered as different from disability

Within UK disability studies there is often a distinction made between impairment and disability. The exact origin of this distinction is contestable but the source most often cited as key is the definition offered by Disabled People's International (DPI), an umbrella group of organisations run by disabled people. They stated (DPI 1982, cited in Goodley 2011, p.6) the distinction as follows:

- *Impairment* is the functional limitation within the individual caused by physical, mental or sensory impairment.
- *Disability* is the loss or limitation of opportunities to take part in the normal life of the community on an equal level with others due to physical and social barriers.

Despite the tautological nature of first part, 'impairment' is clearly positioned as referring to the body and/or the mind, related to individuals and deemed to be a limited, and limiting, state of being. The second part of the distinction, however, repositions 'disability' as something different from impairment. Here, disability refers to the marginalisation of people due to the (unhelpful) ways in which society chooses to respond to those who are deemed 'different-from-the-norm'. Disability is therefore the result of prejudice, oppression and discrimination. The important move which is then made is to argue that too often people are talked of in terms of being isolated and tragic individuals suffering from their impairments (Oliver 1996), when in fact the real difficulties in their lives (which *dis-able* them) are socially created by, for instance, 'inaccessible education, information and communication systems, working environments, inadequate disability benefits, discriminatory health and social support services, inaccessible transport, houses

and public buildings and amenities, and the devaluing of disabled people through negative images in the media' (Barnes 2003, p.9).

For us, this is a useful distinction because it moves the 'problem' from the individual to society. This can be extremely liberating for disabled people as Liz Crow (1996, p.206) has commented, when discussing her feelings on first reading about this distinction:

> This was the explanation I had sought for years. Suddenly what I had always known, deep down, was confirmed. It wasn't my body that was responsible for all my difficulties, it was external factors, the barriers constructed by the society in which I live. I was being dis-abled – my capabilities and opportunities were being restricted – by prejudice, discrimination, inaccessible environments and inadequate support. Even more importantly, if all the problems had been created by society, then surely society could un-create them. Revolutionary! (Crow 1996, p.206)

While whole-heartedly supporting a revolutionary refocus on the social, Crow (1996) goes on to argue that we shouldn't forget impairment or our experiences of the body/mind. She contends that we are mistaken to present 'impairment as irrelevant, neutral and sometimes positive, but never, ever, as the quandary it really is' (Crow 1996, p.208). We agree, and it is how 'impairment' should (or rather should not) be presented to which we now turn.

(b) Impairment categories should not be considered to be 'objective concepts'

Impairment is a quandary, and one which, as we hinted in the introduction, has caused quite a lot of conflict within UK disability studies. These tensions are heightened whenever disability studies engage with an impairment-specific area, such as autism. Debates over whether and how the body, the mind and our subjective experiences of them should be approached within disability studies are ongoing (Mallett and Runswick-Cole 2014; Shakespeare 2006; Thomas 1999, 2007) and for us they matter because how we choose to talk about people and about ourselves matters; it mattered at the airport and it mattered in the lift. We recognise the dangers of 'bringing back' impairment as a valid category of study and would argue that when we do so we need to do so carefully. For us, one of the problems occurs when impairment is mistakenly thought of, and engaged with, as an 'objective concept'.

Crow (1996, p.211) states: 'Impairment, at its most basic level, is a purely objective concept which carries no intrinsic meaning. Impairment simply means that aspect of a person's body does not function or they function with difficulty.' She is attempting to make distinctions between the materiality of flesh and bones

and the personal (and the social) interpretations which make up our experiences. However, we would argue that it 'is not possible to talk about, or experience, the body outside of culture' (Mallett and Runswick-Cole 2014, p.127) and this includes the moments when we talk about flesh and bones. We contend that impairment, and impairment categories such as autism, are not, and should never be considered as, naturally occurring, scientifically discoverable, 'objective concepts' for they are always *within* cultural, as well as social, political and economic, contexts.

In order to support our position, like Goodley (2011), we point to work done on the social construction of other seemingly 'natural' phenomena and to the assertion that rocks are cultural too (Edwards, Ashmore and Potter 1995). As Edwards *et al.* (1995, p.30) note, rocks are:

> ...categorised, included in the definition of the natural world, classified into sedimentary and igneous, divided into grains of sand, pieces of gravel, pebbles, stones, rocks, boulders, mountains, domesticated in parks and ornamental gardens, protected in wildernesses, cut, bought, used and displayed as 'precious stones'; and include as a sub-category 'girls' best friends'; not to mention coolant for vodka!

Similarly, Davis (2002) has suggested that rather than *discovering* pre-existing categories, since the mid-nineteenth century, science and medicine should be seen as *establishing* and giving legitimacy to categories of 'difference' through the circulation of 'medicalised, scientificised discourses'. In other words, science and medicine have been busy creating and authorising impairment categories, one of which is autism, as naturally occurring, scientifically discoverable 'objective concepts'. We briefly explore *how* this is done shortly.

It should be noted that we are not the first to go down this route in terms of impairment: Shelley Tremain (2002, 2005) has interrogated biomedical practices, which have been complicit in the emergence and governance of disability and impairment. In terms of specific categories, work includes: Goodley and Rapley (2002) on learning disabilities; Campbell (2013) on dyslexia; Molloy and Vasil (2002) on Asperger Syndrome; Nadesan (2005) and Bumiller (2009) on autism; Hickey-Moody (2009) on Down syndrome; and Davis (2008) on Obsessive Compulsive Disorder (OCD). These are extremely useful contributions to the field of knowledge we are advocating. However, our specific focus here is on the *capacity* of impairment categories once they come into being. In order to do this, we briefly have to reach back to the moment of construction – the moment of categorisation and definition – because it is the moment when what Goodley (2011, p.113) calls an '*impairment object*' is created that the possibility of commodification is enabled and it is the commodification of impairment which is our ultimate focus.

DEFINING AUTISM: MAKING COMMODIFICATION POSSIBLE

During our exploration of autism as a commodity in academia, we deployed some geographic work on the commodification of nature, in which the geographer Noel Castree (2003) describes *abstraction* as a key process. By abstraction Castree (2003, p.281) is referring to how 'the qualitative specificity of any individualised thing (a person, a seed, a gene or what-have-you) is assimilated to the qualitative homogeneity of a broader type or process'. In other words, how the specifics of one 'thing' come to characterise a bigger 'thing'. We used these ideas to argue that diagnostic categories, such as autism, are *products* of individual people with individual behaviours being absorbed into a broader uniform and standardised 'type' – the diagnostic category of autism (Mallett and Runswick-Cole 2012). To put it another way, through medical and psychological endeavour, diverse biologies and biographies are gathered, smoothed over and labelled as if they were all the same.

We went on to explore a related idea from Robertson (2000), the concept of *functional abstraction*, where individual cases (for us, individual people) are considered *instantiations* of the generic category (for us, autism). It is useful here to consider Robertson's (2000, p.472) exploration of the 'formal assessment methodologies and taxonomic systems', which work to commodify 'wetlands'. In doing so he demonstrates how functional abstraction works, and comments:

> Taxonomic classification systems provide both an imposed order and a common language for scientists [...] assessment methodologies involve paper forms, filled out on a brief visit to a site, which allow the assessor to total up a 'score' for a given site. (Robertson 2000, p.473)

Thinking about the *Diagnostic and Statistical Manual of Mental Disorders* (DSM-5) (APA 2013) and the Autism Diagnostic Interview (ADI) (Le Couteur *et al.* 1989), it is possible to re-read Robertson's account of functional abstraction as a description of the processes which occur during diagnostic assessment. The DSM is described by the APA as:

> the standard classification of mental disorders used by mental health professionals in the United States. It is intended to be applicable in a wide array of contexts and used by clinicians and researchers of many different orientations (e.g., biological, psychodynamic, cognitive, behavioral [sic], interpersonal, family/systems). (APA 2014)

Similarly, the revised version of the Autism Diagnostic Interview (ADI-R) is described by its developers as:

> a standardised, semi-structured, investigator-based interview for caregivers of autistic individuals, which provides a diagnostic algorithm for the ICD-10 definition of autism (World Health Organisation [WHO], 1992) and DSM-IV (American Psychiatric Association [APA], 1993). (Lord, Rutter and Le Couteur 1994, p.660)

And, thus, fulfils 'a need for an instrument that could differentiate autism from other disorders' (Lord *et al.* 1994, p.660). Here, the role of functional abstraction in the process by which individuals are identified, or defined, as having autism becomes clear. The 'taxonomic classification system' contained in the DSM can certainly be said to be imposing an 'order' and offering a 'common language', while the ADI-R is an interview schedule 'filled out' on a 'visit' to the clinician's office allowing 'the assessor to total up' an algorithm. A number of other instruments for diagnosing autism have also been developed and the uptake of these point again to the presence and success of abstraction. Indeed, diagnostic assessment practices only make sense if the process of abstraction is at work and autism has, at some level, been coherently separated out as a 'discrete ontological' entity with its 'own qualitative specificities' (Castree 2003, p.280), identifiable from other entities.

The emergence of autism as a discrete ontological entity is a crucial moment, for it is the moment when it becomes a 'thing' that it becomes consumable and, therefore, amenable to commodification. The moment autism is defined as an identifiable category is the very moment it begins to have potential as a commodity. We will leave it to others in this book to argue over the 'science' of autism, that is to say whether, and to what extent, autism is identifiable from other categories of existence and other ways of being. What we are interested in is how the emerged and used category of 'autism' has become commodified, rather than whether or how 'it' really exists.

AUTISM AS A 'SUCCESSFUL' COMMODITY

By the processes outlined above, it can be argued that all impairment categories have the potential to be consumable and become a commodity. In this sense, autism is not unique. However, not all impairment categories go on to become 'successful' commodities. In this section, we aim to demonstrate the success of autism as a commodity, which is bought and sold at an astounding rate, becoming deeply embedded within the processes and practices of capitalist consumer culture.

We have previously highlighted the educational courses, scientific and academic conferences, research centres and published research which suggests that, over the past decade, the institutional exchange of autism 'knowledge'

has become big business (Mallett and Runswick-Cole 2012). Although we discussed wider concerns, for the purposes of clarity we narrowed our examples, mostly, to UK social science arenas. However, with the lines between academia, government and voluntary sectors becoming increasingly blurred, it is getting harder to distinguish institutional and national boundaries. For instance, at the time of writing, ICare4Autism's African Autism Awareness and Intervention Initiative is preparing to launch a programme in Ghana (ICare4Autism 2014). ICare4Autism is also known as the International Center for Autism Research and Education, Inc. and is a global, non-profit organisation based in New York City, USA. Another example which crosses institutional and national boundaries is the Autism Research and Training Initiative in India (ARTI), which was funded by the USA-based organisation Autism Speaks (Autism Speaks 2014).

It may seem strange to be including academia and non-governmental, non-profit, charity organisations within the scope of 'capitalist consumer culture'. In using this term we are advocating a conceptualisation of the contemporary global world as one 'driven by the social arrangement in which the buying and selling of goods and services is not only the predominant activity of everyday life but is also an important arbiter of social organisation, significance and control' (Mallett and Runswick-Cole 2012, p.37). The pervasive nature of such social arrangements, particularly in the global North, means that academia and non-governmental charity organisations are as implicated in the capitalist logic as big corporate business, in the form of multinational companies such as Starbucks or Google.

This capitalist logic can be seen in the arena of autism therapy. Applied Behaviour Analysis (ABA), Relationship Development Intervention (RDI) and the Son-Rise Program are just some examples of 'therapies' that are available to be bought on the open market. Rather like the now-familiar strap-line in shampoo advertisements, the Son-Rise Program was even voted the 'Best Therapy' at the 2011 AutismOne conference awards. These therapies use academic (often psychological) techniques but are offered through non-governmental, not-for-profit and/or charitable organisations in the form of books, CDs, DVDs and training events. Son-Rise products, for instance, are delivered through the Autism Treatment Center of America (a trade-marked name), but are part of the Option Institute, a non-profit, federally tax-exempt, charitable organisation. A Son-Rise Starter Kit, for example, is currently retailing at $98 and includes three books, four CDs and a DVD (Option Institute 2014).

This isn't to say that big corporate businesses aren't also getting in on the autism act, as established retailers can be seen using 'autism' as a category to sell and package their own products. The store Toys R Us, for instance, offers suggestions in the form of a list of 'Ten Toys that Speak to Autism' (cited in McGuire 2011) and the online retailer Amazon promotes their 'large collection

of sensory toys for autism' (Amazon.com 2014), which includes the 'Tangle Fuzzies Great ADHD/Autism Toy'.

Sometimes what is being exchanged is far less tangible than a book or a fuzzy toy. McGuire (2013, p.99) discusses how in 'the summer of 2007, one of the many places where one could learn about autism and autism advocacy was on the side of a special series of paper Starbucks coffee cups'. That summer, in a coalition of autism, advocacy and capitalist consumer culture, across North America coffee was consumed with a little bit of autism on the side, as over five million Starbucks cups displayed a statement from the founder of Autism Speaks urging the drinker to 'learn the early warning signs of autism' (Autism Speaks 2007, cited in McGuire 2013, p.99). Here, it could be argued, Starbucks is capitalising (pun intended) on the, now well-documented, public fascination with autism (Murray 2008) by using 'category intrigue' (Moore 2006) to sell more coffee. The *use* of autism here is further proof of its increasingly commodified status.

The realm of contemporary popular culture tells a similar story of use and fascination, with many films (e.g. *Mary and Max*; *My Name Is Khan*; *Rain Man*), plays (e.g. *Curious Incident of the Dog in the Night-Time* and *Spoonface Steinberg*), television programmes (e.g. Jonah Jeremiah 'JJ' Jones in *Skins*, Virginia Dixon in *Grey's Anatomy* and Channel 4's *Autistic Gardener*), videogames (e.g. Jade 'The Indigo Child' in *Fahrenheit*) and museum exhibitions (e.g. *Welcome to Our World... Living with Autism*) re-presenting 'autism' for mass entertainment markets. The picture is the same in the publishing industry with a plethora of novels (e.g. Mark Haddon's *Curious Incident of the Dog in the Night-Time*, 2003; Nicholas Sparks' *Dear John*, 2006; Jodie Picoult's *House Rules*, 2010; Margaret Attwood's *Oryx and Crake*, 2003), autobiographies (e.g. Grandin 1996; Higashida 2013; Jackson 2002; Lawson 2000) and newspaper articles across the globe (e.g. Belluck 2014; Doherty 2014; Griffiths 2014; Karambu 2010) displaying a similar fascination with the topic. There are many, many more examples and in all of them some element of 'autism' has been used, packaged and is being exchanged for financial gain. So, with all this selling, *what*, we may ask, is being bought? Our answer utilises the notion of 'promise'.

THE 'PROMISE' OF AUTISM: BUYING A 'NEW' NORMAL

The insights of W.F. Haug (1986) are really helpful here. He discusses how market exchange depends on the consumer's self-acknowledged need for the object. However, at the moment of exchange, the precise object has not yet been experienced; it is instead the *promise* of its use-value that is bought. For Haug the promise is established through its appearance, which helps us to refine the

question: 'What is the *promise* perceived in autism?' We argue that it is the promise of coherence that makes us buy (into) autism.

We can follow this at work in the realm of *autism therapy*. If we consider autism therapies to be essentially a marketplace for autism 'expertise' it is clear it has become a very successful (and, for some, lucrative) area. Interventions and treatment programmes provide a space for the exchange of 'valuable' information for people labelled with autism and their families and offer the 'promise' of remediation, rehabilitation and, perhaps, resolution, in the form of a cure.

As we discussed earlier, predominately biomedical but also social, political and economic practices of abstraction have created a situation where 'expert' professionals coherently produce autism as a 'thing' because they perceive a need for certain behaviours and symptoms to be explained and remedied. Parents and families help (re)produce autism in their interactions with the medical profession and consume autism in order to understand and better care for their loved ones. Indeed, being a 'good parent' depends on consumption of such knowledge. Practitioners and academics consume such knowledge in their efforts to fulfil the perceived need for informed interventions in certain situations (e.g. the classroom). Individuals also consume such knowledge in efforts to better understand themselves. Thus the circular logic of a self-sustaining commodity chain is established through the power of promise.

The power of this 'promise' lies in a consensus on what we have termed elsewhere the 'normal abnormal' or 'new' normals (Mallett and Runswick-Cole 2016). Capitalist consumer logic demands goods that conform and that idiosyncrasies are ironed out (Holt 2002). We suggest that these 'ironed out' 'specificities of impairment labels are revealed as a way to indirectly interact with difference and, in doing so, neutralise its danger by gaining knowledge over it' (Mallett and Runswick-Cole 2016). In other words, when we buy (into) impairment labels, such as autism, we do so in part because they promise to take away the danger of the unknown. They do this not only by helping to explain diversions from 'normal' but, and crucially, by also providing a new set of norms for what it means to be 'normal' *within* the specified subcategory of 'abnormal' – that is, what it means to have 'autism'. However, it doesn't stop there, as medical diagnoses (and the impairment categories they deliver) are also used as essential tourist information (Mallett and Runswick-Cole 2016) for those travelling to or through the land of that particular impairment. Providing the evidence for not being normal is only the starting point; impairment labels also offer information on potential life span, possible behavioural traits, probable co-morbidity factors, quality of life and even the likelihood of finding employment. For instance, the DSM-5 informs readers of the following about people diagnosed with 'autism':

> Extreme difficulties in planning, organisation, and coping with change negatively impact academic achievement, even for students with above-average intelligence. During adulthood, these individuals may have difficulties establishing independence because of continued rigidity and difficulty with novelty.
>
> Many individuals with autism spectrum disorder, even without intellectual disability, have poor adult psychosocial functioning as indexed by measures such as independent living and gainful employment. (APA 2013, p.57)

It may be that when impairment labels are bought into, what is being purchased is the 'promise' of a new 'normal', and a new set of expectations for that new normal; but like all commodities, the promise is never fully fulfilled and the satisfaction is only temporary because what has been delivered is partial and incomplete for it is the result of the process of *abstraction.* Consumers buying into the idea of a new normal (Mallett and Runswick-Cole 2016) therefore find, eventually, that this new category is unable fully to explain or account for the difference they, or those they are close to, experience. A phrase we have often heard from autism advocates and activists alike is 'if you've met one person with autism, you've met one person with autism', begging the question, what's the point of the label 'autism'? While the response might be that it is about *getting to know the individual with autism,* such labelled people often have so little in common with one another that, despite the promise, 'autism' lacks explanatory power.

Although the temporary nature of the initial satisfaction is deeply experienced by many, it is not the death knell it perhaps should be, for within the logic of capitalist consumer culture it becomes a moment of opportunity. The loss of satisfaction is a moment exploited for further market expansion and profit as the consumer's unsatisfied desire is simply channelled in another direction (another therapy, another conference, another DVD, another book chapter) in an increasingly divergent market place.

BRANDING AUTISM: DIFFERENT FEAST, SAME TABLE

Commodities are not fixed or static; rather, they are 'things' in motion that are reinvented – rebranded – often within shifting cultural or temporal locations to suit local and changing sensibilities (Jackson 1999). This, again, is essential to the logic of capitalism and it could be said that autism's ability to be flexible is part of its success. Slater (1997, p.105) associates modern productivity with 'increasing differentiation of goods and increasing refinement and discrimination in tastes, needs and experiences'. Autism as a 'spectrum' of disorders and with its myriad co-morbidity factors allows for further and further differentiation and

refinement, making its strength its ability to fragment and cater for an increasing array of needs and experiences.

Earlier we discussed how consumers' (people labelled with autism; parents/carers; allied professionals) desire for knowledge of this new normal is often channelled through therapy brands such as Applied Behaviour Analysis (ABA), Relationship Development Intervention (RDI) and the Son-Rise Program. All of these can be seen as products of 'differentiation' for they emerged as a response to the perceived inadequacy of existing products, and have since become established 'brands' themselves. These products and brands will last as long as they are *perceived* as 'useful' (fulfilling the promise). But the commodity cycle never rests and sometimes it is consumers themselves who seek to break through the dominance of more established brands and differentiate the market place by creating their own brand, rather than simply consuming that which is foisted on them (Holt 2002).

In relation to autism therapy, Rupert Isaacson, the father of a son labelled with autism, is a good example of consumer turned producer. In his book, *Horse Boy: A Father's Quest to Find his Son*, Isaacson (2009) has developed and trademarked his own autism therapy, the Horse Boy Method. The method 'is not intended or offered as a cure for autism', the website tells us (Horse Boy 2009). However, and tantalisingly, '*ameliorative effects may or may not occur. The method was found to be very useful with Rupert's son Rowan and with other children subsequently. We simply follow what worked for Rowan and others but there is no guarantee of outcome*' (Horse Boy 2009). Despite this overt caveat to the 'promise' of the therapy, there are now Horse Boy Foundations in the USA and UK, Horse Boy Camps you can visit for a short family break and Independent Horse Boy Practitioners who have completed a two-day training programme.

While differentiation helps explain autism's continued success as a commodity (because the promise is never fully fulfilled and temporary satisfaction gives way to the need to consume again and thereby the opportunity to sell again), it also means we are stuck within its logic. Slater (1997, p.125) following Marcuse, speaks to this when he comments: 'identified so utterly with the commodities on offer, modern subjects cannot see alternatives or perceive the limited nature of satisfaction within the commodity system'. For instance, although the branding may be different the essentials of therapy 'products' remain incredibly similar. The Son-Rise Program claims that children can learn to speak, even if they've never spoken (Son-Rise Program, n.d.) whereas the Horse Boy Method talks about a number of techniques that seemed to bring about better verbal communication with Rupert's son (Horse Boy 2009).

It is here we begin our consideration of the implications of autism as a commodity. In the next section we argue that autism is so embedded in the cycle of commodification that even the movement which seeks to resist the

'autism-as-disorder' narrative, by re-using and re-inscribing the category with different meanings, cannot escape capitalist logic.

IMPLICATIONS: RE-INSCRIBING THE BRAND

As the example of consumer turned producer tells us, consumers are not merely cultural dupes or 'passive, nearly inert beings, acted upon as objects' (Holt 2002, p.72). Rather, consumers simultaneously consume, create and shape the meanings of the goods exchanged. Crucially, some consumers seek to 'emancipate themselves from marketer-imposed codes by altering their value to signify opposition to establishment values' (Ozanne and Murray 1995, p.523). The autism self-advocacy movement represents another example of consumers attempting to emancipate themselves from the established codes by challenging the 'autism-as-disorder' brand. Self-advocacy movements have tried to re-inscribe the autism brand with affirmative, oppositional meanings by calling for 'respect for neurodiversity' and 'the development of autistic cultural activities'.

Aspies for Freedom (AFF) identify 'neurodiverse' people as an oppressed minority group and Autism Pride Day is held on 18 June every year to celebrate autistic identity. Autism Pride Day directly challenges the meanings of autism invoked on World Autism Awareness Day (WAAD) held annually on 2 June (McGuire 2011). The difference between a neurodiverse understanding of autism and traditional biomedical approaches is that while self-advocates argue that autism is caused by differently wired brains, this difference is just that – a difference, rather than a 'disorder' (Runswick-Cole 2014). However, despite the attempts to do so, it is difficult to escape the capitalist logic of the markets. Brands work quickly to re-inscribe 'oppositional' meanings back into the dominant brand (Holt 2002) – we only have to think of the way in which 'Fair Trade' has been co-opted by big brands such as Nescafé.

We can see this at work in autism advocacy too. In the UK, for example, the mainstream National Autistic Society has re-appropriated the language of neurodiversity; its advice to media organisations is to use the phrase 'neurotypical' (used by the neurodiversity community) to describe 'normal' people (National Autistic Society, n.d.). The oppositional value of the neurodiversity brand is thus diluted. In order to create new opportunities for resistance, consumers must create alternative meanings as soon as the new meaning has lost its 'oppositional value' (Ozanne and Murray 1995, p.523). However, criticism of the neurodiversity movement from within the critical psychiatry movement suggests that this is certainly not an easy thing to do. As the oppositional value of neurodiversity can be seen only in relation to repositioning difference in more affirmative ways, it therefore keeps the original brand intact. Both Timimi, Gardner and McCabe (2010) and Runswick-Cole (2014) urge the neurodiversity movement to think

through the implications of hanging on to a medical diagnosis that is predicated on an acceptance of autistic difference as a biological/neurological truth.

For us, keeping the commodity intact results in many other issues being left unaddressed. In the rest of this chapter we explore some of these issues. In the next section we discuss the tendency for categories to act as the one and only 'truth' worth knowing, before moving on to highlight the dangers of investing in, and relying on, unreliable labels; and, finally, we suggest that embracing uncertainty may be our only hope.

IMPLICATIONS: DETERMINING DEFINITIONS

A further implication of Robertson's (2000) concept of *functional abstraction* is that individual cases (individual people) are often considered as examples of the generic category which 'stands over and above them' (Castree 2003, p.281). We contend here, as we have done previously (see Mallett and Runswick-Cole 2012), that if the dominance of medical definitions are left undisturbed, individuals, who are labelled with commodified impairments (such as autism) are in danger of being dissolved into inescapable, fixed and totalising impairment-led identities. As Robertson (2000, p.466) states, 'commodification involves an act of reference in which, through exchange, the abstraction is treated by actors as equivalent to the concrete'. The resulting experience of a 'concrete' label being considered before, and at times, instead of everything else that person is, or aspires to be, is all too obvious. For us, this is a form of psycho-emotional disablism as the label places limits on what disabled people 'can do' and 'can be' (Thomas 2007, p.72).

In their 2012 paper, 'Reading Rosie: the postmodern disabled child', Goodley and Runswick-Cole attempt to disrupt the dominance of pathological readings of the lives of disabled children. They tell the story of Rosie, a child they worked with as part of a research project (*Does Every Child Matter, Post-Blair? The Interconnections of Disabled Childhoods*; see Goodley and McLaughlin 2011). Goodley and Runswick-Cole (2012) juxtapose stories of Rosie that draw on orthodox understandings of autism as a biomedical deficit, a social model approach to disability, and a Nordic relational model of disability; as well as telling Rosie's story through a socio-cultural lens. Their aim is to consider the enabling and disabling potential of each of these stories. Rosie, they argue, is a child of whom a thousand stories could be told, and her 'autism' story is only one of many possible accounts (Goodley and Runswick-Cole 2012).

Here, we also seek to trouble the homogenisation of 'impairment subjectivities', which arise once 'impairment objects' (Goodley 2011) are created and legitimised. Academia is as guilty as anywhere in its thirst for 'autism'-specific research on lived experiences and the increasing use of the idea of an 'autistic subjectivity'. Our worry, as stated above, is the inevitable process of reduction that occurs

whenever a person is related to through a pre-existing label or category. The next section moves on to discuss the related danger inherent here: investing in, and relying on, labels which are themselves in flux.

IMPLICATIONS: INVESTING IN A CATEGORY

As we have previously noted, in 2010 six out of the seven editions of the leading disability studies journal *Disability and Society* included an article on either autism or Asperger Syndrome (Mallett and Runswick-Cole 2012). In the process of writing this chapter, we looked over the four years since we had observed this phenomenon and found that something very interesting had happened. In 2011, of the seven editions, four included a main article with 'autism' (or a related term[2]) in its title. The only other specific impairment category to appear more than once was Attention Deficit Hyperactivity Disorder (ADHD), with two mentions. In 2012, two of the seven editions included main articles focusing on 'autism' (although in both cases the editions included two separate pieces), and a further four editions included a 'book review' or a 'current issue' article on the topic, leaving only one edition with no mention of 'autism' in the titles of any of its contents. This seems to be the beginnings of a shift in attention. While the first four editions in 2013 followed a similar pattern (three had main articles with 'autism' in their title and the fourth included a book review) it then all went quiet. 'Autism' does not appear in any of the final four editions of that year. In the two years that have followed, the trend has continued. Of the ten editions published in 2014, only three included a main article featuring 'autism' in its title. In 2015, only two articles focused on autism; both appeared in issue 8. It remains to be seen whether these academic trends continue, but their presence sounds alarm bells as to the dangers of being 'in fashion', because what we know about fashion trends is that they rarely last very long.

The falling-off in autism as a focus does not seem to be due to a new kid on the block. In terms of specific impairments (here we are not including generic terms such as 'mental illness' or 'learning difficulties') there wasn't another category that received anywhere near the same level of attention. The only other specific impairments to be named in a title of a main *Disability and Society* article more than once over the four-year period (2011–2014) were ADHD and dyslexia – with three mentions each. When compared with a total of 12 main articles mentioning autism there isn't much of a contest. For us, the insights offered here are about the dangers of capitalist consumer culture, and the resulting commodification of impairment.

2 By 'related term', we mean other words that are used to also denote the use of the category of 'autism'. These were 'autistic', 'autistic spectrum', 'autistic spectrum disorder' and 'Asperger Syndrome'.

Slater (1997, p.157) describes 'fashion' as 'the constant change in tastes, goods, appearances, lifestyles that characterise modernity' and comments that 'producers intensify and exploit this dynamic, speeding it up through programmed cultural obsolescence and the constant renovation of markets'. In this case, the producers (the academics) do seem to be moving away from autism and into other markets in the hunt for the next big 'thing', which may or may not be tagged onto a specific impairment category. As we have argued, academic knowledge is always contingent on its social-cultural-political-economic contexts (Mallett and Runswick-Cole 2012) and therefore, at this moment in time, it is tied to a capitalist logic. For many the academic interest in 'autism' was welcomed. The boom time produced greater knowledge and understanding of the 'impairment' and the lived experiences of those so labelled. Some good practice was developed in relation to education, social care and technology. But for boom times to continue, the market needs to be constantly renovated. As we discussed above, this is often done by differentiation, and that is a process that wilfully makes one 'thing' useless in order to replace it with more useful 'things'.

While it appears that the boom time in autism is still in existence in many other areas, such as educational interventions, and differentiation is opening up new global autism markets at a rapid rate, the trends within disability studies should serve as a warning for autism's increasing its capitalist credentials. When a category, such as autism, becomes so deeply implicated within capitalism it necessarily comes with 'cultural obsolescence' pre-programmed into it. There is little escape from this capitalist logic; at some point, all useful 'things' become useless so that other useful 'things' can be purchased. There is nothing within the capitalist consumer system that protects autism's status as fascinating and able to turn a profit. For those associated with the category, the problem then becomes a problem of 'investment'. If one has invested (financially and/or emotionally) in something that was thought to have 'use-value' and its value starts to diminish, one is left high and dry.

Neither is there anything protecting the positions of the differentiated subcategories. A good example of this is the debates over the place of Asperger Syndrome (AS) in the recent edition of the DSM. With the publication of DSM-5, the diagnosis of Asperger Syndrome was removed as a separate category and, instead, became part of an umbrella category of Autism Spectrum Disorder (ASD). There was huge controversy over this change with worries expressed over people being undiagnosed and the withdrawal of support services. However, little was said about the impact on individuals of being defined one way only to be redefined through the publishing of a new medical manual. The actual implications of this DSM manoeuvre are yet to be documented, but it serves as a useful reminder of how precarious it is to invest in categories that are externally produced and exchanged.

We are returned here to the partial nature of the *abstraction* process and the (never-to be-satisfied) promises diagnosis offers. Given the persistent and pervasive nature of contemporary consumer culture it is easy to become disheartened and disillusioned with the current global order. In our conclusion, we want to offer some moments of hope and opportunity. We do this by highlighting three Cs: certainty, consciousness and commitment.

CONCLUSION: THE THREE CS

Nirmala Erevelles (2011) describes what it means to attend to the ambiguities of the diagnostic and treatment process when she recounts the experiences of her and her partner, Robert Young. When faced with a diagnosis of a 'Grade IV brain tumour – glioblastoma multiforme (GBM)', Erevelles (2011, p1) recounts how they were thrown into a world in which medical, neurological, economic, political, historical, social, cultural and material matters collided and from which, not only could the purely 'biological' not be separated, but the inherent (and shifting) power relations could not be ignored. As she discusses, while the label deceives by offering a soothing certainty – we 'know' what this is and how to handle it – such a label can never predict or account for the struggle with the US medical insurance company over the availability of a new treatment or the complex historical legacies of race and gender which led to a worry about public reaction to grand mal seizures if they occurred in the 'wrong place' at the 'wrong time'. Erevelles (2011) reminds us that bodies, minds, flesh, bones and behaviour are complicated *because* they are deeply enmeshed in their socio-economic contexts. Her account is poignant, profound and powerful and although it could easily have tipped into painting a very gloomy picture, it refuses to and instead hints at some options for optimism. In emphasising our three Cs we are actively borrowing from her work while also drawing together themes from our own.

1. *Exercise suspicion of* ***Certainty***. A theme throughout this chapter, and a point Erevelles (2011) reinforces, is the need to be suspicious of certainty whenever it is presented to us. As we have discussed, diagnostic categories, impairment labels, treatment regimes, and interventions often offer 'too good to be true' ordered and certain versions of reality. Once one acknowledges that such certainty is a fantasy and a by-product of the commodification process, you can engage with the world anew, and we suggest that this should be through a *conscious* engagement. Crucially, this does not involve a blanket rejection of all commodified things, but rather a *knowing* engagement.

2. *Practise* ***Conscious*** *engagement*. Erevelles (2011, p.7, citing Ebert 1996) posits her analytical framework as:

> a mode of knowing that inquires into what is not said, into the silences and the suppressed or missing. In order to uncover the concealed operations of power and the socio-economic relations connecting the myriad details and representations of our lives.

We too advocate the need to practise a mode of noticing the processes underpinning the situations in which we find ourselves. This book chapter, and our other work around impairment, could be seen within such tradition. In Mallett and Runswick-Cole (2012, p.46) we name this approach as *defetishisation* and describe it as 'the process by which we acknowledge our denial and work through the consequences of that acknowledgement'. The denial we are referring to is the denial of our own complicity in the status quo. In other words, by practising a conscious engagement with the world one must be willing to reflect on one's own role in producing and consuming and seek to do so consciously. Such knowledge can then enable us to, for instance, use and refuse labels at moments that matter for us and those we love and support. We advocate this approach because it aligns with our third C.

3. *Maintain political* ***Commitment***. We follow our explication of defetishisation by suggesting that doing so will 'contribute to the transformation of society' and enable the participation 'in efforts towards the continued emancipation of all disabled people' (Mallett and Runswick-Cole 2012, p.46). Likewise, in asking 'Why do some bodies matter more than others?' Erevelles (2011, p.6) is also revealing her political commitment to enable 'the conditions of possibility' (p.17) that surround the disabled body. We suggest that holding onto political and emancipatory commitments is a key component in the struggle for equality and against prejudice, oppression and discrimination on the basis of a perceived impairment.

Being suspicious of certainty, being consciously engaged and upholding a political commitment to emancipation may just be enough to resist the urge to measure, test, label and commodify and, thereby, ensure increasing respect of difference in its full glory.

REFERENCES

Amazon.com (2014) *Sensory Toys for Autism on Amazon.com.* Available at www.amazon.com/gp/feature.html?ie=UTF8&docId=1000899231, accessed on 9 November 2015.

American Psychiatric Association (APA) (2013) *Diagnostic and Statistical Manual of Mental Disorders, Fifth Edition (DSM-5).* Washington DC: American Psychiatric Association.

American Psychiatric Association (APA) (2014) *DSM.* Available at www.psych.org/practice/dsm, accessed on 9 November 2015.

Attwood, M. (2003) *Oryx and Crake.* London: Virago.

Autism Speaks (2014) *ARTI: The Autism Research and Training Initiative in India.* Available at www.autismspeaks.org/science/grants/arti-autism-research-training-initiative-india, accessed on 9 November 2015.

Barnes, C. (2003) 'What a difference a decade makes: reflections on doing "emancipatory" disability research.' *Disability and Society 18*, 1, 3–17.

Belluck, P. (2014) 'Study finds that brains with autism fail to trim synapses as they develop.' *New York Times,* 21 August. Available at www.nytimes.com/2014/08/22/health/brains-of-autistic-children-have-too-many-synapses-study-suggests.html?_r=1, accessed on 9 November 2015.

Bumiller, G. (2009) 'The geneticization of autism: from new reproductive technologies to the conception of genetic normalcy.' *Signs 34,* 4, 975–899.

Campbell, T. (2013) *Dyslexia: The Government of Reading.* Basingstoke: Palgrave MacMillan.

Castree, N. (2003) 'Commodifying what nature?' *Progress in Human Geography 27,* 3, 273–297.

Channel 4 (UK) (2015) *The Autistic Gardener* [Television Series].

Crow, L. (1996) 'Including All Our Lives: Renewing the Social Model of Disability.' In J. Morris (ed.) *Encounters With Strangers: Feminism and Disability.* London: Women's Press.

Davis, L.J. (2002) *Bending over Backwards: Disability, Dismodernism and Other Difficult Positions.* New York: New York University Press.

Davis, L.J. (2008) *Obsession: A History.* Chicago, IL: University of Chicago Press.

Doherty, E. (2014) 'School locked autistic children in dark room, parents claim.' *Herald Sun,* 18 May. Available at www.heraldsun.com.au/news/victoria/school-locked-autistic-children-in-dark-room-parents-claim/story-fni0fit3-1226921952506, accessed on 9 November 2015.

Edwards, D., Ashmore, M., and Potter, J. (1995) 'Death and furniture: the rhetoric, politics and theology of bottom line arguments against relativism.' *History of Human Sciences 8,* 2, 25–49.

Elliot, A. (dir.) (2009) *Mary and Max* [Film]. Icon Entertainment International.

Elsley, B., and Brittain, J. (creators) (2007–2013) *Skins* [Television Series]. E4 (UK).

Erevelles, N. (2011) *Disability and Difference in Global Contexts: Enabling a Transformative Body Politic.* New York: Palgrave Macmillan.

Goodley, D. (2011) *Disability Studies: An Interdisciplinary Introduction.* London: Sage.

Goodley, D. (2014) *Dis/ability Studies: Theorising Disablism and Ableism.* Abingdon: Routledge.

Goodley, D., and McLaughlin, J. (2011) *Does Every Child Matter, Post-Blair? The Interconnections of Disabled Childhoods.* ESRC end of award report, RES-062-23-1138. Swindon: ESRC. Available at www.scie-socialcareonline.org.uk/does-every-child-matter-post-blair-the-interconnections-of-disabled-childhoods-esrc-end-of-award-report-res-062-23-1138/r/a11G00000017w8VIAQ, accessed on 9 November 2015.

Goodley, D., and Rapley, M. (2002) 'Changing the Subject: Postmodernity and People with Learning Disabilities.' In M. Corker and T. Shakespeare (eds) *Disability/Postmodernity: Embodying Disability Theory.* London/New York: Continuum.

Goodley, D., and Roets, G. (2008) 'The (be)comings and goings of developmental disabilities: the cultural politics of impairment.' *Discourse: Studies in the Cultural Politics of Education 29,* 2, 239–255.

Goodley, D., and Runswick-Cole, K. (2012) 'Reading Rosie: the postmodern disabled child.' *Educational and Child Psychology 29,* 2, 53–66.

Grandin, T. (1996) *Thinking in Pictures: And Other Reports from my Life with Autism.* New York: Vintage Books.

Griffiths, S. (2014) 'Have scientists found the autism GENE? Breakthrough as specific link between DNA and the condition is discovered.' *Daily Mail,* 7 July. Available at www.dailymail.co.uk/health/article-2683127/Have-scientists-autism-GENE-Breakthrough-specific-link-DNA-condition-discovered.html, accessed on 9 November 2015.

Haddon, M. (2003) *Curious Incident of the Dog in the Night-Time.* London: Jonathan Cape.

Haddon, M., adapted by Stephens, S. (2012) *Curious Incident of the Dog in the Night-Time* [Play].

Hall, L. (1997) *Spoonface Steinberg* [Play].

Haug, W.F. (1986) *Critique of Commodity Aesthetics: Appearance, Sexuality and Advertising in Capitalist Society.* Minneapolis, MN: Minnesota University Press.

Hickey-Moody, A. (2009) *Unimaginable Bodies: Intellectual Disability, Performance and Becomings.* Rotterdam: Sense Publishers.

Higashida, N. (2013) *The Reason I Jump: One Boy's Voice from the Silence of Autism.* Trans. D. Mitchell and K. Yoshida. London: Hodder and Stoughton.

Holt, D.B. (2002) 'Why do brands cause trouble? A dialectical theory of consumer culture and branding.' *Journal of Consumer Research 29,* 1, 70–90.

Horse Boy (2009) *Horse Boy Method – Autism.* Available at www.horseboyworld.com, accessed on 9 November 2015.

ICare4Autism (2014) *Autism Africa Initiative.* Available at www.icare4autism.org/global-autism-center/autism-africa-initiative, accessed on 9 November 2015.

Isaacson, R. (2009) *Horse Boy: A Father's Quest to Find his Son.* New York: Little, Brown.

Jackson, L. (2002) *Freaks, Geeks and Asperger Syndrome: A User Guide to Adolescence.* London: Jessica Kingsley Publishers.

Jackson, P. (1999) 'Commodity cultures: the traffic in things.' *Transactions of the Institute of British Geographers 24,* 1, 95–108.

Johar, K. (dir.) (2010) *My Name is Khan* [Film]. Fox.

Karambu, I. (2010) 'How parents can take care of autistic children.' *Business Daily,* 30 June. Available at www.businessdailyafrica.com/How-parents-can-take-care-of-autistic-children/-/539444/948902/-/g1g4w6z/-/index.html, accessed on 9 November 2015.

Lawson, W. (2000) *Life Behind Glass: A Personal Account of Autism Spectrum Disorder.* London: Jessica Kingsley Publishers.

Le Couteur, A., Rutter, M., Lord, C., Rios, P., *et al.* (1989) 'Autism diagnostic interview: a standardized investigator-based instrument.' *Journal of Autism and Developmental Disorders 19,* 3, 363–387.

Levinson, B. (dir.) (1988) *Rain Man* [Film]. United Artists.

Linton, S. (1998) 'Disability studies / not disability studies.' *Disability and Society 13,* 4, 525–540.

Lord, C., Rutter, M., and Le Couteur, A. (1994) 'Autism Diagnostic Interview – Revised: A revised version of a diagnostic interview for caregivers of individuals with possible pervasive developmental disorders.' *Journal of Autism and Developmental Disorders 24,* 5, 659–685.

Mallett, R., and Runswick-Cole, K. (2010) 'Knowing Me, Knowing You, Aha!: Does the urge to know impairment reveal an urge to know normal?' Critical Disability Studies Conference 'Theorizing Normalcy and the Mundane', 12–13 May, Manchester, UK.

Mallett, R., and Runswick-Cole, K. (2012) 'Commodifying Autism: The Cultural Contexts of "Disability" in the Academy.' In D. Goodley, B. Hughes and L.J. Davis (eds) *Disability and Social Theory.* Basingstoke: Palgrave MacMillan.

Mallett, R., and Runswick-Cole, K. (2014) *Approaching Disability: Critical Issues and Perspectives.* Abingdon: Routledge.

Mallett, R., and Runswick-Cole, K. (forthcoming 2016) 'The "Urge to Know" Normal: Theorising How Impairment Labels Function.' In R. Mallett, C. Ogden and J. Slater (eds) *Theorising Normalcy and the Mundane: Precarious Positions.* Chester: University of Chester Press.

McGuire, A. (2011) 'War on Autism: On Normative Violence and the Cultural Production Of Autism Advocacy.' Unpublished PhD thesis, University of Toronto.

McGuire, A.E. (2013) 'Buying time: the s/pace of advocacy and the cultural production of autism.' *Canadian Journal of Disability Studies 2*, 3, 98–125.

Miller, D. (2003) 'Could the Internet defetishise the commodity?' *Environment and Planning D: Society and Space 21*, 359–372.

Molloy, H., and Vasil, L. (2002) 'The social construction of Asperger Syndrome: the pathologising of difference?' *Disability and Society 17*, 659–669.

Moore, J. (2006) *Tribal Knowledge: Business Wisdom Brewed from the Grounds of Starbucks Corporate Culture.* Chicago, IL: Kaplan Publishing.

Murray, S. (2008) *Representing Autism: Culture, Narrative, Fascination.* Liverpool: Liverpool University Press.

Nadesan, M.H. (2005) *Constructing Autism: Unravelling the 'Truth' and Constructing the Social.* Abingdon: Routledge.

National Autistic Society (n.d.) *How to Talk about Autism.* Available at www.autism.org.uk/news-and-events/media-centre/how-to-talk.aspx, accessed on 9 November 2015.

Oliver, M. (1996) *Understanding Disability: From Theory to Practice.* Basingstoke: Macmillan.

Option Institute (2014) *The Son-Rise Program® Starter Kit.* Available at www.optioninstitutestore.org/Autism?product_id=61, accessed on 9 November 2015.

Ozanne, J.L., and Murray, J.B. (1995) 'Uniting critical theory and public policy to create the reflexively defiant consumer.' *American Behavioural Scientist 38*, 516–525.

Picoult, J. (2010) *House Rules.* London: Hodder and Stoughton.

Quantic Dream (2005) *Fahrenheit* [Videogame]. Atari.

Rhimes, S. (creator) (2005–present) *Grey's Anatomy* [Television Series]. ABC (USA).

Robertson, M.M. (2000) 'No net loss: wetland restoration and the incomplete capitalization of nature.' *Antipode 32*, 4, 463–493.

Runswick-Cole, K. (2014) '"Us" and "them"? The limits and possibilities of a politics of neurodiversity in neoliberal times.' *Disability and Society 29*, 7, 1117–1129.

Shakespeare, T. (2006) *Disability Rights and Wrongs.* Abingdon: Routledge.

Slater, D. (1997) *Consumer Culture and Modernity.* Cambridge: Polity.

Son-Rise Program (n.d.) *Treating Autism, Asperger's and Other Developmental Disorders.* Available at www.autismtreatmentcenter.org/contents/other_sections/index.php, accessed on 9 November 2015.

Sparks, N. (2006) *Dear John.* London: Sphere.

Thomas, C. (1999) *Female Forms: Experiencing and Understanding Disability.* Buckingham: Open University Press.

Thomas, C. (2007) *Sociologies of Disability and Illness: Contested Ideas in Disability Studies and Medical Sociology.* Basingstoke: Palgrave MacMillan

Timimi, S., Gardner, N., and McCabe, B. (2010) *The Myth of Autism: Medicalising Men's and Boys' Social and Emotional Competence.* Basingstoke: Palgrave Macmillan.

Titchkosky, T. (2008) *Reading and Writing Disability Differently: The Textured Life of Embodiment.* Toronto: University of Toronto Press.

Tremain, S. (2002) 'On the Subject of Impairment.' In M. Corker and T. Shakespeare (eds) *Disability/Postmodernity: Embodying Disability Theory.* London/New York: Continuum.

Tremain, S. (2005) 'Foucault, Governmentality and Critical Disability Theory: An Introduction.' In S. Tremain (ed.) *Foucault and the Government of Disability.* Michigan, MN: Ann Arbor/The University of Michigan Press.

V&A Museum of Childhood, London (March 2011) *Welcome to Our World...Living with Autism* [Exhibition].

CHAPTER 7

HOW RUDE?

AUTISM AS A STUDY IN ABILITY

Kim Davies

INTRODUCTION

In this chapter I take up the work of Fiona Kumari Campbell (2012) to stalk ableism by stalking autism. I will analyse the representations of autism in dominant medical discourses and use 'autism' as a method for, and contribution to, the emerging field of Studies in Ability. According to conventional tropes, autistic people live in a world of their own, and, like aliens on the wrong planet, are only spectrally present in 'the real world', the world of the 'normal people'. Autistic presence (Murray 2010) is represented as being so strange that it is the antithesis of being human and is itself antithetical to all that is good about humans. According to this normalising view, autistic people exist on the edges of the boundary of human being-ness and lack those very qualities that make people human: empathy and an ability to understand other people's thoughts and feelings. Indeed, autism is about as far away as possible from all that is held to be essential in humans and essentially human. This chapter will crip[1] this deficit Theory of Mind view of autism by rudely asking just who, in the normal–autistic binary, is unable to appreciate Others' ways of being and what happens when the lens of autism is used to focus on the privileges and perpetuation of ableism?

I want to use 'autism' as a tool, a method if you like, for stalking normalcy. Now, you will have noticed that I have placed 'autism' in inverted commas. I have done this to signal to you that I am really quite uncertain about what 'autism' is, if indeed 'it' is anything at all, although it is clear to me that whatever 'autism' may be, it has had widespread impact upon our lives in the West from about the middle of the twentieth century, especially as a diagnostic reflex

1 I use the term 'crip' here as a verb and as another way of describing how autism, as a method of critique, can challenge 'mainstream representations or practices to reveal abled-bodied assumptions and exclusionary effects [...to] expose the arbitrary delineation between normal and defective and the negative social ramifications of attempts to homogenize humanity' (Sandahl 2003, p.37).

(Harwood and Allan 2014) through which we respond to human – behavioural and communication – differences. So while I am uncertain about the existence of 'autism' as a medical condition, I am certain of its existence as a socio-cultural and categorical phenomenon, identity marker and shaper of human possibilities.

'Stalking' is also a somewhat troubling expression since it has connotations of lingering threat and potential violence that make me uncomfortable, even when, as in this instance, we are stalking concepts not people. However, I use the term 'stalking' because I am taking up the work of Fiona Kumari Campbell who first introduced the argument that 'disabilities' are ways in which ableism produces and performs itself (Campbell 2008a, 2008b, 2009, 2012). She described 'stalking' as one way in which this constitutive relationship between normalcy as ableism and 'disability' could be analysed and deconstructed. On a more positive note, stalking does suggest the active way in which we need to hunt for ableism as it seeks to conceal itself, almost invisibly, in the midst of 'disability' and it also implies that our aim in all this searching may be the elimination of that thing we pursue: namely ableist normativity as the dominant discourse shaping *all* of our human subjective possibilities.

I will begin this chapter by outlining Campbell's argument for stalking ableism and then apply this argument to 'autism', in particular to the deficit Theory of Mind (ToM) theory of autism that posits that it is the inability of people diagnosed with autism to appreciate and understand the thoughts and feelings of others that explains the nature and characteristics of autism itself. In making my argument, that is to say, in stalking autism, I will refer to both Asperger's and Kanner's original work describing the children they studied to frame up the existence of 'autistic psychopathy' as a distinct psychiatric diagnosis. I will consider the representations of these children (and their families) as disordered, and the rendition of this 'disorder' as 'autism' within the medicalised framework of individualised, inherent, if ambiguous, pathology. I will draw attention to the absence of contextualisation beyond notions of biological deficit and mal-development, especially the diagnostic elision of institutional contexts – medical and educational – that sought to simultaneously name and contain this emerging 'disorder'. I will conclude my hunt for the ableist normativity hidden at the heart of 'autism' by reasserting the importance of discursive relationality in any frameworks of human understanding and the possibilities for becoming human beyond 'normal' notions of 'us' and 'them'.

STALKING ABLEISM, STALKING NORMALCY

In this chapter I am taking up Campbell's (2008a, para. 3) challenge 'to reverse, to invert [the] traditional approach, to shift our gaze and concentrate on what

the study of disability tells us about the production, operation and maintenance of ableism'. Campbell herself extends McRuer's (2002) work on compulsory able-bodied-ness into what she names *the ableist project* through an invitation to disability scholars and people interested in disability to undertake 'a more nuanced exploration of epistemologies and ontologies of ableism' (Campbell 2008a, para. 2). 'Autism', and in particular deficit Theory of Mind theories of it, will be the focus of my undertaking here as I seek to use autism as a method to stalk normalcy.

Firstly, we should clarify some terms, in particular what I mean when I speak of 'ableism' and 'normalcy'. As I have indicated, I am taking up Campbell's work and applying it to the context of autism. When she speaks of 'ableism' Campbell (2001) is referring to:

> a network of beliefs, processes and practices that produces a particular kind of self and body (the corporeal standard) that is projected as the perfect, species-typical and therefore essential and fully human. Disability is cast as a diminished state of being human. (Campbell 2001, p.44)

She is careful to distinguish this notion of ableism from *disablism*, which is what she considers to be the orthodox, if hegemonic, way of framing up 'disability'. Campbell (2008a) describes disablism as:

> a set of assumptions (conscious or unconscious) and practices that promote the differential and unequal treatment of people because of actual or presumed disabilities. On this basis the strategic positions adopted to facilitate emancipatory social change whilst diverse, essentially relate to reforming those negative attitudes, assimilating people with disabilities into normative civil society and providing compensatory initiatives and safety nets in cases of enduring vulnerability. (Campbell 2008a, para. 6)

So, for Campbell, disablism operates an assimilationist agenda, seeking to measure up and reshape disabled people according to 'normal' human behaviour and standards. Standing in strong contrast is the ableist project, where Campbell refocuses the normative gaze onto the very ideas and practices that construct 'normal' human beings and, in their shadow, as a necessary consequence and casualty, the left-over disabled others.

Campbell (2008b, p.152) cautions us to use the terms ableism and disablism carefully: 'For some the term ableism has been used interchangeably with the term disablism. However, these two words render radically different understandings of the status of disability to the norm.' For me, Campbell's call for the denouncement of disablism and its replacement with an ableist project requires us to reposition ourselves in similar ways to how Whiteness Studies has positioned us in relation

to race and postcolonial projects. Campbell's ableist project is deeply radical, a *critical* disability studies project, where 'disability' is re-imagined and realised differently in post-human times. She works hard to stress that her purpose in theorising ableism is not to replace disability/disablism with another grand narrative that explains disability oppression, but rather to instigate new sites of study and different research questions to expose 'the convergence of networks that produce exclusionary matrices and ontologies' (Campbell 2008b, p.153).

NORMALCY, COMPULSORY ABLE-BODIEDNESS AND STUDYING ABILITY

As I have indicated, Campbell's notion of ableism is built upon and extends McRuer's (2002) work around compulsory able-bodiedness as well as Davis's (1995) seminal notion of normalcy, so it is useful to briefly revisit these before undertaking this specific study in ability using 'autism' as our method. Many people seem willing to accept that what counts as 'normal' human behaviour varies socio-culturally, across time and place. So, for example, citizens are now expected to allow the diverse range of socio-cultural and religious beliefs and practices that form mainstream 'diversity' and 'multiculturalism'. However, while many people will happily concede that what is 'good' and 'right' will vary with society, culture and religion, they will not acknowledge that what counts as 'ability' – and therefore also 'disability' – are also contextually governed. Thus, dis/ability continues to be represented as though it is universal and ahistorical and, as a consequence, the ideological effects of normalcy avoid critical interrogation.

One of the ways that normalcy (Davis 1995) conceals the power of the norm as a social construct is through the ostensible self-evidence of 'normal' human behaviour and 'normal' human development. We take so much about 'normal' human bodies, including 'normal' human brains and 'normal' human minds, at face value and for granted. Conditions such as 'autism' are premised upon 'realities' such as 'developmental delay' and 'neurodevelopmental disorder', and indeed they place such social constructions at the core of their diagnostic frameworks and clinical descriptions. Diagnostic categories such as autism thereby support and sustain the work of normalcy. Disability must exist and be real, we (uncritically) think to ourselves, because there are disabilities such as autism and disabled people everywhere!

When 'disability' is framed in relation to 'normal' human behaviour and the 'normal' human being, 'ability' is positioned as synonymous with 'normal'; and whatever is not 'normal' becomes, necessarily, *dis*-abled and less than fully human. Being disabled or having a disability becomes an undesirable, if pitiable,

way of being in the world. This is how 'ability' and 'disability' are socially constructed and dependent upon each other for their existence. That 'normal' is socially constructed and that the 'norm' is reified slips from notice (and into hiding) as attention and efforts are directed at helping the disabled: fixing what is broken or wonky, or, if that is not possible, recuperating the disabled person into some sort of 'normal' life.

In addition to being the 'natural' human condition, being 'normal' is assumed to be universally desirable; it is also therefore compelling and difficult to resist, even if what we hold to be 'normal' is variable across time and place and even when the price of having 'normal' people is having 'disabled' people, that is, people who are disabled by 'the norm'. It appears almost impossible to live a viable life outside of the abled/disabled binary and we are compelled to take up subjectivities within these parameters in order to seem real to ourselves as well as to others. This is how abledness becomes compulsory (McRuer 2002) and normative (Davis 1995), how we are complicit in its perpetuation and why it seems almost impossible for us to conceive of 'ontologically peripheral lives as distinct ways of being human [...] Ableism's constitutional divide posits two distinct and entirely clear ontological zones: disabled and abled (normate)' (Campbell 2008a, paras. 5 and 11). Thus our human possibilities are constrained – we can be able-bodied and normal, or disabled and not normal, with the latter considered an undesirable, somewhat less than fully human, condition. In short, to be 'normal', it is compulsory to be able-bodied; and to shore up the normalcy of abledness, we are compelled to perform 'abled' and 'disabled' repeatedly in order to bring ourselves into existence and make ourselves socially recognisable and personally intelligible.

Meanwhile, it is this social compulsion to 'be normal', in its illusory interiority (Graham and Slee 2008), that ableism lurks virtually invisible as an 'enforced presumption that erases difference' (Campbell 2008a, para. 8). The naturalised (universal and ahistorical) self-evident, sheer 'common sense', existence of 'disability' is the periphery that secures ableism's empty core and it is through its very absence that, paradoxically, ableism becomes present, from everywhere and nowhere at once, from without and from within ourselves. As Campbell (2008a, paras. 15 and 17) argues: 'charting a criterion of Abled to gain definitional clarity can result in a game of circular reductionism – saying what *is* in relation to what it *isn't*, that which falls away... The disabled body has a place, a place in liminality to secure the performative enactment of the normal.' Ableism can only be unmasked by what McRuer (2002) calls 'crafty reductionisms' and it is in such an attempt to be crafty that we now turn to autism as a method, as a study in ability, of 'how the able, able-bodied, non-disabled identity is maintained' (Campbell 2012, p.215).

AUTISM AS A STUDY IN ABILITY

Nadesan (2005) was one of the first scholars to place autism in its socio-cultural and discursive context. She unveils the myth of 'disability' as an ahistorical and universal phenomenon when she writes:

> Autism is not outside the symbolic waiting discovery. Autism is inscribed and produced through the symbolic and an investigation into these processes of inscription/production reveals current desires, anxieties and opportunities for personhood in the early twenty-first century. (Nadesan 2005, pp.7–8)

'Autism' has always been the site of a discursive struggle over who and what counts as 'human' (Davies 2014), as we shall see as we turn to the work of Hans Asperger and Leo Kanner, the clinicians who conjured 'autistic psychopathy' from a series of child studies in the 1940s and which formed the template for the diagnosis of 'autism'. Kanner's and Asperger's template remains virtually pristine (despite heated debate concerning the removal of Asperger Syndrome) in the diagnostic criteria for autism listed in the latest edition of the *Diagnostic and Statistical Manual of Mental Disorders*, DSM-5 (APA 2013).

It is important to remember that the edifice that is 'autism' was built upon a handful of child studies by both Kanner and Asperger. Kanner worked with eleven children – Donald T., Frederick W., Richard M., Paul G., Barbara K., Virginia S., Herbert B., Alfred L., Charles N., John F. and Elaine C.; and Asperger with even fewer, just four – Fritz V., Harro L., Ernst K. and Hellmuth L. The children and their families were referred for clinical attention (assessment, placement and remediation) by educational and other authorities, a process of ableism that continues to repeat itself in the diagnostic reflex that is such a pervasive practice in Western schooling (Harwood and Allan 2014). The children who were referred to Kanner's and Asperger's hospital-based clinics were all subject to similar processes of initiation into what was to become *their* condition, 'autistic psychopathy'. Referrals for assessment were received, accompanied by authoritative descriptions of the trouble that prompted the desire for expert intervention; detailed family histories were undertaken (and sometimes offered by family members themselves) to identify underlying causes for the evident trouble; batteries of tests were conducted by various other experts to assess the children, most frequently their level of 'intelligence', in order to ascertain if 'feeblemindedness' may be a factor to be taken into account; and finally the children were observed by a range of affiliated experts as well as being subject to the persistent clinical gaze of Kanner and Asperger themselves during the children's hospitalisations or clinic attendances. It was on this basis that these children were diagnosed with 'autistic psychopathy' and it is through their representation in the subsequent work of Kanner and Asperger that we now speak so easily of 'autism' as something 'real' and 'true'.

Now none of this was unusual for its time: diagnosis of pathological individuals by medical experts in sterile clinical locations had, by the early 1940s, become orthodox, although we should acknowledge that Kanner and Asperger were at the very beginnings of its expansion into new child markets. An alternative reading indicates that the children themselves had little in common, beyond the way in which their individual subjectification in their respective case studies was marshalled, in combination, to inaugurate 'autism'. You would think, on the basis of all this expense, time and effort, that we would be able to locate something definitive, coherent, well-articulated and convincing at the centre of this process that could be identified as 'normal' behaviour. However, even with a close reading, 'it' – 'normal' – is difficult to discern. It is ableism that constitutes the illusory interiority that autistic psychopathy/autism shores up.

Let me illustrate this with some examples from Kanner's (1943) and Asperger's (1944) definitive diagnostic publications. Asperger (1944) frames his child studies with this introductory paragraph:

> In what follows, I will describe a particularly interesting and highly recognisable *type of child.* The children I will present all have in common a *fundamental disturbance* which manifests itself in their physical appearance, expressive functions and indeed, *their whole behaviour.* This disturbance results in severe and characteristic difficulties in social integration. In many cases, the social problems are so profound that they overshadow everything else. In some cases, however, the problems are compensated by a high level of original thought and experience. This can often lead to exceptional achievements later in life. With the type of *personality disorder* presented here we can demonstrate the truth of the claim that exceptional human beings must be given exceptional educational treatment, treatment which takes account of *their special difficulties.* Further, we can show that despite *abnormality* human beings can fulfil their social role within the community, especially if they find understanding, love and guidance. There are many reasons for describing in detail *this type of abnormally developing child.* Not the least of them is that *these children raise questions of central importance to psychology and education.* (Asperger 1944, p.37; emphasis added)

From Asperger's account, the children who prompted his invocation of autistic psychopathy (from earlier uses in connection with 'schizophrenia', understood psychoanalytically), and its iteration as a separate clinical diagnosis for particularly disordered children, were fundamentally and irrevocably dis-abled by their shared condition, 'autistic psychopathy'. Despite going on to describe in detail four very different children with varying backgrounds, Asperger is insistent that the school trouble these children experience can be traced to their shared pathology, one that he explains in terms of personality disorder and abnormal

development. While he interrogates aspects of family genealogy, he does not rate as significant any factors outside of the individual child's inherent constitution. The children are wholly and thoroughly disordered by their difference from 'normal' children.

What characterises these 'normal' children of Asperger's (1944) remains elusive, although he deploys Fritz V., Harro L., Ernst K. and Hellmuth L. effectively as living boundary markers writing that Fritz V. was 'utterly indifferent to the authority of adults' (Asperger 1944, p.40) and 'the same boy who sat there listlessly with an absent look on his face would suddenly jump up with his eyes lit up, and before one could do anything, he would have done something mischievous' (Asperger 1944, p.43). Harro L.'s behaviour was problematic for Asperger in a very different way because 'of his contact disturbance' (Asperger 1944, p.56) which entailed his 'extremely limited relationship to his environment. Through the length of his stay on the ward he remained a stranger. One would never see him join in a game with others. Most of the time, he sat in a corner buried in a book, oblivious to the noise or movement around him...such fanatical reading is rare before the age of ten' (Asperger 1944, p.56). According to Asperger (1944), Harro 'did not see the funny side of things and lacked any sense of humour, especially if the joke was on him' (Asperger 1944, p.57). Ernst K. was singled out because 'he liked to tell fantastic stories, in which he always appeared as the hero' (Asperger 1944, p.59) and Hellmuth L.:

> surprised [Asperger by] how clever he sounded. He kept his immobile dignity while speaking and talked slowly, almost as if in verse, seemingly full of insight and superiority. He often used unusual words, sometimes poetical and sometimes unusual combinations. This was consistent with an interest in poetry as reported by the mother. (Asperger 1944, p.66)

I could go on, listing many more descriptions of these case study children that, accidentally it would seem, make them seem very ordinary indeed, especially when shadows of context hint at possible alternative explanations for their apparently problematic behaviours.

Kanner's (1943) account is filled with similar stories of ordinary trouble with many of his case study children reacting to the processes of their diagnosis in similar way to Asperger's (1944) patients. For example, when Donald T. was placed in a tuberculosis preventorium to provide him with 'a change of environment [Kanner reports that he responded with] a disinclination to play with children and do things children his age usually take an interest in' (Kanner 1943, p.3). Similarly, Richard M. surprised Kanner (1943, p.13) by having 'himself led willingly to the psychiatrist's office [where] he engaged at once in active play with toys, paying no attention to the persons in the room' as did Barbara K. when she 'shook hands upon request (offering the left upon coming, the

right upon leaving) by merely raising a limp hand in the approximate direction of the examiner's proffered hand; the motion definitely lacked the implication of greeting' (Kanner 1943, p.16). Alfred L. is singled out for being 'extremely tense during the entire interview, and very serious-minded, to such an extent that had it not been for his juvenile voice, he might have given the impression of a worried and preoccupied little old man' (Kanner 1943, p.24).

I am less surprised by the children's responses to what may have been for them an ongoing interruption to the lives they wished to live, by the grinding routine of parading for strange clinicians, than I am surprised by Kanner's surprise at the children's behaviour. I am not sure what behaviour Kanner and Asperger would have recognised as 'normal' under these circumstances but it is perhaps unsurprising that it remains invisible at the centre of diagnostic disordering of these children.

AUTISTIC PSYCHOPATHY AND ORDERING 'THE HUMAN'

These ordinary stories of trouble, these little details of lives in process and context that may be read quite differently, are, for Kanner and Asperger, only small clues in *their* big story: of 'autistic psychopathy' or 'autism'. For both Kanner and Asperger it is the children's apparent aloofness and disinterest in other human beings, as human beings, that explains and constitutes their 'disorder'. Asperger (1944, p.67) writes that despite 'highly distinctive wide individual differences':

> nevertheless, the essential aspects of the problem remain unchanged. In early childhood there are the difficulties in learning simple practical skills and in social adaptation. These difficulties arise out of the same disturbance which at school age cause learning and conduct problems, in adolescence job and performance problems, and in adulthood social and marital conflicts. Thus, apart from its distinctiveness, it is the constancy which makes autism a highly recognisable entity. *Once one has properly recognised an autistic individual one can spot such children instantly.* They are recognisable from small details, for instance, the way they enter the consulting room at their first visit, their behaviour in the first few moments and the first words they utter. (Asperger 1944, p.68; emphasis added)

There we have it, the instant recognisability of immutable autism, its faultless, unambiguous diagnosis by clinical experts and its entry into the cadre of disorders that police the boundary between 'normal' human beings and others. Indeed, Asperger inaugurates the autistics-as-aliens (and normal people as not strange and at home in this world) metaphor when he depicts the children he studies as sitting preoccupied, perhaps apart in a corner, or even in the middle of a happy,

noisy group of siblings and peers: '*He is like an alien*, oblivious to the surrounding noise and movement, and inaccessible in his preoccupation. He is irritated only if someone breaks his isolation' (Asperger 1944, p.78; emphasis added).

What marks these strangers from 'normal' people? According to Asperger (1944):

> Human beings normally live in constant interaction with their environment, and react to it continually. However, 'autists' have severely disturbed and considerably limited interaction. The autist is only himself (cf. the Greek word *autos*) and is not an active member of a greater organism which he is influenced by and which he influences constantly. (Asperger 1944, p.39)

Here Asperger (1944) is naming the nub of his concern: that the children he identifies as autistic show no interest in living like 'normal' people and their 'shutting off of relations between self and the outside world [is their] fundamental disorder' (Asperger 1944, p.39). The children in Kanner's child studies are represented as similar to Asperger's little aliens. Donald T.:

> Paid no attention to persons around him. When taken into a room, he completely disregarded the people and instantly went for objects... Commands or actions that could not possibly be disregarded were resented as unwelcome intrusions. But he was never angry at the interfering *person*. He angrily shoved away the *hand* that was in his way or the *foot* that stepped on one of his blocks... Once the obstacle was removed, he forgot the whole affair. He gave no heed to the presence of other children but went about his favourite pastimes, walking off from children if they were so bold as to join him. (Kanner 1943, p.5; emphasis in original)

Richard M. is represented by Kanner (1943, p.13) as a child who 'had no contact with people, whom he definitely regarded as an interference when they talked to him or otherwise tried to gain his attention'. According to Kanner (1943, p.15), Richard M. had 'on his side, no affective tie to people' and Virginia S. 'sat among the children, seemingly not even noticing what went on, and gave the impression of being self-absorbed' (Kanner 1943, p.19). Alfred L. used the younger children he played with 'as puppets – that's all' (Kanner 1943, p.24). These representations are Kanner's evidence for the existence of what he named autistic disturbances of affective contact, which aligned neatly with Asperger's autistic psychopathy, and which both clinicians happily reduced to 'autism'. Kanner's (1943) definition mirrors that of Asperger. He writes:

> The outstanding, 'pathognomonic', fundamental disorder is the children's inability to relate themselves in the ordinary way to people and situations from the beginning of life... There is from the start an extreme autistic

> aloneness that, whenever possible, disregards, ignores, shuts out anything that comes to the child from outside. (Kanner 1943, p.33)

'Ordinary' is deployed so casually, so self-evidently, and the children are, as a consequence, placed definitively outside the world of the ordinary. But this is an unreflexive move and one that takes the certainties of ordinary normality at face value. If these children are disordered by autism, then 'autism' itself becomes the way, a method if you like, of ordering the world and marking the borders between the alien world of the autist and the real world, the 'ordinary' world, of 'normal' human beings. This is the illusory interiority (Graham and Slee 2008) that all autistic children help secure and Kanner's and Asperger's case studies help constitute the archives in the epistemologies and ontologies of ableism (Campbell 2012) through the addition of 'autism'.

THEORIES OF MINDS AND CONTESTING WHAT IS NORMALLY 'HUMAN'

Kanner and Asperger's depiction of 'the autist' as an aloof outsider was taken up some decades later in the deficit Theory of Mind explanation for autistic differences and it remains one of the core explanatory frameworks underpinning the diagnosis of 'autism'. According to this theory, lately known as 'mindblindness' and popularised in particular by Simon Baron-Cohen, people diagnosed with autism lack the very qualities that make humans 'human', because they are believed to be deficient in an 'essential' human capacity, a Theory of Mind (ToM). According to Baron-Cohen (2001, p.169): 'a Theory of Mind remains one of the quintessential abilities that makes us human' and refers to the ability 'to infer the full range of mental states (beliefs, desires, intentions, imagination, emotion, and so on) that cause action'. Using primate analogues, Premack and Woodruff (1978, p.515) argue that an individual has a Theory of Mind 'if he imputes mental states to himself and others', which raises the prospects, according to the logic of the theory, that some humans are less 'human' than some primates. Whitten (1993) follows this logic when he argues that it is having Theory of Mind that distinguishes humans, presumably from non-humans, since empathy for other human beings is only enabled, so the theory goes, by a fully functioning Theory of Mind. The irony of positioning autistic people as non-human and unempathic seems to be lost on ToM theorists. ToM theorisation dovetailed smoothly with representations of autistic people as aliens, disinterested inhabitants of the fully and properly feeling world, and it is clear to see how the theory of ToM itself supported and seemed to explain differences characterised as typically 'autistic'.

But ToM is itself a theory, a theory about a construct that is not directly observable. It is problematic to say the least, as are the consequent assertions that

people diagnosed with autism lack theories of mind and therefore empathy for other human beings. Indeed, the theory is premised on a unitary, essentialised notion of what ToM may be, a capacity that is argued to be universally present in 'normal' humans regardless of their locations in time and space: ToM is immune from the effects of culture and history, for example. Moreover, a person either has a fully functioning 'healthy' ToM or not: it is either present or absent. Like the descriptions of behaviour that construct Asperger's and Kanner's representation of their case study children as 'autistic', it is all or nothing regarding ToM, with no room for variability, emergence, reciprocity or relationality in the fixed and essentialised 'natural' abilities of humans, normal and otherwise.

Some have questioned the legitimacy of ToM theory to authorise understandings of 'autism'. Smukler (2005, p.11), for example, draws attention to the importance of 'alternative narratives about autistic minds that incorporate the perspectives of people labelled autistic [arguing that they] are an important counterbalance to the limitations of such professional viewpoints' when he writes that 'the theory [ToM] is "mindblind" with regard to autistic perspectives' (Smukler 2005, p.22). Smukler is highlighting the role of ToM as an epistemology of ableism, although I would argue that stalking ableist ontologies is more complex and difficult than attempting some sort of balance between professional medical perspectives and the narratives of people with autism. Standpoint approaches to autism knowledge are currently very popular, following on from the success of autistic writers such as Temple Grandin and Donna Williams and autistic advocates such as Jim Sinclair, but these narratives also should be troubled for their contribution to essentialising autism as a fixed and immutable biologically based condition, even if it is a condition framed as legitimate difference rather than deficit or disability.

Standpoint is contentious ground upon which to stake knowledge claims since it seriously devalues socio-cultural and historical contexts and the power of dominant discourses to shape available ways of being and doing in our world. As Joan Scott (1991) argued, experience and memory are still discursively situated and mediated, and while they offer a different perspective, it is not necessarily an unproblematic one. Standpoint also assumes a theory of personhood that favours the fixed natures of biological individuals striving to be a particular unitary self, de-emphasising the shifting relational and socio-cultural construction of ways of becoming negotiated across spaces of differences. When people with autism and their supporters claim that they don't just act autistic, they *are* autistic because their autistic behaviours emanate from who they are as people, claims are being made about autism as an ontology that may, ironically, originate in fixed notions of human capacity and being human generated by ableism.

We may embrace autistic self-determination in light of the oppression of ableist discourses but we should also be careful that we are not unnecessarily restricting

our human identities and squandering our human possibilities by subscribing to fixed biological identities, even if they have the advantage of being identities we appear to be choosing for ourselves. So while the ToM explanation for autism may be part of the epistemology that is ableism, we should re-think notions of essential autistic ways of being lest we contribute, in a different way, to our ongoing oppression through ableist ontologies. We can talk back and say 'How rude?' as ToM constructs autism as a cognitive and emotional deficiency and as it authorises the dehumanisation of people with autism as non-empathic, but we can do this without needing, at the same time, to tie ourselves to ontologies that persist in essentialising any and all human beings. When it comes to becoming human, we really are all in it together. Following Runswick-Cole (2014, p.1127), it is time for all of us 'to abandon identity politics in order to pursue a productive politics that moves beyond essentialist binaries' and to disrupt the neoliberal project that requires us to be either 'us' or 'them', one or the other.

GETTING BEYOND AUTISM: CHANGING HOW TO BECOME 'HUMAN'

In this chapter, I have stalked ableism by stalking autism and in the process I have exposed the illusory interiority that lies at its heart. Like Runswick-Cole (2014), I have also troubled the emerging discourses of autism as a way of being, positioned as part of a neurodiverse spectrum of abilities, because they do not replace, rather just reiterate and renovate, the 'us' and 'them' binaries at the heart of normative identity politics. One way forward may be to reconfigure the spaces between all people, not with expanded options of fixed identities called 'identification', but as unfolding and uncertain spaces of becoming, where we can undertake fresh negotiations around who we will allow ourselves to be, for each other. It may be that we can come up with possibilities for human beingness that no longer require my 'ability' to be at the expense of your 'disability'. This would truly be a radical agenda, one that would sidestep intractable identity politics as well as the catch-22 that is 'inclusion'.

REFERENCES

American Psychiatric Association (APA) (2013) *Diagnostic and Statistical Manual of Mental Disorders, Fifth Edition (DSM-5).* Washington DC: American Psychiatric Association.

Asperger, H. [1944] (1991) '"Autistic Psychopathy" in Childhood.' In U. Frith (ed.) *Autism and Asperger Syndrome.* Cambridge: Cambridge University Press.

Baron-Cohen, S. (2001) 'Theory of Mind and autism: a review.' *International Journal of Research in Mental Retardation: Autism 23*, 169–184.

Campbell, F.K. (2001) 'Inciting legal fictions: disability's date with ontology and the ableist body of the law.' *Griffith Law Review 10*, 42–62.

Campbell, F.K. (2008a) 'Refusing able(ness): a preliminary conversation about ableism.' *M/C Journal 11*, 3. Available at www.journal.media-culture.org.au/index.php/mcjournal/article/viewArticle/46, accessed on 10 November 2015.

Campbell, F.K. (2008b) 'Exploring internalised ableism using critical race theory.' *Disability and Society 23*, 2, 151–162.

Campbell, F.K. (2009) *Contours of Ableism: The Production of Disability and Abledness.* Basingstoke: Palgrave Macmillan.

Campbell, F.K. (2012) 'Stalking Ableism: Using Disability to Expose "Abled' Narcissism".' In D. Goodley, B. Hughes and L. Davis (eds) *Disability and Social Theory: New Developments and Directions.* Basingstoke: Palgrave Macmillan.

Davies, K. (2014) 'A Troubled Identity: Putting Butler to Work on the Comings and Goings of Asperger's Syndrome.' Paper presented at the AERA (American Educational Research Association) Disability Studies in Education (DSE) Conference, July, Victoria University, Melbourne.

Davis, L.J. (1995) *Enforcing Normalcy: Disability, Deafness, and the Body.* London: Verso.

Graham, L.J., and Slee, R. (2008) 'An illusory interiority: interrogating the discourses of inclusion.' *Educational Philosophy and Theory 40*, 2, 277–292.

Harwood, V., and Allan, J. (2014) *Psychopathology at School: Theorising Mental Disorders in Education.* London: Routledge.

Kanner, L. (1943) 'Autistic disturbances of affective contact.' *Nervous Child: Journal of Psychopathology, Psychotherapy, Mental Hygiene, and Guidance of the Child 2*, 217–250.

McRuer, R. (2002) 'Compulsory Able-Bodiedness and Queer/Disabled Existence.' In S. Snyder, B.J. Brueggemann and R. Garland-Thomson (eds) *Disability Studies: Enabling the Humanities.* New York: Modern Language Association.

Murray, S. (2010) 'Autism functions/the functions of autism.' *Disability Studies Quarterly 30*, 1. Available at www.dsq-sds.org/article/view/1048/1229, accessed on 10 November 2015.

Nadesan, M.H. (2005) *Constructing Autism: Unravelling the 'Truth' and Understanding the Social.* London: Routledge.

Premack, D., and Woodruff, G. (1978) 'Does the chimpanzee have a Theory of Mind?' *Behavioral and Brain Sciences 1*, 515–526.

Runswick-Cole, K. (2014) '"Us" and "them"? The limits and possibilities of a politics of neurodiversity in neoliberal times.' *Disability and Society 29*, 7, 1117–1129.

Sandahl, C. (2003) 'Queering the crip or cripping the queer? Intersections of queer and crip identities in solo autobiographical performance.' *GLQ: A Journal of Lesbian and Gay Studies 9*, 1–2, 25–56.

Scott, J.W. (1991) 'The evidence of experience.' *Critical Inquiry 17*, 4, 773–797.

Smukler, D. (2005) 'Unauthorised minds: how "Theory of Mind" theory misrepresents autism.' *Mental Retardation 43*, 1, 11–24.

Whitten, A. (1993) 'Evolving a Theory of Mind: the nature of non-verbal mentalism in other primates.' In S. Baron-Cohen, H. Tager-Flusberg and D.J. Cohen (eds) *Understanding Other Minds: Perspectives from Autism.* Oxford: Oxford University Press.

CHAPTER 8

AUTISM AND THE HUMAN

Dan Goodley

INTRODUCTION

The administrative, political, psychological and identity category of autism raises many questions about how we dissect humanity. Is autism a disruption to what it means to be human? Are people with autism considered to be human? Does autism or neurological diversity offer an alternative conceptualisation to the dominant discourse associated with modern(ist) man? Do autism politics support or subvert other forms of human struggle? Does autism contest or reinsert a very familiar notion of the individual that is complicit in the reproduction of neoliberal capitalism? Do autistic activists risk leaving their activism in the language of the oppressor or are they saying something very different and revolutionary? This chapter responds to these questions. The contradictory positions, moves, sways and swerves implicit in the above questions capture the complexities of what the postcolonial writer Sylvia Wynter defines as *the* struggle of our new millennium, which:

> will be one between the ongoing imperative of securing the wellbeing of our present ethno-class (i.e. Western bourgeois) conception of the human, Man, which over-represents itself as if it were the human itself, and that of securing the wellbeing, and therefore the full cognitive and behavioral autonomy of the human species itself/ourselves. (Wynter 2003, p.260)

My starting point is that people associated with the label of autism are fundamentally members of the human species and, simultaneously, the presence of autism demands that we think again about what it means to be a member of humankind. The chapter will deal with the following analytical considerations:

1. Arguing about autism: questions about positionality
2. Postcolonial theory: the case of Sylvia Wynter
3. Autism as human Other: towards a politics of wonder

4. Autism as hyper-ethnoclass man: the curious incident of the male in the blight
5. Autism giveth and taketh away: the biopolitics of autism.

This chapter will assume little to no understanding of postcolonial theory on the part of the reader and will develop this approach as a fruitful perspective to think again about autism and the human.

ARGUING ABOUT AUTISM: QUESTIONS ABOUT POSITIONALITY

Whilst mindful of the essentialist dangers of naming oneself (or not) in relation to a disability identity (e.g. O'Toole 2013) it is important to acknowledge the deeply political nature of autism discourse. The category has been enthusiastically adopted as an identity position by numerous individuals across the globe. Families of children so-labelled have used the category to access key services and forms of support. Activists have extended the phenomenon to elaborate neurological diversity: urging others to recognise and value embodied difference. Others have suggested that autism is nothing more than a myth perpetuated by the biopolitics of psychiatry and psychology; disciplines obsessed with their own sense of entitlement and legacy. Any debate, analytical intervention or rhetorical interrogation of the many faces of autism has the potential to upset somebody. I feel it is important to recognise this at the outset and to acknowledge some anxieties that I have in entering the autism debate.

My own research and activism has long been associated with the lives and ambitions of people with the label of 'learning disabilities' or 'intellectual disabilities'. When I wrote my first book fifteen years ago, I was engaged with the politics of self-advocacy where activists preferred either to be called 'people with learning difficulties' or 'People First' (Goodley 2000). Autism was hardly mentioned by the majority of the self-advocacy activists that I met around the UK. Now, of course, we have established examples of autism self-advocacy in the UK, the United States and Australia, to name but a few contexts. I do worry that self-advocacy's critical approach towards specific impairment labels appears to have been sidelined by the appropriation of the autism category. The history of self-advocacy reveals a commonality of identity (self-advocates) over divergence associated with different impairment labels. It did not seem to matter if someone had the label of 'Down syndrome', 'mild intellectual disability' or 'complex cognitive impairments'; what mattered was a shared sense of being a politicised self-advocate. Today, so it seems to me, one often comes across self-advocates with learning disabilities *and* autism. But, what right do I have as someone not identifying with the label of autism to make such critical observations? Were

we to resituate (at least for a short while) autism as a social and cultural concern (rather than an individually owned identity), then the category becomes a public issue potentially addressed by anyone. This raises questions about why one has entered the autism debate. My own reasons relate to a long-standing commitment to the politics of disability and the interdisciplinary field of disability studies. My own sense is that autism gives much whilst also, potentially and simultaneously, taking many things away. I will return to this observation later.

The main thrust of this chapter will consider autism's relationship with the categorisation of the human being. My analysis uncovers the strange paradox of autism: it is made to sit outside of what is normatively understood as human whilst, at times, recuperated back into the normative milieu as a souped-up, hyper version of that familiar trope of the modern human being: rational man (especially when one is discussing 'high functioning' forms of autism). This duality of function, ambivalence of usage and image of paradox highlights autism's complex relationship with humanness including valued and disavowed versions of what it means to be a valued human being. These are, of course, complex considerations. And like any tricky issue we need some theoretical help.

POSTCOLONIAL THEORY: THE CASE OF SYLVIA WYNTER

In the writing of a recent book I found myself drawn to the potential for postcolonial theory to say much about dis/ability (Goodley 2014). I am, of course, not the first disability studies researcher to find postcolonial theory useful to an analysis of the constitution of dis/ability, the exclusion of disabled people and the reification of the able. Mark Sherry (2007) provided a useful comparative reading of disability and postcolonial studies while the work of writers such as Anita Ghai (2006), Karen Soldatic (Soldatic and Fiske 2009) and Shaun Grech (2013) have accentuated the positive contributions that postcolonial theory brings to understandings of disability especially in social, political and national contexts outside of the domineering Western European and North American countries. I have found the work of Frantz Fanon (1976, 1993) especially helpful for thinking through the ways in which disabled people are constituted as an absolute 'Other' to the dominant ableist imaginary, mimicking the position of people of colour in a racist white world (Goodley 2011). The way I read it is that Fanon is as a game-changer. He brings an analytical concern to the theoretical and political table. He asks, how do black people become negated, erased and made inhuman by dominant white culture? This turning of the gaze back on to the oppressor and the oppressor's conception of the human is a hugely important shift. Not only is the oppressor or racist now the object of theory and analysis, so too are their implicit theories and explicit philosophical assumptions that

they hold around their conception of what it means to be a valued human being in a world mainly geared to fit the demands and ambitions of white people. Postcolonial theorists such as Fanon urge us to make a leap of faith; to give up on comfortable, easy to use and typical ideas about the human being and instead to ask: what other conceptions of the human might exist had the white man not got there first! This is not to deny that humanness has a long, complex history of development (encompassing multi-ethnic contributions) but to think about how the contemporary human might be explained in relation to a number of genealogical origins.

A compelling genealogy is provided by Sylvia Wynter in her 2003 article. I will extensively quote, now, from this piece and urge you – the reader – to stick with me for a few paragraphs. My sense is that a close reading of Wynter is worth it, especially as we shall see later as we move our analysis into a consideration of autism and the human.

In this work she pitches her claim that the contemporary battle for recognition involves, on one side, *those engaged in wider human struggle* (which would include non-white, non-European and disabled people) versus, on the other side, *ethnoclass man* (embodied in the white, heterosexual, American, able, male). Ethnoclass man is normative man; civic-humanist and rational citizen. Whilst presented as a neutral 'descriptive state of the human' (Wynter 2003, p.281), ethnoclass man has a violent and shameful history where 'all other modes of being human would instead have to be seen not as the alternative modes of being human that there are "out there", but adaptively, as the lack of the West's ontologically absolute self-description… With this systemic repression ensuring that we oversee (thereby failing to recognise) the culture and class-specific relativity of our present mode of being human' (Wynter 2003, pp.281–282). 'The new descriptive statement of the human, Man, as primarily a political subject – of, therefore, the West's own self-conception' (Wynter 2003, p.233): 'optimally economic man' (Wynter 2003, p.314) was constituted 'in a law like manner through the systemic stigmatisation of the Earth' (Wynter 2003, p.321). Through the functions of modernity, the Atlantic slave trade and the rise of capitalism, ethnoclass man became 'instituted as the only, universally applicable mode of being human' (Wynter 2003, p.299). 'One of the major empirical effects of "the rise of Europe" was its construction of the "world civilisation" on the one hand, and, on the other, African enslavement, Latin American conquest, and Asian subjugation' (Wynter 2003, p.263). Society 'would remain unable, from then on until today, of conceiving an Other to what they call human' (Wynter 2003, p.299). 'All Others', Wynter argues, 'had to be read through the descriptive statement of the human' (Wynter 2003, p.300).

Ethnoclass man became the prism through which one viewed what it meant to be human. Some 'lucky souls' were included so 'gradations of rationality, civilisation, development, skin shade, caste could account for one's interpellation

in the ethnoclass able-man imaginary' (Wynter 2003, p.300). Many others were rejected from the category, cast off as animal and non-human. Those outside of ethnoclass man were pitched as irrational, uncivilised, deficient others. This resulted in legitimating 'the expropriation and internment of the Indians, the mass enslavement of the Negroes, and the internment of the Mad – all ostensibly as living proof of their naturally determined enslavement to irrationality' (Wynter 2003, p.305). To this we could add, of course, the eugenic segregation and institutionalisation of people with intellectual disabilities.

Constituting ethnoclass man as the idealised modern citizen drew a line between 'on the one hand, divinely created-to-be-rational humans, and on the other, no less divinely created-to-be-irrational animals' (Wynter 2003, p.313). Here we find a 'socio-ontological line now drawn between rational, political Man (the settler of European descent) and its irrational Human Others (the categories of Caliban [i.e. the subordinated Indians and the enslaved Negroes])' (Wynter 2003, p.314). Of course to the latter group of Human Others we can add disabled people. These Human Others were made to occupy 'the matrix slot of Otherness – to be made into the physical referent of the idea of the irrational/sub rational Human Other' (Wynter 2003, p.265); 'the savage Other, the fossil Other, the abnormal Other, the timeless ethnographic Other' (Wynter 2003, p.267). Observing the current socio-political climate in 2003, Wynter (2003, p.260) describes those caught up in the category of the Human Other:

> defined at the global level by refugee/economic migrants stranded outside the gates of the rich countries, as the postcolonial variant of Fanon's category of les damnés (Fanon 1963) – with this category in the United States coming to comprise the criminalised majority Black and dark-skinned Latino inner-city males now made to man the rapidly expanding prison-industrial complex, together with their female peers – the kicked-about Welfare Moms – with both being part of the ever-expanding global, transracial category of the homeless/the jobless, the semi-jobless, the criminalised drug-offending prison population.

The narrative of ethnoclass-man-as-valued-citizen has been told so often that the story has become naturalised: ethnoclass-man-is-human. For any individual to possibly claim a 'normal' North American identity then, this inevitably must entail that individual putting up a 'visible distance between themselves and the Black population group' (Wynter 2003, p.260) or any other Human Other category that is considered to be Other to ethnoclass man. This devastating critique recalls Michel Foucault and also Fanon in terms of its analytical style but goes further, I would suggest, in terms of clearly and carefully outlining *the struggle of our times*: to contest the over-representation that a valued life is one associated with ethnoclass-man. 'The central over-representation', Wynter writes, 'enables the interests,

reality, and wellbeing of *the empirical human world* to continue to be imperatively subordinated to those of the now globally hegemonic ethnoclass world of "Man"' (Wynter 2003, p.262; emphasis added). The empirical human world – peopled by the politically condemned and culturally excluded – constitutes a potentially radical and subversive 'archipelago of Human Otherness' (Wynter's term – 2003, p.321). This means taking back the human from the 'present ethnoclass mode of being human, Man', which is nothing more than an over-representation of the desires and ambitions of 'the Western and Westernised (or conversely) global middle classes' (Wynter 2003, p.313). For Wynter (2003), we need to recognise how we have come to represent the human in such tragically reduced ways and resituate humanness in the archipelago of Human Otherness. We seek to find 'the lost motives, related no longer to Man's but to our human self-interest', that is, 'to come to grips with...still-to-be-explained puzzle of (human) consciousness(es)' (Wynter 2003, p.331). As I have written elsewhere:

> In these post-ethnoclass able-man times, who defines our humanness and humanity? What makes for us all to be human? What kind of humanity do we want to cherish? Can we define our humanness together? (Goodley 2014, p.164)

These questions resonate too with the focus of this chapter: autism and the human. I want to consider the contradictory ways in which autism can be seen to weave in and out of the ethnoclass-man and empirical human world (associated with the archipelago of otherness) described by Wynter. My sense is that autism is a ducker and a diver, a mover and a shaker, a complex friend and foe of humanness. But my sense even now is that re-energising the human category is something I would feel a lot happier with than over-representing autism.

AUTISM AS HUMAN OTHER: TOWARDS A POLITICS OF WONDER

Let us consider autism's relationship with the dominant culture by considering the location of autism as part of that empirical other that Wynter defines as Human Others; those other Others of the dominant same of ethnoclass man. The politics of the Other is evident in autism self-advocacy and autism politics where activists contest the dominant disabling imaginary and ableist symbolic order. Being autistic is cast as deficient Other to the rational, sociable, extraverted ideal of ethnoclass rational citizen. Autism, McGuire (2011; see also Chapter 5) has argued, increasingly terrorises the human, threatening to get into our families, under our skin and into our heads. The individual and collective activism of autism activists in virtual and real spaces demonstrates the potential for political agitation to occur as a consequence of being denied access to the rational heart

of contemporary society. One way of understanding autism activism's potential is captured by Tanya Titchkosky's (2011) wonderful turn of phrase: that thinking about the human being through disability has the potential to spark a *politics of wonder*. Rather than viewing autism as deficient other we are asked, instead, to wonder about disability's productive possibilities. This affirmative reading of activism has connections with the Wynter's plea to find 'the lost motives, related no longer to Man's but to our human self-interest', that is, 'to come to grips with...still-to-be-explained puzzle of (human) consciousness(es)' (Wynter 2003, p.331). In all activist commons debates, differences of opinion will reign. It is impossible to summarise the complexities of what is now a pan-national activist network. I do think, though, it is possible to identify three areas of autism activism that engage with conceptions of autism and the human.

The first activism I will term as ***brain activism***. This is an appeal to recognise human diversity through reference (or deference) to the neurology. This fits with what Bill Hughes (2009) has called the move towards biological citizenship. Borrowing from the work of Nicolas Rose (which we will revisit later on), this activist group is composed of biological or genetic citizens, some of whom claim citizenship in the name of a diagnostic category or condition. As they have come together they have developed a variety of patterns of self-help that include campaigning for recognition and resources to improve the lives of those who live with the condition in question (Hughes 2009). One way in which lives can be improved is if others have more empathy and understanding for those with the condition of autism. Take for example the following definition provided by Stanton (2010) for the *Thinking Person's Guide to Autism: What is Neurodiversity?*:

> The idea of neurodiversity was developed by autistic people in opposition to the pathologising model. According to them autistic people are not disordered. They have a different sort of order. Their brains are differently wired. They think differently. They do not want to be cured. They want to be understood.

The difficulties associated with brain activism can be explained in relation to what we might term *the essentialism paradox*. Whilst an appeal to neurological diversity pitches autism advocacy in relation to the wide expanse of human embodiment there is always a danger that medicalising discourses become the all-encompassing narrative for explaining the difference of autism. One's humanity becomes known in terms of an essentialist understanding of personhood that risks knowing that person solely in terms of a neurological label.

The second form of political activity associated with autism I will define as ***environmental activism***. This is an approach to agitation and organisation that recognises the lack of fit between the person with autism and the wider (disabling) autism-unfriendly world. The appeal here is to make the built environment

friendly, community settings and relational expectations more sensitive to the needs of people identified as having autism. So, if we were thinking about delivering an 'autism-friendly' conference we might think about controlling the brightness of lighting, asking members of an audience to wave their hands rather than applaud and ensure consistent medium volume levels for those speaking. While I was writing this chapter I received an email about the publication of a new book. The email read:

> For people with Autism Spectrum Disorder (ASD), the stresses of coping with a world that often seems alien to them can frequently lead to depression. Written specifically for adults with ASD, this ground-breaking book offers accessible and sensitive advice on how to manage depression and make positive steps towards recovery.

This summary of Dubin's (2014) book perfectly captures an environmental discourse around the causes of depression: that a sense of alienation caused by an intimidating environment might lead to psychological trauma. Such a view is in concert with literature of the social model of disability and the notion of internalised oppression. We know that hate crime against disabled people is rising and this can be experienced as psychologically terrorising, eliciting psychic reactions including the re-injuring of self through internalising discriminatory values (Marks 1999), lowering self-worth and lessening a sense of intrinsic value (Reeve 2008; Thomas 2007). The dangers of such an approach relate to what we might phrase as *the homogenisation problem*: in attempting to construct environments to become more autism-friendly, designers have in mind an autism-typical type of human user. Such a type is a myth and in danger of creating a view of people associated with the label as being essentially all the same.

Moreover, as Mallett and Runswick-Cole (2012) have commented, it is interesting to note that autism appears to work as a high-functioning impairment label (people often think they understand what autism is and what implications it creates) compared with other low-functioning labels (global developmental delay, for example, is rather vague and lacks explanatory power).

The third form of politicisation I will describe as ***divergent activism***. Activists associated with this approach contest the usefulness of the autism category and instead implore others to value the oddness, difference, uniqueness and divergence of humankind per se. This includes respecting individuals' rights to act differently, to prefer different ways of relating and living alongside and with others. Recently, Greenstein (2013, p.49) has argued for a *dis-ability studies* perspective to indicate 'a spectrum or multitude rather than the binary dis/ability which was constructed through power relations and hegemonic beliefs about ideal productive bodies and about notions of usefulness'. This is an interesting post-conventionalist take on the complex terrain of dis/ability through which

humanity is often mapped. The problems of such an approach lies in *the fluidity of diversity*: where it is difficult to settle on a particular identity position in a sea of floating signifiers of difference.

While each of the three activist positions boasts various strengths and potential weaknesses they all demonstrate autism's engagement with the human (and vice versa).

AUTISM AS HYPER-ETHNOCLASS MAN: THE CURIOUS INCIDENT OF THE MALE IN THE BLIGHT

Let us now consider the ways in which autism and ethnoclass man might, potentially, be cut from the same cloth. Autism appears in our culture as a well-known acquaintance. While we are told that autism is a monstrous blight on humanity, simultaneously, autism appears also to occupy an interesting place *in* the world of ethnoclass man. There is something uncanny about autism – it feels strangely familiar. Let us think about those classic stereotypes that whirl around the word autism: alone and anti-social; lacking in empathy; obsessed with routine and order; unhappy with uncertainty and spontaneity; fixed in outlook; clear in focus. I have run an exercise in a class with psychology undergraduates where I present these psychological descriptors. I asked students if these descriptors reminded them of anyone. The two most common responses were 'someone with autism' and 'my father'. Autism seems to say something about maleness and vice versa. Such a coupling has been systematically developed by Simon Baron-Cohen (2002, 2003), Professor of Developmental Psychopathology at the University of Cambridge and Fellow at Trinity College, Cambridge. In his 2002 paper, Baron-Cohen argues the following in his abstract:

> The key mental domains in which sex differences have traditionally been studied are verbal and spatial abilities. In this article I suggest that two neglected dimensions for understanding human sex differences are 'empathising' and 'systemising'. The male brain is defined psychometrically as those individuals in whom systemising is significantly better than empathising, and the female brain is defined as the opposite cognitive profile. Using these definitions, autism can be considered as an extreme of the normal male profile. There is increasing psychological evidence for the extreme male brain theory of autism. (Baron-Cohen 2002, p.248)

Baron-Cohen's research has spawned a research industry around autism and he remains, arguably, the most well-known figure in global autism research. His current work, according to his homepage, is engaged with 'testing the "extreme male brain" theory of autism at the neural, endocrine and genetic levels' (Baron-Cohen, n.d.).

I am sure that the irony is not lost on you that autism's linkage with extreme maleness is being developed in an elite British university that might be conceived as being at the heart of a British empire that historically helped spawn ethnoclass man across the globe. Note too the re-individualisation of autism and maleness: drilling down into the brain, into the neural, endocrine and genetic levels. Interpolating autism into the male-centre of ethnoclass man gives autism a prestige and recognition.

Earlier we considered the ways in which autism self-advocacy had promoted positive conceptions of autism as a neurologically different kind of humanness. In contrast, Baron-Cohen's autism and its easy sit with the extreme male brain of ethnoclass man appear to suggest this: that autism is simply not different enough. There is no doubt that high-functioning types of autism sits easily with modernist notions of rational man. I recall those times at disability conferences and in conversation with parents and professionals when it was expressed with relief that the child has 'high-functioning' autism. There is something rather ableist about this kind of autism discourse. Wolbring (n.d.) defines ableism as 'the favoritism for certain abilities for example cognition, competitiveness or consumerism and the often negative sentiment towards the lack of favoured abilities and has a long history'. Hence, so the stereotypes suggest, while our autistic man might not like to shop, we do know that he likes to think, or systemise as Baron-Cohen would have it. Understanding the peccadillos of male behaviour as a display of autism permits an understanding of the weird, eccentric or strange behaviour to be viewed as approximations of typical or average man as well as an indicator of a psychopathology. Hence, autism works in and against the norms of ethnoclass man: being evoked either as the opposite or an approximation of the male centre.

AUTISM GIVETH AND TAKETH AWAY: THE BIOPOLITICS OF AUTISM

The final analytical consideration I want to explore in relation to autism is its functioning as a biopolitical category. Lauren Berlant (2007) describes biopower as that force which permits something to live or die, the power to regularise life, the authority to force living not just to happen but also to endure and appear in particular ways. Autism appears as life and death and is classically biopolitical in nature. To unpack this further let us borrow on the analyses of Rabinow and Rose (2006). Their analysis suggests that biopower refers to the making of individuals and the population. Biopower is held together by three practices.

First, *one or more truth discourses are produced about the 'vital' character of living human beings*, and an array of authorities are considered competent to speak that truth. Hence whole panoplies of health, educational and social care professionals are called upon to speak with expertise about ab/normal childhood development.

Autism is called upon as an exemplar that speaks of the vital character of child development. Second, *strategies for intervention upon collective existence in the name of life and health* are elicited to identify and address ab/normal child development within the population. Hence in order to define anomalies and abnormalities then there must be some sense of normal child development and behaviour against which autism can be judged to exist as opposite. Autism becomes a key strategy for intervening in the lives and health of child population of a nation. Third, *modes of subjectification*, 'through which individuals are brought to work on themselves, under certain forms of authority, in relation truth discourses, by means of practices of the self, in the name of their own life or health, that of their family or some other collectivity, or indeed in the name of the life or health of the population as a whole' (Goodley 2014, p.61). Autism becomes a most popular and populist discourse for speaking of oneself and others, our own children and other children in general. Hence, we are encouraged to think more and more about an autistic spectrum. The only problem (though some would see this as a benefit) with a spectrum is that one can (and should) place oneself on that register. So, forget the spectrum of the rainbow or the spectrum of humanity: autism is *the* way of capturing the variegated nature of humanity. While this might sound somewhat bleak and reductionist, one needs to keep in mind the excessive nature of biopolitics.

Autism is a biopolitical category that cannot help producing in excess of itself. While many critical observers denounce autism discourse on the grounds of its pathologising and medicalising tendencies, the reality is that like any discourse many things are said and many tales are told about the object of that discourse. We have huge forms of commodity fetishism around autism and the production of a discernible industry described and critiqued by Mallett and Runswick-Cole (2012) as holding the potential to endlessly other, separate and pathologise human difference associated with autism. We also have a label and category that can be evoked on a t-shirt: 'I am autistic, not naughty'. We too have an educational label that can be used by parents to access services and support whilst, at the same time, being at risk of providing a totalising discourse about children. So a child gets extra support from a teaching and learning assistant that broadens their engagement with their classroom. But the presence of the same teaching assistant in the playground negates against children forming organic friendships devoid of adult supervision. The same child might not be invited back to his peers' households for lunch because the parent 'does not know what to do with autistic kids'. The biopolitics of autism are such that as soon as they give with one hand they threaten to take away with the other.

CONCLUSION

Recently I have argued for the development of a distinct intellectual project: *dis/ability studies* – the bifurcated study of co-existing processes associated with dis/ability and disablism/ableism. Disability is always haunted by the spectre of ability. Ability needs disability to be by its side in order to speak of what it is not. Similarly, when I think of autism it is always haunted by the spectre of the human. Is autism antithetical to humanness? Is autism one expression of humanity? Does autism permit us to think again about the human? Or is autism a boundary category constructed by those who obsessively, rigidly and carefully guard the borders of what they consider to be human? My sense is that any study of autism must also engage with the simultaneous study of the human. To consider autism and the human as distinct, unrelated projects would seem to be a major mistake, at least to me. If we all value our common humanity then one needs to endlessly ask what the category of autism gives to or detracts from our shared humanness.

REFERENCES

Baron-Cohen, S. (2002) 'The extreme male brain theory of autism.' *TRENDS in Cognitive Sciences 6*, 6, 248–254.

Baron-Cohen, S. (2003) *The Essential Difference: Men, Women and the Extreme Male Brain.* London: Penguin/Basic Books.

Baron-Cohen, S. (n.d.) *Biography.* Available at www.autismresearchcentre.com/people_baron-cohen, accessed on 10 November 2015.

Berlant, L. (2007) 'Slow death: sovereignty, obesity, lateral agency.' *Critical Inquiry 33*, 754–780.

Dubin, N. (2014) *The Autism Spectrum and Depression.* London: Jessica Kingsley Publishers.

Fanon, F. (1976) *The Wretched of the Earth.* Trans. C. Farrington. London: Penguin.

Fanon, F. (1993) *Black Skins, White Masks* (Third edition). London: Pluto Press.

Ghai, A. (2006) *(Dis)embodied Form: Issues of Disabled Women.* Delhi: Shakti Books.

Goodley, D. (2000) *Self-Advocacy in the Lives of People with Learning Difficulties.* Buckingham: Open University Press.

Goodley, D. (2011) *Disability Studies: An Interdisciplinary Introduction.* London: Sage.

Goodley, D. (2014) *Dis/ability Studies: Theorising Ableism and Disablism.* London: Routledge.

Grech, S. (2013) *Disability, Poverty and the Global South: Critical Reflections from Guatemala.* London: Palgrave Macmillan.

Greenstein, A. (2013) 'Radical Inclusive Pedagogy: Connecting Disability, Education and Activism.' Unpublished PhD thesis, Manchester Metropolitan University.

Hughes, B. (2009) 'Disability activisms: social model stalwarts and biological citizens.' *Disability and Society 24*, 6, 677–688.

Mallett, R., and Runswick-Cole, K. (2012) 'Commodifying Autism: The Cultural Contexts of "Disability" in the Academy.' In D. Goodley, B. Hughes and L.J. Davis (eds) *Disability and Social Theory.* Basingstoke: Palgrave MacMillan.

Marks, D. (1999) *Disability: Controversial Debates and Psychosocial Perspectives.* London: Routledge.

McGuire, A. (2011) 'War on Autism: On Normative Violence and the Cultural Production Of Autism Advocacy.' Unpublished PhD thesis, University of Toronto.

O'Toole, C. (2013) 'Disclosing our relationships to disabilities: an invitation for disability studies scholars.' *Disability Studies Quarterly 33*, 2.

Rabinow, P., and Rose, N. (2006) 'Biopower today.' *BioSocieties 1*, 195–217.

Reeve, D. (2008) 'Negotiating Disability in Everyday Life: The Experience of Psycho-Emotional Disablism.' Unpublished PhD thesis, University of Lancaster.

Soldatic, K., and Fiske, L. (2009) 'Bodies "locked up": intersections of disability and race in Australian immigration.' *Disability and Society 24*, 3, 289–301.

Sherry, M. (2007) '(Post) Colonising Disability.' Special issue of *Wagadu, Journal of Transnational Women's and Gender Studies 4*, Summer, 10–22.

Stanton, M. (2010) *Thinking Person's Guide to Autism: What is Neurodiversity?* [Blog] Available at www.thinkingautismguide.com/2010/06/what-is-neurodiversity.html, accessed on 10 November 2015.

Thomas, C. (2007) *Sociologies of Disability and Illness: Contested Ideas in Disability Studies and Medical Sociology.* Basingstoke: Palgrave MacMillan.

Titchkosky, T. (2011) *The Question of Access: Disability, Space, Meaning.* Toronto: University of Toronto Press.

Wolbring, G. (n.d.) *Ableism and Ability Ethics and Governance: About the Project.* Available at http://ableism.wordpress.com/about-the-project, accessed on 10 November 2015.

Wynter, S. (2003) 'Unsettling the coloniality of being/power/truth/freedom: towards the human, after man, its overrepresentation – an argument.' *CR: The New Centennial Review 3*, 3, 257–337.

CHAPTER 9

AUTISM SCREENING AND DIAGNOSTIC TOOLS

Sami Timimi and Brian McCabe

INTRODUCTION

The use of diagnostic tools and screening instruments has become a central part of the autism industry's methodology for identifying cases. These tools have acquired the status of medical tests, leading many to talk and enquire about 'being tested for autism'. However, these 'tests' are questionnaire-based and can only measure the person answering the questions' perception on those questions at a particular moment in time. They do not provide a validated independent measure of any aspect of biological/physiological functioning. Information gained via subjective questionnaires would not qualify as 'tests' in the rest of medicine. This chapter will examine and deconstruct the most popular diagnostic and screening tools, illustrating how little they add to a more comprehensive understanding of the person in question.

Autism and Autistic Spectrum Disorder (ASD) are behaviourally defined diagnoses, characterised by concluding that there are qualitative 'impairments' in social communication, social interaction and imagination (the core triad of symptoms), as set out in the *International Classification of Diseases*, 10th revision (ICD; World Health Organisation 1992) and the *Diagnostic and Statistical Manual of Mental Disorders*, Fourth edition (DSM-IV; APA 1994). Sensory hypo-sensitivities or hyper-sensitivities to the environment are also said to be common features, but have only been included in the list of symptoms for ASD in the new *Diagnostic and Statistical Manual*, Fifth Edition (DSM-5; APA 2013).

So, in DSM-IV autism is classified as belonging to the 'pervasive developmental disorders' (PDD). There are five subcategories listed under PDD:

- Autistic disorder: see below.
- Asperger Syndrome: relatively good verbal language, with milder non-verbal language problems, restricted range of interests and relatedness.

- PDD-NOS (not otherwise specified): non-verbal language and other problems that do not meet the strict criteria for other PDD disorders.
- Rett Syndrome: a rare neurodegenerative disorder predominantly of girls.
- Childhood disintegrative disorder: another rare neurodegenerative disorder.

In common practice, Rett Syndrome and childhood disintegrative disorder are considered mainstream medical disorders and are not usually dealt with within services for ASDs.

The triad of symptoms described as indicative of autism are:

- *First*, an inability to engage in reciprocal social interaction. A popular idea is that the autistic child fails to develop a 'Theory of Mind' and cannot imagine what other people may think or feel; thus, they lack empathy. Humans, animals and objects are treated alike. The child may become solitary, avoid eye contact and display little of the interested curiosity and exploratory play seen in infants and young children.
- *Second*, communication problems, both verbal and non-verbal. Rather than having a problem with spoken language per se, the autistic child appears not to grasp the point of communication. The affected child may not babble, is often late to speak and has difficulties in understanding what is said to them. This defect in understanding spoken speech may be almost total, or may be subtle and merely take the form of literal interpretation of language. If the autistic child does develop spoken language, then there is sometimes an abnormality in the way it is used, such as echolalia (repeating back what someone has said word for word). Volume, pitch and tone of speech are said to be peculiar. Sometimes the affected child may remember and repeat endlessly whole conversations, but be incapable of explaining the content.
- *Third*, evidence of restricted imagination and a predilection for rigid routines. The autistic child may form strange attachments to certain everyday objects, such as pieces of plastic or stones, or become fascinated with flicking paper or running water from taps. An obsessive need for routine is often found, with temper tantrums resulting from any small change in the usual pattern of their life.

In more severe cases first presentation with symptoms such as delayed language and solitary play is believed to be apparent before the age of three years. Higher-functioning children tend to have behavioural presentations at around four or five years or subtle social problems in later childhood. Concerns about more able

children, or those with Asperger Syndrome, may not develop until children are exposed to the greater social demands of the school environment. Some children may even have been considered well advanced in their development, because of their special interests or precocious vocabulary.

However, according to the new DSM-5 criteria (APA 2013), ASD is no longer based on a triad of symptoms, as detailed above, but instead the DSM-5 guidelines use two criteria domains:

- Language and social communication deficits are grouped into a social interaction criteria domain.
- Repetitive or restrictive behaviours serve as the second criteria domain and include 'sensory behaviours' for the first time.

Furthermore, in DSM-5, the terms 'autistic disorder', 'Asperger disorder', 'childhood disintegrative disorder' and 'PDD-NOS' have been replaced by the collective term 'Autism Spectrum Disorder'. At the time of writing, DSM-5 criteria had not yet filtered into the screening and diagnostic questionnaires, and so this chapter will mainly focus on instruments that have been developed in relation to criteria that predate DSM-5.

THE DEVELOPMENT OF CRITERIA

In 1956, Kanner and Eisenberg provided the first formal set of criteria for the diagnosis of autism. The criteria focused on two dimensions of the condition: a profound lack of affective contact; and repetitive, ritualistic behaviour, which must be of an elaborate kind. Some practitioners found these criteria too narrow, in particular because they omitted the unusual language and communication patterns that seemed to them a core element of the condition. Rutter's (1978) refinement introduced the concept of simultaneous deficits in three behavioural domains: impaired social relationships, impaired language and communication skills, and insistence on sameness. In 1976 Lorna Wing conducted one of the first epidemiological surveys on autism and in 1979, together with Gould, they wrote what is often considered a seminal piece entitled 'Severe impairments of social interaction and associated abnormalities in children: epidemiology and classification' (Wing and Gould 1979). This paper was the first epidemiological study using the now-familiar triad; which together with Rutter's papers laid the foundation for the triad (impaired social relationships, impaired language and communication skills, and restricted imagination) in its various forms becoming the accepted operational definition for autism ever since – until, that is, the arrival of DSM-5, where we are now back to a bi-dimensional construct, albeit somewhat different to Kanner and Eisenberg's two dimensions.

The shift away from the Kanner criteria appears to have broadened the scope of the diagnosis. For example, age of onset is one criterion that has changed over time. Kanner and Eisenberg (1956) implied an age assumption by using the term 'early infantile autism'. Rutter (1978) (followed by DSM-III; APA 1980) set a specific age of onset limit of earlier than 30 months. The DSM-III-R (APA 1987) criteria relaxed this limit, requiring only that the age of onset occur during infancy or childhood. ICD-10 (World Health Organisation 1992) and DSM-IV (APA 1994) set an age limit at 36 months, in part as a reaction to the problem posed by the expanded age definition introduced in DSM-III-R.

At the time of ICD-9 (World Health Organisation 1978), autism appears under 'Childhood Psychoses' and was characterised by an age of onset before 30 months. Also included in ICD-9 under 'Childhood Psychoses' was the subcategory of 'Disintegrative Psychosis', said to be characterised by a regression in development. There was also an 'Atypical Childhood Psychosis' category and a final unspecified category.

In Rutter's influential modernisation of the definition in 1978, three related terms – autism, infantile autism and childhood autism – were used somewhat interchangeably. DSM-III (American Psychiatric Association 1980) used 'infantile autism' as the core descriptor, but also placed autism in the context of 'Pervasive Developmental Disorders' (PDD) for the first time. DSM-III helped the move towards the concept of a spectrum of autistic disorders through classifying autism under PDDs, and also introduced the term 'atypical PDD'.

DSM-III had five classes of what it described as 'Infancy, Childhood or Adolescence Disorders'; these were: intellectual (mental retardation), behavioural (ADD and conduct disorders), emotional (anxiety disorders and other disorders of childhood), physical (eating disorders, stereotyped movement disorders and other disorders with a physical manifestation) and developmental disorders (PDD and specific developmental disorders). It introduced a new way of classifying those who didn't quite reach diagnostic criteria such that each of these subcategories terminated in an 'atypical' category, described as a 'residual' class. It was to be used whenever a person did not quite meet the descriptive criteria for any of the other disorders in that subcategory, but shared some features with them. With regard to the developmental disorders, what differentiates PDD from a specific developmental disorder is that in the case of the former every aspect of development is assessed as being affected. Within the category of PDD there were a further three subcategories: infantile autism, childhood onset PDD and atypical PDD. What appears to differentiate the first two categories is the age of onset – if onset was before 30 months then infantile autism was to be used; after 30 months childhood onset PDD. Atypical PDD was to be used when a

person did not meet the full criteria for the other two, but shared some similarity to them.

In 1987, a revised edition of DSM-III, DSM-III-R (APA 1987), abandoned the term 'infantile autism', in part to allow for cases where the onset of symptoms did not occur in early infancy. DSM-III-R also included a new category of 'pervasive developmental disorder – not otherwise specified' (PDD-NOS). PDDs now had just two disorders: autistic disorder and PDD-NOS.

In ICD-10 (World Health Organisation 1992) the category of PDD has eight subcategories: childhood autism, atypical autism, Rett Syndrome, childhood disintegrative disorder, hyperkinesis associated with mental retardation, Asperger Syndrome, other PDDs and PDD-unspecified. The latter is similar to PDD-NOS and the penultimate category, together with 'hyperkinesis associated with mental retardation', has no DSM equivalent.

DSM-IV (APA 1994), which took a similar approach to ICD-10, used the term 'autistic disorder'. DSM-III-R had introduced the term 'PDD-NOS' and this was retained in DSM-IV. By DSM-IV the PDDs now had three new diagnoses: 'Asperger Syndrome', 'childhood disintegrative psychosis' and 'Rett Syndrome'. DSM-IV therefore has five categories for the PDDs: autistic disorder, Asperger Syndrome, PDD-NOS, Rett Syndrome and childhood disintegrative disorder.

If you found all the above rather confusing to follow, we can assure you that you are not alone. The basis on which the continuous mutation of constructs happened is not only difficult to understand, but also raises a number of issues with regard to obtaining valid and reliable information on the time trends and prevalence rates for autism. Given the changing definitions of autism, accurate comparisons of changing prevalence over time are difficult to make. The three sets of DSM criteria for autism have varied in breadth. Some have argued that the move from DSM-III to DSM-III-R broadened the concept of autism, contributing to an apparent increase in prevalence over time; however, others believe that in the shift from the DSM-III-R criteria to the DSM-IV/ICD-10 criteria, a 'corrective' narrowing occurred, although this is unlikely to have compensated for the changing trends in clinical practice as it came to take seriously the expanded notion of the autistic spectrum. With the advent of yet another change in the criteria in DSM-5, the same debates on whether this will increase or decrease rates of diagnosis are happening. Meanwhile, the frequency of diagnoses of autism continues to rise and the more important debates about why we can't settle on a diagnostic system and criteria are rarely mentioned.

DIAGNOSTIC PRACTICE

Although autism 'experts' are fond of claiming that diagnostic tools are highly reliable and valid and that clinicians using these can be trained to become

'accurate' diagnosticians, there is much reason to doubt this. Given the widening of the diagnostic frame since the notion of ASD became popular, it seems more likely that clinicians have subscribed to the notion of a spectrum that seems ever-widening. It is not surprising that some of the leading clinicians and researchers in this subject have no desire to adhere to diagnostic criteria that could undermine the validity of the wider spectrum that has become embedded in routine practice.

Rutter and Schopler (1987, 1992) discuss some of the thorny issues surrounding diagnosis and classification of autism and PDDs. They disagree with a system that might stipulate a minimum number of symptoms as they feel this might tie the hands of clinicians, but they do not address the issues of ethics, global functioning, or levels of impairment and how diagnosis may be viewed in relation to these. When considering diagnosis without proper reference to the extent and limit of impairments, could this not lead to unnecessary medicalisation and pathologising, with all the subsequent implications of ascribing disability? The authors refer to the importance of cause, course and response to treatment as factors to be considered in the identification and classification of disorders, but come across as untroubled by the lack of any solid evidence to support current ASD categories having developed as a result of clear differences in any of these areas. They also suggest that within a group of disorders it would be better to have too many (even unsubstantiated diagnostic categories), which could later be collapsed with or into each other, than vice versa. This, however, avoids engagement with surrounding problems of what should be the basis on which a variety of aberrant behaviours are grouped together to make a set of disorders and how to differentiate these from other groupings of disorders. They make a case for differentiating autism and related disorders from learning difficulties, specific language disorders and other developmental disorders, though the grounds for doing this rest on a belief in the uniqueness of autism and PDDs, a belief that seems to us based more on circular reasoning than scientific evidence, as establishing where the spectrum begins and ends is just as difficult as differentiating one condition from another within the spectrum.

Rutter and Schopler (1987, 1992) reject the proposal that a lack of 'Theory of Mind' is the main deficit of autism and related conditions. They also (correctly, in our opinion) reject the idea that clinical judgement is a necessary or sufficient criterion for ascribing diagnosis, as all that would yield would be consensus, which is not the basis for a solid empirical scientific foundation. In other words, lumping together disparate behaviours, with possibly different causes and courses, is unlikely to result in good research into cause or interventions or to lead to the sort of scientific foundation necessary to support a system of classification that will be useful for developing a scientific evidence-based approach, as found in the rest of medicine. It is our contention that current theory and practice lacks such a scientific basis and is, as a result, based on ideological developments

reflecting a variety of academics' and clinicians' opinions, which have gradually developed into a series of (often disputed) consensus-based approaches. By Rutter and Schopler's standards, then, we have failed to achieve an adequate scientific basis for current classifications and therefore practice in this area is anything but evidence-based.

Despite none of the ASDs having this solid scientific foundation on which to build sound and ethical clinical practice, the belief that early screening and early diagnosis is essential became increasingly popular in recent decades (e.g. Baird, Cass and Slonims 2003). Given that the internet is awash with suggestions of various famous people, past and present, from scientists to actors to musicians who are deemed to have been (or are) sufferers of some form of autism,[1] then if the prognosis for some children with ASD is to be able to look forward to joining tomorrow's greats, then why not leave well enough alone? One might think that this variability of symptom expression and course and prognosis might be sufficient to allow a note of caution to creep into the professional discourse.

One possible good reason for early screening tools and early diagnosis would lie in this reliably leading to successful interventions; however, as discussed elsewhere (e.g. Timimi *et al.* 2010), we have no good evidence to support this possibility. If symptoms are subject to such variability whether or not 'technical' interventions are applied, then what is the purpose of such a system of classification and attempts at early diagnosis?

Charman and Baird (2002) wonder how accurate and stable the diagnosis of an ASD might be. Although arguing for the stability over time of the syndrome, it is worth noting that in two studies available for their review, one by Gillberg and colleagues (1990) and the other by Lord (1995), both written by strong advocates of the 'lifelong' disorder hypothesis, one child out of 28 and 30 respectively were found to be no longer autistic, according to their criteria, by the age of three years, a year after the first assessment. More recent studies have suggested even greater variability in outcomes the further on that children are followed. Fein and colleagues (2013) looked at 34 young people diagnosed with autism as children (confirmed through examining their early medical records) who no longer met autism's criteria. Anderson, Liang and Lord (2014), in their study, find that 9 per cent of the group improved to the point that they no longer met the diagnostic criteria for autism; with another 28 per cent retaining some mild difficulties in social functioning, but doing very well in several areas, particularly cognitive and academic functioning, with most successfully accessing or completing a college education. Farley and colleagues (2009) examined the adult outcome (average age 32.5 years) for 41 people diagnosed with autism in early childhood. They found half the group were rated as 'Very Good' or 'Good'

1 See, for example, http://autism.lovetoknow.com/Famous_People_with_Autism.

on a global outcome measure. A study of 120 individuals first diagnosed with autism in adulthood (Hofvander *et al.* 2009) found that about a quarter had a college or university degree, about a half were living independently, and more than 40 per cent had a job or were studying. Given this accumulating evidence, the retention of the belief that autism is a lifelong disability/disorder is simply not supported. Furthermore, there is little support found in the above studies that improved outcomes were the result of early intervention, casting further doubt on the utility of early diagnosis, particularly if we continue to tell parents that we are diagnosing a lifelong disability/disorder.

The issue of diagnosing at the other end of the age spectrum – that of diagnosing childhood disorders in adults – is also highly problematic. Children with 'autism', as it used to be defined, are unlikely to have escaped diagnosis by the time they reach adulthood given the accompanying range of disabilities (physical and mental) associated with this previously rare diagnosis. There is a great difficulty in using contemporaneous symptoms as being indicative of childhood problems, or using an adult's retrospective recall of childhood functioning to assess their childhood. The difficulties in detecting symptoms, which may have occurred many decades ago, are all too obvious; but just what kind of behaviour is worthy of scrutiny? Wing (1981) began the trend of using adults to study childhood onset 'autistic' disorders. The case histories outlined by her were procured from adults and it is not clear from her paper whether evidence beyond individual or parental recall of childhood history was obtained. This began not only a trend of using adults to retrospectively investigate possible ASD symptoms in childhood, but also the clinical practice of diagnosing adults (who had not received such diagnoses in childhood) with ASDs.

DIAGNOSTIC QUESTIONNAIRES

Tools such as the Autism Diagnostic Interview – Revised (ADI-R) (Lord, Rutter and Le Couteur 1994) and the Autism Diagnostic Observation Schedule – Generic (ADOS-G) (Lord *et al.* 2000) are increasingly being used in the diagnostic process. If one gets a high score on one of these this usually results in a diagnosis of autism. If a lower score is found, but still above the threshold, then a diagnosis of AS, PDD-NOS or ASD may be given.

The ADI-R (Lord *et al.* 1994) is marketed as a 'clinical diagnostic instrument' for assessing autism in children and adults. It consists of a standardised, semi-structured clinical interview for caregivers. The interview contains 93 items and focuses on behaviours in three content areas or domains: quality of social interaction (e.g. emotional sharing, offering and seeking comfort, social smiling and responding to other children); communication and language (e.g. stereotyped utterances, pronoun reversal, social usage of language); and repetitive, restricted

and stereotyped interests and behaviour (e.g. unusual preoccupations, hand and finger mannerisms, unusual sensory interests). Responses are scored by the clinician based on the caregiver's description of the person in question. The interview then generates scores in each of the three content areas (i.e. communication and language; social interaction; restricted, repetitive behaviours). For each item, the clinician gives a score ranging from 0 to 3. A score of 0 is given when 'behaviour of the type specified in the coding is not present'; up to a score of 3 for 'extreme severity' of the specified behaviour. A diagnosis of autism is given when scores in all three content areas of communication, social interaction and patterns of behaviour meet or exceed the specified cut-offs. The ADI-R is said to require substantial training in administration and scoring, and a 'highly trained' clinician is thought to be able to administer the ADI-R in approximately 90 minutes. There is no requirement for the assessor to observe any of the behaviours the caregiver is reporting.

The ADOS-G (Lord *et al.* 2000) is marketed as a semi-structured assessment for individuals suspected of having autism or other pervasive developmental disorders (PDD). The ADOS-G consists of four modules. Each module is aimed at children and adults of differing developmental and language levels, ranging from no expressive or receptive language to verbally fluent adults. The examiner is allowed to observe the occurrence or non-occurrence of behaviours that are deemed to indicate a diagnosis of autism or other PDDs across developmental levels and chronological ages. The examiner selects the module that is most appropriate for a particular child or adult on the basis of his/her expressive language level and chronological age and then uses structured activities and materials, and less structured interactions, to provide 'standard' contexts in which social, communicative and other behaviours are observed. Within each module, the participant's response to each activity is recorded by the diagnostician, with overall ratings being made at the end. These ratings are then used to formulate a diagnosis. The ADOS-G essentially provides a 30- to 45-minute observation period during which the examiner presents the individual being assessed with planned social situations in which it has been determined in advance that behaviour of a particular type is expected to appear.

The focus of the ADOS-G is on observation of social behaviour and communication. Standardisation lies in the hierarchy of behaviour employed by the examiner and the kinds of behaviours taken into account in each activity during the overall ratings. The examiners have a difficult task, as what the examiners do not do (such as deliberately waiting to see if the participant will initiate an interaction or try to maintain it) is as important as what they do, thus there is implicit acknowledgement that in setting up 'social' scenarios the person and personality of the examiner is unavoidably part of the mix. As such the goal of 'standardisation' seems difficult to achieve. The impact of the observer in any

human situation under study is well recognised in the humanities. Anthropologists, in developing the ethnographic method of investigation, recognised the impact the investigator had not only on an individual, but on a whole community, and as a result developed a methodology that required the investigator to live among those they were studying for months and sometimes years, before they could make observations that went beyond the reactions of the studied to the person studying them.

Thus, both the ADI-R and ADOS-G provide a superficial and subjective way of diagnosing an individual with an ASD. They are examples of judging a book by its cover, and in the case of ADI-R someone else's book. Although supporters of the use of such rating 'instruments' claim that reliability and consistency in scoring can be established by training in use of these instruments, in the real world, however, this rarely translates into practice, which is not surprising given that the so-called 'symptoms' being rated are open to highly subjective interpretations. One of the authors (ST) has found that even within the boundaries of a rural county, in one town the numbers diagnosed with an ASD are plentiful and exceed those that are diagnosed with ADHD and in the next town there are hardly any – all down to the differential diagnostic habits of two clinicians using similar instruments. In his practice, ST has found that when clinically working with those who have been previously diagnosed with 'autism', it only takes a few meetings before far more meaningful narratives have emerged than those attached to the superficial focus of 'symptoms' and 'diagnosis'. Working in this way, without the distraction of trying to categorise behaviours, ST has found that diagnostic-type conversations ascribing experiences to 'autism' (as in 'this is because of his autism') usually disappear and become of little relevance to therapeutic work.

In addition, both tests require considerable time to administer, which has led some (such as Williams and Brayne 2006) to suggest that this undermines their efficacy and practicality in clinical settings, arguing, instead, that we should use shorter screening tests. Others suggest that these 'instruments' should not be used in isolation because they cannot capture the presentation of stereotyped behaviours, meaning a more complete diagnostic history is required. De Bildt and colleagues (2004) specifically looked at the ability of ADOS-G and ADI-R to discriminate between those with autism and learning disability; they conclude that the level of agreement between the two tools was 'fair' but both had poor ability to discriminate between PDD and learning disability in general. Like other authors, they emphasise that neither should be used in isolation; use of both, augmented by as much personal historical detail as possible, is desirable. If that is the case and consensus is arguing that these 'instruments' should be supplemented by thorough history-taking and clinical judgement, one wonders why the well-trained clinician can't just use historical data, without recourse

to cumbersome, superficial tools, open to subjective interpretation and poor discriminatory capacity for conditions within the spectrum and between other potential diagnostic categories.

In 2002 Wing and colleagues devised the Diagnostic Interview for Social and Communication Disorders (DISCO). The authors explain that the purpose of developing the DISCO was to assist clinicians in the diagnosis, differential diagnosis and management of ASD and other development disorders affecting social interaction and communication. Thus, they suggest that the autistic spectrum is wider than that of PDD and accept that this means widening the spectrum further; as a result the list of behaviours in the DISCO exceeds that of the other two tools. The authors are astute enough to point out that any attempt to devise a tool of this nature falls prey to the 'insoluble' problem of 'circularity', but no attempt is made to solve it! We wish to suggest that this circularity is only a vicious one as long as one is committed to both the spectrum and a pre-determined view of what constitutes autism, the spectrum, or normal behaviour. It matters little whether any of these tools have specificity, reliability or validity if the premise (face validity) upon which they are based is flawed. In what appears a self-serving view, the authors suggest that rigid adherence to diagnostic categories will prove detrimental to parents and caregivers.

For those who seek a referral for a diagnosis of AS, some services (and one author, BM, can attest to this through personal experience) send out the Autism-spectrum Quotient questionnaire (AQ) (Baron-Cohen *et al.* 2001). Baron-Cohen and colleagues argue that this instrument has been piloted over several years on adults with AS or High-Functioning Autism (HFA). In their study (Baron-Cohen *et al.* 2001), the authors report that of the 11 individuals who exceeded the 32 cut-off score, all were male and of these seven were deemed to be eligible for a diagnosis of HFA or AS on further assessment. None of these seven had previously received a diagnosis of HFA or AS. The authors report that no diagnoses were actually given to these seven because none of those meeting the criteria complained of any current unhappiness with many of them reporting that within a university setting (the sample was of Cambridge University students) their desire to pursue their narrow interests was not considered odd, and was even valued. Despite this, the authors conclude that the AQ has reasonable validity and also decide that their results show that HFA and AS are found disproportionately among scientists, mathematicians and engineers, which to them suggests a link between these professions and the autistic spectrum. The potential ethical issues raised by a questionnaire that leads to making a potentially serious diagnosis for a group of people that are happy and functioning well is not considered by the authors.

It is well worth looking in further detail at the AQ, to see what behaviours it sets out to try and capture. Here are some of its questions:

- I prefer to do things on my own rather than with other people.
- If I try to imagine something, I find it very easy to create a picture in my mind.
- I often notice small sounds when others do not.
- I usually notice car number plates or similar strings of information.
- I am fascinated by dates.
- I would rather go to a library than a party.
- I find myself more strongly drawn to people than things.
- I don't particularly enjoy reading fiction.
- I notice patterns in things all the time.
- I am not very good at remembering phone numbers.
- I enjoy social occasions.
- I enjoy meeting people.
- I am not very good at remembering people's date of birth.

One may wonder what these questions have to do with the 'core' feature of a lack of empathy. It is also worth pointing out that this list bears more than a passing resemblance to Eysenck's Personality Inventory (Eysenck and Eysenck 1975) which has questions such as: Do you like mixing with people? Do you like working alone? Do you like planning things carefully, well ahead of time? To us this bears more than a slight resemblance to pop psychology questionnaires found in magazines and the subjective, 'open to interpretation' nature of Astrology charts.

SCREENING FOR ASDS

In 2003 a UK National Plan for Autism was published. This plan was implemented by the All Parliamentary Group on Autism, and was developed by the National Autistic Society in collaboration with the Royal College of Paediatrics and Child Health and Royal College of Psychiatrists (National Autistic Society 2003). The plan had ten 'key' action points:

- Easy and transparent access to assessment within a specified time frame.
- Discussion of the diagnosis, taking into account a sensitive framework for sharing information.

- Easy access for families to information and support and relating it to their needs.
- Multi-agency, multidisciplinary assessment and working.
- Appropriate intervention.
- Immediate appointment of a key worker for the family.
- Care plan developed with and for the family.
- Care management for complex situations and ongoing needs.
- Regular ASD-specific training of all professionals working in assessment and provision of services.
- Strategic planning and coordination of ASD services for local populations must be undertaken.

In addition, under the subheading 'Identification' the plan recommends training of all involved professionals in 'alerting' signals of possible ASD both at pre-school and school age, together with 'regular opportunities' (at least at 8–12 months, 2–3 years and 4–5 years) to discuss a child's development with parents as part of 'surveillance' to detect and respond rapidly to any developmental concerns. They also recommend that the detection/diagnosis of all developmental problems including autism/ASD should be audited in each local area. Although whole population screening was not recommended, these recommendations represent a sea change in our approach to autism even though it was acknowledged in the document that these recommendations come from professional opinion with little research being available to support it producing positive benefits to the lives of those 'identified' as autistic at such a young age. The lack of evidential support and the clinical, ethical and potential lifelong implications for those diagnosed was not discussed.

In the UK, as in other parts of the world, we have, in a very short space of time, moved from the realms of vague unsubstantiated hypotheses to political ideology. There are no 'national plans' for dyslexia, ADHD, learning disability, childhood depression, dyspraxia, and so on, so why autism? In the plan there is reference to behavioural features that rarely appear in the academic literature and are not part of the 'symptoms' that lead to a diagnosis, such as biting/hitting peers and being oppositional to adults, but also virtual acknowledgement of what we have been arguing – that, given the available evidence, autism is best understood as a social construct – even though, of course, this cannot be admitted as overtly as that would undermine the whole idea behind a 'National Plan':

> The identification of an ASD is through behavioural 'symptoms'... Yet behaviour by itself is a poor guide to diagnosis and certainly there is no single behaviour or even set of behaviours that unequivocally denote autism, although missing behaviours may be a better guide. Making a diagnosis is, therefore, a clinical judgement, with behavioural 'symptoms' as a guide to that judgement. This task is made more problematic by the fact that most behaviours that are seen as 'characteristic' of an ASD can be seen in other (including normally developing) populations, albeit at times of particular stress or in isolation. A further difficulty for the categorical model of ASD is that the three behavioural domains (communication, social understanding and skill, flexibility in thinking and behaviour) vary dimensionally across both the normally developing and the ASD populations. There is no point (other than an arbitrary one) at which behaviour along any one of these three dimensions can be divided into 'autistic' versus 'non-autistic'... It is also the case that many people with ASD view themselves as part of normal human variation, rather than as having a pathology. (National Autistic Society 2003, p.76)

Reading the above through the eyes of scientific scepticism, it is hard to conclude that even the authors know how to define what they are calling 'autism'. Instead, it is only 'experts' who will be able to categorise this difficult to characterise syndrome (like, of course, the experts who wrote that document).

If you screen a population it is likely to be the case that 'hidden' numbers of people with a disorder will be detected. How many largely depends upon how specific the definition of a case is. A lack of case specificity undermines the argument for the use of screening and screening tools. Unless you can reliably distinguish a case of X from that of Y then the possibility of large numbers of false positives increases. Without adequate definitions of the sort that enable epidemiological studies and surveys to identify cases of 'autism' without recourse to an 'expert' to make the diagnosis in every case, we cannot trust the findings of any studies and figures produced on prevalence. It also causes fundamental problems for screening.

According to the National Screening Committee (2000) certain criteria have to be fulfilled for a population screening tool to be valid. For example, the second criterion states:

> The epidemiology and natural history of the condition, including development from latent to declared disease, should be adequately understood and there should be a detectable risk factor, or disease marker, and a latent period or early symptomatic stage. (National Screening Committee 2000, p.26)

Criterion number 13 states:

> The benefit from the screening programme should outweigh the physical and psychological harm (caused by the test, diagnostic procedures and treatment). (National Screening Committee 2000, p.27)

It is unlikely that diagnostic screening for autism, or the broader ASDs, could meet either of these criteria, or indeed some others in the list. Indeed, the UK National Screening Committee policy on autism and ASD remains that screening is not recommended (NSC 2012) despite strong lobbying for this policy to change from both the National Autistic Society and the British Psychological Society.

Many concerned parents and professionals have been exposed to literature and programmes from lay and professional sources that talk about 'autism' and autistic symptoms and how to recognise them. The authors of this literature and these programmes have a considerable interest in the expansion of behaviours that necessitate interventions from 'experts', who then become vital in oiling the wheels of 'screening'. Parents may be caught in a trap of thinking that the diagnosis will lead to access to goods and services that their child would otherwise be denied. Indeed, many of these (well-intentioned) 'experts' contend that that is one of the rationales behind their proselytising. To us, however, it seems that the people who have most obviously benefited from the increase in the use of tools for screening for and diagnosing of ASDs have been the professionals themselves.

SCREENING QUESTIONNAIRES

The Checklist for Autism in Toddlers (CHAT) was devised by Baron-Cohen and colleagues in 1992. The CHAT is a screening instrument which seeks to identify children aged 18 months who are at risk for an ASD. It is a short questionnaire used by primary health workers (such as community paediatricians) during the 18-month developmental check. The following are examples of questions asked by the CHAT.

Section A – Ask Parent:

Yes or No?

- Does your child take an interest in other children?
- Does your child enjoy playing peek-a-boo/hide-and-seek?
- *Does your child ever pretend, for example, to make a cup of tea using a toy cup and teapot, or pretend other things?

- *Does your child ever use his/her index finger to point, to indicate interest in something?

Section B – Doctor's observation:

Yes or No?

- *Get child's attention, then point across the room at an interesting object and say, 'Oh look! There's a (name a toy)!' Watch child's face. Does the child look across to see what you are pointing at?
- *Get the child's attention, then give child a miniature toy cup and teapot and say, 'Can you make a cup of tea?' Does the child pretend to pour out the tea, drink it, and so on?
- *Say to the child, 'Where's the light?' or 'Show me the light.' Does the child point with his/her index finger at the light?

* Indicates critical question most indicative of autistic characteristics.

Baron-Cohen and colleagues (1996) pinpointed protodeclarative pointing (pointing at an object of interest), gaze monitoring and pretend play as key items to screen for with the CHAT. The conclusion that these, above any other features, when seen at such a young age, are indicative of potential future autism seems to have been arrived at without any robust research evidence to substantiate this idea.

Robins and colleagues (2001a) decided to modify the CHAT. The M-CHAT does not require physicians' observations, just parental self-report. The questionnaire is simply given to parents of a 16–30-month-old infant as a screening tool. The following are examples of questions found in the M-CHAT:

- Does your child take an interest in other children?
- Does your child like climbing on things, such as up stairs?
- Does your child ever pretend, for example, to talk on the phone or take care of a doll or pretend other things?
- Does your child ever use his/her index finger to point, to ask for something?
- Does your child ever use his/her index finger to point, to indicate interest in something?
- Does your child look you in the eye for more than a second or two?
- Does your child smile in response to your face or your smile?

- Does your child imitate you (e.g. you make a face – will your child imitate it)?
- If you point at a toy across the room, does your child look at it?
- Does your child walk?
- Does your child look at your face to check your reaction when faced with something unfamiliar?

Each question is marked by a yes/no answer and the questionnaire can be completed in a couple of minutes. If the child fails two to three items (or more) they should be referred for a diagnostic evaluation. It is not clear whether or why a 16-month-old child not exhibiting these behaviours should raise concerns about developmental delays or problems that are worthy of an autism diagnosis or in what way such behaviours constitute specific risk factors for the development of autism or an ASD. Those of us who are parents can imagine our children 'failing' this 'test' quite easily at 16 months of age or older, particularly our boys (who often develop the type of skills being rated later than girls).

The Robins *et al.* (2001a) M-CHAT produced a critical response by Charman and colleagues (2001), among whom Baron-Cohen is listed as a co-author. Whatever the respective merits of the CHAT and M-CHAT, there appears to have broken out something of a turf war. In neither the Robins *et al.* (2001a) article nor in the subsequent articles of Charman *et al.* (2001) and Robins *et al.* (2001b) do either side spend any time addressing the kinds of ethical criticisms that could be made if they had attempted to judge the merits of their screening tools by the criteria established by the NSC. Given the current state of case definition and knowledge (then and now), it is hardly surprising that they chose not to do so.

In a 2001 paper by Baird and colleagues (that also includes Charman and Baron-Cohen as co-authors) there is a discussion of the case for and against screening for autism. In the paper the authors choose to highlight the importance of parental concerns as if the scientific questions should be dictated by a demand and supply equation. In answer to the question of 'Why screen?' they point to parental concern and early intervention and treatment, although, as they admit, evidence for the efficacy of such interventions improving prognosis is poor to absent. This admission should effectively undermine the whole argument for screening but Baird and colleagues (2001) skate over it. Further, they suggest that another reason for early screening is genetic counselling:

> The risk of a second child having autism when the first has the diagnosis is 5% (one hundred times the reported prevalence), and the chances of a more general problem in social communication or cognitive development are several times higher still. There is no prenatal diagnostic test but parents

> need to have this information as soon as possible if they are to make personal choices about extending their family based on existing knowledge rather than ignorance. (Baird *et al.* 2001, p.469)

As with many papers on this subject the terms autism and ASD are used interchangeably. This is particularly unfortunate when they appear to argue that the prognosis for what had hitherto been called 'autism' is dismal, which as we outline above is far from what the evidence says.

We now turn to the Childhood Asperger Syndrome Test (CAST), which was devised to screen for possible AS. This screening tool was devised by Scott and colleagues (2002a) and includes Baron-Cohen as a co-author. Initially a pilot was devised where 13 children already diagnosed with AS were compared with 37 'typically developing' children aged four to 11 years. The CAST consists of 37 questions with yes/no answers. There are six 'control' questions, so the maximum score is 31. They conclude that, as all of the AS sample scored equal to or greater than 15 on the CAST, while none of the controls did, choosing a provisional cut-off of 15 would not generate too many false positives or lead to many cases needing an assessment for a possible social and communication condition, in a typical mainstream primary-age population. The authors then argue that as a result CAST was suitable to administer as a screening to a wider population, when perhaps more appropriate questions might have been whether such a tool could differentiate from other comparable conditions, and the appropriateness of generalising from a small population of already diagnosed individuals to other populations.

In the subsequent study (Scott *et al.* 2002a, 2002b) the CAST was sent to the parents of 1150 primary-school-aged children in the Cambridge area. An additional screening tool called the Social Communication Questionnaire (SCQ) was also sent to families who returned the initial CAST questionnaire, and this acted as a comparison tool. Further assessment using the ADOS-G was undertaken in those above or near the cut-off scores on the CAST or SCQ. Any individual who was 'discovered' but not already in receipt of an AS diagnosis was not automatically given one, but was given sufficient information to procure one if they wished. Out of the 1150, 199 replied. Of these 199, 25 withdrew consent, leaving 174 of whom 139 also returned the SCQ. Of the 199, 6.5 per cent scored at or above the cut-off point on the CAST. Given that the authors assume that an expected level in the population was 0.5 per cent, this led the authors to conclude that either the score of 15 was too low or that only those parents who already had concerns replied. If one adopted the former view one might have thought that this seriously undermined the validity of the tool as a screening measure. Were one to assume that the tool was a valid one, then it would yield an epidemiological result for AS that far exceeds all current estimates

for ASD prevalence, let alone AS. Yet the authors conclude: 'In summary, these preliminary results indicate that the CAST may be an effective tool for the early screening of primary-school-age (4–11 years) children at risk for AS and related conditions, in a non-clinical sample' (Scott *et al.* 2002a, p.30), but only if the CAST cut-off point is raised to 17.

The papers do not discuss whether those identified did pursue a diagnosis. Serious ethical issues are involved in identifying need where none had hitherto been discerned, but this is not raised as an issue by the authors, who instead conclude that with ongoing development CAST could be established as a UK screener to act:

> ...as an early indicator for those children likely to be at risk for AS or related conditions, who are not achieving their educational potential and who have clinical or educational needs. It needs to be developed using a non-clinical sample as these children may not yet be in touch with clinical services, but it is likely that such children will be the ones for whom there is already parental and/or teacher concerns, but who may be struggling to have their needs recognised, or who are being misclassified as lazy, naughty, disruptive, etc. (Scott *et al.* 2002a, p.30)

In addition to questions about the appropriateness of such conclusions, given the unacceptable mutation of the original study hypothesis (that CAST with a cut-off of 15 is a suitable screening instrument for AS), which clearly (and unsurprisingly) produced unacceptable rates of false positives, it also begs the question of just whom the tool is devised for if 'lazy', 'naughty' or 'disruptive' children are the target population.

The possibility of profound consequences of using CAST as a screening tool makes it worth examining further. The following are examples of questions are as they appear in the CAST:

- Does s/he come up to you spontaneously for a chat?
- Does s/he enjoy sports?
- Does s/he appear to notice unusual details that others miss?
- Does s/he find it easy to interact with other children?
- Can s/he read appropriately for his/her age?
- Does s/he mostly have the same interests as his/her peers?
- Does s/he have an interest which takes up so much time that s/he does little else?
- Does s/he enjoy joking around?

- Does s/he have difficulty understanding the rules for polite behaviour?
- Does s/he appear to have an unusual memory for details?
- Does s/he often do or say things that are tactless or socially inappropriate?
- Can s/he count to 50 without leaving out any numbers?
- Does s/he often care how s/he is perceived by the rest of the group?

Should any of these behaviours warrant concern, never mind diagnosis? One is left with the view that the authors have a predetermined view of AS that essentially becomes circular. In other words: 'What is causing X to find it difficult to interact with other children?' Answer: 'Because X has AS.' 'How do you know X has AS?' Answer: 'Because X finds it difficult to interact with other children.'

Williams and Brayne (2006) make a distinction between primary and secondary screening for ASD. They define secondary screening as an early diagnostic screen for children with a known developmental problem. The authors also report that in a survey they found that 9 per cent of child health teams were already using primary screening (screening all children for potential developmental difficulties). As we have mentioned, once you start with the presupposition that certain behaviours are worthy of diagnosis and are likely to be indicative of a specific condition, you are likely to be caught in a process of circularity; unless you are aware of this, ethical concerns about such a process will pass unnoticed.

Let us take the Webb and colleagues (2003) paper as an example. All mainstream primary schools in Cardiff were invited to participate in a prevalence survey of ASD. Teachers of each class filled in a questionnaire based on ICD-10 criteria for autistic disorders (primary screening). The ASSQ (secondary screening) was completed on children identified with problems from the first questionnaire. A total of 11,692 were screened and 234 (2%) children were identified as requiring an ASSQ – with 151 of 234 (65%) ASSQs returned. Of the 151, 60 children (52 male, eight female; 40 per cent) scored 22 or more on the ASSQ (i.e. deemed above the cut-off for ASD). Their notes and the involved professionals were then consulted. From this 35 children, unknown to specialist services before this time, had an additional assessment. From these, 17 children (all male) were diagnosed as having an ASD. The authors note that they discovered a diverse population who 'had' an ASD, including some who did not fit into the ICD-10 classification they were meant to be using (which makes one wonder what the point of the study having ICD-10 criteria was in the first place). In this situation what differentiates the secondary screening method from the primary one is largely a matter of size (involving smaller numbers being screened with slightly longer instruments). Some children whose symptomology appeared not

to have given previous cause for concern were, by the end of the study, in receipt of a diagnosis; a diagnosis, moreover, of a condition considered lifelong and disabling. Predictably, the ethics of such a process are not discussed.

This is particularly worrying as the authors describe having a protocol that was agreed with the local education authority, who liaised with individual schools. Parents were informed of the survey in writing by their child's school and advised to inform the school if they did not wish to participate. School staff and parents were advised that this was a survey of emotional, behavioural and communication problems, as the authors did not wish to introduce observer bias towards autistic behaviour in the screened population. Given that this eventually led to diagnosing children who had, up until that time, not been candidates for an ASD diagnosis, this raises major ethical concerns. The process that led to diagnosis was not initiated through requests for help from the children or their parents. Instead they found themselves swept along in a process for which initial consent was procured in a way that deliberately obscured a possible outcome – a potentially devastating label being applied to the child.

It seems to us that not only is the bar very low in terms of scientific quality in the autism research community, it is equally (and in our opinion unacceptably) low in ethical terms.

CONCLUSION

In this chapter we have described the current mainstream approach to the classification of ASDs and recounted some of the history behind this. We then critically examined how this relates to the development of diagnostic practice, diagnostic tools and approaches to screening for autism. The literature can be characterised as suffering from concepts with fuzzy boundaries, widening of diagnostic boundaries as behaviours that are difficult to view as pathological per se became included, a poor evidence base to support such changes, and classifications and practices that are subject to relentless circularity (with experts defining behaviours that become the sole criteria for confirming their theories – the behaviour becoming simultaneously symptom, syndrome and cause). Such an ideological basis for classification and practice has led us to conclude that current classifications lack validity and current questionnaires should not be used for diagnosis, screening or clinical practice more generally. We also strongly support the UK National Screening Committee policy that screening for autism and ASD is not recommended and should not be undertaken.

REFERENCES

American Psychiatric Association (1980) *Diagnostic and Statistical Manual of Mental Disorders, Third Edition (DSM-III)*. Washington, DC: APA.

American Psychiatric Association (1987) *Diagnostic and Statistical Manual of Mental Disorders, Third Edition Revised (DSM-III-R)*. Washington, DC: APA.

American Psychiatric Association (1994) *Diagnostic and Statistical Manual of Mental Disorders, Fourth Edition (DSM-IV)*. Washington, DC: APA.

American Psychiatric Association (2013) *Diagnostic and Statistical Manual of Mental Disorders, Fifth Edition (DSM-5)*. Washington, DC: APA.

Anderson, D.K., Liang, J.W., and Lord, C. (2014) 'Predicting young adult outcome among more and less cognitively able individuals with autism spectrum disorders.' *Journal of Child Psychology and Psychiatry 55*, 485–494.

Baird, G., Cass, H., and Slonims, V. (2003) 'Diagnosis of autism.' *British Medical Journal 327*, 488.

Baird, G., Charman, T., Cox, A., Baron-Cohen, S., Wheelwright, S., and Drew, A. (2001) 'Screening and surveillance for autism and pervasive developmental disorders.' *Archives of Diseases in Childhood 84*, 468–475.

Baron-Cohen, S., Allen, J., and Gillberg, C. (1992) 'Can autism be detected at 18 months? The needle, the haystack and the CHAT.' *British Journal of Psychiatry 161*, 839–843.

Baron-Cohen, S., Cox, A., Baird, G., Swettenham, J., *et al.* (1996) 'Psychological markers in the detection of autism in infancy in a large population'. *The British Journal of Psychiatry 168*, 158–163.

Baron-Cohen, S., Wheelwright, S., Skinner, R., Martin, J., and Clubley, E. (2001) 'The Autism-Spectrum Quotient (AQ): Evidence from Asperger Syndrome/High-Functioning Autism, males and females, scientists and mathematicians.' *Journal of Autism and Developmental Disorders 31*, 5–17.

Charman, T., and Baird, G. (2002) 'Practitioner review: diagnosis of Autism Spectrum Disorder in 2 and 3 year old children.' *Journal of Child Psychology and Psychiatry 43*, 289–305.

Charman, T., Baron-Cohen, S., Baird, G., Cox, A., *et al.* (2001) 'Commentary: The Modified Checklist for Autism in Toddlers.' *Journal of Autism and Developmental Disorders 31*, 145–148.

De Bildt, A., Sytema, S., Ketelaars, C., Kraijer, D., *et al.* (2004) 'Interrelationship between Autism Diagnostic Observation Schedule-Generic (ADOS-G), Autism Diagnostic Interview-Revised (ADI-R), and the Diagnostic and Statistical Manual of Mental Disorders (DSM-IV-TR) classification in children and adolescents with mental retardation.' *Journal of Autism and Developmental Disorders 34*, 129–137.

Eysenck, H.J., and Eysenck, S.B.G. (1975) *Manual of the Eysenck Personality Questionnaire (Adult and Junior)*. London: Hodder and Stoughton.

Farley, M.A., McMahon, W.M., Fombonne, E., Jenson, W.R., *et al.* (2009) 'Twenty-year outcome for individuals with autism and average or near-average cognitive abilities.' *Autism Research 2*, 109–118.

Fein, D., Barton, M., Eigsti, I., Kelley, E., *et al.* (2013) 'Optimal outcome in individuals with a history of autism.' *Journal of Child Psychology and Psychiatry 54*, 195–205.

Gillberg, C., Ehlers, S., Schaumann, H., Jakobsson, G., Dahlgren, S.O., and Lindblom, R. (1990). 'Autism under age 3 years: a clinical study of 28 cases referred for autistic symptoms in infancy.' *Journal of Child Psychology and Psychiatry and Allied Disciplines 31*, 921–934.

Hofvander, B., Delorme, R., Chaste, P., Nydén, A., *et al.* (2009) 'Psychiatric and psychosocial problems in adults with normal-intelligence autism spectrum disorders.' *BMC Psychiatry 9*, 35.

Kanner, L., and Eisenberg, L. (1956) 'Early infantile autism 1943–1955.' *American Journal of Orthopsychiatry 26*, 556–566.

Lord, C. (1995) 'Follow-up of two-year-olds referred for possible autism.' *Journal of Child Psychology and Psychiatry 36*, 1365–1382.

Lord, C., Risi, S., Lambrecht, L., Cook, E.H., *et al.* (2000) 'The Autism Diagnostic Observation Schedule – Generic: a standard measure of social and communication deficits associated with the spectrum of autism.' *Journal of Autism and Developmental Disorders 30*, 205–223.

Lord, C., Rutter, M., and Le Couteur, A. (1994) 'Autism Diagnostic Interview – Revised: a revised version of a diagnostic interview for caregivers of individuals with possible Pervasive Developmental Disorders.' *Journal of Autism and Developmental Disorders 24*, 659–685.

National Autistic Society (2003) *National Autism Plan for Children.* London: National Autistic Society.

National Screening Committee (2000) *Second Report of the UK National Screening Committee.* London: Department of Health.

National Screening Committee (2012) *The UK NSC Policy on Autism Screening in Children.* Available at www.screening.nhs.uk/autism, accessed on 10 November 2015.

Robins, D.L., Fein, D., Barton, M.L., and Green, J.A. (2001a) 'The Modified Checklist for Autism in Toddlers: an initial study investigating the early detection of autism and Pervasive Developmental Disorders.' Journal *of Autism and Developmental Disorders 31*, 131–151.

Robins, D.L., Fein, D., Barton, M.L., and Green, J.A. (2001b) 'Reply to Charman *et al.*'s Commentary on the Modified Checklist for Autism in Toddlers.' *Journal of Autism and Developmental Disorders 31*, 149–151.

Rutter, M. (1978) 'Diagnosis and definition of childhood autism.' *Journal of Autism and Developmental Disorders 8*, 139–161.

Rutter, M., and Schopler, E. (1987) 'Autism and Pervasive Developmental Disorders: concepts and diagnostic issues.' *Journal of Autism and Developmental Disorders 17*, 159–186.

Rutter, M., and Schopler, E. (1992) 'Classification of Pervasive Developmental Disorders: some concepts and practical considerations.' *Journal of Autism and Developmental Disorders 22*, 459–482.

Scott, F., Baron-Cohen, S., Bolton, P., and Brayne, C. (2002a) 'The CAST (Childhood Asperger Syndrome Test): preliminary development of UK screen for mainstream primary-school children.' *Autism 6*, 9–31.

Scott, F., Baron-Cohen, S., Bolton, P., and Brayne, C. (2002b) 'Brief Report: Prevalence of Autism Spectrum Conditions in children aged 5–11 years in Cambridgeshire, UK.' *Autism 6*, 231–237.

Timimi, S., McCabe, B., and Gardner, N. (2010) *The Myth of Autism: Medicalising Boys' and Men's Social and Emotional Competence.* Basingstoke: Palgrave Macmillan.

Webb, E., Morey, J., Thompsen, W., Butler, C., Barber, M., and Fraser, W.I. (2003) 'Prevalence of Autistic Spectrum Disorder in children attending mainstream schools in a Welsh Education Authority.' *Developmental Medicine and Child Neurology 45*, 377–384.

Williams J., and Brayne C. (2006) 'Screening for Autism Spectrum Disorders: what is the evidence?' *Autism 10*, 11–35.

Wing, L. (1981) 'Asperger's Syndrome: a clinical account.' *Psychological Medicine 11*, 115–129.

Wing, L., and Gould, J. (1979) 'Severe impairments of social interaction and associated abnormalities in children: epidemiology and classification.' *Journal of Autism and Childhood Schizophrenia 9*, 11–29.

Wing, L., Leekam, S.R., Libby, S.J., Gould, J., and Larcombe, M. (2002) 'The Diagnostic Interview for Social and Communication Disorders: background, inter-rater reliability and clinical use.' *Journal of Child Psychology and Psychiatry 43*, 307–325.

World Health Organisation (1978) *Mental Disorders: Glossary and Guide to their Classification in Accordance with the Ninth Revision of the International Classification of Diseases.* Geneva: WHO.

World Health Organisation (1992) *The ICD-10 Classification of Mental and Behavioural Disorders: Clinical Descriptions and Diagnostic Guidelines.* Geneva: WHO.

Part III

CHANGING PRACTICE

CHAPTER 10

SCHOOLS WITHOUT LABELS

Nick Hodge

INTRODUCTION

It is now 20 years since the Salamanca Statement made the inclusion of children[1] with 'Special Educational Needs' (SEN)[2] in mainstream schools[3] a national commitment for the 94 Governments who adopted it (UNESCO and the Ministry of Spain 1994). However, the development of inclusive learning environments is still experienced by many schools as a challenge (Webster and Blatchford 2015). Academics have provided models of inclusive practice for schools, such as the Index for Inclusion (Booth and Ainscow 2000), but there is clearly a need for academics to offer further support. Some argue that academics should not be prescriptive and dictate how schools should form themselves, that real change can only come when it is teachers rather than academics who decide how inclusion should be enabled within their schools (Burton and Wellington 1998; Crockett 1985). But, like the writer faced with an empty page, the act of imagining can sometimes feel too overwhelming a place to start. It can be helpful therefore to begin with a suggestion that can be reflected upon, critiqued, personalised and then developed. In this chapter I offer a model of inclusive practice through a critical analysis of one significant element within the inclusion process, the practice of diagnosis and labelling. I hope that this model will help the reader to employ a 'sociological imagination' (Mills 1959). This requires the reader to step away from the habitual understandings of the purpose and value

1 The term 'children' is used here for ease of reading. It is intended to also refer to young people up to the age of 18 years. In England this is currently when the period of compulsory education ends (Gov.UK 2014a).

2 The term 'Special Educational Needs' (SEN) is the legal category assigned to children in England who are assessed as having difficulties with learning. SEN can also include perceived difficulties with behaviour, socialisation and physical impairments (Gov.UK 2014b). With the Children and Families Act 2014 (DfE and DoH 2014a) the category has been renamed as Special Educational Needs and Disability (SEND).

3 The term used in England for any school that is not a special school or an independent school (DfES 2001). An independent school is one that is not dependent upon national or local government for funding.

of diagnostic labels that he/she may have assimilated and to reflect on the other possible meanings and impacts of these.

Diagnosis and the attachment of labels to children have concerned me for some years. I was a teacher in England of children with SEND for fifteen years before I became a university-based academic with a specialism in 'autism'. Whilst studying for my Doctorate in Education in the early 2000s I encountered for the first time the social model of disability (defined below). This resulted in me then questioning many of the canons of special education that I had previously accepted without interrogation or challenge. The idea that diagnosis and labelling is always in a child's best interests was one such canon. For seventeen years now as an academic, I have worked closely with teachers and parents and carers and people who identify with the labels of autism as students on academic courses, conferences and workshops, within Local Authority Strategy Groups (UK local governing bodies) and as a school governor. In doing so I have encouraged students to adopt a more critical engagement with labels, to interrogate their function, value and impact. My experience of this, however, is that students are reluctant initially to give up the meanings of labels that they are accustomed to. For some students an identity has been created around a label (Ortega 2013) or as parents they have fought hard to secure a diagnosis for their child and so have invested heavily in this being an enabling act. Others tell me that labels are essential as they are the key to resources or that as practitioners they have to work within legal and professional requirements and labels are positioned as a necessary element of these. Labels certainly seem entrenched in the minds of many of my students as essential to the enablement of children with SEND. Later in this chapter I explore further why this reluctance to let go of labels might occur.

My own concerns with labels actually began many years before I began my doctorate, when I was a young teacher working in special education. I used to meet regularly for 'last orders'[4] with a group of teacher friends. At the start of the new school year I would ask my friends what their new pupils were like. Those working in mainstream schools would respond with, 'I've got Myrth, she's a real character, very funny' and, 'Finn, he's very quiet, gentle, seems a really sweet kid.' But when I asked my friends who worked in special schools[5] they usually replied something like, 'I've got one with Angel Syndrome, two Fragile X, two Down's and two with Autism.' At the time this troubled me, not because my friends used the labels in this way, but because I did not. I used to think of my pupils by name first, their personalities second and their abilities and challenges third. I often struggled to remember their diagnosis. I worried that my lack of focus on labels

4 A tradition in England of meeting in the pub for a drink before service ended at 11pm.

5 Those schools designated exclusively for disabled children.

was a failing for a special schoolteacher. Since then, however, labels have come to trouble me for different reasons. Or perhaps for the same reasons but now as an academic I can situate my felt, instinctive unease with labels within a theoretical context. I now have a conscious understanding of why they are problematic and so I'm able to resist them from a differently informed position.

In this chapter I articulate that position through an analysis of the impact that the processes of diagnosis and labelling have on the educational and life experiences of disabled children. The chapter begins with an historical account of the inception of labelling through which I encourage the reader to identify and reflect on the political, economic and cultural contexts from which labels emerged and in which they now operate. Through this historical review labels are exposed as tools of capitalism that are used to segregate, control and expel to the margins of community those children who are positioned as economic burdens on the state (Oliver 1990). Labels are exposed as agents of 'disablism'[6] and not the essential enablers of children that many teachers assume them to be.

It is important to me that my own academic writing has a clear link to the development of educational practice and that it contributes to the establishment of more equitable and enabling practices in schools for all pupils. To this end the chapter concludes with suggestions as to how teachers, parents and carers and/or disabled people might accommodate labels to minimise their disabling effects whilst not exposing themselves, where relevant, to professional risk. A reader might question whether labels should be the highest priority on the inclusion agenda but the ways in which we conceptualise children govern every aspect of how we engage with them. Within the chapter I illustrate some of these issues with examples from a research study that I conducted for my Doctorate in Education between 2004 and 2006. This study focused on the experiences of three families who were at different stages of negotiating the process of the diagnosis of autism in relation to their children. Marie and John's son Sam was three years old; Ann and Mark's son Ben was four; and Todd, the son of Rachel and Bob, was six years old. I interviewed the parents at regular intervals for a year in order to identify and understand what the process of diagnosis meant to them. Labels carry with them their own set of social values and expectations (Green *et al.* 2005). The families in this study were negotiating those imbued within the label of 'autism'. However, many of the same or similar disabling effects of that label will also apply to other labels that are associated with special educational needs.

6 Disablism is defined by Scope (an organisation based in England and Wales that campaigns for the rights of disabled people) as 'discriminatory, oppressive or abusive behaviour arising from the belief that disabled people are inferior to others' (Scope 2014).

DIAGNOSIS AND LABELLING

Barnes (2004, p.41) argues that, 'the identification and labelling of impairment as socially deviant is subject to ideological, political and cultural forces'. In England, the practice of diagnosis and labelling gained momentum with the rise of industrialisation that began in the eighteenth century. People migrated from their rural communities to the cities, giving rise to concerns about population control and the need to protect the quality of the workforce. The capitalist drive for profit valued only those who could make an economic contribution through industrial hard labour. People became transformed into workers whose worth to society was mainly dependent upon their physical and/or mental capabilities (Erevelles 2000; Hughes 2001; Oliver 1990; Tregaskis 2004). Those who were seen as incapable of this type of work were considered 'a drain on the public purse' (Waltz 2013, p.26). People who were deemed to be 'social deviants', such as those with learning difficulties, mental health issues or criminal tendencies, were also claimed to be prodigious reproducers. This raised fears that these 'non-productive deviants' would take resources from those capable of work and become an unbearable financial burden on society. To be labelled in the eighteenth and nineteenth centuries as 'the idiot' child, later the 'mentally defective' or 'feebleminded' child, was therefore to be positioned as a 'threatening apparition' who needed to be regulated, controlled and prevented from reproduction (Nadesan 2005, p.63). Systems of identification and categorisation started to develop as the authorities sought to segregate these groups. They were to be kept apart and prevented from breeding in the hope that their genetic line would become extinguished (Race 1995; Sheldon 2014). These 'defective biologies' were to be kept from 'contaminating' the workforce (Erevelles 1997) as a 'productivist culture had no place for impaired labour power' (Hughes 2001, p.26).

It can be seen therefore that the practices of diagnosis and labelling have their roots in the protection of the political and economic stability of the state rather than in the welfare of disabled children (Nadesan 2005). Labels only came into being to protect the interests of the powerful. Kliewer and Biklen, writing about American educational policy at the start of the twentieth century and using the terminology of that period, observe that, 'eugenically derived special education was most concerned with controlling morons through segregation' (Kliewer and Biklen 2000, p.193). The use of the term 'moron' is now startlingly offensive and so highlights the objectifying, dehumanising and lethal nature of labels. Although such conceptualisations of disabled children may now seem extreme, in fact little has changed in the twenty-first century: disabled children continue to be positioned as an economic burden on the state and in consequence are subject to marginalisation and expulsion. Ball (2013) identifies the capitalist drivers in today's schools as competition between schools articulated through league tables based on output indicators (5+ GCSE A*–C grades). The ranking

of schools only according to level of academic outputs has produced an 'economy of student worth' (Ball 2013, p.16). Schools are judged by results and perceived poor performance can even result in a compulsory take-over by another school/ organisation. The stakes are extremely high and so it is little surprise that some schools will work to expel children with labels that promise 'poor performance' (Ball 2013). Even today the labelled child is still seen as a threat to the productive future of their communities.

THE DISABLING EFFECTS OF LABELS

Gillman, Heyman and Swain (2000) identify three of the most significant ways in which labels can marginalise and exclude children.

The first of these is that professionals and others use labels to justify intrusive, sometimes painful and often costly interventions that are usually focused upon making disabled children as 'normal' as possible (Nadesan 2005; Shyman 2015). The pathologisation of children as abnormal or disordered gives rise to a plethora of agencies and services whose very existence is dependent upon the maintenance of the notion of developmental conditions that are in need of remediation or cure (Nadesan 2005). Autism-related 'specialist' approaches, interventions and cures are marketed aggressively. Many of their claims are unsubstantiated by research but are made attractive to parents who are made desperate through operating within what Waltz (2013, p.163) terms a 'cure-or-catastrophe model of autism' in which having a child with autism is positioned as a tragic and costly burden (Knapp, Romeo and Beecham 2009; Parsons *et al.* 2011; Research Autism 2012). Paradoxically, disabled children are viewed as both a financial burden and a commodity that can be exploited for profit (Mallett and Runswick-Cole 2012). In the United Kingdom between 2007 and 2011, £21 million was spent on autism research, with the majority of projects funded focusing upon neural and cognitive systems, genetics and other risk factors (Pellicano, Dinsmore and Charman 2014) with the aim of either reducing symptoms or preventing the existence of children with autism. A comparatively small amount of research funding was focused upon addressing the practical requirements of children with autism and their families through improving support services (Pellicano *et al.* 2014). Labels sell and autism is big business (*The Economist* 2014).

The second exclusionary act of labels is the disempowerment of parents and carers and non-medical professionals. The mystique of medical terminology that surrounds a diagnosis creates an authority for the assignment to children of the devalued status of 'deviant', 'disordered', 'different' or 'special' (Goodley 2000; Thomas 2007). These are children whom only doctors can understand and make better. Parents and non-medical practitioners become hesitant and uncertain as to whether they are able support such a child without the 'expert' knowledge of

the particular 'syndrome' that medical professionals assert they have. The system of labelling leads therefore to 'the marginalisation, disqualification and rejection of knowledge and expertise of individuals and their family carers' (Gillman *et al.* 2000, p.396). Marie, a participant in my own study, illustrates this process. In my early visits to Marie she told me of the games and learning activities that she and Sam, her son, did together and of the pleasure that they both received from this. One of my visits followed shortly after the suggestions had been made by 'expert' professionals that Sam might 'have' autism and that the parents should accept the label in order to access the specialist help that a child with autism would need. I could see that Marie was upset and I asked her whether anything in particular was causing her distress. Marie explained that now that Sam had been given the diagnosis of autism she and Sam's father, John, 'don't know what to teach him, how to teach him' (Marie in Hodge 2006, p.148). The label and the medical mystique that surrounds it are so powerful that these overrode the three years of experience that Marie and John had in providing expert learning for their son.

A third effect, articulated by Gillman and colleagues (2000), is that labels can lower the expectations of others. This association of levels of skill with a particular 'impairment' label is termed by Goodley (2001) as a 'relational construction'. This phrase captures how behaviour is interpreted in relation to diagnostic labels and how some labels, such as 'learning difficulties', carry with them lower expectations of potential educational and life success (Goodley 2001). In my study Ben's father, Mark, illustrates this process when he describes his puzzlement that a teacher who had previously engaged very effectively with Ben suddenly stopped spending time with him. This deeply disturbed Mark and so he asked the teacher about this change in behaviour. The teacher explained that she had been visited by the autism specialist support team[7] who had informed her that Ben had autism. Mark perceived the teacher's understanding of autism to be that children like that want to be left alone. This change in the teacher's behaviour was deeply upsetting for Mark who stated, 'I could really see the difference in her, in the way she talked...she is never going to see Ben as a normal child anymore...she (the teacher) is going to stamp Ben as autistic and in her words autism means "Oh, they're just wandering around in their own world"' (Mark in Hodge 2006, p.175). So here behaviours associated with autism in textbooks superseded the teacher's expert knowledge of the child that had been established through her own relationship with him. The power of the label was stronger than the teacher's own experience and the teacher no longer

7 An autism specialist support team is a group of people within education services who have been assigned the status of 'expert' in relation to autism. How they operate varies but usually they will work with families and schools to develop 'appropriate' educational provision for children with autism.

held the same aspirations and expectations for the child's learning that she had prior to him receiving it. The label became all that could be seen of the child and academic success was not something that this teacher associated with autism. A critical element of inclusion is 'how disabled children are valued as learners by non-disabled people' (Aspis 2001, p.29). In this example this child was no longer attributed the same potential for learning.

Green and colleagues (2005, p.201) also refer to this process of value reduction when they state that, 'labelling involves not only the perception that someone is different, but also the assignment of social import to that difference'. Marie, in my study, reflects on this when she states that, 'any label will limit what you do and how people look at you' (Marie in Hodge 2006, p.104). For Marie, giving someone a label is 'the most damaging thing that you could ever do… It could potentially ruin somebody's life' (Marie in Hodge 2006, p.175). As the earlier example with Ben illustrates, the introduction of a label such as 'autism' into the child–teacher relationship can create a 'social awkwardness that interferes with ordinary social interaction' (Green *et al.* 2005, p.202). The effect of labels negating any personal characteristics that a child or young person may have is referred to by Shakespeare (2006, p.71) as 'identity spread': 'The impairment label becomes the most prominent and relevant feature of their lives, dominating interactions.' The label becomes the totality of the child's social identity (Lauchlan and Boyle 2007). The focus is no longer on the child but on a collection of specific impairment behaviours and characteristics that are associated with the particular label. It is these that school staff feel must be constrained and changed and in doing so appreciation of and respect for the child's personhood may be lost (Chappell, Goodley and Lawthom 2001). Children stop having a special need and become the child who is a special need, as in, 'Is your brother a special need?' (Runswick-Cole and Hodge 2009, p.200).

Goodley (2000), reflecting upon his own life as a non-labelled man compared with the labelled lives of the participants in his research, records some of the impacts that labels can bring to a life: 'people being put in a house with strangers, not being asked where they would like to live, prevented from going out because others think they are incapable and of archaic treatments in institutions' (Goodley 2000, p.73). Sen (1999) also critiques these attacks on individual freedom that Sen argues result from 'the terrible burden of narrowly defined identities' (Sen 1999, p.8). The effect of the imposition of these labelled identities on children is that their freedoms to become who they want to be and to live in ways of their choosing are curtailed.

In 2001 UNESCO warned how labels work against the inclusion agenda by positioning the problem of learning as a 'within child' issue, thereby excluding consideration of problems with teaching: 'Indeed their (disabled children's) lack of learning or slow development was put down to their impairment rather than to

the restrictions they experienced in interacting with others and to participating in different environments' (UNESCO 2001, p.22). This conceptualisation of particular ways of being as necessarily a 'problem' and one that is situated within the child is sometimes referred to as the 'individual model of disability' (Oliver 1996). Within this model it is the child who is expected to change or be changed in order to become as 'normal' as possible (Thomas 2004). An alternative model is the 'social model of disability'. This means of understanding disability holds that it is not people's bodies or minds that prevent them from engaging fully with society but discrimination, prejudice and the assemblage of disabling barriers within the economic, social and cultural environments (Shakespeare 2006). For proponents of the social model it is society that is to blame for denying disabled people equality through a variety of practices. These include denying access to employment and thereby making disabled people dependent on charity, preventing physical access to social spaces, not recognising non-spoken systems of communication and segregation through specialised schooling (Barnes 2000). It is not the impairment that excludes the person from taking part in society but these restrictions imposed by society.

Edward Timpson (2013), who at the time of writing was Minister for Children and Families in the British Government, highlighted one of the dangers of labels through suggesting that these can sometimes provide teachers with a scapegoat to justify a pupil's lack of learning. In a 'within the individual' model of disability, problems with learning are often explained away as the result of the child's impairment, thereby excusing teachers from examination of their own practice (Solity 1992). However, some disabled pupils offer an alternative perspective on why they might experience problems with learning. For them the barriers to learning could be 'boring lessons; teachers not understanding their needs; other pupils messing about; and a feeling that no one really expects them to do well' (Aspis 2001, p.130). Timpson promises that the revised Code of Practice for Special Educational Needs and Disability (SEND)[8] (DfE and DoH 2014b), which from September 2014 has directed schools on how to respond to pupils with SEND, 'will be more challenging in urging schools to improve the quality of teaching for all pupils – rather than just label "difficult" pupils as having SEN' (DfE and DoH 2014b, p.1). This shift in focus away from labels would seem a welcome one, but concerns have been raised about whether some children with SEND will be made more vulnerable by the new Code (IPSEA 2014). The suspicion remains that the loss of a label will also result in the loss of entitlement to additional services.

8 The Code of Practice is governmental guidance for schools in England on educational provision for children and young people with special educational needs and disabilities aged 0–25 years.

In fact it is unlikely that the new Code of Practice will do much to reduce the reliance on labels as these have a history of being difficult to disregard, and labels such as autism, dyslexia, dyscalculia, dyspraxia, deaf, deafblind are still referred to within the Code (DFE and DoH 2014b). 'People first' language has for many years attempted to counter the effect of label domination by emphasising the personhood of the child before the label, for example 'child with autism' rather than 'autistic child' (Goodley 2011). Even so, the use of 'with' as in 'a child with social and behavioural difficulties' still encourages people to locate the 'problem' of learning or behaviour within the child and his/her identified 'condition' (Tobbell and Lawthom 2005). To keep practitioners and carers mindful of this, Tobbell and Lawthom (2005) argue for the adoption by services of terms such as 'child labelled as having social and emotional behavioural difficulties'. Tobbell and Lawthom argue that this may help to remind staff of the socially constructed nature of a 'diagnosis' and the need to always examine the context that surrounds the child, including the relationships contained within it.

The disabled people's movement in Britain also emphasises the socially constructed nature of disability through a careful use of terminology. To make explicit that disability is something that is done to you and not something that is an inherent part of you, the disabled people's movement has rejected terms such as 'people with a disability' or 'people with learning disabilities' in favour of 'disabled people' (Mallett and Runswick-Cole 2014). This term is useful in the fight against labels as unlike 'people first' language or the use of 'person with…' there is no reference made to specific impairments. Unfortunately scant attention seems to be made to this important distinction by policy makers and service providers who continue to support a language of people first.

Sinclair (1999) also rejects people first terminology but for different reasons. For Sinclair, being autistic is fundamental to personhood as autism is something that cannot be separated from the person. Brown (2011) argues that the identity of an autistic person is only valued when it is recognised through the use of the term 'autistic'. For Brown, when people first language is used this demeans and devalues the state of being autistic. Hughes (2009) uses the concept of 'biological citizenship' to capture how people can build a sense of identity around their label in this way so that it becomes critical to their sense of who they are and where they belong. Brownlow and O'Dell (2013) note a tension here, however. Using the example of autism they state that 'biomedical understandings enable the positioning of difference in a positive way, through the potential validation of an autistic identity in a positive manner; however, the counterposition is that of individuals being determined by a reductionist, biologised discourse' (Brownlow and O'Dell 2013, p.103). Such academic tensions are problematic for individuals who are renegotiating their identity through the diagnostic process. Ortega

(2013) observes that debate and uncertainty around the constructed nature of 'impairment' can cause stress and anxiety to individuals whose very identity then seems to be contested.

The label of Asperger Syndrome is a useful example of the problematic nature of the social construction of impairment identity. In 1981 Wing effectively created the diagnosis and therefore the identity, only for it then to be delegitimised as an identity with the fifth edition of the *Diagnostic and Statistical Manual of Mental Disorders* (DSM-5) (APA 2013). However, in my own experience, as Ortega argues, students who identify with the labels of autism are sometimes challenged by a view of autism as a social construct, a concept that has been negotiated and agreed by the medical community as opposed to a definite physical 'thing' that they 'have'. Nonetheless, even whilst embracing an identity around a label, it is critical to remain mindful of and guarded against its power to act as a tool of othering, marginalisation, and even expulsion.

LABELS AS TOOLS OF EXPULSION

Sassen (2014) is concerned with the macro-forces within economic, political and social structures that act to marginalise, exclude and even expel members from their own communities. Sassen refers to 'zones of expulsion' to describe the spaces on the 'systemic edge' of communities to which those who are not useful to the capitalist project are effectively banished. Sassen describes the forces that enable these processes of expulsion as 'subterranean trends'. Although these are manifold, all-powerful and cross national boundaries, they are rarely made explicit. They operate insidiously and for the most part unseen. Sassen's work has not yet been applied to micro-environments such as schools but here I argue that zones of expulsion do exist within the education system and that labels are one of the tools through which these are enabled. The 'othering' of children through labels (Rorty 1989), the construction of them as 'different' and 'special' and therefore requiring special provision or staff with special skills or special modes of transport to get to school, all work to justify the exclusion of children from mainstream spaces within schools. Here they will not interfere with the academic success of the high achievers who are the main providers of 'positive' results for the schools. Children who cannot contribute through high academic achievement become problems rather than children experiencing problems. Sometimes exclusion to the margins of the school community takes on the even more extreme form of total expulsion from the school community.

The English Department for Education (DfE) statistics for the number of permanent and fixed-term exclusions from schools in England in the academic year 2012/13 reveal that children with the label of special educational needs

are far more likely to receive a permanent or fixed-term exclusion than children without the label (DfE 2014). Children with statements of special educational needs are around six times more likely to receive a permanent exclusion than pupils with no SEND and around nine times more likely to receive a fixed-period exclusion than children without any identification of SEND. For children with the label of SEND but who do not have a statement these figures rise further in relation to permanent exclusions, with these pupils being ten times more likely to receive one of these than children without this label. Persistent disruptive behaviour is the most common reason given for exclusion (DfE 2014). Tobbell and Lawthom (2005) using the example of 'emotional, social and behavioural difficulties' argue that such exclusions might result from the label itself. If teachers understand difficulties with learning or behaviour as a manifestation of a condition within the child then they might feel powerless to change this through teaching. They may come to see the child as unable to learn and so no longer as the responsibility of the school.

Sassen (2014) is interested in identifying the 'systemic edge', the point where the included become the excluded, as it is here that subterranean trends can be revealed. This review of the impact of labels on the school experience of children and their families identified earlier one such trend as the capitalist performativity agenda of schools. The governmental policy known as the 'standards agenda' is focused upon raising the attainment of pupils in schools. Schools are compared with each other and ranked according to pupils' results in predominantly literacy, numeracy and science. The survival of schools and therefore teachers' jobs is dependent upon achieving high scores for pupil attainment (Ainscow, Booth and Dyson 2006). One result of the pressure to perform well in the rankings is that, 'low-attaining students, students who demand high levels of attention and resource and students who are not seen to conform to school and classroom behavioural norms become unattractive to many schools' (Ainscow *et al.* 2006, p.296). The entry of such pupils into schools may therefore be resisted overtly or through more subtle and often harder to resist means such as suggesting that the school is not in the best interests of the child (Hodge 2006). Pupils already attending school may find themselves excluded. Marginalisation may also take less direct forms. Schools may decide, for example, not 'to "invest" in work with children with special needs where the margins for improved performance are limited' (Ball 2003, p.223). The 'terror of performativity' is such that it becomes transformative in its effects on teachers (Ball 2003). Even those who embrace the inclusion agenda can find themselves supressing or compromising their principles when faced with the prospect of not meeting the expected standards (Ball 2003, 2013). Some teachers may no longer have the personal resources to act as advocates and enablers for pupils with SEND.

THE PERCEIVED VALUE OF LABELS

The section above establishes the problematic and contentious nature of labels. My experience of working with teachers and parents and carers, however, is that they are very reluctant to surrender the labels and to move away from using them. I trust in the commitment of teachers as well as parents and carers to do what they feel is best for their children and so I recognise that for them the labels must be perceived as having some use and value. Labels are imbued with the status and power of the medical profession. Doctors have traditionally enjoyed high social status and a pursuant exclusive authority to assign the status of the 'impaired' or 'disabled' to individuals (Lipworth *et al.* 2013; Thomas 2007). Kuipers (1989, p.100) argues that medical knowledge has traditionally been accepted as the 'unassailable "God's truth"', which makes medical claims difficult to challenge. Jodrell (2010) suggests another reason for support for labels, as claims can be found within the research literature that labels increase knowledge and understanding of individual needs and so provide a service for children. This view is reflected in the UNESCO (2001) inclusion guidance for teachers in its representation of different impairment groups and advice on how to teach 'them'. This guidance, however, appears conflicted on the value of labels. Whilst offering a challenge to labels through an emphasis on the uniqueness and individuality of all children, such as stating, 'No two children are alike' (p.8), the document then goes on to identify the shared characteristics of children within their different impairment groups and presents a number of strategies that this 'type' of child will respond to. So the message for teachers remains that 'these' children are members of a different group and require special provision.

Gillman and colleagues also suggest further reasons for why people might seek out labels for themselves or their dependents. Labels can provide a means of explaining symptoms of 'illness' or 'abnormal' development in order to relieve 'the stress or ambiguity of the unknown' (Gillman *et al.* 2000, p.394). A label can be an explanatory device that can be useful to family carers in their dealings with the general public and an official diagnosis can be a powerful convincer that relieves parents of giving further explanation for their child's behaviour to others (Gray 2002). There is a hierarchy of impairments (Deal 2003) with some labels felt to be more stigmatising than others. This can then lead to a search for a more favourable label.

Avdi and colleagues argue that parents also seek diagnosis as 'official acknowledgement of the "reality" of the problem' (Avdi, Griffin and Brough 2000, p.248), evidence to demonstrate that their concerns were legitimate. For some parents a label comes as a relief because the condition or syndrome is responsible for the child's developmental 'problems' and not their parenting (Ong-Dean 2005). However, this issue could be addressed without resorting to labels. The doctor could present the results of an assessment as, 'We have found

that Mary has strengths in these areas and challenges in these others. Some children develop in this way; that is just how some children are. From what you tell us, Mary seems to learn best when…'

What some parents and carers say that they really want from an assessment of their child's development is to recognise that whoever has carried it out has come to know their child, his/her personality, character, strengths and challenges and can support them as parents and carers with understanding why and how their child's profile might have developed in this way (Hodge 2006). This is what is critical to parents and carers rather than for their child to be made bureaucratically different and subsumed within a medical category (Hodge 2006). However, within the current system of educational provision a label is often the only means of access to specialist support and enhanced financial resources and so parents are compelled to seek it (Hodge 2006; Kelly 2005). This can lead to a bartering between parent or carer and professional where the parent or carer agrees to an unwanted label just to access required support: '…then we agreed the trade-off should be to get him statemented…' (Mother in Hodge 2006). The ability to access resources can therefore make a label a desirable commodity. Because of this Fox and Kim argue that some groups with 'emerging disabilities' are campaigning to acquire a label, 'hoping that medical acceptance will lead to greater social acceptance' (Fox and Kim 2004, p.334) and to more timely and effective medical and social services.

DISRUPTING LABELS

Labels have been established within this chapter as situated within and maintained by historical, political, cultural and economic forces. Halpin (2014) in writing about the position of nurses within autism assessment teams[9] questions what power nurses can really have to disrupt disabling practices considering their standing within the medical hierarchy. The same question can be asked here of teachers as to whether they really have the power to refuse labels when these are so embedded within the fabric of the educational system. In 1992 Giroux questioned the value of his earlier work that focused only on schools without taking account of the wider context because in doing so he 'vastly underestimated both the structural and ideological constraints under which teachers labor' (Giroux 1992, p.1). Ball (2013) identifies some of these constraints on teachers when he states that, 'the Conservative Governments of 1979–97 and Labour and Coalition Governments have all been keen to displace the participation of teacher associations, trade unions and local authorities from the policy process'

9 An autism assessment team in England is usually a group of health practitioners who assess the development of children in relation to being assigned a diagnosis of autism.

(Ball 2013, p.3) and that, 'the daily lives of teachers and learners in school are driven more and more by the extrinsic demands of performance, competition and comparison, putting both under greater and greater stress' (Ball 2013, p.25). Teachers would appear therefore to be under too many pressures already to take on the fight of refusing labels.

Halpin (2014) found that the nurses in her study drew strength from their collective reflection and re-evaluation during the research process of what their profession means to them and the conditions in which they practise it. Through identifying the forces that worked against their professional ethics these nurses found a new resolve for resistance. Giroux (1992) believes in the ability and intent of teachers to become critical pedagogues, to engage critically with theory and to use this to develop their practice. I hope that through this chapter enough of a challenge has been made to the imperious command of labels to enable teachers to come to know them differently. Once teachers come to regard labels through a critical lens, thereby coming to know their true nature and purpose, then like Giroux I trust that teachers will be creative in resisting them, as best they can within the restraints of the performativity agenda.

Goodley and Runswick-Cole (2012) suggest that many of us in our management of labels 'use and refuse' them. When the label can be made to serve a useful purpose for the child such as accessing resources then it is made use of. But if the label would restrict the life opportunities of a child then it is refused. Pupils may come into schools with labels and teachers may note and consider these as one small part of coming to know the child. These labels would then be put into storage. Rather than a school without labels it will be a school with labels filed away. If the label serves an empowering purpose for a child or young person and is felt to be critical to their developing identity then, for that child, the label can be utilised. For many pupils, however, the only labels that teachers would use within the school would be their names.

Resistance to labelling is not a call for an abandonment of assessment. I support fully coming to know children, but as people and not as categories. It is vital that we come to know who children are, what they enjoy, fear, their hopes and aspirations for their future, their worries and concerns, what motivates them and what turns them away from learning. We need to find out what skills children have and which ones would be helpful for them to develop, to learn about which teaching methods might best support this learning and how the environment needs to be structured to most enable this.

Jordan and Jones (1995) attempted to modify the impact of labels by suggesting that they should be thought of as signposts,[10] that they are not to

---

10 The recommendation that the label of autism be considered only as a signpost is attributed in this text to Richard Exley.

become the identity of the child but would alert teachers to a range of impairment-relevant resources and teaching strategies. The problem with this approach is that a signpost inevitably points a teacher towards a range of resources and teaching strategies that would help 'a child like that'. Signposting does not enable the child to escape the othering impact of the label. Nor are signposts effective in directing the attention of teachers to children who do not have the particular label but would benefit from these same resources and strategies. Rather than think children with autism need this and children with Attention Deficit Hyperactive Disorder (ADHD) need another prescriptive set of provisions, teachers would serve pupils better if they could select from a toolbox of approaches, strategies and resources the ones that would most enable that particular child. Teachers will still need to know about and be able to use a full range of teaching methods but they will rely on their knowledge of a child's character and personality to use them and not his/her label. So in the school without labels the teacher might think, 'Erin places her hands over her ears a lot when the class is all together. I know that some children can find noise particularly painful – I wonder if that is happening for her' or, 'Ned doesn't seem to predict what will happen next in class and he gets upset when it is not what he is expecting. I know that some children find picture timetables useful. Perhaps that might help Ned.'

CONCLUSION

Within this chapter I have argued that the practices of diagnosis and labelling emerged as a response to historical economic and social forces. These practices were intended to serve the interests of capitalism and to help control the perceived threat to political and economic order. They were not introduced to support and enable disabled children, contrary to the role of labels as perceived by many teachers and parents and carers. Some of the dangers of labels have been identified and illustrated. Embedded within the individual model of disability, labels have been revealed as locating the 'problems' of development within the child or young person thereby removing any need for assessing and changing the impact of the social and educational environments. Labels promote the idea of the disabled child being the problem and that it is the child who needs to change to become more 'normal'. Rethinking this from a social model of disability perspective has been shown to shift the 'problem' from the child to the environment with an expectation that it is the school and the practice of teaching that needs to change. Labels have been positioned within this chapter as dehumanising attacks on personhood that expel children to the margins of their school community and even beyond.

In the tradition of Critical Pedagogy (Giroux 1992), I have called upon teachers in schools to resist these effects by recognising and celebrating the

individuality of children, responding to them as people with their own way of learning rather than as members of an impairment group who all are and learn the same. Teachers are also subject to political and cultural pressures that they may feel powerless to overcome. Therefore I have argued for resistance, a using and refusing of the label, rather than total rejection as the most practical strategy for schools. Children will come into schools with labels already attached to them. These can be used for maximising access to resources but the disabling effects of these labels must also be recognised, discussed and addressed. Labels should be kept within locked drawers, only to be removed in necessity, with care and the certainty that this is in the best interests of the child. We may not yet be ready for schools without labels but it is time for schools that recognise and resist their disabling effects.

REFERENCES

Ainscow, M., Booth, T., and Dyson, A. (2006) 'Inclusion and the standards agenda: negotiating policy pressures in England.' *International Journal of Inclusive Education 10*, 4–5, 295–308.

American Psychiatric Association (2013) *Diagnostic and Statistical Manual of Mental Disorders, Fifth Edition (DSM-5)*. Washington, DC: APA.

Aspis, S. (2001) 'Inclusive Education, Politics and the Struggle for Change.' In L. Barton (ed.) *Disability Politics and the Struggle for Change*. London: David Fulton.

Avdi, E., Griffin, C., and Brough, S. (2000) 'Parents' constructions of the "problem" during assessment and diagnosis of their child for an autistic spectrum disorder.' *Journal of Health Psychology 5*, 2, 241–254.

Ball, S.J. (2003) 'The teacher's soul and the terrors of performativity.' *Journal of Education Policy 18*, 2, 215–228.

Ball, S.J. (2013) *Policy Paper – Education, Justice and Democracy: The Struggle Over Ignorance and Opportunity*. Centre for Labour and Social Studies (CLASS). Available at www.classonline.org.uk/pubs/item/education-justice-and-democracy, accessed on 11 November 2015.

Barnes, C. (2000) 'A working social model? Disability, work and disability politics in the 21st century.' *Critical Social Policy 20*, 4, 441–457.

Barnes, C. (2004) 'Reflections on Doing Emancipatory Disability Research.' In J. Swain, S. French, C. Barnes and C. Thomas (eds) *Disabling Barriers – Enabling Environments* (Third edition). London: Sage.

Booth, T., and Ainscow, M. (2000) *Index for Inclusion: Developing Learning and Participation in Schools*. Bristol: Centre for Studies in Inclusive Education (CSIE).

Brown, L. (2011) *The Significance of Semantics: Person First Language, Why It Matters*. Autistic Hoya. Available at www.autistichoya.com/2011/08/significance-of-semantics-person-first.html, accessed on 11 November 2015.

Brownlow, C., and O'Dell, L. (2013) 'Autism as a Form of Biological Citizenship.' In M. Orsini and J. Davidson (eds) *Worlds of Autism*. London: University of Minnesota Press.

Burton, J., and Wellington, K. (1998) 'The O'Banion model of academic advising: an integrative approach.' *NACADA (National Academic Advising Association) Journal 18*, 2, 13–20.

Chappell, A.L., Goodley, D., and Lawthom, R. (2001) 'Making connections: the relevance of the social model of disability for people with learning difficulties.' *British Journal of Learning Disabilities 29*, 2, 45–50.

Crockett, D.S. (1985) 'Academic Advising.' In L. Noel, R. Levitz, D. Saluri and Associates (eds) *Increasing Student Retention.* San Francisco, CA: Jossey-Bass Publishers.

Deal, M. (2003) 'Disabled people's attitudes toward other impairment groups: a hierarchy of impairments.' *Disability and Society 18*, 7, 897–910.

Department for Education and Skills (DfES) (2001) *Inclusive Schooling: Children with Special Educational Needs.* Available at http://webarchive.nationalarchives.gov.uk/20130401151715/http://www.education.gov.uk/publications/eOrderingDownload/DfES-0774-2001.pdf, accessed on 11 November 2015.

Department for Education (DfE) (2014) *Statistical First Release: Permanent and Fixed Period Exclusions in England: 2012 to 2013.* SFR/2014 July 31. Available at www.gov.uk/government/collections/statistics-exclusions, accessed on 11 November 2015.

Department for Education (DfE) and Department of Health (DoH) (2014a) *Children and Families Act 2014.* Norwich: The Stationery Office. Available at www.legislation.gov.uk/ukpga/2014/6/pdfs/ukpga_20140006_en.pdf, accessed on 21 January 2016.

Department for Education (DfE) and Department of Health (DoH) (2014b) *Special Educational Needs and Disability Code of Practice: 0 to 25 Years.* DfE-00205-2013. Available at www.gov.uk/government/publications/send-code-of-practice-0-to-25, accessed on 11 November 2015.

Erevelles, N. (1997) 'Re-constituting the "Disabled" Other: Historical Materialism and the Politics of Schooling.' Paper presented at the Annual Meeting of the American Educational Research Association, Chicago, IL, March 24–28, 1997. Available at http://eric.ed.gov/?id=ED461148, accessed on 11 November 2015.

Erevelles, N. (2000) 'Educating unruly bodies: critical pedagogy, disability studies and the politics of schooling.' *Educational Theory 50*, 1, 25–47.

Fox, M.H., and Kim, K. (2004) 'Understanding emerging disabilities.' *Disability and Society 19*, 4, 323–337.

Gillman, M., Heyman, B., and Swain, J. (2000) 'What's in a name? The implications of diagnosis for people with learning difficulties and their family carers.' *Disability and Society 15*, 3, 389–409.

Giroux, H.A. (1992) *Border Crossings: Cultural Workers and the Politics of Education.* London: Routledge.

Goodley, D. (2000) *Self-Advocacy in the Lives of People With Learning Difficulties: The Politics of Resilience.* Buckingham: Open University Press.

Goodley, D. (2001) 'Learning difficulties, the social model of disability and impairment: challenging epistemologies.' *Disability and Society 16*, 2, 207–231.

Goodley, D. (2011) *Disability Studies: An Interdisciplinary Introduction.* London: Sage.

Goodley, D., and Runswick-Cole, K. (2012) 'Reading Rosie: the postmodern disabled child.' *Educational and Child Psychology 29*, 2, 53–66.

Gov.UK (2014a) *School Leaving Age.* Available at www.gov.uk/know-when-you-can-leave-school, accessed on 11 November 2015.

Gov.UK (2014b) *Children with Special Educational Needs.* Available at www.gov.uk/children-with-special-educational-needs/overview, accessed on 11 November 2015.

Gray, D.E. (2002) '"Everybody just freezes. Everybody is just embarrassed": felt and enacted stigma among parents of children with high functioning autism.' *Sociology of Health and Illness 24*, 6, 734–749.

Green, S., Davis, C., Karshmer, E., Marsh, P., and Straight, B. (2005) 'Living stigma: the impact of labeling, stereotyping, separation, status loss, and discrimination in the lives of individuals with disabilities and their families.' *Sociological Inquiry 75*, 2, 197–215.

Halpin, J. (2014) 'The Role of the Nurse in Preschool Autism Assessment.' Unpublished PhD thesis, Sheffield Hallam University.

Hodge, N. (2006) 'Disabling Families: How Parents Experience The Process of Diagnosing Autism Spectrum Disorders.' Unpublished EdD thesis, Sheffield Hallam University.

Hughes, B. (2001) 'Disability and the Constitution of Dependency.' In L. Barton (ed.) *Disability Politics and the Struggle for Change.* London: David Fulton.

Hughes, B. (2009) 'Disability activisms: social model stalwarts and biological citizens.' *Disability and Society 24,* 6, 677–688.

Independent Parental Special Education Advice (IPSEA) (2014) *Response to the revised draft SEN Code of Practice.* May. Available at www.ipsea.org.uk/news/2014/ipsea-responds-to-the-revised-draft-sen-code-of-practice-may-2014, accessed on 11 November 2015.

Jodrell, D. (2010) 'Social-identity and self-efficacy concern for disability labels.' *Psychology Teaching Review 16,* 2, 111–121.

Jordan, R., and Jones, G. (1995) *Meeting the Needs of Children with Autistic Spectrum Disorders.* Abingdon: David Fulton.

Kelly, S. (2005) 'A different light: examining impairment through parent narratives of childhood disability.' *Journal of Contemporary Ethnography 34,* 2, 180–205.

Kliewer, C., and Biklen, D. (2000) 'Democratizing disability inquiry.' *Journal of Disability Policy Studies 10,* 2, 186–206.

Knapp, M., Romeo, R., and Beecham, J. (2009) 'Economic cost of autism in the UK.' *Autism 13,* 3, 317–336.

Kuipers, J.C. (1989) '"Medical discourse" in anthropological context: views of language and power author(s).' *Medical Anthropology Quarterly, New Series 3,* 2, 99–123.

Lauchlan, F., and Boyle, C. (2007) 'Is the use of labels in special education helpful?' *Support for Learning 22,* 1, 36–42.

Lipworth, W., Little, M., Markham, P., Gordon, J., and Kerridge, I. (2013) 'Doctors on status and respect: a qualitative study.' *Journal of Bioethical Inquiry 10,* 2, 205–217.

Mallett, R., and Runswick-Cole, K. (2012) 'Commodifying Autism: The Cultural Contexts of "Disability" in the Academy.' In D. Goodley, B. Hughes and L.J. Davis (eds) *Disability and Social Theory.* Basingstoke: Palgrave MacMillan.

Mallett, R., and Runswick-Cole, K. (2014) *Approaching Disability: Critical Issues and Perspectives.* London: Routledge.

Mills, C.W. (1959) *The Sociological Imagination.* New York: Oxford University Press.

Nadesan, M.H. (2005) *Constructing Autism: Unravelling the 'Truth' and Understanding the Social.* Abingdon: Routledge.

Oliver, M. (1990) *The Politics of Disablement.* Basingstoke: Macmillan.

Oliver, M. (1996) *Understanding Disability: From Theory to Practice.* Basingstoke: Macmillan.

Ong-Dean, C. (2005) 'Reconsidering the social location of the individual model: an examination of disability in parenting literature.' *Journal of Medical Humanities 26,* 2/3, 141–158.

Ortega, F. (2013) 'Cerebralizing Autism Within the Neurodiversity Movement.' In M. Orsini and J. Davidson (eds) *Worlds of Autism.* London: University of Minnesota Press.

Parsons, S., Guldberg, K., MacLeod, A., Jones, G., Prunty, A., and Balfe, T. (2011) 'International review of the literature of evidence of best practice in educational provision for children on the autism spectrum.' *European Journal of Special Needs Education 26,* 1, 47–63.

Pellicano, E., Dinsmore, A., and Charman, T. (2014) 'What should autism research focus upon? Community views and priorities from the United Kingdom.' *Autism 18,* 7, 756–770.

Race, D. (1995) 'Historical Development of Service Provision.' In N. Malin (ed.) *Services for People with Learning Disabilities.* London: Routledge.

Research Autism (2012) *Interventions, Treatments and Therapies for Autism.* Available at www.researchautism.net/autism-interventions, accessed on 11 November 2015.

Rorty, R. (1989) *Contingency, Irony and Solidarity.* Cambridge: Cambridge University Press.

Runswick-Cole, K., and Hodge, N. (2009) 'Needs or rights? A challenge to the discourse of special education.' *British Journal of Special Education 36,* 4, 198–203.

Sassen, S. (2014) *Expulsions: Brutality and Complexity in the Global Economy.* London: The Belknap Press of Harvard University Press.

Scope (2014) 'Lesson plan: Disablism: prejudice against disabled people.' Available at www.scope.org.uk/support/professionals/teaching-disability-history/lesson-plans/disablism, accessed on 11 November 2015.

Sen, A. (1999) *Development as Freedom.* Oxford: Oxford University Press.

Shakespeare, T. (2006) *Disability Rights and Wrongs.* London: Routledge.

Sheldon, A. (2014) 'Women and Disability.' In J. Swain, S. French, C. Barnes and C. Thomas (eds) *Disabling Barriers – Enabling Environments* (Third edition). London: Sage.

Shyman, E. (2015) *Besieged By Behavior Analysis for Autism Spectrum Disorder: A Treatise for Comprehensive Educational Approaches.* London: Lexington Books.

Sinclair, J. (1999) *Why I Dislike Person First Language.* Available at http://jisincla.mysite.syr.edu, accessed on 11 November 2015.

Solity, J. (1992) *Special Education.* London: Cassell.

The Economist (2014) 'Treating autism: In development. Companies struggle to meet soaring demand for autism treatments.' December 13. Available at www.economist.com/news/business/21636064-companies-struggle-meet-soaring-demand-autism-treatments-development, accessed on 11 November 2015.

Thomas, C. (2004) 'How is disability understood? An examination of sociological approaches.' *Disability and Society 19,* 6, 569–583.

Thomas, C. (2007) *Sociologies of Disability and Illness: Contested Ideas in Disability Studies and Medical Sociology.* Basingstoke: Palgrave Macmillan.

Timpson, E. (2013) 'Rewriting the code.' *SEN Magazine.* Available at www.senmagazine.co.uk/articles/articles/senarticles/rewriting-the-code, accessed on 11 November 2015.

Tobbell, J., and Lawthom, R. (2005) 'Dispensing with labels: enabling children and professionals to share a community of practice.' *Educational and Child Psychology 22,* 3, 89–97.

Tregaskis, C. (2004) *Constructions of Disability: Researching the Interface between Disabled and Non-Disabled People.* London: Routledge.

United Nations Educational, Scientific and Cultural Organisation (UNESCO) and the Ministry of Spain (1994) *The Salamanca Statement and Framework for Action on Special Needs Education.* Available at www.unesco.org/education/pdf/SALAMA_E.PDF, accessed on 11 November 2015.

United Nations Educational, Scientific and Cultural Organisation (UNESCO) (2001) *Understanding and Responding to Children's Needs in the Inclusive Classroom: A Guide for Teachers.* Paris: Inclusive Education. Available at http://unesdoc.unesco.org/images/0012/001243/124394e.pdf, accessed on 11 November 2015.

Waltz, M. (2013) *Autism: A Social and Medical History.* Basingstoke: Palgrave Macmillan.

Webster, R., and Blatchford, P. (2015) 'Worlds apart? The nature and quality of the educational experiences of a pupil with a statement for special educational needs in mainstream primary schools.' *British Educational Research Journal 41,* 2, 324–342.

Wing, L. (1981) 'Asperger's syndrome: A clinical account.' *Psychological Medicine 11,* 1, 115–129.

CHAPTER 11

DOES A DIAGNOSIS OF ASD HELP US TO HELP A PERSON WITH INTELLECTUAL DISABILITIES?

Graham Collins

INTRODUCTION

The question this chapter will consider is: does the label of autism add anything at all to the approaches that services put together to help someone with an intellectual disability? The focus is on approaches which aim to help people by teaching them new ways of behaving and understanding their world and supporting them in everyday life – often called psychosocial/educational approaches.

Intellectual Disability (ID) is commonly defined in terms of deficits in intellectual ability and social functioning, which are present throughout the person's life. For example, the World Health Organisation defined Intellectual Disability as: 'a significantly reduced ability to understand new or complex information and to learn and apply new skills (impaired intelligence). This results in a reduced ability to cope independently (impaired social functioning), and begins before adulthood, with a lasting effect on development' (WHO 2010, p.4). Other present and past terms for Intellectual Disability include Intellectual Impairment, Learning Disability and Mental Retardation.

Intellectual Disability itself is a socially constructed category, which covers people who have a wide range of features and disabilities. For example, the common criterion that a person's Intelligence Quotient (IQ) should be two standard deviations below the mean (i.e. IQ less than 70) is an arbitrary figure. It is now widely recognised that both intellectual ability and social functioning are multifactorial concepts, which cannot easily be defined by a single number, and that we should be more sophisticated in how we conceptualise them (see Schalock 2011 for discussion). However, there is a large body of research and experience relating to people with this label, which has resulted in the development of specialist Intellectual Disability services with skills and knowledge in how to

improve people's lives. This chapter will investigate whether the autism label adds anything to our ability to help people with the ID label.

There is a strong association between the diagnosis of Autistic Spectrum Disorder and Intellectual Disability. For example, in their 2010 review paper, Emerson and Baines concluded, 'we estimate that between 20% and 33% of adults known to Councils with Social Services Responsibilities as people with learning disabilities also have autism. Across England, this suggests that between 35,000 and 58,000 adults who are likely users of social care services have both learning disabilities and autism. The number of adults in the population who have both learning disabilities and autism (including those who do not use specialised social care services) is likely to be much higher' (Emerson and Baines 2010, p.12). It was estimated that 40–60 per cent of children diagnosed with autism also had an ID diagnosis. Because of this strong association, this chapter will primarily consider people labelled with Intellectual Disability (ID) and Autistic Spectrum Disorder (ASD), though similar questions about the treatment implications of an autism diagnosis can be asked for people with abilities in the 'average' range of intellectual ability.

There are generally accepted concepts of diagnosed conditions:

- A person shows signs and symptoms, which suggest a known condition.
- We do tests to confirm this.
- Once we are sure the person has the condition, we then can help them using tried and tested methods that work for those with the condition.

A lot of effort and energy is often put into determining whether a person merits a diagnosis of autism. Many resources are expended to provide highly trained teams of professionals to determine a diagnosis. There are many formal assessment tools, some requiring intensive training to master, for example the Diagnostic Interview for Social and Communication Disorders (DISCO) (Wing *et al.* 2002).

They aim to give a valid and reliable decision about whether a person is autistic, or not, and maybe which subdivision of the autism spectrum they inhabit. However, when it comes to devising programmes to help the person, this chapter will argue that the value of this diagnostic label seems questionable. It is argued that most suggested treatment approaches and programmes are applicable to anyone who has ID whether they have an ASD diagnosis or not. This chapter will consider whether it is therefore right and helpful for clinicians to use precious resources on a diagnostic process when these resources could be better employed working therapeutically with people experiencing difficulties in their lives.

DOES THE DIAGNOSIS HIGHLIGHT SPECIFIC UNIQUE PROBLEMS FOR SOMEONE WITH ASD?

Autism is widely characterised by the 'triad of impairments' first proposed by Wing and Gould (1979). If this triad of impairments is the fundamental defining characteristic of people with autism, it might be thought that this would signpost services to help a person's needs in a way that is specific to ASD.

People with autism are said to have difficulties of:

- Social communication (e.g. problems using and understanding verbal and non-verbal language, such as gestures, facial expressions and tone of voice)
- Social interaction (e.g. problems in recognising and understanding other people's feelings and managing their own)
- Social imagination (e.g. problems in understanding and predicting other people's intentions and behaviour and imagining situations outside their own routine).

(Department of Health 2010, p.12)

The third element of the triad (difficulties of social imagination) is described differently in some accounts, for example as 'restricted, stereotyped, repetitive behaviour' by the World Health Organisation (1992, p.181) in the *International Classification of Diseases*, Tenth Edition.

There are questions that can be raised about the triad of impairments. For example, do these elements of the triad always appear together, and are they confined to people with an ASD diagnosis? There is evidence that the answer to both these questions is 'No'. For example, Happé and colleagues reported: 'In our population-based studies, using data from over 3,000 twin pairs assessed between the ages of 7 and 9, we have found modest-to-low correlations between autistic-like behavioural traits in the three core areas' (Happé, Ronald and Plomin 2006, p.1218). They found that many of the children in their study showed just one of the triad of impairments, with 59 per cent of the children with social impairments only showing this one and not the other elements of the triad. Therefore it seems questionable whether the core deficits of autism are something people with the ASD label have in common. This has led to the development of the 'fractionable autism triad theory', as described by Brunsdon and Happé (2014), which suggests that the three features of the autism triad have different genetic, environmental and cognitive origins, and may occur separately in different individuals.

Let us now look at each of these defining characteristics of autism, and consider whether they are also present in the wider group of people with ID.

The first two elements of the triad, social communication and social interaction, are issues that have long been known to be problematic for people with ID. However, the area of social functioning is complex. Cook and Oliver (2011) carried out a wide review of research on defining and measuring sociability in children with ID. Overall they conclude that there is a substantial body of research indicating that compromised social functioning for individuals with ID has far-reaching implications for their quality of life. However, they suggested that there is currently a lack of agreement on key concepts in the area. They proposed four constructs of sociability: social cognition, social skills, social behaviour and social competence.

Social cognition includes the abilities to read and interpret verbal and non-verbal social cues, knowledge about social behaviours and their consequences, and the ability to make accurate attributions of the other person's mental state. People with ID have been shown to have difficulties in this area. For example, Rojahn, Lederer and Tassé (1995) reviewed research which looked at people's abilities to recognise facial expressions. They concluded that compared with non-ID controls, subjects with ID had difficulty recognising emotion and this disability is more prevalent the lower the person's level of intellectual ability.

Social skills is described by Cook and Oliver (2011) as a very broad area and they suggest that it refers to socially acceptable learned behaviours that people exhibit in specific situations in order to perform competently on social tasks. Many studies have shown social skills deficits for children and adults with ID. For example, Agaliotis and Kalyva (2008) found that children with ID made fewer non-verbal initiations of social interactions than matched non-disabled peers. In a different example Pina and colleagues (2013) compared the performance of children with ID with non-disabled peers on a social stories task. The task asked the children to choose the best resolution to socially difficult situations. Children with ID were more likely to choose what they termed as 'dysfunctional' strategies (either aggressive or passive) than their controls.

Social behaviour is also a broad concept on which Cook and Oliver (2011) found no agreement in the literature. There are so many different ways people behave socially, for example cooperation, altruism, friendship, and assertiveness, that it is not possible to give one overall definition.

Social competence is another broad term referring to the ability to integrate thinking feeling and behaviour to achieve social tasks and outcomes valued in society. It includes elements of social skills and social behaviours. An indicator of how people with ID have difficulties with social competence is the widespread finding that they are less likely to develop friendships and more likely to experience loneliness than non-disabled people. For example, in their review of

social inclusion and community participation of individuals with ID, Amado and colleagues (2013) report that people with ID have fewer friends than others and those considered to be friends are likely to be family members or paid staff.

So, while social communication and social interaction are broad concepts, we can see that as well as individuals with an ASD diagnosis, people with ID are also likely to experience difficulties in these areas.

When it comes to the third element of the triad, repetitive behaviours have long been known to be associated with people with ID. For example, one study found that 57 per cent of residents of a facility in Ireland for people with ID showed stereotyped behaviour (Walsh 1994). There is some interesting evidence that different genetic syndromes may be associated with subtly different patterns of repetitive behaviours. Moss and colleagues (2009) developed the Repetitive Behaviour Questionnaire. This rated 17 different behaviours, which they combined into five subscales: Stereotyped behaviour, Compulsive behaviour, Restricted preferences, Insistence on sameness, and Repetitive speech. Data was collected on individuals with ID and from a number of different genetic syndromes: Angelman, Cornelia de Lange, Cri du Chat, Fragile X, Lowe, Prader-Willi and Smith-Magenis. They discovered different patterns of behaviours depending on the syndrome. They found, for example, that individuals with Cri du Chat syndrome were most likely to have repetitive behaviours attached to objects, whereas those with Smith-Magenis syndrome were more likely to show attachment to people. They included a group which they described as having 'heterogeneous intellectual disabilities'. They found an indistinctive profile of repetitive behaviour within this group. They suggested that the heterogeneous ID group could be considered to be the central point of a spectrum of repetitive behaviours on which some participant groups such as the Angelman syndrome group score below this and others such as the Fragile X syndrome group score above, with the other participant groups placed at various points on items and subscales within this spectrum. They did not have a separate group of individuals with an ASD diagnosis, but used the Autism Screening Questionnaire to measure autistic features in each of the groups. They found no association between autistic spectrum phenomenology among three of their five syndrome groups, with some specific correlations in two of the groups: Cri du Chat and Fragile X. According to their study, therefore, repetitive behaviours are not confined to people with an autism diagnosis and are common in people with intellectual disabilities.

Whatever the diagnosis of the person, it seems essential that an individual analysis of the functions of such behaviours are made, as it is not possible to generalise what the function of each behaviour is. For example, Joosten, Bundy and Einfeld (2012) looked at the functions of stereotypic and repetitive behaviours for children with ID with and without a diagnosis of ASD. Although

they found some differences between the groups on the likelihood of behaviours having certain functions, the context of the behaviour had a bigger influence. For example, for both groups, sensory enhancement was a more likely motivator in free time and anxiety reduction was a more likely motivator during transition between activities. Once again, the message seems to be 'generalise at your peril'.

In addition to the triad of impairments, there are also a number of other problems that are commonly associated with autism. These include sensory dysfunction. For example, 'Many people with autism may experience some form of sensory sensitivity or under-sensitivity, for example to sounds, touch, tastes, smells, light or colours' (Department of Health 2010, p.10). Some conditions, such as auditory hypersensitivity, are so closely associated with the common view of autism that 'autism friendly' cinema showings are put on with lower sound levels and more ambient lighting.

So what is the evidence that autism is associated with over- or under-responsiveness to sensory stimuli, preoccupations with sensory features of objects or unusual reactions to sensory stimuli? In one study, Ying-Hua Tan and colleagues (2012) compared various sensory differences of 156 children with an ASD diagnosis with 141 children with other language delays. They found that 49 per cent of the children in the ASD group showed auditory hypersensitivity; however, 28 per cent of children with language delay also reported this. It seems therefore that knowing a person has autism does not imply that they must also have auditory hyper-sensitivity, just as the absence of a diagnosis does not mean the person does not have this hyper-sensitivity.

In their review of the evidence for sensory dysfunction in autism, Rogers and Ozonoff (2005, p.1255) reached equivocal conclusions: 'sensory symptoms are more frequent and prominent in children with autism than typically developing children, but there is not good evidence that these symptoms differentiate these children from other developmental disorders.'

Chronic hypo-arousal or hyper-arousal has been used as an explanation for rigid and repetitive behaviours. For example, one theory suggests that stereotypic behaviours and general withdrawal from the social world develop as a way of preventing further over-arousal. Rogers and Ozonoff (2005, p.1255) also reviewed the evidence supporting the various theories of sensory dysfunction, but again came to equivocal conclusions:

> in reviewing the evidence relevant to two theories of sensory dysfunction in autism, over- and under-arousal theory, we find that there is very little support for hyper-arousal and failure of habituation in autism. There is more evidence that children with autism, as a group, are hypo-responsive to sensory stimuli, but there are also multiple failures to replicate findings and studies that demonstrate lack of group differences.

To summarise, then, each of the features of ASD may not be shown by someone with an ASD diagnosis, but may be shown by someone with an ID (see Table 11.1). For each 'symptom' the severity and nature of any difficulties will vary by individual more than by diagnosis.

TABLE 11.1 COMPARISON OF FEATURES OF PEOPLE WITH ASD AND ID

Features	People with ASD	People with ID
Social impairments	Likely to have these impairments, nature varies with individual	May have these impairments, nature varies with individual
Communication impairments	Likely to have these impairments, nature varies with individual	May have these impairments, nature varies with individual
Repetitive/ restricted behaviours and interests	Likely to have these impairments, nature varies with individual	May have these impairments, nature varies with individual
Sensory sensitivities	May have hyper-, hypo- or no sensitivities	May have hyper-, hypo- or no sensitivities

Is there really then little difference between people with ID with or without an ASD diagnosis? As we have seen, there is a great deal of commonality between the two conditions. However, there have been many attempts to identify the specific profile of difficulties for people with an ASD diagnosis. For example, Matson, Wilkins and Ancona (2008) carried out an empirical study to describe symptom patterns in adults with autism and severe intellectual disability. They compared 57 adults with ID who met ICD-10 diagnostic criteria for autism, with 57 matched controls with ID only. They found that the adults with autism showed a clear and distinct symptom profile compared with matched controls. Significant correlations were found between items on the scales they used and the diagnosis of autism. These were so marked that, by combining the items together, they could predict the diagnosis correctly in 90 per cent of the cases.

This study raises the interesting general question when we are considering whether the autism diagnosis is helpful when it comes to treatment implications, which is: does a finding of average group differences actually predict what an individual's needs are? In their study, Matson and colleagues found the five most frequently endorsed symptom items for the people with autism were: awareness of the rules of play; interest in social activities; interest in what other people say;

peer relationships; and limited number of interests. The percentage of the autistic group rated as having problems for these items ranged from 98 per cent to 91 per cent. These were significantly higher than the non-autistic group. However, if we look at the control group who did not have an autism diagnosis, the percentage rated as having problems on these items ranged from 68 per cent to 47 per cent. So, a large proportion of the non-autistic group also had problems in these areas, while a small minority of the autistic group did not. Even when there are statistically significant differences between groups of people labelled autistic and others who are not, this does not imply that we know which problems a specific individual with the label will have and that individuals who don't have the label, don't have the problems.

DOES THE LABEL 'AUTISTIC' HELP US TO KNOW HOW TO HELP THE PERSON?

For Autistic Spectrum Disorders, a lot of effort and resources are put into the diagnostic process. Local teams may not have the expertise to provide the definitive diagnostic assessments and people may be referred out of their locality, or to private services, which may charge thousands of pounds for a diagnosis. It is often assumed that the point of diagnosis is to make sure that the appropriate help is given to the person, for example: 'this is the case even for those who are already receiving support for a learning disability or mental ill-health: diagnosis of autism can change the way they are treated' (Department of Health 2010, p.33).

However, in practice, once we have the ASD diagnosis, does this actually add to our ability to help the person?

In the United Kingdom the National Institute for Health and Care Excellence (NICE) provides national guidance and advice on health and social care interventions. NICE produces what it claims are evidence-based guidance and advice for health, public health and social care practitioners, and has produced guidelines on autism in both children and adults (NICE 2012). These include guidance on best practice in psychosocial interventions, based on a review of the research.

The guideline on adults on the autistic spectrum suggests a range of psychosocial interventions. It is interesting that these are based on the individual presenting problems of the person, rather than using the diagnosis as a guide (NICE Guideline 142, 2012, sections 1.4, 1.5, 1.6, pp.24–31):

- For social communication difficulties it recommends a group or individual social learning programme focused on improving social interaction. Social learning programmes to improve social interaction should typically include: modelling, peer or individual feedback, discussion and

decision-making, explicit rules, and suggested strategies for dealing with socially difficult situations.

- For adults with autism who are socially isolated or have restricted social contact, consider a group or individual based structured leisure programme focusing on interests and abilities of the individual with structure and support.
- For people with anger problems, provide an anger management intervention including a functional analysis of anger and anger-provoking situations, coping and problem-solving skills and relaxation training.
- For challenging behaviour, provide interventions for any physical disorders, and then do a functional analysis of behaviour, using this to plan a behavioural intervention.

This is sound guidance, but is no different to the guidance which would be given about anyone with an intellectual disability, whether they 'had autism', or not.

Interestingly, when developing this guidance, the group used 25 research studies for treatment options, 15 of which were on people with ID, three were on people with ID and ASD, while only seven were with people diagnosed with ASD alone. It appears that evidence supporting condition-specific treatments for people with a diagnosis of an ASD is hard to find.

ARE SPECIAL TREATMENTS FOR AUTISM SPECIAL?

There are a number of treatment packages which are frequently used by specialist autism services. Three common approaches are Treatment and Education of Autistic and Related Communication Handicapped Children (TEACCH), Picture Exchange Communication System (PECS) and Applied Behaviour Analysis (ABA).

Treatment and Education of Autistic and Related Communication Handicapped Children (TEACCH)

TEACCH was founded in the University of North Carolina in 1972. It claims to be a family-centred, evidence-based practice for autism, based on a theoretical conceptualisation of autism, supported by empirical research, enriched by extensive clinical expertise, and notable for its flexible and person-centred support of individuals of all ages and skill levels.

The principles and concepts guiding the TEACCH system are listed as:

- *Improved adaptation:* through the two strategies of improving skills by means of education and of modifying the environment to accommodate deficits.
- *Parent collaboration:* parents work with professionals as co-therapists for their children so that techniques can be continued at home.
- *Assessment for individualised treatment:* unique educational programmes are designed for all individuals on the basis of regular assessments of abilities.
- *Structured teaching:* it has been found that children with autism benefit more from a structured educational environment than from more 'free' approaches.
- *Skill enhancement:* assessment identifies emerging skills and work then focuses upon these (this approach is also applied to staff and parent training).
- *Cognitive and behaviour therapy:* educational procedures are guided by theories of cognition and behaviour suggesting that difficult behaviour may result from underlying problems in perception and understanding.
- *Generalist training:* professionals in the TEACCH system are trained as generalists who understand the whole child, and do not specialise as psychologists, speech therapists, and so on.

Virues-Ortega, Julio and Pastor-Barriusoc (2013) carried out a meta-analysis of studies of TEACCH in practice and found overall only small effects on communication and activities of daily living, though larger gains in social behaviour and decreases in maladaptive behaviour. The mixed results may partially reflect the difficulty in assessing the impact of a multi-component package, when many of the parts of it may be present in other approaches. TEACCH therefore is an individualised programme of skill development, therapy and environmental manipulation based on a holistic view of the individual derived from an individual assessment of their strengths and needs. However, would this not perfectly describe the sort of approach that is desirable for any person with an intellectual disability, whether on the autistic spectrum or not?

Picture Exchange Communication System (PECS)

PECS was developed in 1985 in Delaware as a unique augmentative/alternative communication intervention package for individuals with ASD and related developmental disabilities. It uses the theories of B.F. Skinner to teach communication skills by reinforcing the exchange of pictures for objects

or actions. It develops from this to teach more advanced language strategies. The approach has been successful in improving communication by children and adults who have little or no speech, whether this deficit is related to autism or other developmental disabilities. For example, Hart and Banda (2009) reviewed 13 single-subject studies which included 39 individuals with developmental disabilities, 56 per cent of whom also had an ASD diagnosis. They found that most subjects, with or without ASD, showed improvements in communication skills, although improvements in speech were only shown by a small minority. PECS seems to be a useful aid to communication training, but seems applicable more broadly than just to those with an ASD diagnosis. Again there is no clear rationale for why this would not be good practice for all with ID who maybenefit.

Applied Behaviour Analysis (ABA)

Though widely talked of as if it is a specialist intervention for people on the autistic spectrum, in fact ABA has for decades been an approach applied to all aspects of human behaviour. Again rooted in the behaviourist approach of Skinner, it obtained a focus with the first publication of the *Journal of Applied Behaviour Analysis* in 1968. It has most widely been used with children and adults with ID. For example, in a review of 30 years of use of ABA with challenging behaviour, Beavers, Iwata and Lerman (2013) found that 88 per cent of their studies were on people with an ID diagnosis, whilst 37 per cent were with people with an ASD diagnosis. Applied Behaviour Analysis is therefore another treatment that is not autism-specific.

What do specialist services provide?

If the attributes of someone with an ASD diagnosis aren't unique to that condition, and the specialist treatments developed for ASD do not contain any special methods, what do autism specialist services provide?

Harker and King, in a 2004 report for the National Autistic Society, said that features of specialist provision should be:

- individual person-centred planning
- understanding problems of communication, social awareness, stress and anxiety
- teaching independence and behavioural skills
- using schemes for structuring an environment to be autism-friendly
- awareness of physical standards and design issues

- risk and risk management practice
- helping developing social networks and social inclusion
- ensuring there is some specific training for staff on Autistic Spectrum Disorders
- setting appropriate service standards.

Much of this list is open to questioning. For example, if we believe that people with an ASD label may have hyper- *or* hypo-sensory sensitivities in a range of modalities, and that these may also occur in others with ID, what does an 'autism-friendly' environment actually mean? Most of the list, however, would be applicable to any service provision for people with ID.

The guidance on autism from NICE says the following:

> If residential care is needed for adults with autism it should usually be provided in small, local community-based units (of no more than six people and with well-supported single person accommodation). The environment should be structured to support and maintain a collaborative approach between the person with autism and their family, partner or carer(s) for the development and maintenance of interpersonal and community living skills. (NICE Guideline 142, 2012)

It goes on to encourage individualised approaches to facilitate integration in the community. It is hard to argue that these approaches are not desirable, but it is equally hard to argue that the same approaches would not benefit people with ID and, indeed, people who require forms of residential care generally.

Perhaps specialist autism services are better because they group together people with the same needs. There is a general argument that there are advantages in grouping people with similar disabilities together. For example, Mansell and colleagues suggest: 'Sometimes functional grouping in community settings reflects an explicit attempt to provide specially tailored support and care for individuals with similar needs' (Mansell *et al.* 2003, p.170). They then go on to point out that there have been mixed results from research into functional grouping of people in community settings. Hatton and colleagues (1995) found that there were advantages in grouping together people with visual impairments. However, there is evidence that, for people with severely challenging behaviour, functional grouping in specialist homes may offer no advantages or may even result in worse outcomes (Emerson *et al.* 1992; Mansell 1995; Mansell *et al.* 2003).

When considering the ASDs, one could hypothesise that grouping together people with communication difficulties and problems in understanding social behaviour may actually make life harder for them. What will they see to model

effective communication on? How will they learn widely accepted interpersonal behaviours? Alternatively, one could argue that specialist environments give the chance to devise 'autism-friendly' physical environments and allow staff to develop special expertise in skills relevant to those with autism. However, as we have seen, it is debatable that there is one 'special' type of environment that will be friendly to everyone with autism. Do you keep it quiet to avoid overstimulation or will this make life harder for those with auditory hypo-sensitivity? One could also question what 'special expertise' staff will develop, when we have seen that the 'special treatments' all have something to offer people with ID including those who do not have an autism diagnosis.

The evidence on the effects of grouping people with autism together in specialist services is limited. Felce and Perry (2012) studied 76 residences for people with ID which they classified as having either 'congregate groups' of people with autism or not. To be classified as a congregate group, at least 60 per cent of the home's residents had to have had an ASD diagnosis (as classified on a battery of assessments). They described 50 of the 76 residences as 'congregate groups'. They assessed various lifestyle outcomes for the residents, including involvement in the community, participation in everyday activities and staff attention. They found some differences in the residence management between the groups. Non-congregate settings tended to be larger, with better organised working methods. However, when the residents were matched for levels of ability and challenging behaviour, there were no significant differences in resident outcomes between the types of settings.

CONCLUSION

This chapter set out to look at how the diagnosis of autism helps us to help the individual. Having a reliable and valid diagnosis should help us to:

- understand the person's problems
- know the best way to help them
- help us to set up services that provide for the specific needs of the group with the diagnosis.

What we have seen, however, is that the impairments and other features of people with an ASD diagnosis are not unique to those individuals, but are also found in other people with ID without an ASD diagnosis. Official guidance on treatment for people on the autistic spectrum is based on treatments and general research that also helps people with ID. I have also discussed how specialist service models for people on the autistic spectrum do not seem to provide anything that a good service for people with ID shouldn't also provide.

Despite this, vast resources are invested in diagnosing people with an ASD and setting up special services for them. It seems that the evidence that points to the diagnosis telling us very little about the individual or how to help them is treated as irrelevant.

There are three disadvantages for this state of affairs continuing:

- We are in danger of wasting scarce resources on a diagnostic process which has little benefit to the people it serves or their families.
- We are in danger of creating a two-tier service for people with intellectual disabilities, with those who have an ASD label getting access to more resources than those who don't. Emerson and Baines (2010) estimated that between 20 per cent and 33 per cent of adults with ID could also be diagnosed with an ASD. This means that specialist teams, day centres, schools, residential provision, and so on, are being set up which are denied to 70–80 per cent of people with ID even though they are also likely to benefit from them.
- We are in danger of providing block treatments for people based on their diagnostic label rather than an individualised assessment of need and a corresponding treatment/management programme.

What then is the alternative? We seem to be in an era of increasing specialisation of health and social services with the emphasis being on precision of diagnosis together with 'evidence-based' treatment pathways. Yet there is also an increasing concern with the holistic needs of the person and of treating the individual in a person-centred way, with dignity and compassion (see for example the Francis Report 2013). The study of the concept of autism, and of people who are given that label, has stimulated many fruitful ideas and techniques. Our challenge is now to make the benefits available to all who need them regardless of diagnosis, and to develop forms of help that are based on the individual's needs and strengths.

In terms of assessment, then, we need to ask a series of questions for each person with an ID, whether they have an autism diagnosis or not. These would cover social interaction, communication, repetitive and restricted behaviours, and also how they sense the world. Do they have difficulties with social interactions? What exactly are these difficulties? Do they have difficulties recognising and responding to emotions? Do they have difficulties learning social rules? What do they understand about non-verbal behaviour and body language?

In terms of communication, speech and language therapists have developed many useful assessments of verbal and pre-verbal communication competences, both expressive and receptive. As well as these we need to be aware of more subtle difficulties, for example misunderstandings of similes and metaphors, or taking colloquial phrases literally. In terms of restricted interests and repetitive

behaviours, we need to carry out a functional analysis of these – what function do they appear to serve? When are they most or least frequent? What seem to be setting factors and triggers for them? In terms of possible sensory issues, what do we know of the person's auditory sensitivity, or their visual acuity, or taste, or smell? If the person behaves in ways described as 'challenging' we need to complete a full functional analysis of the behaviour as the first step.

After a full assessment of the person's individual pattern of difficulties, we can create a formulation of their problems. It should be pointed out, that many features often described as 'autistic' may not be problematic at all. Restricted interests may make a person an expert in a particular field. A person may have idiosyncratic social interactions, but still survive happily in their local community. Personal characteristics will only become major problems if they inhibit the person's wellbeing and quality of life. A formulation will link up what we know of the person's pattern of strengths and needs with what we know of their history and current behavioural influences. For example, an odd way of interacting may have led to bullying in the past, which has led to the development of current unbearable anxiety when confronted by any but the most familiar people. Having formulated the person's major problems, this should lead on to the implications of this in how to help the person. This would include aspects of their physical and social environment, as well as techniques for supporting them in having a full quality of life experience. There may also be implications for particular educative or therapeutic techniques. All this work is applicable to anyone with an ID.

This chapter has not considered people in the average or above range of intellectual ability who are labelled as having an ASD. While some of the specific assertions would not apply, many of the general arguments are the same. Fundamentally, we would want to see an individual assessment of each person to produce a formulation of their needs, and packages of help built around these.

The UK Autism Strategy *Fulfilling and Rewarding Lives* asserts:

> Diagnosis alone is not enough: the fundamental change we want to see is that diagnosis leads to a person-centred assessment of need, in line with the NHS and Community Care Act 1990. (Department of Health 2010, p.39)

What is unclear is why we need the diagnosis in the first place for this person-centred response the guidance seeks.

REFERENCES

Agaliotis, I., and Kalyva, E. (2008) 'Nonverbal social interaction skills of children with learning disabilities.' *Research in Developmental Disabilities 29*, 1–10.

Amado, A.N., Stancliffe, R.J., McCarron, M., and McCallion, P. (2013) 'Social inclusion and community participation of individuals with intellectual/developmental disabilities' *Intellectual and Developmental Disabilities 51*, 5, 360–375.

Beavers, G.A., Iwata, B.A., and Lerman, D.C. (2013) 'Thirty years of research on the functional analysis of problem behaviour.' *Journal of Applied Behavior Analysis 46*, 1, 1–21

Brunsdon, V.E., and Happé, F. (2014) 'Exploring the "fractionation" of autism at the cognitive level.' *Autism 18*, 1, 17–30.

Cook, F., and Oliver, C. (2011) 'A review of defining and measuring sociability in children with intellectual disabilities.' *Research in Developmental Disabilities 32*, 11–24.

Department of Health (DoH) (2010) *Fulfilling and Rewarding Lives: The Strategy for Adults with Autism in England.* London: DoH.

Emerson, E., Beasley, F., Offord, G., and Mansell, J. (1992) 'An evaluation of hospital-based specialized staffed housing for people with seriously challenging behaviours.' *Journal of Intellectual Disability Research 36*, 291–307.

Emerson, E., and Baines, S. (2010) *The Estimated Prevalence of Autism among Adults with Learning Disabilities in England.* Improving Health and Lives: Learning Disabilities Observatory. Public Health England.

Felce, D., and Perry, J. (2012) 'Diagnostic grouping among adults with intellectual disabilities and Autistic Spectrum Disorders in staffed housing.' *Journal of Intellectual Disability Research 56*, 12, 1187–1193.

Francis, R. (2013) *Report of the Mid Staffordshire NHS Foundation Trust Public Inquiry.* London: The Stationery Office.

Happé, F., Ronald, A., and Plomin, R. (2006) 'Time to give up on a single explanation for autism.' *Nature Neuroscience 9*, 10, 1218–1220.

Harker, M., and King, N. (2004) *Tomorrow's Big Problem: Housing Options For People with Autism – A Guide for Service Commissioners, Providers and Families.* London: National Autistic Society.

Hart, S.L., and Banda, D.R. (2009) 'Picture Exchange Communication System with individuals with developmental disabilities: a meta-analysis of single subject studies.' *Remedial and Special Education 31*, 6, 476–488.

Hatton, C., Emerson, E., Robertson, J., and Henderson, D. (1995) 'The quality and costs of residential services for adults with multiple disabilities: a comparative evaluation.' *Research in Developmental Disabilities 16*, 6, 439–460.

Joosten, A.V., Bundy, A.C., and Einfeld, S.L. (2012) 'Context influences the motivation for stereotypic and repetitive behaviour in children diagnosed with intellectual disability with and without autism.' *Journal of Applied Research in Intellectual Disabilities 25*, 3, 262–271.

Mansell, J. (1995) 'Staffing and staff performance in services for people with severe or profound learning disability and serious challenging behaviour.' *Journal of Intellectual Disability Research 39*, 3–14.

Mansell, J., Beadle-Brown, J., Macdonald, S., and Ashman, B. (2003) 'Functional grouping in residential homes for people with intellectual disabilities.' *Research in Developmental Disabilities 24*, 170–182.

Matson, J.L., Wilkins, J., and Ancona, M. (2008) 'Autism in adults with severe intellectual disability: an empirical study of symptom presentation.' *Journal of Intellectual and Developmental Disability 33*, 1, 36–42.

Moss, J., Oliver, C., Arron, K., Burbidge, C., and Berg K. (2009) 'The prevalence and phenomenology of repetitive behavior in genetic syndromes.' *Journal of Autism and Developmental Disorders 39*, 572–588.

NICE (2012) *Autism. The NICE Guideline on Recognition, Referral, Diagnosis and Management of Adults on the Autism Spectrum.* National Clinical Guideline Number 142. London: The British Psychological Society and The Royal College of Psychiatrists.

Pina, F., Flavia, M., Laura, S., and Luana, S. (2013) 'Learning disabilities and social problem solving skills.' *Mediterranean Journal of Clinical Psychology 1*, 2, 1–23.

Rogers, S.J., and Ozonoff, S. (2005) 'Annotation: What do we know about sensory dysfunction in autism? A critical review of the empirical evidence.' *Journal of Child Psychology and Psychiatry 46*, 12, 1255–1268.

Rojahn, J., Lederer, M., and Tassé, M. J. (1995) 'Facial emotion recognition by persons with mental retardation: a review of the experimental literature.' *Research in Developmental Disabilities 16*, 5, 393–414.

Schalock, R.L. (2011) 'The evolving understanding of the construct of intellectual disability.' *Journal of Intellectual and Developmental Disability 36*, 4, 223–233.

Tan, Y., Xi, C., Jiang, S., Shi, B., Wang, L., and Wang, L. (2012) 'Auditory abnormalities in children with autism.' *Open Journal of Psychiatry 2*, 33–37.

Virues-Ortega, J., Julio, F.M., and Pastor-Barriusoc, R. (2013) 'The TEACCH program for children and adults with autism: a meta-analysis of intervention studies.' *Clinical Psychology Review 33*, 940–953.

Walsh, P.G. (1994) 'A survey of stereotyped behaviours exhibited by adults with learning disability living in a residential centre in the west of Ireland.' *British Journal of Learning Disabilities 22*, 3, 90–93.

Wing, L., and Gould, J. (1979) 'Severe impairments of social interaction and associated abnormalities in children. Epidemiology and classification.' *Journal of Autism and Developmental Disorders 9*, 11–29.

Wing, L., Leekam, S., Libby, S., Gould, J., and Larcombe, M. (2002) 'Diagnostic interview for social and communication disorders: background, inter-rater reliability and clinical use.' *Journal of Child Psychology and Psychiatry 43*, 307–325.

World Health Organisation (WHO) (1992) *International Classification of Diseases: Diagnostic Criteria for Research, Tenth Edition.* Geneva: WHO.

World Health Organisation (WHO) (2010) *Better Health, Better Lives: Children and Young People with Intellectual Disabilities and Their Families. The Case for Change.* Background paper for the Conference, World Health Organisation Regional Office for Europe.

CHAPTER 12

CRITICAL SYSTEMIC THERAPY

AUTISM STORIES AND DISABLED PEOPLE WITH LEARNING DIFFICULTIES

Mark Haydon-Laurelut

INTRODUCTION

Autistic Spectrum Conditions (ASCs)[1] are a boom industry (Timimi, Gardner and McCabe 2010) from academia (Mallett and Runswick-Cole 2012) to the world of fiction (Hacking 2009). Biomedical understandings of ASCs are a powerful story in contemporary health and social care services for disabled people with learning difficulties,[2] in health and social care more generally, and in the wider culture of the global North. Autism is most commonly clinically framed as a neurodevelopmental disorder.[3] However, a dramatically different perspective is elaborated by Timimi and colleagues (2010) who interrogated the makings of autism and found, in line with the sparse scientific evidence for autism as a biogenetic disorder, that autism functions as a:

> metaphor for focusing on a disparate range of behaviours that suggest a lack of the type of social and emotional competencies thought to be necessary for the functioning of societies dominated by neoliberal economic and political foundations. (Timimi *et al.* 2010, p.7)

This bracing view is that the construct of autism is culturally and historically specific and also tells us more about gender relations in late capitalism than it does about biology: 'it is boys who are increasingly unable to fulfil the cultural expectations of an essentially non-gendered childhood' (Timimi *et al.* 2010,

1 This chapter employs the term Autistic Spectrum Conditions as opposed to Autistic Spectrum Disorders in acknowledgement that for some persons so labelled and their supporters their experiences are not appropriately reflected in the potentially stigmatising term 'disorder'.

2 This chapter uses this term to imply that those referred to are people first who are disabled by oppressive social environments. Other terms in use include Intellectual Disabilities (in a North American and Australasian context) and Learning Disabilities (in a UK context).

3 A neurodevelopmental disorder is impairment in the functioning of the brain or central nervous system that develops as the individual grows.

p.215). This situates ASCs as developing in relation to mutable cultural norms. Writing about reading difficulties, now commonly medicalised as dyslexia, Campbell (2014) notes that impairment categories shift in their proximity to the norm over time. Bodies now labelled as autistic were perhaps closer to the norms of the late nineteenth and the early to mid-twentieth century. These bodies and their characteristics are increasingly distant from the kinds of humans – those of the 'agile' or 'flexed' workforce, narcissistic, hypersocial and so on – demanded from the second half of the twentieth century to the present day by the changing socio-economic conditions of neoliberal capitalist cultures and a service economy.

This chapter focuses on psychotherapy and, in particular, systemic or family therapy with disabled people with learning difficulties and ASCs. What might be the response of therapists working with disabled people with learning difficulties to the labels and knowledge(s) developed around ASCs? What might a critical (including a focus on the importance of power) and systemic (the importance of context, meaning and connection) therapy have to offer? According to Hoffman (1990), systemic therapy is an art of lenses – it concerns contextual artistry (Pearce 2011), the playing with differing viewpoints, differing frames. For example, a view of a particular person with learning disability (let's call her 'Megan') as having 'aggressive challenging behaviour' may be understood differently when placed alongside understandings that put to one side this kind of service language. So we might ask: 'If you were to talk about this person without using these words, how would you talk about what is going on? Is the person lonely? Frightened? Angry?'

We can ask questions that frame the issue in socio-economic contexts and ask: 'What power does Megan have to influence the conditions of her life right now, be a member of this community...did Megan choose to live here?'

And we can frame this behaviour as a (important) communication and enquire: 'So you feel her behaviour is "attention seeking"? What kind of attention might Megan need right now and how might it make sense for her, given the environment she finds herself in, to seek this in this manner?'

In co-creating multiple frames, a critical systemic therapy relativises and problematises the dominant biomedical frame. There are always alternative ways of describing, engaging and making the social world.

I work in community learning disability teams as a systemic therapist and a proportion of those I meet also have an ASC diagnosis. The next section of this chapter introduces the literature on systemic therapy, disabled people with learning difficulties and ASCs.

SYSTEMIC THERAPY: DISABLED PEOPLE WITH LEARNING DIFFICULTIES AND AUTISTIC SPECTRUM CONDITIONS

In the global North, disability and disabled people with learning difficulties and autism are predominantly framed through the dominant individual medical model (Oliver 1990) requiring individual medicalised or psychologised cure, rehabilitation or remediation. Given systemic therapy's focus on the relational – that problems develop in the space between people – it is unsurprising that there has been relatively little literature on systemic therapy and ASCs and less still on those with learning difficulties who also have a label of ASC; autism is viewed predominantly as an individual cognitive issue. Additionally, echoes of the mother-blaming past of early family approaches to autism may still cast a shadow (Simon 2004).

Psychotherapeutic approaches for people with learning difficulties have more generally been neglected (Linington 2002). There is, however, a steadily growing literature on systemic therapy and disabled people with learning difficulties (Baum 2007; Baum and Lynggaard 2006; Daynes *et al.* 2011; Fidell 1996, 2000; Haydon 2009; Haydon-Laurelut, Bissmire and Hall 2009; Haydon-Laurelut and Nunkoosing 2010; Haydon-Laurelut and Wilson 2011; Jenkins and Parry 2006; Purdy 2012; Webb-Peploe and Fredman 2015). Additionally, a number of systemic therapists have written about their work with people with ASC though these are not necessarily persons also labelled with learning difficulties.

Simon (2004; see also Chapter 15) described her work with families with a child with Asperger Syndrome. Simon immerses herself in the child's area of special interest, showing how it is meaningful to them and how the content of their special interest may be used metaphorically to guide the session with the family. Munro (2010) describes a model of working with teenagers with Asperger Syndrome incorporating family therapy, narrative therapy, cognitive behavioural therapy and other therapeutic methods to produce an integrated approach. Migerode (2009) explored the place of diagnosis in systemic couple therapy and characterises diagnosis as a meaning and an opportunity to belong to a community as well as a path to exclusion. Migerode, Vander Elst and Rober (2010) examined the way that couples with one member with autism talk about autism. They found that though couples often did find the diagnosis useful – in creating some understanding about what was 'wrong' with the partner – it was, however, not without problems for the couple, for example when conflict was created by one partner agreeing with the diagnosis and the labelled partner not agreeing with it. The research suggests that the label might provide initial relief from questions, insecurities and self-blame (particularly for the partner of the person diagnosed); however, this leads to further questions, insecurities and

problems about how to manage new identities – for example occupying the sick role (Parsons and Fox 1952) – for the diagnosed person. Diagnosticians may well be less likely to witness these later issues, resulting in a biased opinion about the impact of diagnosis. There seems no reason to believe that this will significantly differ in couples of disabled people with learning difficulties and ASC.

SYSTEMIC THERAPY: CORE CONCEPTS AND PRACTICES

In order to explore what a critical systemic approach might offer, it is important first to introduce some core contemporary systemic therapy concepts and practices.

Critical

Systemic therapists may work with an individual, yet more often work will occur with couples, family groups, relational networks or organisations (Hedges 2005). Systemic therapy focuses on what happens between people – how they interact with one another and one another's ideas. Contemporary systemic therapy views these processes as constituting people-in-relationship; that is, we are made by and through the communications. Systemic therapy is thus well placed to act as a critical voice amongst psy-professionals and the autism industry as it has, to some extent, created space between itself and the contemporary Western focus on the individual bioself – the model that informs much psychological practice[4] – as foundational.

Context

Context is a central component. Meaning emerges out of the things we do together (stories lived) and the way we narrate these things (stories told) (Pearce 2007). Meaning is both created in context and is a context for other meanings. Diagnoses may be powerful contexts and invite therapists to ask themselves and others questions such as:

- 'What autism stories are organising meaning and action in this family/couple/organisation?'

4 However, there is emerging evidence that in relation to disability, at least in terms of its contemporary literature, the profession stills draws predominately upon medical model ideology (Haydon-Laurelut 2013).

- 'What is "autism" a context for (episodes, identities, relationships and so on) and in what contexts (home, clinic, club, shop) is this understood?'
- 'Does this make preferred ways of being-in-relationship?'
- 'What if we imagined other stories?'

For example, we might consider the ASC as the primary concern when focused on the difficulties a young man is experiencing, thus occluding other important contexts such as socio-economic inequality, disablism, service quality, the contribution of others to relational difficulties, or issues of age, race, gender, sexuality and identity more generally.

For systemic therapy there are always multiple stories that can be told about any pattern of action, and redescribing those leads to the possibility for new actions. This frees therapists from finding the 'true' description of events. Often people in the system of concern (Lang and McAdam 2014) hold very different ideas about the nature of a problem. A father may believe his daughter's self-harm is 'attention seeking', a sibling view it as an aspect of a 'syndrome', a psychologist may focus on the need for parental consistency and so on. Systemic therapists view all of these as stories or 'punctuations' (Selvini *et al.* 1978). In such situations, exploring and supporting coherence and coordination (Pearce 2007) of stories (including stories about autism) between the person and significant others may be part of systemic therapy. For example, dialogue may be supported between a service, let's call them 'The Pines', who hold a strong biomedical neurodevelopmental view, and parents of a person with an ASC label who may reject the label and attribute 'challenging behaviour' to poor service quality and other personal characteristics of their son whom they believe to be 'attention seeking'. In such a situation the use of mediation skills, such as helping system members to connect with one another's common intentions (providing a good quality of life for the person), may support a context where moving forward becomes possible.

Circularity

Systemic therapists hold a circular and dynamic position on social realities where causes and effects become punctuations made by observers or participants in interactional sequences. In the patterns of action that make up life, one person may be viewed as beginning the pattern (cause) and one as responding to the 'cause'. This can lead to one person being seen as more blameworthy than another, depending on the punctuation of the interactional sequence. Labels that describe some people as falling away from social norms may invite punctuating at those labelled as the causes of problems, as in, 'he causes problems in the family

because his ASC means he doesn't see others' points of view', which then frames possible solutions as being concerned with changing, or at least coping with, the labelled person's behaviour. The invitation of the systemic therapist is likely to be of the order of 'what patterns do we wish to create together' and 'who needs to do what in order to create this'. Conflict may occur where different people in a family punctuate the interactional sequence at different points. In our earlier example, 'The Pines' may be blamed for its lack of attention to the person's individuality and the parents for their lack of knowledge about or rejection of autism. Systemic therapists, assuming blame and shame constrain the creation of good outcomes, adopt the interactional, circular perspective and ask:

- 'What are the patterns of interaction between service and family (and person) and what do they produce?'
- 'What are the hopes and dreams of the person, the family, the service?'
- 'What are the logical connotations of the patterns?'

Systemic therapists will often positively or logically relate current patterns to show that – despite unwanted outcomes – each person's behaviour has logic given an understanding of their position in context.[5]

Difference

Difference is a resource, and therapists will seek differences that make a difference to the system (Bateson 1972). Therapists will talk with families and ask family members to talk with each other in ways that are similar enough to make sense to them and yet different enough to provide new information that might be of interest to them. Therapists in this way attempt to both exercise and provoke curiosity (Cecchin 1987). They may enquire about how people have come to have the ideas they have about themselves and others:

- 'When did this word autism enter your life and what did it tell you about your son and you, then and now?'
- 'When is it useful and when does it need to be put to one side?'

Curiosity leads therapists to enquire about the 'rules' around actions and beliefs (Pearce 1994). Family members are invited to become an audience to their own actions and beliefs so that they may have greater abilities to comprehend and effect change in their lives.

5 There may of course be an issue with service quality that requires addressing (including perhaps a need to work on their abilities in working in partnership with families).

Social construction and reflexivity

Contemporary systemic therapists have engaged with social constructionist ideas (Gergen 1999). For social constructionists, social reality (thoughts, emotions, selves, relationships, family, organisations, culture) is made in social communication (Pearce 1999, 2007). Diagnoses such as autism are no exception to this. This idea has profound consequences for therapeutic work as therapists hold response-ability for the realities co-constructed with clients. When professionals speak uncritically of autism as if its existence was pre-discursive, they take part in reproducing a version of the world with all its attendant consequences – they do not merely report on the 'facts'. Additionally, therapists may view family and cultural realities as intertwined with hegemonic discourses of race, gender, disability, sexuality, age and so on being negotiated in family life. If social communication constitutes emotion, narrative and meaning then therapists should be constantly alert to how they are feeling, what they are saying, how they are listening, and tune into feedback about the impact these feelings, words, choice of questions, facial expressions, beliefs and so on are having on their clients. To engage reflexively (Burnham 1992) is to become attuned to what we are being organised by, what the therapy is creating and to the part one is playing in this. It is to critically interrogate our own culturally situated responses to ASCs and disability more generally:

> We only need to consult our feelings and thoughts about disability – feelings and thoughts gleaned from our culture – to 'know' that disability is a condition of 'abnormalcy' that should be removed from both individuals and society; these thoughts and feelings about disability also tell us that if disability cannot be removed, it must be coped with and adjusted to, and that such practices are second best. (Michalko and Titchkosky 2009, p.4)

Noticing, interrogating, disrupting, and relativising internalised disablism is an aspect of critical reflexive engagement. This is a radically different position from the positivist notion of clinician as dis-covering the reality of the client or the myth of the objective 'God's eye' clinician in control of the therapeutic reality.

Systemic practices

Therapy will usually begin with developing an agreement about the expectations of the work and how it will proceed. As systemic therapists work with systems, decisions will need to be made about whom to invite. Attention is paid to the referrer, who will generally be spoken with and possibly invited to the first meeting. This is unusual in counselling and psychotherapy; however, they are the person who has produced a written narrative about which they will presumably be concerned. We ask:

- 'Who else is concerned?'
- 'About what?'
- 'Why now?'

Regarding convening, disabled people with learning difficulties and ASCs will often have large support systems including family members, personal assistants, group home staff, day centre staff, other health and social care professionals, and peers or friends, making the task of who to invite and how best to include the person a very important one. After many years of working with these decisions, I do not have any fixed rules about this other than that the default option is that the referred person is invited to attend and that the service receiving the referral must have a conversation about who is invited as a 'one size fits all' approach is not useful in unique situations. For example, we might not meet with a person together with some members of the significant system if we have reason to believe this will be an aversive experience for the person.

Teams and pairs

Systemic therapists are more likely to work in teams or with co-therapists. A team allows for more stories/perspectives. In a pair, one person may speak with the family and the other observe the therapist and family interact. At particular points in the session the observer(s) will be asked to comment on what they have noticed. If there is more than one observer they will usually have a conversation with each other. If there is one observer then a conversation will usually occur with the therapist. In this way the family are invited to be an audience to their own stories, hearing themselves spoken about as characters in those stories – 'I was struck by the way John from "The Pines" and Megan's mother showed their determination to seek the best outcome for Megan. I wonder what they noticed about the conversation so far?' This conversation should model exploring a number of ideas and no attempt is made to 'sell' a single idea. The reflecting conversation attempts to connect to the family's conversation and ideas and offer something different enough to spark their curiosity. At the end of the reflecting conversation, the therapist asks the family if there is anything they wish to comment on.

Systemic therapy may involve anything from a single session to many sessions over an extended period. The constitution of the sessions may change over time as, for example, a parental consultation becomes important for a couple to talk together without the children present, or perhaps an individual consultation with the person who finds it easier to discuss his concerns without others present. Persons may bring their key-worker or workers who can act as a resource to the person outside of the sessions. As the work continues, the therapist will check in at least

once per session about how the therapy is progressing for each member – 'Are we talking about the things we need to talk about? What do we need to do more of?' – and seeks to notice the effects of the conversations. Often a set number of meetings will be agreed so families know what time is available. Therapy often ends with a letter, sometimes jointly written with the family, that records aspects of the work that was important to them.

SYSTEMIC THERAPY IN PRACTICE

> The language of pathology is necessary for the functioning of institutions. (Cecchin, Lane and Ray 2010, p.22)

The people I see for therapy or consultation come with various labels, including but not limited to:

- Learning (intellectual) disabilities
- Autism
- Pervasive Developmental Disorder Not Otherwise Specified (PDDNOS)
- Asperger Syndrome
- Attention Deficit Hyperactivity Disorder (ADHD)
- Down syndrome
- Challenging behaviour
- Tourette syndrome
- ODD (Oppositional Defiance Disorder).

Living together with the labels and referral storylines are of course unique individuals with unique histories, families and support networks. An outgoing and engaging young man concerned about friendships and the complexities of using social media; an engaging and humorous young man whose unconventional behaviour leads others to be concerned about him; a person who feels lonely since they have moved from a 'group home' to a flat on their own where they receive several hours of community support each week; a survivor of institutional abuse who seeks security in the label as a hope that she will receive better care if the label is understood by others; an articulate man struggling with starting adult life; parents bemused by their daughter's behaviour and wondering if the label might offer some certainty and the 'correct' treatment; an elderly man who lived with his father till late in his life who is supported by young female carers, the man is said to be 'obsessed' by some of the carers; parents bemused at their

daughter's condition and struggling to think about their part in the patterns for which they have sought professional help; carers worried that their son may be vulnerable to abuse in the community; parents who are concerned that they may have to move as they have a spare bedroom and wonder if another label may help;[6] a man, most likely abused in institutional settings, who repetitively mentions a word that appears to relate to these experiences.

I see people who have been bullied; people who are angry or confused about their diagnosis; relatives and workers concerned about the person and their behaviour, that may include harming themselves and others; people living in unsuitable environments; people negotiating a number of life transitions, including the involuntarily dislocation of 'out of area placements'. In the adult community learning disability teams in which I work, many of these transitions include young adults leaving the family home.

Thematically there are those I see who are 'inducted' by professionals into a medical model of ASCs; those who are 'curious' about ASCs; the 'pragmatic' that are wondering if the label might secure resources and interventions; and the 'resistant' that oppose the label. The threads linking those I see with whom ASC is an issue is that the person has been to a previous clinician who has diagnosed them as having an ASC or they have come across the term in the media and wonder if it applies to their adult son or daughter with learning difficulties as they seek to understand their behaviour. There indeed appears to be a spectrum of persons who receive the label autism; this, however, is not the same as saying there is an autism spectrum. In sum, a diagnostic frame foregrounds the individual's ASC characteristics as the highest context marker through which life events and difficulties are then viewed, subjugating the contextual power of episodes of commutation, identity, family history, stories, beliefs, patterns and legends, community and the shifting norms and specifications of the wider culture. As Timimi and colleagues (2010) note, the diagnosis stands in the way of understanding that many paths are possible to difficulties that may appear similar.

Let us consider an example of systemic therapy with 'James'.[7]

---

6 The biomedical view of Autism may have dismissed the notion of parental behaviour as a cause of the ASC of their child; however, it exposes them to further risk – first, the risk of being thought to be genetically implicated in their child's condition; second, to the disciplinary practices of the psy-professions (Rose 1985) involved in the ASC industry. With a diagnosis comes the prescriptions of the psy-professions for certain understandings and actions that parents must have and perform. Behaviour problems may be viewed as being caused in some measure by parental failure to subject themselves to current professionally formed behaviours and beliefs. Parents are people who must now 'manage' their son or daughter. It is up to them to do their utmost (via the latest therapies, for example) to ensure that their autistic son's or daughter's unruly body is contained.

7 Consent sought and obtained from 'James', which is not his real name.

JAMES

James, a man in his late sixties, was described in the referral as having a mild learning disability and a diagnosis of Asperger Syndrome. He lived in a residential service in a rural area. James was described by the referral as using 'maladaptive' strategies to avoid following rules he did not like. The 'strategies' included setting fires, damaging property (it was noted that he had not done these things for some years) and 'going on at people'. The referral, from a health worker (from the part of the UK from which James had recently relocated) and the social worker, felt James would very likely value having someone to speak with about his anxieties and behaviours.

James wished to meet with me by himself. We had eight meetings and for most of the meetings a trainee clinical psychologist also participated. James spoke at speed, moving quickly between past and present. At times we had difficulties understanding what James wanted us to hear. Gradually a picture emerged of a person who had received poor care from both family members and staff in institutions. James had spent much of his life in services, including the large institutions before the 'community care' reforms of the 1980s. James spoke of serious physical and psychological abuse.[8] James told us he wanted to work on 'anxiety' and 'urges' as well as where he wanted to live. It also appeared that he valued having a place where we could be witnesses to his experiences.

We explored the life of 'urges' and 'anxiety'. James held a strong story that 'urges' (e.g. to smash a window) occurred due to Asperger Syndrome. In working systemically with James we were less focused on either/or logics (e.g. was Asperger Syndrome the correct diagnosis) and more on both/and logics concerning the meanings, place and life of these words for James and others. James had found in Asperger's a way of framing biography, and in particular a way of making sense of those who had maltreated him and his response to this and to living in institutions more generally. James had a strong story that those who did not understand the syndrome had maltreated him. Asperger's also relieved James of responsibility for his actions; they were due to the syndrome. As it said in the letter I wrote with James' support at the end of our sessions:

> I understood that Asperger Syndrome (AS) allows you to feel less blamed (more safe) for problems and behaviours that you engaged in as you 'can't help' having AS. You said to me: 'I wasn't naughty – I was ill, I know the difference.'

Asperger Syndrome as a biomedical label helped James make meaning out of events that seemed unjust and that I felt he was very angry about. James appeared not to feel permitted to express directly anger about his maltreatment; perhaps it

---

8 Communicated appropriately, with James's consent, to the appropriate parties.

did not feel safe. It seemed to me to be entwined with 'urges' that were protests – they could be understood as displays of anger and defiance at what was happening and had happened in his life.

The label Asperger Syndrome minimised the abuse; it was just a lack of education on the part of the staff. We offered James a difference – that is, that regardless of what staff and others knew about ASCs the events he described should never have happened – they were wrong. We didn't at any point challenge the diagnosis – though there were question marks raised by other team members. The diagnosis did, however, seem to be less of a topic of discussion as we moved to discussing what James wanted and how he might go about getting it.

As mentioned, James did not want to be punished for the acts he described – such as setting fire to buildings and smashing windows. We developed a story/hypothesis with James that helped us to understand this request as a way of letting us know that he was fearful of being 'sent back' to an institution where he would receive harsh treatment and not be 'allowed' to engage in his favourite pastime – travelling all day on buses and trains.[9]

Curiosity: multiple frames, multiple James

James and others told a story of James having a strong dislike of rules, and this was also employed as a way of accounting for past behaviours and current 'urges'. This appeared as a 'blocked' stuck story. A story that says this is how this person is. The story also supported the connected story of James as inherently problematic and these had been both connected with the rigid-thinking ASC story and accepted by James and his service providers. But could James and I become curious about this story? If we stepped into other relational framings it turned out that James was also quite a respecter of rules. When I asked James for a unique outcome – a time when a rule was 'OK' – he told me about Mr Griffiths from many years ago whose rules he respected. James was 'allowed' to go out on the buses if he followed 'his' rules.[10] Further work with James on rules helped us to develop some rough criteria as to the kinds of rules, and from whom, he would be more likely to follow. This included the often-overlooked issue of age and gender as James had problems being – as he saw it – told what to do by women young enough to be his grandchildren. This seemed to soften his story

9 Stories about time can be a key aspect of therapy and we (myself and the trainee I was working with) hypothesised that James's sense of time was particularly fluid and that the past and present were closely interconnected places through which he traversed.

10 My embodied response to this story informed me that this broke a 'rule' in a strong story I had about what James's basic rights were. He was an adult, so why was he 'allowed'! This was quite different from the tone of James's story. At these points of difference privileging my stories would be at best unhelpful and unethical given that James was telling me of something he clearly remembered fondly.

about always not liking the rules of others. What had happened in this moment to James's ASC-driven inflexible thinking? Who was being inflexible in their thinking?

Self-reflexivity: a route to new understandings

In one of our later sessions James said to me that he wanted to control people. I noticed feeling uncomfortable as I heard James say this. At moments such as this, self-reflexivity – a noticing of the stories that are organising the therapist's hearing, feeling and responding (my discomfort with 'wanting to control others' as a goal) – is an important systemic skill. Developing my own curiosity about this story supported listening to James in a way that facilitated James to tell this story and to make connections. He spoke of wanting others, particularly professionals, to stay with him. Staying with a person for the long term was something he saw as being professional, and he also wished to create what he described as a kind of 'foster family' where he could be looked after (in the way he had never been, perhaps). This seemed to me to paint a somewhat different picture of someone who sought family and safety and belonging rather than a thin story of a controlling man.

The letter at the end of therapy stated:

> You have developed ways of coping including being in a 'power struggle'. I understand James that services need to focus on how to support you to feel safe and also how to find a way of having rules that you are more likely to respect – particularly respecting your age and the experience that comes with it.

The focus of the work was not to cure James of irrational thoughts or behaviours (Cognitive Behavioural Framework) or to find the 'correct' diagnosis for him (Psychiatric Bio-Medical Framework), but rather a systemic frame where the work was to support him to develop his stories about his experiences, to include the critical frame of power, crucial to ethical narratives of disabled life, and to support, with James's agreement, a sharing of these stories with those who would have power in his life after our meetings had finished. At the end of therapy James invited me to his review meeting to support his telling of our work.

Asperger Syndrome in James's life

Asperger Syndrome in James's life helped simplify his biography, helped him to feel that his actions were morally legitimate; as well as (as long as others knew about AS) helping him to feel there was a possibility of future safety. However, seeking this safety through the diagnosis had its drawbacks; the framing of a life

through Asperger's robbed James of a sense of agency, offered him an identity as everlastingly 'ill', and appeared to temper his sense of legitimate protest at maltreatment as a human being. It was also fragile and at risk of being discredited, as different clinicians are encountered and diagnostic fashions change.[11] Moreover, it supported thin stories of his personal characteristics (not liking rules/anxious and controlling) that were subsequently troubled and nuanced by the therapeutic process.

WORKING WITH DIAGNOSES

Questions and debates around diagnosis have raged for decades and these questions are perhaps as urgent as they have ever been, particularly in the case of ASCs given the phenomenal rise in diagnoses from what was formerly considered a rare condition.

Diagnosis is part and parcel of medical model dominated services. Various contexts combine in medicalised services to support the rush and rise in diagnoses of ASCs including the pseudo-health market encouraging the branding of services with the simple authoritative labels that diagnoses such as ASC provide. Autism is characterised by deficit and the status of 'patient'. That some welcome the diagnosis and others talk of 'difference not disability' does not alter this. The logic of normalcy (of the included and fully human and the excluded and not fully human) is not challenged and there are darker ways in which this plays out. The culture of ableism (Campbell 2009) is illustrative of this. The internet shows sites, videos and so on where people with an ASC diagnosis attempt to distance themselves from and malign people with learning disabilities. Indeed, the term 'high-functioning' is often heard at conferences and read on social media, and appears to function as a way of distancing oneself or one's relative from the 'learning disabled' position. Whilst this may be a useful strategy for individuals, we might well ask who is ultimately responsible for this dilemma, this distancing, this continuing stigma and denigration? We might also ask what kind of culture is being created and with what consequences. Does it mean continued discrimination against people with learning disabilities and a culture where for those for whom the current version of normal or valued citizen is out of reach, in order to be valued (or at least less devalued) each person needs to seek to obtain the next 'best' medical label for themselves or their family member? Moreover, is it a satisfactory state of affairs that professional groups employ a naïve realist position to justify the diagnosis as 'fact', which is merely uncovered, or employ a consumerist metaphor to point out that some individuals appear 'happy' with

11 For example, during our work DSM dropped Asperger Syndrome from its classificatory system. Also at the end of our work I understood that another clinician was considering another diagnosis for James.

'their' label? To what extent do clinicians and services have a responsibility to aggregate the cultural consequences of their day-to-day clinical practices and to ask the question, 'What are we making?' The autism-as-difference paradigm, for example, has been critiqued for resulting in a continuing binary of 'them' and 'us' that fails to challenge the commodification of difference and continues to cast some as 'other' (Runswick-Cole 2014).

Assessing the risks of diagnosing

Given this chapter's concern that an ASC diagnosis for disabled people with learning difficulties may be a powerful context (for example, shaping understandings of life; shaping social identity; being of limited clinical value; a source of distress to some diagnosed; an artefact of a market-driven ideology), this raises questions regarding consent to diagnosis of disabled people with learning difficulties. What are the risks of diagnosis – to the individual, to their family, to the community and the wider culture? How as clinicians should we be assessing these risks? How is capacity to give or withhold consent to the diagnostic process negotiated with adults with more severe learning difficulties? Professionalised spaces are often assumed to be safe spaces and risk as something that is 'out there' (Hatton 2014), allied to naïve realist ontology and the power of professional groupings. This is an area that needs further reflection and research.

CONCLUSION: CRITICAL SYSTEMIC THERAPY WITH PERSONS WITH ASCS

Biomedical stories dominate the professional world of assessment, diagnosis and treatment services. Medicine may be useful if you are ill; the problem is that medicine finds a home everywhere (Michalko 2012). When ASC stories achieve salience in a network, ASCs may become a powerful organising context for making sense of life. There are often repeated revisions as multiple diagnoses are applied over a lifetime, reflecting the individual proclivities of clinicians as well as the mutable fashions of the psy-professions. The critical therapist attempts to bracket these constructs to locate the local, relational, genealogical stories that White and Epston (1990) have described as 'experience-near descriptions'. Furthermore, therapy can be a place to explore positioning around these discourses; the stories of autistic spectrum theorists are but one way of describing the world amongst many possible, and possibly more fruitful, others.

Questions remain. Given the lack of biological markers for ASCs (Timimi *et al.* 2010) one might legitimately question the use of such scientifically doubtful labels by clinicians. However, in the context of the therapeutic encounter, to reject the label would be to do further injustice to those who have found it

a useful way of managing and making sense of their lives as well as ignoring the coercive power of professional diagnostic categories. That said, listening with a diagnostic ear risks therapeutic violence as a person's experience is appraised in relation to an external 'big other' hegemonic norm, colonising it rather than seeking to understand it in local terms. A critical systemic approach involves curiosity (Cecchin 1987) and irreverence (Cecchin *et al.* 2010) about psychiatric labels. We ask what this or that use of 'autism' makes. For example, the autism industry as a whole contributes to making impairment-talk (talk about biomedical causes of loss or difference in an individual's functioning) rather than disability-talk (talk about problems encountered when a person with impairment attempts to take their place as a member of their community and encounters social, environmental and psycho-emotional barriers). More generally, critical therapists, acknowledging and responding to power, may hold open a space for marginalised stories of disability as culture, as spiritual, as socio-economic oppression and so on (Roosen 2009) and be sensitised to all forms of dis/ableism (Goodley 2014). Therapists may play their part in expanding stories of disabled life, holding diagnostic hegemony to account and resisting the ever-shrinking parameters of the normal. In sum, systemic therapists and other professionals might ask themselves what kind of home is therapy going to be for ASC stories.

REFERENCES

Bateson, G. (1972) *Steps to an Ecology of Mind.* London: Ballantine Books.

Baum, S. (2007) 'The use of family therapy for people with learning disabilities.' *Advances in Mental Health and Learning Disabilities 1*, 8–13.

Baum, S., and Lynggaard, H. (eds) (2006) *Intellectual Disabilities – A Systemic Approach.* London: Karnac Books.

Burnham, J. (1992) 'Approach-Method-Technique: making distinctions and creating connections.' *Human Systems 3*, 1, 3–26.

Campbell, F.K. (2009) *Contours of Ableism.* Basingstoke: Palgrave Macmillan.

Campbell, T. (2014) 'The Political Anatomy of Ableism: Bio-Politics and the Numerical Plotting of the Population.' Keynote paper: 5th Annual International Conference, Theorising Normalcy and the Mundane: More Questions of the Human, University of Sheffield, 7–8 July.

Cecchin, G. (1987) 'Hypothesizing, circularity, and neutrality revisited: an invitation to curiosity.' *Family Process 26*, 4, 405–413.

Cecchin, G., Lane, G., and Ray, W. A. (2010) 'Eccentricity and intolerance: a systemic critique.' *Human Systems: The Journal of Therapy, Consultation and Training 21*, 1, 7–26.

Daynes, S., Doswell, S., Gregory, N., Haydon-Laurelut, M., and Millett, E. (2011) 'Emergent cake: a plurality of systemic practices.' *Context 114*, 21–25.

Fidell, B. (1996) 'Making family therapy user-friendly for learning disabled clients.' *Context 26*, 11–13.

Fidell, B. (2000) 'Exploring the use of family therapy with adults with learning disabilities.' *Journal of Family Therapy 22*, 308–323.

Gergen, K.J. (1999) *An Invitation To Social Construction.* Thousand Oaks, CA: Sage.

Goodley, D. (2014) *Dis/ability Studies: Theorising Disablism and Ableism.* London: Routledge.

Hacking, I. (2009) 'Autistic autobiography.' *Philosophical Transactions of the Royal Society B: Biological Sciences 364,* 1522, 1467–1473.

Hatton, C. (2014) *A Place of Greater Safety? Risk and People with Learning Disabilities.* Available at www.chrishatton.blogspot.co.uk/2014/03/a-place-of-greater-safety-risk-and.html, accessed on 17 November 2015.

Haydon, M. (2009) 'Systemic therapy and the social-relational model of disability: enabling practices with adults with intellectual disability.' *Clinical Psychology and People with Learning Disabilities 7,* 6–13.

Haydon-Laurelut, M. (2013) 'Critical: Therapy and Disability.' Presented at 8th European Family Therapy Association Congress, Istanbul, Turkey, 24–27 October.

Haydon-Laurelut, M., and Nunkoosing, K. (2010) '"I want to be listened to": systemic psychotherapy with a man with intellectual disabilities and his paid supporters.' *Journal of Family Therapy 32,* 73–86.

Haydon-Laurelut, M., and Wilson, C. (2011) 'Interviewing the internalized other: attending to voices of the "other".' *Journal of Systemic Therapies 30,* 1, 24–37.

Haydon-Laurelut, M., Bissmire, D., and Hall, H. (2009) 'Systemic staff consultation in staffed accommodation – what do we mean by systemic? What do we mean by working systemically?' *Human Systems: The Journal of Therapy, Consultation and Training 20,* 35–50.

Hedges, F. (2005) *An Introduction to Systemic Therapy with Individuals: A Social Constructionist Approach.* London: Palgrave Macmillan.

Hoffman, L. (1990) 'Constructing realities: an art of lenses.' *Family Process 29,* 1, 1–12.

Jenkins, R., and Parry, R. (2006) 'Working with the support network: applying systemic practice in learning disabilities services.' *British Journal of Learning Disabilities 34,* 77–81.

Lang, P., and McAdam, E. (2014) 'Referrals, Referrers and the System of Concern: A Chapter about Good Beginnings.........Designed to Lead to Quicker Endings!' Available at www.taosinstitute.net/Websites/taos/Images/ResourcesManuscripts/McAdam-lang-%20Referrals,%20Referrers%20and%20the%20System.pdf, accessed on 17 November 2015.

Linington, M. (2002) '"Whose handicap?" Psychotherapy with people with learning disabilities.' *British Journal of Psychotherapy 18,* 3, 409–414.

Mallett, R., and Runswick-Cole, K. (2012) 'Commodifying Autism: The Cultural Contexts of "Disability" in the Academy.' In D. Goodley, B. Hughes and L.J. Davis (eds) *Disability and Social Theory.* Basingstoke: Palgrave Macmillan.

Michalko, R. (2012) 'Who does the WHO have in mind?' Keynote paper at Disability and the Majority World Seminar, Manchester Metropolitan University.

Michalko, R., and Titchkosky, T. (2009) 'Introduction.' In R. Michalko and T. Titchkosky (eds) *Rethinking Normalcy: A Disability Studies Reader.* Toronto, Ontario: Canadian Scholars' Press.

Migerode, L. (2009) 'What is a diagnosis? On "autism" in couple therapy.' *Human Systems: The Journal of Therapy, Consultation and Training 20,* 24–40.

Migerode, L., Vander Elst, L., and Rober, P. (2010) 'Speaking of autism in sessions of couple therapy.' *Human Systems: The Journal of Therapy, Consultation and Training 21,* 2, 270–284.

Munro, J.D. (2010) 'An integrated model of psychotherapy for teens and adults with Asperger Syndrome.' *Journal of Systemic Therapies 29,* 3, 82–96.

Oliver, M. (1990) *The Politics of Disablement.* Basingstoke: Macmillan.

Parsons, T., and Fox, R. (1952) 'Illness, therapy and the modern urban American family.' *Journal of Social Issues 8,* 4, 31–44.

Pearce, W.B. (1994) *Interpersonal Communication: Making Social Worlds.* London: Harper Collins.

Pearce, W.B. (1999) *Using CMM: The Coordinated Management of Meaning.* Available at www.pearceassociates.com/essays/cmm_seminar.pdf, accessed on 17 November 2015.

Pearce, W.B. (2007) *Making Social Worlds: A Communication Perspective.* Oxford: Wiley-Blackwell.

Pearce, W.B. (2011) At Home in the Universe with Miracles and Horizons: Reflections on Personal and Social Evolution. Available at http://pearceassociates.com/essays/documents/AtHomeintheUniversewithMiraclesandHorizonsv3-1.pdf, accessed on 21 January 2016.

Purdy, L. (2012) 'How to fail as a family therapist working with adults with learning disabilities: a paradoxical literature review.' *Journal of Family Therapy 34,* 419–430.

Roosen, K. (2009) 'From tragedy to "crip" to human: the need for multiple understandings of disability in psychotherapy.' *Critical Disability Discourse 1,* 1–25.

Rose, N.S. (1985) *The Psychological Complex: Psychology, Politics, and Society in England, 1869–1939.* London: Routledge and Kegan Paul.

Runswick-Cole, K. (2014) '"Us" and "them"? The limits and possibilities of a politics of neurodiversity in neoliberal times.' *Disability and Society 29,* 7, 1117–1129.

Selvini-Palazolli, M., Boscolo, L., Cecchin, G., and Prata, G. (1978) *Paradox and Counter-Paradox: A New Model in the Therapy of the Family in Schizophrenic Transaction.* London: Aronson.

Simon, G. (2004) 'Systemic family therapy with families with a child who has a diagnosis of Asperger Syndrome.' *Human Systems: The Journal of Systemic Consultation and Management 15,* 4, 257–274.

Timimi, S., Gardner, N., and McCabe, B. (2010) *The Myth of Autism: Medicalising Men's and Boys' Social and Emotional Competence.* Basingstoke: Palgrave Macmillan.

Webb-Peploe, H., and Fredman, G. (2015) 'Systemic empathy with adults affected by intellectual disabilities and their families.' *Journal of Family Therapy 37,* 2, 228–245.

White, M., and Epston, D. (1990) *Narrative Means to Therapeutic Ends.* Dulwich Centre, Adelaide, South Australia: Norton.

CHAPTER 13

CRITICAL AUTISM AND CRITICAL NEUROSCIENCE

TOWARDS A SCIENCE OF RESEARCH AND PRACTICE

Tom Billington

INTRODUCTION

> The whole place was wobbly and rockly with noise and everything was moving, there was big smells and all the things were different, it was full of dark noise and light noise and echoes and growly voices. (John, in Billington 2000, p.120)

John wrote this description of his experience of a school classroom aged nine which I incorporated originally within a psychological assessment. During the course of such assessments (in education and the family courts in England) it has seemed to me that the lexicon for exploring what we have been thinking of as autism and its place in the world is incomplete and often unsatisfactory. Professional discourses in autism have tended to position any young person diagnosed with autism not just as different but as deficient (see Diagnostic Criteria, DSM-5), as perhaps lacking in imagination, friendless, isolated, as a *less than* version of a human. This isolation, it is assumed, takes the form of a kind of non-permeable membrane supposedly existing between the young person and their (social, cultural) environment which somehow makes aspects of that environment unknowable to them, constructing the young person as knowable to others only in the context of their autism.

However, during professional practice, such a membrane, if it exists at all, often seemed highly permeable and the young person could on such occasions present not as isolated but as hypersensitive to their environment, for example, to sensory stimuli – sight, hearing, taste, smell and touch – and often to people. The young person could then seem to be almost overwhelmed by their experiences, when internalising aspects of the external world. A young person who had been

presenting as otherwise content could suddenly become so agitated/distressed/ excited by some kind of sensory stimulus in the environment (human or otherwise) that he or she would appear defenceless against the materiality of the sensation(s). The seemingly overwhelming nature of the sensations would prompt questions in me concerning the young person's experience, and I would be reminded of Freud's observation that 'protection against stimuli is an almost more important function for the living organism than reception of stimuli' (Freud [1920] 1984, p.299). However, while the young person might struggle to protect themselves, as a practitioner psychologist I have been well-wadded against such exploratory possibilities, armed with ways of talking or writing about autism which have been informed primarily by the authority of medicalised discourse (Billington 2006; Timimi, Gardner and McCabe 2010). I have long since come to see such authoritative discourse as a means by which, as a professional, I can defend myself and in the process obscure accounts which might engage with the young person's experience.

It is perhaps important for you as reader to know that from professional training through to practice as an educational and child psychologist, engagement with 'experience', either my own or the experience of 'clients' (for example, children, parents, teachers), has rarely been encouraged. This is not merely an ethical concern but also a scientific one since, while professional practice is supposedly built upon scientific principles, any scientific approach to consideration of experience or indeed relationships has been lacking. I have continued to aspire to scientific principles in practice of course, questioning, hypothesising, testing out, formulating and reformulating as part of any assessment. However, there has been an unhelpful disconnect between the theoretical models of the human implicit within clinical models of the person and the actual people with whom I have worked. (*Note:* My argument is that the customary model of science adopted is one which has been borrowed from the natural sciences and this is not always appropriate when contemplating persons – see Harré 2004.)

In addition, increasingly, assessment practices which allow themselves to be restricted by diagnostic discourse at the level of the individual have seemed inadequate (Billington 2000; Timimi *et al.* 2010) not least since the processes involved seem oblivious to external factors, for example the socio-cultural context, the processes of governmentality (Rose 1988) or indeed a human relationality (Gergen 2009). I have become dissatisfied therefore, in particular, with the incompleteness of the science and the failure to engage with what might be termed the human (Goodley and Runswick-Cole 2014), a position shared by other practising psychologists, for example:

> I discovered within a few years of earning my Doctorate that models of clinical practice based upon a scientific approach to practice were insufficient

(sometimes woefully inadequate) in assisting many of the clients with whom I worked. (Adams and Miller 2008, p.376)

Professional practices have tended to ignore more complex theoretical models of human relationality in favour of an individualised psychopathology. In this chapter I seek to challenge the biomedical model of autism and in the process encourage other kinds of professional activity; for example, I refer briefly to phenomenology (Bergson [1911] 1998; Rowlands 2010) and then neuroscience (Damasio 2011). Ultimately, however, I rely on an emerging critical approach to neuroscience in order to find ways of knowing which are sustained by a particular scientific attitude to practice, one which sees the human in the form of actual persons and which possesses a capacity for socio-political critique (Rose 2006; Rose and Abi-Rached 2013), not least since 'critical neuroscience emphasises the politics implicit in scientific practice' (Slaby and Choudhury 2012, p.31).

My motivation to write about autism, since first being 'hit in the stomach' (Fitzgerald 2013, p.134) by the realisation of what I was encountering, is a result of the 'clinical encounters' shared with the many young people with whom I have worked and who have been in receipt of the diagnosis (Costa and Shimp 2011).

PROFESSIONAL/RESEARCH PRACTICE

During early work as a practitioner, I became concerned that some professional accounts of autism might be unacceptable in terms of changing social mores – for example, regarding the ways in which professionals could disallow the 'voice' of young people – due to an inability to conceptualise persons and their experiences. I did not want to contribute to a process in which young people's difficulties were subject to discourses of deficit, but I certainly did not want to do this on the basis of what seemed to be an imperfect and incomplete knowledge base. The following five 'critical questions' arose out of that experience:

How do we speak of children?

How do we speak with children?

How do we write of children?

How do we listen to children?

How do we listen to ourselves (when working with children)?

(Billington 2006, p.8)

These questions have proved a useful resource in resisting the deficit discourses and also as a means of thinking about a more scientific approach to consideration of the relational processes implicated in the 'clinical encounters', in accordance

with Bion's dictum that 'the science of relationships has yet to be established' (Bion 1970, p.64).

However, too often in work with young people, their families and teachers, the narratives of a deficit model of autism being circulated in the processes of diagnosis are already so firmly established that it has been difficult to conceptualise any other aspects of the young person. Young people can all too easily be trapped in a process of 'classificatory looping' (Hacking 1995) in which all those surrounding them are engulfed by conceptually restricted accounts of autism and which the young person might ultimately imbibe: 'classification can be taken up into the self-understanding of those classified' (Choudhury and Slaby 2012, p.8).

I found that, as a practitioner, once I engaged, not with a young person, but primarily with conventional autistic narratives, I closed down opportunities for developing or keeping alive all kinds of other stories, other selves, which the conventional autism narrative could deny. Accessing and deploying new critical materials thus became crucial to the ways in which I was evaluating my practice. This chapter is part of that self-evaluation, a further attempt to find alternative ways of addressing the above five 'critical questions'. The following extracts taken from earlier research (Billington 2000) provide an example of how, as a practitioner psychologist, I could look beyond the confines of a narrow understanding of a non-human 'science' in order to engage with other possibilities, of 'transforming scars into data' (Stengers 2011, p.310).

Jim

During my visit to Jim's home on a cold winter's evening, he stood quietly at the window and stared out at the darkness. The moon was bright but my memory recalls that as we gazed together at the heavens Jim spoke briefly of the distances between earth and various other objects in the night sky. He seemed to be conceptualising space in an attempt to locate himself within an external world of objects but in the process demonstrating the capacity to engage meaningfully with his surroundings. The qualitative nature of such experiential possibilities would invariably be beyond the scope of most autism or behaviour-specific checklists, yet the intensity of his participation in our sparse conversation suggested that we were sharing a meaningful engagement to which we were both contributing spontaneously.

The occasion I recollect was characterised by a calmness and thoughtfulness on Jim's part, which had been little in evidence at his school. Of course, the

situation was one with many variables. I had already met Jim several times; familiar objects at home surrounded him, and I had developed a warm relationship with his parents over a period of time. I wondered what a different, arguably more scientific approach to practice with persons would look like in this otherwise most human, most intrinsically social of scenarios?

Tom

Tom was six years old and had received his diagnosis of autism about four years previously. His parents, Bridget and Cary, were said to be unhappy about Tom's special school and at our first meeting I encouraged them to talk. During a number of subsequent meetings they expressed their sense of frustration, which was not only due to the sheer practical difficulties of living with their son, but also due to the difficult experiences they had had in working with professionals. The parents were concerned, not just by day-to-day management issues caused by Tom's behaviour but also about a problem caused by professionals. Bridget and Cary simply did not want to *see* Tom in the way that some of the professionals were seeing him and nor did they want to *talk* about him in the way that some professionals were talking about him (Billington, McNally and McNally 2000). To Bridget and Cary, Tom was far more than a psychopathology, an agglomeration of deficits, or indeed a suitable subject for a behavioural analysis; he was their son who possessed all kinds of individual qualities and characteristics which they recognised and which prompted in them different emotions and feelings.

During the visit to Tom's special school, I observed that the class housed far too many children, many of whom were presenting the adults with major management problems. The children, all of whom had some kind of significant special need, at times moved around the small class space in a seemingly haphazard fashion and the noise could be unbearable. Tom meanwhile had found his own solution to the assaults on his sensory (auditory) equilibrium. At first sight he seemed cocooned, isolated from his environment, and gave no sign whatsoever of any kind of sensory recognition relating to anyone or anything in his surroundings. However, when introduced to the quiet rattling sound made by one of his favourite toy cars, he turned his head immediately. So Tom *could* hear. Also, in his own movements about the class, Tom's unerring ability to avoid collisions without actually looking directly at any obstacle indicated that he could also see. He was thus being selective in his attention, choosing to acknowledge or ignore, accept or reject. His sensory information processing thus seemed located in a personal sense of time and space which was inherently psychological and emotional, since he appeared to be taking steps to protect himself from the sensory overload which may have been a source of distress.

Some initial reflections

Such observations do not appear immediately to assist in managing the learning or behaviour of either Jim or Tom; especially, should behaviour or learning objectives be required to address simplistic targets, stripped of meaning or quality. However, while there are good practical reasons not to reject simple target-setting, we should not overlook the possibility of a different kind of professional attitude. It is argued here that a finer, more sophisticated balance needs to be achieved between what, for example, a professional can claim to know ('knowledge') and what he or she might experience, which (currently at least) lies beyond the scrutiny of any traditional scientific method.

Just as Jim seemed to be fascinated by conceptualisations of his place in the cosmos, so Tom was attempting to function in relation to the space in which he found himself. They had both, in their own ways, exhibited an awareness of aspects of their environment and their responses reflected an understanding of some inner principles of action in time and space. While the examples cited here could be dismissed as mere narratives, the brief accounts suggest possibilities for how, as practitioners or researchers, we might fine-tune our understandings of the ways in which some young people diagnosed as autistic might be engaging with the world and experiencing their lives.

PHENOMENOLOGY AND NEUROSCIENCE

> Minds emerge from process and interaction, not substance. In a sense we inhabit the spaces between things. (Broks 2003, p.56)

Henri Bergson was a phenomenological philosopher who was sceptical about the capacity of a purely positivist science to answer the most profound of questions relating to the nature and peculiarity of human lives. He was more interested in the kinds of human inquiry which were less amenable to measurement and thus critical of attempts to apply such techniques in situations for which it was ill-equipped:

> Physics, whose particular function it is to calculate the external cause of our internal states, takes the least possible interest in those states themselves... (Bergson [1913] 2001, p.70)

Bergson believed that all we can do is measure the space between objects or events and that in the process we fail to engage with the experiential phenomena of the human lives which exist in these very spaces – in between the points of measurement. In addition, any consciousness is in-relation-to the existential presence of others and thus beyond simple measurement. Margaret Lock (Lock

and Nguyen 2010) considered 'conventional dichotomies between the "inside" and "outside" of the human body' (Slaby and Choudhury 2012, p.33) and in the process challenged traditional assumptions about individual personhoods, the self and, not least, our supposedly bounded minds and bodies. Indeed, arguments borrowed both from contemporary phenomenological philosophy and critical neuroscience would suggest that the experiences of Jim and Tom would, as for all, depend not only on the interdependence of mind and body but also on the influence upon them as organisms by dynamic external forces.

An emerging principle in critical neuroscience is that 'mental life requires more than the brain' (Kirmayer and Gold 2012, p.314). A concept, which some philosophers and neuroscientists have been focusing upon, is the '4ea' model of mind, which attempts to account for mental phenomena and their interdependence on both internal and external processes. For example, it is suggested that 'embodied' mind is made up of wider extra-neural structures and processes within the body; that mind is 'embedded', functioning in a specific environment; that mind is 'enacted' in the world; and that mind is 'extended' in ways which are taken into, and received from, the environment (see Gallagher 2005; Rowlands 2010). Finally, mind is considered as inherently and unavoidably 'affective' (i.e. emotional; Protevi 2009) not least since 'minds without emotion are not really minds at all' (Le Doux 1998, p.25).

Contemporary neuroscience has fast been expanding the scope of its activities and the technology exists now to provide a window into the inner biological workings of the brain (for example, Le Doux 1998; Linden 2007; Rose 2006; Zeki 2009). Indeed, the knowledge it is producing may make important contributions to individual wellbeing in the future. Damasio (2011), for example, provides detailed and iridescent analyses of the neurobiological processes of the brain and makes a number of helpful distinctions, for example between brain (as a material part of the organism) and mind (as process). However, while the forms of knowledge neuroscience is producing may make important contributions to individual wellbeing in the future, Damasio usefully challenges the Cartesian legacy that for humans thinking takes primacy (which has been the assumption of most research and practice in the human sciences) and instead, like Le Doux and others, has begun to see that it is emotion which has as an a priori function at all points within the temporality and spatiality of mind.

Damasio is insistent that any underlying unity within mind is 'the secret behind the "binding" of separate regions [of the brain] by space and time... timing may well be key to relating' (Damasio 2011, p.87). However, he proposes that the map-making processes of mind are not merely cognitive, narrowly conceived, since 'map-making brains have the power of literally introducing the body as content into the mind process' (Damasio 2011, p.89).

While there are pressures which have been directing neuroscience to construct itself according to narrow Cartesian principles, some neuroscientists are being attracted outside the conventional boundaries of their science. For example, in tracing the origins of the very particular forms of investigation adopted in the human sciences back to Descartes, Damasio challenges the self-imposed limitations of scientific approaches that are predicated on a necessary schism between mind and body (Damasio 1994; see also Ryle 1949). He acknowledges his debt to Spinoza ([1677] 1989), the philosopher who, three centuries previously, had testified as to their indissolubility (Damasio 2004).

Damasio challenges what he regards as the Cartesian schism between mind and body and does so by suggesting that mind-map processes are intrinsically imbued with sensorily-informed emotionality which we in turn process into human feelings: 'how perceptual maps are felt and experienced – is not only central to the understanding of the conscious mind, it is integral to that understanding' (Damasio 2011, p.101). Damasio's ideas link to those of Bergson in seeing our 'emotional state unfolding in time' (Damasio 2011, p.111). Time, space and emotionality are thus inextricably linked in both phenomenology and neuroscience as processes of mind, underpinning our experience of ourselves, whether neuro- or a-typical.

Contemporary neuroscience is currently host to a number of important conceptual dichotomies. For example, the nature–nurture debate is constantly revisited, and there is often uncertainty as to whether any 'neurological discrepancies are a cause or an effect of the disordered behaviour' (Timimi *et al.* 2010, p.122). There are also problems in containing the activities of the brain within the 'modular' structure which would make analysis and categorisation much more straightforward for diagnosticians. For example, 'different people may use different regions of the brain to solve the same task, making the idea of localising functions...very difficult' (Timimi *et al.* 2010, p.132). Indeed, the discourses of an astonishing interconnectivity permeate many neuroscientific accounts of the brain and thus resist any simplistic psychological categorisation; while a focusing upon a neural plasticity likewise challenges any reductionist attempts to fix any model of mind/brain in the form of a static, non-dynamic and thus non-changeable psychopathology. The importance of the environment, of socio-historical context, and the dynamic nature of the functions of the brain seem to be creating an approach to knowledge which is intolerant of old ways of constructing psychopathology, but is rather an approach to knowing which can tolerate the notion that 'the genome is a linear and stable sequence [while] the brain is a dynamic structure organised in three dimensions of space and one of time' (Rose 2012, p.55).

CRITICAL NEUROSCIENCE

> We agree with Ian Hacking that science, medicine, education and other institutions and powerful areas of social practice and policy are key contributors in 'creating' kinds of people. (Choudhury and Slaby 2012, p.8)

Neuroscience is being used increasingly to inform understandings of what it is to be human in almost the same way that psychology had been doing previously during the last one hundred years or so. Media reports are now frequently found to be claiming to reveal the 'infant brain', the 'adolescent brain', but perhaps more problematically, the 'ADHD brain', the 'brain of an abused or neglected infant', or indeed the 'autistic brain'. The technology now exists to picture both our brains and our bodies – computerised axial tomography (CAT scans), positron emission tomography (PET scans) and functional magnetic resonance imaging (fMRI). Neuroscience has thus been extending the scope of its activities beyond the brain to consideration of the whole body and indeed beyond, to the 'conditions' in which it functions, for 'the brain is not the sole producer of the mind but a relational organ that mediates the interaction between the organism and its complementary environment' (Fuchs 2012, p.341).

The nature of popular headline claims made on behalf of neuroscience reinforces an over-zealous reductionism in attempts to seduce the reader to believe that the brain images produced by scanning are realist accounts of the person. What we actually see in such images are, of course, invariably not real brains but mere images, representations of a brain which are the products, not solely of a scientific inquiry, but also of a creative partnership in which algorithms of brain functioning are transformed into media artefacts by artists and designers of computer graphics. Even before we begin to critique the nature of the science, therefore, we need to make a conscious effort to critique first the actual technologies being used, their strengths and limitations, and second, the techniques being used to represent the inner workings of brain and body, for any representations are just that, mere 'images...[which are] consciously selected to enhance the textual argument' (Dumit 2012, p.219).

Dumit (2012) informs us that the images of brains we see in popular culture are invariably not actual brains, of course, but representations, texts which have been produced and which can be read in much the same way as this book, and thus subject to different principles of reading and interpretation. The schism between the actual brains and the means by which those brains are represented thus provides a space which allows for all kinds of other ideas about the human to be inserted. These ideas will be shaped, not just by neutral science, but also by cultural, social, political and economic forms of influence – by ideology.

There is an even further distance to cover should we seek to fill the void between the compelling coloured images of electrical activity in the brain and

the actual experience or feelings of the person, which remain even less accessible to forms of scientific empiricism. Indeed, 'neuroscience lets us down. Somehow, bursts of electricity in the wetware of the brain don't seem adequate to the exquisitely structured mind that I, and you, have' (Tallis 2008, p.158). While contemporary neuroscience has access to technologies of which previous generations of philosophers, scholars and scientists could scarcely have dreamt, the technologies have located, not mind, only brains; indeed, a crucial distinction is made since some neuroscientists claim that 'mind is a process not a thing' (Damasio 2004, p.183).

However, the pursuit of the 'normal' still remains strong in this new science. Allied disciplines which have constructed themselves upon deficit models of the human are likely to be attracted by the emerging knowledge, in particular those disciplines which are linked to processes that can lead to various kinds of social exclusion – cultural, political or economic. Psychology, for example, will find the promise of revitalised accounts of the ideal human difficult to resist and the old psychopathologising tendency will then be waiting to reassert itself, to reinforce epistemological boundaries and to diminish the narrative accounts of persons to deficits. There are many difficulties remaining in translations between neuroscientific accounts and the category, but there is also a need for vigilance, not least regarding the danger that the 'textual manipulation of imaging texts, if without challenge, will permit an otherwise untheorised collapse from scan to diagnosis' (Dumit 2012, p.221).

'Neuroscience is increasingly being called upon to build prescriptions about how to live' (Choudhury and Slaby 2012, p.5) and the tendency is for an expectation that contemporary science will be able to 'reveal' the disordered brain and to create models of the person in the forms of categories by comparison with some notion of the ideal human. There is thus a danger that neuroscientists in the future, as psychologists in the past, will merely create 'a baseline definition of "normal" [which is actually] both a physiological and a social judgment' (Dumit 2012, p.200). Should this again prove to be the case, new ideals or models of personhood will be created from which future generations of young people, as those before, will be at risk of becoming medicalised and diagnosed, excluded and 'othered', that is, as imperfect humans. Any ideas we might have as to what is 'normal', therefore, need to be argued not only by neuroscientists but also by social scientists and, not least, I argue here, by those who will be at the receiving end of such theories.

With this in mind I take the view that critical neuroscience could perform a useful function and, in particular, might usefully 'renew(s) the possibility for critical commentators to be engaged with, rather than estranged from, laboratory science' (Slaby and Choudhury 2012, p.42). Indeed, 'a comprehensive understanding of the nature of the human mind and behavior is impoverished

without a theoretical and empirical approach that incorporates…multiple layers of analysis' (Chiao and Cheon 2012, p.290).

FINAL REFLECTIONS FOR RESEARCH AND PRACTICE

I have argued: 1) that there have been theoretical constraints upon the ways in which autistic mind and experience can be conceptualised; 2) that professional discourses (practitioner and research) have evolved on the basis of an incomplete and sometimes inappropriate kind of scientific activity; and 3) that the theoretical resources upon which professionals have been expected to base their work with young autistic people and their families have been limited because they have failed to engage with the *quality* of human experience.

Neuroscience has been reminding us that processes of mind are beyond measurement, since they are 'constructing qualities' (Damasio 2011, p.97). I argue that in relation to Jim and Tom it was more important that I remained committed to their *qualities*, not as autistic, but as human beings in shared moments of time and space, in their home or school. Damasio, Tallis, Rose and other neuroscientists have made explicit not only a distinction between brain and mind (as process), but also a connectivity between our brain and bodies – in mind. They point towards the importance of avoiding the pitfalls of a 'neuroreductionism…[and want to ensure that] human beings are not thought of as identical with their brains' (Rose and Abi-Rached 2013, p.163).

There is a long tradition in philosophy both before Bergson (for example, Spinoza) and after (Gilbert Ryle and more recently Mark Rowlands) in which the study of what it is to be human has endeavoured to tolerate a sensory model that is intrinsically connected to our affective lives. To Bergson and Damasio there would be an umbilical cord between our emotionality and our processes of mind and a belief in a lived experience that eludes measurement through its existence in time and space.

Bridget and Cary had known that their son, Tom, was suffering in class. As professionals we had not utilised theoretical resources which were sufficiently sensitive to respond to the parents' belief that Tom was exhausted by his efforts to cope with the distress of existing in the time and space of his classroom.

While direct communication was still difficult for Jim, during this particular observation he tolerated his sensory world and processed the feelings experienced during those moments of more conventional social interaction and shared attention. Jim was beginning to behave differently in response to his own experience, using spoken language to express his thoughts and feelings in relation to the time and space of his experiential being.

The professional mode adopted with these two boys was not one of technician or diagnostician but that of a theoretically inquisitive practitioner, resisting any mere busy-ness or utilitarianism. I argue that both practitioners and researchers need to be sensitive to matters of time, space and experience in order that any future work can be based on more sophisticated understandings of relational quality and of affective human personhoods. Approaches to critical autism and critical neuroscience could support the development of scientifically informed research and practice which does not shirk from the conundrum posed so eloquently by John's experience of the classroom described at the start of this chapter and captured here by the neuroscientist:

> There is an abyss between [our] knowledge and [their] experience that cannot be bridged scientifically. (Damasio 2000, p.308)

REFERENCES

Adams, J.B., and Miller, R.B. (2008) 'Bridging psychology's scientist vs. practitioner divide: fruits of a twenty-five year dialogue.' *Journal of Theoretical and Philosophical Psychology 28*, 2, 375–394.

Bergson, H. [1911] (1998) *Creative Evolution.* New York: Dover.

Bergson, H. [1913] (2001) *Time and Free Will: An Essay on the Immediate Data of Consciousness.* New York: Dover.

Billington, T. (2000) *Separating, Losing and Excluding Children: Narratives of Difference.* London: Routledge Falmer.

Billington, T. (2006) 'Working with autistic children and young people: sense, experience and the challenges for services, policies and practices.' *Disability and Society 21*, 1, 1–13.

Billington, T., McNally, B., and McNally, C. (2000) 'Autism: working with parents and discourse in experience, expertise and learning.' *Educational Psychology in Practice 16*, 1, 59–68.

Bion, W. (1970) *Attention and Interpretation.* London: Karnac.

Broks, P. (2003) *Into the Silent Land: Travels in Neuropsychology.* London: Atlantic.

Chiao, J.Y., and Cheon, B.K. (2012) 'Cultural Neuroscience as Critical Neuroscience in Practice.' In S. Choudhury and J. Slaby (eds) *Critical Neuroscience: A Handbook of the Social and Cultural Contexts of Neuroscience.* Chichester: Wiley-Blackwell.

Costa, R.E., and Shimp, C.P. (2011) 'Methods course and texts in psychology: "Textbook science" and "tourist brochures".' *Journal of Theoretical and Philosophical Psychology 31*, 1, 25–43.

Choudhury, S., and Slaby, J. (eds) (2012) *Critical Neuroscience: A Handbook of the Social and Cultural Contexts Of Neuroscience.* Chichester: Wiley-Blackwell.

Damasio, A. (1994) *Descartes' Error: Emotion, Reason and the Human Brain.* New York: Quill.

Damasio, A. (2000) *The Feeling of What Happens: Body, Emotion and the Making of Consciousness.* London: Vintage.

Damasio, A. (2004) *Looking for Spinoza.* London: Vintage.

Damasio, A. (2011) *Self Comes to Mind: Constructing the Conscious Brain.* London: Vintage.

Dumit, J. (2012) 'Critically Producing Brain Images of Mind.' In S. Choudhury and J. Slaby (eds) *Critical Neuroscience: A Handbook of the Social and Cultural Contexts of Neuroscience.* Chichester: Wiley-Blackwell.

Fitzgerald, D. (2013) 'The affective labour of autism neuroscience: entangling emotions, thoughts and feelings in a scientific research practice.' *Subjectivity 6*, 2, 131–152.

Freud, S. [1920] (1984) *Beyond the Pleasure Principle: On Metapsychology.* London: Penguin.

Fuchs, T. (2012) 'Are Mental Illnesses Diseases of the Brain?' In S. Choudhury and J. Slaby (eds) *Critical Neuroscience: A Handbook of the Social and Cultural Contexts of Neuroscience.* Chichester: Wiley-Blackwell.

Gallagher, S. (2005) *How the Body Shapes the Mind.* Oxford: Oxford University Press.

Gergen, K. (2009) *Relational Being: Beyond Self and Community.* Oxford: Oxford University Press.

Goodley, D., and Runswick-Cole, K. (2014) *Becoming Dishuman: Thinking about the Human through Dis/ability.* Discourse: Cultural Politics of Education. Open Access. Available at www.mcgill.ca/igsf/files/igsf/becoming_dishuman_copy-libre.pdf, accessed on 17 November 2015.

Hacking, I. (1995) 'The Looping Effect of Human Kinds.' In D. Spencer and A.J. Premack (eds) *Causal Cognition.* Oxford: Oxford University Press.

Harré, R. (2004) 'Staking our claim for qualitative psychology as science.' *Qualitative Research in Psychology 1*, 1, 3–14.

Kirmayer, L., and Gold, I. (2012) 'Re-socializing Psychiatry: Critical Neuroscience and the Limits of Reductionism.' In S. Choudhury and J. Slaby (eds) *Critical Neuroscience: A Handbook of the Social and Cultural Contexts of Neuroscience.* Chichester: Wiley-Blackwell.

Le Doux, J. (1998) *The Emotional Brain.* London: Phoenix.

Linden, D. (2007) *The Accidental Mind: How Brain Evolution Has Given Us Love, Memory, Dreams and God.* Cambridge, MA: Belknap Harvard.

Lock, M., and Nguyen, V.K. (2010) *An Anthropology of Biomedicine.* Chichester/Oxford: Wiley-Blackwell.

Protevi, J. (2009) *Political Affect: Connecting the Social and the Somatic.* Minneapolis; MN: University of Minnesota Press.

Rose, N. (1988) *Governing the Soul: The Shaping of the Private Self.* London: Routledge.

Rose, N., and Abi-Rached, J-M. (2013) *Neuro: The New Brain Sciences and the Management of Mind.* Princeton, NJ: Princeton University Press

Rose, S. (2006) *The 21st Century Brain: Explaining, Mending And Manipulating The Mind.* London: Vintage.

Rose, S. (2012) 'The Need for a Critical Neuroscience: From Neuroideology to Neurotechnology.' In S. Choudhury and J. Slaby (eds) *Critical Neuroscience: A Handbook of the Social and Cultural Contexts of Neuroscience.* Chichester: Wiley-Blackwell.

Rowlands, M. (2010) *The New Science of Mind: From Extended Mind to Embodied Phenomenology.* Boston, MA: MIT Press.

Ryle, G. (1949) *Concept of Mind.* London: Penguin.

Slaby, J., and Choudhury, S. (2012) 'Proposal for a Critical Neuroscience.' In S. Choudhury and J. Slaby (eds) *Critical Neuroscience: A Handbook of the Social and Cultural Contexts of Neuroscience.* Chichester: Wiley-Blackwell.

Spinoza [1677] (1989) *Ethics.* Trans. G.H.R. Parkinson. London: Dent.

Stengers, I. (2011) *Thinking with Whitehead: A Free and Wild Creation Of Concepts.* Cambridge, MA: Harvard University Press.

Tallis, R. (2008) *The Kingdom Of Infinite Space: A Fantastical Journey around Your Head.* London: Atlantic.

Timimi, S., Gardner, N., and McCabe, B. (2010) *The Myth of Autism: Medicalising Men's and Boys' Social and Emotional Competence.* London: Palgrave Macmillan.

Zeki, S. (2009) *The Splendours and Miseries of the Brain: Love, Creativity and the Quest For Human Happiness.* Chichester: Wiley-Blackwell.

CHAPTER 14

EARLY DIAGNOSIS OF AUTISM
IS EARLIER ALWAYS BETTER?

Ginny Russell

INTRODUCTION

In the medical literature, earlier diagnosis of autism and accompanied early intervention is uncritically equated with 'better' than late diagnosis and no intervention. The chapter will set out three reservations to the early diagnosis/ intervention paradigm.

First, although the rationale for diagnosis given in these arguments is that intervention is essential for improved outcomes, the literature on effectiveness of early intervention for children with autism is far from conclusive. Some methods seem to work for some children some of the time, but often at huge time investment. Methodologies of assessing benefits are frequently flawed. Finally, both the autism community and the scientific establishment have sometimes denounced previous interventions as inappropriate.

Second, there are some studies that show that children with serious symptoms of autism may improve to subclinical levels as they mature without intervention. It is difficult to tell at very young ages which children will go on to have lifelong difficulties, and the younger the child, the more difficult it is to differentiate.

Third, there are potential iatrogenic effects and other inadvertent negative effects from attaching diagnostic labels to children. The early diagnosis/ intervention paradigm springs from the notion of 'plasticity', that there are sensitive periods of brain development early in a child's life, and it is important to intervene before these windows have closed. However, the same notion of plasticity could be applied to any negative consequences of diagnostic labelling: an early label of autism may affect a very young child more. I will also briefly discuss the function of autism diagnosis from a parent's point of view.

To conclude, when interventions are not proven, and when iatrogenic effects of labelling are not disproven, the benefits of the early intervention paradigm for childhood developmental disorders should be questioned, at least until there is concrete evidence of real benefit.

RATIONALE FOR EARLY DIAGNOSIS OF AUTISM

Early intervention and diagnosis for Autism Spectrum Disorder (here referred to simply as autism) has become a recognised research priority. The implicit assumption behind much research is that the earlier a diagnosis of autism is made (in other words, the younger the child's age when diagnosis is made), the better (Crais *et al.* 2006; Filipek *et al.* 2000). Early intervention aims to ameliorate development of symptoms of autism, so that intervention minimises the development of impaired communication, promotes social interaction and minimises repetitive behaviour in children. Language acquisition and the promotion of cognitive and functional skills are often secondary goals. The early intervention paradigm is emphasised across many child health conditions, and for autism, the importance of early intervention is the consensus view. This quote from the book *Overcoming Autism* reiterates this point:

> I can't stress strongly enough the importance of diving into action immediately. Every expert in the field agrees that early intervention is essential and critical. The 'wait and see' approach is detrimental to your child. Children with autism tend to avoid things that are difficult, and communication is difficult for them, so they avoid situations where they might be expected to communicate. As a result, they become more isolated and withdrawn. So it's critical that you get a program started right way. (Koegel and LaZebnik 2005, p.38)

Many autism studies have put early identification of autism as a core objective (Watson *et al.* 2007). Guidelines from health institutions and charities also push the early diagnosis/intervention agenda. For example, Autistica's report *One in a Hundred* emphasises the importance of diagnosis at the youngest possible age, and promotes early intervention (Wallace, Parr and Herd 2012). Autistica is a charity which funds medical research to understand the causes of autism, improve diagnosis, and develop new treatments and interventions. Their report is fairly typical of policy guidelines released in the United Kingdom and United States.

In her very thoughtful analysis McGuire (2013) describes how slow development and/or developmental delay of autism is framed as an underlying biomedical problem that must be corrected as early as possible as it threatens the productivity of neoliberal societies. She shows how far the notion of early intervention as crucial has travelled into the public realm: in 2007, Starbucks released five million takeaway coffee cups across North America displaying a statement from Autism Speaks, a parent-led charity that aims to cure autism. The statement read as follows:

> Every 20 minutes – less time than it will take you to drink your coffee – another child is diagnosed with autism. It's much more common than

> people think, with one out of every 150 children diagnosed. Learn the early warning signs of autism, and if you're concerned about your child's development, talk to your doctor. Early intervention could make a big difference in your child's future. (Autism Speaks 2007, cited in McGuire 2013)

McGuire argues that the statement works to produce the non-normatively developing child as non-valuable and, perhaps even, as non-viable in the contemporary market-driven economy. It certainly illustrates the point that early intervention is the received wisdom and accepted as imperative in the public domain.

The reason early diagnosis is recommended for autism in particular is connected to the concept of developmental plasticity. Plasticity only occurs during an age-limited developmental stage in the early life of the child when he/she has the ability to acquire a particular skill, which can influence later development (Dennis 2000). It is a well-established concept in the case of the acquisition of language and the development of the visual cortex, with both human and animal studies showing that limiting environmental stimuli leads to lack of brain development. Developmental plasticity means that children are attuned to learning; and generally speaking, younger children are more responsive, and the younger the child, the less fixed a developmental pathway may be. Neuroplasticity describes how experiences reorganise neural pathways in the brain. Long-lasting functional changes in the brain occur when children learn new skills. The concept of developmental plasticity is a conspicuous theme in child development, and it establishes an early time frame in which deterministic shaping of neural networks is carried out.

After sensitive periods in development, plasticity diminishes as a result of changes in the structure or function of developing neural circuits. Language development, for example, undergoes a so-called 'critical period' between the ages of one and six years (White *et al.* 2013). A sensitive period in development is a similar, but less well defined by time, period which begins and ends gradually, and constitutes a period of maximum sensitivity to acquisition of social skills, language acquisition, and sensory and motor abilities. The idea of a sensitive period was popularised by many developmental psychologists and educators in the early twentieth century, including Maria Montessori in her influential book *The Absorbent Mind*, which is still in print (Montessori [1949] 2009).

From birth until about the age of six, children become skilled at numerous activities without formal instruction. According to supporters of the idea of critical periods, this occurs because it is very easy for children to acquire certain abilities during a specific period. Also, once a period is passed, the development of the brain has progressed past the point where that specific ability can be easily

attained. After this, the ability must be formally taught, it will take effort to learn and will not be as readily acquired by the child (Knudsen 2004). Language acquisition is the classic example: children who are not exposed to language before a set developmental stage will miss the window of opportunity to acquire it (Snow and Hoefnagel-Höhle 1978). Likewise, an early child–parent attachment period is thought to be crucial for later social development of the infant (Pastor 1981). Research suggests that children who have not developed strong attachment as infants have major difficulty with social skills and relationships later (Bohlin, Hagekull and Rydell 2000). Although Bowlby's theory of attachment as a cause of autism (see Bettelheim's 'refrigerator mother' theory, 1967) has now been discredited, early diagnosis and intervention for a child with autism is still seen as crucial. Autism is described by some as a 'critical period disorder' (LeBlanc and Fagiolini 2011). One underlying conviction is that intervention for autism should take place before critical age-dependent periods of development have passed and abnormal developmental pathways become fixed (Zoghbi 2003), hence, in this reading, early diagnosis is crucial.

Early intervention is a concept and form of practice that plays a key role in major public health, mental health, and educational policies in the UK and the USA. However, little attention has been paid to how cultural contexts change considerations of the ethics of early intervention. Early diagnosis is widely endorsed for autism because it is assumed that the younger the child, the more chances there are of succeeding with treatment. Treatments take the form of highly structured behavioural programmes such as Applied Behaviour Analysis (ABA), Speech and Language Therapy, Occupational Therapy, the Picture Exchange Communication System (PECS), Alternative and Augmentative Communication (AAC), Sensory Integration Therapy and the school-based Treatment and Education of Autistic and Related Communication Handicapped Children (TEACCH) method. The belief is that the earlier the diagnosis is made, the greater the chances of success in 'normalising' a child's developmental trajectory, before windows of opportunity have closed.

RECENT TRENDS

Over the last twenty years, the age at which autism diagnosis is made in children has been pushed earlier and earlier (Parner, Schendel and Thorsen 2008). One US study has shown the prevalence of autism increasing rapidly between 1997 and 2003, with a simultaneous drop in the mean age of children's autism diagnosis (Liu, King and Bearman 2010). It is not uncommon for children as young as 18 months old to receive an autism diagnosis in the USA (Hertz-Picciotto and Delwiche 2009), and an autism diagnosis at age two is not unusual in the UK (Jick and Kaye 2003). Some research now claims that babies as young as eight months

old can be identified with symptoms of autism (Ibañez, Grantz and Messinger 2013), and other studies claim that children can be identified with autism aged six months, four months or even at birth (Teitelbaum *et al.* 1998). Teitelbaum and colleagues claim that early behaviour indicating autism 'are present at birth and that they can be used to diagnose the presence of autism in the first few months of life' (Teitelbaum *et al.* 1998, p.13982). They claim that their findings 'indicate the need for the development of methods of therapy to be applied from the first few months of life in autism' (Teitelbaum *et al.* 1988, p.13982).

The first studies describing how autism emerges during infancy were based on home videotapes recorded before a diagnosis of autism was made, for example based on early differences in social attention. Many have utilised non-blinded rating of children's behaviours in the light of a known research diagnosis, a practice which is questionable (e.g. Maestro *et al.* 2002). Often studies use developmental screening tools such as the First Year Inventory, a retrospective parent-report questionnaire to identify infants at 12 months who might be at risk for autism. However, parents' retrospective recall may be inaccurate as it could be influenced by later diagnosis (Russell *et al.* 2014). Frequently, children who are identified as at risk for autism by parents are invited for in-person diagnostic evaluations. Typically, findings of studies that seek to identify the early signs of autism are described as 'promising' (e.g. Dawson 2008) and advocate early screening as a way to identify infants who are 'at risk' for a diagnosis of autism (e.g. Woods and Wetherby 2003). Landa (2008, p.138), describes how 'early detection of – and intervention to treat – autism is crucial because it is likely to lead to an improved outcome'. An improved outcome for autism would be an increase in social-communication ability which is seen in a group who are given the specific intervention versus less improvement in the group who are not.

Some US organisations are now pushing for population-wide screening for autism in children as young as 18 months. For example, the American Academy of Pediatrics (2010) recommends that physicians routinely screen for autism at this age. These calls are apparently well supported by research, which is sometimes financed by parent-led charities. For example, the charity Autism Speaks provides financial backing for:

> new methods for early detection and more effective treatments… Prevention will entail detecting infants at risk before the full syndrome is present and implementing treatments designed to alter the course of early behavioural and brain development. (Dawson 2008, p.775)

The underlying assumptions made in much of the early diagnosis literature seem to be:

1. There is a fixed core disorder called autism that is present from birth and can be correctly identified soon after birth.
2. Treatment and amelioration of symptoms is a desirable outcome.
3. Early intervention is effective.
4. Those children identified early as autistic will not 'get better' without intervention.
5. Diagnosis itself will not have a negative impact on children and their families.

I have caveats to the last three of these assumptions. The first two are outside the scope of this chapter but have been discussed elsewhere in this book.

Caveat 1: Is early intervention for autism effective?

The rationale for early diagnosis of any child developmental disorder assumes that once children are correctly identified with an underlying disorder, appropriate interventions can be put into place to treat symptoms of that disorder (Committee on Children with Disabilities 2001). From a medical perspective, the goals of treatment for autism and other developmental disabilities are delineated clearly by several guidelines. The US paediatrics guideline cited above describes the goals of autism intervention thus:

> To improve the overall functional status of the child by promoting the development of communication, social, adaptive, behavioral, and academic skills. (American Academy of Pediatrics 2010, p.1225)

Interventions for autism are not normally pharmaceutical but generally take the form of behavioural interventions and, later in life, increased educational resources. 'Symptoms' of autism, of course, are behaviours also. Autism diagnosis is often framed as a way for parents and children to access important health and educational services and other forms of support (Russell and Norwich 2012). Mansell and Morris (2004) provide a useful summary of typical interventions and services that are adopted after an autism diagnosis is given in the UK. These include extra educational support in the classroom or special schooling, parents' support groups, speech and language therapists, school psychologists, psychiatrists, respite care and focused access to information such as books and academic journals. Special units and schools were rated as the most useful source of support. Early intervention models are normally intensive, requiring concentrated one-to-one work of adults with a child for up to forty hours a week (Myers and Johnson 2007).

Rigorous randomised controlled trials (RCTs) to assess such early interventions are rare. One exception was a RCT of a parent-mediated communication-focused intervention, which found that there was no significant decrease in autism symptoms for the group assigned to the intervention (Green *et al.* 2010), although facets of children's relationships with parents did improve. Another widely cited RCT for early intervention that tested the Early Start Denver Model (ESDM), an intensive behavioural programme for toddlers, found that children who received the ESDM showed significant improvements in IQ and adaptive behaviour (Dawson *et al.* 2009). Even in this case, core autism symptoms did not always improve.

The rationale often given for diagnosis is that intervention is essential for improved outcomes. However, the literature on effectiveness of early intervention for children with autism is far from conclusive. Some methods seem to work for some children some of the time, but often with huge time investment by parents or therapists. Overall, there is a lack of consensus on the most successful intervention strategies (Feinberg and Vacca 2000). Several systematic reviews for early intervention have concluded there is no established 'cure' for autism. A comprehensive systematic review published in *Pediatrics* established that there is little evidence for positive effects of pharmaceutical or behavioural interventions for autism (Warren *et al.* 2011). They found an overall lack of evidence that autistic-like behaviours of young children improved substantially after diagnosis and subsequent intervention:

> One powerfully replicated finding across the available literature is that many children who receive early intensive intervention, across methodologies, will not demonstrate dramatic gains in social, cognitive, adaptive, and educational functioning. (Warren *et al.* 2011, p.e1309)

Other reviews have confirmed that the field does not yet have interventions that meet the criteria for well-established and efficacious treatments (Francis 2005). Warren and colleagues' systematic review of early interventions concluded that the available evidence suggests that some interventions might work for some subgroups of children, but which children these will be remains under-researched, so that it would currently not be possible for a clinician to confidently recommend a particular treatment for a particular child.

Early intervention research in autism is also beset by methodological concerns; the strength of the evidence base is insufficient to low. Overall, the evidence for effectiveness of early intervention is weak (Myers and Johnson 2007). Despite such concerns, reviews usually conclude that there are enough positive outcomes to warrant some form of intervention and this is translated into policy and guidance. The US National Institute of Health, for example, emphasises that 'the urgency of early identification and treatment puts the quest

for infant screening and diagnostic instruments at the forefront of our priorities' (Bristol-Power and Spinella 1999, p.435). What is not often acknowledged is that early interventions for autism are high-cost both in terms of financial and time commitment and may be exhausting for parents and children alike, especially when a better outcome remains uncertain.

There seems to be a disjunction between the level of actual evidence for effectiveness of early interventions for autism, and what I would term as the rhetoric of early intervention that is frequently espoused. Perhaps it is a question of interpretation – glass half full or glass half empty, as argued by Charman (2011). Early intervention research has not found a 'cure' for autism, despite decades of trying. Indeed, in the recent past some types of intervention for autism have been denounced as cruel and unsuitable by members of the autism community, including forms of Applied Behaviour Analysis (Dawson 2004). Therapy for very young children can involve between 25 and 40 hours a week of intensive training to 'maintain desirable adaptive behaviours' (Myers and Johnson 2007, p.1164). Other forms of intervention, once mainstream, are now well-established as having been inappropriate. Holding therapy, for example, has been shown to be potentially physically harmful to children (Pignotti and Mercer 2007). It is hard to predict whether all the autism interventions that are utilised today will be acceptable to future generations.

Caveat 2: Improvement with no intervention?

A second counter-argument to early diagnosis is that in early childhood behavioural traits display huge variability from child to child (and from situation to situation). Thus it is difficult to distinguish a two-year-old who cannot speak because s/he may continue to display symptoms of autism later in life from a two-year-old that cannot speak because he is slower and will catch up later (Landa 2008). According to some, 30 per cent of children who are given diagnosis at age two no longer meet criteria for ASD diagnosis at age four (Turner and Stone 2007). My own work has compared two groups of children with severe autistic-type traits measured at age two; one group who received an autism diagnosis later, and the other who did not (Russell *et al.* 2012). Children without an autism diagnosis did better on a range of outcomes as adolescents, which suggested it was difficult to distinguish pre-school age children who have autistic-like traits but improve, without having been diagnosed, from those who go on to develop lifelong impairment. This shows that children with serious symptoms of autism may improve to subclinical levels as they mature without intervention. In these cases, 'wait and see' may be the best strategy.

Overall, the evidence of the age at which autism can be reliably diagnosed is unclear (Stone *et al.* 1999). The psychiatry and medical literature centres on

how reliably an early diagnosis can be made, and the accuracy of screening checklists as tools. Early diagnosis leading to better treatment outcomes is the mantra, but even if this were true, accurate early diagnosis of autism is also more difficult, given that children vary more widely in their level of development at younger ages. There is great uncertainty about future trajectories when screening procedures for autism begin before age two (Rutter 2006).

Caveat 3: Could diagnosis influence outcome in a negative way?

Once told about a specific childhood diagnosis, it has been shown that perceivers tend to interpret behaviour in the light of the diagnostic frame (Fogel and Nelson 1983). But little work has been done that disentangles the perceivers' negative expectancies that are based on an early 'autism' diagnostic label, and expectancies based on the actual behaviours of the child. Concrete evidence that labelling of a child – putting a name to a condition, or in this case giving an early autism diagnosis – could potentially have a negative or positive impact is scarce.

I now review some research in self-fulfilling prophesies (SFP) in older children, and some research from expectancy bias studies in social psychology and education. Some of this work is very dated, and some more recent, but it does suggest that iatrogenic effects of early autism diagnosis are at least possible. Both SFP and expectancy bias studies are founded on labelling theories that were often touted by sociologists, radical psychiatrists and psychologists in the 1960s and 1970s.

Edgerton (1967) pointed out that nearly all of the enormous amount of literature in the field of cognitive impairment was from the perspective of social workers, psychiatrists, psychologists and other medical specialists. In such circumstances, he elucidated, people with intellectual disabilities are only ever professionally 'known' in terms of their 'disabilities' or 'abnormalities'. This, then, informs the way that such people are perceived and treated, leading to objectifying them. The anthropologist Goode (1984) also argued that the focus on labels does not allow entry into the world of an intellectually disabled person. He attempted to eradicate the professional distance between himself and his subjects. He shunned research techniques that objectified children as research subjects, and developed a relationship with a severely intellectually impaired deaf/blind girl on her terms. Recently researchers have attempted to address the issue of who is allowed into the conversation about childhood disability by focusing on children's voices (Singh 2013) or stories (Curran and Runswick-Cole 2013).

Research has documented SFPs in both the lab and the real world. Rosenthal and Lawson told students who were training rats to run round a maze that their animals were either clever or stupid. Although rats were actually randomly assigned, the 'clever' rats learned the maze quicker. Students' beliefs about

their rats were self-fulfilling (Rosenthal and Lawson 1964). In Rosenthal and Jacobson's (1966) influential, much criticised yet highly cited, 'Pygmalion' study the researchers posed as educational psychologists, went to a school and tested a class of pupils. They then told the teacher that 20 per cent of these pupils were 'intellectual bloomers': potentially brighter than the others, despite these 20 per cent actually being selected quite randomly. When the children were retested a year later the 'bloomer' pupils really did do better in intelligence tests. Once an expectation is set, they argued, even if it isn't accurate, people tend to act in ways that are consistent with that expectation. The result is that the expectation comes true.

The work of Rosenthal and his colleagues provoked a flurry of work on SFPs, and in 1978 Rosenthal and Rubin reviewed 345 separate studies dealing with the phenomenon, which confirmed its existence. The effects of SFPs have been noted in many settings, including in the classroom amongst stigmatised groups (Jussim and Harber 2005). The expectancy of worse outcomes for a target group has been also shown to be self-fulfilling. Teacher perceptions were shown to predict achievement more strongly for low achievers than for high achievers (Madon, Jussim and Eccles 1997). Rist (2000) showed how a pre-school teacher placed children in reading groups that reflected their class backgrounds, and how subsequent teacher expectancy mediated learning.

Bogdan (1982) drew on work in semantics to suggest that people labelled 'mentally retarded' were covered with a 'cloak of incompetence' that is virtually impossible to discard. They thus become prisoners of the explicit and implicit meanings attached to these labels. Bogdan argued that the label 'mentally retarded' creates a barrier to understanding people on their own terms. It prevents others from seeing and treating people so defined, as human beings with feelings, understandings and needs. Such work was instrumental in the replacement of derogatory terms with politically correct language that attempts to refer to disabled groups in a more positive way.

Fogel and Nelson (1983) found that disability labels could bias teachers' behavioural checklist scores. In their ingenious study, teachers who watched a video of a child and were told about the child's learning difficulties attributed more characteristics of cognitive impairment to the child than teachers who were not aware of the diagnostic label for the same child.

A comprehensive review of expectancy bias and stigma at the beginning of this century only identified two studies looking specifically at expectancy bias in relation to childhood diagnostic labelling (Jussim *et al.* 2000). In these experiments, boys were paired as partners and one in each pair was led to believe that the other had an attention deficit hyperactivity disorder (ADHD) diagnosis. Partners perceived ADHD-labelled boys as having more symptoms, and they talked less to them, were colder and gave them less credit in shared tasks. The

boys with bogus ADHD labels felt that their partners were 'meaner' to them than the non-labelled boys did. This has interesting implications for autistic children, where social communication may be a problem, indicating that the diagnostic tag actually made attempts at social communication less likely. However a follow-up study showed that the effect of *actually* being diagnosed as ADHD had a far greater effect than being incorrectly labelled by experimental manipulation, even when the perceivers were unaware of the diagnostic labels. This was interpreted as showing that the actual behaviour of a boy had a far greater effect than a bogus label (Harris *et al.* 1992).

A more recent study with potential implications for diagnostic labelling of children with ADHD-type behaviours was conducted by Sayal and colleagues (2010). These researchers conducted a randomised controlled trial where one group of children who displayed high levels of inattention/hyperactivity were identified as having high probability of having ADHD to teachers. A second group with equivalent symptoms were not identified to teachers. The researchers found that children in the 'identified to teachers' group were twice as likely as the other group to have high scores in inattention/hyperactivity at follow-up five years later. The authors discuss labelling theory and teacher expectancy as one possible reason for these outcomes, although another could be reporting bias.

Applied to autism, labelling theory hypothesises that diagnosing and labelling a child as autistic will lead to shifts in expectancy and attitudes of those in contact with the child, as well as altering the self-identity of the child, and this will serve to reinforce the 'abnormal' autistic behaviour. Labelling theory has been influential in social policy and the practices of schools and asylums. Today, in the UK, psychiatric training still cautions professionals about the dangers and consequences of labelling patients too early, while educational research into the impact of streaming children has informed the development of the comprehensive system in Europe (Slattery 2003). The early autism label, then, could produce negative perceptions and reduced expectations in parents, teachers, peers and even, later, in the children themselves, leading to self-fulfilling outcomes. Meta-analysis of all work on SFPs found effects, real but small, of about 0.1–0.2 in terms of correlation or regression coefficients (Jussim *et al.* 2000). However, the size of the effect varied in different situations and contexts.

Although SFPs are real, there are probably more powerful factors at work in maintaining problematic interactions for families whose child has autism-type behaviours than an autism diagnosis itself. My point is, however, that research does suggest that the treatment of children with an autism diagnosis by the health professionals involved in the child's care is likely to be influenced by his or her autism diagnosis. This treatment by the professional, in turn, may, in some way, influence outcomes. Although adverse labelling effects from autism diagnosis are certainly not proved, neither are they disproved. If autism is the lens

through which a child is viewed from an early age, and there is aforementioned plasticity, the malleable period when the young child is particularly sensitive to intervention will also mean they may be equally sensitive to potential negative impacts of labelling-based interactions on their development.

WHAT DO PARENTS GAIN FROM THEIR CHILD'S EARLY AUTISM DIAGNOSIS?

In her detailed analysis of a cross-cultural study of ADHD, Malacrida (2004) notes a tradition of cultural resistance to labelling in the UK, in contrast to the Canadian medicalised model. She argues that this reflects the influence of the anti-psychiatry movement in the UK. A picture emerges of a trade-off between potential positive and negative outcomes, as parents weigh up the likelihood of risks and benefits before making a decision to get a diagnosis. We carried out a study interviewing parents of children who had either pursued or rejected an autism diagnosis for their child (Russell and Norwich 2012). Parents faced considerable dilemmas when confronted with the prospect of an autism diagnosis. Although diagnosis may lead to services, respite and a partial explanation for a child's behaviour, parents also considered the potential devaluation, stigma and rejection that may result. Diagnosis *may* lead to services, but often does not, thus often operates as a 'promise' that may or may not be fulfilled. A diagnosis can vindicate and blame, can legitimise or stigmatise, as Jutel and Nettleton (2011) point out. The autism diagnosis therefore represents a double-edged sword for many parents.

An early autism diagnosis, or indeed autism diagnosis at any point in childhood, allows others to deploy biomedical explanations for a child's behaviour (Farrugia 2009). Grinker (2008), the father of an autistic child, compared approaches to autism across cultures as his family moved from Korea, to South Africa and India. He found that the biomedical definition was a useful tool to explain his daughter's behaviour in order to deflect culturally situated definitions. For example, autistic symptoms might be attributed to demonic possession in some cultures. His work demonstrates that the deployment of the biomedical explanation by the parent is in part a response to the cultural context that the child inhabits. Grinker (2008) also wondered whether an autism diagnosis is sometimes more for the parent's needs rather than the child's, enabling the parent to feel they are doing something constructive to help – a point made by more forcibly by Fitzpatrick (2008). Singh (2004) elaborates on the impact a diagnosis can have in shifting attribution of behaviour – from mother-blame to brains – even going so far as to describe the 'sacrifice' of the son (via ADHD diagnosis and treatment) to protect the mother.

CONCLUSION

Diagnostic labelling is sometimes treated as if it were 'good' or 'bad'. Some scholars have seen labelling as an unnecessary and wholly destructive process. In my view, as in that of Riddick (2002), there are many aspects to labelling, both positive and negative. Potential positive outcomes of diagnosis are appropriate and helpful treatment, and alteration to the environment, together with obtaining better resources through funding and legislation. These can be offset against potential negative outcomes. Quicke and Winter (1994) adopt an interactionist perspective to show that labelling can lead to discrimination or positive outcomes depending on the type of label and its context, and the tensions between these effects.

However, any balance between good and bad vis-à-vis early autism diagnosis does not seem to be reflected in the literature. A cursory glance at the intervention literature and that on screening and the development of diagnostic tools, all burgeoning areas of autism research, reveals no questioning of the overwhelming benefit of early diagnosis and intervention. 'The earlier intervention can begin, the better the outcome' (Woods and Wetherby 2003, p.180) is typical of the assumptions found in both academic and lay literature. This assertion of benefit seems to me to be founded on fairly flimsy evidence. Methodologies for assessing effectiveness of early interventions are frequently flawed. There is no robust data favouring one approach over others. While some interventions that support social skills do have some empirical support, for example the Early Start Denver model (Dawson *et al.* 2009), there is a lack of consensus on the most successful intervention strategies. Some approaches work for some children, in controlled settings, but it is not possible to make predictions about efficacy for all children diagnosed with autism. Al-Qabandi, Gorter and Rosenbaum (2011) point out that if long-term outcome is not modified, emphasis on the importance of early diagnosis and intervention for autism may be misplaced.

Early diagnosis is essential, it is argued, so that diagnosis is made during a critical period in a child's life when the child is more sensitive to environmental influences or stimulation than at other times during his/her life. However, this notion of developmental plasticity could also be applied to any negative aspects of labelling, and even potential adverse effects of very early intensive behavioural training. I would argue that 'the early diagnosis imperative' has become a form of dogma in autism intervention research, and to some extent in policy and practice. As time passes, more and more children are being diagnosed with autism and the earliest age of autism diagnosis continues to drop. When the effects of intensive, early interventions are not conclusively known, and when iatrogenic effects of labelling are not disproven, in my view the benefits of early diagnosis/intervention for autism should be scrutinised in more depth before becoming accepted practice.

REFERENCES

Al-Qabandi, M., Gorter, J.W., and Rosenbaum, P. (2011) 'Early autism detection: are we ready for routine screening?' *Pediatrics 128*, 1 e211–e217.

American Academy of Pediatrics (2010) *Autism Alarm.* Available at www.aap.org/en-us/about-the-aap/Committees-Councils-Sections/Council-on-Children-with-Disabilities/Documents/AutismAlarm.pdf, accessed on 21 January 2016.

Bettelheim, B. (1967) *Empty Fortress.* New York: Simon and Schuster.

Bogdan, R. (1982) *Inside Out: The Social Meaning Of Mental Retardation.* Toronto: University of Toronto Press.

Bohlin, G., Hagekull, B., and Rydell, A.M. (2000) 'Attachment and social functioning: a longitudinal study from infancy to middle childhood.' *Social Development 9*, 1, 24–39.

Bristol-Power, M.M., and Spinella, G. (1999) 'Research on screening and diagnosis in autism: a work in progress.' *Journal of Autism and Developmental Disorders 29*, 6, 435–438.

Charman, T. (2011) 'Commentary: Glass half full or half empty? Testing social communication interventions for young children with autism – reflections on Landa, Holman, O'Neill, and Stuart (2011).' *Journal of Child Psychology and Psychiatry 52*, 1, 22–23.

Committee on Children with Disabilities (2001) 'The pediatrician's role in the diagnosis and management of Autistic Spectrum Disorder in children.' *Pediatrics 107*, 5, 1221–1226.

Crais, E.R., Watson, L.R., Baranek, G.T., and Reznick, J.S. (2006) 'Early identification of autism: how early can we go?' *Seminars in Speech and Language 27*, 3, 143–160.

Curran, T., and Runswick-Cole, K. (eds) (2013) *Disabled Children's Childhood Studies: Critical Approaches in a Global Context.* Basingstoke: Palgrave Macmillan.

Dawson, G. (2008) 'Early behavioral intervention, brain plasticity, and the prevention of Autism Spectrum Disorder.' *Development and Psychopathology 20*, 3, 775–803.

Dawson, G., Rogers, S., Munson, J., Smith, M., *et al.* (2009) 'Randomized, controlled trial of an intervention for toddlers with autism: The early start Denver model.' *Pediatrics 125*, 1, e17–e23.

Dawson, M. (2004) *The Misbehaviour Of Behaviourists: Ethical Challenges To The Autism–ABA Industry.* Available at www.sentex.net/~nexus23/naa_aba.html, accessed on 18 November 2015.

Dennis, M. (2000) 'Developmental plasticity in children: the role of biological risk, development, time, and reserve.' *Journal of Communication Disorders 33*, 4, 321–331.

Edgerton, R.B. (1967) *The Cloak of Competence: Stigma in the Lives of the Mentally Retarded.* Berkeley, CA: University of California Press.

Farrugia, D. (2009) 'Exploring stigma: medical knowledge and the stigmatisation of parents of children diagnosed with Autism Spectrum Disorder.' *Sociology of Health and Illness 31*, 7, 1011–1027.

Feinberg, E., and Vacca, J. (2000) 'The drama and trauma of creating policies on autism.' *Focus on Autism and Other Developmental Disabilities 15*, 3, 130–137.

Filipek, P.A., Accardo, P.J., Ashwal, S., Baranek, G., *et al.* (2000) 'Practice parameter: screening and diagnosis of autism. Report of the Quality Standards Subcommittee of the American Academy of Neurology and the Child Neurology Society.' *Neurology 55*, 4, 468–479.

Fitzpatrick, M. (2008) *Defeating Autism: A Damaging Delusion.* London/New York: Routledge.

Fogel, L.S., and Nelson, R.O. (1983) 'The effects of special education labels on teachers.' *Journal of School Psychology 21*, 3, 241–251.

Francis, K. (2005) 'Autism interventions: a critical update.' *Developmental Medicine and Child Neurology 47*, 7, 493–499.

Goode, D.A. (1984) 'Socially Produced Identities, Intimacy and the Problem of Competence Among the Retarded.' In L. Barton and S. Tomlinson (eds) *Special Education and Social Interests.* London/New York: Croome Helm.

Green, J., Charman, T., McConachie, H., Aldred, C., *et al.* (2010) 'Parent-mediated communication-focused treatment in children with autism (PACT): a randomised controlled trial.' *The Lancet 375,* 9783, 2152–2160.

Grinker, R.R. (2008) *Unstrange Minds: Remapping the World of Autism.* New York: Basic Books.

Harris, M.J., Milich, R., Corbitt, E.M., Hoover, D.W., and Brady, M. (1992) 'Self-fulfilling effects of stigmatizing information on children's social interactions.' *Journal of Personality and Social Psychology 63,* 1, 41–50.

Hertz-Picciotto, I., and Delwiche, L. (2009) 'The rise in autism and the role of age at diagnosis.' *Epidemiology 20,* 1, 84–90.

Ibañez, L.V., Grantz, C.J., and Messinger, D.S. (2013) 'The development of referential communication and Autism symptomatology in high-risk infants.' *Infancy: The Official Journal of the International Society on Infant Studies 18,* 5, 1–21.

Jick, H., and Kaye, J. A. (2003) 'Epidemiology and possible causes of autism.' *Pharmacotherapy: The Journal of Human Pharmacology and Drug Therapy 23,* 12, 1524–1530.

Jussim, L., and Harber, K.D. (2005) 'Teacher expectations and self-fulfilling prophecies: knowns and unknowns, resolved and unresolved controversies.' *Personality and Social Psychology Review 9,* 2, 131–155.

Jussim, L., Palumbo, P., Chatman, C., Madon, S., *et al.* (2000) 'Stigma and Self-fulfilling Prophecies.' In T. Heatherton, R. Kleck, M. Hebl and G. Hull (eds) *The Social Psychology of Stigma.* New York: The Guilford Press.

Jutel, A., and Nettleton, S. (2011) 'Towards a sociology of diagnosis: reflections and opportunities.' *Social Science and Medicine 73,* 6, 793–800.

Koegel L.K., and LaZebnik, C. (2005) *Overcoming Autism: Finding the Answers, Strategies, and Hope That Can Transform a Child.* New York: Penguin Books.

Knudsen, E.I. (2004) 'Sensitive periods in the development of the brain and behavior.' *Journal of Cognitive Neuroscience 16,* 8, 1412–1425.

Landa, R.J. (2008) 'Diagnosis of autism spectrum disorders in the first 3 years of life.' *Neurology 4,* 3, 138–147.

LeBlanc, J.J., and Fagiolini, M. (2011) 'Autism: a critical period and disorder?' *Neural Plasticity,* e921680.

Liu, K., King, M., and Bearman, P. S. (2010) 'Social influence and the autism epidemic.' *American Journal of Sociology 115,* 5, 1387–1434.

Madon, S., Jussim, L., and Eccles, J. (1997) 'In search of the powerful self-fulfilling prophecy.' *Journal of Personality and Social Psychology 72,* 4, 791–809.

Maestro, S., Muratori, F., Cavallaro, M.C., Pei, F., *et al.* (2002) 'Attentional skills during the first 6 months of age in Autism Spectrum Disorder.' *Journal of the American Academy of Child and Adolescent Psychiatry 41,* 10, 1239–1245.

Malacrida, C. (2004) 'Medicalization, ambivalence and social control: mothers' descriptions of educators and ADD/ADHD.' *Health 8,* 1, 61–80.

Mansell, W., and Morris, K. (2004) 'A survey of parents' reactions to the diagnosis of an autistic spectrum disorder by a local service: access to information and use of services.' *Autism: The International Journal of Research and Practice 8,* 4, 387–407.

McGuire, A.E. (2013) 'Buying time: the s/pace of advocacy and the cultural production of autism.' *Canadian Journal of Disability Studies 2,* 3, 98–125.

Montessori, M. [1949] (2009) *The Absorbent Mind.* Minooka, IL: BN Publishing.

Myers, S.M., and Johnson, C.P. (2007) 'Management of children with Autism Spectrum Disorders.' *Pediatrics 120,* 5, 1162–1182.

Parner, E.T., Schendel, D.E., and Thorsen, P. (2008) 'Autism prevalence trends over time in Denmark: changes in prevalence and age at diagnosis.' *Archives of Paediatrics and Adolescent Medicine 162,* 12, 1150–1156.

Pastor, D.L. (1981) 'The quality of mother–infant attachment and its relationship to toddlers' initial sociability with peers.' *Developmental Psychology 17,* 3, 326–335.

Pignotti, M., and Mercer, J. (2007) 'Holding therapy and dyadic developmental psychotherapy are not supported and acceptable social work interventions: a systematic research synthesis revisited.' *Research on Social Work Practice 17,* 4, 513–519.

Quicke, J., and Winter, C. (1994) 'Labelling and learning: an interactionist perspective.' *Support for Learning 9,* 1, 16–21.

Riddick, B. (2002) 'An examination of the relationship between labelling and stigmatisation with special reference to dyslexia.' *Disability and Society 15,* 4, 653–667.

Rist, R.C. (2000) 'Student social class and teacher expectations: the self-fulfilling prophecy in ghetto education.' *Harvard Educational Review 70,* 3, 266–301.

Rosenthal, R., and Jacobson, L. (1966) 'Teachers' expectancies: determinants of pupils' IQ gains.' *Psychological Reports 19,* 1, 115–118.

Rosenthal, R., and Lawson, R. (1964) 'A longitudinal study of the effects of experimenter bias on the operant learning of laboratory rats.' *Journal of Psychiatric Research 69,* 61–72.

Rosenthal, R., and Rubin, D.B. (1978) 'Interpersonal expectancy effects: the first 345 studies.' *Behavioral and Brain Sciences 3,* 377–386.

Russell, G., and Norwich, B. (2012) 'Dilemmas, dilemmas and destigmatization: parental perspectives on the diagnosis of autism spectrum disorders.' *Clinical Child Psychology and Psychiatry 17,* 2, 229–245.

Russell, G., Golding, J., Norwich, B., Emond, A., Ford, T., and Steer, C. (2012) 'Social and behavioural outcomes in children diagnosed with autism spectrum disorders: a longitudinal cohort study.' *Journal of Child Psychology and Psychiatry 53,* 7, 735–744.

Russell, G., Miller, L.L., Ford, T., and Golding, J. (2014) 'Assessing recall in mothers' retrospective reports: concerns over children's speech and language development.' *Journal of Abnormal Child Psychology 42,* 5, 825–830.

Rutter, M. (2006) 'Autism: its recognition, early diagnosis, and service implications.' *Journal of Developmental and Behavioral Pediatrics 27,* 2, 4–58.

Sayal, K., Owen, V., White, K., Merrell, C., Tymms, P., and Taylor, E. (2010) 'Impact of early school-based screening and intervention programs for ADHD on children's outcomes and access to services: follow-up of a school-based trial at age 10 years.' *Archives of Pediatrics and Adolescent Medicine 164,* 5, 462–469.

Singh, I. (2004) 'Doing their jobs: mothering with Ritalin in a culture of mother-blame.' *Social Science and Medicine 59,* 6, 1193–1205.

Singh, I. (2013) 'Brain talk: power and negotiation in children's discourse about self, brain and behaviour.' *Sociology of Health and Illness 35,* 6, 813–827.

Slattery, M. (2003) *Key Ideas in Sociology.* New York: Nelson Thornes.

Snow, C.E., and Hoefnagel-Höhle, M. (1978) 'The critical period for language acquisition: evidence from second language learning.' *Child Development 49,* 4, 1114–1128.

Stone, W.L., Lee, E.B., Ashford, L., Brissie, J., *et al.* (1999) 'Can autism be diagnosed accurately in children under 3 years?' *Journal of Child Psychology and Psychiatry 40,* 2, 219–226.

Teitelbaum, P., Teitelbaum, O., Nye, J., Fryman, J., and Maurer, R.G. (1998) 'Movement analysis in infancy may be useful for early diagnosis of autism.' *Proceedings of the National Academy of Sciences of the United States of America 95,* 23, 13982–13987.

Turner, L.M., and Stone W.L. (2007) 'Variability in outcome for children with an ASD diagnosis at age 2.' *Journal of Child Psychology and Psychiatry 48*, 8, 793–802.

Wallace, S., Parr, J., and Herd, A. (2012) *One in a Hundred.* Autistica. Available at www.autistica.org.uk/wp-content/uploads/2014/10/One-in-a-Hundred-Autisticas-Report.pdf, accessed on 18 November 2015.

Warren, Z., McPheeters, M.L., Sathe, N., Foss-Feig, J.H., Glasser, A., and Veenstra-Vanderweele, J. (2011) 'A systematic review of early intensive intervention for Autism Spectrum Disorders.' *Pediatrics 127*, 5, e1303–e1311.

Watson, L.R., Baranek, G.T., Crais, E.R., Reznick, J., Dykstra, J., and Perryman, T. (2007) 'The first year inventory: retrospective parent responses to a questionnaire designed to identify one-year-olds at risk for autism.' *Journal of Autism and Developmental Disorders 37*, 1, 49–61.

White, E.J., Hutka, S.A., Williams, L.J., and Moreno, S. (2013) 'Learning, neural plasticity and sensitive periods: implications for language acquisition, music training and transfer across the lifespan.' *Frontiers in Systems Neuroscience 7*, 90.

Woods, J.J., and Wetherby, A. (2003) 'Early identification of and intervention for infants and toddlers who are at risk for Autism Spectrum Disorder.' *Language, Speech, and Hearing Services in Schools 34*, 3, 180–193.

Zoghbi, H.Y. (2003) 'Postnatal neurodevelopmental disorders: meeting at the synapse?' *Science 302*, 5646, 826–830.

CHAPTER 15

THINKING SYSTEMS
'MIND' AS RELATIONAL ACTIVITY

Gail Simon

INTRODUCTION

> All new knowledge comes from people on the margins and they tend not to be from within institutional/ised knowledge and resources. (Whitfield and Simon 2014, p.24)

In this chapter, I propose how, as professionals, we need to shift our skills from diagnostic activities to relational curiosity to develop collaborative ways of conversing with people who have been diagnosed with Asperger Syndrome and others in their networks. Through immersing ourselves in dialogue with people and their social and professional networks, we can bring forth evidence of people with Asperger Syndrome having unique and useful expertise, which can play a part in resolving concerns and improving communication between those in their networks. Not only is it socially productive, but it is also ethical for professionals to shift their focus from an exploration of 'mind', as commonly believed to exist solely within an individual person, to the relational contexts so influential on what we are constructing with each other through talk and how that shapes what is able to be recognised and developed.

By foregrounding dialogue over diagnosis, we see how experimenting with user-friendly talk can provide opportunities for symptoms and features of high-functioning autism/Asperger Syndrome (Wing 1981; Gillberg 1991) to be understood as meaningful communications in which the 'disabled' person is experienced as able and enabling. The individualised account of the person having been diagnosed as having Asperger Syndrome is exchanged for descriptions of an interactive social system. I will illustrate how we can relocate 'mind' from the cognitive brain to the social opportunistic space created between people.

RELATIONAL OPPORTUNITIES

> 'So, you take this case and I will make notes and we can discuss it afterwards. Okay?' The supervisor takes herself behind the one-way screen and the nervous trainee clinical psychologist goes to fetch the family to the consulting room. Once back in the room, the psychologist quickly gives up on conversation with the child suspected of having Asperger Syndrome who gives responses not apparently connected to her questions. Instead, she asks the parents questions about the child's physical, emotional and social history going back to birth. She fends off questions from the child which she feels are inappropriate and distracting and completes her information gathering exercise. After a break to discuss the case with her supervisor, she negotiates spending some time alone with the child and proceeds to conduct some tests, one of which is the Sally–Anne test. At the end of the session, the trainee says to the parents that she will let them know the outcome of the assessment and says a nice goodbye to the child. The trainee and her supervisor agree that the child could be diagnosed as having Asperger Syndrome and they arrange for a diagnostic letter to go out to the parents and for the parents to be invited to a group for parents with children who have Asperger Syndrome. (Extract from composite diagnostic interview)

So what did we hear from the parents in this diagnostic interview? We heard that mealtimes and bedtimes are hell; that they are worried about neglecting other children in the family; that they are arguing with each other about how best to respond to the child in question; that they are concerned with how the school is responding to their child; and what the neighbours must think. But what we end up with is a report focused on the child with parental information being lined up to reinforce a story of an individual with cognitive and communication difficulties. The family is seen as a victim of unfortunate circumstances and offered information and advice to cope with their child. The professional system, with *its* limited cognitive framework, fails to see that the family is a *system* struggling with communication challenges and that it is resourceful, creative and open to collaborative approaches. There is no expectation that the family can teach the professionals anything. They provide supporting information for diagnostic purposes. The family is shuffled into a passive service 'user', advice-recipient position. There is no consideration that the family may be able and interested in sharing or creating knowledge with the professional system, or that they could be part of the knowledge innovation for resourcing the wider community.

The problems parents and children want help with occur almost exclusively in the context of relationships. Communication difficulties are the most common presenting concern in therapy. Parents want to talk about how to manage mealtimes, changes of routine, arguments between family members, co-parenting

communications, dealing with the frequent fall-out from school and other 'Now what?' episodes.

AREAS OF SPECIAL INTEREST AS RELATIONAL SYSTEMS

Systemic lines of inquiry have been successful when treating the child's area of special interest as a resource (Simon 2004). For a start, it is the one thing that is likely to engage the young person with a diagnosis of Asperger Syndrome: 'Their special interest is often their sole topic of conversation. Asperger individuals seem to love talking about their interest, regardless of whether one has heard it all before' (Frith 1991, p.11). Whether one has heard it all before is not simply to do with repetition by the person with the interest. It is matter of how others listen, understand and engage with the conversation. Obsessive behaviour of the symptom-spotter – and here I am talking about the diagnostic clinician – results in lost opportunities to hear about relational functioning within an area of special interest. This can also transfer itself to parents emulating what the professionals consider to be good practice.

A person with an area of special interest is likely to have in-depth knowledge about complex relational activities, which make up communicating systems. Talking about them creates and brings forth new ways of relational being and relational knowing. Exploration of the area of special interest of the child diagnosed as having Asperger Syndrome might bring forth a description of a meaningful, communication system. By understanding the area of special interest as such a system, the therapist and family can be invited to communicate at times with each other through the metaphor of the area of special interest. This system might be useful in generating a language to describe the workings of that family, which all family members can use. This may facilitate and help understand processes of communication, change and what makes a difference. Compare these two conversations:

Example 1

Parent: The teachers tell him off because he charges across the playground and doesn't stop in time. Then he crashes into one of the younger children and hurts them. And he gets in trouble.

Professional: What game were you playing when you were running so fast?

Will: The Sir Nigel Gresley is an A4 Pacific locomotive 4468.

Parent (to professional): He's train mad.

Parent (to child): You can't be a train in the playground. You will crash into people like you did into that young child. And hurt them.

Professional: Did you see the other child cry?

Will: It broke the record in 1938. It went at 126 miles an hour.

Professional: When you crashed into the little girl, what did she do?

Parent: She cried, didn't she? Because you bumped into her.

Will (in flat monotone voice): She fell over.

So what is happening here? The professional is asking about perception, noticing and trying to activate the child's cognition as though it can be awakened through noticing questions. The professional is in a bind. On the one hand, they are seeing evidence of fixed characteristics typical of Asperger Syndrome: lack of cooperation in difficult conversations, possible cognitive difficulties, apparent inability to imagine and empathise with another person and so on. On the other hand, the professional, like the parent, is trying to effect change with those same, apparently unmovable features. And nothing new emerges, so reinforcing the story of fixed characteristics. What is fixed or repetitive is the pattern of communication between those in the room. Behind this pattern is the contradictory belief that the professional will be able to change the fixed problematic behaviours of the person with Asperger Syndrome.

Let's look at another excerpt in which the professional shifts their approach and becomes curious about the relational coordinations between parts of the system.

Example 2

Professional: So how does the Sir Nigel Gresley get to go that fast?

Will: Its engine.

Professional: Does it just go like that immediately or does it build up speed?

Will: Builds up speed.

Professional: How does it build up speed? Can you tell me how it all works? I am interested to know. I like steam trains but I don't know that much about them.

Will: Well, it doesn't just start going at 128 mph.

Professional: Okay.

Will: It depends on how much coal goes into the furnace.

Professional: What does the coal do in the furnace?

Will: It heats the water to make steam, which makes the engine go faster.

Professional: How does the fireman know when to put coal in to the furnace?

Will: The driver tells him.

Professional: And what happens when the driver wants the train to slow down?

Will: The train has to reduce its steam and apply the brakes.

Professional: How does the driver let the fireman know to put on less coal to make less steam?

Will: He tells him.

Professional: How come the fireman does as he is told?

Will: He just does. Or the train would crash.

Professional: Okay. So they don't want the train to crash. And who tells the driver how fast to go?

Will: The signals.

Professional: So who works the signals?

Will: Outside York, there are seventeen signal boxes. We've got one near us.

Professional: And how do the signalmen know when to switch the levers?

Will: It depends. It could be to make sure the train goes in the correct direction at a junction or it may be to avoid a collision especially on single tracks where they need to use sidings for trains to pass each other safely.

Professional: Yes, I see. Why does the train driver agree to follow the rules of the signals?

Will: Well, they would derail if they didn't slow down and crash into another train.

Professional: And if they derailed?

Will: It takes four cranes to get one engine back onto the track. We saw it up in Shap.

Professional: Do people sometimes get hurt?

Will: Yes, if they are carrying passengers.

Professional: And why do drivers sometimes hoot before a crossing?

Will: To warn pedestrians and cars.

Professional: Of what?

Will: Of a train coming...

Professional: So they don't go on the tracks?

Professional: And what would happen if they didn't hoot?

Will: There would be risk to life and limb.

Professional: You know a lot about how things work, how train drivers and fireman and signalmen all work together to get places and keep people safe, don't you?

Parent: I guess when you are charging about the playground, you have to be the driver, the fireman and the signalman all in one! It's great hearing you talk about trains in this way. You know so much.

Several things appear to be going on here:

1. The child's answers start cautiously and appear to confirm non-sequitur responses typical of Asperger Syndrome but this behaviour changes when the professional changes their behaviour. The child starts to see there are other forms of talk on offer than being required to change or being tested.
2. In this excerpt, the professional repositions herself as a learner. She listens and asks as if for the first time, without trying to create any evidence. The repositioning by the professional brings forth a story of the person with Asperger Syndrome as having knowledge and expertise.
3. This knowledge and expertise is about the moving parts of a communicating, interactive system with a feedback loop. The narrative describes a relationally responsive system (train, driver, fireman, signalman, signals, pedestrians, passengers) in which all the component parts/people are cooperative and sensitive to communications. Conversational participants have to recalibrate their expectations and learn to leave their expectation of hearing repetitive, decontextualised facts so they can be receptive to noticing a narrative of a system at work in the area of special interest.
4. The knowledge and expertise of the child is clearly not simply a list of decontextualised facts. The child demonstrates both contextualised

knowledge and hypothesising abilities. A coherent narrative is made visible by having an interested enquirer.

5. The parent has an unusual experience of not feeling bored by the repetitive nature of the area of special interest and leaves with increased admiration for their child's abilities.

6. The professional and parent are careful not to rush into advice giving and making connections to the playground activity which might well have alienated the child from collaborating in the conversation further. But they are now equipped with a meaningful metaphor which is of immediate interest to the young person and which they will be able to draw on further in future conversations.

Areas of special interest often contain a communicating system between the characters or component parts. These areas of special interest often seemed to be connected to a subject in which there is a system at work, such as trains, computers and electricity. Within these cybernetic systems are feedback loops, mechanisms for managing cyclical or unusual events, rule-bound *and* rule-creating ways of being.

By foregrounding relational curiosity, the area of special interest ceases to be constructed as symptomatic of an embodied condition and instead becomes a social opportunity dependent on others becoming engaged in understanding and meaning-making. The area of special interest might be used both by the person diagnosed as having Asperger Syndrome and by others close to him as a means through which to connect, to communicate:

> I act not simply 'out of' my own plans and desires, unrestricted by the social circumstances of my performances, but in some sense also 'in to' the opportunities offered to me to act, or else my attempts to communicate will fail or be sanctioned in some way. (Shotter 1989, p.144)

When exploring a person's area of special interest in detail, it is common for friends and families to become totally engrossed – as if for the first time of hearing – and often elaborate with questions of their own. Viewed in this way, rather than listening for sameness, we can listen for difference with all the novelty that a first hearing brings (Shotter 2008b). We immerse ourselves within the area of special interest and take an alongside position with the other speakers. We approach the subject with openness and wonder. We surrender our preconceived knowing and, with it, the inevitable about-ness position which sites us outside of the others' world, so scuppering the possibilities of new ways of knowing how to go in the conversations.

Within a systemic social constructionist framework, the child's special area of interest could be thought of as a narrative or collection of connecting narratives – as a way of languaging – and therefore as a potential resource to the therapeutic process and to the family or other social relationships. An important contextualising factor in systemic therapy would involve understanding how family members interact with the child around their area of special interest, exploring the stories they bring to this feature and looking at the contexts in which these stories have arisen.

For example, it can be useful to ask about:

- roles of individuals or individual parts
- means of communication
- patterns of communication
- power relations between parts/people
- rule-bound or rule-creating systems
- patterns of change
- alliances
- decision-making
- movements between parts/people.

In creating a shared means of talking about relationships, which had not previously existed for families and professionals, there emerges a useful resource that enables family and friends to access some of narratives about the workings of the world of the person diagnosed with Asperger Syndrome. Of course, this kind of conversation also feels more relevant to the person with the area of special interest and it can be a pleasure for them to experience genuine attention and interest of others in areas of their world that are important to them. They also have the experience of not being positioned in a mono-dimensional way as the problematic person or the identified patient but as an authority in an area which others in the room know only a little about and as someone with something useful to contribute.

CONCEPTUALISING 'MIND' AS RELATIONAL ACTIVITY

When people first hear the expression 'Theory of Mind', they often believe that this refers to a broad philosophical debate on what counts as 'mind'; an understandable response. However, in the field of child psychology and child psychiatry, there is

assumed to be only one Theory of Mind and it dominates the field with a limited set of assumptions about what 'mind' is. This cluster of ideas plays a central part in explaining and diagnosing autistic spectrum conditions (Baron-Cohen, Leslie and Frith 1985). Theory of Mind centres individual cognition at the heart of its hypothesis. This reflects a wider trend of decontextualising human behaviour within contemporary mental health which dominates the field theoretically and therefore has implications for what forms of treatment are available. The problem is that the dominant approach focuses only on the individual. It relies on an idea that it is the individual who has the problem *in them*. This approach reflects an attachment to a deficit model of human beings and discourages a focus on people's relational world. This model does not foreground the exploration of relational possibilities and drawing out evidence of resourcefulness in people. Hickok (2014) situates what are perceived as cognitive deficits in people with autism not so much as to do with individual cognition but reflecting limited opportunities for mirror neuron systems. McGuire and Michalko situate autism within a relational system: 'Rather than conceiving autism as an individualising medical problem, we understand autism as a complex interactional process. We treat autism as belonging squarely in the realm of the social and not in the realm of the individual' (McGuire and Michalko 2011, p.164).

In the working fields of autism, professional theory has focused on the individual participants in the conversation. A family of three may be conceptualised as one plus one plus one, for example. Separate entities. The individual parts are separated from the whole. The prominence of an embodied self in the literature arises out of the early biological sciences, which investigated the inner workings of the human body to correct any perceived problems whether manifesting as physical or social. The physical body is still used as the metaphorical container and site for investigation and treatment of physical and 'mental' problems, as is the case for professional activities with people who are diagnosed as being on the autistic spectrum. To speak about 'mental health' or 'learning disability' is a way of individualising experience and communications. It takes the person out of their social world and locates 'issues' within a notion of physical self made up of organic matter. The brain is frequently understood as the organic container and structural influence of something called the 'mind'. This model proposes that mind is damaged by atypical neurological differences which impact on the individual's social functioning.

Timimi and colleagues are concerned about the production of knowledge associated with autism and how it is presented: 'Perhaps more than any other child and adolescent psychiatry category, autism is viewed as the product of sound science with knowledge arising from…the "positivistic" or technical approach' (Timimi, Gardner and McCabe 2010). Brownlow and O'Dell (2009) critically review the literature on Theory of Mind and conclude that the research

has been carried out by outsiders and makes fundamental assumptions about neurotypicality, which undermines new knowledge emerging about ability and the whole person. Autism research is almost exclusively dedicated to proving this connection and to finding a cure to prevent 'atypical' neurology. It is a strategy which overlooks the cultural and relational contexts and which sidesteps any invitations to reflexivity, which could be of use in considering what kinds of talk, for example, count and are valued and what are not.

Leppington says that the constructivist concept of 'thought' is not proof of the individual mind but of the social world. The question is not so much 'How does the individual rational consciousness account for the social world?' but 'How, in a social world, to account for culturally specific notions of the individual?' (Leppington 1991, p.86). Nevertheless, the term 'Asperger Syndrome' exists, to date, as a *description* of a 'state of mind' and of behaviours associated with that state of mind. Gergen and Gergen (2002, p.80) reflect that, 'We differ from the constructivists in that what is imported into the situation is not a "state of mind" but an array of linguistic capacities. These capacities emerge primarily as we acquire the language of the culture.'

A significant element in the diagnosis of Asperger Syndrome and autism involves the Theory of Mind test (Baron-Cohen *et al.* 1985), which assesses the ability to conceptualise beliefs and attribute them to another. The Sally–Anne test (Baron-Cohen *et al.* 1985) is meant to show that the child who has Asperger Syndrome is not capable of a kind of third party thought (to empathise with another, imagine what another thinks, and so on) and the learning that can arise from that. In the test, there are two dolls, Sally and Anne. Sally has a marble, which she puts in her basket and then leaves the room. Anne has seen this and while Sally is out the room, Anne takes the marble and hides it in a box. When Sally comes back in the room, the tester asks the child, 'Where will Sally look for her marble?' The correct answer is Sally's basket. Children with Asperger Syndrome are less likely to come to this conclusion, pointing instead to the box.

Gregory Bateson's ideas about the importance of situating actions within context are essential for understanding people. He says:

> 'Context' is linked to another undefined notion called 'meaning'. Without context, words and actions have no meaning at all. This is true not only of human communication in words but also of all communication whatsoever, of all mental process, of all mind, including that which tells the sea anemone how to grow and the amoeba what he should do next. (Bateson 1972, p.15)

It would be interesting to experiment with this test across cultures, ages and with variations and see what 'evidence' they produced. One of the problems here is that, while the test may be interesting, the conclusions drawn from it are attributed solely to the cognitive abilities of the individual child. Another problem is the

acceptance of 'thought' as existing in isolation of human relationships. McGuire and Michalko critique the Sally–Anne exercise as decontextualised and creating only a partial picture which has much undermining evidence about its reliability from other studies (McGuire and Michalko 2011). Unless we study play in other contexts, the apparent lack of creative play or ability to empathise might not be occurring across the board or may be a feature, for example, characteristic of family relationships. In the examples above and below, we see how people reorganising their expectations of communication open up new opportunities for self and other. 'We do not treat "Theory of Mind" as a "thing-in-the-brain". Instead, we understand intentionality, shared and otherwise, as a method whereby people, all people, attribute motives to one another as a way to make sense of human interaction' (McGuire and Michalko 2011, p.173).

Systemic theory and practice is interested in what counts as 'knowledge'. In the context of the social world, information is not seen as a free-floating and gatherable set of objective facts but as contextually produced and subjective narratives. Reflexive epistemological knowing is understood as a process rather than end product. Professionals often ask, 'What can be observed and therefore known about X?' This is an ontological question to which modernist science expects answers and that, from here, generalised conditions, syndromes, and so on will be generated. The question 'How do I observe and know about X?' is an epistemological question about methods of knowing. But to take a step further into 'What are the contexts which are likely to be influencing what I think I know about X and how am I looking?' invites another level of critical reflexivity in which the enquirer takes responsibility for the inevitability of their bias. Further questions might also be useful: 'Whose voices am I listening to in this inquiry?' and: 'How am I allowing my relationship with my hypothesis to open or restrict what we can together achieve?' These last two questions are important in that they invite ethical reflexivity about not only ontological knowing but about the methodological influences on one's interpretation and responses to data.

The child diagnosed as having Asperger Syndrome may set great value on knowing about their area of special interest, as do professionals on theirs. The question 'Does the child diagnosed as having Asperger Syndrome have the ability to move between what they know and how they know what they know?' is based on a particular notion of ability-deficit located in individual mind. Asking instead, 'What do we need to do to create the dialogical conditions which bring forth co-creative conversation?' orientates the professional away from looking for evidence to experimenting with relational solutions.

Maturana suggests that every family member is a 'scientist' – in as much as people generate explanations for behaviour (Maturana 1991). He speaks of the *passion* in human beings to attempt to understand, relate parts of a system, but points out that we can only generate explanations (descriptions) of workings

within the limits of our area of structural determinism (Maturana 1991). One could then say that all the participants in collaborative action research (professionals, person diagnosed as having Asperger Syndrome and other family members) are living systems and are part of other living systems which are determined by culturally generated linguistic structures, such as going to the doctor if you have a worry and entering into a certain kind of individualised talk about the history and symptomology of that worry. Systemic social constructionists, as opposed to constructivists, might say that we act in to and out of the limits of the language and stories available to us and the opportunities to tell them (Shotter 1989).

According to Maturana, the only possible outcome of human interaction is that professionals and families are more likely to generate explanations and meanings coherent with the limits of their life experience as explained to themselves (Maturana 1991). From a systemic social constructionist understanding of human systems as linguistic systems, we not constrained by *experience* so much as by *conversational opportunities.*

GETTING OVER DETERMINISM AND DIAGNOSIS

The neurological story of connection creates a theory of inevitable causality. It determines that the individual is the site for treatment and draws on medical ideas to understand and to treat the problem, which is firmly located within the individual. It does not allow for social, cultural and political influences. Nor does it allow for opportunities to: 1) make sense of behaviours and communications within relational contexts; and 2) to work with those relational contexts to create more opportunities for better communications between participants.

Following diagnosis, professional interventions encourage 'neurologically atypical' people to correct or adapt their communication styles to fit in with the dominant culture. Such interventions are based on behavioural correction with tailored cognitive learning.

Ideas about 'treatment' have been developed within a modernist scientific discourse in which it is assumed that it is possible for one person to acquire more knowledge on a subject than the people coming for 'treatment'. In a scientific model, there is an assumption that it is possible and desirable to achieve objective information by remaining impartial to the subject. This model does not allow for the ideological bias of the professional, nor of the familial, socio-cultural and economic influences on the information that is generated by examinations of the person to be assessed.

The information to diagnose a condition and inform a 'treatment' method is generated by a series of questions designed by professionals in relation to a hypothesis. This hypothesis is inevitably a product of the information available at the time and arises out of hidden and therefore unquestioned ideology based on

all manner of social, cultural, political and economic influences on methodological assumptions. Diagnostic questions trace the history and symptomatology of a condition and focus on the life of the condition and little on the circumstances in which people are or have been living.

Diagnostic formats restrict the imagination of professionals and families to be curious about what makes a difference to a person's lived experience and their relationships. Instead, there is the risk of enacting a rule-bound format of assessment. This is likely to produce a description of an individual which is limited and linear. Such an assessment pays little attention to family culture or school resources so there is no room for a circular analysis of how interpersonal behaviours are maintained or changed. It follows that what you ask influences what you find and, therefore, what you do – so medical model stories are likely to influence the methods of 'treatment' and result in a plan for managing the individual under scrutiny. Because diagnosis focuses on an individual's cognition, it neglects the collaborative aspects of communication in which others are also responsible for how dialogue can take place and for what kind of talk counts. Instead of the meeting with professionals becoming an opportunity to experiment with what kind of talking and listening makes a difference, the process of diagnosis sets the professional and service users apart in different camps and reifies their positions.

Professionals engaged in diagnostic symptom-spotting often appear to mirror monological ways of talking reminiscent of people talking about an area of special interest. This symmetrical form of communication results in the creation of misinformation because it is a one-way activity by the collector of information and precludes the possibility of dialogue. Dialogue is problematic in monological discourses, such as those often found in modernist sciences, as it requires etiquette of being in relation with people and finding ways of going on in conversation without having a map or a set of instructions. Instead, in a dialogue, participants are required to work at coordinating with each other to get from a to b, to work out how to communicate in ways that are meaningful, appreciative, and carry a sense of possibility in going forwards. Professionals need permission to not know in order to find new ways of communicating with people in ways that feel productive. Current prescribed diagnostic procedures are: 1) restricting professionals' ways of speaking and being with families; 2) not enabling professionals to explore new ways of being and therefore learning with families what kinds of talk make a positive difference; 3) leading to important opportunities being missed by the emphasis on diagnosis over exploratory interventions.

It has been my experience that normally sparky and empathic professionals can fall into demonstrating a lack of imagination when acting in relation to their area of special interest – diagnostic criteria; and that they can fail to empathise sufficiently with the person in front of them to find out how they do think, how

they are communicating and what their abilities are. The clinic becomes the corridor for monological behaviour and single stories, which sadly emphasise deficit and inability. Diagnostic procedures become restrictive to happening upon new ways of knowing and being.

LINGUISTIC SYSTEMS AND RELATIONAL KNOW-HOW

A shift from a reverent demonstration of knowledge about the area of special interest to a shared world of imaginary play can result in a more ironic relationship with the area of special interest and more know-how in relationships.

The following example demonstrates my re-creating of a difficulty when I ask six-year-old Jamie to pretend to be something. I am struggling with competing narratives about how to be with Jamie. On the one hand, I am looking for confirmation of evidence that Jamie has Asperger Syndrome; on the other hand, I am trying to find ways of coordinating with Jamie in the moment of play. In effect, I am in two systems simultaneously: the professional system of diagnostic linguistics and the *making it up as we go* system of being in spontaneous knowledge-creating relationships. The system in focus eventually becomes the relationships in the room between people and play objects.

The process of using questions with Jamie is immediately problematic. He appears not to like being asked questions. In addition to conversation with Jamie proving difficult, there does not seem to be an obvious interactive system in his area of special interest, dinosaurs:

Therapist: Can you pretend to be a dinosaur?

Jamie: I'm not a dinosaur.

Therapist: Do like you're pretending.

Jamie: I'm not a dinosaur.

Jamie: I'm Godzilla.

Therapist: Okay, why don't you pretend to be Godzilla?

Jamie: I-don't-know (sing-song, looking elsewhere).

I don't think Jamie had a problem with understanding the concept of 'pretend play' as would be suggested by the criteria for diagnosing Asperger Syndrome. I was asking him to act in isolation. I think he may well have pretended to be a dinosaur if I had asked the grandparents to join in, me too perhaps, and we had all pranced around making noises and talking to each other as dinosaurs. In effect, I was asking Jamie to give a solo performance – and in the context of the

House of Tests (the clinic) where he had been initiated into diagnostic tests in the recent past. Shotter is intrigued by:

> our immediate *sensing* of the qualitative 'shape' of *how* the others around us are *responding* to us, *spontaneously*, and the influence of that on how safe and secure we feel in being who we are to them, and how the 'shape' of that *feeling* arouses anticipations within us as to what next might come from them – anticipations as to how they will treat us as being *this or that* kind of person in the world. (Shotter 2015, p.2)

In this following example from a subsequent play session, I had learned that I needed to enter into the play and be in the relational interactions, take leaps myself, and create both in and out positions.

> *Therapist:* I wonder what a Gigantosaurus moves like? Okay. Here comes the Gigantosaurus. It's taking gigantic leaps. *(Makes leaping noises)*
>
> *Therapist (as Gigantosaurus):* 'Hello Jamie! How are you today?'
>
> *Therapist:* Look, the Gigantosaurus spoke.
>
> *Jamie fetches the T-Rex and makes it roar at the Gigantosaurus.*
>
> *Gigantosaurus:* Oh, I'm frightened!
>
> *T–Rex roars.*
>
> *Gigantosaurus:* Eeek!
>
> *Jamie:* It's a T-Rex!
>
> *Therapist:* It makes a big roar. The Gigantosaurus says, 'It makes a big roar.'
>
> *Gigantosaurus:* Are you friendly?
>
> *Therapist:* Maybe the Gigantosaurus wants to be friends with the T-Rex. Do you think he wants to be friends or not?
>
> *Jamie:* He wants to be friends.
>
> *Therapist:* Does the T-Rex want to be friends?
>
> *Jamie:* Yes, he is.
>
> *Therapist:* Maybe that's his way of saying hello – doing a big roar.

Playing didn't only enable Jamie to extend his range of communication, it enabled me to extend mine – playing in this way created an 'us'. I moved between different person-positions and so did Jamie. My earlier questions to Jamie constructed an 'I–you'. These early questions were influenced by my relationship with diagnostic

criteria and created a discord in our attempts to communicate with each other. When I entered into and created a shared world with Jamie, this made for a more collaborative and creative culture which seemed not only to make for connection but which brought forth evidence of non-Asperger Syndrome abilities. The imaginary and interactive play going on here is with both parties initiating contact and responding to each other. We are creating a new linguistic system in which we are talking about talking and reflecting on relationships. We both know that we are ourselves and yet are pretending to be another creature. We have created a meaning-making system and have moved away from the rule-bound naming, describing and collecting relationship with dinosaurs:

> When one person acts 'into' a jointly constructed setting rather than 'out of' his or her own plans or desires, an outcome is produced which is independent of any of the individuals involved and 'belongs' only to the collectivity they constitute. (Shotter 1989, p.147)

In shifting the focus from the child to communicating systems, Jamie's family started to follow Jamie's lead in any imaginary play, elaborated themselves and enjoyed the intimacy arising out of this play. But the family also found it hard to step out of the naming games, the question–answer ways of speaking that they had witnessed and felt was expected by professionals in the clinic – just as I had done.

Human beings have no innate ability to make sense of complex interactions. They are very difficult to learn to interpret, as we are not usually aware of the contexts people are acting out of or think they are acting into. We often feel nervous while we are still in the process of sense-making or when we have misunderstood the other. We have to learn to be patient while we wonder what is going on and we have to learn to act respectfully while we are trying to work this out. The world of human interaction is awash with uncertainties:

> Instead of understanding autism simply as a puzzle, we treat it as an example of the fundamental human features of uncertainty, of the incompleteness and partiality of communication, of the constant risk presented by the potential undoing of the tie that makes you and I a 'we'. (McGuire and Michalko 2011, p.164)

FROM EXPERT PROFESSIONAL KNOWING TO A LEARNING CULTURE OF COLLABORATIVE ACTION RESEARCH

Rather than rush to a position of expert knowing from without a relationship, the invitation here is for professionals to develop a new culture akin to collaborative

action research. Professional knowledge becomes a process of collaborative learning. Learning happens from within the living moment of interaction *with* people and not through theorising without and about them. It is a pragmatic response, which foregrounds strengths and abilities over the culturally specific products of evidence of disability and communications difficulties. It is also an ethical response to one of the persistent bastions of the psychiatric, psychological and psychotherapeutic professions: the belief that the professional expert has more relevant knowledge than the client and their social network.

A collaborative action research approach repositions the identified patient as someone with a contribution to make to therapeutic conversations. Their expertise and abilities can be recognised in contrast to how the knowledge of the patient has become de-centred and peripheral (Foucault 1980). Lather's concept of 'catalytic validity' proposes turning a symptom of disorder into a resource for both an identified patient and their family (Lather 1991). Professional expertise has a facilitative and creative function in finding ways of incorporating the contribution of all family members and in encouraging the activities and attitudes needed to achieve new ways of seeing and being with each other. This form of dialogue brings forth and showcases the ability of the person with a diagnosis of Asperger Syndrome to explain and develop lineal and circular accounts of complex relational systems. Conversation is not understood as a means to collecting knowledge so much as a means of generating knowledge. The shift, both for the person diagnosed with Asperger Syndrome and for the professional, facilitates new ways of knowing how to go on in conversation with less repetitive, rule-bound ways of talking.

CONCLUSION

The invitation in this chapter is to understand that diagnosis is usually a monological activity by one person about another. Dialogue, on the other hand, leads to improved communication with people and to better coordination with them.

By entering into a collaborative inquiry with people with Asperger Syndrome and their families, professionals can extend repertoires of communicating with people described as having autistic spectrum conditions and their families and friends. If we resist being governed by Compulsive Diagnosing Behaviours (CDB) and Symptom Spotting Tendencies (SST), we can open ourselves up to new ways of being with people in therapeutic play and conversation. We can encourage a reflexive curiosity about what makes a difference in what we are doing with each other that opens or closes opportunities for meaningful and fruitful dialogue. The study of grammar in both professional and family systems

might generate more descriptions of connectedness than would otherwise be available to family members.

For professionals to point to parts of the brain and insist the knowledge will emerge in the future about the cause of autism is not of much use to people who want to be appreciated and enter into easier communications. Such lineal causality reduces people with Asperger Syndrome or high-functioning autism to people with something inherently wrong with them and, by doing so, further isolates them from others. This results in entire research budgets being diverted to the task of locating a mythical organic cause followed by a cure. In the meantime, many possibilities yet to be explored with people diagnosed as having Asperger Syndrome and their social networks, on how to improve everyday communications, and with that, their quality of life, are missed. Given how many families crave meaningful interaction with their child with Asperger Syndrome and desire improved harmony across their family, there is much to commend a relationally oriented systemic approach in which all participants are positioned as collaborative action researchers.

REFERENCES

Baron-Cohen, S., Leslie, A.M., and Frith, U. (1985) 'Does the autistic child have "Theory of Mind"?' *Cognition 21*,1, 37–46.

Bateson, G. (1972) *Steps to an Ecology of Mind.* Chicago, IL: University of Chicago Press.

Brownlow, C., and O'Dell, L. (2009) 'Challenging understandings of "Theory of Mind": a brief report.' *Intellectual and Developmental Disabilities 47*, 6, 473–478.

Foucault, M. (1980) 'Subjugated Knowledge.' In C. Gordon (ed.) *Power/Knowledge – Selected Interviews and Other Writings 1972–1977.* Brighton: Harvester Press.

Frith, U. (ed.) (1991) *Autism and Asperger Syndrome.* Cambridge: Cambridge University Press.

Gergen, K.J., and Gergen, M. (2002) 'Ethnography as Relationship.' In A. Bochner and C. Ellis (eds) *Ethnographically Speaking. Autoethnography, Literature, and Aesthetics.* Walnut Creek, CA: AltaMira Press.

Gillberg, C. (1991) 'Clinical and Neurobiological Aspects of Asperger Syndrome in Six Family Studies.' In U. Frith (ed.) *Autism and Asperger Syndrome.* Cambridge: Cambridge University Press.

Hickok, G. (2014) *The Myth of Mirror Neurons: The Real Neuroscience of Communication and Cognition.* London: Norton.

Lather, P. (1991) *Getting Smart.* New York: Routledge.

Leppington, R. (1991) 'From constructivism to social constructionism and doing critical therapy.' *Human Systems: Journal of Systemic Consultation and Management 2*, 2, 79–104.

Maturana, H. (1991) 'Science and Daily Life: The Ontology of Scientific Explanations.' In F. Steier (ed.) *Research and Reflexivity.* London: Sage.

McGuire, A.E., and Michalko, R. (2011) 'Minds between us: autism, mindblindness and the uncertainty of communication.' *Educational Philosophy and Theory 43*, 2, 162–177.

Shotter, J. (1989) 'Social Accountability and the Social Construction of "You".' In J. Shotter and K. Gergen (eds) *Texts of Identity.* London: Sage.

Shotter, J. (2008) *Conversational Realities Revisited: Life, Language, Body and World.* Ohio, OH: Taos Institute Publications.

Shotter, J. (2015) 'Ontological risks and communication anxieties – on what and whom others will "allow" us to be.' *International Journal of Collaborative-Dialogic Practices 6.*

Simon, G. (2004) 'Systemic family therapy with families with a child who has a diagnosis of Asperger Syndrome.' *Human Systems: The Journal of Systemic Consultation and Management 15,* 4, 257–274.

Timimi, S., Gardner, N., and McCabe, B. (2010) *The Myth of Autism: Medicalising Men's and Boys' Social and Emotional Competence.* Basingstoke: Palgrave Macmillan.

Wing, L. (1981) 'Asperger's syndrome: a clinical account.' *Psychological Medicine 11, 1,* 115–129.

Whitfield, G., and Simon, G. (2014) *Notes for Pink Practice working paper.* Unpublished.

CHAPTER 16

THE ETHICS AND CONSEQUENCES OF MAKING AUTISM SPECTRUM DISORDER DIAGNOSES

Saqib Latif

This chapter engages with an ethical view of how people's ideas are modified and influenced by the dominant classification systems, which in a capitalist market has been driving toward a technically based biomedical model of mental wellbeing. Whilst such a model may be good for expanding markets, problems of feeding disproportionate demand against limited resources arise in universal public health systems such as the United Kingdom National Health Service (NHS). A consequence of this biomedical model is that psychiatric diagnoses operate in practice as categorical, like other medical or surgical diagnoses, where an illness 'exists' or 'does not exist'. Such a categorical approach is valid in surgery where there is a fracture or no fracture, or in medicine where cancer cells are either present or absent. However, in psychiatry, there is significant theoretical and empirical support for the concept of dimensionality that encourages a view of presentations as being variations of traits and states of mind that are present on a continuum. Arguments about 'whether Autism Spectrum Disorder (ASD) exists' are essentially semantic as it is more a matter of the use of specific language to describe certain presentations amongst professionals and the public, resulting in these presenting behaviours being bestowed with a certain meaning, rather than an 'uncovering' of some essential truth about the nature of the presenting behaviours. There is no dispute about the existence of ASD behaviours; instead the dispute is about whether these behaviours amount to a discrete naturally occurring category that the diagnostic label represents. Is it fair, necessary or useful to reduce down to a one-dimensional construct of ASD the evolving personality, experiences, diverse histories and contexts of a growing child with a highly plastic brain?

The neoliberally driven desire to encapsulate diverse presentations into medical model reductionist frameworks has resulted in the constantly changing nature of ASD definitions. Whereas the medical model has worked well for most medical specialities, this has produced some major conceptual difficulties with highly dynamic mental health presentations such as ASD. First, thresholds for diagnosis are highly variable and have changed multiple times since the inception of the term. Second, the element of subjectivity cannot be taken out from the diagnosis despite the development of multiple diagnostic instruments, as receiving the diagnosis depends largely on *who* you ask and *who* asks the questions, rather than the nature of actual problems encountered by the person. Third, there remains significant and unaddressed cross-cultural variability, which is yet to be explored due to the relative lack of data from most parts of the world.

Instead of basing practice on such a narrow reductionist territory, I will argue in favour of value-based approaches (Fulford 2009). Human behaviour involves social and moral dimensions, and cannot be understood without taking into consideration the values of that individual, their family and indeed their broader cultural milieu. Any attempt to 'treat', without consideration of these aspects, risks sliding into attempts to exert paternalism and social control through the medium of politically sanctioned state institutions.

INTRODUCTION

The boundaries of psychiatric disorders are fluid and their understanding is evolving. As a result, psychiatric classification systems have long been the subject of controversies. A number of diagnostic terms have been removed from the classifications systems. For example, homosexuality was part of psychiatric classification until 1973, and many new diagnoses have found their way into current diagnostic systems (APA 2013; Blashfield 1998). This continuous changing in diagnostic categories is something one would not find in recent decades in any other 'medical' speciality.

It was around the turn of twentieth century that an interest in discrete categorisation of mental health problems became more evident. Bleuler (1911) first used the term 'autistic' to denote a withdrawal from interest in the outside world in individuals diagnosed with schizophrenia. Carl Jung ([1923] 1971) suggested severe introversion as characteristic of this autistic withdrawal, though he was not in favour of strict classification as he believed that all people have tendencies in different directions. In the context of autism, Leo Kanner (1943) and Hans Asperger ([1944] 1991) are key individuals, who around the same time, though living in different parts of the world (USA and Austria respectively), published their research with children and suggested they presented with a syndrome of autism (Kanner 1943) or autistic psychopathology

(Asperger [1944] 1991). This became the foundation for future definitions in this contentious area.

It is important to note the changes in the understanding of the construct of autism, where once 'idiocy' (probably referring to what we now call intellectual disability) was viewed as an integral part of autism and an overlap was believed to exist with the construct of 'childhood psychosis' (Creak 1951). This is no longer the case. Further modifications in this construct over the next several decades led to an expansion of the concept of autism from a rare and specific set of behaviours to a 'spectrum' that extends from a helpless non-communicative person to some of the most eminent contributors to human progress, such as Newton and Einstein, who have retrospectively been said to have features of autism. One wonders, given that there is such a massive variation, whether it should be called a 'disorder' spectrum, or just a 'human' spectrum. There is a high level of heterogeneity in the symptoms, and partly due to lack of clarity about the boundaries of this construct, the definition of autism has been widened over time, leading to an 'autism epidemic' (Timimi, Gardner and McCabe 2010). With such a wide spectrum and variations in the construct over time and across various cultures of the world, does this label of 'ASD' add anything to our understanding and how to help those labelled with it?

The classification was originally devised as a means of communication amongst professionals, but it has served to strengthen the medical model, which in turn has led to increased paternalistic practices and an increase in the accompanying stigma. I propose that a move towards a social model of understanding and value-based practice is more helpful, and more sustainable, than the current reductionist biomedical model. I must make it clear here that my scepticism is only about the stability of a distinct something called 'autism', and not about the subjective distress of the people with difficulties who may be labelled as such.

IS AUTISM A 'MENTAL DISORDER'?

In the past four decades, the concept of mental disorder has been viewed in different ways by differing philosophical orientations, leading to a questioning of the biomedical model. They include critical psychiatry, anti-psychiatry, post-psychiatry and the social constructivist movement. All these movements have in common that they criticise the biomedical model of mental illness, and advocate something which tends to get missed when adopting such a model, which is the use of a more context-rich biopsychosocial approach to understanding the presentations. The norms that define mental disorder in psychiatry are not primarily medical or even scientific, but are really social norms disguised by the involvement of the medical profession and partly under the influence of political and societal pressures (Bolton 2008). The tension around the reliability

and validity of ASD diagnoses is one manifestation of this inadequacy of the biomedical model.

Various movements critical of psychiatry have existed in its history, with strong 'anti-psychiatry' critiques made by sociologist Erving Goffman (1968) and philosopher Michael Foucault (1965), who questioned the nature and social/political function of psychiatric institutions. Amongst psychiatrists themselves, R.D. Laing (1960) and Thomas Szasz (1974) argued against understanding of mental illness in terms of brain pathology. Szasz (1974) argued that mental illness is no more than a metaphor because it does not have any identifiable basis in physical pathology and is best understood as a way of communication about the distress of an individual. Szasz (1974) was vocal and explicit about the (ab)use of the concept of 'mental illness' as a method of avoiding responsibility by individuals, and its use by the society and the courts to avoid punishment; at the same time as enabling social control over individuals deemed non-conformist to a narrowing concept of 'normal'. He proposed that what is called 'mental illness' is better thought of as 'problems of the living'. A similar moral–medical boundary is of course apparent with bodily disorders, with illness excusing one from responsibility, such as when a doctor gives out an 'off work' certificate, but the boundary is far more problematic in psychiatry. Szasz (1974) faced considerable opposition from pro-biological psychiatrists such as Kendell (1975) who have argued that mental illness must be viewed as no different from any bodily disorders. Though it is claimed that recent research into autism spectrum disorders has shown biological determinants, closer examination of such claims reveals that causative mechanisms or biological abnormalities have not been found for autism, and it would be fair to say that the idea came before the evidence, and the evidence is now being 'shaped' to fit the idea (Timimi *et al.* 2010).

The current problematic state of diagnostic classifications has been aptly summarised by one of the DSM Panel's own members:

> The point is not that decisions about what is normal are riddled with personal biases and political considerations, but rather that, by dint of a handful of influential professional efforts, those subjective determinants of diagnoses masquerade as solid science and truth. (Caplan 1995, cited in Hill 2013, n.p.)

Let me next try and define the term 'disorder'. The American Psychiatric Association (APA 1994) uses the term disorder to imply the existence of a clinically recognisable set of symptoms or behaviours associated in most cases with *distress* and with *interference with personal functions.* It recognises that disorder is not an exact term, and is only used to avoid even greater problems that are inherent in the use of terms such as disease and illness. The World Health Organisation in its guidelines notes that, 'social deviation or conflict alone, without personal

dysfunction, should not be included in mental disorder' (WHO 2004, p.351). The definition thus highlights 'distress' and 'personal dysfunction' as important elements. In clinical practice this may not be seen in cases of autistic spectrum, and, more often than not, it is the distress of parents, families or teachers that bring the young person to medical attention. In my view, labelling a person with a mental disorder, without the elements of personal distress and dysfunction, because they are struggling to conform to some culturally accepted norm could be viewed as unethical.

If we agree to call highly impressive people from history as disordered, then perhaps we all would want to be disordered! But what should we tell a young person getting diagnosed with ASD about which bracket she or he is being put in – are they with the Einstein group or in the group labelled with intellectual disability? Being 'different' should not necessarily mean being 'disordered'.

It is generally accepted that the symptoms of autistic spectrum conditions can and do exist in the general population. It is a combination of those behaviours up to and beyond a certain threshold that leads to the behaviours being symptoms of a 'disorder'. But who should be given the power to decide on where that arbitrary cut-off lies? Those who are given the power to decide are faced with the challenge of developing 'objective' approaches to diagnosing it as a categorical disorder, despite it being acknowledged that the behaviours are present on a continuum. Given the wide range of behaviours examined, the act of making a diagnosis ultimately comes down to the subjective judgement of a professional who decides, on the basis of information provided at that time, whether the person reaches that threshold or not. If it is agreed that we are dealing with a dimensional construct and that there is a continuum between normal aspects of personality and autistic features, why should a classification system treat it as a categorical condition with a 'yes she has it', 'no she doesn't' binary?

Autism is considered to be a 'neurodevelopmental' disorder (i.e. problems with the development of the nervous system), and much of the research has been done on young people under the age of 18 years. Very few long-term studies have been done to show what the longer-term prognosis is for people diagnosed with an ASD, so we know little about how they would function as adults. Longer-term outcomes are likely to be dependent on many variables including family and educational support, personal strengths and weaknesses, and so on. What is achieved by labelling someone with a disorder if it doesn't really predict outcomes and can lead to increased stigma? Little has been written about the impact of messages of pessimism, hopelessness and 'chronicity' and of thinking about autism as a lifelong 'disorder'.

Even if we imagine that mankind has been able to develop a perfect tool to diagnose ASD which has high levels of reliability, what is that tool going to measure? The validity of the concept itself is fluid, and changes with time and

culture. We know that the ability to understand the emotions of others, often considered a core deficit in autistic spectrum conditions, is affected significantly by intrinsic factors including age, intelligence, academic abilities, vocabulary, mood and physical illnesses, and extrinsic factors including culture, nature of the relationship or 'attachment', recent losses and life events. On many occasions I have seen cases where, for instance, the mother of a young boy gives a different picture in support of that child presenting with autistic spectrum behaviours, against a father who claims not to have seen such features when the boy is with him. One of the problems of any interview assessment is that it is based on the assumption that the information is gathered from an 'objective' source without any bias, whereas in reality personal perceptions of people vary enormously. If the information depends largely on who you ask the questions to, then the diagnosis based on such information will be equally subjective and potentially invalid.

Not only does it depend on who you ask, it also depends on who asks the questions. Generally the remit of clinical diagnosis is limited to medically trained doctors, whereas in the case of autism not only clinical psychologists but also educational psychologists, speech and language therapists, nurses and even teachers can make or recommend a diagnosis. All these different clinicians will be using their own judgements driven by their training backgrounds and personal preferences in reaching a decision about saying 'yes' or 'no' to a diagnosis of autism; consequently setting the threshold for this dimensional concept at different levels across different clinicians, teams and locations.

Advocates for conceptualising autistic spectrum as a 'disorder' often believe that it is imperative to have a formal diagnosis, so that the difficulties can be recognised and appropriate support could be sought from educational, social or health services. Whilst this may help procure needed services, the risk is that the young person ceases to be seen as a unique individual as from henceforth they will be recognised primarily by their 'autism' label. In my opinion, we should argue for better services for those young people who are struggling in the areas (for example) of social interaction at schools or other places, but this should be done without resorting to a lifelong label.

As the term 'autism' has become part of our language, it has come to be understood in today's culture as a sign of a serious 'lifelong disorder'. Thus use of this label can function as a 'ticket' to access specialist resources. It is a shame that reliance on a specific label of disorder is necessary for schools to put in place the right support for a child's unmet needs. On the other hand, the label is often used as a 'defence' or 'distraction' for behaviours that may have nothing directly to do with the construct of autism. Many times I have heard the phrase 'he behaves in this way because he is autistic' and then the attempts to help with that behaviour may be dropped.

INTERNAL STIGMA

An important consequence of medical model thinking is the resulting 'internal stigma', associated with lack of hope and an expectation of poor outcomes for the person with the label. When a person is labelled with a lifelong disorder by an 'expert' and is given some medication (for example to control a behaviour), the burden of responsibility is shifted from the person to the presumed 'illness'. Now she knows she is not to be blamed because an agent over which she has no control (in this case the 'disorder' of autism) is the cause. This may give the patient and/or their family a sense of relief and indebtedness to the expert, and become a source for the expansion of the expert's business. Responsibility is taken away from the person and those around the person – there is no expectation that the person takes responsibility for their behaviour, and expectations for them to change as they grow and develop may be permanently altered.

When we take away the control from the person by saying, 'It's not you, it's the "illness"', we are not only inculcating a sense of disability with its connotation of helplessness and dependence, we are also projecting the sense that you have no conscious control over what you do. This leads to reduced expectations and ambitions. The use of labels can therefore lead to people becoming trapped in a limiting way by their own beliefs and by the reactions and behaviours of those around them to the label. It is therefore important, in my opinion, to loosen the coupling between diagnosis and disability, with any assessment for disability being based on the level of impairment and context-dependent needs (e.g. in schools) rather than the diagnosis. A psychosocial model instead would acknowledge that not everything is within any person's control (diagnosis or no diagnosis) and focus on the social context.

When it comes to treatment, there are no known evidence-based treatments available that are specific for 'autism' (Timimi *et al.* 2010) and we are thus far from any 'cure'. What is the point of attaching a disorder label to a young person when the cause is not known, it does not predict outcome and there is no cure? There are some potentially serious negative consequences for the child in the future, as it may influence employers against giving a job to a person who has had a diagnosis of Autism Spectrum Disorder. We are neither doing any favours to the young person nor to society by labelling a significant proportion (about 1%, according to Baird *et al.* 2006) of our future workforce as 'disabled' with an ASD diagnosis.

AUTISM AS AN INDUSTRY

Some researchers have blamed genetics, whereas others thought the environment (such as vaccines) was to be held responsible for causing autism. The list of controversies associated with autism seems endless, but there is still no clarity on the question of causation. The later retracted study associating the MMR vaccine with autism (Wakefield 1998) led to thousands of children not being vaccinated and society then paid the price of a measles epidemic (Press Association 2013). In the past Bruno Bettelheim thought autism was caused by the pathological behaviour of parents, in particular what he termed 'refrigerator mothers' (Timimi *et al.* 2010), and more recently the theory that autism is the extreme end of the male continuum of behaviours has been put forward (Baron-Cohen 2003). These debates and controversies have proved to be a blessing for some, as they have inflated autism's media profile and helped bring money for research and patients to willing practitioners, which further increases the interest of a growing class of professionals and the public in keeping the category of autism as a medical disorder. One of the consequences of this has been the discrepancy between society's expectations from the medical model of ASD and the current service provision within the financially struggling UK National Health Service, which has led to some prolonged waiting lists for assessments.

Since the autism diagnosis is viewed by some as a means to gain financial or educational advantage – for example, financial benefits such as Disability Living Allowance (a disability-related benefit) in the UK, or for insurance purposes in the USA – there has been an increasing number of requests for a diagnostic assessment. It is this type of 'partly non-purposeful' misuse of diagnosis, where the diagnoser is not fully aware of the factors influencing their decision-making, that is becoming more common. While talking about the beauty of diagnosis as a solution to human problems, Reich (1980, p.10) says:

> With remarkable ease diagnoses can turn the fright of chaos into the comfort of the known; the burden of doubt into the pleasure of certainty; the shame of hurting others into the pride of helping them; and the dilemma of moral judgement into the clarity of medical truth.

It is in this capacity of the diagnosis to apparently explain, and even justify, all types of behaviours which are odd or considered socially unacceptable that the lure and power of diagnosis lies; but it is also this perception about diagnosis which can lead to its abuse.

This lure often leads to increasing pressure from society on psychiatric and other medical professionals to do more, diagnose more ASD, and provide more explanations for behaviours deemed socially unacceptable. This growing pressure can be hard to resist. On the one hand, it can lead to research and developments in the field of mental health; on the other hand, it can lead to

over-diagnosis, easy labelling of behaviours which are out of social norms, and overuse of unnecessary and potentially harmful treatments.

What is happening today is that a generation of psychiatrists and paediatricians have been trained according to a narrow biomedical model, using classification systems that ignore psychosocial aspects and that have little evidence that they reflect biological reality. All too often medical and other professionals end up diagnosing ASD due to the wishes of schools and families in order to get additional educational and/or social support; and not necessarily because this is what the young person wants and without good evidence that the diagnosis will lead to better outcomes for anyone. This is, in my opinion, unethical.

Psychiatry continues to be perceived as unscientific, and keeps getting associated with violence, stigma and untreatability (Allott, Loganathan and Fulford 2002). The medical model, which has a narrow focus on within-person experiences and the biology of the individual, creates a decontextualised and simplistic idea of the problem, disengaging us from our social responsibility as a society, and enhancing our dependence on doctors as 'experts', rather than trying to use our own problem-solving skills. The alternative of a values-based biopsychosocial model embraces broader conceptualisations of the origins of complex behaviour.

VALUES-BASED PRACTICE

Several forces are inherent in capitalist culture that creates high expectations of people, instilling a 'false' sense of having control over their environments (the current insurance-driven and risk-averse culture is an example of that). Society's high expectations lead to disappointments and alienation, with social consequences including family breakdowns, high divorce rates, crime, domestic violence, child abuse and neglect, alcoholism and drug abuse, and general feelings of isolation and frustration; these often then result in depression and many other mental health problems (Gasper 2010). In a capitalist society, the main discourse around mental health problems is biological, where any behaviour which is deviant from the narrow acceptable range is deemed as 'pathological', with the problem then internalised into the person, ignoring their environmental, social and political contexts (Prilleltensky and Gonick 1996). Capitalist markets value productivity, competitiveness and independence, with anyone who 'falls short' in these areas struggling to survive (emotionally and financially). Mental health care is itself part of these macroeconomics; hence the agenda is driven by those with the money, such as big pharmaceutical companies with vested interests in promoting diagnosis. These powerful institutions use the 'expert' model of doctors as a mechanism for profit-making through the labelling of individuals.

The analytic philosopher Gilbert Ryle (1967) proposed a conceptual model of mental disorder and argued that, except for dementia and learning disabilities, mental illnesses cannot be called medical illnesses, rather they are moral problems of living. Others such as Christopher Boorse (1975) and Richard Hare (1952), through their contributions in the linguistic-analytical model, helped our understanding to move from a fact-centred medical model to a fact-plus-values model; one in which evaluative and factual elements are woven through the conceptual fabric of medicine. Wakefield (2000) also played an important role in the broader understanding of the concept of mental disorder.

It is the practical application of these ideas in the form of values-based practice that I believe to be the future, as it emphasises and builds on the diversity of individual human values, in the areas of experience and behaviour with which psychiatry is concerned. There is no 'right outcome' in values-based practice, rather it relies on 'good process' as a basis for balanced decision-making in partnership with service users (Fulford 2009). In the appropriate clinical application of evidence-based as well as values-based practice, both facts and values must be taken into account at the time of assessment and throughout treatment.

Instead of following the biomedical model that can lead to practice with a poor evidence and ethical basis, mental health practitioners can be guided by the principles of working in partnership with people and their families, with a shared goal of their individual and collective development and empowerment. They will see themselves as helpful allies in a joint project, rather than as revered experts. They will move their practice beyond the approach of focusing on identifying pathologies in favour of one that elicits competencies. Persons with mental health problems have skills, resilience and capacities to grow. As the social and psychological world of the child has a critical influence on their wellbeing and development, a more systemic approach to practice should be followed. It is time for psychiatrists and other mental health practitioners to recognise that diagnosis in psychiatry is not a values-neutral scientific process, and it is time to more actively take into account the role of values in order to work in genuine partnership with the service users (Fulford 2009).

My final thought is that very few people have spoken up as advocates on behalf of those children and young people who are at the centre of it, because usually it is the professionals, parents and teachers around them, who will, with their own agendas, speak on their behalf. If given a choice between getting a lifelong label of a disorder with all the possible repercussions for the rest of their life, or getting support without the diagnosis, who would want to get a label? It is indeed a shame that in today's world, appropriate support cannot be sought without having first to resort to a label of 'disorder'. It is our ethical duty, whether we are clinicians, parents, teachers or politicians, to change this.

REFERENCES

Allott, P., Loganathan, L., and Fulford, K.W. M. (2002) 'Discovering hope for recovery.' *Canadian Journal of Community Mental Health 21*, 13–33.

American Psychiatric Association (1994) *Diagnostic and Statistical Manual of Mental Disorders, Fourth Edition (DSM-IV)*. Washington, DC: APA.

American Psychiatric Association (2013) *Diagnostic and Statistical Manual of Mental Disorders, Fifth Edition (DSM-5)*. Washington, DC: APA.

Asperger, H. [1944] (1991) 'Autistic Psychopathy in Childhood.' In U. Frith (ed.) *Autism and Asperger Syndrome*. Cambridge: Cambridge University Press.

Baird, G., Simonoff, E., Pickles, A., Chandler, S., *et al.* (2006) 'Prevalence of disorders of the autism spectrum in a population cohort of children in South Thames: the Special Needs and Autism project (SNAP).' *The Lancet 368*, 9531, 210–215.

Baron-Cohen, S. (2003) *The Essential Difference: The Truth about the Male and Female Brain*. New York: Basic Books.

Blashfield, R.K. (1998) 'Diagnostic models and systems.' *Comprehensive Clinical Psychology 4*, 57–59.

Bleuler, E. (1911) 'Dementia Praecox oder Gruppe der Schizophrenien.' In G. Aschaffenburg (ed.) *Handbuch der Psychiatrie*. Leipzig: Deuticke.

Bolton, D. (2008) 'What is Mental Disorder?' In D. Bolton (ed.) *An Essay in Philosophy, Science and Values*. Oxford: Oxford University Press.

Boorse C. (1975) 'On the distinction between disease and illness.' *Philosophy and Public Affairs 5*, 49–68.

Creak, M. (1951) 'Psychosis in childhood.' *Journal of Mental Science 97*, 545–554.

Foucault, M. (1965) *Madness and Civilisation: A History Of Insanity in the Age of Reason*. New York: Random House.

Fulford, K.W.M. (2009) 'Value, Science and Psychiatry.' In S. Block and S. Green (eds) *Psychiatric Ethics*. Oxford: Oxford University Press.

Gasper, P. (2010) 'Marxism, capitalism and alienation.' *International Socialist Review 74*. Available at http://isreview.org/issue/74/capitalism-and-alienation, accessed on 19 November 2015.

Goffman, E. (1968) *Asylums*. Harmondsworth: Penguin.

Hare, R.M. (1952) *The Language of Morals*. Oxford: Oxford University Press.

Hill, V. (2013) 'Conference Introduction.' At Medicalisation of Childhood Behaviours: The Need for a Paradigm Shift Conference, Manchester, June. Available at www.bps.org.uk/events/division-educational-child-psychology-one-day-event-medicalisation-childhood-time-paradigm-sh, accessed on 19 November 2015.

Jung, C.G. [1923] (1971) *Psychological Types*. London: Routledge and Kegan Paul.

Kanner, L. (1943) 'Autistic disturbances of affective contact.' *Nervous Child 2*, 217–250.

Kendell, R.E. (1975) 'The concept of disease and its implications for psychiatry.' *British Journal of Psychiatry 127*, 305–315.

Laing, R.D. (1960) *The Divided Self*. Baltimore, MD: Penguin.

Press Association (2013) 'Swansea measles epidemic: 620 cases confirmed.' *The Guardian*, April 9. Available at www.theguardian.com/society/2013/apr/09/swansea-measles-epidemic-620-cases, accessed on 19 November 2015.

Prilleltensky, I., and Gonick, L. (1996) 'Politics change, oppression remains: on the psychology and politics of oppression.' *Political Psychology 17*, 127–148.

Reich, W. (1980) 'Psychiatric Diagnosis as an Ethical Problem.' In S. Bloch and S. Green (eds) *Psychiatric Ethics* (Fourth edition). Oxford: Oxford University Press.

Ryle, G. (1980) *The Concept of Mind*. London: Penguin.

Szasz, T. (1974) *The Myth of Mental Illness* (Revised edition). New York: Harper and Row.

Timimi, S., Gardner, N., and McCabe, B. (2010) *The Myth of Autism: Medicalising Men's and Boys' Social and Emotional Competence.* London: Palgrave Macmillan

Wakefield, A. (1998) 'Ileal-lymphoid-nodular hyperplasia, non-specific colitis, and pervasive developmental disorder in children.' *The Lancet.* Retracted.

Wakefield, J.C. (2000) 'Aristotle as socio-biologist: the function of a human being, argument, black box essentialism, and the concept of mental disorder.' *Philosophy, Psychiatry and Psychology* 7, 17–44.

World Health Organisation (2004) *Pocket Guide to ICD-10 Classification of Mental and Behavioural Disorders.* London: Churchill Livingstone/Elsevier.

CHAPTER 17

EXAMINING LANGUAGE AND COMMUNICATION IN AUTISM SPECTRUM DISORDER – IN CONTEXT

Tom Muskett

INTRODUCTION

As is the case for all psychiatric disorders, the diagnostic process for Autism Spectrum Disorder (ASD) involves the matching of particular presenting behaviours against those listed in agreed clinical definitions of the condition. Many of such behaviours are related to language and communication; by definition, the diagnosis is associated with some level of apparent difficulty in relation to reciprocal conversational interaction. Numerous specific language and communication behaviours are also diagnostically relevant (for a complete description, see Rapin and Dunn 2003). These include: pronoun reversal (i.e. use of second person 'you' where first person 'I' is grammatically expected) and other pronoun misuse (e.g. use of third person 's/he' to refer to oneself); echolalia (i.e. immediate or delayed repetition of previously heard language); idiosyncratic language use, including apparently self-generated words; apparent failure to answer, and/or mis-answering of, questions; stereotypical language (i.e. unusual, and often ostensibly repetitive, use of 'chunks' of language); and a range of non-verbal communication issues in relation to eye gaze, gesture, and use of the body and space during interaction.

In psychiatric diagnostic frameworks, the behaviours that are specified in clinical criteria are described as being *signs* that index the 'mental disorder' in question. Hence, echolalia, pronoun reversal, idiosyncratic language and so forth can be considered signs of ASD. In reflection of psychiatry's lineage, this terminology has been appropriated from medicine where 'sign' refers to an externally observable physical phenomenon indicative of an underlying physiological problem. As an internet search indicates, describing ASD explicitly

in terms of signs and symptoms[1] is commonplace. Accordingly, it is typically assumed that language and communication behaviours such as those listed above can legitimately be represented in these terms.

In this chapter, I argue that there are problems associated with conceptualising language and communication behaviours within this kind of framework. These arguments are congruent with an established line of critical thinking that is commonly applied to diagnoses such as depression and schizophrenia. It is notable that these well-rehearsed arguments are not typically considered in relation to ASD, despite it having emerged from the same frameworks and methods of practice as other psychiatric diagnoses. Regardless, it will be demonstrated that such critiques are directly relevant for critical consideration of current thinking about language and communication in ASD.

This chapter is organised as follows. First, I briefly present the aforementioned critical arguments that have been made more generally in relation to psychiatric diagnosis. As will be described, these arguments problematise the manner in which psychiatric diagnostic frameworks construct human behaviours and experiences as if endogenous (coming primarily from within the person) products of underlying mental disorder, which can therefore legitimately be interpreted and discussed out of context (be this subjective, social, cultural or otherwise). These arguments will then be adapted in order to challenge dominant descriptions of language and communication in relation to ASD. Finally, I illustrate how the aforementioned signs of ASD can be repositioned as contextually meaningful, through presenting a socially oriented analysis of two real interactions involving diagnosed children.

THE PROBLEMS OF CONTEXT WHEN DEFINING DISORDER

The routes by which diagnostic categories are proposed, defined and subsequently accepted by professional communities are often taken for granted within medical disciplines themselves. Outside of these disciplines, however, there is ongoing interest in understanding these matters as complex and contestable social processes worthy of examination in their own right. In relation to medicine, many theorists have sought to deconstruct hegemonic means of describing the body, health, ill health and physical disease (Brown 1995), as well as the

1 In medicine, 'symptoms' refers to a patient-reported subjective phenomenon, which cannot be independently observed by a clinician. For example, chronic thirst is a symptom of diabetes. These are distinct from 'signs', which are argued to be objectively verifiable. In psychiatry, patient self-report of symptomatology is a distinct part of the diagnostic process, but symptoms and signs are often conflated when profiles of conditions are presented. For consistency, only 'signs' will be used in this chapter.

lived experiences of those classified as ill (e.g. Conrad and Barker 2010). This work has powerfully demonstrated that Western concepts of disease, whose universality and objectivity may be taken for granted, when viewed outside of the uni-disciplinary lens of medical science can alternatively be understood as culturally specific, socially situated and subjectively experienced. An overlapping body of work within critical psychology and psychiatry specifically focuses on 'psychiatric disorders' as definitional apparatus for the classification of apparently problematic behaviours, thoughts and experiences. These perspectives charge that such frameworks, in spite of their veneer of scientific neutrality, inevitably propagate particular culturally – and historically – situated sets of ideas about people, what people (should) do, and how people (should) interact with one another and the broader social world. These ideas are shared across the definitions of all psychiatric disorders, as they are inexorably embedded within the classification frameworks and professional practices though which such conditions are described and identified.

To identify the specific world-views that are central to Western psychiatry, one can turn a critical eye to the published diagnostic criteria themselves. For instance, Crowe (2000) conducted a discourse analysis of the DSM-IV in terms of its organisation, structure and the forms of language used therein. Through this analysis, common tacit themes underpinning psychiatric disorders as *particular ways of thinking about people and their behaviour* (rather than as 'medical problems' per se) were identified. One of these themes is particularly important for the discussions presented in this chapter. Just as, for instance, the rash associated with measles is tacitly understood in medicine as an emergent consequence of a specific viral infection internal to the ill person's body, in psychiatry the signs listed on diagnostic criteria are similarly interpretable as comparably emerging from an underlying specific *mental* disorder internal to the affected individual. As Crowe discusses, this individually focused approach to definition inevitably overlooks other possible interpretations of the same issues:

> It excludes the possibility that [troubling behaviour/experience] may be a response to external events. The definition of mental disorder assumes that identification of disorder is determined by a subjective experience of distress and that this subjective experience of distress is a symptom of some disorder. This is a self referential process dependent upon classifications of disorder and then a pursuit of signs that could be interpreted as symptoms in order to validate a subjective appraisal of disorder. (Crowe 2000, p.72)

So, through a process of circular thinking (see also Boyle 1999), signs of disorders can primarily be interpreted as merely indexing the presence of the disorder itself. It is suggested that such a theorising of human functioning, reinforced through the individually focused presentation of clinical criteria, provides a specific

interpretative framework which leaves little space for interpreting behaviours, thoughts and experiences as possessing contextual and/or subjective meaning.

Such concerns underpin many critiques of the decontextualised manner in which psychiatric discourses represent certain aspects of human experience and similarly have spurred efforts to highlight contextualised alternative interpretations of the same phenomena. For example, some theorists have sought to position experiences associated with diagnoses such as depression (e.g. misery, pervasively negative thinking) and schizophrenia (e.g. reporting seeing or hearing things, holding apparently unusual beliefs) as meaningful contextualised responses to subjective experience (e.g. Thomas, Bracken and Leudar 2004). Conversely, a far broader interpretative context is made relevant by community-orientated psychologists, for whom such issues are considered in relation to shifting socio-economic trends and the accompanying nexus of change in labour markets and social governance institutions. From this perspective, forms of distress currently thought of as psychiatric conditions are reconstructed as meaningful individual responses to the structural and economic inequality and social upheaval associated with neoliberal systems of government (e.g. Curtis and Curtis 2012).

In this chapter, a similarly contextualised interpretive framework will be argued for in relation to language and communication in ASD. Where this differs from the arguments described above is that its interpretive focus falls upon a different form of context – I argue below that the language and communication signs of ASD must be re-thought in terms of the specific social, interactional and relational circumstances in which they might be observed. Let us now explore some issues with existing decontextualised accounts of language and communication in ASD, by deconstructing an exemplar of a relevant sign associated with the diagnosis.

DECONSTRUCTING LANGUAGE AND COMMUNICATION IN ASD

Consider the following communication-relevant criterion for ASD as listed in the DSM-5 (APA 2013): the 'failure of normal back and forth conversation' (see DSM-5, ASD criteria A.1). Following Crowe (2000), through inclusion in diagnostic criteria this phenomenon is presented as a problem demonstrated by an individual, which is indexical of the presence of ASD within the individual. But to what extent is this construction sustainable? Is it legitimate to understand a 'failure' of conversation as an individual matter, isolated from the social contexts in which it occurs?

One way to approach these questions is by considering more precisely what could constitute 'normal back and forth conversation', and indeed 'failure' of this. Implicit in the description of this sign is what is described in psychology as

pragmatic ability, defined as an individual's overall supposed competence to use language socially. Lists of pragmatic skills and difficulties are often provided in work about ASD; for instance, Baron-Cohen (2001, p.178) notes the following as potentially compromised in ASD, all of which presumably fall under the umbrella of 'normal back and forth conversation':

1. Tailoring one's speech to a particular listener.
2. Adapting the content of one's speech to what your listener already knows or needs to know.
3. Respecting conversational maxims [...] such as being truthful, relevant, concise, and polite.
4. Turn-taking appropriately so that there is space for both participants in the dialogue.
5. Being sensitive to the other person's contribution to the conversation.
6. Recognising what is the wrong or right thing to say in a particular context.
7. Staying on topic.
8. Appropriately helping your listener to follow when a topic change is occurring.

The tone of this list (and the many others like it) is easy to take for granted, but note that its approach to conceptualising communication is markedly decontextualised. None of these descriptions of everyday aspects of communication behaviours (other than possibly item 6) include references to contextual issues such as where speakers might be, who (or how many people) they may be talking to, what they might be talking about, or what they might be doing more broadly through their talk. Instead, these points are presented as 'abilities' that an individual can possess or, potentially, not possess. Yet everyday experiences of language and communication suggest that whatever a 'failure of normal back and forth conversation' might constitute differs according to *social and interactional context.*

Take item 4 on the above list about 'turn-taking appropriately so that there is space for both participants in the dialogue'. It is common sense that the distribution and nature of speakers' contributions to an interaction varies depending on context. Social encounters in many settings may be asymmetrical, in that one speaker is positioned to do or say more than the other. There are many examples of normative asymmetry in interaction, including encounters between teachers and pupils, doctors and patients and so forth, where there are differential rights associated with who can ask questions and demonstrate knowledge (Heritage

2004). There are even social settings (e.g. meetings, wedding receptions, lectures) where there exists prior agreement about who speaks, when, and to do what (see Sacks, Schegloff and Jefferson 1974). Evidently, what could be judged as 'appropriate' (or a failure of) turn-taking differs across each of these contexts, to the extent that behaviours said to represent a problem in one setting may not be identified as such, or manifest at all, in another.

Comparable arguments about context-specificity are applicable to all of the language and communication phenomena listed in the first paragraph of this chapter. For example, at what point does repetition, forms of which are commonplace in everyday interaction, become pathological? Similarly, when might language become idiosyncratic, for whom, and in what contexts? If these signs legitimately represent endogenous manifestations of underlying disorder, it follows that they should be possible to define precisely out-of-context, yet clearly this is challenging. Such challenges are further illustrated on considering the various 'failures' in relation to conversations that are experienced by all people relatively frequently in their day-to-day lives. For instance, it is part of everyday social experience that people sometimes are not concise, are (advertently or inadvertently) impolite, insensitive to what is the 'right or wrong thing to say', or (advertently or inadvertently) speak over another person. Such incidents do not immediately indicate the presence of disorder. Hence, during the diagnosis of ASD, judgements must be made about whether these issues occur in such a way that an implicit threshold for 'a-typicality' is reached. These judgements are both subjective and culturally specific. As Daley (2002) discusses, diagnostic decision making varies significantly across cultural contexts, even when based upon common clinical definitions. It seems that context appears central to interpretation, even at the seemingly decontextualised level of diagnosis.

In spite of these issues, language and communication phenomena are typically presented as endogenous in most textual accounts of ASD. This reflects a historically powerful hegemony; as noted above, individualised and decontextualised description represents a common feature of psychiatric classification, and in disciplines outside of psychiatry there is a comparably long history of individualised and asocial theorising of language and communication. For example, within Western psychology, language has traditionally been theorised as a window into a private realm of mental states, as opposed to a social phenomenon (Potter and te Molder 2005). This perspective is isomorphic, or corresponds, with the decontextualised methods of description in psychiatric diagnostic frameworks, as is reflected by most theoretical accounts of language and communication in ASD. Here, such behaviours are consistently presented as individual psychological phenomena that can be considered in isolation from social or interactive contexts (Sterponi, de Kirby and Shankey 2015), as they are meant to reveal deficits in supposed cognitive, neurobiological (e.g. De Fossé

et al. 2004) and/or genetic (e.g. Bartlett *et al.* 2014) substrates of language and communication.

Whilst the separation of language and communication from context is taken for granted across the majority of clinical, research and popular accounts of ASD, there are implications of these forms of knowledge and description. Following the critical psychology perspectives outlined earlier, it is inevitable that decontextualised frameworks restrict the range of meanings and interpretations that can be conferred onto communication behaviours potentially describable as signs of ASD. For instance, in the case of echolalia, it could be that the echoed phrases in question have a personal meaning for an individual and/or those around them, or only manifest in particular affective, situational, interpersonal or relational contexts – or, indeed, are responded to as meaningful by those around the individual, and thereby perform a social function. It is unclear how such interpretations could sit within the narrow parameter of description associated with a decontextualised, signs-based account of the same phenomena, which would primarily emphasise the diagnostic relevance of the behaviour.

In summary, I argue that to construct certain language and communication behaviours as merely signs of ASD may obfuscate personal, contextual, experiential or social meanings for the phenomena in question, in favour of upholding a persisting medical analogy that appears logically contestable. Few practitioners who work with people with ASD would disavow the importance of facilitating the social participation of diagnosed individuals. Whilst 'participation' can have many meanings, one relevant interpretation relates to whether an individual is assumed and/or positioned by others to contribute meaningfully at any moment in a given social encounter (Shakespeare 1998). Hence, if it is that interpretation of language and communication behaviours as individual markers of pathology can stymie the attribution of competence and agency to diagnosed individuals, it appears reasonable to respond to such interpretations as actions that are potentially damaging and dangerous, both to individuals and to a broader inclusive society.

RECONSTRUCTING LANGUAGE AND COMMUNICATION IN ASD – IN CONTEXT

Decontextualised perspectives on language and communication in ASD dominate descriptions of the condition, and hence influence representations of diagnosed individuals. However, as suggested above, a dominant voice is never the only voice. By re-examining such matters from alternative perspectives there exist possibilities to develop alternative accounts of language and communication in ASD. Helpfully, there has been considerable criticism of the dominant individualised, asocial and decontextualised academic positions on language and

communication more broadly. Some of these criticisms are aligned to particular methodological approaches for analysing language and communication, which model these as social phenomena rather than as products of individual psychology. Such *discursive* approaches typically focus on examining language in the specific interactional, social, cultural and/or ideological contexts of its usage. When applied to so-called communication disorder (including with relation to ASD) these methods can yield powerful alternative representations of behaviours and diagnoses, which usefully triangulate the arguments presented above. In the remainder of this chapter, I illustrate these possibilities by applying a specific discursive methodology, Conversation Analysis (CA), to generate alternative contextualised accounts of two language and communication phenomena associated with ASD.

CA uses recordings of real social encounters to generate micro-detailed qualitative accounts of the organisation of social interaction. Analysis focuses not on individual speakers' behaviours in isolation, but instead on sequences of turns produced by all those in an interaction. CA is based on the fundamental principle that the meaning of any turn can be interpreted inductively according to what the next speaker does subsequently – hence, in terms of the *context* of its production. To provide a basic example, a 'hello' can be interpreted by the analyst as a greeting if reciprocated by another speaker. This principle leads to a strict analytic focus on what the participants in the interaction themselves demonstrate to be relevant (or indeed problematic) at any moment in an encounter. Therefore, the analyst avoids projecting personal post-hoc assumptions about the meaning or function of people's talk or behaviour, in favour of examining its treatment in context, at a specific point in time, by those who were involved then and there.

CA has been used to examine social interactions across a broad range of contexts (for an accessible introduction, see Wooffitt 2005). A small but growing field of work specifically focuses on encounters in which one or more participants are categorised as disordered (see Antaki and Wilkinson 2013), including in terms of ASD (for a review, see Garcia 2012). For example, several CA studies have examined recordings of interactions involving apparently echolaic language (e.g. Sterponi and Shankey 2014; Stribling, Rae and Dickerson 2007; Wootton 1999). This work has consistently indicated that such language manifests variably in response to particular interactional contexts, and is not inevitably treated as problematic or meaningless by other speakers. This is incongruent with the dominant construction of the same behaviour as a mere index of underlying disorder.

I now present an example of such analysis in terms of another language and communication phenomenon associated with the diagnosis. The short extract below comes from a play-based therapy session involving Jonathan, an eight-year-old boy with a diagnosis of ASD, and Rachel, a 19-year-old speech and language therapy student, which was recorded as part of a larger research

project.[2] Following the session, Rachel commented that Jonathan's language appeared strikingly repetitive. As described above, 'repetition' is a language and communication sign associated with ASD, and therefore could be interpreted as a behaviour merely indexing ASD, or alternatively reflecting underlying cognitive deficits. However, a CA examination of the session indicated that not only was Jonathan's repetition variable (in terms of what was repeated, when, and how) but was also systematic, in that it emerged at particular interactional junctures. Most intriguingly, it appeared to serve a contextualised social function.

In the following extract, Rachel and Jonathan are seated at a table with a set of Thomas the Tank Engine toys, which Jonathan is removing from a bag and arranging on the table. During this section of recording, which lasts less than 30 seconds, Jonathan repeats a name of one of the toys – 'Diseasel' – six times over a short stretch of interaction in a manner that is impressionistically repetitive (as marked with sideways arrows). A transcription glossary is included at the end of the chapter.

Extract 1: 'Diseasel'

1	R	**who's**	**{that one**	
2			{*(points to specific train)*	
3	(..)			
→4	J	**the new (.) Diseasel**		
→5		**(.) Diseasel (.) Duhseasel**		
6	R	**oh right (.) can**		**{I have a look at him**
7				{*(R reaches out for train)*
8		(..)		
9		*(R looks to J)*		
10	R	**is that alright**		
11	J	*(points at toy)*		
→12		**it's (.) Diseasel (.) Duyseasel**		
13		*(J lifts train to R's face)*		

2 Full informed consent to participate in this project was provided by the adults and the parents/guardians of the children. The children were appropriately supported to provide assent by a familiar individual independent of the project. All names used in this chapter are pseudonymous.

14		**meet him**
15		*(R leans back and addresses train)*
16	R	**oh (.) hello**
17		**he's nice isn't he**
18		**he's bigger than** [***(inaudible)***
19	J	[**and his name is**
→20		**Diseasel**
21	R	**Diseasel (.) that's different isn't it**
22	J	**it's told by Ringo Starr**
23		*(J looks at trains)*
24		**mmmuh (.) now (.) it's Toad now**
25		*(J picks up new train)*

I will now discuss this extract line by line. In lines 4–5, 'Diseasel' represents an appropriate response following R's question in line 1; what is more impressionistically unusual is its repetition. However, in line 6 R does not indicate there to be any problems regarding J's answer, despite being positioned to do so as asker of the question (Schegloff 1992). In fact, line 6 explicitly accepts J's answer as adequate ('oh right') in spite of the apparent repetition, before moving the interaction forward.

What happens next is interesting. J does not respond to R's suggestion about looking at the Diseasel toy (an omission that R herself indicates in line 10), but instead repeats the word again twice in line 12. Whilst appearing impressionistically repetitive, compare this turn against lines 4–5: whilst the former is grammatically incomplete (beginning with 'the new'), the latter is a complete sentence with a grammatical subject ('<u>it's</u> Diseasel…'). This modification is potentially significant, as speakers typically produce increasingly grammatically precise repetitions of prior talk in a bid for clarification when interlocutors have not responded in the desired manner (see Schegloff, Jefferson and Sacks 1977). This raises the interesting possibility that, from J's perspective, R's response in line 6 may not have been what was anticipated by lines 4–5.

Following this second repetitive turn, J immediately lifts Diseasel to R whilst directing her to 'meet him' (line 14). R provides a response in lines 17–18, but J then speaks over her to retake the floor for further repetition. This turn (lines 19–20) is again grammatically different from those previous. First, it links to R's half-completed response with 'and', thereby ratifying the appropriateness

of her prior turn in spite of this interruption. Second, it contains only a single iteration of 'Diseasel'. Finally, it is more precisely worded than line 12, explicitly establishing that 'Diseasel' is the *name* of the toy (compare 'and his name is Diseasel' against 'it's Diseasel' and 'the new Diseasel').

Above, I noted that speakers typically use increasingly precise repetitions to provide clarification when the intended action of an earlier turn has apparently not been realised. The subsequent sequence provides evidence that this may be the case here. In line 21, R herself uses 'Diseasel' in her talk for the first time. What happens next is striking: J desists repeating 'Diseasel', before ultimately shifting focus to another toy (lines 23–24) and thereby closing this part of the interaction. This desistance suggests that, from J's perspective, any unfinished interactional business has now been resolved. Hence, in this short extract, it appears that J's repetition represented an attempt to prompt R to acknowledge explicitly the name of the toy. Regardless of whether this is an unusual aim for J to pursue, the means by which he did so (through repetition and progressive reformulation of turns) constitute typical interactional practices, which moreover appear ultimately to have worked in this context.

Strikingly, J's other repetitive language during the recorded session similarly desisted once R had ratified something in J's immediately prior talk. Such dynamically variable, active and functional use of repetition, which has demonstrable contextual meaning for both participants, cannot be accounted for if it is merely described as a sign of ASD. Instead, the above account positions repetition as a social route through which J contributed to an interactional exchange shaped by both he *and* R.

There are further implications of this final point. From a CA perspective, an individual's ostensibly problematic communication and/or behaviour must, to a greater or lesser extent, be analysed in terms of the context established by prior turn(s) of co-participant(s). Hence, it follows that co-participant(s) may have a role (albeit unintentionally) in the subsequent manifestation of behaviours that could be described as signs of the condition. This is not to suggest that J's behaviour in the above extract is the 'fault' of R, but instead that all human behaviour – be it interpreted as atypical or otherwise – can be considered as socially mediated and contextually specific.

Such a position, which is enabled by approaches such as CA, presents a challenge to decontextualised sign-based constructions of language, communication and behaviour in diagnoses such as ASD. The late critical psychologist Mark Rapley, in relation to adults categorised as intellectually disabled, made powerful arguments of this nature. For instance, Rapley (2004) used a CA approach to demonstrate how several so-called dispositional tendencies endogenously associated with intellectual disability (such as acquiescence; see Sigelman *et al.* 1980) are, when examined in context, apparent interactional by-products of the institutional/professional

communications that such individuals tend to experience. My colleagues and I adopted this standpoint in work about a child with a diagnosis of ASD who appeared impressionistically inflexible during play work conducted by me (Muskett *et al.* 2010). Using CA, we demonstrated that this inflexible behaviour occurred at junctures in the interaction where I was attempting (often intrusively) to play with the child. However, analysis also indicated that the child may not have been setting out to play at all, but instead was apparently attempting to tell a story using toys. Therefore, my play-focused interjections were arguably inappropriate. Following this insight, in later sessions I negotiated explicitly the nature of the activity as play rather than storytelling, and in this context the child's seemingly inflexible behaviours were not evident.

The second extract below illustrates these themes. The participants are Leon, an 11-year-old with a diagnosis of ASD, and Teresa, a 21-year-old speech and language therapy student. In this case, during her work Teresa reported that she found Leon's conversation style to lack reciprocity. Leon was interested in a television programme about dinosaurs called *Walking with Beasts*, and was reported to often adopt the style of the programme's narrator during conversation. Teresa experienced this as exclusionary, rendering her unable to contribute to the interaction.

As with Jonathan's repetition, Leon's conduct could therefore be legitimately described as a sign of ASD – the aforementioned 'failure of normal back and forth conversation'. However, on examining the interaction using CA, a more complex picture again emerged. Just as Jonathan was reported to be repetitive but did not repeat everything, Leon did not always talk like the narrator of *Walking with Beasts.* CA therefore enabled exploration of the circumstances in which he did adopt this style and with what consequences. In the case of this interaction, Leon began speaking as if a narrator from approximately 40 seconds into the recording (see line 38 below), facilitating identification of what may have precipitated a transition into this style.

Extract 2: 'Walking with Beasts'

T **so you are a bit of a palaeontologist**
(.)
L **no (.) I just listen (.) and read**
like about the (.) books
and (.) listen on the (.) DVD
it's a- usually in complete series
and usually I get some(.)thing from

	(.) the vi- (.) on (.) taped on video
	(0.5)
T	**really (.) so (.) d'you-**
	(0.4)
	so d'ya like watching films about dinos[aurs
L	**[uhhh**
	(0.5)
	not exactly with Jurassic Park (.) no
	(0.4)
T	**it's not very accurate (.) is it Jurassic Park**
	(.)
L	**no**
	(0.5)
L	**too- (.) {raahwrr**
	{(L makes 'monster' gesture)
	(0.5)
L	**too much (.) scary (.) things**
	(L looks up, maintains eye contact with T)
	(0.7)
L	**{su-**
	{(T nods, maintaining eye contact)
	(L breaks eye contact)
	(1.4)
	(L looks around)
L	**errrr I didn't-**
	(0.4)
L	**soooooo (.) the thingy (.) erm**
	(1.1)
	(L makes brief eye contact with T)
L	**I'll say-**
	(.) so after the death of the dinosaurs-
	err (.) took millions of years to recover

The first person to speak on the recording is Teresa, with her turn establishing that 'dinosaurs' is the live topic for forward discussion. Correspondingly, between lines 9 to 24 L and T engage in a (somewhat stilted) conversation on this topic. Whilst the interaction lacks fluidity, note that at this point L is not acting as if a narrator, but instead is providing subjectively fitting answers to T's questions.

Following these question–answer pairs, the interaction changes in line 24. First, L looks to T with sustained gaze (line 25). Typically, such gaze serves to nominate a next speaker (Lerner 2003), but here T does not take the floor. Following another period of silence and as L begins to speak again (line 27), T nods. This nod can be interpreted as a very minimal floor-take from T, deferring speaking rights back to L. L is therefore nominated as speaker again, positioning him as responsible for driving the interaction forward. There are two further occasions (lines 33 and 35–36) where T could take a next turn but similarly does not. Strikingly, it is following these three occasions that L segues into the style of narrator from *Walking with Beasts* (lines 38–39), following an apparent marking of this transition in line 37.

From an onlooker's perspective, the socially awkward segment of interaction corresponding to lines 1–37 might legitimately be described as a 'failure of normal back and forth conversation'. However, as indicated by the above analysis, it would be misrepresentative to locate these issues as emanating solely from Leon. Teresa repeatedly defers the opportunity to initiate new conversational topics or otherwise progress the existing context forward, which in itself fails to uphold normative social practices (see Stivers and Robinson 2006). In this sequential context, L's transition to narrator achieves (not necessarily consciously) a progression out of an otherwise socially difficult interactional rut. Of course, there probably are less impressionistically unusual methods by which to achieve this (such as initiating talk around a socially neutral shared topic such as the weather; see, for example, Jefferson 1988, p.433), but as the above indicates, unusual does not equate to meaningless or essentially dysfunctional. To describe Leon as a child who presents with a 'failure of normal back and forth conversation' (or alternatively a 'fixated interest' in *Walking with Beasts*) is therefore not a conclusion that does credit the apparent social function and contextual significance of the phenomena at hand.

CONCLUSION

In this chapter, a deconstructive critique of the dominant decontextualised signs-based clinical perspective on language and communication in ASD has been provided. Drawing upon critical perspectives that problematise the methods of description associated with psychiatric frameworks, I argued that it is logically unsustainable to describe communication behaviours as if mere decontextualised

indices of underlying individual disorder. Moreover, I suggested that the glossing over of context when interpreting and describing such behaviours may contribute to damaging representations of diagnosed individuals, which both overlook communicative competency and underestimate capacity for social participation. As was demonstrated, it is possible to generate alternative contextualised accounts of such phenomena. These have the potential to broaden discourses around ASD, and moreover underpin professional practices oriented towards interactional participation rather than remediation of individual deficit (Muskett *et al.* 2010).

Whilst many within critical psychology and psychiatry would positively emphasise the importance of broadened perspectives on psychiatric disorders, the potentially negative consequences of the hegemonic position on language and communication in ASD cannot be understated. Critical psychologist Thomas Teo (e.g. 2010) problematises unitary interpretations of human activity and ability that may negatively impact upon groups when 'equally plausible interpretations of the data are available' (Teo 2010, p.296). Above, I argued that the dominant interpretation of language and communication in ASD may reduce scope for attributing meanings to communication behaviours. I also empirically demonstrated, in Teo's words, an 'equally plausible interpretation' of two examples of such behaviours. As Teo argues:

> Interpretations of inferiority, or problematisations [...], are never determined by empirical results; yet, they have a negative impact on the Other. Thus, interpretations are the actions of a subject against an object that one must label as violent. (Teo 2010, p.298)

I argue that such violence in interpretation, even if inadvertent, is a risk inherent in application of any unitary framework to describe an individual's competencies and needs. As explored throughout this chapter, the repertoires offered by psychiatric discourses and the profound cultural importance of language and communication add layers of complexities – and therefore risks – to this base position. Hence, whilst I have not considered how the above arguments interface with other critical and radical representations of ASD, a clear congruence between this chapter and others in this volume is its reflexive questioning of dominant clinico-medical discourses about the condition. After all, as long as theorising of the diagnosis remains 'silo-ed' within the frameworks of description and causation offered by contemporary psychiatry and developmental psychopathology, representations of those who live with the label will remain unduly restricted.

APPENDIX: TRANSCRIPTION GLOSSARY[3]

[	Overlapping talk
{	Used to indicate synchronisation between talk and non-verbal action
(description)	Description of non-verbal action
(.)	A micro-pause, hearable but too short to measure
(..)	A longer, subjectively notable pause under 0.5 seconds
(...)	A pause of over 0.5 seconds
(1.0)	A pause of, for example, 1.0 seconds
Eh-	Hyphen indicates rapid cut-off of talk.

REFERENCES

American Psychiatric Association (2013) *Diagnostic and Statistical Manual of Mental Disorders, Fifth Edition (DSM-5).* Washington, DC: APA.

Antaki, C., and Wilkinson R. (2013) 'Conversation Analysis and the Study of Atypical Populations.' In T. Stivers and J. Sidnell (eds) *Handbook of Conversation Analysis.* Chichester: Wiley-Blackwell.

Baron-Cohen, S. (2001) 'Theory of Mind in normal development and in autism.' *Prisme 34,* 174–183.

Bartlett, C.W., Hou, L., Flax, J.F., Hare, A., *et al.* (2014) 'A genome scan for loci shared by autism spectrum disorder and language impairment.' *American Journal of Psychiatry 171,* 1, 72–81.

Boyle, M. (1999) 'Diagnosis.' In C. Newnes, G. Holmes and C. Dunn (eds) *This is Madness: A Critical Look at Psychiatry and the Future of Mental Health Services.* Ross-on-Wye: PCCS Books.

Brown, P. (1995) 'Naming and framing: the social construction of diagnosis and illness.' Journal of Health and Social Behaviour 35(S), 34-52.

Crowe, M. (2000) 'Constructing normality: a discourse analysis of the DSM-IV.' *Journal of Psychiatric and Mental Health Nursing 7,* 67–77.

Curtis, C., and Curtis, B. (2012) 'The Operation of a Suicidal Cohort and its Socio-economic Origins.' In C. Walker, K. Johnson and L. Cunningham (eds) *Community Psychology and the Socio-economics of Mental Distress.* Basingstoke: Palgrave.

Daley, T.C. (2002) 'The need for cross-cultural research on the pervasive developmental disorders.' *Transcultural Psychiatry 39,* 4, 531–550.

De Fossé, L., Hodge, S.M., Makris, N., Kennedy, D.N., *et al.* (2004) 'Language-association cortex asymmetry in autism and specific language impairment.' *Annals of Neurology 56,* 6, 757–766.

Garcia, A.C. (2012) 'Medical problems where talk is the problem: current trends in conversation analytic research on aphasia, autism spectrum disorder, intellectual disability, and Alzheimer's.' *Sociology Compass 6,* 4, 351–364.

3 Adapted from Jefferson 2004.

Heritage, J. (2004) 'Conversation Analysis and Institutional Talk.' In R. Sanders and K. Fitch (eds) *Handbook of Language and Social Interaction.* Mahwah, NJ: Erlbaum.

Jefferson, G. (1988) 'On the sequential organization of troubles-talk in ordinary conversation.' *Social Problems 35,* 4, 418–441.

Jefferson, G. (2004) 'Glossary of Transcription Symbols with an Introduction.' In G.H. Lerner (ed.) *Conversation Analysis: Studies from the First Generation.* Amsterdam: John Benjamins.

Lerner, G. (2003). 'Selecting next speaker: the context sensitive operation of a context free organization.' *Language in Society 32,* 2, 177–201.

Muskett, T., Perkins, M., Clegg, J., and Body, R. (2010) 'Inflexibility as an interactional phenomenon: using Conversation Analysis to re-examine a symptom of autism.' *Clinical Linguistics and Phonetics 24,* 1, 1–16.

Potter, J., and te Molder, H. (2005) 'Talking Cognition: Mapping and Making the Terrain.' In H. te Molder and J. Potter (eds) *Conversation and Cognition.* Cambridge: Cambridge University Press.

Rapin, I., and Dunn, M. (2003) 'Update on the language disorders of individuals on the autism spectrum.' *Brain and Development 25,* 3, 166–172.

Rapley, M. (2004) *The Social Construction of Intellectual Disability.* Cambridge: Cambridge University Press.

Sacks, H., Schegloff, E.A., and Jefferson, G. (1974) 'A simplest systematics for the organization of turn-taking in conversation' *Language 50,* 4, 696–735.

Schegloff, E.A. (1992) 'Repair after next turn: the last structurally provided defense of intersubjectivity in conversation.' *American Journal of Sociology 97,* 5, 1295–1345.

Schegloff, E.A., Jefferson, G., and Sacks, H. (1977) 'The preference for self-correction in the organisation of repair in conversation.' *Language 53,* 2, 361–382.

Shakespeare, P. (1998) *Aspects of Confused Speech: A Study of Verbal Interaction Between Confused and Normal Speakers.* London: Erlbaum.

Sigelman, C.K., Schoenrock, C.J., Spanhel, C.L., Hromas, S.G., *et al.*(1980) 'Surveying mentally retarded persons: responsiveness and response validity in three samples.' *American Journal of Mental Deficiency 84,* 5, 479–486.

Sterponi, L., and Shankey, J. (2014) 'Rethinking echolalia: repetition as interactional resource in the communication of a child with autism.' *Journal of Child Language 41,* 2, 275–304.

Sterponi, L., de Kirby, K., and Shankey, J. (2015) 'Rethinking language in autism.' *Autism 19,* 5, 517–526. Available at http://aut.sagepub.com/content/19/5/517.full.pdf, accessed on 19 November 2015.

Stivers, T., and Robinson, G. (2006) 'A preference for progressivity in interaction.' *Language in Society 35,* 3, 367–392.

Stribling, P., Rae, J., and Dickerson, P. (2007) 'Two forms of spoken repetition in a girl with autism.' *International Journal of Language and Communication Disorders 42,* 4, 427–444.

Teo, T. (2010) 'What is epistemological violence in the empirical social sciences?' *Social and Personality Psychology Compass 4,* 5, 295–303.

Thomas, P., Bracken, P., and Leudar, I. (2004) 'Hearing voices: a phenomenological-hermeneutic approach.' *Cognitive Neuropsychiatry 9,* 1/2, 13–23.

Wooffitt, R. (2005) *Conversation Analysis And Discourse Analysis: A Comparative And Critical Introduction.* London: Sage.

Wootton, A.J. (1999) 'An investigation of delayed echoing in a child with autism.' *First Language 19,* 3, 359–381.

FUTURE DIRECTIONS

Katherine Runswick-Cole,
Rebecca Mallett and Sami Timimi

The contributors to this radical text have set out a number of challenges to the orthodox ways in which autism is typically understood in a variety of twenty-first century global locations. The challenges fall under three main themes, which are reflected in the organisation of the text: the science of autism; the cultural life of autism; and the professional interventions and practices of autism. These themes are not discrete entities; rather they intersect with one another as is demonstrated by the ways they have been taken up by different authors throughout the text. However, we take a moment here to consider each of these themes in turn, before considering future directions for what a genuinely critical approach to autism studies might offer to the lives of people who have been labelled with various autisms and their allies.

Within the book, authors have mounted a sustained challenge to the science of autism including: questioning the validity of autism as a scientific category (Timimi and McCabe, Chapter 2); pointing to the problem of heterogeneity (Hassall, Chapter 3); problematising screening and diagnostic techniques (Timimi and McCabe, Chapter 9; Russell, Chapter 14); and drawing on critical neuroscience analyses (Billington, Chapter 13). Each of these critiques disrupts the often taken-for-granted assumption that autism can simply be understood as a biomedical disorder.

The book is also concerned with the cultural production of autism. It is clear that autism is a cultural artefact whose presence provokes a host of meaning-making. Relationships with autism, as cultural artefact, are revealed as shifting and complex (Runswick-Cole, Chapter 1). The cultural production of autism is closely connected to real, symbolic, structural and systemic violence in the lives of people labelled with autism (McGuire, Chapter 5). Discussions of autism also

speak to broader questions of the human (Davies, Chapter 7; Goodley, Chapter 8) and to identity politics (Ortega, Zorzanelli and Rios, Chapter 4). A discussion of the commodification of autism (Mallett and Runswick-Cole, Chapter 6) reveals yet another troubling facet of the cultural production of autism and the impact that this has on people's lives.

The interventions and practices associated with autism are questioned and challenged within this book. Crucially, labelling and the diagnosis of autism has been consistently identified by authors within this text as acting in disabling, rather than enabling, ways in the lives of people labelled with autism (Hodge, Chapter 10; Collins, Chapter 11; Haydon-Laurelut, Chapter 12; Russell, Chapter 14; Simon, Chapter 15; Latif, Chapter 16; Muskett, Chapter 17).

As Ramilow (2006, cited in Runswick-Cole 2014, p.8) has noted, neoliberal politics is consumed by a concern to maintain the boundaries between 'us' and 'them'. In the United Kingdom in contemporary times, this approach is exemplified by the current preoccupation with sorting the 'scroungers' from the 'strivers' – the feckless and work-shy from the responsible and hard-working. Only the 'worthy poor' (an ever-shrinking category) will benefit from the redistributive policies of the welfare state. In England, as in many other countries, diagnostic labels such as autism do crucial boundary work: first, to maintain the categories of 'us' and 'them', the 'ab/normal' and the 'dis/ordered', but also to maintain the distinction between the 'un/worthy' poor 'scrounger' and the 'striver'. A diagnosis can seem to offer to smooth the path to access to services and support in neoliberal times – although as the authors reveal in this text, this is often far from the case.

Our stated aim is to challenge the pseudo-scientific claims upon which autism as biological disorder and difference are premised as well as exploring how autism is produced, consumed and commodified, and for what purposes, in the twenty-first century. At the same time we are mindful of the impact of these debates on the lives of people labelled with autism and their families and other allies. In a time of austerity, we are acutely aware of the risk that our work could be misappropriated and taken up by those who might want to exclude people from the services and support that they need. However, our aim is that, by moving away from diagnosing autism, this might instead act as the starting point for improving service provision for those who experience the type of difficulties that could lead to such a diagnosis and, indeed, those who experience difficulties but do not meet the criteria for diagnosis.

Challenging any orthodoxy is a risky business, made even more so when one challenges an orthodoxy in which people are so heavily invested emotionally, politically and financially. We would like to thank the contributors to this edited book, and our publishers, for taking that risk and hope that this book will be received in the spirit that it was written – one of openness and inquiry.

REFERENCE

Runswick-Cole, K. (2014) '"Us" and "them"? The limits and possibilities of a politics of neurodiversity in neoliberal times.' *Disability and Society 29*, 7, 1–13.

THE CONTRIBUTORS

Tom Billington is Professor of Educational and Child Psychology in the School of Education at the University of Sheffield, where he belongs to a community of critically-inclined psychologists and educationists, researchers and practitioners, and also students from around the globe; he also frequently works internationally. His single-authored books are *Separating, Losing and Excluding Children: Narratives of Difference* and *Working with Children: Assessment, Representation and Intervention.* Tom's current research projects concern the development of critical approaches to ADHD, autism and also neuroscience. He is a Fellow of the British Psychological Society.

Graham Collins qualified as a clinical psychologist from Liverpool University in 1980. Since that time he has worked as Head of Specialty for Intellectual Disabilities at Barnardo's, St Helens and Knowsley Health Authority and Nottinghamshire Healthcare Trust. He has also worked for a number of independent sector care providers, and currently works in Nottinghamshire for a residential care provider for people with intellectual disability, mental health problems, and acquired brain injury. Graham has taught on the Liverpool, Sheffield, Leicester and Trent Clinical Psychology training courses, and presented at a number of conferences. He has a variety of interests in the field of intellectual disabilities, and has published papers on challenging behaviour, client satisfaction, autism, service evaluation, and sexuality and relationships.

Kim Davies is a doctoral student in the School of Education at The University of Queensland, Australia. She has previously worked as a teacher educator at Monash University, Australia. She is concerned with the socio-cultural politics of schooling and her teaching and research focus on critical engagement with theories and practices of 'difference', 'diversity', 'disability' and 'inclusion' and their implications for educational policies and teaching practices. Her work is informed by poststructuralism, especially by the theories of Mikhail Bakhtin and Judith Butler, the research of Deborah Youdell, as well as critical disability scholars Tanya Titchkosky, Dan Goodley and Katherine Runswick-Cole. She teaches in the areas of diversity and inclusive education as well as critical disability studies in primary and secondary pre-service teacher education programs.

Dan Goodley is Professor of Disability Studies and Education at the University of Sheffield. He has written a number of books contesting and theorising the dual processes of ableism and disablism including *Dis/ability Studies: Theorizing Disablism and Ableism* and *Disability Studies: An Interdisciplinary Introduction.* With colleagues in Sheffield and Manchester Metropolitan Universities he is currently exploring a new form of theory and activism (see www.dishuman.com).

Richard Hassall is a qualified clinical psychologist, now retired. He has previously worked in child and adolescent mental health and intellectual disability services in Surrey, Merseyside, the West Midlands and Oxford. His most recent full-time post was in Leeds where he developed a mental health service for children with intellectual disabilities and their families, and also participated in an autism diagnosis team. He has published research into factors associated with stress in parents of children with disabilities. Following retirement, he completed an MA in philosophy and is currently working on a PhD in the same subject at the University of Sheffield. He is interested in conceptual issues associated with psychiatric diagnostic categories and how much scientific value can be attached to these.

Mark Haydon-Laurelut is a Senior Psychological Therapist in the National Health Service where he works with adults with intellectual disabilities (learning disabilities) and their systems of significant relationships. Mark is also a Senior Lecturer in Psychology at the University of Portsmouth where his teaching includes the MSc Applied Psychology of Intellectual Disabilities programme. Mark is particularly interested in the intersections between therapy and disability and critical therapeutic practice.

Nick Hodge is Professor of Inclusive Practice at The Autism Centre, Sheffield Institute of Education, Sheffield Hallam University. Prior to joining the university in 1998, Nick's professional background was in supporting disabled children and their families in schools for over 15 years. His research interests focus on the issues that impact on the education and wellbeing of disabled children and young people and their families. More information on Nick is available at www.shu.ac.uk/research/ern/sp_nick_hodge.html.

Saqib Latif is consultant in child and adolescent psychiatry and acting Clinical Director of Kent and Medway Children's Mental Health Services. He is employed by Sussex Partnership NHS Foundation Trust, and has helped develop integrated care pathways to deliver child and family centred services. He did his core training at Guy's, King's and St Thomas, higher specialist training from the Institute of Psychiatry, at South London and Maudsley NHS Foundation Trust, and carried on to do a Masters at King's College London in Medical Ethics and Law. He is particularly interested in developmental disorders and the aetiology of psychiatric disorders.

Rebecca Mallett is a Principal Lecturer in Education and Disability Studies at the Sheffield Institute of Education (Sheffield Hallam University). Her main areas of research include 'disability' in popular culture, the constitution and regulation of interpretative strategies within cultural disability studies and, more recently, the commodification of impairment. She is on the editorial board of *Disability and Society*, is a Fellow of the Higher Education Academy, and coordinates the Disability Research Forum (www.disabilityresearchforum.wordpress.com).

Brian McCabe is of Scottish descent, a fact which he believes is significant in explaining his temperamental idiosyncrasies. Brian has experienced a considerable amount of mental health issues including a descent into and then out of alcoholism. He has sought 'treatment' for his mental turmoil and in doing so he has acquired a plethora of diagnoses including Asperger Syndrome, ADHD, a personality disorder, as well as depression and anxiety. His last diagnosis was dysthymia. In the end Brian feels that his mental health issues are probably a concomitant of his personality and that he has suffered as much from the attentions of mental health professionals as he has his issues. He believes that his diagnoses and treatments have been both ineffective and inefficacious and that these interventions have been of more benefit to those who have made them than himself. He believes that, diminished in severity though they are, he will carry his mental health issues to the grave. He is co-author of *The Myth of Autism: Medicalising Men's and Boys' Social and Economic Competence.*

Anne McGuire is a Lecturer in the Equity Studies Program at New College, University of Toronto, Canada. Her teaching and research draw on interpretive perspectives in disability studies and cultural studies and focus on such themes as biopolitics, race and disability, capacity, vitality and precarity, systemic ableism, normalcy and violence. Her forthcoming book, *War on Autism: A Culture of Normative Violence*, analyses the cultural production of autism and the ideological and material effects of contemporary discourses of autism advocacy. She has published articles in *Journal of Educational Philosophy and Theory*, *Canadian Journal of Disability Studies*, *Disability Studies Quarterly* and *Atlantis: A Women's Studies Journal.*

Tom Muskett is a Senior Lecturer in Critical and Social Psychology at Leeds Beckett University. Tom's professional background is in speech and language therapy (SLT). He has worked in clinical and educational roles with children with diagnoses of autism and their families, and until recently led a clinical SLT training programme at the University of Sheffield. Informed by his experiences in these roles, Tom's current research aims to explore how alternative approaches to studying language and communication can generate critical/radical accounts of diagnoses such as autism, and how these accounts might underpin novel and progressive approaches to professional practice.

Francisco Ortega is Associate Professor at the Institute for Social Medicine of the State University of Rio de Janeiro. He is also Visiting Senior Research Fellow at the Department of Social Science, Health and Medicine of King's College, London. His research examines the many emerging 'neuro-disciplines' such as neuroethics, cultural neuroscience, neuroaesthetics, and the cerebralisation of autism and other psychiatric disorders. In addition, he has undertaken qualitative research on the mechanisms of social and personal identity formation in individuals diagnosed with autism and Attention Deficit Hyperactivity Disorder (ADHD) in Brazil. His main books include *Corporeality, Medical Technologies and Contemporary Culture* and (with Fernando Vidal) *Being Brains* and *Neurocultures: Glimpses into an Expanding Universe.*

Clarice Rios is a postdoctoral research fellow at the Institute for Social Medicine, at the State University of Rio de Janeiro (UERJ). She has a BA in Psychology from PUC-Rio, an MA in Social Sciences from the University of Chicago and a PhD in Sociocultural Anthropology from the University of California, Los Angeles. In her work she uses methodological and theoretical approaches from psychological anthropology to address the challenges and questions raised by the field of collective health in Brazil. Clarice's current research explores the biopolitics of autism treatment through the lens of person-centred ethnographic research. She is particularly interested in the notion of expertise and the ways in which parents and professionals become experts in autism.

Ginny Russell is an interdisciplinary Research Fellow at the University of Exeter Medical School where she is affiliated to the Exeter Centre for Study of Life Sciences (Egenis). Her research encompasses epidemiology, developmental psychology, health services research and sociology. Ginny initially trained as a researcher at the BBC's Natural History Unit in Bristol, becoming a television producer/director. She has also freelanced as a reporter for Radio 4's *Natural History Programme* and *Science in Action* on the BBC World Service. Since embarking on an academic career in 2011, with a PhD that focused on implications of autism diagnosis, she has published around 20 original journal articles, and written for various publications including *The Times Educational Supplement* and *Britain in 2015.*

Katherine Runswick-Cole is Senior Research Fellow in Disability Studies and Psychology at Manchester Metropolitan University. She locates her work in a critical disability studies perspective that aims to understand and challenge exclusionary and oppressive practices associated with disablism, as well as considering the ways in which disability intersects with other forms of marginalisation including hetero/sexism, racism, poverty and imperialism. Much of her work has focused on the lives of disabled children, young people and their families. More recently, she has been working with partners asking how people with the label of learning disability are faring in a time of economic austerity

in the UK (www.bigsocietydis.wordpress.com). Katherine is the mother of two young adults, one of whom has been labelled with autism.

Gail Simon has worked for many decades with children with a diagnosis of Asperger Syndrome and their families, developing ways of communicating through play and hobbies, which improve family relationships. She runs a symposium for research into systemic therapy with people living with autism and has published on the subject. Gail leads the Professional Doctorate in Systemic Practice at the University of Bedfordshire. She has presented at national and international conferences on systemic practice research, autism, and how therapy and research can offer social and political interventions. She is registered with the United Kingdom Council for Psychotherapy (UKCP) and the Association for Systemic and Family Therapy (AFT). She is a member of the Professional Affairs Committee for the Association for Systemic and Family Therapy (AFT) and has written the AFT guidance for Commissioners of Family and Systemic Therapists.

Sami Timimi is a Consultant Child and Adolescent Psychiatrist and Director of Medical Education in the National Health Service in Lincolnshire and a Visiting Professor of Child Psychiatry and Mental Health Improvement at the University of Lincoln. He writes from a critical psychiatry perspective on topics relating to mental health and childhood and has published over a hundred articles and tens of chapters on many subjects including childhood, psychotherapy, behavioural disorders and cross-cultural psychiatry. He has authored four books including *Naughty Boys: Anti-Social Behaviour, ADHD and the Role of Culture*, co-edited three books including (with Carl Cohen) *Libratory Psychiatry: Philosophy, Politics and Mental Health*, and co-authored two others including (with Neil Gardner and Brian McCabe) *The Myth of Autism: Medicalising Men's and Boys' Social and Emotional Competence.*

Rafaela Zorzanelli received a PhD in Public Health at State University of Rio de Janeiro. Her research program includes contested illnesses and medical diagnosis, with focus on emergent psychiatric diagnosis in Brazil. A secondary line of research examines uses and misuses of psychotropic drugs as neuroenhancers in Brazil. Raraela teaches Fundamental Concepts of Public Health and Qualitative Research Methods.

SUBJECT INDEX

ABA (Applied Behaviour Analysis) 82–3, 214, 255
ability
  autism as study in 132, 137–40
  and disability 135–6, 144, 148, 157
  studying 135–6
able-bodiedness, compulsory 135–6
ableism
  definition 155
  and disability 133–5, 155
  and disablism 134–5
  and illusory interiority 138, 142, 144
  normalcy, compulsory able-bodiedness and studying ability 135–6
  referral as process of 137
  stalking 133–5
  terminology of 133–4
  Theory of Mind as epistemology of 143–4
abstraction
  functional 116–17, 124
  partial nature of process 127
  as process of commodification 116–17
  producing autism as a 'thing' 120
  result of 121
activisms 151–4
adoption studies 34–5
amygdala 38
areas of special interest *see* interests, special
Asperger Syndrome
  assimilated into 'autistic spectrum' 54
  as broader ASD diagnosis 34
  characteristics typical of 272
  childhood test 176–8
  comparison with Wing's cases 32, 40, 54
  eliminated from DSM category 31, 50, 53, 54, 56, 102, 126, 161, 194
  example of person diagnosed with 231–4
  expertise of people with 269
  first introduction as category 54
  interactive social system account 269–70
  listed in ICD-10 53, 163
  need for exploration on how to improve everyday communication 286
  as PDD subcategory 159
  relational system example 272–5, 285
  special interests of people with 271–6, 279
  term existing as description of 'state of mind' 278
  Theory of Mind and Sally-Anne tests 278
  working with children diagnosed with 223
Aspies for Freedom (AFF) 123
attachment disorder 40–1
Attention Deficit Hyperactivity Disorder (ADHD) 41, 125, 247, 261–3
autism
  becoming an expert on 22–3
  as behaviourally defined diagnosis 159, 172
  and being human
    biopolitics of 155–6
    as human other 151–4
    as hyper-ethnoclass man 154–5
    positionality 147–8
    postcolonial theory 148–51
  as belonging to pervasive developmental disorders 159–60
  as biogenetic disorder 221
  as brain difference, not disorder 23–4
  branding 121–3
  in Brazil
    CAPS system 69–70
    construction of diagnosis in virtual community 80–5
    as disability 70–5
    psychiatric reform 68–9
    representations of, in printed media 75–80
  changes
    in conceptualisation of 52–7
    in nature of definitions 289
    in understanding of construct of 290
  communication and language in
    deconstructing 303–6
    reconstructing 306–13, 315
  as contemporary cultural construct 24–8
  crisis in diagnosis 30–1, 45–6
  cultural production of 317–18
  defining, for commodification 116–17
  diagnostic criteria for 50, 52–3, 56–7, 102–3, 161–3
  'disability studies' perspective 45
  early diagnosis of *see* diagnosis: early
  epidemic of increased visibility 76–80
  getting beyond 144
  heritability of 33, 35

autism *cont.*
history of development of, as diagnosis 31–4
implications of commodification 123–7
as industry 295–6
and intellectual disability
association with 41, 205
comparison with 206–11, 216
'living with' 94–9
as mental disorder 290–3
models of 7–8
as 'natural kind' 59–64
as neurodevelopmental disorder
contemporary thought 30
definition 221
different perspective 221–2
evidence supporting 34–8
few studies on long-term prognosis 292
refuting claim 40, 44–5, 49
no single, distinctive disorder represented by concept of 49–51, 55
as not the story 27
personal stories of 110–11
politics of 42–4
'promise' of 119–21
psychological theories of 57–9
science of
genetic studies 34–7
neuroimaging 37–8
severity of 101–2
as socially/culturally produced phenomenon 9
specialist services 212–17
studies of
critical, targeting 7–9
cross-disciplinary nature 7
as study in ability 132, 137–40
as successful commodity 117–19
symptoms indicative of 160–1
and systemic therapy 222–4, 235–6
this *thing* called 19, 21, 24–5, 28, 106–7, 111, 117, 120
treatments, prognosis and heterogeneity 39–42
Autism Diagnostic Interview – Revised (ADI-R) 116–17, 166–8
Autism Diagnostic Observation Schedule – Generic (ADOS-G) 167–8, 176
'autism spectrum'
change to definition of 44–5
as distinct from spectrum of persons who receive autism label 230
emergence of concept 54
genes acting on 32–3
moral hierarchy of 103
spectral quality of 103
Autism Spectrum Disorder (ASD) *see* autism
Autismspectrum Quotient questionnaire (AQ) 169–70
autistic aloneness 50, 58
autistic psychopathy 133, 137–8, 140–2

biological markers for autism 62, 74, 172, 235
biomedical model *see* medical model of autism
biopolitics of autism
being human 155–6
in Brazil 67–86
boy culture 43–4
'boyhood,' cultural space of 42–3
brain activism 152
brain deficit 40
brain development 252, 254–5
brain studies 37–8, 245–9
branding autism 121–4
Brazil
autism wars
autism as disability 70–5, 85
autism at CAPS 69–70
Brazilian Psychiatric Reform 68–89
construction of autism diagnosis in virtual community 80–1
analytical considerations 83–4
method 81–2
results 82–3, 85
representation of autism in printed media 75–6, 85
epidemic of increased visibility 76–80
business, autism as 117–18, 189, 295–6
see also commodification of autism

capitalist logic 118–19, 123, 126
CAPS system, in Brazil 67, 69–70, 73–5
CAST (Childhood Asperger Syndrome Test) 176–8
CDD (childhood disintegrative disorder) 52–3, 160–1, 163
cerebellum 38
certainty, exercising suspicion of 127
CHAT (Checklist for Autism in Toddlers) 173–5
circularity 225–6
collaborative action research, moving towards 284–5
commitment, maintaining political 128
commodification of autism 25–6, 110–13
aggressive marketing 189
branding 121–3
buying a 'new' normal 119–21
certainty, conscious engagement and commitment 127–8
defining impairments 113–15
implications
determining definitions 124–5
investing in category 125–7
re-inscribing brand 123–4
making possible 116–17
successful 117–19
communication
and areas of special interest 271–6
assessment of 217–18
context for 278
diagnosis neglecting collaborative aspects of 281

dialogue leading to improved 285
difficulties
dialogue problematic in monological discourse 281–2, 285
most common presenting concern in therapy 270–1
study of grammar to improve 285–6
encouraged to adapt to fit in 280
with feedback loop 274
individualising 277
and language
behaviours related to 300–1
deconstructing, in autism 303–6
importance of context 313–14
negative consequences of hegemonic position on 314
problems of context 301–3
reconstructing, in autism 306–13
linguistic systems 282–4
reorganising expectations of 279
user-friendly talk 269, 272–4, 283–4
Compulsive Diagnosing Behaviours (CDB) 285
confidentiality 21, 27
conscious engagement, practising 127–8
consent 20–1, 179, 235
context
importance of, in communication and language 313–14
problems of, when defining disorder 301–3, 306
reconstructing communication and language in 306–13
situating actions within 278
in systemic therapy 224–5
Conversation Analysis (CA) 307–13, 316
Copy Number Variants (CNVs) 36
critical neuroscience *see* neuroscience
critical systemic therapy *see* systemic therapy
cultural obsolescence 126

Dawes, Jason 99–106
defetishisation 128
deficit model 7, 242, 248, 277
determinism 280–2
diagnosis
ability to highlight specific, unique problems 206–11, 216–17
abuse of 295–6
assessing risks of 235
and behaviours 174–5, 178–9, 193
construction of, in Brazilian virtual community 80–4
crisis in 30–1, 45–6
criteria for 50, 52–3, 56–7, 102–3, 161–3
early
effectiveness 257–9
improvement with no intervention 259–60
influencing outcome negatively 260–3
and labelling 252, 260–4
and parents 263
rationale for 253–5
recent trends 255–7
reservations to 252
effects of 64
ethics and consequences of 288–97
expenditure of resources on 205, 211, 217
getting over 280–2
history of 31–4
and labelling 186–90, 193, 196–7, 199, 264, 318
linguistics of 280–4
loosening coupling with disability 294
power of professionals 63–4
practice 163–6
questionnaires, use of 166–70, 179
and screening for autism 170–3, 179
'silo-ed' theorising 314
standing in way of understanding 230–4
template for 137
use of, in systemic couple therapy 223–4
variable thresholds for 289, 292–3, 305
working with 234–5
Diagnostic and Statistical Manual 30–1, 50, 52–7, 102–3, 116–17, 120–1, 126, 137, 159–63, 194, 234, 239, 302–3
Diagnostic Interview for Social and Communication Disorders (DISCO) 169, 205
difference 7–8, 23–4, 45, 49–50, 63–4, 74, 113–14, 152, 155, 191, 196–7, 226, 292
disability
and ability 135–6, 148, 157
and ableism 133–5, 155
autism as, in Brazil 70–5, 85
as different from impairment 113–14
disablism
and ableism 134–5
definition 134, 187
labels as agents of 187, 189–94, 318
noticing internalised 227
psycho-emotional 124
urge to return to 'basics' of 19
divergent activism 153–4
DSM *see Diagnostic and Statistical Manual*

education, feminisation of 43
empathy, lack of 40–1, 98, 170
environmental activism 152–3
essentialism 44, 152
ethics
of diagnosis
autism as mental disorder 290–3
categorisation of mental health problems 289–90

ethics, of diagnosis *cont.*
changes in understanding of construct of autism 290
example 178–9
influence of dominant classification systems 288–9
dilemma of 20–1
of early intervention 255
of nurses 198
ethnoclass man 149–51, 154–5
'extreme male brain' theory 34, 58, 154–5

'false-belief' tasks 57
family studies 36
feminisation of education 43
fiction featuring autism 119
films featuring autism 21–2, 119
fractionable autism triad 55, 63, 206
Fragile X syndrome 208

genetic counselling 175–6
genetic studies 34–7
Graves disease 60

heterogeneity 39–42, 50, 63, 290
high-functioning autism 53, 58, 153, 155, 169, 233, 234, 269, 286
homogenisation 153
'human'
and autism 146–57
autistic presence as antithesis of being 132
changing how to become 144
contesting the normally 142–4
less than version of 135–6, 239
normalcy 134–6
ordering the 140–2
Other 146, 148–54
passion to understand 279–80
professional failure to engage with 240–1
hypersensitivity 159, 209, 239–40

ICD-10 (International Classification of Diseases) 53, 56, 117, 159, 162–3, 178
illusory interiority 136, 138, 142, 144
impairment
category
capacity of 111–12, 115
example of functioning in different ways 110–12
as not 'objective concepts' 114–15
specific, in disability literature 125
defining
as different from disability 113–14
'objective concepts' 114–15
'subjectivities' 124–5
infantile autism 31–2, 54, 162–3
Institute for the Study of Neurotypicals (ISNT) 23–4
Intellectual Disability (ID)
assessment of 217–18
association with autism 41, 205
comparison with autism 206–11, 216
definition 204
heterogeneous 208
as socially constructed category 204–5, 207
interests, special
example of ironic relationship with know-how 282–3
monological behaviour 281–2
as relational systems 271–6
within systemic therapy 223
value placed on 279
internal stigma 294

James, case study 231–2
Asperger Syndrome 233–4
curiosity and multiple frames 232–3, 236
self-reflexivity 233
Jim's case 242–5, 249

labels
as agents of disablism 187, 318
calls for resistance to 200
challenge created by limiting use of 45
concerns with 186–7
and diagnosis 188–9
disabling effects of
autism as 'big business' 189
disempowerment of carers 189–90
justification for lack of learning 192, 293
reliance on labels and terminology 193–4
value reduction 190–1
working against inclusion agenda 191–2
disrupting 197–9
and early diagnosis 252, 260–4
feelings about 27
impairment
autism as 112–13
buying into 120–1
exponential growth in 111
implications of 26, 124
internal stigma 294
and systemic therapy 229–30, 236
as tools of expulsion 194–5, 199
value of
perceived 196–7
possible 211–12
language *see* communication
linguistic systems 282–4
'living with' autism 94–9
looping effect 61–2

malaria 51, 60
male/man
boy culture 43–4
ethnoclass man 149–51, 154–5
masculinity and cultural space of 'boyhood' 42–3
McCarron, Katie 99–106
medical model of autism 7–8, 223–4, 230, 234, 281, 288–92, 294–7
mental disorders
and autism 290–3
and CAPS, in Brazil 69–70, 74

DSM, as standard classification of 116
as natural kinds 61, 64
'mind' as relational activity
areas of special interest as relational systems 271–6
conceptualising 276–80
dialogue over diagnosis 269
from expert professional knowing to learning culture of collaborative action research 284–5
getting over determinism and diagnosis 280–2
improved communication 285–6
linguistic systems and relational know-how 282–4
relational opportunities 270–1
mind-reading 57–8
mind, theories of 142–4
mindblindness 57–8, 98, 142
'mommy blogs' 20–1
mothers
of disabled children 20
'duty' of 24
in mother-child dyad 21
'refrigerator' 21, 98, 255, 295
murders
of Jason Dawes and Katie McCarron 99–101
making sense of 101–6

natural kinds
autism as 59, 61–3
mental disorders as 61, 64
in science 51, 60
neoliberal cultures/societies 43–4, 98, 106, 221–2, 253
neoliberal marketisation 25–6
neoliberal politics 9–10, 144, 289, 303, 318
neurodiversity, definition 152
neurodiversity movement 23–4, 123–4
neuroimaging 37–8, 247
neuroscience
contemporary
challenging Cartesian principles 246
expanding scope of activities 245, 247
host to important conceptual dichotomies 246
critical
call to support research and practice 250
'emphasising politics implicit in scientific practice' 241
'mental life requires more than the brain' 245
mind and brain 247–9
and neuroimaging 37–8, 247
neurological story of connection 280
pursuit of the 'normal' 248
non-fiction books on autism 22, 97, 122
normalcy
and compulsory able-bodiedness 136
concealing power of norm as social construct 135
in the human 134–6
logic of 234
stalking 133–5
terminology of 134

online social networks in Brazil 80–5
oppositional value 123

pathologisation of autism 97–8, 101–3
PECS (Picture Exchange Communication System) 82–3, 213–14, 255
'person with autism' phraseology 95–7
pervasive development disorders (PDDs) 34–5, 52–3, 159–64, 167, 169, 229
phenomenology 245–6
politics of autism
activisms 151–4
biopolitics, in Brazil 67–86
boy culture 43–4
essentialism 44
feminisation of education 43
masculinity and cultural space of 'boyhood. 42–3
neoliberal 9–10, 144, 289, 303, 318
working environments 43
positionality 147–8
postcolonial theory 148–51
print media, representation of autism, in Brazil 75–80, 85
professional practice
approaches to critical autism and neuroscience 250
engagement with 'experience' 240, 249–50
engaging with other possibilities
Jim's case 242–3, 249
reflections on 244
Tom's case 243, 249
evolving on basis of incomplete scientific activity 249
examples of communication approaches 271–6
expert knowledge
determinism and diagnosis 280–1
moving towards collaborative action research 284–5
failure to engage with the human 240–1
focus on family as separate entities 277
ignoring human relationality in favour of individualised psychopathology 241
interest in what constitutes 'knowledge' 279
with limited cognitive framework 270
linguistic systems 282–4
tolerating sensory model 239–40, 249
values-based 296–7
ways of conceptualising young people 241–2
prognosis 39, 55, 175–6, 292
psychiatric reform in Brazil 68–9, 75

'quasi-autism' 37
questionnaires
diagnostic 166–70
screening 173–9

reflexivity 227
'refrigerator mothers' 21, 98, 255, 295
relational functioning
  conceptualising 'mind' as relational activity 276–80
  determinism within 280–1
  from expert knowledge to collaborative action research 284–5
  relational know-how 282–4
  relational opportunities 270–1
  relational systems, areas of special interest as 271–6
repetitive and restricted behaviours and interests (RRBIs) 52, 54–6, 58–9, 208
Rett Syndrome 52–3, 102, 160, 163

Sally–Anne test 23, 57, 270, 278–9
schizophrenia 30–1, 289, 303
schools
  in Brazil 73, 79–80, 82
  capitalist drivers in 188–9
  description of experience in 239
  example of special 243
  feminisation of education 43
  inclusion of children with special educational needs as national commitment 185
  inclusive practices 185–6
  labels in
    concern about 186–7
    disabling effects of 189–94
    as influential 262
    modifying impact of 197–200
    perceived value of 196–7
    as tools of expulsion 194–5
  as most useful source of support 257
  screening questionnaire in 176–9
science
  of autism 34–8, 317
  medical, role of, and autism 84–5
  natural kinds in 51, 60
screening and diagnostic tools
  autism disorders and symptoms indicative of 159–61
  development of criteria 161–3
  diagnostic practice 163–6
  diagnostic questionnaires 166–70
  screening
    for autism 170–3
    as not recommended 173, 179
    primary and secondary 178–9
    questionnaires 173–9
self-advocacy movement 100, 123, 147–8, 151, 155
self-reflexivity 233
SEND (Special Educational Needs and Disability) 185–6, 192, 195
sensory dysfunction 209–10
severity of autism 101–3
signposts 198–9
social behaviour 207
social cognition 207
Social Communication Questionnaire (SCQ) 176
social competence 207–8
social construction
  'ability' and 'disability' 135–6
  autism best understood as 11, 171, 194
  and child's areas of interest 276
  concept of 'thought' 278
  at core of diagnostic frameworks 135, 193
  critical of biomedical model of mental illness 290
  of disability 193
  of impairment identity, labels as example of problematic nature of 194
  intellectual disability 204–5, 207
  language and stories 280
  of natural phenomena 115
  power of norm as 135–6
  and reflexivity 227
  and systemic therapy 227
social imagination, impairment of 56, 206
social model of disability 23–4, 75, 124, 153, 192, 199, 290
social motivation deficit 58–9
social skills 207
specialist services
  ABA 214
  disadvantages 217
  effects of grouping people together 215–16
  PECS 213–14
  provision 214–15
  TEACCH 212–13
stigma 45, 64, 82, 196, 261–3, 294
symptom heterogeneity 40–1
symptom spotting 271, 281, 285
systemic therapy
  as an art of lenses 222
  core concepts and practices
    circularity 225–6
    context 224–5
    critical 224, 235–6
    difference 226
    social construction and reflexivity 227
    systemic practices 227–8
    teams and pairs 228–9
  diagnosis
    assessing risks of 235
    working with 234–5
  disabled people with learning difficulties and autistic spectrum conditions 223–4, 235–6
  in practice
    case of James 231–4
    labels 229–30

TEACCH (Treatment and Education of Autistic and Related Communication Handicapped Children) 82, 212–13, 255
television programmes 97, 119
theoretical journey
  autism as contemporary cultural construct 24–8
  becoming an autism expert 22–3

beginning 21–2
concept of 19–20
ethics 20–1
neurodiversity movement 23–4
social model of disability 23
Theory of Mind (ToM) 33, 133–4, 142–4, 160, 164, 276–9
therapeutic violence 26, 236
therapy
autism, as commodified 118, 120, 122
critical systemic 221–36
thinking systems *see* 'mind' as relational activity; Theory of Mind (ToM)
Tom's case 243–5, 249
treatment
and autism therapy 120
in Brazil 70–5, 78–80, 82, 84–6
for early diagnosis 255, 260
lack of specific and differential help 39, 217, 294
within modernist scientific discourse 280–1
none solely applicable to autism 51
packages 212–14
triad of symptoms 23, 32–3, 54–7, 63–4, 160–1, 206–9
twin studies 35, 206

UK National Plan for Autism 170–2

values-based practice 296–7
violence against autistic people
cultural logic of 93, 100–1, 103–7
'living with' autism 94–9
making sense of
rational calculus of life and death 103–6
severity of autism 101–2
spectrum of pathologies 102–3
murders of Jason Dawes and Katie McCarron 99–101

working environments 43
World Autism Awareness Day (WAAD) 123
'worthy poor' 9–10, 318
Wynter, Sylvia 148–51

zones of expulsion 194

AUTHOR INDEX

Adams, J.B. 241
Agaliotis, I. 207
Ainscow, M. 185, 195
Al-Qabandi, M. 264
Allan, J. 133, 137
Allen, J. 173
Allott, P. 296
Amado, A.N. 208
Amarante, P. 68
Amazon.com 118–19
American Academy of Pediatrics 256–7
American Psychiatric Association (APA) 30, 50, 52, 54–5, 103, 116–17, 121, 137, 159, 161–3, 194, 289, 291, 303
Anagnostou, E. 38
Ancona, M. 210–11
Anderson, D.K. 165
Andrade, M. 71
Andreasen, N.C. 61
Angell, M. 30
Antaki, C. 307
Archer, C. 20
Ariel, C.N. 81
Ashmore, M. 115
Asperger, H. 32, 54, 137–43, 289–90
Aspis, S. 191–2
Attfield, E. 94
Attwood, M. 119
Attwood, T. 22
Autism Association of Western Australia 94
Autism Speaks 118–19, 253–4
Autistic Self Advocacy Network (ASAN) 93, 100

Bagatell, N. 81
Baggs, A. 100
Baines, S. 205, 217
Baird, G. 31, 165, 175–7, 294
Baker, D.L. 81
Ball, S.J. 188–9, 195, 197–8
Banda, D.R. 214
Barnes, C. 19, 114, 188, 192
Baron-Cohen, S. 7, 23, 33–4, 52, 55, 58, 98, 142, 154–5, 169, 173–6, 277–8, 295, 304
Barros, D. 68
Bartlett, C.W. 306
Bateson, G. 226, 278
Baum, S. 223
Bearman, P.S. 255
Beavers, G.A. 214
Beecham, J. 189
Belluck, P. 119
Bergson, H. 241, 244, 246, 249
Berlant, L. 155
Bertilsdotter Rosqvist, H. 81
Bettelheim, B. 21, 98, 255, 295
Biehl, J. 68–9, 78
Biklen, D. 188
Billington, T. 239–43
Bion, W. 242
Bissmire, D. 223
Blashfield, R.K. 289
Blatchford, P. 185
Bleuler, E. 31, 39, 98, 289
Block, P. 69–71
Blume, H. 80
Bodfish, J.W. 56
Bogdan, R. 261
Bohlin, G. 255
Bolton, D. 290
Bonniau, B. 81
Boorse, C. 297
Booth, T. 185, 195
Boyle, C. 191
Boyle, M. 302
Bracken, P. 303
Brayne, C. 168, 178
Bristol-Power, M.M. 259
Brittain, J. 119
Broderick, A. 94
Broks, P. 244
Brown, L. 93, 95–6, 193
Brown, P. 85, 301
Brownlow, C. 81, 193, 277–8
Brunsdon, V.E. 206
Bumiller, G. 115
Bundy, A.C. 208–9
Burlandy, L. 68
Burman, E. 43
Burnham, J. 227
Burton, J. 185

Cameron, C. 23
Campbell, F.K. 132–6, 142, 234
Campbell, T. 115, 222
Carvalho, S. 79
Cascio, A. 80
Cass, H. 165
Castree, N. 116–17, 124
Cavalcante, F. 69–71
Cecchin, G. 226, 229, 236
Çevik, K. 93, 100
Chamak, B. 81, 83
Channel 4 119
Chappell, A.L. 191
Charman, T. 74, 165, 175, 189, 259
Cheon, B.K. 249
Chevallier, C. 58
Chew, K. 93
Chiao, J.Y. 249
Choudhury, S. 241–2, 245, 247–8
Clarke, J. 80
Collins, H.M. 83–4
Committee on Children with Disabilities 257
Connell, R.W. 42
Connor, S. 94
Conselho Nacional de Secretários de Saúde (CONASS) 68
Cook, F. 207

Cooper, R. 61
Costa, R.E. 241
Couto, M. 70
Crais, E.R. 253
Creak, M. 290
Crespi, B. 36
Crockett, D.S. 185
Croft, H. 36
Crow, L. 114
Crowe, M. 302–3
Csillag, C. 68
Curran, T. 260
Curtis, C. & B. 303

Daley, T.C. 305
Damasio, A. 241, 245–6, 248–50
Davidson, J. 80–1
Davies, K. 137
Davis, L.J. 115, 135–6
Dawson, G. 256, 258, 264
Dawson, M. 259
Daynes, S. 223
De Bildt, A. 168
De Fossé, L. 305–6
de Kirby, K. 305
Deal, M. 196
Deer, B. 83
Delgado, P. 68, 70
Delwiche, L. 255
Dennis, M. 254
Department for Education and Skills (DfES) 185
Department for Education (DfE) 185, 192–3, 194–5
Department of Health (DoH) 185, 192–3, 206, 209, 211, 218
Dias, I. 71
Dickerson, P. 307
Dillon, K.M. 94, 97
Dinsmore, A. 189
Doherty, E. 119
Douglas, H.R. 31
Dragulinescu, S. 60
Duarte, C. 70
Dubin, N. 153
Dumit, J. 247–8
Dunlop, B. 43
Dunn, M. 300
Durbin-Westby, P. 100
Dyson, A. 195

Dziobek, I. 38

Easter Seals 94, 97
Eccles, J. 261
Economist, The 189
Edgerton, R.B. 260
Edwards, D. 115
Einfeld, S.L. 208–9
Eisenberg, L. 31–3, 161–2
Elia, L. 72
Elliot, A. 119
Elsley, B. 119
Emerson, E. 205, 215, 217
Epstein, S. 83
Epston, D. 235
Erevelles, N. 127–8, 188
Evans, R. 83–4
Eyal, G. 76, 81
Eysenck, H.J. & S.B.G. 170

Fagiolini, M. 255
Fanon, F. 148–50
Farley, M.A. 165–6
Farrugia, D. 263
Fein, D. 165
Feinberg, E. 75, 258
Feinstein, A. 98
Felce, D. 216
Fidell, B. 223
Filipek, P.A. 253
Fiske, L. 148
Fitzgerald, D. 241
Fitzgerald, M. 39
Fitzpatrick, M. 263
Fogel, L.S. 260–1
Folkman, S. 22
Folstein, S. 35
Foucault, M. 285, 291
Fox, M.H. 197
Fox, R. 224
Frances, A. 30
Francis, K. 258
Francis, R. 217
Franco, S. 74
Fredman, G. 223
Freehling, A. 94
Freitag, C.M. 34
French, S. 23
Freud, S. 240
Frith, U. 7, 23, 52, 271, 277
Fuchs, T. 247
Fulford, K.W.M. 289, 296–7

Gallagher, L. 36
Gallagher, S. 245
Garcia, A.C. 307
Gardner, N. 19, 26, 33, 36, 38–9, 45, 54, 64, 123–4, 165, 221, 230, 235, 240, 246, 277, 290–1, 294–5
Gasper, P. 296
Gergen, K.J. 227, 240, 278
Gergen, M. 278
Ghai, A. 148
Ghaziuddin, M. 53
Gilbert, R. & P. 42
Gillberg, C. 56, 165, 173, 269
Gillet, J. 83
Gillman, M. 189–90, 196
Giroux, H.A. 197–9
Goffman, E. 291
Gold, I. 245
Goldberg, J. 69
Gonick, L. 296
Goodley, D. 19, 26, 111, 113, 115, 124, 147–8, 151, 156, 189–91, 193, 198, 236, 240
Gordo-Lopez, A. 43
Gorter, J.W. 264
Gould, J. 32, 55–6, 161, 206
Gov.UK 185
Graham, L.J. 136, 142
Grandin, T. 119, 143
Grantz, C.J. 256
Gray, D.E. 196
Grech, S. 148
Green, J. 258
Green, S. 187, 191
Greenstein, A. 153
Griffiths, S. 119
Grinker, R.R. 263
Guerry, Y. 94

Hacking, I. 61–2, 81, 221, 242, 247
Haddon, M. 119
Hagekull, B. 255
Hall, H. 223
Halpin, J. 197–8
Happé, F. 31, 50, 53, 55–7, 63, 206
Harber, K.D. 261
Hardan, A.Y. 38
Hare, R.M. 297

Harker, M. 214–15
Harré, R. 240
Harris, M.J. 262
Hart, S.L. 214
Harwood, V. 133, 137
Haslam, N. 51, 61, 64
Hatton, C. 215, 235
Haug, W.F. 119–20
Haydon-Laurelut, M. 223–4
Hedges, F. 224
Herd, A. 253
Heritage, J. 304–5
Hertz-Picciotto, I. 255
Heyman, B. 189–90, 196
Hickey-Moody, A. 115
Hickok, G. 277
Higashida, N. 119
Hill, V. 291
Hilpern, K. 30
Hodge, N. 190–1, 195, 197
Hoefnagel-Höhle, M. 255
Hoffman, L. 222
Hofvander, B. 39, 166
Holt, D.B. 120, 122–3
Horse Boy 122
Hughes, B. 7, 152, 188, 193
Hughes, V. 36
Hyun Uk, K. 25

Ibañez, L.V. 256
ICare4Autism 118
Independent Parental Special Education Advice (IPSEA) 192
Isaacson, R. 122
Iwata, B.A. 214

Jaarsma, P. 7
Jackson, J. 20, 22
Jackson, L. 22, 119
Jackson, P. 121
Jacobson, L. 261
Jaunay, E. 81
Jefferson, G. 305, 309, 313, 315
Jenkins, R. 223
Jick, H. 255
Jodrell, D. 196
Johar, K. 119
Johnson, C.P. 257–9
Jolly, K.A. 94
Jones, G. 198–9
Jones, R.M. 53, 55, 59, 63
Joosten, A.V. 208–9
Jordan, R. 198–9
Joseph, J. 35–6
Julio, F.M. 213
Jung, C.G. 289
Jussim, L. 261–2
Jutel, A. 263

Kalyva, E. 207
Kanner, L. 7, 31–3, 38, 50, 52, 54, 57–8, 98, 137–43, 161–2, 289–90
Kapp, S.K. 7
Karambu, I. 119
Kaye, J.A. 255
Kelly, S. 197
Kendell, R.E. 291
Kenway, I.M. 80
Kim, K. 197
Kimmel, M. 42
King, M. 255
King, N. 214–15
Kirmayer, L. 245
Kliewer, C. 188
Knapp, M. 189
Knudsen, E.I. 255
Koegel, L.K. 253
Kras, J. 7
Kuipers, J.C. 196

Lai, G. 38
Laing, R.D. 291
Lam, K.S.L. 56
Lamont, L. 99, 101, 103–4
Landa, R.J. 256, 259
Lane, G. 229, 236
Lang, P. 225
Lange, N. 38
Lather, P. 285
Lauchlan, F. 191
Lawson, R. 260–1
Lawson, W. 119
Lawthom, R. 191, 193, 195
Lazarus, R. 22
LaZebnik, C. 253
Le Couteur, A. 116–17, 166
Le Doux, J. 245
LeBlanc, J.J. 255
Lederer, M. 207
Leppington, R. 278
Lerman, D.C. 214
Lerner, G. 313
Leslie, A.M. 23, 277
Leudar, I. 303
Levinson, B. 21–2, 119
Levy, N. 58
Liang, J.W. 165
Linden, D. 245
Linington, M. 223
Linton, S. 95–6, 111
Lipworth, W. 196
Liu, K. 255
Lobato, L. 68
Lock, M. 244–5
Loganathan, L. 296
Lord, C. 53, 55, 59, 63, 117, 165–7
Lotter, V. 32
Lovaas, O.I. 98
Luciano, P. 105
Lynggaard, H. 223

Madon, S. 261
Maestro, S. 256
Malacrida, C. 263
Mallett, R. 19, 25, 94, 111–18, 120–1, 124–6, 128, 153, 156, 189, 193, 221
Mandy, W.P.L. 55
Manifest 73
Mansell, J. 215
Mansell, W. 257
Marks, D. 153
Mateus, D. 69
Matson, J.L. 210–11
Maturana, H. 279–80
McAdam, E. 225
McCabe, B. 19, 26, 33, 36, 38–9, 45, 54, 64, 123–4, 165, 221, 230, 235, 240, 246, 277, 290–1, 294–5
McGuire, A.E. 22–4, 95, 98, 106, 118–19, 123, 151, 253–4, 277, 279, 284
McLaughlin, J. 124
McMartin, P. 94
McNally, B. & C. 243
McRuer, R. 134–6
Mello, A.M. 71
Mercer, J. 259
Merikangas, A. 36
Messinger, D.S. 256

Michalko, R. 23, 95–6., 102, 106, 227, 235, 277, 279, 284
Migerode, L. 223
Miller, D. 112
Miller, R.B. 241
Mills, C.W. 185
Ministério da Saúde 69, 72
Mitchell, D.T. 93
Mletzko, T. 43
Molloy, H. 115
Montessori, M. 254
Moore, C. 20, 22
Moore, J. 119
Morello-Frosch, R. 85
Morgan, S.H. 94
Morris, K. 257
Morrison, A. 20
Moss, J. 208
Munro, J.D. 223
Murphy, S. 31
Murray, J.B. 123
Murray, S. 119, 132
Muskett, T. 311, 314
Myers, S.M. 257–9

Nadesan, M.H. 21, 38, 115, 137, 188–9
Naseef, R.A. 81
National Autistic Society 39, 123, 170–3, 214
National Screening Committee 172–3, 179
Ne'eman, A. 94
Nelson, R.O. 260–1
Nettleton, S. 263
Nguyen, V.K. 244–5
NICE Guidelines 31, 211–12, 215
Norwich, B. 257, 263
Nunes, F. 70–1
Nunkoosing, K. 223

Ochs, E. 76, 81
O'Dell, L. 81, 193, 277–8
Oliver, C. 207
Oliver, M. 23, 113, 187–8, 192, 223
Ong-Dean, C. 196
Option Institute 118
Orsini, M. 83
Ortega, F. 19, 80–1, 83, 186, 193–4, 318
Osteen, M. 81
O'Toole, C. 147
Overboe, J. 95–6
Ozanne, J.L. 123
Ozonoff, S. 209

Parner, E.T. 255
Parr, J. 253
Parry, R. 223
Parsons, S. 189
Parsons, T. 224
Passos, I. 68
Pastor-Barriusoc, R. 213
Pastor, D.L. 255
Pearce, W.B. 222, 224–7
Pellicano, E. 189
Perry, J. 216
Pettigrew, S. 20
Picoult, J. 119
Pignotti, M. 259
Pina, F. 207
Pinto, R. 70
Piven, J. 56
Plomin, R. 57, 206
Potter, J. 115, 305
Premack, D. 142
Press Association 295
Prilleltensky, I. 296
Protevi, J. 245
Purdy, L. 223

Quantic Dream 119
Quicke, J. 264

Rabinow, P. 155
Race, D. 188
Rae, J. 307
Rapin, I. 300
Rapley, M. 115, 310
Ray, W.A. 229, 236
Reeve, D. 153
Reich, W. 295
Research Autism 189
Rhimes, S. 119
Riddick, B. 264
Rist, R.C. 261
Rober, P. 223
Robertson, M.M. 116, 124
Robins, D.L. 174–5
Robinson, G. 313
Roets, G. 111
Rogers, S.J. 209
Rojahn, J. 207
Romeo, R. 189
Ronald, A. 50, 55–7, 63, 206
Rones, N. 94
Roosen, K. 236
Rorty, R. 194
Rose, N.S. 155, 240–1, 249
Rose, S. 241, 245–6
Rosenbaum, P. 264
Rosenberg, C.E. 67
Rosenthal, R. 260–1
Ross, D.S. 94
Rowlands, M. 241, 245, 249
Rubin, D.B. 261
Runswick-Cole, K. 9, 19–20, 23–6, 94, 111–18, 120–1, 123–6, 128, 144, 153, 156, 189, 191, 193, 198, 221, 235, 240, 260, 318
Russell, G. 256–7, 259, 263
Rutter, M. 32–3, 35, 37, 39–40, 50, 53, 59, 63, 117, 161–2, 164–6, 260
Ryan, S. 20
Rydell, A.M. 255
Ryle, G. 246, 249, 297

Sacks, H. 305, 309
Sadato, N. 37
Sainsbury, C. 22
Sampier, K. 99, 104–5
Sandahl, C. 132
Sassen, S. 194–5
Sayal, K. 262
Schalock, R.L. 204
Scheff, T. 45
Schegloff, E.A. 305, 309
Schendel, D.E. 255
Schopler, E. 39–40, 164–5
Scope 187
Scott, F. 176–7
Scott, J.W. 143
Selvini-Palazolli, M. 225
Sen, A. 191
Shakespeare, P. 306
Shakespeare, T. 19, 114, 191–2
Shankey, J. 305, 307
Sheldon, A. 188
Sherry, M. 148
Shimp, C.P. 241
Shotter, J. 275, 280, 283–4

Shyman, E. 189
Siebers, T. 45
Sigelman, C.K. 310
Silverman, C. 76, 83
Simon, G. 223, 269, 271
Sinclair, J. 95–6, 107, 143, 193
Singh, I. 260, 263
Skuse, D.H. 55
Slaby, J. 241–2, 245, 247–8
Slater, D. 121–2, 126
Slattery, M. 262
Slee, R. 136, 142
Slonims, V. 165
Smith, J. 93, 100
Smith, M. 83
Smukler, D. 143
Snow, C.E. 255
Snyder, S.L. 93
Soldatic, K. 148
Solity, J. 192
Solomon, O. 81
Son-Rise Program 118, 122
Souza, R. 68
Sparks, N. 119
Spinella, G. 259
Spinoza 246, 249
Stanton, M. 152
Starr, E. 36
Stengers, I. 242
Stephens, S. 119
Sterponi, L. 305, 307
Stivers, T. 313
Stock Kranowitz, C. 22
Stone, W.L. 259
Stribling, P. 307
Swain, J. 23, 189–90
Szasz, T. 291
Szatmari, P. 31, 34, 39

Tallis, R. 248–9
Tan, Y. 209
Tassé, M.J. 207
Taylor, C. 76
Taylor, M.J. 38
te Molder, H. 305
Teitelbaum, P. 256
Tenório, F. 68
Teo, T. 314
Thomas, C. 114, 124, 153, 189, 192, 196
Thomas, P. 303
Thorsen, P. 255
Timimi, S. 19, 26, 30, 33, 36, 38–9, 43–5, 54, 64, 123–4, 165, 221, 230, 235, 240, 246, 277, 290–1, 294–5
Timpson, E. 192
Titchkosky, T. 95–6, 111, 153, 227
Tobbell, J. 193, 195
Tregaskis, C. 188
Tremain, S. 115
Tsai, L.Y. 36, 53
Tuinier, S. 37
Turner, L.M. 259

UNESCO 185, 191–2, 196

V&A Museum of Childhood 119
Vacca, J. 75, 258
van Amerom, G. 80
Van Der Burgt, I. 37
van Krevelen, D.A. 54
Vander Elst, L. 223
Vasil, L. 115
Verhoeff, B. 50, 52, 55, 62–4
Verhoeven, W.M. 37
Virues-Ortega, J. 213
Volkmar, F.R. 31, 74

Wakefield, A. 83, 295
Wakefield, J.C. 297
Wallace, S. 253
Walsh, P.G. 74, 208
Waltz, M. 188–9
Warren, Z. 258
Wassink, T.H. 36
Watson, L.R. 253
Webb, E. 178
Webb-Peploe, H. 223
Webster, R. 185
Wellin, S. 7
Wellington, K. 185
Wetherby, A. 256, 264
White, E.J. 254
White, M. 235
Whitfield, G. 269
Whitten, A. 142
Wilkins, J. 210–11
Wilkinson, R. 307
Williams, J. 168, 178
Williams, S.C. 36
Wilson, C. 223
Winfrey, O. 94, 97
Wing, L. 32, 54–6, 63, 161, 166, 169, 194, 205–6, 269
Winter, C. 264
Wolbring, G. 155
Woodruff, G. 142
Woods, J.J. 256, 264
Wooffitt, R. 307
Wootton, A.J. 307
World Health Organisation (WHO) 53, 69, 117, 159, 162–3, 204, 206, 291–2
Wynter, S. 146, 149–52

Yergeau, M. 98

Zachar, P. 51, 61
Zavestoski, S. 85
Zeki, S. 245
Zoghbi, H.Y. 255

CPI Antony Rowe
Chippenham, UK
2019-03-08 10:24

ANALYZING TALK in the SOCIAL SCIENCES

ANALYZING TALK in the SOCIAL SCIENCES

Narrative, Conversation & Discourse Strategies

Katherine Bischoping
Amber Gazso

SAGE
Los Angeles | London | New Delhi
Singapore | Washington DC

SAGE

Los Angeles | London | New Delhi
Singapore | Washington DC

SAGE Publications Ltd
1 Oliver's Yard
55 City Road
London EC1Y 1SP

SAGE Publications Inc.
2455 Teller Road
Thousand Oaks, California 91320

SAGE Publications India Pvt Ltd
B 1/I 1 Mohan Cooperative Industrial Area
Mathura Road
New Delhi 110 044

SAGE Publications Asia-Pacific Pte Ltd
3 Church Street
#10-04 Samsung Hub
Singapore 049483

Editor: Jai Seaman
Assistant Editor: James Piper
Production editor: Katie Forsythe
Copyeditor: Christine Bitten
Proofreader: William Baginsky
Marketing manager: Sally Ransom
Cover design: Shaun Mercier
Typeset by: C&M Digitals (P) Ltd, Chennai, India
Printed and bound by CPI Group (UK) Ltd,
Croydon, CR0 4YY

MIX
Paper from responsible sources
FSC www.fsc.org FSC® C013604

First published 2016

Library of Congress Control Number: 2015938458

British Library Cataloguing in Publication data

A catalogue record for this book is available from the British Library

ISBN 978-1-4462-7248-0
ISBN 978-1-4462-7249-7 (pbk)

To our students

Table of Contents

About the Authors xi
Acknowledgements xiii

1 Introduction 1

Why You Should Read This Book 1
Why Talk Data? Why These Three Strategies? 3
Our Approach 4

PART I ANALYZING NARRATIVES 7

2 Broad Strokes Approaches to Narrative Analysis 9

Knowing the Past through Oral History 10
Knowing the Present through Oral History 15
Studying the Processes of the Life Course 19
Studying the Self as Essence or as Narrative Process 23
Chapter Summary 27

3 Fine-grained Analyses of Meaning 29

Analyzing Emplotment, Up Close 30
Discerning the Language of Agency 33
Observing Uses of Imagery and Figurative Language 36
Listening to the Sounds of Stories 39
Chapter Summary 42

4 The Interview in Narrative Analysis 43

Being Reflexive about Standpoint and Representation 44
Being Reflexive about Embodiment 50
Being Reflexive about Notions of a 'Good' Story 54
Chapter Summary 63

PART II ANALYZING TALK-IN-INTERACTION 65

5 The Basics of Conversation Analysis 69

The Founding Insight of Conversation Analysis 69
Understanding the Conversation Analysis Paradigm 72
Analyzing the Mechanisms of Everyday Talk 75
Chapter Summary 86

6 Conversation Analysis Approaches to Social Categories 87

Introducing Membership Categorization Analysis 87
CA and Categories: Debating the Alternatives 93
Chapter Summary 96

7 Institutional Talk-in-interaction 97

Learning the Basics of Institutional Talk-in-interaction 97
Analyzing How Institutional Work Gets Done in Stages 99
Studying Turn-taking within Institutions 102
Analyzing Other Mechanisms of Institutional Talk 104
Chapter Summary 109

8 The Interview in Conversation Analysis 111

Pinning Down the Qualitative Research Interview 112
Asking What Talk about Categories Accomplishes 118
Studying Focus Groups through a CA Lens 122
Chapter Summary 127

PART III ANALYZING DISCOURSE 129

9 Foucauldian Discourse Analysis 131

Introducing Foucault 131
Unpacking Power, Knowledge, and the Subject 134
Doing Foucauldian DA 138
Chapter Summary 142

10 Critical Discourse Analysis 143

Understanding the Principles of CDA 144
Doing CDA 148
Chapter Summary 154

11 Garden-variety Discourse Analysis 155

Understanding the Discourse–Society Dialectic 155
Unraveling Identities and Subjectivities 157

Analyzing Power and Discourse 160
Working with Time 164
Chapter Summary 165

12 The Interview in Discourse Analysis 167

Being Reflexive about Power in DA 168
Being Reflexive about Performativity and Performance 174
Being Reflexive about Positioning 178
Chapter Summary 180

13 Conclusion 181

Now That You've Read This Book 181
What You've Learned about Talk 182
Remember Those Scenarios? 185
Why You Should Close This Book 187

References 189
Index 217

About the Authors

Katherine Bischoping (PhD, University of Michigan) is an Associate Professor of Sociology at York University. Her intellectual trajectory from statistics to applied survey research, and then to qualitative approaches in sociology and beyond, including poetry and playwriting, has been informed by her abiding fascination with research methods. Katherine's projects examine the behind-the-scenes work of methodologists, the role of narration and memory in oral history methods, gendered discourses in cultural narratives, and cultural work and workers. She has been published in such journals as *Public Opinion Quarterly, Holocaust and Genocide Studies, American Journal of Political Science, Canadian Review of Sociology and Anthropology*, and *Sex Roles*.

Amber Gazso (PhD, University of Alberta) is an Associate Professor of Sociology at York University. Her main areas of research interest include: citizenship; family and gender relations; research methods; poverty; and the welfare state. Much of her research explores family members' relationships with social policies of the neo-liberal welfare state and has been published in such journals as the *Canadian Journal of Sociology, Citizenship Studies, Journal of Family Relations, Journal of Family Issues*, and the *International Journal of Sociology and Social Policy.* Amber works comfortably with a mixed methods approach (quantitative and qualitative) in her research but has shifted to greater application of qualitative methods more recently. This first book, in some ways a consolidation of her knowledge of qualitative analysis, has deepened her interest in this field of study.

Acknowledgements

We could not have written this book without the feedback provided by colleagues from York University and other universities who were willing to be readers for us. We are incredibly grateful for your time and expertise. You include Jeffrey Aguinaldo, Renee Anspach, Greg Bird, Matthew Clark, Susan Ehrlich, Laura Funk, Susan Levesque, Ryan McVeigh, Carmela Murdocca, Riley Olstead, and Roberto Perin. We also thank Logan Donaldson and Elizabeth Quinlan for permitting us to use excerpts from their data.

We also could not have written it without our graduate students, who read whole or partial chapters or simply talked with us about some dilemma we faced as we were writing. We particularly thank Kritee Ahmed, Bojan Baća, Krista Banasiak, Megan Butryn, Selom Chapman-Nyaho, Ian Davidson, Julianne DiSanto, Erkan Ercel, Zhipeng Gao, Markus Gerke, Duygu Gül Kaya, Caitlin Janzen, Azar Masoumi, Shihoko Nakagawa, Marc Sinclair, Gökbörü Tanyıldız, and Jason Webb, as well as students in our graduate courses in Interviewing Methods and Qualitative Methods. For meeting the challenges of research assistance and support, we thank Rawan Abdelbaki, Daniel Blais, Angelina Duhig, and Adam King.

We thank the team at SAGE for believing in this project. We thank our family and friends who encouraged and inspired us. Our final thank-yous are for the places that made the writing easier. The New York Public Library reminded us of Patience & Fortitude, Lake Simcoe and Sir Winston Churchill Park brought us respite and perspective, and the tree window that Michael built framed our writing with the changing of the seasons.

ONE

Introduction

WHY YOU SHOULD READ THIS BOOK

Picture these scenarios:

1. As a graduate student, you've conducted 45 interviews. You have over 1000 pages of near verbatim transcripts of the interviews to analyze. You panic when you look at these pages. You panic more when your supervisor tells you that simply 'coding your data for themes' will not help you at your defense or at the job talks you hope will follow.
2. As a researcher, you've encountered numerous challenges in recruiting the 30 participants you've planned for your study. Between timelines and funding troubles, you've had to wrap up your data collection with only 12 interviews completed. You now have talk data, but not enough for the kinds of analytic strategies you're used to. You don't know what to do.
3. As a professor, you're responsible for mentoring students to their successful completion of their degrees. You have a meeting with a promising student who has obtained ethics approval for videotaping marital counseling sessions. When you ask him, 'What method of analysis are you planning to use?', he says, 'I don't know what you mean.'
4. One of your doctoral students intends to do research on understanding the experience of surviving cancer. When you meet to discuss her research proposal, she explains that she thought using a Foucauldian approach would give her work cachet.
5. You've never been completely satisfied with how you've been analyzing data. You do the same things you always do and, frankly, you're bored. You wonder how you might spice things up.

What would you do in each of these scenarios? Our answer is that you should read this book. We wrote it for our advanced students and for researchers like us, for those curious about how to use new approaches and for those who are overwhelmed, exhausted, stuck, or confused and in need of help – quick help, not the kind of help where you realize you'll have to read hundreds of books and

articles to get some purchase on what your options are. We read *for* you, aiming to pinpoint strategies you could find useful.

We present Narrative Analysis (NA), Conversation Analysis (CA), and Discourse Analysis (DA) strategies, representing three of the social sciences' most powerful and popular qualitative approaches for analyzing **talk data**. A straightforward definition of **strategies** is that they are careful plans or methods to achieve a goal. Our primary goal is to provide readers with examples of NA, CA, and DA strategies in order that they can achieve their research objectives. We write from the assumption that the broad goal of many readers of this book is to write their own qualitative analysis article, book, assignment, thesis, or dissertation. But the strategies we write of here can also be directed toward narrower goals of faculty, students, and other researchers alike, including: fine-tuning the link between your primary research question and your methods; ensuring that your theoretical stance coheres with your methods; and organizing your analysis in a way that will be recognizable to intellectual communities of narrative, conversation, or discourse analysts.

There are quite a few other important things we ask you to keep in mind in reading this book. We assume that you have already collected data in the form of talk, following a research design, in order to answer a research question related to the wider literature relevant to your topic, and to how you distinctively theorize it. We also assume that you have some basic sense of how to code qualitative data. We're not going to review all that. Instead, what this book *is* about is directing your analysis of talk data strategically. It is about helping you to focus your coding and analysis in a direction guided by NA, CA, or DA. Toward that end, we answer the following questions for each of the overarching strategies:

- What is it good for? What kinds of research questions, settings, or forms of talk data is it especially suited to?
- What is its intellectual history? Who are the founding thinkers, and what are the key works? Is there a canon – or active opposition to formulating one?
- Have scholars in particular disciplines contributed key insights? Have they been talking to one another in the process?
- What are its social theoretical underpinnings? What are you assuming about the nature of knowledge if you use it?
- What standards does it set for a rigorous analysis?
- What are its key concepts and analytic foci?
- Are there key debates or sticking points you should be aware of? Are there concepts or terms that tend to be used confusingly in the literature? (We'll flag these for you!)
- How does it compare or contrast with the other overarching strategies? Are there points at which they discuss the same thing?

You may also find that you read some but not all of this book. No problem. We quite liked imagining readers who would take up the chapters of most interest to them. We worked carefully to design this book so that it could be read by holistic or selective readers alike.

WHY TALK DATA? WHY THESE THREE STRATEGIES?

At some point in their careers, most researchers in the social sciences will find themselves working on a project that involves talk data, in which at least two parties interact, whether from interviews, from recording naturalistic talk in everyday or institutional settings, or from media, including television talk shows, political speeches, or newspaper articles that quote laypersons and experts. The popularity of talk data has burgeoned since World War II – not only because tape recorders became inexpensive, but also in response to social, political, and intellectual currents.

You will see that some of the strategies that this book presents carry forward the spirit of civil rights, feminist, queer, decolonization, and other movements and identity politics, all of which are concerned with ordinary people and their communities. Post World War II narrative analysts distinguish themselves here for their efforts to recuperate subjugated histories, and for their humanist emphasis. That is, they are particularly interested in individuals' perceptions, experiences, and interpretations of their circumstances, with their quests for meaning, and with experiential, rather than expert, knowledge. In some circles of NA this 'interpretive turn' came in response to the limitations of research that emulated scientific models of inquiry.

Although many of today's conversation analysts take up social problems, the founding insight of CA had nothing to do with social problems. Instead, it was to hail ordinary talk as the foundational site of shared meanings and the very basis of the social order. In so doing, CA set itself apart from earlier linguistics projects, which had looked askance at the messy spontaneities of ordinary talk, and treated such talk as an impure and inconsequential form of language. It also distinguished itself from earlier sociological work that took a top-down approach to questions of how social order is possible.

Discourse analysts, meanwhile, have always been concerned with power dynamics or material and social inequalities. As you will see, they are not humanist in their emphasis in the same way as narrative analysts and they do not see talk as solely foundational. They see talk as part of wider webs of meanings and practices – or discourses – that are implicated in producing social problems.

In this book, you will find that CA strategies always pay heed to what makes talk so distinctive. NA and DA strategies are less consistent about this, in that some literary-based NA strategies work equally well for spoken and written narratives, while DA strategies conceptualize talk as one of many forms of social text. Therefore, throughout our discussions of strategies, you may find us making reference to any or all of talk's distinctive bundle of features:

1. We talk in ways that are socially available to us: we use language, an imperfect way to represent experience; we employ conversational mechanisms; and we draw upon discourses that may free or coerce us.

2. Talk is uttered by individuals who have agency (or seem to).
3. Talk emerges in the moment.
4. Although talk is ephemeral, vanishing with the passing moment in which it occurs, through research methods it becomes fixed in transcripts.
5. Talk is embodied, involving gesture, tones, rhythms, and more, although the social sciences struggle for a vocabulary through which to capture that.
6. In this embodied medium, speakers' bodies can act as signifiers.

For each of NA, CA, and DA, you will see an entire chapter devoted to the site of talk that is the interview, one of the most common data collection methods and one of the best-theorized. Importantly, in each of the three strategies, rather than treating interviews and other data collection methods as neutral tools, the talk in research encounters has come to be recognized as socially constructed. Method, too, has become an object of study and is seen to play a role in the knowledge that analytic strategies produce.

OUR APPROACH

Upon first glance, you may think that this book is simply a bulky literature review. It is not. In meeting our goal of providing other researchers with analytic strategies, we read a lot. We read research articles and books with the intent of uncovering the multitude of purposes to which NA, CA, and DA were used and distilling strategies from them. As well, we complement our analysis of others' scholarly discussions of talk and methods of analyzing it with primary data from each of our own independent qualitative research projects and some examples from popular media. We sometimes write about articles as narrative analysis when their authors see them as a mix of narrative and discourse analysis and we often focus on only a few lines of a conversation analysis when, of course, the author's analysis was deeper and more extensive. In each instance, our intent was to pull out the analytic significance of a piece for our purpose of showing the reader how one might go about *doing* NA, CA, or DA. We included works that we admired and considered exemplary.

While writing this book, we listened a lot. From our discussions with students in Education, Film, Law, History, Philosophy, Psychology, Social Work, Sociology, and Women's Studies, we learned that students across the disciplines often struggled to define their core concepts or to relate their theories to their analytic strategies. Students raised questions that challenged us, and that illustrated that working with qualitative analytic strategies is not a matter of black or white, but of shades of grey.

If you are looking for the 'Bischoping and Gazso model of analysis,' you will not find it here. We saw our role as synthesizing sprawling and interdisciplinary literatures, curating strategies with wide application to readers across the social

sciences, and mapping out debates while clearly signaling the rough patches. In our syntheses, we deliberately use common language such as 'fine-grained' narrative analysis or 'garden-variety' discourse analysis rather than inventing elaborate typologies. We do not want our language to get in the way of your finding of strategies that work for you. What we do want to emphasize is the importance of remembering the paradigms about the nature of knowledge that underlie any application of these strategies.

In this, we are influenced by Guba and Lincoln (1994) whose work revealed to each of us that ontology, what can be known, and epistemology, how we know, and the standards for rigorous analysis should all go hand in hand in choosing and using an overarching analytic strategy. For this reason, we devote sections of each Part of this book to setting these paradigms forth. So the reader will find that, in simplest terms, we write about how NA, CA, and DA strategies can be varyingly positioned along a continuum between realism, in which a reality is thought to exist though it may never be perfectly apprehendable, and constructionism, where reality is a construct of persons and groups. Realists might be interested in what really happened in the past or about the real consequences of material inequalities. Constructionists might take up how the past is diversely understood or how experience is constituted by larger meaning-making systems. And there's more than one flavor of each of these as well as blends in between. With these understandings in hand, you can be confident and crafty, meaning to have good craftsmanship, in adopting analytical strategies that best fit your theoretical leanings and research interests in a particular project. There is considerable freedom and even fun to be found in eclecticism.

We write as sociologists. This means that throughout the book, we are inevitably drawn to strategies that speak to one of the central concerns of our home discipline: the relationship of the individual to society, what is sometimes called the micro–macro link or the relation of agency to structure. Our book cannot exhaustively cover all approaches to NA, CA, and DA in the social sciences, let alone all the cross-overs of these overarching strategies into the humanities. Importantly, we are not linguists. We slice the pie of talk differently from linguists. Some linguists would say all naturally occurring, non-hypothetical talk is discourse. Therefore they would say that conversation analysis falls under the discourse analysis umbrella rather than being separate from it. Sociologists, however, see discourse as encompassing naturally occurring talk, scripted talk, text, practices, ideology, and power and, for this reason, distinguish conversation analysis, which is solely about talk, from discourse. Our disciplines have agreed to disagree.

Our book is written in three parts: Analyzing Narratives; Analyzing Talk-in-interaction; Analyzing Discourse. Each part begins with an introduction to its intellectual project and then explains the subsequent chapter contents. We will not go into this here. For a flavor of each, see Textbox 1.1.

Textbox 1.1: If It Were a Game ...

Narrative analysts treat narrative as though it were Solitaire, the game for the contemplative player, with or without an onlooker. The player contemplates the relations among cards, the meaning of their sequences, the ways her game has turned out or could have turned out if played differently. At the same time as the player has agency, she is constrained by the structure of possibilities offered by the cards. Similarly, narratives involve searching for meanings in relation to the flow of events over time. A narrator can replay his story, or arrange its events differently to find new meanings. He has agency at the same time as he is structurally constrained. And, he might tell his story differently depending on who's present.

Studying talk as a conversation analyst would be like studying Slapjack, a card game in which players take turns at laying down a card, face up. Everyone watches with eagle eyes for a Jack to be laid down, because whoever slaps it first moves ahead in the game. The fun comes from the game's fast pace and the players' hair-trigger responsiveness to what the last player has done – in these characteristics, it is like conversation, with its rapid fire coordination among speakers, its speakers' responsiveness to the most recent utterances, and its chaotic orderliness. Finally, this game is child's play, involving taken-for-granted competences.

Analyzing discourse would be like analyzing a game of Scrabble. Our vocabulary permits our action in a competitive game where knowledge is power. In Scrabble, letters materially ground the words we can possibly construct, just as economic and political circumstances ground the discourses to which we contribute. Your performance in Scrabble hinges on what is made discursively available to you by preceding moves in the game: as a skilled wordsmith or a three-letter wonder. Likewise discourses constrain or produce possibilities, setting conditions on their agency. Further, playing the game of Scrabble and life well involves performing according to norms – or the Scrabble dictionary – or risk being disciplined.

You will find each chapter may introduce as many as ten or more strategies, marked in italics. We use **bold** to denote key concepts or terms and provide definitions of these in the course of the text. Further, the astute reader will soon realize that some of these concepts or terms seem alike but are used in different ways in different over-arching strategies. For example, 'authority' is used in different ways in NA and CA. We use the icon to the left to highlight these potentially confusing concepts or terms throughout the book. As you browse through this work, we hope that you find strategies that inspire you. And, one last thing before you turn the page: a good work can be done by choosing just one or two strategies, just as a delightful meal can consist of two courses or even one if it truly suits your tastes.

Part I

Analyzing Narratives

Is narrative analysis right for my data? What is a narrative and how is it different from a story? How do I go about narrative analysis? What do I look for? These are some of the questions that concern us when we have collected talk data and are considering whether or not narrative analysis is a suitable strategy with which to approach it. We speak to these concerns in this chapter.

Narrative analysis will appeal to you if you are a **humanist**, interested in understanding individuals' and communities' quests for meaning. Narratives tell us about the perceptions individuals and communities have of everyday life experiences and about how what is meaningful is expressed. You might equally be intrigued by how narratives reflect social norms, mores, and values about what the form and content of a 'good story' should be, as well as larger, more abstract social structures, and institutions. Because narratives are told in interaction between two or more people, at the same time as they are situated in wider and changing contexts, both local and global, narrative analysis will offer you distinctive opportunities to examine the theoretical juncture of the micro and the macro.

While there have been many scholarly waves of interest in narrative analysis, it is presently rising on the same tide as the social and political rights movements and identity politics of the 1960s onwards. Narrative analysis is valued because it can reveal diverse lives, including those that may be bracketed as unusual or socially deviant, those that are broadly perceived as normative, and those that are largely unsung or overlooked. To present the stories of the subjugated can be a means of witnessing and drawing attention to the social inequalities and oppression they experience. As we read for this part of the book, seeking out examples, we felt spoiled for choice, as voices and personalities came powerfully and vividly to the fore. Narrative analysis, if done well, can captivate your readers and persuade them in a distinctive manner.

Narrative analysis offers unique charms for the methodologically minded, too. The strategies we discuss in this part of the book are derived from an extraordinarily wide range of disciplines, each bringing something to the party. You will find historians and

psychologists, philosophers and journalists, poets and geographers, anthropologists and more, jostling noisily and happily. The challenge is largely to synthesize their offerings. Many typologies of narrative analysis are available, most notably that developed by American sociologist Catherine Kohler Riessman (2005). But, when we compare her fourfold typology to those outlined by United Kingdom (UK) health researchers Phoenix, Smith, and Sparkes (2010) or South African education researchers Rogan and de Kock (2005), or UK psychologist Nollaig Frost (2009) we find the same terms, such as 'structural' or 'performative' narrative analysis, to have inconsistent or even contradictory meanings. Our solution has been to avoid choosing amongst the mid-range theorizing that these typologies represent. Instead, we situate NA research questions, concepts, and analytic strategies in relation to their ontological and epistemological underpinnings.

So, what is a narrative? We begin by defining **stories** or **narratives**, two terms we use interchangeably, as recountings of experiences that have taken place over time. Time is an essential element of narratives, whether we are thinking of talk about a specific period, such as this afternoon, about what has been continuous over time, such as our habit of having tea together, or about change, such as what happened after 9/11. Time matters because when narrators turn the vast complexity of their experiences into the stories that they tell, they are mustering what they now understand to be most important about what happened into a parsimonious sequence. To analyze a story is to analyze the consequences, the meanings explicit or implicit in it, to understand how narrators are answering questions such as: What is the essence of what happened? Was what happened ethical? Was it desirable – and by what system of values? Why did it happen? What caused things to differ from 'the usual'? How did I understand it then? What does it mean for me, and others, now? What is to be learned?

We begin with a chapter on 'broad strokes' strategies of working with oral histories or life histories, using narratives to understand the past, or treating narratives as speaking to the perspectives of the present. The next chapter of 'fine-grained' narrative analysis strategies take a magnifying lens to stories and the surrounding text, drawing on literary and psychoanalytic perspectives. It is in Chapter 4, on interviewing, that we shift from thinking of stories as texts to thinking of them as told in the moment of the interview, jointly constructed by narrators and listeners who come to the interview from different social locations, and are caught up in each others' presences as stories emerge. The interdisciplinary party that is narrative analysis smiles on all of these strategies, combining them freely, mixing grain and grape in a way that you will not see elsewhere in this book.

TWO

Broad Strokes Approaches to Narrative Analysis

Broadly different research questions and different ways of conceiving of time inform how we have divided this chapter into sections. We start off with the oral historian's question: 'What exactly happened?' The strategies for answering all orient to time as though it were a river that flows clearly forward from a fixed, knowable past into the present. As we will explain, to believe that this question can make sense in the first place is to rely on positivist/realist paradigms.

Next, we take heed of how time can instead be conceived of as a river's eddy. That is, from the standpoint of the storytelling present at the eddy's center, narrators can be thought of as looking back upon their past experiences. What they see there informs how they gaze toward the future; likewise, what they today imagine or hope their futures will be whirls back to inform how they look back upon their pasts (see Ricoeur, 1984). With this conception of time, narratives do not track the 'real' course of the past, but instead speak to the perspectives of the present and to projections of the future. Exploring narratives in this way involves shifting – to various degrees – toward a constructionist paradigm for research, one that values the multiplicity of narrators' possible subjective interpretations and meanings, and the processes by which they arrive at them. The three broad strokes strategies that we set forth use narratives to explore: present-day meanings of the past; the transitions, turning points, and interconnectedness of lives; and the relation of narrative to the self and its mutability over time.

KNOWING THE PAST THROUGH ORAL HISTORY

Ontology and Epistemology in the Realist Paradigm

Within the discipline of history, the 1960s and 1970s saw a fresh blossoming of **oral history** research, in which personal narratives were recognized as a valuable source of information about overlooked or obscured aspects of the past. At the outset of that new blossoming, historians had predominantly endorsed **positivism**. In response to the **ontological** question, 'What can be known?' positivist historians would say, 'Facts about what took place in the past.' (Historians have likewise tended to be **realists**, which means that they believe some real past does exist, independent of anyone's observing it. If a tree falls in a realist's forest, it always makes a sound.)

With regard to the **epistemological** question, 'How do we know?' positivist historians would answer that they are objective knowers, ones who observe the past from a neutral, value-free position. Thus, although many practitioners of oral history had avowedly political motivations for posing research questions about the hidden histories of subjugated groups, positivism informed how those in history departments defended the validity of their sources and analyses to colleagues accustomed to scrutinizing written sources. 'Our analyses are valid because memories *can* be accurate,' the oral historians would have said, falling back to the position that if the vagaries of oral narrators' memories and ephemerality of talk had tainted their data, so too had the subjectivity of the document writers of times past.

It was historian Luisa Passerini who, in 1979, made a significant intervention into her discipline's paradigm with her interviews about Italy under fascism. Passerini (1979) maintained that the conflicted feelings that her working class narrators recounted did not taint her project of discovering the objective truths of the past so much as they served as truths of a qualitatively different character. That her narrators had felt their labor to be a moral duty at the same time as they found it alienating helped to explain why they initially did not revolt against fascism, but later did: their subjectivity held the seeds for revolt. Since Passerini's intervention, oral historians in history departments have been far less apologetic about working with subjective data. In so doing, those seeking out the truths of the past have not had to abandon their positivist paradigm. As Guba and Lincoln (1994) explain, positivism can be stretched to incorporate and welcome subjective data, treating it as commensurate with what more objective sources offer. Thus, to technical analyses of the 1984 Bhopal, India industrial disaster, Mukherjee (2010) adds the voices of survivors as they recount their first glimpses of the strange white mist that would change their lives, their harrowing stampede for survival, and the continuing ordeal of unpredictable health conditions that they experience as monstrous.

Strategies for Rigorous Realist Analysis

Within both positivism and realism, reliance on talk data gathered well after events have passed means that errors of memory are seeping in, muddying oral

historians' views into the past. Important criteria for such an analysis are whether it minimizes such errors and assesses whether data reliably point to clear conclusions: every single strategy we outline is concerned with achieving **rigor** by that definition. A first strategy is to *take into account oral historians' experiences with the reliability of various kinds of oral evidence.* Finnegan (2006) provides a most helpful summary of the reliability of key data involved in tracking individuals. While people's memories of place names tend to be highly reliable, memories of first names and of dates are fraught with error, owing to nicknaming, mix-ups with similar names, differences between baptism and birth years, and the like. Attending to respondents' comments about the accuracy of their memories of various kinds of information may be useful if they themselves can make comparisons to other sources of data, such as personal notebooks (e.g., Turnbull, 2000); otherwise, say Neisser and Libby (2000), it would be illogical to depend upon respondents' memories of how good their memories are.

When talk data are about long past events or from cultures that rely more upon the knowledge technologies of orality than those of literacy (see Ong, 2012), additional considerations may come into play. Rather than calling your data oral history, you may speak of it as part of **oral tradition.** That is, consisting of cultural knowledge such as laws, legends, proverbs, origin myths, and children's play songs, that have been passed down without having been recorded in writing. The foundational text to consult is Jan Vansina's (1985) *Oral Tradition as History*, which provides additional strategies for assessing the messages from the past, such as asking whether maintaining the reliability of these messages has been culturally rewarded, or whether there are material objects, such as treasured heirlooms or marred landscapes, that serve as **mnemonic devices.**

Psychologists' studies of memory can also be useful to oral historians – but within limits. Oral historians are interested in memories based in natural settings, be they factories, homes, or battlefields. Most psychologists, however, prefer to study memories created in laboratory settings, where they can control the stimuli to which subjects are exposed. Oral historians are often interested in long-term memories accrued over the years. However, few psychologists study such long-spanning **autobiographical memories.** In fact, psychological studies of autobiographical memory need not cover years of lived experience. Studies of it can assess how well subjects remember events that might be only a few hours past. (Psychologists distinguish such memory from **working memory**, which lasts for just the few seconds needed to write down a telephone number.) Thus, relatively few cognitive psychological studies can help us understand particularities of how the more remote past is remembered.

To assess sources, we can factor in these studies' insights about the broader processes by which memories of personal experiences tend to stay stable or alter. Autobiographical memory researchers have found that memories of events are generally more likely to be accurate when the events are more recent, distinctive, or highly emotionally charged (Bauer, 2007), and when the memories have frequently been retold (Neisser and Libby, 2000). Further, in what's termed the **reminiscence bump**, events experienced between the ages of 10 and 30 are more available and

reminisced about than others, perhaps because these ages include distinctive and important changes in social roles (see Bauer, 2007). Meanwhile, common errors of memory include **hindsight**, which makes us believe we always could have foretold what has come to pass, **consistency bias**, wherein we tend to remember our past selves in ways that make them more predictive of our present ones (see Albright, 1994), and **misattribution**, wherein we cease to unite information about an event into a whole, and thus confuse one event with another (Schacter, 2001).

As an example, we can consider how co-author Katherine's mother Johanna once said that she remembered gathering with her family around the radio so as to listen to the first shots of World War II being fired on Poland (see Bischoping, 2014), a distinctive event, but one that was over 30 years past by the time that Johanna told Katherine about it. Johanna's memory does not entirely make sense, since German radio would hardly have announced a surprise attack as part of its programming. However, it's possible that she had mixed elements of this event up with a subsequent radio dramatization. Indeed, it is sometimes to an astonishing extent that what narrators report as vivid personal autobiographical memory can turn out to be filled in with media and mass cultural depictions (for example, see Figes, 2008).

Moving beyond errors in memory, Martha Howell's (2001: 60–8) *From Reliable Sources: An Introduction to Historical Methods* can be consulted for its excellent overview of historians' strategy of *assessing the accuracy of sources through several criteria.* These include **trustworthiness** (i.e., whether narratives are shaded by vanity, fear, political preferences, and the like), **competence** (i.e., the term that covers how factors such as individual interests, expertise, and capacity for comprehension can influence accounts), and **authority** (i.e. whether the writer was an eyewitness to an event or providing a hearsay account). Whether the account is internally consistent and plausible in light of other information is assessed too.

To see how these criteria of competence and authority work in practice, we focus again on Johanna's not-quite-plausible story of what she had heard on German radio. It makes sense to wonder about Johanna's competence to understand what she might have heard on the radio: born in 1935, she had been not quite four years old on the day that Germany began its attack. Further, because Katherine had herself heard this story in her childhood, her own competence to understand it can be questioned. Finally, we have the issue of Katherine's authority in transmitting Johanna's story second-hand. Although precisely what had been playing on the radio cannot be known, stepping back from that matter, the story can be thought of as offering a vivid and plausible fragment of information about how one German family had understood the importance of the attack on Poland.

For a stronger claim to be made would require additional narrators' voices, but all that Johanna's older sister could remember is that they had been away on a northern island, convalescing with whooping cough. When multiple narrators speak to the same events or era, you can *consider the criteria discussed above*

as you pick out their stories' common thread, a process called ***triangulation.*** More specifically, we can use Denzin's (1989a) labels of **data triangulation** in instances when cross-checks are made among narrators, across spaces, or over time, and of **methodological triangulation** when cross-checks are made among kinds of data sources, be they narrators, documents, monuments, mementos, mass graves, or scars. As you triangulate, be explicit about how you are choosing among differing possibilities and how confident your choices are. Alagoa (2001: 100) does so very clearly in explaining that his rule of thumb for working with oral histories of the Okpoama community in Nigeria was to accord greater credence to a narrative of an eyewitness that was corroborated by at least one other narrator and that was plausible in relation to other known information, with ties broken by looking for the greatest consensus.

The Case of Testimonio

A specific genre of oral history to which the positivist paradigm fits less than easily is that of **testimonio**, originating in the Liberation Theology-informed social movements of Latin America. In testimonio, '[t]ruth is summoned in the cause of denouncing a present situation of exploitation and oppression or in exorcising and setting aright official history' (Yúdice, 1991: 17). In this definition, we see that testimonio is decidedly positivist, laying claim to truth with a capital 't.' Readers may be leery of putting this label on testimonio, because positivism and related Enlightenment sciences have been used to promulgate other so-called Truths that now appear repellent, such as racial categorization schemes.

However, Hardt and Negri (2000: 155–6) turn this concern on its head, arguing that Enlightenment means of seeking Truth become quite palatable when they can be put to the ends of justice. This formulation displaces the standpoint of positivism's knower from one that is objective and neutral to one that is simultaneously objective *and* avowing an ethical and political position. In one way, this change in standpoint works. When vast ominous silences have been produced by the destruction of (or failure to create) archives, the fabrication of data, or harm to would-be narrators, a positivist faith in incrementally discovering truth by relying on the sources that are most plausible 'in light of other information' appears naïve. But, this formulation has built-in contradictions, which come most to the fore when narrators' testimonies come under close scrutiny. When narrators are speaking to extraordinarily painful experiences, such gentle doubts as we earlier cast on Johanna's memory of hearing the first shots fired on Poland could well seem heartless, undermining, and unethical. And yet, truth claims in positivism depend on rigorous scrutiny of their bases.

The social sciences' most famous instance of this conundrum revolves around the testimonio *I, Rigoberta Menchú: An Indian woman in Guatemala* (Menchú, 1984), in which Menchú depicted herself as an illiterate peasant and eyewitness to the

politically motivated murder of two family members during the Guatemalan Civil War. Some years later, after Menchú had become a Nobel Peace laureate, David Stoll (1998), an American political science graduate student, interviewed other Guatemalans who said that Menchú had been attending a Catholic boarding school during these events, and that it was a family conflict that had motivated her father's murder. A storm of controversy broke out about these discrepancies and several others that Stoll discovered (see Arias, 2001). Many who had been moved by Menchú's testimonio returned to its first chapter to mull over the passage: 'My name is Rigoberta Menchú. I am twenty three years old. This is my testimony. I didn't learn it from a book and I didn't learn it alone. I'd like to stress that it's not only *my* life, it's also the testimony of my people' (Menchú, 1984: 1). Some testimonio scholars attempted to defend Menchú, for example, by saying that this passage pointed to a shared authority for the events she had related, and that the work spoke to the truth of others' lives, if not entirely Menchú's own. Others, however, felt betrayed and devastated.

The analytic tension that Stoll's discovery brought to such a breaking point has been manifest in other projects where the stakes are high and the audience extends well beyond the local, such as in the testimonio on the Stolen Generations of Aboriginal children in Australia (Attwood, 2008) or the 'Comfort Women' forced into prostitution for Japan's military during World War II (Kimura, 2008). Can or should a paradigm exist wherein testimonio's claim to capital-t Truth is sustained without subjecting narrators to positivist-style scrutiny? Your analytic strategy may be *to address this tension*. Recently, commentators have done so by arguing that narrators should not be conceived of as victims who passively transmit information for historians to judge. Instead, they should be regarded as active political subjects and interpreters in their own right or as people whose political **subjectivity**, whose self-understandings and self-perceptions as political actors, is being formed by the very process of testifying (see Kennedy, 2006; Kimura, 2008; Uehara, 2007). For example, Choi (2011: 31) describes how a survivor of a Korean War massacre, frustrated by being given only 20 minutes to testify upon her visit to the USA, surprised herself by plucking out her glass eye to make her point.

Textbox 2.1: A Summary of Strategies for Knowing the Past

- Use oral historians' past experience to assess the reliability of various types of oral evidence.
- Use cognitive psychologists' insights to understand whether the memories being studied are likely to be stable or changeable.
- Assess sources in terms of trustworthiness, competence, and authority.
- Triangulate among sources, being explicit about how you resolve ties.
- In testimonio research, address the tension between assessing truth claims and treating narrators ethically.

KNOWING THE PRESENT THROUGH ORAL HISTORY

Ontology, Epistemology, and Rigor in the Constructionist Paradigm

We now make a transition from using narratives to look back in time, to focusing on what narratives about the past reveal about the perspectives of the present, which include projections about possible futures. The different strategies of doing so involve various degrees of shifting away from positivism and realism toward a **constructionist** paradigm. What is the **ontology** of such a paradigm, that is, what can be known through it? Are stories still regarded as routes to an objective reality, as they had been in the positivist/realist paradigms? The short answer to the latter question is that it is not the right question. Following Berger and Luckmann's (1966) *The Social Construction of Reality*, narrative analysts understand themselves to know the social world through their research participants' subjective reconstructions of their experiences of 'knowing' and 'being,' whether in speaking with others, or – as Frank (1979) points out – simply in talking to themselves.

Some constructionists, such as sociologist George Herbert Mead (1934) would go so far as to say that it is through language and interaction that meanings are formed, altered and disseminated: we narrate and therefore we are. Others such as Neisser (1994) and Collins (2010) would call this too strong a view, pointing out that we have experiences that we do not put into narrative or even language form. How girls experience their clitorises before having a name for them (Waskul et al., 2007) is a case in point. But constructionists all would agree that narrators engage in a host of interpretive processes before a word of a story crosses their lips. To perceive something as 'experience,' to recollect some aspects of it and not others, to ponder it, and to begin to express it in language, let alone to make sense of it in storied form, is to layer interpretation onto interpretation (Neisser, 1994; Ochs and Capps, 1996).

Further, any story we tell is contingent on the moment of its telling and cannot be expected to be the narrator's last word, even if the narrator herself thinks it is. Boje's study of how stories circulate in an office-supply company emphasizes that '[e]ach performance is never the completed story; it is an unraveling process of confirming new data and new interpretations as these become part of an unfolding story line' (1991: 106). For the epistemological question 'How do we know via narratives?' the answer is intimately linked to ontology – we know through our relations with others. Stories must be understood to be socially constructed or 'literally created' (Guba and Lincoln, 1994: 111) by a teller and a listener who might never arrive at a shared understanding (Scheurich, 1995). This occurs within a social setting that influences what is salient or tellable, as well as in a broader socio-political context in which stories are inter-subjectively compared.

Given that constructionists revel in the profusion of interpretations, and that analysis is itself an act of interpretation, constructionist notions of rigor are far removed from those of realists, who aim to show that they have reduced error and are closing in on the truth. Donald Polkinghorne (2007) maintains that

constructionists should seek to persuade their audiences that their conclusions about narrators' interpretations are plausible – a softer claim than realists', but not a simpler one. To warrant it, says Polkinghorne, involves the strategy of *explaining how you've addressed the likely gaps between the meanings that narrators experienced and the narratives that they've provided.* For example, if you have interview-based data, you will want to reflect on how well your interviewing methods addressed the inadequacies of language to fully and easily convey meaning, and your capacity to elicit and be trusted with narrators' self-reflections. Being able to say that you conducted repeated interviews with your narrators, gave them the opportunity to comment on transcripts, or reflected on the differences between theirs and your standpoints (see Chapter 4) would be assets here. Moreover, says Polkinghorne (2007), you'll want to provide an analysis that does not merely reiterate what narrators have said, but instead delves into its meaning, with claims being grounded in your data. Chapter 3 will outline strategies for orienting to spoken narratives as though they were literary texts.

Plural Pasts and their Present-day Meanings

Within the discipline of history, it was literary scholar Alessandro Portelli's (1981/1991) study of memories of the death of an Umbrian factory worker named Luigi Trastulli that most eloquently made the case that a constructionist paradigm could be used to support research questions of an altogether new nature. Portelli discovered that although police had killed Trastulli in 1949 while he was participating in an anti-NATO protest, 30 years later, his co-workers would systematically shift the context of his death to their momentous labor protests of 1952 and 1953. They desired Trastulli's death not to have been in vain, Portelli maintained, and turned it into a symbol of their greatest struggle. Further, since the workers had become pro-NATO by the time they were interviewed, that Trastulli had died protesting NATO had become awkward.

Portelli thus came to the realization that oral histories possessed an untapped potential to explain how the longings and politics of the present shaped memories and narratives of times past. In pressing oral histories into the service of envisioning the past, positivist historians had been discarding as errors the very meanings that Portelli proposed to cherish. It is important to note that with this radical suggestion, he was not taking a purely constructionist position of the type that Trouillot (1995: 4–6) says would call all accounts of the past equal fictions, and thereby depoliticize them. Rather, in contextualizing his analysis with the newspaper report that set Luigi Trastulli's death in 1949, Portelli's constructionism was firmly anchored in realism.

Since Portelli's study, narrative researchers with oral history data in hand *choose to what extent to focus on the past versus on its present-day meanings and the social processes that influence them.* Sometimes the data will almost choose for you, as is our reading of Johnson's (2005) analysis of an oral history-based report on New Zealand's Whanganui River. She describes a passage of the report as follows:

> [it] offers many 'reasons' for the lack of fish in the rivers such as sewage discharge, farm run-off, sedimentation and so on. Any discussion of possibly supernatural or non-scientific explanations is excluded from this list. Yet turn the page and under another heading, 'sacred waters', we are told of the 'moving accounts' offered concerning the river's purifying and healing powers. (2005: 266)

With no unified 'real' truth about the Whanganui River's history in sight, the jarring differences in the narrators' ontologies cried out to be investigated. But in other instances, as Kennedy argues (1998), the two choices can be complementary. Kennedy shows how oral histories with lesbian narrators can both establish a fact about the past, such as that a working-class lesbian community had been publicly visible in Buffalo, New York in the 1930s, and reveal how narrations were configured by the myth that no one could have been openly homosexual in the US until the 1969 Stonewall demonstrations.

While realist historians treat memories as though they are retrieved from some haphazard, corruptible archive of the brain, constructionists' understandings of memory align with more recent work in cognitive psychology, in which the act of remembering is posited to entail a creative process of reconstruction, carried out by a generative, ever-changing brain in response to circumstance and social context (Brockmeier, 2010). *To explore how reconstructions of the past change in changing contexts* has proven an effective strategy for illuminating this. Portelli's 'The Death of Luigi Trastulli' essay can also be read as an exemplar of this strategy because it compares what had been documented in 1949 to how it was reconstructed by numerous narrators 30 years later.

This strategy can be extrapolated in a number of ways, for instance, to focus on the history of multiple reconstructions of the past that are made by a single individual. An exemplar here is Curaming and Aljunied's (2013) perceptive study of the public statements made by Jibin Arula, who was the sole survivor of a group of mutinying Filipino military recruits who were massacred by their trainers. Curaming and Aljunied emphasize that the statements Arula made between 1968 and 2010 were largely consistent, especially those depicting the massacre and his life as tragic struggles; in realist terms, he could be considered a generally reliable narrator. Arula's overall reliability makes the instances of variations in his statements all the more interesting. At one point, he emphasized that the mutiny had been class-based; at another, that it was based on the recruits having been Muslim; and at yet others, he expressed remorse for having told anyone what he had gone through. Arula's shifting reconstructions, Curaming and Aljunied propose, could be related to the emergence of a myth that Christians in the Philippines had long been attempting genocide against Muslims, and to an escalating and deadly inter-religious conflict.

Other strategies for examining how the meanings of the past are inflected by the social pay less heed to individual-level memories. More attention is instead given to **collective memory**, a tremendously influential concept developed by French philosopher Maurice Halbwachs (1950). Collective memory, Halbwachs theorized, transcends and extends beyond the memories of the

individual members of a group, and is profoundly affected by social location. A strategy derived from this conceptualization is *to map out and seek to understand the divides in collective memory and, hence, between the groups involved in remembering.* Carole McGranahan's (2010) research on the role of Tibetan women in battles against China in the 1950s and onward is an excellent illustration. Although McGranahan consistently found Tibetan men to deny that women had any role in these battles, several Tibetan women narrated that they had indeed fought. McGranahan interpreted this difference in relation to patriarchal views that women's fighting emasculates men and to Buddhist views that menstrual blood is a dangerous pollutant. It should be noted that this strategy can be applied to investigate the differences between researchers' and research participants' interpretations of the past, an issue that has especially interested feminist oral historians who are uneasy about privileging their own interpretation over participants' (Arat, 2003; Sangster, 1994). We will be taking this up in Chapter 4.

Another common strategy for oral historians is to explore the dynamic between a state's **official history**, i.e., its public narrative of its history, which it bolsters with commemorations, museums, monuments, and so forth, and a multiplicity of possible **histories from below**. Such histories are based on memories of the everyday lives of disenfranchised groups or – in postcolonial contexts – of **subalterns** who fall outside the power structures of both the colony they inhabit and their colonizers' homeland. In some instances, such as Johnson's (2005) Whanganui River example, mentioned above, a history from below unambiguously contests an official account: there is no singular past here, but rather, pasts that are plural, local, and contingent. (For an accessible discussion of the postmodern vision of multiple histories to which this is related, we recommend Keith Jennings's (2003) *Re-Thinking History.*) But, in other instances, dominant narratives are so constraining that histories from below do not emerge fully fledged so much as in ambivalent fragments, contradictions, and silences, for which an analyst should be alert (Jennings, 2004: Loh, 2013; Stoler and Strassler, 2006). If the relations of power to knowledge and to what can be expressed interest you, then so will the Part III discussions of discourse analysis strategies, which can be applied to oral history data.

Following from the formulation of Halbwachs and those working in his tradition, when autobiographical memories turn out to differ from official history, a useful tactic may be to *examine whether families, distinctive for combining an intergenerational structure with passionate bonds and day-to-day transmission of memories, shape how the differences are negotiated* (see Assmann, 2008; Erll, 2011; Mason, 2008). In Dhooleka Sarhadi Raj's (2000) valuable formulation, this might be better expressed in terms of the transmission of ignorance, than of memory. Studying Hindu families in Delhi whose first generations had arrived as refugees from Pakistan at the time of British India's Partition, Raj shows how the refugee generation avoided speaking of the hardships of their displacement. She traces

this generation's strategy of deliberate forgetting to its desire for successive generations to fall in with India's official history, which depicts state formation as a glorious moment of independence. Although Raj's example is of a generation forcibly aligning the memories it transmits with what official history would endorse, such is not always the case. In other settings, as in post-World War II Germany, family loyalties and affections have fostered narratives in which family members are glowingly painted in terms that contradict an official history critical of the Third Reich (Welzer et al., 2001). Within families, it may be the weak, those positioned as most easily disturbed by harsh truths, who paradoxically are positioned as holding the greatest power over what is narrated in other settings.

Textbox 2.2: A Summary of Strategies for Knowing the Present through Oral Histories

In any use of a constructionist paradigm:

- Explain how you've addressed the likely gaps between the meanings narrators have experienced, and the narratives they've provided.
- Choose whether your focus is the past vs. its present-day meanings and the social processes influencing them.

To study plural pasts and their present-day meanings:

- Explore how reconstructions of the past change in changing contexts.
- Map out and seek to understand the divides in collective memory and the groups involved in remembering.
- Compare a state's official history to histories from below.
- Examine families as sites in which official and autobiographical memories may differ.

STUDYING THE PROCESSES OF THE LIFE COURSE

As researchers, our goal instead may be to analyze talk data for stories that illustrate lives as they unfold and change, through planned or unexpected role transitions or turning points, or when one person's experiences ripple into the lives of others. While the previous chapter considered how oral history data speaks of the past or its resonance in the present, in this chapter we more commonly speak of **life history** or **life course** data.

These terms may look confusingly similar, and statements that blur them together – as when Harris and Parisi speak of using a life history calendar technique to capture 'the timing and sequence of life course events' (2007: 40) – may look all the more bewildering. However, we consider the two approaches to have converged and their labels to now be interchangeable. Both are rooted in the

Chicago School of Sociology (see Dewilde, 2003; Stanley, 2010), which had a central concern with how social interaction was shaped by the urban environment, a constructionist approach known as **symbolic interactionism**. In this approach, humans are perceived as exercising agency, ongoingly constructing their social worlds and transforming their environments through shared symbols and acts of meaning-making.

The term 'life history' can be traced to W.I. Thomas and Florian Znaniecki's (1918–1920) landmark Chicago School study, *The Polish Peasant in Europe and America*, which used Polish immigrants' autobiographies and letters to preserve and represent the meanings they gave their experiences (Luken and Vaughan, 1999). Thomas was later to become renowned for the dictum that, 'If men define situations as real, they are real in their consequences' (Thomas and Thomas, 1928: 571–2). This dictum neatly sums up how perceptions and interpretations, rather than objective reality, can hold great sway in determining social action.

The life course perspective, which includes both qualitative and quantitative methods, originated decades later with the work of Glen Elder (1974, 1978, 1994). His signal contribution was to propose that any research on how an individual's passage through life unfolds must factor in that person's socio-historical context, family context, and the relation of the family to other institutions (see Brettell, 2002; Dewilde, 2003). Individuals' choices and their opportunities to exercise personal agency, Elder maintained, are simultaneously conditioned by these contexts and by the lives of others to whom they are linked. For instance, soldiers' decisions to desert must be understood in the contexts of the war they have been waging, their families' attitudes toward their options, and the legal, financial, employment, and social repercussions they and their families will face. Coupling the insights of these perspectives, we understand a life history to be an individual's story of the course of their life – a story that must be understood to be created through individual perceptions and agency at the same time as it is shaped by social structure.

Before we start discussing strategies, it is important to observe that Elder's approach, with its emphasis on socio-historical contexts and social structures, is rather more realist than Thomas and Znaniecki's. That the life course perspective to which Elder contributes includes qualitative methods alongside decidedly positivist/realist quantitative ones also means that life course studies are taken up more often by policy developers seeking 'hard evidence.' But, in our review of the recent literature, we found little discussion of the ontological and epistemological divide that this might seem to suggest. Instead, the two strategies blurred together, with an **ontology** and **epistemology** that we would again call constructionism anchored in realism. Strategy-wise, life history and life course researchers seem, like good sisters, to be glad to share what's in their closets.

Life history/life course researchers may focus on the story of one person or several. One concern may be how sharply marked, consequential moments of **role transition**, such as becoming jobless, entering university, becoming a

parent, migrating, caring for an ailing partner, or living under a new regime, are negotiated. Exciting contributions to life course research can come via the strategy of *uncovering how a group of respondents experiencing the same consequential transition turn out to be following one or a few* ***conventional plots***. Among the social sciences' best-known projects of this kind is Elizabeth Kübler-Ross's (1969) interview-based discovery that, among terminally ill patients, grieving moves through five stages, from denial to anger, and then to bargaining, depression, and acceptance in turn.

An exemplary analysis in which two conventional plots emerged is Anya Ahmed's (2013) study of UK retirees who migrated to Spain as 'lifestyle migrants,' i.e., for non-economic reasons. Ahmed found some migrants to narrate a 'quest' plot, in which a calling to move to Spain was succeeded by unanticipated obstacles upon arrival. Although the climate proved harsh, the housing was not in a village but in a pre-built residential area, contacts with Spanish people were few, yet the 'quest' narrators prevailed over these obstacles by finding companions who shared their purpose. Other migrants, however, narrated a 'voyage-and-return' plot, in which obstacles brought them to realize that their true companions had been at home in the UK all along. A life course perspective on these plots involves observing how the narrators' agentic choices were conditioned by the lives of the companions and others with whom they interacted, as well as structural and cultural factors, such as the trajectory of Spanish urban development, the romanticized images the narrators had held of Spain, and the cultural availability of quest and voyage-and-return plots.

You can also analyze life histories for whether they support or dispute the plotline for a role transition that another researcher has set forth. Critics of Kübler-Ross's model, for example, have observed that the dying may skip various stages that she had predicted, experience the stages out of order, or cycle amongst them; any stage model prescribing a lock-step sequence is open to such critiques. Another critically oriented strategy is to question to whom a plotline applies or under what conditions. For instance, while a sizable body of research shows that women with young children cannot necessarily conform to expectations that people on welfare become employable, co-author Amber's most recent, as-yet-unpublished research nuances the understanding of the gendered character of welfare-to-work transitions by showing how criminalized men who are recovering from addiction face similar barriers.

Instead of focusing your analysis on the transitions or life stages that social scientists have deemed significant, you might prefer to *examine how research participants speak of the events that they themselves consider to have radically disrupted or changed their life courses*. UK sociologist Anthony Giddens developed the concept of **fateful moments** to refer to the times when individuals reach 'crossroads' (1991: 143) in their lives, and must make choices with consequences both for the future and for how they understand their identities. In related work, American sociologist Norman Denzin had defined **epiphanies** as 'interactional

moments and experiences which leave marks on people's lives' (1989b: 70) over time and which might take a number of forms, e.g., major epiphanies pervade all aspects of one's life, while relived ones involve arriving at a new insight about a past experience.

As Goodey (2000) discusses, good social scientific analysis of such turning points involves *connecting them to their cultural and institutional contexts*. Berger (2008) does so in presenting the life history of Melvin, an undergraduate and American Paralympian who had been involved in gang sub-culture until being shot and becoming paralyzed from the waist down. Rather than casting Melvin as the hero of an individual struggle to overcome obstacles against all odds, Berger deftly shows how Melvin's adaptation to his disability and his actions were facilitated by structural conditions, such as a strong rehabilitative program and a supportive basketball program, as well as by experiences prior to becoming paralyzed that he was able to transpose onto his new reality (see 2008: 327).

Finally, following from another of the central theoretical principles of the life course perspective, we can *probe how individual experiences are linked with what transpires in the lives of others* (McDaniel and Bernard, 2011). For example, Amber uses a life course perspective in research on how 'families by choice' manage their low income through the instrumental and expressive supports that they give and receive from one another. In this research, participants did not define 'family' in strictly kin terms. Rather, their perception of others as family, especially others who were not kin, was informed by having shared specific kinds of life experiences (Gazso and McDaniel, 2015). In families by choice comprised of groups of lone mothers who were not blood relations, the mothers' senses of one another as 'family' stemmed from how their life courses had followed similar and interconnected paths, including disruptions such as divorce and alcoholism in their childhood homes, and experiences of teen homelessness and poverty as lone parents. Says one such mother: 'because we all are the strays, so we are just kind of family to each other. So that's basically where my family that I have created kind of comes around, we've all been the black sheep of our family [of origin].'

Textbox 2.3: A Summary of Strategies for Analyzing Life Course Processes

- Establish whether a group of respondents experiencing the same transition are following one/a few conventional plots.
- See whether your data support or dispute a plotline that another researcher has already found.
- Examine how research participants speak of the events they regard as epiphanies/fateful moments.
- Probe how individual experiences are linked with what transpires in the lives of others.

STUDYING THE SELF AS ESSENCE OR AS NARRATIVE PROCESS

In addition to illuminating the courses of lives and their interconnection, stories about experiences can shed light on a longstanding philosophical puzzle about the self. How can the self be thought of as responding to change in 'a perpetual state of becoming' (Chandler, 2000: 211), and, yet, as continuous over time, as somehow identical from one day to the next? A light-hearted example is that of Helen, a Brisbane, Australian interior designer who is positive that she is changing, in that she expects her tastes to become 'less cottagey,' at the same time as she's confident that she'll always love the cream-colored cottagey chair in her bedroom, meaning that it will always reflect her sense of self (Woodward, 2001: 126). The question is also a serious one. It's only because your self is understood to have continuity that people can lay plans with you and hold you accountable for your deeds. Otherwise, as Craig (1997) points out, a war criminal could give a 'That wasn't really me' defense. What, then, is the basis of this continuity?

As Chandler (2000) discusses, one tradition of Western thought would reply that the **self is an essence**. That is, we each possess some inner core, whether it be a soul, a destiny, a Cartesian ego who declares 'I think therefore I am,' or a bundle of persisting personality traits. Such a reply does not explain how Helen can foresee herself becoming 'less cottagey.' It fails to capture the sense that time or change matter. A contrasting reply posits that the self is not so much a noun as a verb, **a process of narration.** This reply builds on the thought of sociologist and symbolic interactionist George Herbert Mead (1934) and philosopher Paul Ricoeur (1984). Mead says that the self has two components, a *me* comprised of the attitudes and meanings we perceive others to hold of us, and an impulsive *I* that makes sense of the *me*. Meanwhile, Ricoeur says that the past is always understood from the perspective of the present and with an eye to the future. Douglas Ezzy (1998) fused these two theories to propose that a present-day narrative self continually updates its own unfinished story. The *I* strives to interpret the meanings of the *me*'s history and to project that *me* into a future. It is through this process that Helen can both affirm her past acquisition of the cream-colored chair and coherently project a future in which her tastes will change.

An initial analytic strategy arising from all this is to *ask whether research participants think of their selves as essences or as processes of narration?* 'I made one of my participants cry,' Jodi Kaufmann (2010: 104) writes at the outset of her article about how Jessie, a male-to-female transsexual, had responded to a draft analysis depicting her gender as fluid, as a narrative-in-progress that disrupted binaries of sex and gender. Jessie responded, 'You have taken away the identity I have worked all my life to build ... Who am I if you take this away?' (p. 104). Although Jessie had spent nearly 80 percent of her life history interview speaking of how she had been mistakenly born in a male body – i.e., of her self as having a female essence – Kaufmann

had initially considered these passages less relevant because they seemed to her to reproduce heteronormative expectations and the criteria by which psychiatric gatekeepers decide who is eligible for sex-reassignment surgery. Jessie's desire to live her female essence would repudiate any outsider's notion of her gender as fluid.

Note that, with the above question and example, we have shifted into research with a fully constructionist orientation. Even though Jessie, war criminals, and other individual selves may be understood to be anchored in continuity in a realist sense, we have let that anchoring slip, and are engaging more fully with our narrators' self-constructions. We now mark a second shift, into strategies concerned with the connection of narratives to wellbeing or psychological adjustment.

A first such strategy *asks how respondents are affected by the view of self as a narrative or by particular narratives about their selves.* Can thinking of the self in narrative terms offer them resilience in the face of an uncertain or foreshortened future? Chandler et al. (2003) observed that among adolescents in a Canadian psychiatric unit, those who spoke of the self as a narrative process were at lower risk of committing suicide than those who spoke of the self in essentialist terms. Studies of people diagnosed with life-threatening or chronic conditions have similarly explored which kinds of narratives about the future give them the most hope. Ezzy's (2000) landmark study of people living with HIV/AIDS (PLWHA) in Australia found that they narrated their experiences in three ways. In what Ezzy called 'linear chaos narratives', PLWHA expressed the belief that 'there is no future' (p. 612). In 'linear restitution narratives', they denied the inevitability of death and expressed hope by attempting to 'colonize the future' (p. 615) by making long-term plans such as home-buying. Finally, in 'polyphonic narratives' that were full of contradictions, PLWHA embraced uncertainty and expressed a hope that it could enrich the present, as in this interview excerpt:

> It's a bit cliche maybe that it's probably the best thing that ever happened to me. Something like a sentence of death concentrates the mind wonderfully. ... Previously I was wasting a lot of time in that you can, you can always find heaps and heaps of things to do in your life to avoid the, the larger issues. (p. 614)

What happens when the process of narration is disrupted by a past trauma that has breached the self? Here, the psychotherapeutic model for addressing trauma through narrative holds tremendous sway. In it, trauma is understood to disrupt comprehension, remembrance, and the ordinary forgetting required for narration to occur. In the flashbacks of post-traumatic stress disorder (PTSD), memories too painful to be accessed verbally thrust themselves cruelly, vividly, and uncontrollably to the fore, transforming what had been 'there and then' into the 'here and now' (see BenEzer, 1999; Kraft, 2004). If a person with PTSD can externalize a traumatic experience by expressing it verbally to a trustworthy listener, the argument goes, then a narrative can be formed that permits the past and present meaning of the experience to be considered, and that will reduce its intrusions into the future.

Exciting work is being done that *inquires into the generalizability of the psychotherapeutic model*. Such work assesses whether healing need always be language-based (Gheith, 2007; Kidron, 2012), questions whether the communal and enduring injuries of mass political violence are best remedied by treating trauma as an individual pathology (Kagee, 2004; Summerfield, 1999), and scrutinizes claims, such as the South African Truth and Reconciliation Commission's, that narration can further healing at a national level (van der Merwe and Gobodo-Madikizela, 2008; van der Walt et al., 2003). The last of these points brings to light how differently the various strategies we have been looking at would approach data about the same period of the past. While positivist researchers are asking, 'Exactly what happened during apartheid?', and researchers interested in histories from below are asking 'How do marginalized groups' accounts of this period differ from what had been official history?', some researchers interested in the self would ask 'Can what helps individuals to heal also help a nation?'

More broadly speaking, we can *observe how narratives serve to explain the breaches, turmoil, discontinuities, or glitches in our lives*. Järvinen (2001), for example, analyzes the justifications and excuses in the life histories of two male alcoholics in Copenhagen to show how they are turning their amoral behavior into moral tales that say more about who they want to be than who they have been becoming. Another strategy holds that the narratives we generate in such circumstances are drawn from **cultural repertoires**, that is, the conventional narratives available in a specific cultural context (Linde, 1993). This focus somewhat echoes our earlier mention of how narrating epiphanies in one's life are linked to cultural and institutional contexts but here we see more specific emphasis on how these narratives are culturally constituted and perhaps constrained. Among Soviet Gulag survivors, Figes found some to offer what he called a 'Survival' narrative of transcending troubles through individual struggle (2008: 126). Although this is a narrative that will be familiar in many cultural contexts, Figes also found survivors to offer a distinctively 'Soviet' narrative (p. 16) of taking consolation in thinking that their forced labor had contributed to the Soviet victory in the Great Patriotic War (World War II) or to the Soviet economy, creating the industrial towns in which they and former Gulag administrators continued to live and in which they take pride. 'It is our little Leningrad,' (p. 131) says one such survivor of her fume-ridden Arctic mining town.

Within a familiar setting, we may take repertoires for explaining discontinuity, and even for identifying what constitutes a discontinuity, so much for granted that they become invisible. Charlotte Linde (1993) proposes that a strategy for locating discontinuities and repertoires is to *hone in on what narrators take the most pains to explain and how they go about doing so*. Applying this strategy to white middle-class Americans' career histories, Linde (1993) observed that her subjects offered copious explanations of how they found silver linings in the accidental turns their careers had taken. They also exerted themselves to explain how apparent discontinuities in their careers could actually be understood as continuities at some deeper level. These narrators achieved coherence by using cultural repertoires that emphasized the persistent exercise of agency, not to mention having a job.

Linde's strategy is thus alert to the values accentuated in particular contexts and to the hazards of appearing to fail to embody them. (If this appeals to you, then Part III's discussions of discourse analysis should, since cultural repertoires might equally be called 'discourses.')

As this review of strategies for studying narrative's relation to the self draws to a close, we note that it has been preoccupied with projects of self-understanding in which bounded individualism and rationality are valorized (see Bordo, 1986). If individuals can understand themselves and tell their stories, the logic goes, they can become happier. Much as the urge to self-expression may be being experienced as natural, who has been schooled to tell what to whom, and to what end, reflects social inequalities (Tilly, 2006). Steedman (2000) also makes this case through her 300-year history of the project of self-narration, in which she draws parallels between the recent flourishing of pedagogy about self-expression and the requirement in place in England since the eighteenth century that the poor confess their troubles as a condition of obtaining social assistance. Freund (2014) even cautions that oral histories can compel narrators to construct selves as something to be known, to be fixed, and to be surveilled. In Chapter 9, we will see such themes again emphasized by philosopher Michel Foucault.

Moreover, cross-cultural studies have long pointed to alternate conceptions of the self that emphasize relational and communitarian values (e.g., De Craemer, 1983; Markus and Kitayama, 1991). In certain contexts, neither the concept of the self as an essence nor that of the self as a process of narration holds up. Further, citing examples from their own and others' ethnographies around the globe, in which narrators who had been asked for life stories presented information about myths, taboos, or their lineage, sometimes in song, sometimes in dramatic performance, and sometimes by handing over their identity cards, Kratz (2001) and Giles-Vernick (2001) argue that the life story – and the conception of the self that it entails – is far from universal. *If your respondents explicitly or implicitly question the logic by which you understand the self,* consider making that the focus of your investigation.

Textbox 2.4: A Summary of Strategies for Studying the Narrative Process

- Explore whether your narrators think of their selves as essences or as processes of narration.
- Ask what the implications are of viewing one's self as a narrative (or by a particular narrative about their selves).
- Inquire into how well models relating narrative to breaches of the self can be generalized.
- Observe how narratives serve to explain the breaches, turmoil, discontinuities, or glitches in our lives.
- If your respondents question the logic by which you understand the self, consider focusing your investigation there.

CHAPTER SUMMARY

Table 2.1 Broad strokes approaches to narrative analysis

Are your data...	*Some typical data*	*Paradigm*
A window into the past	Oral histories Testimonio	Positivism/realism
Offering a perspective on the multiple meanings that the past holds in the present	Oral histories	Constructionism, anchored in realism
Offering a perspective on how life course transitions, turning points, or interconnected lives are experienced	Life histories Narratives about specific transitions, e.g., career/migration/school Narratives about turning points	Constructionism, anchored in realism
Offering a perspective of the nature of the changing self	Life histories Narratives about uncertain future Narratives about past trauma, including testimonio	Constructionism, sometimes anchored in realism

People are storytellers engaged in a search for meaning, their memories and constructions of their experiences intimately linked to the flows or eddies of time. Table 2.1 sums up the relation between how data is viewed, what typical data are, and the paradigm informing analysis. In broad strokes, if we think of time as flowing forward like a river, talk data can help realist analysts piece together the answer to the question 'what happened?' If we think of narratives as constructed in the present, but eddying into the future and back into the past, then we have many choices for how analysis of talk data can proceed. Each of these is profoundly humanist in its orientation, valuing the individual search for meaning and capacity to re-evaluate the past, rather than seeing these as impediments. Through talk data, we can aim to understand the present-day meanings of the past, and how and why communities and sub-communities may remember the past in ways that align with or be distinct from official histories. Alternately, we can analyze talk data to understand how individuals experience the course and stages of their lifetimes, in terms of how their agency is conditioned by various social structures and of how their lives are linked to those of others. Our final broad strokes analytic strategies take up how the self can be understood to have continuity, yet be able to change, through its narrative essence. The structure of a narrator's story thus becomes a clue to the state of the narrator's self.

THREE

Fine-grained Analyses of Meaning

So far, we have painted narrative analysis in broad strokes, outlining strategies for comparing sizable samples of narratives and lengthy segments of interview transcripts in order to find their common themes, orientations, or storylines. We now turn to literary, linguistic, and psychoanalytically based strategies for focusing more closely on the miniscule, and the meanings it conveys. These will be especially useful in three situations:

- If you're thinking, 'I just have stories! I don't think my project fits into any of the broad strokes approaches discussed so far!' Okay. Then try these. You may need only one or two strategies, pursued in depth, for your project to work.
- If you're thinking, 'Sure, I have some stories, but storytelling isn't *all* that my respondents did.' Your transcripts might include many passages that are not related to time at all, such as lists, descriptions, rhetorical statements, or explanations of procedures. While it would be odd to present a narrative analysis that altogether neglects narrative, other aspects of talk that help to elaborate the meanings that matter to narrators are fair game for analysis.
- If you have very small samples or short stories. When you have so little data that comparing and contrasting among respondents is impossible, then look at your data close up. Although these strategies are suited to working with samples comprised of even only one narrator, short segments of transcripts, and the smallest of parts of speech, they also can complement any of the broad strokes approaches that we've been discussing.

These strategies can be of help whether you're using a realist paradigm or a more constructionist one. In the former situation, they can give you insight into a narrator's possible biases; in the latter, as Polkinghorne (2007) had suggested, they can bring nuance and enhanced validity to your understanding of a narrator's interpretations. Bauer and Thompson's (2004) review of works on Jamaican transnational migration warns us to go about this with a grain of salt, *being aware*

of how culturally available and historically grounded forms of expression (or what Part III will speak of as discourses) may be mistaken for distinctive and telling individual ones. They give the example of how,

> when a woman describes herself as a stepdaughter treated as a Cinderella, she may be using this ancient metaphor not only to convey her childhood sufferings, but also to indicate the obstacles she has successfully overcome. It would be very dangerous, without looking at an interview as a whole, to assume that because she spoke of herself as a Cinderella child, the woman's sense of self was as a Cinderella. (2004: 347)

A final observation before we launch into these strategies is that the imagery and other devices that we might interpret as narrators' expressions of subconsciously held meanings, following Freud (1900/1999), are also used consciously as rhetorical devices by politicians and creative writers. It is probably best to *be more cautious about claims as to whether a narrator uses a rhetorical device consciously or subconsciously*, and more bold about claims as to how it affected you as a reader or listener.

Textbox 3.1: A Summary of Strategies for Beginning Fine-grained Analysis of Meaning

- Remember that the expression of meanings is filtered or expressed through culturally available discourse.
- Be cautious about attributing intention to speakers' use of literary and rhetorical devices.

ANALYZING EMPLOTMENT, UP CLOSE

Labov and Waletzky's Model of the Story

Emplotment is a term that speaks to narrators' choices about what to include within their stories' plots. The social sciences' pre-eminent strategy for understanding emplotment was developed by sociolinguists William Labov and Joshua Waletzky (1967; see also Labov, 1997). In their model, because stories place events in sequence, that sequence must be understood to contain an argument for why those events occurred. The tiny story 'Alice ate an orange and then got sick' suggests that the orange caused Alice's illness, while 'Alice got sick and then ate an orange,' proposes that Alice thinks the orange will help her. Labov and Waletzky's model also posited that all **stories** had essentially the same formal structure, consisting of the following sequence of elements (plus one more that we'll take up shortly):

- an optional **abstract** that briefly sums up the story's most newsworthy event.
- **orientation** to the who, what, when, and where of events.

- **complicating action**, a sequence of events that are implicitly causally related and relevant, and that include the event announced in the abstract.
- an optional **resolution**, explaining the consequences of the most newsworthy event.
- an optional **coda** that signals that the narrator considers the story complete.

To think through aspects of how this model works, we use the story of 'Mollie's worst job' (see Textbox 3.2), told by a Toronto actor with whom Katherine conducted a career history interview. Mollie's story initially abides nicely by Labov and Waletzky's model, with an abstract in line 1 that signals that a restaurant's failure to close when a customer died is the story's most newsworthy event. Mollie orients us in line 2 to the story's setting. By line 6, the restaurant's failure to close has occurred. Mollie's decision in line 10 to quit the job seems on track to be the story's resolution. But, then, the model becomes confusing to apply. In line 13, Mollie orients us to a new character, that of a customer who asks to speak to the manager. Are we still in the same story? Are we in a new story whose abstract Mollie has opted not to provide, but at which she hints with 'That's never a good sign'? (line 14). Does it even matter?

These questions illustrate the frustrations of working with the sequential stages of Labov and Waletzky's model, which often winds up being used as a foil. Countless studies have 'discovered' that stories may lack beginnings, middles, or ends, and that they do not all march stalwartly forward through the fields of time. More creative projects take the strategy of *investigating why, or with what consequences, groups of narrators tell stories that systematically diverge from the model*, either by making them more elaborate or by omitting elements altogether. Etter-Lewis (1993) does so in discovering that, as path-breaking African American women professionals told their life histories, they often embedded stories about significant others within their longer stories. Etter-Lewis maintained that by elaborating their stories in this way, her respondents were underscoring their sense of self as self-in-community. Meanwhile, Burnell and colleagues (2010) show that British veterans who recount their traumatic war stories with less coherence – e.g., by omitting orientations to the stories' characters and locales, or by presenting contradictory complicating action – are those who garner less social support and perhaps therefore find it more difficult to cope with their traumas.

Another strategy starts off by modifying or discarding elements of Labov and Waletzky's model, to arrive at a looser definition of story. Stanley (2008: 437) employs a working definition that includes 'an account of things that have happened (usually, to some people), which has a beginning, middle and end, although not necessarily in this order; which involves some form of emplotment so that the story develops or at least has an end,' while Frost (2009: 15) even writes of 'identifying those sections of text that sounded, looked or simply "felt" like stories.' Labov and Waletzky might shudder at this. However, these amendments let Stanley, Frost, and other researchers move on to the remaining component of Labov and Waletzky's model, one that is not locked into any sequence. They *concentrate on the narrator's **evaluation** of what has happened.* Like Frost (2009), we regard Labov and Waletzky's emphasis on identifying and isolating evaluations to be the finest of their contributions to NA.

Textbox 3.2: Mollie's Worst Job

1 I also worked as a hostess in a restaurant where someone quite literally died in the restaurant and they didn't close the dining room.

2 An elderly lady came in with her son and her daughter-in-law, and it was a big room, like twice the size of this, and that was just the back dining room; it was a restaurant across from the Convention Center.

3 This woman had a heart attack and fell over.

4 When the waitress came to take her order, she's on the floor.

5 The family is sobbing, the waitress is in shock, the people at the next table are ordering another round of beer, and the staff – the manager said just [*makes a 'big round nothing' with her fingers*].

6 They didn't shut the dining room.

7 The paramedics were, they literally intubated her and were pumping [*makes CPR motions*], and people were still eating, and they carried her out with a blanket over her face.

8 Through the front dining room.

9 You'd think it was something out of a movie, that you couldn't possibly have this happen in real life.

10 That was the day I decided to leave that place.

11 That was a defining moment.

12 That guy was unbelievable.

13 And that night, a customer came in as we were closing down and said, 'Can I speak to the manager?'

14 That's never a good sign.

15 And I got the manager and the manager asked what the trouble was, and he said, 'I was here when the lady' – and trailed off – 'and I called 911 on the cell phone.'

16 The guy wanted some sort of compensation that his dinner was interrupted.

17 And he wanted some kind of compensation from the restaurant.

18 I've never been so appalled by, sort of, your average human being.

19 I have no words to even assess that.

20 It was ... It was awful.

21 But it's like the type of thing you would see in a TV show, as a black comedy.

22 You would think it would never happen in real life and it did.

Source: by permission of K. Bischoping and E. Quinlan

Returning to Mollie's story, we see her offering evaluations at numerous points, in both direct and subtle forms. She explicitly describes the customer's compensation-seeking as appalling and awful (lines 18, 20), and the manager's decision as 'unbelievable' (line 12), while conveying her view that the manager

was callous by means of her hand gesture (line 5). Her dismay at their profit motives and her decision, in this 'defining moment' (line 11), to quit the restaurant job connects to the money-versus-art struggle that she, like other cultural workers in the study, references elsewhere in her interview (Bischoping and Quinlan, 2013). Mollie's effort to come to terms with the seeming unreality of what happened is also couched in terms familiar in the theatre, i.e. in her questioning of whether this was 'real life,' a movie, a TV show, or a black comedy (lines 7, 9, 21, 22). (In sharing this story in a graduate course on Interview, Katherine proposed to her students that Mollie's use of 'literal' (lines 1, 7) could also be marking the reality/unreality question. The students, who were of Mollie's generation, contended that 'literal' no longer had this meaning, and was simply a culturally available way of marking emphasis.)

A life course researcher might observe that the evaluations in Mollie's emplotment are intrinsically related to her social position as a cultural worker. Differently positioned characters in the story might give very different evaluations of what had happened. For example, as Mollie went on to recount ironically, the family members wrote to the restaurant saying, 'Thank you for all your help. It was our mum's favorite restaurant.' Meanwhile, a narrative analyst interested in the relation of narrative to Mollie's self might focus on how her persistent interest in the reality, believability (line 19), and speakability (lines 15, 19, 20) of what happened could be manifestations of trauma. Such a researcher would note that although Mollie says she has no words, she continues to look for them, finding some value in the process of telling the story.

Textbox 3.3: A Summary of Strategies for Analyzing Emplotment

- Investigate why, or with what consequences, groups of narrators may tell stories that diverge from Labov and Waletzky's model.
- Concentrate on narrators' evaluations.

DISCERNING THE LANGUAGE OF AGENCY

To what extent do narrators regard themselves as sole authors of their own fates, as members of a collective, or as pawns in others' games? Where do they think responsibility for the triumphs and disasters of the past lie? *Attention to the agents whom narrators highlight in their stories* can point to the answers to such questions. Returning to Textbox 3.2, we can notice that Mollie absents herself from her own story between line 1, when she says that she worked as a hostess in the restaurant, and line 10, when she reveals that she decided to quit this job. During lines 2 through 8, other characters are depicted as responsible for every

single one of the story's actions. Others die, sob, are in shock, order beer, say nothing, intubate their patient, eat, or fail to close the dining room. Mollie's complete self-effacement maintains that the events of lines 2 through 8 were not of her making. It could additionally be read as an indication of their traumatic nature, as she seems to dissociate herself, her thoughts, and her feelings from what was happening around her.

Sociolinguists and literary analysts alike have several additional strategies for identifying how narrators take up questions of agency and responsibility; here, we will give you a flavor of two of them. In English and many other languages, *attending to the pronouns that narrators use to refer to the actors in a story* can be a powerful strategy for pinning down how they evaluate their agency and responsibility, and others'. An exposition of this strategy is to be found in Timor and Landau's (1998) study of Israeli ex-convicts who had begun to attend yeshivot (religious academies) for rehabilitation:

- Narrators use the **first person singular pronoun**, *I*, to identify themselves as the prime movers of events. Timor and Landau found narrators to speak of their reputable present selves in the first person singular, with its spirit of self-determination: 'Today if I open a small synagogue, it would be wonderful' (p. 368).
- Narrators use *we*, the **first person plural pronoun**, to present a collective story emphasizing solidarity or diffusing agency and responsibility. Timor and Landau's narrators tended to recount their criminal pasts in the first person plural, e.g., 'Before, we used to judge a guy by the laws of crime. [...] We didn't respect anyone honest. In the unwritten law of crime, we considered informers garbage, not humans' (p. 368).
- Narrators can also use the **second person pronoun**, *you*, to diffuse responsibility by maintaining that any reasonable listener would perceive things in the same way and feel the same way about them. For example, one of Timor and Landau's narrators explains his past crimes with, 'You see people dressed nicely, then you become jealous. Then you try to steal some money' (p. 369).
- Finally, when narrators use **third person pronouns**, describing what *he*, *she*, *it*, or *they* have done, they portray their own agency as diminished, circumstances as beyond their control, and events occurring willy-nilly.

Narrators also offer interpretations of agency and responsibility for events by means of what's called the **voice** of their verbs and by whether actions are described using verbs versus nouns. We give the vocabulary for talking about this in Textbox 3.4, using the title of the Bob Marley (1973) song, 'I shot the sheriff' as our example. Applying its vocabulary, we can say that when one of Timor and Landau's narrators refers to his past with, 'In general there was violence and people were hurt' (1998: 369), it is by using nominalization, followed by an agentless passive construction. The effect is that he is blurring over what happened, distancing himself from his actions and eliding responsibility for them.

Textbox 3.4: Voice and Nominalization

1. 'I shot the sheriff'	We say that Bob Marley's song title is in the **active voice** because the subject, *I*, is the character who is the agent of the sentence's action, *to shoot*. If this title were taken tobe answering a question, that question would be, 'Who shot the sheriff?'
2. The sheriff was shot by me.	Here, we move to **passive voice**: the sentence's subject, *the sheriff*, is the passive recipient of another's agentic action. If this sentence were answering a question, the question would be 'What happened to the sheriff?' The assailant, *me*, begins to slip out of the picture, with his or her responsibility sharply diminished (see Henley et al., 1995).
3. The sheriff was shot.	In **agentless passive voice**, the agent of the action disappears altogether.
4. The shooting of the sheriff occurred.	When we replace the verb *to shoot* with a noun, *shooting*, we have done what's called **nominalization**. This turns attention away from what's fluid, active, and changing (i.e., the act of shooting) toward a situation that's static, and therefore more inevitable and remote.

Pronouns and voice can also be important cues to understanding how narrators experience or represent the degree of agency that they have in institutional settings. Lapum et al. (2010) give the example of an open-heart surgery patient named Joseph, who recounts his experience as follows:

> What they did as soon as you enter the hospital, they take all the information, they give you a robe and put you in bed, they want to prepare you ... she gave me a pill, she said, 'Put under your tongue.' ... and she said, 'Okay we're going to take you to the operating room.' 'Thank god,' I said, 'We're finally going.' (p. 757, authors' emphases)

Analyzing this quotation, Lapum et al. emphasize how Joseph experiences himself to be giving over his agency to the medical practitioners and technology surrounding him. By the end of the quotation, he is subsumed into their 'we.' The patients that Lapum et al. studied tended to speak of themselves as 'I' again as they spoke of recovering from surgery and becoming less dependent on others and technology for their survival. But importantly, Anspach (1988) shows that even medical practitioners, whom we might think of as holding more institutional power than patients, are prone to turning technology into the agent in their talk. She explains that when doctors presenting case histories make statements such

as 'the MRI revealed a growth' as opposed to 'the radiologist interpreting the MRI data saw a growth,' the effect is to transform their, and other practitioners', subjective opinions into objective scientific fact.

In a strategy that doesn't hinge on grammar, Marie-Françoise Chanfrault-Duchet (1991) recommends that a narrator's ***key phrases*** *can be used to analyze how a narrator understands and problematizes the link of self to normative social models,* making a micro to macro link that intrinsically involves the narrator's agency. Key phrases can indicate that the narrator accepts, denies, resists, or is ambivalent about these models. Amber's grandmother, for example, used to cap off stories of hardships, such as of a family member's difficulty in obtaining adequate health care, with the phrase 'That's just the way it is.' This phrase would turn stories that could otherwise have been read as outright criticisms of the social model into resigned acceptance of it.

Textbox 3.5: A Summary of Strategies for Discerning the Language of Agency

- Notice which agents stories highlight.
- Use pronouns and voice as clues about agency.
- Observe what key phrases reveal about how a narrator problematizes the link of self to social norms.

OBSERVING USES OF IMAGERY AND FIGURATIVE LANGUAGE

Although time and sequence, and related ideas about perspective, cause, and effect, are all essential to storytelling, there is good reason to pay attention to the ways that narrators talk that are not all about plot. Stoler and Strassler (2006) press narrative analysts to recognize this by contrasting how Javanese people who had been servants spoke of working for Japanese occupiers versus Dutch colonizers. These narrators spoke spiritedly about the Japanese occupation of Java, but told few eventful stories about injustice they had experienced at Dutch colonizers' hands. Rather than expressing their interpretations of colonial relations through plot, they mentioned fragments of concrete sensory memories of employers who would pat them on the head, scold them, or eat only 'potatoes, potatoes, always potatoes, potatoes with this, potatoes with that ... potatoes, potatoes, potatoes non-stop ... with steak' (p. 34). Stoler and Strassler thus propose that submerged meanings, judgments, and markers of difference were surfacing through **imagery**, that is, through vivid descriptions that appeal to the senses. The same can be proposed of **figures of speech**, defined as words or phrases whose meaning extends beyond its literal interpretation, such as metaphors, catchphrases, and proverbs.

In oral histories with women who left Ireland in the 1930s, Louise Ryan (2002) noted how frequently the narrators mentioned clothing, whether in references to wearing an undershirt made of flour sack during adolescence, having painful and squeaky shoes while training in England to become a nurse, or buying a 'bottle green' (p. 50) outfit to wear for a first trip back home. One power of such imagery, and thus one reason to look out for it, is that it invites a narrative's audience to partake in the narrator's experiences and evaluations. If reading about a story of squeaky shoes led you to imagine hearing a squeak or to feel vicarious embarrassment, then this image has begun to draw you into sympathy with the narrator's point of view. Further, by recounting detailed images such as the precise shade of a green suit, narrators can persuade their audiences that they still feel close to their earlier lived experiences and are able to recall them faithfully (Ross and Buehler, 1994). According to Tannen (2007), narrators who voluntarily divulge detailed images are also showing that they are at ease with their audience. This sign of a narrator's trust can be used by constructionist researchers to strengthen the claims to rigor that Polkinghorne (2007) discussed, i.e., the claim that a narrative reflects experienced meanings. For all these reasons, *considering whether detailed images have been provided, and how and why they affect you,* can be a useful strategy.

Further, you might *test whether the meanings of a narrative's imagery corroborates what you have observed about the narrative's plot.* Ryan (2002) observed that her narrators repeatedly mentioned clothing as a symbol of their life transitions, tensions about family relationships, and experiences of belonging or being an outsider in Ireland and England, all elements directly relevant to the analytic concerns typical in a life course perspective. In our reading of Mollie's story in Textbox 3.2, one of its most commanding images is that of the dead woman being 'carried out with a blanket over her face' (line 7). The relation between this woman's dead and covered face, and Mollie's new and clear-sighted awakening to the realization of her employer's profit motive, is very nearly one in which a death leads to a figurative rebirth. Because Mollie's distinctive and personal experience is expressed in a widely available vocabulary for speaking of epiphanies (DeGloma, 2010), the imagery of her story corroborates its epiphany theme.

The strategy of *paying particular attention to narrators' uses of metaphors* is worthwhile because of the wealth of meanings that such expressions reveal. Metaphors work by taking mental associations about a **source domain**, one that is usually concrete and readily accessible, and mapping them onto a **target domain** that is usually more abstract or unfamiliar. Take this statement that Kamal, a Biology undergraduate at a large Canadian university, made at a focus group on first-year university experiences conducted for our colleague Logan Donaldson:

> The first time I was at [X University], I walked into Stavener Hall and you just see a bunch of ants going everywhere, so it's not ... I wouldn't say it's a home but it's not horrible either.

Here, Kamal uses 'ants' as the source domain in his metaphor for the people in Stavener Hall, who are his target domain. He thus invites readings of these people as rational, purposeful, and industrious individuals, scuttling in an undifferentiated and not especially gregarious mass within an environment that dwarfs them. Had Kamal instead chosen lemmings or cats, sled dogs, dinosaurs, or robots as his source domain, a host of different evaluations, again condensed into a single word, would have been implied.

In *Metaphors We Live By,* linguist George Lakoff and philosopher Mark Johnson (2003) explain how metaphors are socially shared and can direct understandings (also see Gibbs, 2008). We can be on the watch for metaphors that become **extended** throughout a narrative or narratives, linking associations into an argument. An example is of how adolescent Bosniak girls born of war rapes speak of themselves as cancers whose malignant contamination of healthy tissue (i.e., their loved ones) can be destroyed only by bloodletting (i.e., suicide) (Erjavec and Volčič, 2010). To assess the universality of a metaphor can also be helpful.

Textbox 3.6: Translating Talk of Self-love and 'Jihad'

When I was working in sales at Lucky Brand Jeans, one of my colleagues had a fascination with language. 'Teach me something in Arabic,' he'd say, 'and I'll teach you something in Portuguese.'

After a while of this, he asked me for help with a tattoo he wanted to get. He was going through a process of self-discovery and had found a perfect Buddhist saying to express it: 'You, yourself, as much as anybody in the entire universe, deserve your love and affection.'

At the same time, he wanted a tattoo that would have an element of mystique, and that would express the saying in a way both visible and private. So, he asked me to translate it to Arabic. In one way I could do it. I could produce a word-for-word faithful translation.

But, I had to say to this colleague, this doesn't convey the same meaning. To talk of self-love is not a dominant discourse in Arabic-speaking countries as I've experienced them. To speak in that way would convey a level of narcissism and individualism that would not pay heed to the collective. The expectation in these countries is that love and affection comes from those around us, not from ourselves. A faithful translation of this phrase could not be a transparent one.

A different challenge comes from the Arabic word *jihad*, which has entered the English vocabulary. Reading and writing 'jihad' in the West, many take for granted what it transparently means: a holy war. However, among Arabic speakers, the essence of *jihad* is struggle. Among us, it is a word that can be used in many contexts – for example, without any exaggeration at all, I could say to a friend, 'I *jihad*ed to write my essay!'

Thus, 'jihad' may seem transparent, but its use is unfaithful. What Samuel P. Huntington (1993) has called the Clash of Civilizations, the theory that post-Cold War conflict will be driven by religious and cultural identities, is shaping *jihad*'s dominant meaning in the West.

Source: Rawan Abdelbaki, in Abdelbaki et al., 2014

When Henry (1999) explored how Hmong migrants to the US understood measles, she found that many of them metaphorically equated their bodies with landscapes, and measles with agricultural crops that responded to changes in weather and the seasons. In contrast, American health care professionals metaphorically equated measles and other diseases with an enemy in warfare. These differences directed profoundly different understandings of how measles should be treated. For instance, Henry explains that Hmong could understand a fever as a way for a rash, equated with seed, to grow and run its course, as in this narration about a child's illness: 'maybe the measles start on her body – that's why the body is kept hot – for it to come out. Otherwise you make the body cool and measles [will be] dead inside and [this] will cause a problem for the body' (p. 41).

Working with imagery and figurative language poses especial challenges when research requires translation between languages. *Identifying the challenges and explaining how they affect narrators' apparent meanings* is important in a rigorous analysis. Often social scientists, like professional translators, choose to aim for what is called **transparency**, rendering the meaning of the original in a way that readers will readily grasp, rather than for **fidelity**, a word-for-word rendering that might confuse readers. But, it's not always simple, as Halai (2007) shows in an outstanding account of how globalization is implicated in the translation issues she encountered when working with bilingual (Urdu–English) data that she had collected in Pakistan. Among Halai's tactics is to present a key word or phrase in its original language (perhaps **transliterating** to the audience's writing system), and then to discuss why it resists straightforward translation. It is this strategy that our graduate student colleague Rawan Abdelbaki models in Textbox 3.6.

Textbox 3.7: A Summary of Strategies for Observing Imagery and Figurative Language

- Consider whether detailed imagery has been provided, and what its effects are.
- Test the relations of a storyteller's imagery to what you know about the story's plot.
- Attend to narrators' uses of metaphors.
- Identify the challenges of translation and explain how they affect narrators' apparent meanings.

LISTENING TO THE SOUNDS OF STORIES

> The sound must seem an echo to the sense.
>
> Alexander Pope (1711)

Because we have been well schooled in reading silently, we may not be attuned to such echoes of the stories' original sounds as our transcripts retain, or know how to express their resonance to others (Lanham, 2003). In this section, we offer strategies

for doing so that are drawn from literary and linguistic analyses alike. Let's begin with a statement made by LeeAnn, a member of the same first-year undergraduate focus group in which Kamal, of the ants metaphor, had participated. 'I come here, I study, and I leave,' said LeeAnn, expressing a sentiment of disengagement from the social life of the university that several respondents in the group shared. What is it that makes her sentence stick in the mind? On a technical level, an answer can be teased out by observing how the sentence involves repetitions of four kinds:

- **Assonance** is the repetition of nearby vowel sounds. Omitting LeeAnn's consonants, her sentence reads 'I uh ee, I uh ee, a I ee,' or, in the phonetics notation used by linguists, 'aɪ ʌ ɪ, aɪ ʌ ɪ, ə aɪ ɪ.' Repetition of nearby consonants would be called **alliteration**.
- **Rhythm** is created in English when stressed (i.e., emphasized) syllables alternate with unstressed ones in a repeated pattern, or **meter**. Marking LeeAnn's stressed syllables with italics, we see that she starts off with a pattern of 'I *come* here' that is repeated in 'I *study*,' though 'and I *leave*' departs from this pattern.
- **Parallel structure** occurs when clauses, sentences, paragraphs, or larger units have related organizations. Here, each of LeeAnn's clauses begins with the subject 'I,' followed by a verb: come, study, leave.
- **Intertextuality** refers to how a text takes a different meaning when it moves into a different context. Whether LeeAnn intends it or not, the form of her 'I come here, I study, and I leave' is nearly identical to that of Julius Caesar's 'I came, I saw, I conquered,' inviting their contrast. LeeAnn's anti-climactic and detached experience of university becomes more striking through the contrast with Caesar's triumphant ownership with the lands he surveyed.

The overarching analytic strategy deriving from these points is one of *observing the effects of repetitions*. Linguist Deborah Tannen (1987, 1998, 2007) explains that repetitions influence audience, first, by drawing them into the narrator's perspective. When a pattern of sounds, syllables, clauses, or larger units is repeated, its logic takes on a satisfying familiarity, coherence, and ease – the same pleasure we feel when we sing the chorus of a song. Second, repetitions highlight what matters to a narrator, for instance, by mimicking the passage of time, as in 'potatoes, potatoes, always potatoes' (Stoler and Strassler, 2006: 34). Third, even the number of items in a repeated structure can communicate meaning. LeeAnn's trinity of clauses feels complete, whereas a four-clause sentence would have begun to feel like a list that could go on endlessly (Clark, 2006; Jefferson, 1990). However, Kratz's (2001) analysis of life history interviews that she conducted among Okiek in Kenya adds a grain of salt to this conclusion. Kratz hypothesized that her narrators chose to organize their stories into four parts because four is an auspicious number that Okiek use in rituals and poetic structures; how numbers are read can thus be culturally specific.

Importantly, once a pattern of repetitions has been established, breaking from it can seize the audience's attention and mark a shift in meaning. Sociolinguist Jan Blommaert (2008) illustrates this with his analysis of the testimony of Mrs Maureen Cupido, a 'colored' woman telling the South African Truth and Reconciliation Commission about the night that her son, Clive, had been murdered in a political

riot. In Textbox 3.8, a key passage, with Blommaert's system of highlighting repetitions preserved, shows how Mrs Cupido's parallel structure of 'and (then)' phrases propels her narrative forward – until the structural break and wobble in time that marks her son's demise. **Poetics** is the name sometimes given to such methods, which parse a transcript into what resembles a poem on the page, using line breaks to separate clauses, pauses, or perhaps breaths, and stanza breaks to separate topics (Gee, 1991; Woodley, 2001; though see Lanham, 2003 for an alternative format), all in order to facilitate analysis of how the structure of sound amplifies its meaning.

Textbox 3.8: And then

Clive came home early –
eleven o'clock the morning
and then he told me
this march is going to have a lot of trouble.
Little knowing that he is going to be killed

and then he went to this friend
and he sat –
he first then have supper
and then he went to his friend,
and that was early hours, early.

And then we – we wait for Clive to come home,
because my husband never sits, waits for his children,
I am the only one.

And then suddenly I just fell asleep
and then I stood up
and I went to my bedroom
and as I went to my bedroom to get onto my bed,
I heard the shots,
because before the shots,
(my heart) gave three – three thumps
I just – my heart just went you know.

Source: Blommaert, 2008: 434, author's emphases

Textbox 3.9: A Summary of Strategies for Listening to Sounds of Story

- Observe the effects of repetitions on listeners and in conveying meanings.
- Watch for what breaks in repetition do.

CHAPTER SUMMARY

The premise of our 'fine-grained' strategies is one dear to psychoanalysts and literary scholars alike: that people drop clues to their perspectives in the minutiae of their narratives. Strategies based on this premise can stand alone, or can complement any of the broader strokes analyses of the last chapter. In particular, realists can use them to pick up what they would think of as narrators' biases, while constructionists can embrace narrators' interpretations as objects of analytic interest in their own right. The strategies include focusing on how narrators adhere to or depart from the Labov and Waletzky model of storytelling, or on how narrators use the language of agency to reveal their evaluations of who a story's prime movers are. They also include examining how interpretations are conveyed by a story's imagery and figurative language, and on the meanings inherent in a narrative's rhythms and repetitions. These fine-grained strategies sometimes take for granted that a narrative has an audience, for example, one that might be persuaded by repetitions or trusted enough to be given the details. But, for the most part, they treat stories as texts, rather than as embodiedly told, in the moment, to a listener whose responses shape the telling.

FOUR

The Interview in Narrative Analysis

In this chapter, we address why and how narrative analysts take into account the contexts in which stories are told. The context of the research interview is our focus because much NA work relies on interview data and because many narrative analysts have applied themselves to understanding this context. If your narrative data does not come from interviews, we encourage you to consider whether the principles we discuss here are still relevant in your work.

The central question, usually referred to as one of **reflexivity**, asks how one's self and one's methods are implicated in the knowledge one produces. Rather than assuming that interviews are a one-way transmission of narrators' thoughts, feelings, experiences and intentions to interviewers, narrative analysts understand them to involve what Elliot Mishler (1991: 52) and subsequent sociologists have called a **joint construction of meaning**. In the discipline of history, Michael Frisch (1990) coined the related term **a shared authority** to highlight how researchers' interpretations hinge on what narrators offer or hold back. We've already seen the term authority in Chapter 2, as a term used to distinguish firsthand knowledge from secondhand and so forth. Frisch instead uses it to assert that researchers and narrators share authorship of interview data, and that their process affects how authoritative audiences will understand the resulting analysis to be.

In the first section of this chapter, we take up feminist critiques of androcentric knowledge, as well as the anti-colonial critiques that emerged in the discipline of anthropology. These two bodies of critique share strategies for reflexive inquiry into how what one claims to know depends on one's standpoint, i.e., one's consciousness, as informed by social location, cultural context, and political forces. But, as you'll see, these bodies of critique don't always overlap, and their differences are ontological ones. For instance, a realist feminist claim that women could research women's experiences more accurately than men could, would fly in the face of

post-structuralism, a variant of constructionist thought that produced a crisis in the discipline of anthropology. Post-structuralists maintain that no knowledge claim is certain and that all so-called facts are fictions linked to configurations of power. We will see that post-structuralists' strategies for dealing with issues of representation sometimes differ from those of realists.

The second part of this chapter is motivated by the observation that much is lost as we move from the lived experience of an interview to the transcribed words on a page. The two are as different as butterflies in flight are to a pinned one. We will draw on feminists', anthropologists', and cultural geographers' scholarship to provide a conceptual vocabulary for naming how the experienced interview and the transcript differ and for recognizing how bodies, emotions, and uses of spaces inform what we 'know' – once we abandon dichotomies such as mind vs. body, thought vs. emotion, or person vs. environment. These insights lead into strategies interviewers can use to reflexively recuperate knowledge that transcends the words on a transcript's page, for instance, when they are faced with respondents who seem to be communicating through silence, or when they experience their relationships with respondents as microcosms of the greater phenomenon under study.

Finally, this chapter asks how it matters that the interview data that narrative analysts interpret quite often takes the form of stories. Many of our students who have not yet been exposed to narrative analysis have a default understanding of a story as a monologue that a teller delivers to a listener. If stories are instead to be understood as joint constructions in which both tellers' and listeners' notions about what stories *should* be like can come into play, then it is essential for narrative analysts to ask the reflexive question of whether those notions are shaping their data. In our reading of the NA literature, we repeatedly find emphasis on four interconnected norms about stories. Stated in layperson's terms, they are that stories should be newsworthy, should not discombobulate their listeners or tellers, should be coherent, and finally, should be 'true.' We set forth how narrative analysts of various stripes have labeled these four notions, unpacked how each one affects *both* interviewers and respondents, and formulated strategies for considering their impact on knowledge production.

BEING REFLEXIVE ABOUT STANDPOINT AND REPRESENTATION

Until the 1980s, the interviewer–respondent relationship was most commonly problematized by asking whether the interviewer was an insider to the main social category defining the group of respondents. (Simmel's [1908/1950] essay on 'The stranger' provides an early formulation of this question.) Yet, **insider/outsider** accounts seem without fail to come to the same conclusions. Researchers expecting to be recognized as 'insiders' come to realize that no singular identity can account

for all that transpires in their research. For instance, in Temitope Oriola's (Oriola and Haggerty, 2012) study of kidnappings of foreign oil workers in the Niger Delta, he found that his expected insiderhood as Nigerian was not as meaningful as his ethics review committee had expected. Once he had arrived in Nigeria, at various instances, other social categories emerged as more important. His familial connections and Yoruba ethnicity helped him to make contacts, while his unfamiliarity with the customs of the Delta region and the interpersonal aloofness he had acquired during graduate studies in Canada proved to be hindrances (see also Narayan, 1993; Schütz, 1945/1970). Meanwhile, researchers expecting to take an outsider position tend to be startled to experience belonging or rapport during interviews, as feminist Donna Luff (1999) illustrates with reference to her study of British anti-feminist women lobbyists. We recommend that instead of referring to insider/outsider status, you avail yourself of the newer, more analytically nimble **standpoint theory**.

The Basics of Standpoint and Representation

Standpoint refers to how a person's consciousness and interpretations develop according to the experience of being socially located in particular categories, performances, and intersections of race, class, gender, sexuality, citizenship, ability, and so forth (Intemann, 2010; Sprague and Zimmerman, 1993; Weedon, 1999). A standpoint is not given, so much as achieved through critical, community-based reflection of how one's knowledge is shaped by prevailing power structures and cultural conditions (Hartsock, 1983/2003; Intemann, 2010). For our purposes in this section, standpoint is the position from which one is knowingly reflexive about the interview and about the larger process of knowledge production of which it is part. **Positionality**, meanwhile, refers to the relative positioning of researchers and participants, in which knowledge is situated (Alcoff, 1988).

Feminist standpoint theory was inspired by Hegel's discussions of the relationship between the master and the slave and Marx's subsequent interest in the standpoint of the proletariat (Harding, 1986; Hekman, 1997). Feminists of the late 1970s onward called for knowledge to be grounded in the standpoint of women – in their lived experience of social and material relations (Hekman, 1997). Philosopher Nancy Hartsock (1983/2003), who is among the three most influential early standpoint theorists, argued that bringing women's knowledge out of the shadows was a necessary corrective to patriarchal and phallocentric institutions and ideology. Philosopher Sandra Harding (1986) argued that androcentric bias characterized all aspects of science: problem formulation, concepts, theories, methods, and interpretations. And sociologist Dorothy Smith (1987) set her discipline on its head by arguing that all its earlier knowledge had been written by men privileged by their position in the ruling relations of society. For women's subjugated position to be deliberately represented in knowledge coming from a woman's standpoint would make knowledge more accurate, in the realist sense, and would have liberatory potential.

Feminist standpoint theory has since grown. In particular, Black feminist standpoint theory introduced the idea that Black women experience their lives within multiple systems of oppression, in what's termed an **intersectionality matrix** (Few, 2007) and thus deliberately injected Black women's ways of knowing into research conducted with them (Collins, 1989). This intervention was among the efforts made to rearticulate standpoint through a **politics of difference**, instead of through a master narrative of a universal woman's experience (Hekman, 1997; Tuana, 1993). In such a politics, women do not uniformly experience themselves as patriarchally oppressed and can themselves oppress other women across lines of race, class, (dis)ability, sexuality, religion, nationality, and so forth. Because of the scope intersectionality could have, some researchers would say that the knowledge available from any standpoint must be understood as partial – and for them, standpoint theory has taken leave of its realist origins. However, for other researchers, such as those working with testimonio, certain intersectional locations are thought to possess subjugated knowledges that are necessary to bring to wider audiences. These more realist researchers would speak in terms of 'truths.'

At the same time as feminist standpoint theory was being developed, anthropology began to confront what it termed the **crisis of representation** (Marcus and Fischer, 1986). This crisis has dual aspects, known as **power and poetics** (Clifford and Marcus, 1986). The power aspect is analogous to early feminist standpoint theorists' concerns about the androcentrism of knowledge. Anthropologists were becoming newly concerned that their discipline's habit of casting a 'knowing' gaze upon, and representing, distant Others' cultures had made it complicit in projects of empires, up to and including American imperialism (Rosaldo 1989; Said 1978, 1989). Globalization, transnational population flows, and new borderland and hybrid identities (Anzaldúa, 1987; Bhabha, 1994) meant that anthropologists could no longer hold themselves apart from their informants and could no longer tidily divide themselves from the Others whom they studied (Rosaldo, 1989). In sum, the fundamentals of anthropology's disciplinary project were in doubt.

The **poetics** aspect of the crisis is related to the decidedly post-structuralist argument, found in anthropology and literary studies alike (e.g., Ebert, 1986), that all language is rife with insupportable claims to certain knowledge. If so, then anthropologists' fieldnotes – the bedrock of their discipline – could no longer be taken as concrete, objective representations of reality, and instead turned into subjective tissues of fiction (Clifford, 1986; Rabinow, 1986). The 'objective' tone of earlier anthropological writing was no longer necessary; worse yet, it was beginning to sound pompous, unevocative, and just plain dull (Rosaldo, 1989). (Note that we now have a broader meaning of poetics than we'd seen in Chapter 3: instead of referring to theories about how the structure of sound affects a poem's interpretation, poetics now refers to broader theories about how the forms of texts influence how they are interpreted.) Because the fundamentals of what anthropology had been doing and could claim to do were both in doubt, anthropologists, like feminists, sought new analytic strategies.

Strategies Based on Standpoints

Whereas researchers using standpoint theory might initially have romanticized the interview as a site of egalitarian sharing between women, they now understand the interviewer–respondent encounter to be inevitably shaped by relations of power and privilege, and require analytic strategies amenable to investigating and ameliorating those relations. Post-structuralist anthropologists are of the same mind. Although their ontology differs from that of some feminist standpoint theorists, the two groups share strategies for understanding how standpoints and academic privilege are implicated in knowledge production.

Inquiring into which positionalities of researchers vis-à-vis research participants are relevant to the stages of knowledge production is a starting point. Proclaiming your standpoint, for example, as a 'white feminist woman economist' won't cut it. Instead, this strategy involves asking what difference differences made as you formulated your research questions, designed your study, sought respondents, carried out the interviews, and made sense of the data. A simple example is Nollaig Frost's (2009) discussion of her realization that, in an interview on mothering, she cut off a respondent who was speaking about mothering decisions uncomfortably different from her own. Despite having British nationality, whiteness, and class in common, differences in mothering practices emerged and constrained the data that Frost collected.

A more extended example is Urvashi Soni-Sinha's (2008) study of 'chain work,' the name given to the jewelry-making industry in West Bengal. Soni-Sinha found that women participants were initially in awe of her academic status, apprehensive about participating, or comfortable with being interviewed if they received something in exchange. However, over the course of several meetings with some women, she found that they began to relate more to her on the basis of their shared Indian ethnicity, and appeared to see the story-collecting purpose of their meetings as secondary. Meanwhile, Soni-Sinha found that her access to child laborers was inhibited because they perceived that their jobs would be at risk if they were to be interviewed by a female researcher, and a non-Bengali one at that. Importantly, Soni-Sinha connects her conclusions about participants' standpoints to assessments of the quality and representativeness of the data that she could gather. Note also that her conclusions are made more compelling by her use of comparisons, i.e., between child and women workers, and between early and later interviews with women. As you'll see, this strategy of *drawing comparisons to bolster standpoint-related conclusions* will appear repeatedly in this section.

Mauthner and Doucet (2003) point out that not only social categories but also ontology and epistemology inform a researcher's standpoint. For researchers approaching their data through a realist lens, tensions can arise between wanting to respect participants' memories and interpretations of their experiences and wanting to stick to what are understood to be the facts. Take, for example, Marxist feminist Joan Sangster's (1994) study of women's experiences of a 1937 textile

mill strike in Peterborough, Canada. In Sangster's reading of written sources about Peterborough's labor history, the strike had been significant as a first effort at industrial unionization and for its violent intensity. Yet, some former workers whom she interviewed many years later remembered the strike in altogether inconsistent ways. One downplayed its importance, another called it 'almost a heyday' (p. 18), and a third focused on the wedding plans she had been making at the time. To Sangster, resolving the dilemma by adopting only a post-structuralist view of knowledge would be tantamount to 'abandon[ing] the concept of experience, moving toward a notion of a de-politicised and "unknowable" past' (p. 22). Instead, she opted to explore how the seeming contradictions between the oral and written sources systematically revealed a larger context of capitalist and patriarchal values and dominant notions of women's roles. In so doing, Sangster blends post-structuralist insights and realist aims to her advantage.

In many research projects, academic privilege is seen as a problem to be addressed. If your research design included a concerted effort to do so during data collection, you should *assess how well it worked.* An important example is that of focus groups, in which participants outnumber researchers and can more freely introduce topics. However, focus groups are no panacea for privilege. The politics of differences among focus group members, or between members and the moderator, can still become manifest (Braun, 2000; Kitzinger, 1994). Further, participants may feel vulnerable, mutually suspicious, or ashamed to be associated, as Farnsworth and Boon (2010) observed in their study of poverty in New Zealand. As focus group guru David Morgan (1996) wryly notes, it's not easy to predict when a focus group will go wrong. If your efforts went badly, we recommend that you analytically connect the unintended consequences to the social problem that your research takes up.

In some other studies, focus groups or other privilege-leveling efforts have proven advantageous. For instance, in studying how marginalization had affected Black Canadian women in prison, Shoshana Pollack (2003) compared focus groups to individual life course interviews. She found that in the groups, participants shared their experiences of systemic racism and being socially excluded, with one recounting how a halfway house staff member had unduly emphasized how much education she would need to raise her income – advice that this participant called, 'like kicking me in the ass. "Oh, Negro, you can never do that".... So get used to this life and go back to eight dollars an hour' (p. 469). In contrast, within the life history interviews, participants often blamed themselves for the paths their lives had taken in a society that they depicted as egalitarian, in that 'if you believe in yourself enough, you can get anything you want out of life, whether you are pink, black, brown, or purple' (p. 467). Pollack concluded that her focus groups permitted participants to address issues of racism more freely than they could in a one-on-one interaction to a white interviewer, and thus were more effective.

Finally, switching gears, there's the strategy of *offering a critique of standpoint-based approaches.* Jocelyn Hollander (2004) points out an important avenue for such a critique

when she says that emphasizing similarities and differences in the social categories to which interviewers and respondents belong has meant that the relational context of interviews receives short shrift. We know little, says Hollander, about the implications of conducting interviews amongst friends, neighbors, or co-workers. If your work involves such a context, you can discuss how past or future relations shape your sampling, your questions, the answers you receive, the conclusions you draw, and what you choose to publish. In this spirit, Jodie Taylor (2011) explains how, in studying queer culture in Brisbane, her pre-existing friendships meant that she received an invitation to an unlicensed warehouse party, that she had at least some respondents (i.e., her friends) who were willing to speak freely about topics such as public sexual behavior, and that she independently decided to take certain statements off the record if they could damage reputations.

Strategies Linking Analysis to Representation

A quite different strategy for taking up questions of academic privilege is *to* ***decenter*** *an analysis.* This means giving research participants a role in determining how an analysis will represent them, and making the researcher's claims to knowledge less central. Decentering methods fall along a continuum. At one end, researchers ask participants for feedback on draft analyses but reserve the final say in what is published. Such a feedback process may go seamlessly, may lead to massive rethinking or appendices of alternative interpretations (Borland, 1991; Kaufmann, 2010), or may reveal irreconcilable differences between researchers and participants or amongst groups of participants (Ferguson, 1991). Midway along the continuum, researchers and respondents collaborate in analysis and writing (e.g., West, 2013), an option Brettell (1991) had considered to be generally most feasible in intensive life history projects with few participants. However, at the farthest end of our continuum, **action research** has emerged as a strategy in which communities and researchers collaborate fully on all stages of research, from designing research questions to disseminating findings (Maiter et al., 2008; Mandell and Whittington-Walsh, 2004; Minkler et al., 2008). But, post-structuralists, beware! Although action research draws on several paradigms, it doesn't sit so well with the post-structuralism's relativism as with more humanist, meaning-oriented forms of constructionism (Reason and Bradbury, 2006).

Although anthropologists wrote of poetics as part of the crisis of representation, they also saw it as a potential solution. If you wish *to write up an analysis in a way that draws attention to different views of truth, and undermines certainties,* poetics can lead to strategies for doing so. For instance, the strategy of writing **polyphonously**, in works that set multiple and contradictory voices into discussion (Horwitz, 1993), is exemplified by Sangster's presence alongside her participants in the labor history article discussed above. Writing as 'I' rather than in the third person is another way to implicitly acknowledge that you don't have an omniscient standpoint from which

to survey and make proclamations about respondents' experiences. And, turning interview transcripts into poems and ends in themselves, presenting poems accompanied by an explanatory essay, or crafting analyses in poetic form (Richardson, 1992; Tedlock, 1991) are among the more imaginative ways of reminding readers that your analysis is not a presentation of objective fact, but has an author.

While there are certainly other creative strategies (e.g., Atkinson, 1990; Centre for Imaginative Ethnography, n.d.), we will concentrate briefly on poetry because it is among the approaches that has been most discussed. A number of motivations have inspired poetry experiments. Barker (2010) began to use poetry to represent her Australian Aboriginal community's distinctive voices more authentically after feeling alienated from how her transcribed voice appeared in interview transcripts. Kendall and Murray (2005), who hope to sensitize doctors and nurses in training to cancer patients' experiences, propose that the emotional expectations that readers bring to poetry mean that words will be read with more feeling if laid out in stanzas rather than in paragraphs. Poetry draws readers in, proposes Richardson (1992), because it is read with the body and not merely the eye. Meanwhile, critics of the poetry strategy say it can treat poetry as though it involved no craft of its own, deter ordinary readers who might regard poetry as inaccessible, and let analysts abscond from their responsibility to academic readers to explicitly interpret data (Schwalbe, 1995). We concur with Michael Schwalbe's bottom line: 'It all depends on what our readers need, want, can use, and can be affected by' (1995: 400).

Textbox 4.1: A Summary of Strategies for Analyzing Standpoints and Representation

- Inquire into positionalities of researchers and research participants that are relevant to the stages of knowledge production.
- Draw comparisons to bolster standpoint-related conclusions.
- Assess how well efforts to address privilege during data collection worked.
- Critique standpoint theory, for example, by asking how relational contexts affect knowledge production.
- Decenter analyses by giving respondents a role in determining how they're represented.
- Write in ways that destabilize claims to certainty.

BEING REFLEXIVE ABOUT EMBODIMENT

Both the poetry-writing strategies that we've just mentioned, and Chapter 3's strategies for analyzing how rhythm and repetition convey meaning, have the premise that it somehow matters that the words fixed in our transcripts were heard by and originated in living bodies that were caught up in one another's presences, and that may have interacted in a shared physical space. To further understand how **embodiment** (this grounding in corporeal materiality) conveys meaning as

we tell or listen to stories, we begin with Siobhán McHugh's (2012) powerful exposition of the impact of sound alone. McHugh provided research participants with a transcript and then a radio clip in which Australian journalist Jan Graham narrates how a soldier who had been wounded by a landmine in Vietnam mistook her for his wife as he lay dying. The transcript is sad; the radio clip is harrowing. The difference, McHugh explains, lies in the 'pact of intimacy' (p. 206) forged by listening to speech in real time, by hearing 'the many and changing tonal aspects of [Jan Graham's] voice; her taut delivery, her uneven breathing, her gulps and sniffles as she struggles to describe what happens' (p. 196).

McHugh's claim that something about Graham's and the listeners' bodies matters involves two important premises. The first pertains to poetics. Although McHugh's point is that sound accomplishes what text cannot, her careful choice of words such as 'taut' and 'gulp' shows that we can give text a fighting chance of communicating evocatively with readers. The second, coming from our feminist and anthropologist friends, is that the Cartesian splits of body from mind and thought from emotion don't make much sense (Lutz, 1988; Rosaldo, 1984). McHugh demonstrates that witnessing other people's facial expressions, glances, posture, gestures, breathing, and the multiple qualities of their voices rouses **emotions** in us. And, as anthropologist Michelle Z. Rosaldo (1984) conceives of them:

> Emotions are thoughts somehow 'felt' in flushes, pulses, 'movements' of our livers, minds, hearts, stomachs, skin. They are *embodied* thoughts, thoughts seeped with the apprehension that 'I am involved'. (p. 141)

We often experience our own emotions as inalienable or 'natural' truths, even though we've actually been socialized within our cultural contexts about when to feel ashamed, happy, envious, and so forth.[1]

Our own emotions therefore play an often unacknowledged part in what we know, serving as a cultural lens through which we rightly or wrongly read others' displays of emotions, which may reflect or conceal how they actually feel. Using our selves as our research instruments, we interpret others' meanings and judge their persuasiveness, authenticity, and more. The challenge is to *make explicit how these interpretations and judgments are based on emotions and embodiment.* One way to identify what you're taking for granted in this regard is to give interview transcripts or excerpts to others to read aloud. When Katherine tried this recently, she discovered that in her readers' renditions, a respondent whom she heard as offering helpful answers came across as resentful, while a wry, frustrated respondent sounded matter-of-fact.

---

[1] When the term **feeling** is used, how it differs from emotion varies among authors. Rosaldo (1984) interchanges the terms; Hochschild (1983: 244) agrees that they are interchangeable but associates feelings with fainter physical sensation; Besnier (1990) says that feelings refer to internal states while emotions are on visible display.

Accompanying quotes with 'stage directions' or touches of description can help to flesh out sparse dialog and convey its meanings to readers. For example, Krista Banasiak (2014) describes how a belly dancer whom she interviewed criticized an instructor by imitating her 'stand[ing] and perform[ing] a lazy hip accent with an uncharacteristic lack of control in her upper body, putting on the pouting face of someone attempting to be overtly sexy and moaning "Uhhhh ... Uhhh ... Uhhh ..."' (2014: 9). By depicting her respondent's embodiment, Banasiak animates a transcript that, if restricted to words alone, would read only 'Uhhhh ... Uhhh ... Uhhh...' (In one of the funnier moments in our work on this book, we each tried to make these 'uhhh' sounds, with Katherine making low, guttural moans, and Amber producing pornographic yips.)

Notably, the use of embodied knowledge, connected to the text of what has been said and its wider context, can even permit narrative analysts to plausibly claim that silences speak. Such claims can make way for inarticulate or relatively unresponsive individuals to be represented in research. (Dis)ability researchers show how questions can be asked in ways that offer words to respondents, such as in yes/no questions, which are atypical in qualitative interviewing (Booth and Booth, 1996; Owens, 2007). Because these interviewing methods could raise new questions about representation and about whether the interviewers are, in effect, setting their words into respondents' mouths, an analytic strategy of reflexively detailing how the participants' embodied messages are being received is crucial.

Silences can likewise be said to speak for articulate individuals who cannot narrate specific experiences. Jehanne Gheith (2007) contends that narrating about the Soviet Gulags is next to impossible for many survivors because their experiences had been traumatic and because the Soviet Union had banned such narration for many years. Survivors may be silent but meanwhile convey meanings through actions. When observing a survivor caring for the dog that he had named after Joseph Stalin, Gheith was able to understand the survivor to be simultaneously protesting a regime that had quashed memory and mourning, exerting a will to power over the historical Stalin, and integrating a harsh past with a nurturing present that included the four-legged Stalin. Elsewhere, narrative analysts offer embodiment-based accounts of how they came to judge silence as the product of uncomprehending shock or a shared sorrow (Ghorashi, 2008), a show of tact (Knudsen, 1990), and more.

To enrich our understanding of storytelling as embodied, we can incorporate cultural geographers' insight that it is also **emplaced** (Anderson and Jones, 2009). That is, we don't tell stories within **space**, understood as an abstract, depopulated void, but within a **place**, rich in personal, cultural, and political meanings (Lefebvre, 1974/1991). We can generalize to other settings what French philosopher Michel de Certeau (1984: 98) had observed in his essay on 'Walking in the city,' namely, that while a **spatial order** offers a walker both constraints and options for her route, the walker invents new possibilities and thus transforms this order. In using space as a medium for narration, narrators reveal the meanings that turn space into place.

A strategy resulting is *to observe what emplacement indicates about the options, constraints, creativity, and meanings of narrators*. Social work researcher Chih Hoong Sin (2003) recounts how a side table's disrepair became evident as he was setting his tape recorder up in the home of Jane, a participant in a project on social support networks of older people in the UK. Jane made a stoic remark, typical of the several that she would make about how her home and garden were deteriorating because of her ill health. However, Sin also heard – and observed – that Jane was reclaiming her sense of agency by crafting the embroidery, stuffed toys, and knitted cushion covers that decorated her home. Sin's observations of Jane's emplacement thus complemented and enriched his interpretations of her lived experience.

Another project that we read as illustrating this strategy is Hanna Herzog's (2005) study of women peace activists living in Israel. When respondents who were Palestinian citizens of Israel were asked where they wanted to be interviewed, Herzog found that they chose varied sites in which to meet interviewers who were also Palestinian, but chose their homes as interview sites when their interviewers would be Jewish. Because these participants asked their Jewish interviewers, 'Is this your first time in an Arab village?' 'You weren't afraid to come?' 'It wasn't hard for you to find your way around here?' (p. 34) and the like, Herzog understood them to be asserting that they had consciously chosen to ask members of the Jewish majority to traverse a social boundary that was ordinarily left to Palestinians to negotiate. Their emplacement of the interview was thus a political act with democratizing intent, pertinent to their activist engagement.

So far in this section, we've been writing about the embodied, emplaced interview only from the perspective of a receptive, observant interviewer. But, of course, participants simultaneously use their embodied, emplaced knowledge to interpret interviewers' responses. Suzanne MacAulay (2004) proposes *analyzing this interviewing relationship as a microcosm of the phenomenon under study*. MacAulay carries this strategy out with fascinating, fine-grained analyses of passages of interview transcripts, including one from her interview with Dejan, a fellow ex-pat living in New Zealand, who is telling her about his recent visit to a dentist. Dejan's language in the passage included quite a bit of **reported speech**, that is, speech that purports to quote directly from what he and others had said. Such speech is generally worth seeking out in transcripts because it marks moments of enlivened performance: it can bring new characters into a story's mix, generate suspense about how the characters will get along, and fold time and space by claiming to re-enact the past (Tannen, 2007). Yet, reported speech is also **heteroglossic**, says philosopher Mikhail Bakhtin (1935/1981: 428). That is, it does not simply reproduce past utterances but instead inflects them with the speaker's intentions.

Now, back to Dejan. At the dentist's, Dejan told MacAulay, staff mispronounced his name, froze at the news that he was from Serbia, and made faces that might have been suitable had he been a war criminal instead of an ordinary client. What made this story especially engrossing for MacAulay was that, when Dejan recounted

what he had heard and seen at the dentist's, he used his gaze and gestures to cast her as his story's antagonists. By inflecting the reported speech in this way, Dejan was able to relish MacAulay's discomfort at the same time as he was seeking her sympathy for being treated like a criminal. MacAulay read this as a power play symptomatic of Dejan's frustration with the global politic in which he remained caught up, despite having migrated from the distant and former Yugoslavia to New Zealand. Thus, MacAulay was able to use Dejan and her joint experience as a data point in an analysis of how global transnational population shifts are experienced in local, intimate settings.

Textbox 4.2: A Summary of Strategies for Being Reflexive about Embodiment

- Be explicit about how embodiment has contributed to your understandings.
- Use emplacement to learn about narrators' options, constraints, and creativity.
- Observe whether the relationship negotiated by interviewer and narrator is an instance of the phenomenon under study.

BEING REFLEXIVE ABOUT NOTIONS OF A 'GOOD' STORY

The bulk of the data narrative analysts use consists of stories or, more broadly speaking, of narration. How these data are analyzed often relates to notions about what constitutes a 'good' story that are widely held among laypersons and that have been painstakingly studied by academics – the newsworthiness of a story, among them. In this section, we look at four such notions.

What does this have to do with reflexivity about one's role as researcher? As consumers of movies, books, and other narratives, we easily understand the goodness of a story to be contingent on what the teller does in his multiple roles. As Werner and colleagues (2004) explain, the storyteller is an author, producing an emplotment that conveys his argument about what meaning the story has. He is the story's performer, responsible for animating the story world. He is often the protagonist in the story or at least a character in it, and thus what he narrates about his past has implications for how his present-day self is regarded. But, what's less obvious is that the goodness of a story depends equally on the listener, in her roles of understanding and assessing the argument, being compelled or bored by the performance, and being in sympathy with or rejecting the character. Thus, our interest is in developing strategies that enable researchers to reflect about how ideas about good stories shaped their interview processes and the resultant data.

A Good Story's Reportability

Kathy, a story has to start with a *problem*.

– Maddy, age five

The notion of a story's **reportability** (Labov, 1972) or **tellability** (Sacks, 1995) is what journalists call its **newsworthiness**. A story is reportable if its narrator would be able to defend having shared it if he were asked, 'Why are you telling that?' Common defenses include that event being reported was unusual, unexpected, or contrary to norms. To explain the last of these criteria, Charlotte Linde (1993: 22) gives the example of being cheated by a used car salesperson. Although this would be neither unusual nor unexpected, it would warrant telling because it doesn't seem right. Literary theorist Jean-François Lyotard puts this another way, by saying that everyday, personally told stories, unlike the grand narratives of cultures, destabilize certainties, feed on conflict, and unsettle 'the order of "reason"' (Browning, 1992: 287). All this sets up a paradox around reportability: if a respondent tells a good story with an emplotment that throws certainties or norms into question, the respondent must surmount the obstacle of the interviewer's disbelief by performing it compellingly (Labov, 1997).

Emplotting an engaging, reportable story doesn't come to us naturally, but is something that we are schooled in. This point was driven home to Katherine on the afternoon that she listened to her young friend Maddy tell herself a long story in which a bunny met a series of friends and ate a series of picnic foods: 'and then they had pickles and then her friend Sarah came and then they had ice cream' is a sample of the kind of story Maddy found satisfying. (Had this been an interview, Katherine would have found it difficult to listen well.) Toward the end of the afternoon, though, Maddy turned to her homework assignment of dictating a story. Instead of writing about the bunny, she churned out a tale in which she had no interest whatsoever, but that met her teacher's requirement that a story 'start with a problem' for a protagonist to overcome.

But we can be schooled, as tellers and listeners, in other notions of satisfying stories. For instance, in kishōtenketsu, a Japanese storytelling genre, the emphasis is not on the build-up and resolution of a character's conflict, so much as contemplation of how incongruous elements all contribute to a whole. (For an adorable example, see the blog 'still eating oranges', 2012.) *If you and your research participants seem to have different criteria for what makes a story reportable, then map those out and discuss how they affect the extent of your data collection.* This strategy isn't only about notions of a reportable story as an engaging one. For instance, to whom a story belongs and who is authorized to tell it is a consideration we saw arising in studies involving Indigenous participants, sometimes in conjunction with the political contexts of settler societies (Johnson, 2005; Ochs and Capps, 1996).

Moreover, a skilful narrator such as Dejan can perform in a way that engages a listener, carrying forward the plot at the same time as carrying along the audience's

interest, so that even a slight or tremendously technical story remains reportable. In contrast, we all know people who can't tell a joke well. But, importantly, it's not all up to the narrator, as Bavelas and colleagues (2000) so brilliantly demonstrate. They conducted an experiment in which participants were asked to tell stories about their experiences of a 'close call' to listeners, some of whom were secretly required to be mentally tallying the number of days till Christmas. These distracted listeners tended to offer storytellers more generic, distanced 'um' and 'mhm' reactions as the stories were being told. In return, the poor storytellers told their tales more disjointedly, sometimes rambling on or breaking off abruptly. One storyteller even began to stumble through a justification of why he had imagined his narrow escape in a life-threatening logging accident to be worthy of mention. This experiment suggests a reflexive analytic strategy of *assessing whether an interviewer has become an invested co-teller of a story,* offering specific feedback and showing an appreciation of the story's implications. If not, then respondents have not been invited to express themselves and their meanings fully.

A Good Story's Liveability

Although reportability is a criterion for a good story, a story can also go too far, crossing over to the terrain of news reports that alert readers to their graphic content (Norrick, 2005). Viewers, readers, and listeners also think of a good story as having a plot and argument they can live with, and characterizing a world they can bear to live in. Hence, a good story can be understood to mean a **liveable** one.

When interviewers hear stories that they find unliveable, they can embodiedly react to the stories' events or arguments and to the narrators themselves. Earlier in this chapter, we'd mentioned that Frost (2009) found herself cutting off respondents whose mothering decisions disagreed with her own. In other works we read, interviewers were angered by trauma survivors who were telling stories about their ordeals (Laub and Felman, 1992), shocked by a grandparent who told a story about incest (Sands and Krumer-Nevo, 2006), and repelled by a sex worker's client who began to masturbate while being interviewed (O'Connell Davidson and Layder, 1994: 215–17).

These embodied responses deserve attention. The threats here can be understood to be simultaneously individual/psychic and social/discursive, arising because certain knowledges, experiences, values, and ways of presenting the self are legitimized through what narrative analysts call **master narratives** (Sands and Krumer-Nevo, 2006), or what discourse analysts would simply call dominant discourses. The trauma survivors' stories, for example, are out of synch with what McAdams (2006) calls the narrative of **the redemptive self**, in which a committed protagonist struggles successfully to overcome obstacles. Because this emplotment is popular in North America, and indeed is the very narrative that Maddy had been schooled to produce, it is easy for many North American listeners to engage with.

The effect, in sociologist Pierre Bourdieu's (1999) terms, is that even humanist researchers intending to respect respondents' meanings can do **symbolic violence** in preferring the moral arguments of some stories, and groups, to others.

Identifying the master narratives that make a respondent's story unliveable to you is one strategy we propose here. A corollary is to be wary of stories that too smoothly and palatably confirm your social scientific expectations. In what Bourdieu (1999: 615–17) calls **false collusive objectification**, narrators can subtly resist the experience of being objectified by research by turning themselves into objects that they see and know from your standpoint. They therefore collude with you in that they falsely deliver precisely the emplotment and moral argument that will please you. You'll also smugly feel that you've managed to level your differences. Bourdieu goes so far as to throw such data out.

Narratives can, of course, also undo their narrators. In lieu of speaking of a narrative as unliveable for a narrator, we can equally speak of a narrator's lack of **composure**. This term gained traction through oral historian Alistair Thomson's (1994) observation that the Australian myth of World War I as a moment of egalitarian nation-building left no space for veterans to articulate their experiences of post-war marginalization. Thomson theorized that we become discomposed when we lack a publically available language (or master narrative) through which to compose and tell the story of an experience. The narrative and the self suffer this lack alike. Alternately, we can use Hollway and Jefferson's (1997) psychoanalytically and sociologically inflected concept of the **defended subject**, a narrator rather more anxious than Thomson's, and more set on defending his private experiences from scrutiny and on protecting his psyche.

An analytic strategy to apply in these instances is *to ask how conclusions are affected by working with traumatized, discomposed, or defended subjects with unliveable narratives* – choose a term and stick to it. An example comes from Christina Sinding's (Sinding and Aronson, 2003) effort to link struggles to provide end-of-life care for friends and family members to the inadequacies of health policy and the decline of the Canadian welfare state. 'We want to disrupt the collective "making do" with fewer and less responsive services; we want to challenge the notion that health professionals "doing their best" in a context of health system constraint constitutes adequate care,' Sinding and Aronson (2003: 115) write. Yet, Sinding's participants uniformly clung to narratives in which their loved ones had died 'good deaths.' For ethical reasons, she could not probe for active criticisms of the health care system, as such criticisms would have threatened the participants. Narrators' impetuses to produce liveable narratives can pose great analytic dilemmas for researchers of a realist bent.

To follow either of the above strategies, we can also draw on psychoanalytically informed scholarship that helps us to recognize defended subjects (Hollway and Jefferson, 1997, 2000; Rosenthal 1993, 2003). The idealization that Sinding's narrators employ is one such defense. Others are exemplified in Antoinette Errante's (2000) study of how education had contributed to Mozambique's decolonization

movement. Because the 1975 independence had been succeeded by years of economic instability and political violence, many Mozambicans grieved the betrayal of their dreams. In Textbox 4.3, we see a prototypical transcript on the left, and on the right, Errante's labeling of the narrator's defensive strategies.

Textbox 4.3: What's to tell

A = Antoinette Errante

N = narrator

A:	What did you do after independence?	
N:	After independence, well I continued teaching for a while and then I quit.	
A:	Can you tell me about your experiences teaching after independence?	
N:	Humph . . . What's to tell. I continued to do my job that's all. Then I had enough. I did not want to teach anymore.	Irritation Denial
A:	You got tired of teaching?	
N:	Humph. They got tired of me. We were [*lower volume*] colonial collaborators. We had been part of the system, so now everything we did was suspect. Eh . . . I just got tired of seeing them burning down everything, [*lower volume*] all those beautiful books.	Irritation Abstraction Mitigation

Source: Errante, 2000: 23

Psychoanalytically informed scholarship also provides models for conducting effective interviews with defended subjects. Because the interviewer's role as data collector can become merged with that of therapist or witness, this gives rise to the analytic strategy of *assessing how well the interviewer enacted their complex role,*

according to concrete lists of dos and don'ts. According to Rosenthal (1993, 2003) and to Hollway and Jefferson (1997, 2000), for a defended subject, a good storytelling experience demands an empathetic listener – one who, among other things, reflects the narrator's emotions back to her, permits the narrator's logic to guide the flow of the interview, avoids 'why' questions that require her to account for her courses of action, refrains from poking at contradictions, and ensures that she is not in crisis when the interview concludes.

A Good Story's Coherence

A powerful indication that a story may be unliveable is its incoherence. As we've observed in Chapter 3, a traumatized teller may present a plot unclearly, failing to orient listeners to the characters and setting of his story or to convey a basic sense of the sequence of events. The performance of storytelling can also go awry, as traumatized tellers can confuse past events with the present of the interview or seem unaware that a listener is trying to make sense of events (Burnell et al., 2010). Stories told thus are 'bad' stories both for being unliveable *and* for being incoherent, that is, for having plots and/or performances that don't hold together for their listeners.

To our set of notions of a good story, we now add that of coherence, one that again depends on the nexus of teller, story, and listener. An analytic option is *to consider how you as a listener/researcher can be implicated in incoherence and what the impact of that is.* Jan Blommaert (2001) gives the example of how African asylum-seekers in Belgium have narratives that are coherent, which he defines in plot-related terms of including orientations, presenting new (and not redundant) information, and drawing clear conclusions for listeners. However, says Blommaert, asylum-seekers face considerable narrative inequality because telling their stories to Belgian listeners requires them to speak in what is often a second or third language, in which their command of verb tenses, pronouns, vocabulary, and so forth, is imperfect. The asylum-seekers are also continually required to clarify their home countries' political contexts in side stories that disrupt the main story's flow. Because the asylum-seekers are required to address listeners who are so differently positioned, their coherent stories risk being heard as incoherent.

As mentioned earlier, (dis)ability researchers make related arguments about how the stories of people with learning difficulties risk being overlooked if interviewing and analysis strategies fail to accommodate them. Michael Angrosino (1992) illustrates the strategy of *finding the central regularities in a narrative that might otherwise be read as incoherent.* Among his research participants is Larry, a man whose talk is characterized by fluid, arbitrary shifts in topic, and by ambiguous use of pronouns. Textbox 4.4 shows an excerpt from the interview, in which Larry is speaking of wrestling star Hulk Hogan, nicknamed 'the Hulkster.'

Textbox 4.4: Me and the Hulkster

Everybody knows me and the Hulkster we're real tight pals, even though he don't come around much no more, he being traveling to Japan and California and all them other foreign countries. And so he keeps on going down to the ring, and everybody's yelling now and it's real hot in there and everybody's yelling, and I remember I seen a picture of the Hulkster and he was driving that big Cadillac car just like the one I used to have before I got locked up. All the girls love a man in a big car, just like me and the Hulkster. Jerry says the best car is a Mercedes but I don't buy it. I mean, you take Elvis. He gave to all his fans, too, you know, give 'em cars just 'cause they asked. Just like I used to do. But mine was pink and his was white just like his robe. I could get one like that – I know where to buy them. I'll get you one too next time I go shopping. I just don't like to go down there – all the girls is just all over me. You know how they hang out down there with nothing better to do. Of course, the Hulkster don't go shopping himself no more neither. He got the same problem like me. Of course his is bigger.

[Researcher: What's bigger?]

His robe. Of course it is. I just lost a lot of weight while I been in this place. Me and him's really the same size but not for that, and that's why we both do so good fighting. He don't take no crap from nobody. You seen how that guy [the opponent] done him? They was partners but then this guy stabbed him in the back. I bet it was because the Hulkster stole his wife – what woman wouldn't want to be with the Hulkster instead of with this other guy.

Source: Angrosino, 1992: 180–1

Although Angrosino mentions the ways in which this narration could seem incoherent, his analytic goal is to discern its unity. Larry's narration is thematically organized around his sense of himself as sexually powerful; note in the Textbox how Larry effects this directly by speaking of girls as 'all over me' or 'loving a man in a big car, just like me and the Hulkster,' as well as through his identification with the Hulkster. Angrosino's analysis thus shows Larry to possess and communicate a consistent self-image.

Finally, this strategy appears in works that swim against the tide of research in which sounding incoherent or self-contradictory to one's audience is a symptom (or even a cause) of speakers' troubles. A narrator engaged in a consistent process of self-questioning may produce stories that shift and contradict one another, says McVee (2005), who studies the seven ways that a white teacher-in-training in the USA told a tale of being shocked to see a mural of a black Jesus in a Catholic school. Changing one's story or having a temporarily incoherent story can be celebrated for permitting a narrator to make sense of new circumstances and adapt to them (Polonoff, 1987; Sools, 2012). If our selves are inherently narrative, the logic goes, then our narratives must be able to change.

A Good Story's Fidelity

A reader of McVee's (2005) analysis might aggravatedly ask, what does this teacher-in-training really think? Can any of her stories be trusted? When a listener seeks a good story, her final criterion is that it possess fidelity – that it be faithful to experience. This criterion should immediately strike a chord in you because it's so closely tied to the ontologies and epistemologies we've been discussing. If you're a realist, or have an ontology at all anchored in realism, the chord will sound sweet; it will sound sour if you're an outright constructionist.

Constructionists, we'll start with what this means for you. A prime example of constructionist work on fidelity is American anthropologist Janneli Miller's (1996) study of her interview with Lucia Soc, a Guatemalan Maya woman who told Miller of a time when she had been enspelled and, even though she didn't believe in witchcraft, subsequently expelled a frog from her stomach. When Miller told Lucia's story to others and observed their reactions, she embarked on the strategy of *showing how listeners' standpoints affect their assessments of the story's **plausibility***, i.e., of whether it *could* have fidelity. Specifically, Miller found that some Anglo listeners to this story immediately judged it to be a mythologized account of an abortion. In contrast, an American Indian woman thought that Lucia's story made sense because she'd heard of a similar enspellment. Despite having mentioned this Anglo vs. American Indian difference, Miller is reluctant to conclude that standpoints are determined by static, mutually exclusive categories of 'culture.' Instead, she employs herself as an example of an Anglo person willing to respectfully adopt a 'beginner's mind' and permit Lucia to represent herself unchallenged.

If you pursue this strategy, a valuable read would be communications researchers Busselle and Bilandzic's (2008) framework for how audiences assess whether fictional narratives are realistic. In brief, it goes like this: When we listen to a story we make sense of it in part by unconsciously using as a baseline our experience with whatever genre the story seems to fit into, and with whatever cast of characters that genre typically involves. (Some of the listeners to Lucia's story did not have relevant experience with stories of the enspellment genre, it seems.) With that comfortable baseline in place, we can become so engaged as to feel **transported** into the **story world**, into its time and place – especially if it is vividly detailed (Cho et al., 2012). There, we come to identify with the perspective of the narrator and follow along with his project of meaning-making. Crucially, when the story's working, we're too immersed in it to be aware of any of this. What we do notice is when we're jarred out of the story world by a frog, or another detail that doesn't make sense. We stop feeling transported, we stop identifying, we stop thinking the story could be realistic.

Realists, or researchers at all anchored in realism, can feel torn by stories that lack fidelity. A commitment to having participants represent themselves can be pitted against a commitment to truth and to populations whom it could serve. We've noticed in our readings that this dilemma is most acute when the researcher and interviewer are one and the same, but dwindles when someone

else has conducted the interview. Why is this? We suggest that reasons include the interviewer's experience of identifying with the narrator after being transported into that person's story world, the intimacy and ethical framework of interviewing, the neutrality to which interviewers often aspire, and the dynamics of ordinary talk, in which outright disagreements are avoided (see Chapter 5). Having avoided disagreement during our interviews can make us feel craven for disagreeing with respondents on paper after the fact.

Michael Frisch's (1990) concept of a shared authority, introduced at the outset of this chapter, reframes the interviewer's dilemma. Instead of choosing between disrespecting or respecting participants, says Frisch, researchers are choosing between treating memories as inert objects to be classified and shelved and treating remembering as a spirited activity involving oral historians and participants alike (Thomson et al., 1994: 35). More generally, analyses of infidelities that are anchored in realism generally *seek to understand what they mean, or do, for a listener, a narrator, or a community of narrators*. They may:

- Produce coherence. If Katherine were to tell a story about her Aunt Hanna, she'd be sparing her listeners a confusing, coherence-threatening truth: that Hanna wasn't genuinely her aunt, but her grandfather's second wife's best friend.
- Make a story more liveable, as when Sinding and Aronson (2003) implausibly found each caregiver they interviewed to claim that their loved one had died a 'good death.'
- Turn a drab story into a reportable one. When stories are told in talk, the embodiment of this performance medium means that the effects of embellishments on listeners can be quickly gauged. Moreover, because talk is more ephemeral than print, infidelities may seem less consequential than they would in writing.

That infidelity links to all of our notions of a good story shows, once again, how interconnected these notions are.

Textbox 4.5: A Summary of Strategies for Being Reflexive about a 'Good' Story

- When narrators and the research audience have different criteria for a reportable story and its telling, map these criteria out.
- Assess whether interviewers engage with narratives in ways that invite narrators to express themselves fully.
- Link stories experienced as unliveable to master narratives.
- Ask how conclusions are affected when narratives are unliveable.
- Assess how well the interviewer enacted the empathetic role of therapist/witness.
- Show that a listener is implicated in incoherence, and the impact of that.
- Find the central regularities in a narrative that could seem incoherent.
- Show how listeners' standpoints affect their assessments of a story's plausibility.
- Ask what functions or meanings unfaithful remembering has.

CHAPTER SUMMARY

It is in this chapter that we see the interviewer, as listener, enter the analytic frame, actively taking part in constructing what is narrated and how. We introduce the concept of reflexivity, and the value of examining how the knowledge that we produce depends on our research methods and on our selves as researchers. (In keeping with the humanist emphasis of much of narrative analysis, the researcher's introspections are more intimately examined here than anywhere else in this book.) The first strategies for reflexivity look at standpoints and the positionality of the interviewer vis-à-vis the narrator, alert to the power imbalances of research and to poetics questions about the capacities of language to represent experience. The next strategies for reflexivity take into account how talk emerges in the moment, and how the embodiment, emplacement, and emotions of interviewers and respondents matter. The final strategies highlight how narration is conditioned by criteria for a 'good' story, i.e., reportability, liveability, coherence, and fidelity (or variants thereof). Although narrators are usually held responsible for whether their stories meet these criteria, we demonstrate how thoroughly the listener is implicated in each of them.

Part II

Analyzing Talk-in-interaction

In our discussion of narrative analysis, talk has been treated in a rich and contradictory variety of ways: as transparently communicating what happened; as thick with cues to narrators' conscious and subconscious interpretations of experience; as a means by which narrators engage, disturb, confuse, or persuade listeners; and as a joint construction between narrators and listeners. In contrast, in **conversation analysis** (CA) any unscripted, naturalistic talk between two or more people is regarded as action. Take, for example, Toronto Mayor Rob Ford's answer in City Council to the question put to him 5 November 2013:

> 'Mayor Ford, have you purchased illegal drugs in the last two years?'
>
> [*Eight seconds passed*]
>
> 'Yes, I have,' answered the Mayor. (*The New York Times*, 2013)

In a thematic analysis such as we've sometimes seen in the NA part of this book, in which talk straightforwardly renders experience, the Mayor's answer could be taken to communicate a simple fact about his illegal drug purchase. But international media and the public dwelled upon the gap that the Mayor let pass between hearing the question and giving his answer. The gap was taken to render the Mayor perplexing, ambivalent, unfocused, ludicrous and more, to somehow undermine his admission (e.g., *Toronto Star*, 2013). The gap was heard as consequential, as a form of action. The gap is what would intrigue a conversation analyst.

What talk (including its gaps) enacts, according to CA's founder, Harvey Sacks (1995), is the order of an everyday world that is not at all self-evident or concrete, yet it is taken for granted as being so. In the CA perspective, this taken-for-grantedness is socially constructed, and it permits an order to be achieved in talk that, in turn, makes any social institution or larger order possible. As Emanuel Schegloff (2006: 70), one of

Sacks's principal collaborators, put it, though Communism has crumbled, the achievement of social order via interaction is here to stay. CA is thus a systematic inquiry into how order is achieved through **talk-in-interaction**, a term that captures CA's initial interest in ordinary conversation (unscripted naturalistic talk in mundane contexts), as well as its rapidly emerging interest in talk in institutional settings, such as in doctors' offices, television talk shows, and airplane cockpits.

What criteria can you use to decide whether CA suits your talk data, you, and your questions? In a minority of instances, online exchanges or reported talk in newspapers have become the stuff of certain kinds of conversation analyses. But the vast majority use spoken interaction, for which audio or video recordings are essential in order that details can be captured; in Sacks's theory, a universe of social and moral ordering is visible in every instant of talk (Schegloff, 1995). Accordingly, Sacks's other principal collaborator, Gail Jefferson, devised an extraordinarily meticulous transcription convention that accords attention to the length in tenths of a second of a pause and to the precise syllable at which two speakers' talk overlapped (Jefferson, 2004; for a simplified version see Atkinson and Heritage, 1984). On pages 67–68, you'll find a list of the transcription symbols used in the examples we quote.

Transcribing a minute of talk can take 20 minutes or more, depending on the number of speakers (Wiggins and Potter, 2008: 83), which brings us to another criterion for deciding whether to choose CA. The transcription process will transform your subjective experience of time. You may come to experience it as a meditative practice in which close engagement with data fuses with detachment from them, assisting you in tackling the challenge of detecting the taken-for-granted. (You may even unintentionally generate a running conversation or analytic commentary on the talk around you. Idly sipping apple tea and listening in on a friend's 900-Euro encounter with a carpet dealer in Turkey, one of us found herself identifying several sales tactics with no effort at all.) But, you may chafe at the extraordinary patience and attention to detail that CA demands, or object, as Smith et al. (2005) do, to how it circumscribes what features of language or the experience of interaction qualify as data. In that case, CA won't be for you.

CA strategies are ideal for research that asks how talk-in-interaction works, seeking to understand how speakers go about orienting to and creating social order at its most basic level of achieving shared understandings. These strategies might be a happy fit if you have come away from data collection with your interest piqued by a trifle of talk, for elegant conversation analyses can start small, by wondering about the meaning of 'oh' or about when a 911 call went wrong. Because CA strategies seek to strip away preconceptions of what matters, they are ideal for curious, open-minded, and even uncertain listeners, for those interested in noticing a loose thread in talk-in-interaction and tracing it back to the social fabric.

CA strategies are also especially suited to researchers working in certain kinds of settings. That CA is at an intellectual juncture of sociology and linguistics makes it inviting for analyzing the resources that languages offer for creating and orienting to social order in everyday life around the globe, and for engaging in debates about which aspects of language are culturally based and which are universal (see Moerman, 1988; Sidnell, 2009). CA is also a good fit to studying how children interact, in part because it

does not require them to participate in the formal apparatus of interviewing, and in part because it recognizes the sophisticated competences they bring to everyday activities such as imaginative play (Hutchby, 2005). Finally, CA is often to be found investigating institutional settings, in projects that are frequently rich in application.

As feminist conversation analysts have demonstrated, CA can respond astutely to research questions motivated by concerns about social inequalities. A caveat is that if your heart is set on such questions, CA will suit you only if you're willing to suspend your politics as you go about the analysis. Conversation analysts and the discourse analysts whose approach you'll find in the next part of this book have disputed this practice at bitter length. Conversation analysts are characterized as mesmerized by their data and shirking responsibility for their conclusions, while discourse analysts are deemed to impose their politics onto the very people whose voices they claim to represent (e.g., see Aguinaldo, 2012; Billig, 1999; Schegloff, 1997, 1999; Widdicombe, 1995). Because profound ontological and epistemological differences underlie this debate, conversation analysts see little rapprochement possible here. If doing a fine-grained analysis of talk as action interests you, contrasting this part to Chapter 10 on Critical Discourse Analysis will help you to choose.

This second part of our book will begin with an overview of the history and paradigm of CA. CA's singular, recent, and radical foundational insight speaks to questions at the intersection of philosophically-minded sociology and linguistics. As such, it has a far more unified perspective and a much greater proclivity to defend it than the gregarious, pluralistic interdisciplinary sprawl that is NA - and also takes more time to set up. We will then turn to a review of CA strategies for working with everyday talk, which revolve around analysis of how turn allocation and the sequential organization of talk-in-interaction achieve order. The following chapter will address ways in which categories figure into talk-in-interaction, either in what is called Membership Categorization Analysis (MCA) or within studies focused on gender, race, and other categories of longstanding interest to social scientists. Next comes a chapter on strategies for CA in institutional contexts. We close with a chapter that turns CA lenses on the talk of the research interview.

LIST OF SOME TRANSCRIPTION SYMBOLS

::	Intonation occurs
_	Underscore 'punches' up the sounds under which it occurs
↓↑	Shifts into high or low pitch
.hhh	An in-breath. Without dot, h indicates outbreath.
^	Pitch rises
(0.0)	Time elapsed in tenths of seconds
(.)	A brief interval (a tenth of a second) between utterances
(words)	Said doubtfully

(( ))	Contains transcriber's descriptions
<	A 'left push,' indicating a hurried start, e.g. compressed onset of utterance
< >	Uttered more slowly than rest of utterance
> <	Uttered more rapidly
,	Continuing intonation
[	The point of overlap onset in talk
=	No break or gap
*	End of overlapped speech
→	Utterance of interest

Adapted from: Heritage and Clayman (2010) and Jefferson (2004). Consult original sources for more information.

FIVE

The Basics of Conversation Analysis

THE FOUNDING INSIGHT OF CONVERSATION ANALYSIS

Harvey Sacks began developing CA in the 1960s, when the prevailing sociological model of Talcott Parsons had been asking, 'How is social order, rather than chaos, possible?' and had been answering by depicting individuals as internalizing cultural values and trotting off to enact them in the social system. For example, Parsons's model would say that in a culture that values learning, children internalize that value and therefore attend school; nothing about talk or the qualities of interaction at school is at issue here.

Sacks and his collaborators were part of an intellectual community of American sociologists who argued otherwise. From Erving Goffman (1967, 1983; cf Schegloff, 1995), with whom Sacks studied for a time, CA drew the insight that interpersonal interaction should matter to sociologists because the **interaction order** *is* social order in its own right, and the base upon which other social institutions function. Further, CA shares Goffman's vision of the social order as simultaneously a moral one. Whereas NA has an implicit model of a social actor who mulls events over and ponders their singularity, CA adopts Goffman's model of a social actor on a perceptive hair-trigger, ordinarily oriented to self-respectingly preserving her **face** – defined as 'the positive social value a person effectively claims for himself by the line others assume he has taken during a particular contact' (Goffman, 1967: 5) – and to considerately maintaining the face of others. Such an actor, Goffman reasoned, must exist in order for the interaction order to be at all possible.

In Goffman's theory, the opposition between a macro, cultural or structural level of analysis and a micro, individual and agency-oriented one, which we have so repeatedly seen in NA and which we will return to in DA, turns into a synthesis. Face, with its conventional positioning as the property of an individual, is here configured as a universal and ongoing prerequisite and accomplishment of interaction, and as a social property on loan to the individual (Goffman, 1967: 10). Identity, too, is understood as an ongoing social accomplishment. Taking things to an extreme, Goffman would have said that because your **identity** as a friend, professor, or barista, is only in play in your interaction with others, when you're alone you lack identity. As Widdicombe (1998) discusses, this model of identity resonates with the more recent thought of cultural theorist Stuart Hall, who posits that different facets of our identities become salient as we move from one setting to another.

The second chief influence on CA was Harold Garfinkel (1967), who criticized mainstream sociology for depicting people as **cultural dopes**, programmed to enact cultural values. CA draws from how Garfinkel took up the German philosophers Alfred Schütz and Edmund Husserl's project of **phenomenology**, which unpacks how people experience what's called the **lifeworld**. The word 'experience' may sound familiar from NA, in which people actively reflect on their pasts. But there's a difference: here, the experiences of the lifeworld are those we unquestioningly take for granted. We take as self-evident the concrete reality of the tree outside the window, the ground beneath our feet, and the familiarities of family.

Well, why shouldn't we? As part of unpacking what actually makes such knowledge flimsy and tentative, phenomenologists point out that on one hand, we can see that what's outside the window is a tree because we already know what the abstraction 'tree' is. On the other hand, this knowing hinges on past contexts in which we and others have pointed to various tangibles and come to agree that they're examples of trees. Phenomenologists call the 'seeing what we already know' part of the endless loop **reflexivity**, and the 'knowing by having pointed and agreed' part **indexicality**. (Yes, phenomenologists have a different definition of reflexivity than the one relating methods to knowledge production, introduced in Chapter 4, and used everywhere else in this book.)

Each of us routinely lets it go unremarked that his or her **subjectivity** – in CA, one's understanding of the social and physical worlds – is an inescapably fragile, working understanding. Instead, we habitually assume that our understandings are shared with others, in what's called shared **intersubjectivity**. Garfinkel exposed this assumption in a series of what he called **breaching experiments**, such as having students act as boarders in their own homes or repeatedly question the meaning of what others were saying. His experimental subjects became unhinged. They strove repeatedly to make sense of what the students were doing (e.g., being rude to their parents by being unaccustomedly polite), rather than doubting what they assumed to be shared beliefs about the workings of

family life and conversation. Garfinkel's experiments gave force to the question of how Goffman's interaction order is possible, for how can we go about interacting with others and calibrating our working knowledge with them, while sustaining our faith in a coherent, self-evident reality?

Garfinkel called his project **ethnomethodology**, meaning the systematic description of ethnos' (Latin for 'the people's') routine methods of jointly making their social interactions intelligible by recognizing each other's contributions and making contributions that will be recognizable to others. Conversation analysts would borrow Garfinkel's naming of interactants as **members** to underscore that they had acquired the same competences for interaction. They'd also borrow his reference to what is recognizable as **accountable**, in order to capture the spirit of being able to understand and account for it and to convey that members hold one another morally accountable to follow their unacknowledged rules (see Heritage, 1998: 180); note how here, as in Goffman's thought, the social order is a moral one. In a kindergarten classroom, for example, we expect that the teacher will not take a nap. But if she did, rather than doubt that it is possible to understand what teachers are or do, we would exert ourselves to make her nap accountable. Perhaps she is modeling napping for the children, is ill or is dead; perhaps she is just a 'bad teacher.'

Putting all this together, it was Sacks (1972) in the revolutionary paper, entitled 'An initial investigation of the usability of conversational data for doing sociology,' who argued that for members to organize their talk, turn by turn, was a momentous accomplishment in which fine-tuning reciprocal understandings, Garfinkel-style, was part and parcel of creating Goffmanesque emergent social action. At the same time, Sacks departed from their methods. Rather than adopting Garfinkel's fieldwork or his harrowing experimentation or Goffman's beguiling pastiche of field and literary examples, Sacks proposed a systematic analysis of everyday, naturalistic conversations.

Although he would pass away in 1975 at the age of 40, Sacks's intervention produced a legacy at the intersection of sociology and linguistics. Many sociologists were drawn to his re-envisioning of the question 'How is social order possible?' into a pinpoint focus on how members go about their talk-in-interaction and to what effect. The linguists of Sacks's day, meanwhile, had been on their own quest for the basis of linguistic order. Although they had been pursuing this quest by using hypothetical sentences so as to abstract what Noam Chomsky (1965) termed the deep structure of language, they were drawn to Sacks's realization that all everyday talk, in all its seeming imperfections, was actually methodical and sophisticatedly ordered. (Sacks's conception of the whole gamut of everyday talk as consequential also intrigued those linguists who had been making forays into the **performativity** of speech by exploring specific acts, such as the promise (following Austin, 1962 and Searle, 1975).) Psychology, communication, education, and computer science number among the disciplines in which substantial and rising use of CA has since been found (Förster, 2013).

UNDERSTANDING THE CONVERSATION ANALYSIS PARADIGM

Ontology and Epistemology in CA

So, what can be known in CA? Conversation analysts' aim to understand the workings of talk-in-interaction is a fundamentally **realist** one. Yet, they are aware that how they apprehend these workings unavoidably involves idealization, just as the statement that 'a tree that falls in the forest makes a sound' involves idealizations such as 'tree,' 'forest,' and 'sound.' That awareness does not cause conversation analysts to lurch toward a constructionism that regards all 'truths' as equal fictions and members as eager creators and promoters of whichever fiction they prefer. The reason is that the truths about the lifeworld that conversation analysts seek are not ones that members consciously experience as Coke® vs. Pepsi® preferences or other matters of debate. This leads conversation analysts to an epistemology, or way of knowing, that strips away the intrusions of social scientists' presumptions and interpretations into analysis, ideally proceeding by induction.

Throughout, CA is strictly **empirical**, grounding its conclusions closely in the data – that is, in the interaction itself. This means:

- Eschewing claims about what the researcher 'knows' to be relevant about the talk's context, unless it can be demonstrated to meet joint criteria that Schegloff (1991, 1997) calls **relevance and procedural consequentiality**.[1] An example of a claim that can pass muster with these criteria is that being in a court-in-session matters. The claim can succeed, Schegloff says, if the members present can be demonstrated to refer to being in court (meaning that they make the claim relevant) and to orient to court session-specific rules about who speaks when and in what manner (meaning that it is procedurally consequential). An example that doesn't pass muster would be the claim that gender matters whenever a man interrupts a woman. If neither party refers to gender, Schegloff would say that gender is not demonstrably relevant here. We discuss the debate related to this conclusion in Chapter 6.
- Rejecting data that come from non-naturalistic social scientific processes, such as experimental tasks conducted in laboratory settings, as these are already thoroughly imbued with researchers' understandings. CA initially did not use interview data, but has come to do so, either to investigate talk-in-interaction within the institution of the research interview (see Chapter 7), or by treating such talk like any other.
- Refraining from explanations rooted in individual personalities, attitudes, or intentions, for only what people do – e.g., what they say, where they gaze, how they move – and with what effect are demonstrably manifest (Heritage, 1991). Considerations of face can be used in explanations, because it is understood to be a social property, and not an individual one.

---

[1] The feasibility of this is contested by Moerman (1988), whose much-cited analysis of Thai and American talk-in-interaction emphasizes that a capacity to interpret culturally specific meanings – whether of the type of rice a Thai person eats, or of how American cabs and buses share the road – pervades all talk-in-interaction. This begs the question, from what position can we stand outside our cultures and identify all the ways that culture infuses our talk?

Rigor in CA

The procedures and standards for a rigorous conversation analysis have become firmly established, much more so than the standards for narrative or discourse analysis. Analysis typically begins with audio or video recordings that are transcribed according to CA convention. This isn't gruntwork, for in CA, transcription is an analytic strategy unto itself, a first step in a practice that Sacks called ***unmotivated looking**, i.e., attuning to the data and being open to possibilities* (Ehrlich and Romaniuk, 2014). The convention reminds analysts of the thickets members must disentangle as they go about mundane talk (Bogen, 1992) and assists analysts in avoiding **glosses**, i.e., unwarranted interpretations of what is happening, by means of a specialized vocabulary and notation system. What might be glossed as a gasp, for example, is termed an audible in-breath and denoted '.h', what is glossed as a correction comes to be among the acts termed a repair, and so forth.

Using the recordings and the **corpus** – the linguistics term for dataset – of transcripts, the next step is to isolate segments containing some recurring way of using talk, other vocalizations, gaze, gesture, posture, or use of objects/the environment that intrigues you. Once such segments have been isolated, Hutchby and Wooffitt (2008: 93) say, an overarching CA strategy is to describe how the members show themselves to orient to a specific device, tool, or rule for talk-in-interaction, and to make patterned use of it. It is by further articulating what members are thereby doing, that this description becomes elevated to analysis. Journal articles using CA typically present meticulous discussion of three to six extended transcript excerpts, such as those in this chapter.

There are some complexities to the inductive tenor of this aim that are worth mentioning. First, as conversation analysts and their critics have discussed, there is no such thing as pure induction, uninformed by a researcher's prior knowledge. But to this, the conversation analysts would say that some methods are nonetheless more inductive than others; Stevanovic's (2013) charming study of humming-in-interaction illustrates how it is possible for a researcher to notice something in a fashion entirely unexpected and fresh. Second, in the decades since CA was founded, a substantial base of knowledge about talk-in-interaction has been built up. It is not uncommon to see deductive CA projects that set out to assess whether discoveries hold across languages or in the realm of computer-mediated communication. Throughout this part of the book, you will see several projects that *test the generalizability of CA findings.*

Finally, it is deduction and not induction that conversation analysts use in a method of warranting claims that is more definitively specified than most in NA or DA. The idea is that researchers and members alike arrive at and demonstrate their understandings of what talk is oriented to on a turn-by-turn basis. Each turn someone takes, researchers and members ask **'why that now?'** (Schegloff, 1998: 413) and formulate hypotheses about what the talk has been orienting to and accomplishing. A member does so in real-time. He uses his best hypothesis about the past turns – and especially the immediately previous one – to formulate a next turn that will display his understanding and **project** what the subsequent turn

will contain (see Sacks et al., 1974). The member's turn allows the researcher to *test the more leisurely understandings she has formulated about what the member could plausibly do next; thus, it's called her* ***next-turn proof*** *strategy.*

This strategy is illustrated in the following exchange, in which Amber's three-year old daughter Mac shows Katherine a toy.

Mac: This is brow::n bunny.

As researchers asking 'why that now?' about Mac's turn, we can notice that she speaks of the toy as 'brow::n bunny' and not as 'a brow::n bunny.' This distinction, made now, can be conjectured to designate the toy as having a proper name, Brown Bunny. 'This is' suggests that Brown Bunny might be being presented for Katherine's commentary or being introduced to Katherine, who could now introduce herself to Brown Bunny or greet it. The emphasis in 'brow::n' opens up the possibility of an alternate topic Katherine could pursue, i.e., that of other, non-brown bunnies among Mac's toys. We can test these four hypotheses, which project commentary, self-introduction, greeting, or a segue to the topic of other bunnies, against Katherine's next turn:

Katherine: Dyou have o::ther bunnies?

This supports the fourth hypothesis about what Katherine understands Mac's turn to be doing. Meanwhile, in real time, Katherine waits for Mac's next turn to see whether her understanding is warranted:

Mac: Blue bunny. Black bunny, da::k brown bunny. This is li::ght brown bunny.

Note that though 'next-turn proof' suggests that an utterance can *prove* a hypothesis, really conversation analysts use utterances to support or disprove hypotheses. Moreover, utterances many turns later may also reveal what members' understandings had been.

Textbox 5.1: A Summary of Strategies for Understanding the Basic CA Paradigm

Approaches throughout CA:

- Use transcription as a strategy for unmotivated looking.
- Find segments in which the pattern(s) of talk-in-interaction can be described.
- Move from describing how talk is proceeding in these segments to analyzing the action that talk accomplishes.
- Ground analysis strictly in the talk data, appealing to context only when necessary.
- Ask 'why that now?' and use the next-term proof strategy to test your understanding of what members are orienting to and doing.
- Consider testing the generalizability of CA findings.

ANALYZING THE MECHANISMS OF EVERYDAY TALK

We now present some basic mechanisms of everyday talk that conversation analysts have thus far discovered, and identify the analytic strategies associated with them. Here, we use a mix of everyday and institutional examples, emphasizing the essential commonalities in turn-taking and other mechanisms that members use in sequentially organizing talk. In Chapter 7, on institutional talk-in-interaction, we direct our attention to where differences lie.

Taking Turns in Everyday Talk

Sacks et al.'s (1974) ground-breaking analysis of everyday talk-in-interaction takes up earlier findings about how speech exchange happens. For the most part, only one person speaks at a given time. Overlaps of speakers' talk are usually brief and somehow managed, so that all but one speaker will prematurely leave off speaking when an overlap occurs; Levinson (1983) says that less than five percent of conversational time is comprised of overlaps. And though talk need not be continuous, the gap between when one person leaves off speaking and another starts can commonly be measured in fractions of seconds. This may seem ho hum. But for conversation analysts, that's exactly the point! How, they ask, does this miracle of mundane and taken-for-granted turn-taking order come to pass? How do members know who is to speak next, and how do they go about projecting when the current speaker's turn will end? How do they accomplish a sense of shared intersubjectivity?

Sacks and colleagues sought answers that would apply regardless of the topic, context, or number of people present, and that would apply even if a person took a turn of a single word. They found that:

- Turns are comprised of **turn-construction units**, which can roughly correspond to syntactical units such as words, phrases, clauses, and sentences, or of gestures such as a shrug.
- Turns can contain a variety of devices by which speakers indicate that they are not yet done, such as rushed speech or grammatical constructions such as an 'if,' which can signal that a 'then' will be forthcoming.
- Turns also contain **transition-relevance places**, i.e., recognizable places, such as pauses, at which a turn-construction unit is done and a new speaker can jump in. Members have strategies for projecting that these places are coming up. Heritage and Clayman (2010: 264–5) cite the example of how the pauses award show hosts can use before announcing winners permit an audience to project that their turn to applaud is nearing.

At transition-relevance places, Sacks and colleagues found a sequence of rules to apply. First, if the current speaker's turn has projected that he will choose his successor, then that's who the next speaker ought to be. Second, if the current speaker hasn't chosen a successor, then that person will self-select from among the current speaker and others present. Third, if more than one person

self-selects, whoever started speaking first conventionally continues to speak, while the others end their turns prematurely. It's by orienting to this sequence that members can manage turn-taking as seamlessly as they do, even under the pressure of a general preference for turns to be shorter, as many may want to hold the floor (Schegloff, 1982). (Of course, things can go wrong, in which case members hold one another accountable.[2])

Strategies for analyzing turn-taking identify devices for prolonging turns, marking transition-relevance places, and projecting the next speaker, commonly with an eye to the broader social action this accomplishes. For example, Ignasi Clemente (2009) analyzes the devices by which child patients, aged 10 to 18, succeed in managing the floor for multiple turns when clinicians ask them case history questions that stump them. In Textbox 5.2, a doctor, an 11-year-old patient, and the patient's grandmother are present. Their topic is the patient's pain.

In this example, we see the child patient prolong her turns in lines 5 and 8 by leaving turn-construction units grammatically incomplete, as well as by extending the word 'like' into 'like:'. Clemente explains that in line 10, the patient uses the device of turning her head – but not her lower body toward her grandmother. She thereby signals a transition-relevance place and selects the grandmother as next speaker. But, importantly, by keeping her lower body turned toward the clinician, the patient also signals that she is turning toward – and ceding a turn to – her grandmother only temporarily, and that the clinician's subsequent questions should once again be hers to answer. Because the clinicians, family members, and child patients all oriented to such devices, the children were able to remain the primary informants on their illnesses.

Although the turn-taking model outlined makes it sound as though normatively only one person should speak at a time, conversation analyses can also *focus on how, and with what consequence, speakers orient to resources that permit a primary speaker to take turns whilst other speakers overlap with them* (see Schegloff, 2000). When you are getting directions to a train station, for example, your simultaneous 'uh huhs' and repeatings back, and the quick questions that you interject are not oriented to as cutting short the direction-giver's turn-taking. Rather, these devices support and confirm the direction-giving process, making it a mutual achievement, rather than the direction-giver's alone. In a fascinating

---

[2] Schegloff (2007) discusses this in terms of **relevance rules** to which members orient. These rules, based on the sequential organization of talk, set the terms for how silences can become conspicuous and for how talk is to be interpreted. If Amber is part of a group that is casually conversing, she might be inconspicuously silent throughout, without that being remarked upon or giving rise to any interpretations. But, once she has been projected to become the next speaker, taking her turn is a way that she shows herself to be oriented to contributing to a shared intersubjectivity. If Amber is silent, that suddenly becomes relevant. She now becomes accountable for not talking, meaning that inferences will be made about her silence.

Textbox 5.2: When was it the worst?

DOC = doctor

PAT = child patient

GMA = patient's grandmother

1	DOC:	.hh when was it (0.4) the worst.
2		(2.6)
3	PAT:	Probably (in the middle).
4		(0.7)
5	PAT:	Like, (0.4)
6	DOC:	About when.
7		(0.3)
8	PAT:	Uh like:, (0.3)
9	DOC:	What month. <Do you [remember about?,
10	PAT: →	[((turns head from clinician to grandma))
11	GMA:	Befo:re Christmas I think.<Just before Christmas.

Source: Clemente, 2009: 880

example of the social consequences of overlapping talk, Wooffitt and Clark (1998) demonstrate how such talk sustains the identities of spiritual mediums. Overlaps between mediums' and their clients' talk about their situations and loved ones permit the mediums to sound so attuned to a spiritual world that they can echo or anticipate their clients' thoughts, a jointly accomplished hallmark of a medium's identity.

That said, how to distinguish an interruption from an overlap has long dogged conversation analysts and others studying talk data; Schegloff (2000) even calls 'interruption' a gloss to be avoided. Julia Goldberg (1990) corrects our last paragraph's simplified premise that an overlap is an **affiliative** act (i.e., one that aligns the two speakers) that endorses the primary speaker's continuation of a turn. An interruption, by implication, is a **disaffiliative** bid for the primary speaker to relinquish a turn. Taking all overlaps as her object of study, Goldberg identifies seven continua along which they can be placed, including whether they would redirect the topic vs. the specific content of the talk, and whether they are focused on the speaker vs. the recipient. That Goldberg and others have observed a large and muddy middle ground here helps us to understand why members also can dispute whether a certain utterance constitutes an interruption.

As another analytic strategy, several studies have tested whether Sacks, Schegloff, and Jefferson's model of turn holds for everyday talk across cultures. Broad support for the model is to be found in Stivers et al.'s (2009) ten-language statistical comparison and in a far-ranging cross-cultural collection edited by Sidnell (2009). Hiroko Tanaka's (2000) work provides a model comparison of how the upcoming end of a turn is signaled in English and in Japanese. She finds that although the English subject–verb–object sentence order makes it easier for members to spot the imminent end of a turn than the incrementally developing sentence order of Japanese does, Japanese offers numerous markers that a sentence is final, akin to the 'you know' and 'eh?' of English. Therefore, while the resources for ending a sentence differ in the two languages, Tanaka finds speakers of both languages to utilize them, supporting the generalizability of the model.

Valuable challenges have also been posed to the Sacks, Schegloff, and Jefferson model. A sympathetic one comes from Garcia and Jacobs (1999), who attempted to extend it in a realm that its 1974 originators could not have imagined – that of internet chat communication. They found that the model's premises that members vie for turns and are ordinarily either speakers or recipients of talk cease to apply. Less sympathetically, O'Connell et al. (1990) protest that the model prescribes a norm in which a smoothly flowing conversation is considered more effective than one whose speakers fulfill their conversational goals, however chaotically. Jones and Thornborrow (2004) doubt that speakers universally orient to a norm of one person at a time holding the floor. They present original empirical findings from junior school classrooms, and cite studies of administrative meetings, women's friendship groups, and Deaf signers in conversation, to propose that more collaborative, flexible conversational floors are possible.

Two-turn Sequences in Everyday Talk

If we return to Textbox 5.2 and the succession of questions that the doctor in Clemente (2009) poses about the timing of the child patient's worst pain, we see something about timing to be the projected answer (line 1), followed by approximate timing (line 6), followed by a month (line 9, first half), and then a yes/no (line 9, second half). Here and elsewhere, as members take their turns, they use – whether consciously or not – various resources to funnel down their projections of what the next turn could plausibly contain. We now introduce two powerful mechanisms for projecting: the adjacency pair and preference design. These are among the ways that talk is organized into **sequences**, that might be as few as two turns long, or as long as a story, or an institutional interaction such as a doctor's visit with its several stages.

Adjacency pairs are sequences of two turns by different speakers, in which the first speaker's turn sets in motion a specific requirement for how the second speaker is immediately obligated to reply. Among the common **first-** and **second-pair parts** are:

Question–answer	Proposal–assessment
Invitation–accept/decline	Command–response
Compliment–acknowledge	Accusation–denial
Greeting–greeting	Farewell–farewell

The doctor's turns in Textbox 5.2 exploit this rule, for all of them are questions, making the patient obligated to answer. Of course, she and other recipients of first-pair parts may do nothing of the kind, in which case they are accountable for it, meaning that inferences will be made about their inaction. The patient orients to this obligation in second-pair parts that are accountable as efforts to produce an answer (lines 5, 8). These culminate in the turn to her grandmother (line 10). Had this patient remained silent or not turned, the account that she was making an effort would have been less plausible.

One analytic strategy involving adjacency pairs is to *identify novel patterned pairs and analyze the actions that they accomplish*. For example, in what Levin (2014) calls 'the Bathroom Formula,' speakers who announce that they are about to use the toilet quite frequently are met with no response or only minimal responses such as 'okay.' Levin maintains that this formula lets the first turn-takers account for their departures, while permitting the second turn-takers to avoid unseemly talk of bodily functions.

Because adjacency pair obligations are so powerful, *instances when a first-pair part by one speaker is not met with a second-pair part by another seize analysts' attention*. For instance, Goodwin (2002: 725) analyzes the utterance of one fourth-grade girl, named Ruth, to another named Angela, who was approaching her:

Ruth: Hi Angela! Bye Angela! ((raising right hand, palm toward Angela))

to show how it is Ruth's breach of the adjacency pair expectation and her appropriation of Angela's turn therein that make Ruth's turn accountable as bullying. Duneier and Molotch (1999) present an extended example of such violations in diagnosing how interactions between Greenwich Village, Manhattan residents and street men go painfully awry. They found a street person named Mudrick to pepper his talk with residents with the first-pair parts of adjacency pairs, such as greetings, questions, and compliments. When a resident would design a disaffiliative move of not responding as obligated, Mudrick would continue to put forth first-pair parts, designing moves that deepened the disaffiliation. The authors reason that such 'interactional vandalism' by the street men was occasioned by the continual disaffiliative climate in which residents would fail to look them in the eye.

We now take up the device of **preference**, which is used in turn design to the effect of indicating which of the projected responses would be the most affiliative or face-saving. When the doctor in Textbox 5.2 asks the child patient about the month of her worst pains, no preferred month is specified. For all we

know, March would be as well-received an answer as October. However, when the doctor asks whether the child can remember the answer to the pain question (line 9), suddenly more is at stake: CA research has established a 'yes' answer to a yes-or-no question to commonly be preferred, though grammar, intonation, and numerous other devices are used to fine-tune inferences about preference (Raymond, 2003). While the doctor's line 9 'Do you remember' conveys a preference for the patient to agree, a question 'Don't you remember?' would make this preference starker.

When a speaker's turn has signaled what response is preferred, its recipient is accountable as acting affiliatively if she produces it promptly and unqualifiedly. When a recipient gives a dispreferred response, she risks being accountable as disaffiliative, but can mitigate that in various ways, such as delaying the turn, using softening prefaces (e.g., 'oh'), **hedges** (e.g., 'I wish I could but'), or stating alternate accounts. The analytic strategy of *investigating how inferences about preference are made or acted on, and to what effect* is exemplified by Kitzinger and Frith's (1999) pointed criticism of how date-rape prevention programs that tell women to 'just say no' overlook the everyday complexities of refusing *any* request.

A small body of works challenges the cross-cultural generalizability of CA findings about adjacency pairs or preference. Diana Eades (1982), a white middle-class Australian (WMCA) who conducted fieldwork among Aboriginal speakers in South-east Queensland, learned that her research participants did not feel obligated to answer most kinds of direct questions. Rather, they were embarrassed for and apologized for one of their own number who had asked Eades a series of direct questions; thus, it was a question-*asker,* rather than a person who failed to answer, who was treated as accountable. Eades proposes that WMCA value dissemination of knowledge whereas these Aboriginal speakers valued its control. Here, she appeals to context in a way that does not meet conversation analysts' criteria of relevance and procedural consequentiality.

Repair in Everyday Talk

Talk-in-interaction is marked by frequent trouble sources, including misunderstandings, mispronunciations and mishearings of words, confusions over names and facts, silences, contradictions, and the like (Sacks et al., 1974; Schegloff et al., 1977). An important focus in CA has been on mechanisms of **correction** or **repair**. The two terms are often used interchangeably, but Schegloff came to prefer 'repair' because it encompasses instances in which a speaker revises an utterance even without having made a factual error (Keating, 1993).

If we return once again to Textbox 5.2, we can observe that a trouble source first becomes apparent after the child patient's 'Probably (in the middle)' description of when her pain was worst (line 3). We can surmise that it is trouble because the doctor and patient are silent (line 4); were the doctor satisfied with the answer,

line 4 would be the ideal moment for posing a question on a new topic, but instead, the doctor begins to ask the patient variations on the same question. From line 4 until line 11, an unbroken sequence of talk repairs the patient's line 3 answer. Nested within this, in line 9, we may also be seeing the doctor repair a possible confusion arising from how the timing of the worst pain is being sought. The answer to a timing question could, after all, be anywhere from a date, to a time of day, to a circumstance such as 'after I've eaten,' and only in line 9 does the question become more specific.

Repair helps in a multitude of ways to maintain the order of talk-in-interaction. If the doctor in our example were indifferent, no repair would be sought: repair displays that parties to the talk are attentive and engaged (Norrick, 1991), putting what they hear to a next-turn proof and finding that it comes up short. Speakers can also withhold information so that others will seek repair, with the effect of distributing responsibility for the continued discussion of a topic, such as gossip (Besnier, 1995). Repair restores intersubjectivity and a shared orientation to the world; working on this chapter, we noticed how thoughts such as 'are we on the same planet?' could come to us when we talked at cross-purposes.

But repair can perturb the flow of talk. Once initiated, it becomes an immediate priority of the member, and thus requires a change in **footing** – Goffman's (1981) term for a shift, understood to be temporary, in how a speaker aligns to herself or a situation. (An aside is one example and putting a topic on hold for repair for eight lines of a transcript, as in Textbox 5.2, is another.) And, repair that is avoided or deferred can fail, as Ulichny (1997) shows in her analysis of 'mismanaged misunderstanding' (p. 243) between English speakers from the UK and English as a Foreign Language speakers from Italy. Having one's talk require repair, especially when others perform it, can also be face threatening, as it may be for the child-patient in our example. Thus, *patterns in the whos, whens, and hows of repair bristle with consequences* worth examining.

In such studies, it has often been useful to be able to categorize repairs according to:

- When they are initiated and effected: We can distinguish **same-turn** repair, initiated and carried through by one speaker within one turn, from **next-turn** repair, which is effected by the speaker whose turn follows the trouble source, and third-turn repair, and so on. The child-patient's repair could be said to be of the next-turn variety, if the silence in line 4 is counted as the doctor's turn.
- Who initiates them: Repairs are **self-initiated** more often than **other-initiated**, a finding that Ulichny (1997) has found to hold in several cultures. The doctor initiates the repairs in our example.
- What form an other-initiated repair takes: Certain devices are typical, such as silence, **Wh-** questions such as 'Who?', partial repetition of part of the trouble, or 'Y'mean' followed by a statement of what's partially understood. The doctor initiates repairs of the patient's turn with silence, and with Wh- questions.

- Who performs them: **Self-repair**, such as the doctor may be doing, is strongly preferred to **other-repair**. Norrick (1991), however, maintains that in some relationships, such as parent–child, other-repair is common on the part of the person with the greater ability to carry the conversation forward. In our example, the grandmother, once allocated a turn by the child patient, performs the repair of her answer.

The doctor and child patient's sequence serves well to illustrate other-initiated repair and self-repair. We turn now, briefly, to an unusual case in which it is the ambiguity about whether repair is underway or not that is consequential. It comes from Nakane's (2011) study of English-speaking police interrogations of Japanese-speaking suspects in Australia. Ordinarily, suspects who do not reply to interrogators' questions become accountable to interrogators as guilty or uncooperative. But when interpretation of the interrogation is required, suspects can also become silent as a way to initiate repair of interpretation errors. The multiple meanings of silence complicate both the interrogation and the interpretation processes.

Extended Sequences in Everyday Talk

We now look at strategies for investigating how more extended sequences of talk-in-interaction can be designed or emergent. In contrast to the compact structure to which members orient in adjacency pairs, and the urgency with which members approach repair work, looser and less predictable possibilities now appear. Researchers have found several longer sequences of talk-in-interaction to be rich in analytic potential. These include various types of heralding utterances, as well as the story – a conceptual category familiar from NA but examined here from fresh angles.

Utterances such as 'Can I ask you a question?' and 'Are you doing anything Friday night?' are called pre-questions and pre-invitations, respectively, and the list goes on. Types of **pre-s** prick up conversation analysts' ears because speakers and recipients alike treat them as preludes or prefaces to questions, invitations, and announcements with marked affiliative/disaffiliative potential. Such turns project that a recipient may want not to be asked a question or may refuse an invitation and can design a response that averts or sidesteps the disaffiliative turn that is in the offing. *Noticing various types of pre-s is a strategy for identifying possible interactional trouble and understanding how it is managed.*

In an analysis that problematizes how members come to interactively establish some – but not all – new information as 'news,' Douglas Maynard (1997) gives the case study of the talk between Andi and Betty that is shown in Textbox 5.3. Maynard points out that a pair of preannouncements (lines 4, 6) by Andi, received with questions by Betty (lines 5, 7), help to produce Andi's line 8 announcement as news, calling for a response, as we see Betty begin to give in line 9.

Textbox 5.3: Well we have some news for you

1 Andi: .hhh well: speaking of bot^toms are you sitting
2 down?
3 Betty: Ye^ah.
4 Andi: Well we have some news for you.
5 Betty: What?
6 Andi: .hhh that may come as a bit of a surprise ehhh!
7 Betty: I see- what are you telling me?
8 Andi: hhhh! Bob and I are going to have a baby.
9 Betty: Oh my good^ness!

Source: Maynard, 1997: 99

Stories, too, have prefaces. While in Chapter 3 we had seen narrative analysts find much fault with the chronological ordering of Labov and Waletzky's (1967) stage model of delivering a narrative, conversation analysts find merit in the model's idea of an abstract containing the story's most newsworthy event. The difference arises because the narrative analyses that we have seen so far have concerned themselves with questions of 'what happened?', 'what does it mean now?', and 'is this a "good" story in the sense of being newsworthy?' whereas conversation analytic strategies *ask about the 'hows' of storytelling and their consequence.* These can range from how a speaker creates moments of emphasis to how a speaker comes to tell a story in the first place. Sacks and colleagues (1974) understood a would-be storyteller's presentation of a preface – a category into which Labov and Waletzky's abstract would fit – to be a turn design projecting that others could request that her story be told. Such a request would putatively allocate her the floor. Notice that in this model, a story is marked out as exceptional. It is outside of the ordinary flow of talk, suspends the normal mechanism of turn allocation, and privileges one teller who follows a clear path through to the end of her telling.

But another view of story as more habitual, jointly and even competitively produced, possibly small and possibly leading in indeterminate directions also is to be found in CA. Gail Jefferson (1978) ascertained that not all stories are heralded by what she called 'elaborate prefaces,' such as '*He* can be a bastard too, he uh one-one day we' (p. 225). Other stories, which tend to be shorter, have more succinct prefaces that quickly underscores how a story is connected to the speakers' environment ('Oh that teeshirt reminded me') or the preceding talk ('Saying dahlias, I just cut some fresh dahlias'), or that accounts for the lack of such a link ('Incidentally') (pp. 221–2). Moreover, Jefferson observed that one story can trigger another, and

that in all but extraordinary cases, recipients of a story offer some commentary on it. She thus began to conceptualize the story as part of the flow of the talk and the environment surrounding it, rather than as a rupture from it.

Alexandra Georgakopoulou (2007) follows through on this line of thought magnificently in her research on **small stories**, which include projections of the future, breaking news, fleeting and oblique references to shared experience, and mentions of stories to be told later. Employing this eclectic definition, she observed a trio of young Greek women to tell 341 stories in 20 hours of their talk-in-interaction, iteratively shaping a shared history, projecting a future, and sustaining their identities within the group, e.g., as good at school or bold with men. The divide between the teller and listener identities dissolved into a joint venture of initiating stories, contributing to their plots, ratifying others' contributions, and stating evaluations. Georgakopoulou used this phenomenon to critique views of story as an individually centered search for the meaning of the past, conducted in monologic form. Thus, she is innovatively advancing a strategy of *interrogating the nature of narrative and narrative identities.*

Topics in CA

In conversation analysts' understanding, putting a story – or, indeed, any – topic on the floor generally furthers the agenda of the member who puts it there. How topics are helped onto the floor or prevented from getting there, how members' utterances in relation to a topic can promote their agendas further, and how topics are drawn to a close are therefore of interest.

A typical CA strategy is to establish what rules, resources, or other devices available in talk-in-interaction help or hinder a speaker to do so, and to what effect. We begin with a cheerful device that might seem irrelevant to the serious question of how a topic comes to prevail: the greeting. Early anthropology had treated greetings as examples of what they called **phatic communion**, a weighty designation for content-free talk that serves to assert sociability (Malinowski, 1923). Sacks (1995), however, cleverly showed that greetings could do far more. For instance, because they come in adjacency pairs, whoever greets first ordinarily will receive a greeting in reply. Although Sacks said that a greeting sequence typically goes on for six or seven turns, whoever breaks with it first will be able to raise the first topic.

As Jefferson (1980) established in her work on how members negotiate their way from a 'How are you?' greeting into the telling of their present troubles, strategies for raising delicate, face-damaging topics involve more interactional labor. Take, for example, a transgressive topic such as the grocery store employees who defile meat. Coupland and Jaworski's (2003) research on how it becomes possible for groups of friends to talk about such topics found members to first go through a process of shifting their footing toward the topic. Thus, a speaker who initially characterizes the topic of defiling meat as 'really quite grim when we're eating'

(p. 90), displays her shift toward a transgressive footing by laughing as references to it continue to be made, and soon after participates in sharing stories. Later, the footing shifts again, as the same speaker again denounces the topic as 'grim' (p. 91). There are norms, Coupland and Jaworski say, about how to transgress norms.

A second general analytic strategy looks to talk about a topic as it is ongoing, and *asks about the resources members utilize and recognize for promoting and contesting views.* In Chapter 2, we had seen oral historians use the notion of **authority** to distinguish reports based on personal experience from those based on experience at second-hand, and so forth; now, in CA, we see questions about how members go about claiming, challenging, and recognizing others' **epistemic authority**, a somewhat broader term that permits claims to have diverse bases (see Mondada, 2013; Sidnell, 2005). For instance, studying how the phenomenon of burnout was discussed by focus groups, Hydén and Bülow (2003) found the group of social workers to locate epistemic authority in their personal experience, while the group of doctors located it in their professional knowledge of whether burnout was a recognized diagnosis.

While far more could be said about the topic of topics, we will close it with another strategy that engaged Sacks and his collaborators: that of *attention to the* ***closing*** *of conversations and topics.* How, they wondered, do speakers manage to jointly coordinate their activity so as to fall silent? How is it that one person's turn no longer leads to another, and that silences cease to be accountable? Schegloff and Sacks (1973) found several devices in common use. For example, speakers can employ adjacency pairs such as farewells to close off a conversation. They can also use a pre-closing such as 'Right,' which takes a turn without adding content to the topic under discussion. The subsequent turn-taker, Schegloff and Sacks reason, no longer has new content to address and is thus projected to either raise a new topic or prolong discussion of the current one.

Textbox 5.4: A Summary of Strategies for Analyzing the Mechanisms of Everyday Talk

- Identify devices used in turn-taking, per Sacks and colleagues' (1974) model, and the social ends thereby accomplished.
- Identify how, and with what consequence, speakers orient to the resource of overlap.
- Identify novel adjacency pairs or be alert for times when a second-pair part isn't uttered. Either way, analyze the effect.
- Investigate how inferences about preference are made or acted on, and to what effect.
- Investigate who does repair, when, how, and in what patterned circumstances – and with what consequences.
- Seek out recurring sequences (e.g., types of pre-) and the work that they do.
- Interrogate the nature of narrative and narrative identities within talk-in-interaction.
- Identify how topics are helped or hindered onto the floor, and to what effect.
- Study the resources that members utilize and recognize for promoting and contesting views.
- Inquire into how a conversation or topic is brought to a close.

CHAPTER SUMMARY

In contrast to narrative analysts, conversation analysts take no interest in individuals, let alone in narrators' subconscious meanings or researchers' reflexive introspections. Instead, conversation analysts understand individuals to be members of a community that shares interactional competences. Unscripted talk among members is understood as an analytic marvel, a means by which, turn by turn, members ongoingly manage to shore up their taken-for-granted assumption that a shared intersubjectivity is possible. CA strategies reveal how this is done through talk's sequential organization, which includes: how turn-taking is so seamlessly achieved; how sequences of talk, ranging from two-turn adjacency pairs to lengthy ones such as stories, are accomplished; and how repairs are effected. CA strategies are empiricist, with conclusions stringently grounded in the infinitesimal details of what is visible or audible in embodied talk, such as a rise in its pitch or the pursing of a lip. Importantly, conversation analysts refuse to read social contexts and forces into talk. Instead, they believe that it is through talk that members continually produce the interaction order on which all social order is based.

SIX

Conversation Analysis Approaches to Social Categories

A running joke of Kathy's father was to speak ironically of his everyday happenings as though they were momentous headline news. If her father was short-changed at the grocery store, 'Pensioner Cheated of Last Nickel' would be his announcement; if he got a parking ticket, his story would become 'Immigrant Violates Canadian Law.' Her father shared with conversation analysts a fascination with the precise social actions that talk can accomplish when members devise and use categories of persons, places, or things – the fascination that **membership categorization analysis** (MCA) pursues. In this chapter, we begin by discussing how MCA has been conceptualized, and illustrating the specific strategies that it offers. Second, we consider strategies arising from conversation analysts' debates about how to engage with social scientific research questions about how inequalities related to gender, sexuality, race, and other analytical categories are manifest in, and reproduced by, talk. The distinction between these two approaches is a subtle but significant one. Whereas in MCA, we look to the categories that members generate in their emergent talk-in-interaction, in the social sciences more broadly, analysts frequently use their own categories as the starting point.

INTRODUCING MEMBERSHIP CATEGORIZATION ANALYSIS

The Basics of MCA

In CA, as we've seen so far, what is fundamental about talk is that it is sequentially organized, permitting intersubjective understandings to be calibrated and

order to become emergent. In **membership categorization analysis** (MCA), proposed by Harvey Sacks in his lectures, sitting at the right hand of sequential organization is the device of putting people, places, or objects into categories. In phenomenologists' terms, this device matters because our everyday use of typifications and categories simplifies the lifeworld (see Schütz, 1962, 1964). At the same time, Sacks (1995: 40) theorized, categories store up members' knowledges and are thus 'inference-rich.'

In what has become the most iconic of CA examples, Sacks (1995: 244) used a child's utterance, 'The baby cried. The mommy picked it up.' Listeners who can make sense of this, Sacks maintained, do so because they can infer that baby and mommy are somehow connected, with particular expectations and obligations arising from that relationship. In formal terms, what Sacks called **membership categorization devices** (MCDs) link **standardized relational pairs** such as mommy and baby or captain and crew (or some larger set of categories, such as positions in an orchestra, pieces of cutlery, or ethnic groups) to a store of related **predicates**, i.e., knowledges, interests, motives, obligations, entitlements, actions, or other characteristics. In the baby–mommy sentence, a 'family roles' membership categorization device is being used. The category of baby has the predicate of being entitled to maternal care, while that of mommy has the predicate of the obligation to provide it.

Sacks (1995: 223–66) observed that we use these devices in conversation according to a number of criteria, including:

- The **principle of economy**: the person who picked the baby up might be 37, of Hungarian descent, a professor, and phobic of clowns, but it's not necessary – and indeed it is impossible – to enumerate all the categories to which she belongs. A single category can suffice, and here it is 'mommy.'
- The **hearer's maxim**: once a category has been used in talk, if members are able to recognize other categories as consistent with the same MCD, then they will do so. Since 'mommy' *can* be taken to fit into an MCD alongside baby, it *will* be.
- The **viewer's maxim**: in Sacks's example, a speaker who has seen a female person picking up a crying baby has inferred that person to be 'the mommy.' Likewise, if we see someone performing brain surgery, we may infer that this person is a brain surgeon, and not Hannibal Lecter. In formal terms, if a characteristic is understood to be bound to a category as one of its predicates, then when that characteristic is on display, the viewer infers that the category is applicable.

MCDs, thus, are among the devices by which members achieve context in conversation.

What makes members' use of categories a matter of analytic interest is that there is no set menu of possibilities from which they select. A person standing on the curb of Queen Street can be fleetingly categorized as 'person waiting to cross Queen' and might be about to become 'traffic fatality.' Likewise, even

though categories are rich in predicates, how tightly or conventionally a predicate is bound to a category is not a given: mommies are not alone in picking babies up. In MCA, to ask how members make sense of Schegloff's 'why that now?' question is to ask how their orientation to the context of the moment informs how they hear, construct, and use categorization devices. The MCA strategies we outline also ask what speakers do by using MCDs, with important possibilities including identity-related work and the making of moral claims.

Strategies for Doing MCA

The strategy of *demonstrating how categories and MCDs can be produced in sequentially organized talk and to what end* is an important one, based in the CA contention that categories and their groupings do not reflect idealized, pre-existing truths, but instead are practical consequences of talk. Eglin and Hester (2003) provide a valuable exemplar in *The Montreal Massacre*, a study of media reports – including talk data in the form of quotations – of the 6 December 1989 shooting and killing of Geneviève Bergeron and 13 others at L'École polytechnique in Montreal, Canada. Eglin and Hester trace the shifts in the categories produced to refer to both the persons involved in this event and the event itself, which was variously termed an act of terrorism, an emergency, a disaster, a tragedy, horror, mass murder, and violence against women. That the Massacre came to be widely typified as the final of these categories was consequential in producing calls for commemoration and redress that were gender-based and not particular to students, Montrealers, or gun control.

Adopting this strategy involves looking closely at the particulars of how and why sequentially organized talk attaches predicates to possible categories. Take for example, this exchange, occurring as Amber's daughter, Mac, was playing a game with Katherine:

Katherine: I'm gonna take another card=

Mac: =No! I::'m the tea::cher.

We see that Mac picks up the notion of entitlement to take a card, mentioned in Katherine's turn, and tacks it onto the category of teacher as one of its predicates. This is a creative act: the predicate Mac uses is not bound by convention to the category of teacher, and nor is teacher a category routinely evoked during a domestic game. Rather, Mac's 'I::'m the tea::cher' stakes the claim that all this is plausible and relevant, and thereby warrants her objection, softening the sharpness of her '=No!'

Of concern to many conversation analysts, and likely to appeal to many others in the social sciences, are strategies for *examining how membership categorization*

devices are used to do identity work. For instance, if we continue to study Mac's turn, we can see that it makes a series of interconnected claims about identities. In referring to 'the teacher,' not 'a teacher,' Mac asserts that only one person in the situation can be incumbent in the identity category of teacher. In emphasizing 'I::'m,' Mac avows this incumbency to be hers. Then, in emphasizing 'tea::cher,' Mac chides Katherine for having mistaken her for something else, something not-a-teacher – and here, it's the standardized relational pair of pupil–teacher that beckons. If Mac is the teacher, by implication, Katherine is her pupil, someone who ought to heed her.

Some research using this strategy asks how claims to incumbency in identity categories, such as Mac's claim to 'teacher,' are made and sustained in sequentially organized talk. For instance, King (2013) shows how a young woman in the UK speaks of herself as being a 'kid' before she took her gap year, and by such devices – and the agreements of her interlocutor – accomplishes a new, more adult age identity. Meanwhile, Maheux-Pelletier and Golato (2008) present an analysis hinging on how a French speaker from Quebec claims a linguistic membership identity by persisting in using *bleuet* as the word for blueberries, even after her interlocutor, who hails from France, has questioned *bleuet*'s meaning and put forth *myrtille* as the correct word. At stake here and in other of these authors' examples is the legitimacy of linguistic identities that are based on the non-normative variants of French spoken outside France.

In these projects, as in conversation analysts' understandings more generally, we reiterate that an identity is not considered to be fixed and internal to an individual, so much as a work-in-progress, situated in interaction. This work-in-progress need not proceed smoothly. Van de Mieroop and Clifton (2012) give the intriguing case of an interview that a black folklorist conducted in Mississippi in 1941 with George Johnson, a former slave. While asking Johnson about his life experiences and musical tastes, the folklorist used an MCD in which liking blues music and feeling favorable toward 'colored people' were predicates tightly bound to the 'colored people' category. However, Johnson contested this MCD in instances when he voiced preferences for big band music and spoke disparagingly of 'niggas.' This study illustrates how 'group memberships are talked into being' (Van de Mieroop and Clifton, 2012: 180).

As Lena Jayyusi (1984) explains in *Categorization and the Moral Order*, categories can sometimes serve as a resource that speakers and listeners use to make moral claims and draw moral inferences. Jayyusi attunes our ears to the distinction between calling someone a 'bad friend' and calling that person a 'bad squash player.' Because the category of friend is predicated on a **moral performance**, i.e., on meeting obligations and fulfilling commitments, to describe a person as 'bad friend' is to simultaneously judge that person's character in its entirety. A 'bad friend' is bad. By contrast, a 'bad squash player,' such as Katherine, is simply bad at performing the competences involved in squash.

Textbox 6.1: Worse than *When Harry Met Sally*

T = Terry, the host of the *Central Weekend* chat show

M = Margaret, the chat show guest

AUD = the audience

T:	well when you say you've not heard anything like it (.) what sort of
	[noise did you (.) forgive me for prying [but I mean=
AUD:	[HHhhhhhhhhh [HHHHHHHHHHHhhhhhhhhhhhhhhhhh
M:	=well it was just sort of (.) what you do see portrayed on film or on
	television today (.) do you want a demonstration?=
T:	=well n-n- [no (1.0) w- w- what are you going to do? you know I mean
AUD:	[HHHHHHHHhhhhhhhhhhhhhhhhhhh
	(.) this is When Harry Met Sally isn't it=
M:	=I yes well tw- twenty times worse than When Harry Met Sally (.) I can
	assure you I mean it was a case (0.5) I did try and I was always (.) I
	never really lost my temper with her and I tried to do everything
	the right↓ way (.) the so called civilised [way
T:	[so what did you do in the
	end?
M:	well I used to go down and ring a doorbell (.) [and ask if she could
T:	[while she was em
M:	keep it [down the noise down
AUD:	[HHHHHHHHHHhhhhhhhhhhhhhhhhhhh
T:	what was her response to you?
M:	it was a case of the fact that (.) er (.) I had reached the age where
	I'd forgotten what it was like to be ↑young and [etcetera etce↑tera
T:	[so she was verbally
	abusive towards you=
M:	=wh-? oh yeah I mean in the end it just got so impossible that er I I
	just (.) well I had to move in the end it was a case of er getting out
	and=
T:	=well it's outrageous that you've had to move (.) I mean perhaps a
	bucket of water might've been the answer
M:	that's what they do to dogs
T:	[HHHhhhhhhhh
AUD:	[HHHHHhhhhhh

Source: Stokoe, 2003: 333–4

A fascinating example of MCA that builds on Jayyusi's conception is Elizabeth Stokoe's (2003) study of UK television chat shows on the theme of complaints about neighbors. Textbox 6.1, above, is an excerpt of a transcript from one such show. In it, the show's guest, Margaret is talking with a host about a neighbor whom she has already characterized as a woman with multiple boyfriends and whose lovemaking she can overhear. Analyzing this transcript, Stokoe points to features such as:

- How the host's 'forgive me for prying' (line 20) implies that it's a breach for sexual sounds to become public. So too does Margaret's calling the neighbor's sounds 'worse than When Harry Met Sally' (line 27), and the audience's laughter (lines 21, 25, 36) when the topic of the sounds is pursued. The neighbor, thus, is touted as being of dubious moral character.
- How 'forgive me for prying' also acclaims Margaret as someone who would not discuss these sounds unbidden, affirming her to be of higher moral character. Margaret's 'the civilised way' (line 30) and the host's 'outrageous' (line 45) also make this point.
- How the host's 'a bucket of water' (line 46) brings into play the category of 'dogs,' which Margaret, via Sacks's hearer's maxim, then takes up (line 47), abetted by the host and audience's laughter (lines 48, 49). 'Dogs,' Stokoe notes, can be synonymous with 'sluts' in the UK context.

Stokoe's conclusion is that 'in juxtaposing the category "young woman" with "extreme" or overt expressions of sexual activity, Margaret has warranted both a recategorization of her neighbor as a "slut" and her own complaint' (2003: 225). To be categorized as a bad woman here becomes grounds for being called a bad neighbor.

While some MCDs are comprised of collections of categories that work together, such as positions in an orchestra, others – such as 'colored' and white, noisy and quiet neighbor, and the variants of French spoken inside and outside France – can come to be constructed as morally laden binaries (Jayyusi, 1984). Housley and Fitzgerald (2002) propose that such **contrast devices** merit particular analytic attention because they can be used to simplify individuals' complexity, generate stark difference, separate 'us' from 'them' and, via a sequential logic, argue that the blameworthy should be punished. And, if the blameworthy are not punished, they must either carry out interactional and moral repair work or risk appearing indifferent to moral principle. Among the examples that Housley and Fitzgerald (2009) give is that of an Australian government that appeared blameworthy because it had failed to meet certain campaign promises. In its attempt at repair work, this government designated the promises that it had met as 'core' and called the others 'non-core.'

Textbox 6.2: A Summary of Strategies for Doing MCA

- Demonstrate how MCDs are produced in sequentially organized talk and to what end.
- Investigate how MCDs are used to do identity work.
- Investigate how MCDs are used in moral claims and inferences.

CA AND CATEGORIES: DEBATING THE ALTERNATIVES

In the preceding sections, researchers had the agenda of determining how members use categorization devices in answering their 'why that now?' question. Now, suppose the agenda was to understand how social inequalities related to categories such as gender, sexuality, and race became manifest in talk-in-interaction. Many social scientists who pose such questions have been attracted to the nuances of CA methods, but the very feasibility of posing and answering these questions from within a CA paradigm has been hotly disputed. Several analytic strategies have been the offshoots of these debates.

The study that sparked debate is Don Zimmerman and Candace West's (1975) 'Sex roles, interruptions and silences in conversation,' which set forth a strategy new to CA:

1. *Select a certain kind of utterance as a dependent variable.* In this study, interruptions were one of the dependent variables of interest.
2. *Count the number of these utterances with the intent of making a statistical comparison.*
3. *Pre-establish the categories of people whose use of this utterance you want to compare.* In this study, the independent variable was gender. The study thus set out to compare how men and women speak in cross-gender conversations.

Zimmerman and West concluded that men's greater control over how commodities were distributed at a societal level was manifest at the interactional level in men's overwhelmingly and significantly greater control over the distribution of time and attention in talk. (For other important exemplars of this strategy, see Fishman, 1978, as well as Ridgeway's body of work on status in group processes, e.g., Ridgeway, 1997.)

Although Zimmerman and West called their study a conversation analysis, many other conversation analysts begged to differ. Point by point, the objections have included:

1. That it ran the risk of glossing utterances that were superficially similar. Recall that in Chapter 5, we'd seen Goldberg (1990) take up the complexities of working with overlaps and interruptions; in fact, she'd done so as part of questioning Zimmerman and West's conclusions. Some researchers from outside the CA paradigm have responded to such objections by *borrowing more from CA so as to add greater nuance to the categories of utterances that they're comparing* (e.g., Gibson, 2008; Okamoto and Smith-Lovin, 2001) ...
2. ... but conversation analysts don't borrow back. The objection here is that, as mentioned earlier, in CA's established epistemology, a universe of moral ordering can be revealed by looking carefully enough at a single grain of sand (Schegloff, 1995), an isolated 'huh' or out-breath. Many conversation analysts regard statistical comparison of aggregated data as beside the point, or acceptable only when it doesn't involve glossing.

3. That to presuppose that social scientists' categories are the ones that matter flies in the face of CA's disciplined curiosity about what members orient to. Schegloff had articulated the criteria of relevance and procedural consequentiality partly in response to Zimmerman and West, pressing the question we mentioned earlier: if a man interrupts a woman and neither demonstrably orients to gender, who's to say that it's gender that matters?

This last point has proven the most vexing, causing some feminists to question whether CA, thus formulated, can be germane to their aims (see Speer, 1999). Among them, Margaret Wetherell (1998) has asked whether it is truly possible or worthwhile for CA to set itself apart from earlier social scientific thought. And, Michael Billig (1999) has asked: if a man rapes a woman and neither of them speaks in a way that demonstrably orients to gender, could a conversation analyst recognize that gendered relations of power are pertinent to the rape? Billig's question illustrates a view you will see is typical among discourse analysts: that power relations are pervasive, even if they are not instantiated in a specific moment of talk.

However, many feminists consider feminism and CA to be complementary. In an influential article, Celia Kitzinger (2000) points out that Billig does not hold a monopoly on feminism. She reasons that ethnomethodology, CA, and an important strand of feminist thought have converged in understanding gender to be situationally produced and performed, rather than an essence that inheres in individuals (e.g., Butler, 1990; Garfinkel, 1967: 116–85, 285–8; West and Zimmerman, 1987). Kitzinger maintains that an insistence on identifying members' orientations requires feminists to squarely address an issue long troubling to them, namely, that the women whose accounts of experience they wish to respect and validate do not always speak of themselves as oppressed. Further, Kitzinger offers an example of how Sacks's (1995: 185–6) attentive analysis of a conversation between two white women about a 'colored' lady showed their talk to orient to white privilege even though they did not name this phenomenon themselves. Via this example, Kitzinger endorses CA's tenets, at the same time as she reminds conversation analysts of the subtlety with which the most canonical of CA works had applied them.

The strategy that has emerged from all this retains from Zimmerman and West (1975) the element of preselecting a variable that matters to social scientists. But, instead of setting out to compare how different categories of speakers talk, the strategy is *to investigate how members orient to this variable, and with what consequence*. Some studies focus on the pervasiveness of assumptions of heterosexism (e.g., Braun, 2000; Land and Kitzinger, 2005) or, in the United States and United Kingdom, of whiteness (e.g., Whitehead and Lerner, 2009; Wilkinson, 2011). Closely related is the concept of the **omnirelevance** of gender, a term that Garfinkel used to characterize how gender is treated as ubiquitously salient in daily activities. Research in this vein is exemplified by Weatherall's (2002) study of talk-in-interaction in a crèche in New Zealand, where four-year-old boys repeatedly repaired how they spoke of one of the figurines in a toy train set (see Textbox 6.3).

Textbox 6.3: It's a her

246 BON: [see he's]dead eh? have to take him to
247 your [hospital eh?]
248 ROS: [.hhh that's] a her
249 BON: him=
250 ROS: =it's a her (2)
251 BON: did your cousin say?
252 ROS: yeah (.) so it's a her

Source: Weatherall, 2002: 773

This and other instances of the children's talk supported Weatherall's conclusion that repair was a mechanism through which gender's omnirelevance became demonstrable to CA standards.

The sensitivities of talk about race and sexualities, and how speakers negotiate them, have also attracted analysts. Kitzinger (2000) provides a valuable discussion of how lesbians utilize turn construction and topicalization devices so as to come out unobtrusively in the midst of turns that quickly open up another topic. Doing so, Kitzinger theorizes, forestalls others' blundering commentary and accusations that the lesbian speakers are parading their sexuality. Regarding race, Whitehead (2009) alerts us to the competing demands on today's normatively non-racist speakers: to not subscribe to essentialist notions of race, to reference race when it's relevant to social inequalities, and to anticipate how others' categorization of one's own race will figure into how one's talk is heard. Whitehead demonstrates how these demands give rise to devices such as mentioning race as though it were an afterthought, and thereby help to publicly reproduce racial structures even if they're privately disavowed.

While this approach has seemed to satisfactorily integrate the CA paradigm with feminist and similar research agendas, *the debates continue*. Susan Ehrlich (2002), for example, has used transcripts from a Canadian sexual assault case that poses a pair of enigmas for feminist conversation analysts. The first is that, in shades of Michael Billig's scenario, the complainant and defendant did not demonstrably orient to gender in their testimony. The second is that the judge – a non-speaking recipient of this testimony – nonetheless did orient to gender in his judgment. How was it that he heard gender to be relevant when a conversation analysis did not? Ehrlich's study, while firmly based in the CA paradigm and its standards, suggest that in sticking to what the speakers demonstrably *say*, something of what they *do* or *mean* may be lost.

Textbox 6.4: A Summary of Strategies for Engaging with CA and its Alternatives

- Preselect categories of speakers and statistically compare their uses of various types of utterances. (Though, be aware that this is not generally considered CA!)
- Select a social inequality variable and observe how members orient to it, and with what consequence.
- Contribute to the debates about the use of social inequality categories in CA.

CHAPTER SUMMARY

Many social scientists pose research questions related to gender, race, sexuality, class, (dis)ability, and other social categories, and are interested in applying conversation analysts' nuanced analytic strategies to these questions. This chapter has sketched out the main avenues for doing so. As proposed by Harvey Sacks in his lectures, the membership categorization analysis avenue is attentive to how categories emerge in interaction, how members negotiate the predicates attached to categories, and how they thereby do moral, identity, or other interactive work. The second avenue begins with a caution sign, erected by conversation analysts as they debated Zimmerman and West's (1975) strategy of quantitatively comparing groups' use of a mechanism of talk, and linking that comparison to social forces. Though this strategy has been adopted elsewhere in social scientific studies of interaction, conversation analysts reject it. Instead, they prefer to observe the multiplicity of ways that members may orient to a social category as they talk, and to understand the consequences.

SEVEN

Institutional Talk-in-interaction

CA's shift in focus from everyday conversation to all talk-in-interaction has opened the door into many institutions, from classrooms to airplane cockpits, doctor's offices to talk radio shows, helplines to Alcoholics Anonymous Meetings, and more. A remarkable amount of the work of institutions gets done primarily through talk, and it's hard to imagine work that gets done without any talk at all. As Maynard and Clayman (1991) explain, the central research questions guiding studies of institutional talk-in-interaction are: How is talk-in-interaction implicated in getting the work of institutions done? How are the mechanics of institutional talk consequentially like or unlike those of ordinary conversation?

LEARNING THE BASICS OF INSTITUTIONAL TALK-IN-INTERACTION

To answer either question is to again begin with an analytic stance of curiosity, of initially suspending what one 'already knows' about an institution. Conversation analysts resist the social sciences' tendency to conceive of institutions as fixed structures where power and authority concentrate. Rather, in CA, institutional contexts such as 'the classroom' are understood to emerge through the turn-taking and sequential organization of talk-in-interaction, and thus are open to negotiation, conflict, and surprises. Take, for example, the March 2013 BBC interview in which presenter Chris Stark confessed to his guest, Hollywood star Mila Kunis, that he was terrified about interviewing her (BBC Radio 1, 2013). Kunis began to ask Stark sympathetic questions about his anxiety and, within seconds, was

learning his friends' nicknames and their favorite drink. For several minutes, the two ceased to talk 'the media interview' into being, to borrow Van De Mieroop and Clifton's (2012) expression.

In many analyses, the answers to research questions about institutional talk use ordinary conversation, such as Kunis and Stark lapsed into, as a baseline.[1] Asking precisely what's the same and what's different can help to focus an analysis. Importantly, in keeping with their conception of all social and institutional order as based upon the order of everyday talk-in-interaction, conversation analysts emphasize that much of how talk is sequentially organized does turn out to be the same as we had seen in Chapter 5: turn-taking, turn design, adjacency pairs, repair, extended sequences, and so forth are all to be found in institutions, though inflected in distinctive ways. Some of the differences that commonly matter are that institutional talk:

- Tends to be more explicitly goal-oriented, specialized, and attentive to the passage and meaning of time than ordinary talk. The express purpose of Stark and Kunis's encounter was for him to interview her about her recent film, for an audience's consumption during a program of specified duration.
- Is more explicitly oriented to rules pertaining to turn-taking and turn type than is everyday talk, whose mechanisms are taken more for granted. Among the earliest oddities of the Stark–Kunis interaction was that she, a guest, was putting a non-repair-related question to him, a media presenter.
- Involves participants whose identity categories are not collections of equals. Rather, categories such as media presenter and Hollywood star are predicated on asymmetries in knowledges, entitlements, obligations, and so forth. As we've seen in the discussion of MCA in Chapter 6, the predicates of categories, and the relevance of a given category to a given moment, are fluid and negotiable.
- The lexical choices – that is, choices of vocabulary – are sensitive to how speakers may be representing an institution or to how they orient to the institutional work to be done. In asking Stark a question about 'football,' Kunis overtly distinguishes it from 'soccer,' demonstrating that, although she is American, she is orienting to Stark as the representative of a UK institution.

The densely layered knowledges of some institutions have given rise to the analytic strategy of *drawing on members' accounts of what they are doing through their talk, and why*. (This would be odd in CA of everyday talk, in which members are not expected to be wise to the infinitesimal details of their ways.) Leudar et al. (2008: 168) demonstrate how this strategy enhanced their analysis

---

[1] Arminen (2000) comments that conversation analysts have found it difficult to define **institution**. They end up defining **institutional talk-in-interaction** by what it isn't: **ordinary conversation**, with its freedoms of topic, turn allocation, and turn lengths (Arminen, 2000: 442).

of how a therapist responded to a boy named Abu, who had been banging at his modeling clay and roaring at other children in his play therapy group. On their own, the conversation analysts had been able to gather that the therapist considered Abu to be behaving aggressively. However, by reading the diary of a trainee therapist who'd been on the scene, the conversation analysts came to realize that therapists would account for Abu's behavior not only in terms of aggression, but also of compulsion and fear. Returning to the recordings, the conversation analysts could then perceive how this interpretation was procedurally consequential in nuancing the therapist's utterances to Abu and the other children.

It's important to note that this strategy does not have to swallow members' insights, hook, line, and sinker. Instead, Peräyklä and Vehviläinen (2003) show that it can lead to productive and sometimes startling *comparisons between what members do and what's prescribed in their* ***stocks of interactional knowledge***, i.e., institutional training materials, such as manuals and other forms of instruction. An example is Tamah Sherman's (2010) use of instructional materials in which Mormon missionaries are told that referring to their faith in their opening statement will be an effective way to proselytize to a new contact. Sherman, however, found that the missionaries whom she studied in the Czech Republic uniformly refrained from utilizing this device, and instead hedged toward the faith topic, avoiding an oppositional us-versus-them dynamic. Thus, in the field, the missionaries were setting aside a prescription contained in their stock of institutional knowledge.

Textbox 7.1: A Summary of Strategies Based on Understanding the Basics of Institutional Talk-in-interaction

- Make use of members' accounts.
- Compare what happens in interaction to what's prescribed in stocks of interactional knowledge.

ANALYZING HOW INSTITUTIONAL WORK GETS DONE IN STAGES

If we were to map out the stages of an ordinary conversation, we wouldn't get far: there are usually greetings, there is the raising of a first topic... and what might happen between that and the farewells is anyone's guess. In contrast, working through institutional goals can involve orienting to, and 'talking into being,' various more predictable stages of interaction. In acute care visits to doctors, typical stages are the opening, presentation of a problem, the gathering

of data through history taking and an examination, diagnosis, treatment, and the closing, though there can be variations, e.g., when a patient presents more than one problem (Heritage and Clayman, 2010). A call to an emergency service typically proceeds from an opening in which the complaint-taker and caller align their identities to the service, to a request/complaint, to a joint understanding of the trouble, to a response/remedy offer, and finally a closing (Zimmerman, 1984).

Studying *how parties to an interaction orient (or don't orient) to the stages of an established model, and to what effect,* is a common analytic strategy. We can look at examples for the pair of stage models we have just mapped out. In the diagnostic interview, Gill and colleagues (2010) discover how patients, alert to the brevity of medical visits and oriented to their conventional stages, may go about 'frontloading' their requests, i.e. presenting their own interpretations of their symptoms while the doctor is still at the phase of taking the history. Meanwhile, Garcia and Parmer (1999) use Zimmerman's model of emergency call-stages to unravel how a 911 emergency service call went so wrong that police took 45 minutes to arrive at the scene of a reported shooting of a pair of undercover officers. Although blame for the delay was heaped on the call-taker's head, Garcia and Parmer show the citizen caller, Melvin Smith, to have played a substantial part in it, especially in the crucial opening phase (see Textbox 7.2).

Textbox 7.2: Nine one one?

CT = call taker

MS = Melvin Smith

1 CT: ((click)) =*<u>nine</u> one one.*

2 (0.4)

3 MS: nine one one? 'h=needs U::H (0.2) .h I need=uh (0.3)

4 uh shots fired at twenny two west hanover street.

Source: Garcia and Parmer, 1999: 310

Garcia and Parmer observe that Smith begins his first turn by initiating a repair ('nine one one?') that does not convey the urgency typical of 911 calls. He later switches from a turn construction unit in which he seeks help for himself ('I need') to a turn construction unit about a problem ('shots fired') for which he does not. Moreover, Smith's turn is indistinguishable from what he might say if he'd heard a car backfiring. Garcia and Parmer's analysis is enriched by facts that

they import from outside the talk-in-interaction, specifically, that the shots had been fired into people who were in Smith's view, indoors, and within his own apartment. These facts and Smith's aim of obfuscating his relation to the shooting become procedurally consequential, in this first turn of his and then repeatedly as the call proceeds.

When a new institution is being investigated, mapping the stages of its interactions with the public can be a substantial contribution of itself. A study we mentioned earlier – Sherman's (2010) analysis of how Mormon missionaries from the USA proselytize to strangers in the Czech Republic – is fascinating because it troubles the boundary between ordinary and institutional talk-in-interaction: at first only the missionaries, but not their contacts, are aware of the institutional goal in play. Sherman discerns an initial stage in which the missionaries come to be recognized as members of identity categories unrelated to faith, e.g., as stranger, foreigner, or volunteer. Then comes a stage of their being recognized as missionaries – the one that the missionaries, as mentioned, hedge toward. Next comes a stage in which the missionaries attempt to topicalize faith, for Sherman also notices how their mentions of their jobs do not suffice to make faith a topic. In the final stage, the missionaries seek to ensure future contact.

Throughout Sherman's study, it is the cusps between stages that stand out as analytically rich. But maybe that's putting it the wrong way. Maybe a stage model does not always discover stages that are already there but instead makes analytically salient those moments that are most fraught, that involve the most interactional accomplishment and effort. Sherman could easily have proposed a model in which the first two stages were collapsed into 'introduction,' or the second and third were collapsed into 'mentioning faith,' but that would have been far less interesting. Heritage and Clayman (2010: 110–17) likewise draw our attention to complexities of how doctors and patients transition from a problem presentation to a history taking.

Finally, emphasis on talk that moves institutional goals forward might be taken to suggest that other talk, of the small talk or phatic communion variety, obstructs those goals. Rather, we recommend the strategy of considering *how such talk is oriented to institutional talk-in-interaction*. For instance, Zimmerman (1998) has shown that in emergency service calls, callers who give conventional greetings and make small talk become accountable by call-takers as lacking in urgency. In other settings, changes of footing in and out of small talk attract attention. Beck and Ragan (1992) show how, while conducting a physical exam, a nurse practitioner can shift frames between person-oriented and medical-oriented talk, as shown in lines 68–69 of Textbox 7.3.

Beck and Ragan theorize that the nurse practitioner is effecting an affiliative move in a situation full of potential discomforts. Projects such as this can be linked to feminist sociologist Arlie Hochschild's (1983) insight that emotional labor is a significant form of labor.

Textbox 7.3: Moving to Denver

P = patient

NP = nurse practitioner

64	NP:	Um:m (.) best time though >like I said< is check one=
65		=week after your period >cuz right before< your=
66		=period your breasts >gets more lumpy anyway< (.)=
67		=but tha week after (.) and your breasts >are less=
68		=lumpy < okay^ (.) there ya go. (.2) okay (.2) you're =
69		=moving to Denver^
70	P:	Mm hmm
71	NP:	(Blood pressure pump sound) (.4) o:h (hhh) I bet you're=
72		=(.) just >can't wait<

Source: Beck and Ragan, 1992: 52

Textbox 7.4: A Summary of Strategies for Analyzing How Institutional Work Gets Done in Stages

- Study how parties to an interaction orient, or don't orient, to what an established stage model predicts, and to what effect.
- Map out a stage model for a new institution.
- Consider the relation of small talk to talk that is explicitly oriented to institutional goals.

STUDYING TURN-TAKING WITHIN INSTITUTIONS

Contrasting turn-taking in an institution's talk-in-interaction to that of ordinary conversation, and asking whether and how it achieves the 'normal' functioning and constitution of the institution is a reasonable strategy for the conversation analyst. In ordinary conversation, turns are said to be allocated locally (Sacks et al., 1974: 729–30), i.e., sorted out in the moment amongst those present. As Heritage and Clayman (2010) explain, in many institutional contexts, members orient to specialized systems of turn-taking and allocation that configure opportunities for action. In some systems, such as in courtroom trials, the

actions and turns are **pre-allocated** in relation to institutional norms. In other systems, such as that of a chaired meeting, a specific individual mediates the allocation of turns. Turn allocation systems can also combine the two, as in marriage counseling in which a counselor questions the couple and 'referees' their talk.

Heritage and Clayman's (2010) discussion of news interviews is especially valuable for showing how the different components of turn-taking and sequential organization entwine. Because the paramount institutional goal is to gain information, the news interviewer scripts her talk using question–answer adjacency pairs to bring this goal to fruition. Orienting to this convention can inhibit interviewees' responses. In ordinary conversation, they could leap in at transition-relevance places but in a news interview, they tend to align with the institutional goal and wait for questions to finish being posed. Moreover, it is common for interviewers to use **statement-prefaced questions**, i.e., to preface their questions with background information so as to be clear to interviewees and to inform the overhearing audience. As Heritage and Clayman explain, the ancillary goal of orienting to an overhearing audience also shapes the interviewer's neutrality, to the point that the interviewer ideally does not even offer **acknowledgement tokens** such as 'oh' (Heritage, 1984), because judgments may be read into their intonation. As we will be discussing extensively in Chapter 8, the research interview has its own distinctive turn-taking rules, related to the institutional goals of data collection and subsequent analysis.

How turn-construction units, transition-relevance places, silences, and overlaps have institution-specific consequences can also be a focus of analysis. In Chapter 5, for instance, we'd seen reference to how a spiritual medium and her client systematically use overlaps in ways that produce the medium's identity. In another example, Ford and Stickle (2012) alert us to the multiple modes of work that members do in order to obtain a turn and others' recipiency in workplace meetings in which a chair mediates turn-allocation. In the meetings they studied, leaning forward or clearing one's throat were oriented to as signs of a desire to speak. Pausing at length after beginning to speak was a tactic they observed being used to garner other members' attention; interestingly, in ordinary conversation, in which turn allocation is not mediated, this could instead signal a transition-relevance place in which other members could begin turns.

Ford and Stickle's example also reminds us of the importance of gesture as a component of talk-in-interaction, and leads into a question that ethnomethodologists, the intellectual cousins of conversation analysts, have raised: whether what is encompassed by talk-in-interaction always suffices as an object of inquiry. All talk is action, but not all action is talk, they argue – a point that is key in studies centered on *work*, rather than on the contrasts between ordinary and institutional *talk* (see Maynard and Clayman, 1991, for a discussion).

A compelling proponent of this point is Maurice Nevile (2004), who explains how airplane pilots go about an approach briefing, i.e., reviewing their plan for a safe landing. The two pilots' interaction involves not only the pilot-flying's talk but also their writing of notes and setting of markers on the equipment displays, in what can be understood to be a series of embodied and accountable claims to the other pilot. In the turn-taking system, the pilot-flying's silences are not transition-relevance places but filled with action, while the other pilot's silences do not mark him as passive, so much as attentively participating in joint work that prevents an airplane crash. The analytic strategy here, which is not limited to turn-taking matters per se, is to *complement CA with observation-based ethnomethodological analysis of sense-making practices.* Because conversation analysts often shun the researcher glosses that observation involves, scholars going this route address the two methods' distinct contributions, rather than stealthily uniting them.

Perhaps the examples presented so far will give the impression that CA is more prone to look in a functionalist spirit for a close concordance between institutional goals and turn-taking systems than to look for discord. Not so. Schegloff (1988/89) famously studied a CBS news interview-turned-confrontation that occurred between anchor Dan Rather and then-US Vice President George H.W. Bush. Schegloff showed how, even when they were loudly talking on top of one another and appeared to commentators to have abandoned the interview project, they were nonetheless attending closely to one another's utterances. Schegloff, like Chris Stark and Mila Kunis, reminds us of the proximity of institutional talk to ordinary conversation.

Textbox 7.5: A Summary of Strategies for Studying Turn-taking within Institutions

- Contrast turn-taking in institutional talk-in-interaction to that of ordinary conversation, asking whether and how it achieves the 'normal' functioning and constitution of the institution.
- Complement CA with ethnomethodological analyses of non-talk actions, noting that these are distinct methods.

ANALYZING OTHER MECHANISMS OF INSTITUTIONAL TALK

One analytic avenue is to observe how the usual mechanisms of sequentially organizing talk-in-interaction are systematically put to specific institutional ends. Speer and Parsons (2006) give the following example of a psychiatrist who is posing a question to a patient seeking sex/gender-reassignment surgery.

Textbox 7.6: It is only theoretical

14	Psy:→	[R:ight. [Now at this stage
15		I have a th:eoretical question to put to you.
16		(.)
17	Patient:	Yes.
18	Psy:	And it is only th:eoretical.
19	Patient:	Yes please do:
20		(0.6)
21	Psy: (1)→	Just suppo:se (0.6) th't (0.4) o:n surgical
22	(2)→	assessmen[t
23	Patient:	[Yes.
24		(0.2)
25	Psy:	Th't a reason emer:ged (.) that made it
26		impossible for you to go an- forward for surgery
27		(0.6)
28	Psy: (3)→	.Hh What would you do:

Source: Speer and Parsons, 2006: 793

In this sequence, Speer and Parsons say that the psychiatrist uses the mechanism of the pre-question to mark the potential sensitivity of what is to be asked. Indeed, by using a pre pre-question (lines 14–15), followed by a pre-question (lines 21–27), he gives this sensitivity extra emphasis. Importantly, his turns, including the pause at line 16, involve the patient, who comes to acknowledge that a question will be forthcoming and to align to the project of its being asked (lines 17, 19). The psychiatrist's reiterations that the question is 'theoretical' and the associated use of 'Just suppose' (line 21) cast the question onto safer terrain. This is ironic, Speer and Parson observe, given that the patient's answer will be used in the psychiatrist's gatekeeping about eligibility for gender/sex reassignment surgery.

A second analytic strategy asks whether the institutional talk-in-interaction shows a patterned use of distinctive mechanisms or ones that are uncommon in ordinary conversation. For instance, returning to Textbox 7.2, we can note that this emergency call service uses a greeting of 'nine one one' that turns out to be standardized. In contrast to the varied greetings possible in ordinary

conversation, this is an opening that simultaneously serves as an identification and moves the work of emergency service gatekeeping along. Meanwhile, Bailey and colleagues (2006) found that members of the bridge team of a merchant ship frequently used a novel adjacency pair of giving orders or information and then repeating them back. These researchers maintain that this adjacency pair makes it possible for members of the team to intersubjectively coordinate their work of maneuvering the ship, to which each of them is making a distinctive contribution.

A great deal of institutional work is done through questions and answers, from asking City Hall how to go about paying taxes to answering a doctor's question of whether a pain is dull or sharp. In many instances of institutional talk, as in ordinary conversation, we understand there to be an **epistemic gradient** in which questions are asked because the asker is **K-** (lacking in specific knowledge) and projects that the person being asked is **K+** (possessing that knowledge). And thus, the questioner might commonly offer an acknowledgement token, to show that the epistemic gradient has been leveled. An analytic strategy is to *observe how epistemic gradients are consequential.* For instance, in educational talk-in-interaction that uses the Socratic method, the epistemic gradient can run in the opposite direction. An instructor understood to be K+ poses questions to students who might be either K+ or K-, and follows up the answer with an evaluative third turn that has educational functions (McHoul, 1978). Here and elsewhere, what is distinctive about the sequence can reflect institutional goals.

One of the most interesting devices that appears more often in institutional talk-in-interaction than in ordinary conversation, save for conversations between adults and children (Forrester and Reason, 2006), is the **formulation**, an utterance in which a speaker re-presents what has been said earlier. A formulation can put the speaker's spin on the content, gisting it selectively, as when a therapist reframes a client's concerns or an attorney gives his summing up. In talk shows, as Hutchby (1996) explains, formulations become a powerful third turn in question–answer sequences. When a host takes a first turn that asks a caller for a second-turn opinion or information, the host is then poised to attack the caller's utterance in a third-turn formulation that produces talk radio's incendiary character. For an illustration, return to Textbox 6.1: Worse than *When Harry Met Sally*. Here, we can understand both lines 40–41, in which the neighbor is labeled abusive, and lines 45–46, in which the host proposes dousing her with water, as third-turn formulations that dramatically heighten the conflict being discussed.

In Ilkka Arminen's (1996) study of personal narratives given at Alcoholics Anonymous (AA) meetings, we see how turn allocation considerations and uses of the formulation entwine to institutional ends. Consider Textbox 7.7, which comes from the narrative of an AA member named Tapsa.

Textbox 7.7: Nothing to do with my disease

1 I was born into a: (0.3) working- hh class family (1.2) in which my father

2 was .kch a factory worker (3.0) and (0.5) that of course was

3 (.) how we lived (0.5) There wasn't much money at all(h) (0.6)

4→ but of course that .kch has nothing to do (0.8) with ↑my: disease

5 (.) And, of course, I was growing up in the middle of all that, u:h

6 up to age of ten, of which I recall very little. My mother . . .

Source: Arminen, 1996: 461, translation his

Analyzing this excerpt, Arminen brings in the Alcoholics Anonymous principle of taking responsibility for one's recovery, and shows it to be relevant and procedurally consequential. Specifically, Tapsa uses a formulation of 'but of course that .kch has nothing to do (0.8) with ↑my: disease' to orient to his listeners, anticipating the possibility that they might be hearing him to be blaming his alcoholism on his background. That Tapsa inserts this formulation into his talk, rather than waiting to hear what his listeners might say, Arminen explains in terms of the AA practice of taking long, monologic, uninterrupted turns. (Incidentally, the use of 'disease' in this example is also a lexical choice in keeping with the Alcoholics Anonymous medical model.)

The most applied strategy of all is *to use CA diagnostically*. Booth and Perkins (1999) provide a valuable case study in their analysis of the interactions between two men: JB, who had acquired aphasia after his aneurysm ruptured, and his brother, RB. These researchers wanted to understand what was constraining JB from putting topics on the floor when he spoke with RB. They found that repair of JB's utterances occupied a majority of the brothers' conversational turns. For instance, when JB mispronounced 'physiotherapy' as 'sðwðz/ therapy or somethin' erm' (ð being the phonetics symbol for the 'th' sound in 'this'), RB attempted to elicit a correct pronunciation from him, leading into 79 turns of repair. RB's emphasis on protracted other-correction, in concert with JB's impaired speech production and comprehension, meant that JB's identities as aphasic and as a pupil in need of correction were perpetually talked into being; his identity as a conversant who might want to raise a topic fell by the conversational wayside. After a CA-guided intervention, the brothers learned to effect repairs more collaboratively and only as necessary, reducing the situational production of JB's aphasic identity.

Diagnostic research can also assess how talk-in-interaction is implicated in whether institutional ends are being met. We've already referred to an instance of this in Chapter 5: Nakane's (2011) exploration of why police interrogations go awry when an interpreter is involved. Greatbatch and Dingwall's (1999) analysis of how the topic of violence between spouses can come to be marginalized in mediation

sessions is another instance. Using the content in Textbox 7.8, these authors propose that the mediator's marginalization of this topic can be understood to be picking up on the wife's.

Textbox 7.8: If you can sort of hit your wife

H = husband

W = wife

M2 = one of two mediators

H I think this is where we inevitably hit the stumbling
block and sort of
(1.2)
W I th- I think another point is that .hh if you can sort of hit
your wi:fe .hh for what's ((Clears throat)) considered
(0.5) uh:m
M2: .hhh Jane I'll stop you there. You- you- you're going into
what went wrong between you and not really where you're
both going now as parents. .hh and
continue to be as parents. .h Whoever gets custody.|
W: Mm:

Source: Greatbatch and Dingwall, 1999: 178

In Greatbatch and Dingwall's analysis, the wife's 'I think' and 'sort of' (line 13) can appear to dilute her commitment to the topic, her use of 'your wi:fe' rather than 'me' (line 14) has the effect of distancing her from the violence, and her 'if' trails away without a consequential 'then' being delivered (lines 13–15). In classic CA form, the authors concluded that what might on the surface appear to be a failing of the mediator was constructed in concert between the mediator and the wife. Rather differently from how discourse analysts might see it, Greatbatch and Dingwall contend that the mediators aren't marginalizing violence because of the power of their position or institution, so much as because violence is a marginalized topic in ordinary conversation. Observing this pattern repeatedly, these researchers present recommendations for how mediators could be better trained, e.g., to recognize how sensitive topics and violence in particular tend to be spoken of in tentative and minimizing ways. Thus, their work exemplifies the applied potential of institutional CA.

Our third applied example comes from Frith and Kitzinger (1998), who take up the social problem of women having unwanted sex with men. They use CA to critique assertiveness-training programs that address this problem by encouraging women to cease to do the emotional work of managing men's emotions, i.e., to cease to have sex out of feelings of guilt or generosity. Frith and Kitzinger observe that *what* young women say about unwanted sex makes these programs sound sensible and justified, but *how* they say it in interaction suggests otherwise. The young women studied depicted men as needy caricatures, while positioning themselves as emotionally capable and strong. In so doing, say Frith and Kitzinger, the women may be resisting how programs routinely depict them as victims for having unwanted sex. If women's talk of doing emotional labor is understood as a means of resisting assertiveness-training programs, then it fails to justify such programs. The authors conclude that in order to support women, programs of a different nature would be needed.

Textbox 7.9: A Summary of Strategies for Analyzing Other Mechanisms of Institutional Talk

- Observe how ordinary conversational mechanisms for sequentially organizing talk can systematically create institutional contexts or be put to institutional ends.
- Ask how distinctive or uncommon mechanisms are used toward institutional ends.
- Examine how epistemic asymmetries are consequential.
- Use CA to diagnose why talk-in-interaction fails to meet an institution's goals.

CHAPTER SUMMARY

That members' talk-in-interaction can constitute institutions ranging from mediation sessions to police interrogations makes CA a powerful tool for social scientists studying institutions. Conversation analysts have found members to use much the same mechanisms to sequentially organize their institutional talk-in-interaction as they use in their ordinary conversation; for instance, questions are still in an adjacency pair with answers. Thus, some CA work emphasizes how institutional talk-in-interaction hasn't fallen all that far from the tree of ordinary talk. Other CA strategies investigate what's distinctive about institutional talk-in-interaction. The answer to this question always is in terms of members' orientations to the existence of institutional goals, whether they subscribe to those goals or not. CA strategies show that this orientation is carried forth in how talk tends to get institutional work done, i.e., in how talk is organized into broad stages, in how specific turn-taking rules facilitate goal achievement; in how goal-related devices that would be atypical in ordinary talk-in-interaction are used; and more. Excitingly for applied researchers, CA can be used for the strategy of diagnosing how an institution can better meet its goals.

EIGHT

The Interview in Conversation Analysis

We saw in Chapter 4 that narrative analysts embrace the interview as an opportunity to access respondents' meanings, as co-constructed with interviewers. They inquire reflexively into how to better document meanings that are embodiedly transmitted and received in the interview, and into the impact of positionality and notions of a 'good story' on meanings. Although issues of representation and privilege trouble narrative analysts, their enthusiasm for the interview has not flagged.

Conversation analysts agree that interviews are joint productions. But, they would be skeptical about many NA strategies for studying how that works. Consistent with NA's overarching emphasis on humanism and on individuals' quests for meaning, narrative analysts' reflexivity tends to value the 'me' in 'methods,' including researchers' experiences of the interview and its Gestalt (see Smith et al., 2005). In contrast, conversation analysts reject data consisting of introspection about embodiment or about feelings that a story is newsworthy or liveable. In CA, data are strictly what's audible or visible in recordings, while introspection is put to the purpose of concertedly avoiding glosses or preemptive conclusions. On the whole, conversation analysts value a disciplined, detached form of **reflexivity**, according to the Chapter 5 definition of observing how one's self and one's methods are implicated in knowledge production.

Moreover, conversation analysts are rather cooler and more judicious than narrative analysts in their approach to the interview. What is it, they ask: Animal, vegetable, or mineral? Conversation or a form of institutional talk-in-interaction? Naturalistic or contrived? Useful or useless? The first set of strategies in this chapter reflect how these questions arose among conversation analysts and their intellectual kin, including those who draw on the interaction ritual of Erving Goffman, or on the ethnomethodology of Harold Garfinkel, which focuses on members' accounting practices.

Reading narrative analysts' conclusions that standpoints and positionality affect interviews, conversation analysts would reiterate the concerns of Chapter 6. Specifically, they would consider it ironic of researchers to foist academic categories onto respondents' talk at the very moment that they claim to be stricken about their privilege to represent others. Conversation analysts would instead demand evidence that members are indeed making what we've been calling social categories relevant and procedurally consequential as they talk. Conversation analysts also use membership categorization analysis strategies to discern what categories come to be mentioned in interviews, how the meanings of these categories and their predicates are negotiated, and what these processes accomplish in the local moment of interaction. All this gives rise to the second set of strategies that this chapter outlines. In them, you'll see that conversation analysts' detached reflexivity can definitely be put to value-laden, feminist ends.

For researchers with group interview data, conversation analysis and related approaches are extraordinarily helpful. Narrative analysts often seem to speak in general terms about the emotional climate of focus groups, the processes such as sharing or exclusion that can happen in them, and the contrasts between what group members reveal on their own versus in the group. The third set of strategies in this chapter draw on an important CA critique of analyses that prioritize the individual over the social, and examine how the niceties of group interaction have consequences for knowledge production.

PINNING DOWN THE QUALITATIVE RESEARCH INTERVIEW

The first landmark contribution that conversation analysts made to the study of the interview was not about qualitative interviewing, but about survey research. Suchman and Jordan (1990) demonstrated how the goals of standardized data collection and interpersonal interaction came into conflict. For instance, they showed how the rigors of questionnaire structure and wording prevented members from drawing on ordinary interactional resources, such as the capacity to determine the topics of talk and to design questions tailored to their recipients. Novice qualitative researchers who are put off by survey interviewing often assert that their new method will collect better data and meet the feminist criterion of being more egalitarian because these interviews are more like conversations. But are they?

Eleven co-authors who pondered their interview experiences with Erving Goffman in mind lead us to one avenue for thinking through the answer. Warren et al. (2003) discuss how interactions between interviewer and respondent typically change footing once the interviewer has posed all her questions. A respondent might change the topic to one that is relevant to both the interviewer and himself, such as to talk about their personal connection; a respondent might decide to pursue his agenda, speak off the record, prolong the interaction with a sudden revelation, or bolt away. The very fact of such a sea

change, propelled by the respondents, tells us that the interview is no ordinary conversation. Its timing, topics, and turn-taking are not entirely spontaneously and emergently negotiated between two or more members. If your objective is to conduct interviews as conversationally as possible, then a rough-and-ready Goffmanesque strategy for testing your success is to *check for changes in footing after the interview.*

Looking at the differences more minutely, conversation analysts would characterize a qualitative interview as institutional talk-in-interaction. That it might take place outside the academy, as you sit at a kitchen table or lie on the grass of a park, makes it no less institutional. The point is that the institution of the interview is 'talked into being' by interviewers and respondents, who orient to conventions that are distinct from those of ordinary conversation. Here are a few of them:

- The likely duration of many qualitative research interviews is set forth in informed consent documents.
- The talk is occasioned by the research goals of the interviewer, even if these are so loosely sketched as 'finding out your experiences of owning ferrets.'
- In a focus group, even if respondents do begin to talk amongst themselves, the moderator has more of an entitlement than other participants to allocate turns.
- The talk's sequential organization involves many questions posed by the interviewer (Rapley, 2001). As in the survey interview, these need not be preceded by pre-questions, even if the topics are delicate ones.
- Questions are the first pair part of an adjacency pair, so respondents are strongly expected to produce the second pair part – the answers. Otherwise, the respondents become accountable. They might account for not answering in a number of ways, such as by asking for clarification (a form of repair) or by saying 'I don't want to answer.' Although ethics documents specify that refusing to answer is possible, it's not interactionally structured to be the default.

What interviewers do once a respondent has uttered an answer to a question is a goldmine of analytic interest to conversation analysts. It's at this juncture, say Mazeland and ten Have (1996), that tensions emerge between whether the respondent's utterance is to be understood as a way in which she makes sense of her lifeworld, or as a turn in the present interaction, or as a datum for future analysis. As Mazeland and ten Have explain, because qualitative interviewers are usually trained to enact neutrality in the 'good interview,' they conventionally reply to respondents with turns such as:

- Remaining silent. Doing so at a transition-relevance place acts as a **continuer**, signaling to the respondent that she should continue with her turn. Interviewers take turns that invite fuller, more extensive answers because at the analysis stage, the length of an answer serves as a proxy for its validity.
- Saying 'uh huh,' or recycling part of the answer. These turns signal that the knowledge is already shared or that it can readily enter the stock of shared knowledge. These turns again act as continuers.

- Saying 'oh' – an answer receipt that acknowledges that the respondent's utterance was newsworthy ... and, yes, it's another continuer.
- Providing a formulation that summarizes or interprets the respondent's answers. As the first pair part of an adjacency pair, the interviewer's formulation calls for the respondent to provide the second pair part, a decision about the formulation's adequacy. Therapists often use rapport-building formulations (e.g., 'that must have been upsetting'), while debaters and lawyers often use confrontational ones. But in research interviews, neutral-sounding formulations are popular, with the preferred decision being one of agreement. In using these formulations, interviewers orient to the future analysis of the interview data, during which summaries and interpretations that the respondent has already validated will come in handy.
- Avoiding comments such as 'I totally agree with you!' Interviewers don't commonly overtly agree with respondents, although they do often ask respondents to concur with their formulations (Koole, 2004).

Despite all this, as Rapley (2001) puts it, 'there is a difference between "doing facilitative and neutral" and "being facilitative and neutral"' (p. 316). Therefore, conversation analysts are quite interested in reflexively *exploring how members' orientations to the conventions of interview shape the knowledge an interview produces.* Rapley (2001) offers the elegant example of a teenage respondent who goes from speaking of types of drugs in general terms to confessing his past drug use only because the interviewer prompts him with 1.4 seconds of silence.

Textbox 8.1 shows an extended illustration from an interview conducted with Alfredo, an English as a Foreign Language student in the United States. In Roulston and colleague's (2001) analysis of this transcript, Alfredo initially presents a strong complaint that culminates in saying that Americans '<u>think</u> the US is the world' (line 36). As the interview proceeds, we see this complaint becoming softened by degrees. The interviewer presents Alfredo with a gentler formulation, 'you don't feel like they're open mi:nded' (line 37), which elicits his decision to agree (line 38). Then, the complaint becomes reconfigured so that it points the finger at American institutions, rather than at Americans per se. The interviewer is fully involved in inviting and co-producing this reconfiguration. She offers frequent 'mm's that serve as continuers (lines 41, 43, 45), and even begins to pin the blame on elementary and high school education (line 47).

Conversation analysts sometimes employ this strategy to demonstrate the flaws of **thematic analysis**, an approach in which the main ideas of what respondents say are summarized, while the supposedly neutral questions and probes of interviewers are swept under the analytic rug. Kathryn Roulston (2001, citing ethnomethodologist Smith, 1974), uses this strategy to demonstrate how thematic analysis goes about abstracting a person's talk from its social context, finding norms or other kinds of order in the aggregate of this talk, and then tautologically 'discovering' that order as the cause of what people say. Meanwhile, Jeffrey Aguinaldo (2012) applies it to propose that although thematic analysis might appear to address dilemmas of representation, such as we discussed in Chapter 4,

Textbox 8.1: You don't feel like they're open minded

A = Alfredo, the respondent

R = the interviewer

33.	A	=they don't know wh- what language is speaking but (here)
34.		they do not they just know about the US
35.	R	mm
36.	A	and they <u>think</u> the US is the world
37.	R	mm you don't feel like they're open mi:nded and
38.	A	yes
39.	R	mm hmm
40.	A	yes sometimes they try they try to [be friendly with with foreign [people
41.	R	[mmuhhuh [mm
42.	A	but it's not their fault [(.) it's not their fault
43.	R	[mm mm hm
44.	A	maybe the the the problem is their tk educational [program in the US
45.	R	[mm
46.	A	they don't receive a good education in
47.	R	elementary [and high school
48.	A	[in the elementaria high school maybe they have to
49.		improve their history and geography
50.	R	mm hmm

Source: Roulston et al., 2001: 764–5

by putting respondents' voices front and center, conversation analysis is superior at detecting how those voices are contingent on the interactional context in which they're elicited.

At the same time as thematic analysis has been criticized by conversation analysts for its inadequate reflexivity, discursive psychologists have been saying the same of conversation analysts who use interviewing data. We'll explain this critique shortly. But first, some explanations for readers wondering, 'Who are discursive psychologists? Don't they belong in the discourse analysis part of this book?' Yes, we'll meet them again there, but they are also relevant here.

Discursive psychology was developed by Derek Edwards and Jonathan Potter (1992), psychologists who distrusted their discipline's **cognitivism**, i.e., its assumption that attitudes, beliefs, personality traits, knowledges, values, intentions, and so forth were fixed properties of individual minds, ready for psychologists to extract. Instead of administering a test that shows someone to be an introvert, for example, discursive psychologists would ask what is accomplished in interaction when someone is called introverted, or when the notion of personality is invoked. Discursive psychologists have one foot in the CA camp because they borrow from CA's meticulous tools for studying how *forms* of talk (such as pauses or formulations) constitute action. They put these tools to the purpose of asking what talk with psychologically related *content* accomplishes. This interest in the relation of content to social action gives them a foot in the DA camp as well.

Some discursive psychologists have been examining how the psychologically related content of interviews is implicated in shaping knowledge production (Potter, 2002; Potter and Hepburn, 2005). These researchers point out:

- Asking about respondents' thoughts, feelings, and attitudes infuses the interview with cognitivism, and detracts from what's relevant to the respondent within his lifeworld. One's stated thoughts and feelings about owning a ferret are hardly the same as one's lived experience of it. This criticism gives a pinpoint focus to an earlier CA suspicion that interviews are too imbued with researchers' categories to be useful.
- The qualitative interviewer is generally understood to be invested in the topic that they're asking about. But, when we consider that interactants manage questions of investment or stakes as they talk, it's implausible to expect respondents to report dispassionately on a topic to an interviewer who plainly has much at stake in it.
- The identity category that respondents understand themselves to have been recruited to fill can impact knowledge production, e.g., ferret owners might speak differently if they understand themselves to be participating in interviews as ferret aficionados, than if they are recruited as illegal possessors of ferrets. (Bischoping and Dykema [1999] have similarly remarked that focus group participants may well take cues about what social category they are expected to represent by looking around the room at the other participants.)

The list goes on, its complexities compounding – so much so that Potter and Hepburn (2005) propose that interviews are too contrived to be a viable source of data about any topic other than methods.

Earlier, Potter (2002) had even contended that social scientists should prefer naturalistic data that passes his **dead social scientist's test**, which asks, 'would the data be the same, or be there at all, if the researcher got run over on the way to work?' (p. 541); the interview would clearly be excluded. This is definitely a provocation to the discipline of psychology, in which interview data are ubiquitous and reflexivity is in short supply. However, many conversation analysts would say it's jumping the gun. Among them, Susan Speer (2002a, 2002b) rejects Potter's plan to make a priori judgments about whether data is naturalistic or contrived and therefore useful or worthless, and instead advocates following the CA tradition of being curious about whether members orient to the interview method as procedurally consequential.

Textbox 8.2: I've got dodgy ankles

Mod 1 = the moderator, Speer

Ben = the respondent

→ Mod 1: >What do you think o' that one ↓then?<
(1.0)
Ben: Lovely
(0.8)
→ Mod 1: Well what's going on in it?
(0.6)
Ben: It's a male ballet dancer
(.)
→ Mod 1: Ri↑ght (1.2) Would you do ↑that?
(0.6)
Ben: Er:m (1.4) no I've got dodgy ankles.
Mod 1: Hhhmm
(2.0)
Ben: But if I ↑could, (.) then I prob'ly would. (1.6) If I:
(1.0) was interested in it.
→ Mod 1: Do you think though that it breaks stereotypes at
all?
(.)
Ben: No
(.)
→ Mod 1: It doesn't?
(.)
Ben: [No]
→ Mod 1: [I] mean some people would say that he's a 'poof ' or
something.
(0.4)
Ben: I think that some people would.
(.)
→ Mod 1: But you wouldn't?
(.)
Ben: ↑No.

Source: Speer, 2002c: 795

Speer (2002c) applies this tradition in a strategy of *assessing interviewing methods that attempt to level researcher's privilege vis-à-vis respondents*. Her examples come from discussions, individual interviews, and focus groups in which participants were given photo prompts showing men and women breaking, or abiding by, gender stereotypes. The limitations of this method are revealed in Speer's reflexive analyses of passages such as Textbox 8.2, in which the interview moderator has prompted a respondent named Ben with a photo showing a male ballet dancer.

In Speer's analysis, Ben's minimal comment of 'Lovely' (line 3), the moderator's waiting silence (line 4), and the line 5 prompt, which conveys that Ben has not yet met the moderator's expectations, immediately signal that there is interactional trouble at hand. The moderator's line 9 'Would you do ↑that?' further presses Ben to either envision himself in the picture or to give a dispreferred response of 'No.' When Ben utters that dispreferred response (line 11), he is accountable for doing so. His account of having 'dodgy ankles' (line 11) is conspicuously neutral about men as ballet dancers. That the moderator interprets it as hedging is seen in how she then embarks on a multi-turn effort to elicit a gendered commentary from Ben (lines 16 to 29), but his hedging continues. Ironically, it is the moderator who introduces the homophobic term 'poof' (line 24) into the talk. All in all, Speer concludes, this talk-in-interaction reads as though Ben's character is being put to a test, and not as though his opinions are being invited to flow free. The photo prompt method here proved antithetic to its feminist objective.

Textbox 8.3: A Summary of Strategies for Pinning Down the Qualitative Research Interview

- If your objective is to conduct a 'conversational' interview, check for changes in footing after the interview.
- Explore how members' orientations to conventions of interview talk, and particularly to interviewers' performances of neutrality, shape the knowledge produced.
- Use discursive psychology to examine how psychology-related factors such as cognitivism and stakes/interests affect knowledge production.
- Assess interviewing methods that seek to level privilege.

ASKING WHAT TALK ABOUT CATEGORIES ACCOMPLISHES

The MCA strategy of *asking how, and to what effect, the attachment of predicates to categories is negotiated*, is a valuable one for reflexivity because when interviewers

or respondents put forth such attachments, they are making knowledge claims. Amber's interview with a woman named Sam, conducted as part of her study of the support networks of people living in poverty, contains an example (see Textbox 8.4).

Textbox 8.4: A little squarehead

Sam: I started using hard core illicit drugs. And you know one day my
mom showed up at my door, she goes 'I know you're using, I don't
want to hear it, get me a 50 piece.' So, 'you didn't tell my little
brothers did you?' No, she didn't tell my little brothers. So I got
her a 50 piece and she stayed.
Amber: What's a 50 piece? [You have to
Sam: [It's crack cocaine.
Amber: Got it, you've got to fill me in here.
Sam: We have a little squarehead.
Amber: I totally am. Believe me I think the most I ever did in my life was
marijuana and that was really fun. That was it. I fully admit it, that's
why you've got to fill me in.
Sam: Okay. Yeah.

In this passage, Sam's answer (lines 1–5) does not lead Amber to ask about a new topic, but rather to initiate a request for Sam to repair her confusion about what a '50 piece' is (line 6). Looking at this, we can first recall that self-initiation of repair is preferred, while other-initiation of repair, as Amber enacts here, is a mild snub, pointing to Sam's failure to maintain the shared intersubjectivity. Further, that Amber requires this specific repair draws attention to Sam and her different alignments to the membership category of crack user. If one of the predicates of this category is knowledge of what '50 piece' means (see Baker, 2004), another unstated but readily available one is that crack users are bad people. Amber's question thus alludes to the possibility that she, as a non-user, would make a judgment threatening Sam's face.

Sam duly provides the repair in line 7. Amber's line 8 acknowledgement token, 'got it,' and her 'you've got to fill me in here' both underscore their different alignments to crack use. It's in line 9 that Sam breaks from the convention in which as respondent, she is the answerer. Her utterance, 'We have a little

squarehead,' is a formulation that proposes that non-users have the predicate of being immaturely or childishly rule-bound. In this utterance, Sam's 'we' argues that this predicate is one a larger audience or collective would endorse. In short, Sam is throwing down a gauntlet. Were Amber to disagree with the squarehead formulation, we could speculate that the continuation of the interview would be at stake. But instead, Amber agrees with Sam, saying 'I totally am' (line 10). This utterance is what Pomerantz (1986) called an **extreme case formulation**, in which an extreme such as 'totally' or 'never' emboldens a claim, and locates truth in the object being discussed, rather than in the eyes of the beholder. (Arguably 'We have a little squarehead' was also an extreme case formulation.) Amber is agreeing that anyone would call her a little squarehead. She thus endorses Sam's predicate for non-users.

Amber doesn't stop there. Her reference to marijuana use as 'really fun' can be seen as another affiliative move. Further, that she offers this reference, and studs it with the phrases 'Believe me,' 'I fully admit,' and 'That was it' (lines 10–11) – phrases that would be suitable if she were a defendant being interrogated in court – suggests that at this juncture she positions Sam as a moral authority to whom an explanation for not having used crack is owing. This passage therefore shows how crack user can become negotiated to have the predicates of free, mature, knowledgeable, and moral – a work of knowledge production that has the effect of saving Sam's face, and perhaps the interview. It is of further interest in relation to other passages in the interview in which Sam states that she is concerned about her mother's crack use. Is there a contradiction here? Only if you think that Sam's attitudes toward crack use ought to be fixed, rather than allowing that they are produced in talk-in-interaction.

Another of our favorite MCA examples is Kyoko Murakami's (2001) analysis of how British veterans who'd been prisoners of war in Japan talked about rice during her interviews about their experiences (Textbox 8.5). As Murakami points out, in line 18, one of the respondents allocates a turn to her and in it, ethnifies her as Japanese, and thus knowledgeable about *bento* boxes.

Having associated Murakami with Japanese food posed an interactional problem as the topic turned to the veterans' poor diets in the camps. Looming over the interview was the possibility that Japanese food preferences would be stereotyped as bad, implicating Murakami. She further shows how she and the veterans together managed to skirt it through talk that divided rice into copious sub-categories, such as 'the best rice' that camp guards ate, versus the lime-treated or seed rice, still unhulled, that was given to prisoners. This is significant, says Murakami, for showing how knowledge about culture does not exist in a perfect encapsulated form, ready to be gathered in the interview. Instead, the members' knowledge, in the form of their categories and subcategories of rice, emerged as a means of negotiating the stakes that Murakami and the respondents had in talking about the war and about being Japanese.

Textbox 8.5: Your *bento*

Int = Murakami, the interviewer

All others = respondents

4.	Ted:	>got a< little or- a little box of that we used to you know
5.		We got breakfast out o' a little brown bowl (2.) pap rice
6.		[(.)a uh and it was rice (.) crushed ((clapping sound))=
7.	Charlie:	[aye
8.	Int.:	=um huh
9.	Ted:	in water (.) and they called it like porridge [you know
10.	Int.:	[Yeah
11.	Ted:	Just a little brown bowl like that. That's what we got.
12.		That was at five o'clock in the morning
13.		[was it six o'clock about
14.	Charlie:	[ye that was six o'clock
15.	Ted:	a six o'clock then you went
16.		[( ) then you got a (.) your little box (.)
17.	Int.:	[hummm
18.	Ted:	your *bento*, was it?
19.	Int.:	hum, lunch [box

Source: Murakami, 2001: n.p.

The other main strategy for working with categories that we saw in Chapter 6 was, of course, *to begin with a social scientific category and proceed by asking whether or how it ever becomes relevant to participants*. For reflexive analysis of interviews, the third step here is to analyze the impact of that relevance for knowledge production. An exemplar is Virginia ('Ginny') Braun's (2000) study of how heterosexism was produced in the focus groups that she conducted with women on the topic of the vagina. For instance, in her final turn in Textbox 8.6, Braun's utterance that women lack opportunities to compare vaginas overlooks the opportunities afforded by lesbian sex. Braun uses her analysis of how participants and she expressed heterosexist presumptions through commission or omission in order to exhort researchers to regard interviews as a site in which they can work to address prejudice.

Textbox 8.6: Women don't have any kind of comparison

Ginny = interviewer

All others = respondents

Ginny:	like guys can compare with each other if they you know so choose
?:	((laughs))
Ginny:	when they're at the urinal or when they're you know in a communal shower or something I know they're not supposed to look but you
?:	mm
Ginny:	I think they probably do
Tara:	they do
	((laughter))
Tara:	of course they do
Julia:	of course they do
Ginny:	I mean I bet they do exactly um but you know know for women women don't have that kind of any kind of comparison

Source: Braun, 2000: 134

Textbox 8.7: A Summary of Strategies for Analyzing what Talk about Categories Accomplishes

- Ask how, and to what effect, the attachment of predicates to categories is negotiated.
- Question whether and how a social scientific category becomes relevant to participants.

STUDYING FOCUS GROUPS THROUGH A CA LENS

Among conversation analysts and other researchers using focus group data, it's commonplace to acknowledge that the caprices of group dynamics make groups, rather than individuals, the appropriate unit of analysis: eight focus groups with five participants apiece are not a sample of 40 individual participants, but of eight groups. So far so good. However, reflexively-minded conversation analysts take the question of how to think about individuals in relation to groups much farther.

Their thinking about it is most easily explained by looking at the road not taken – at a strategy for analyzing focus group data that's common elsewhere, but

that is shunned by conversation analysts. It's the strategy of asking whether what respondents said in the focus group is more or less true than what they'd say if asked individually. For example, Paula Meth's (2004) study of women's experiences of fear and violence in Durban, South Africa contrasts focus group and individual diary-writing methods. Meth observes that in focus groups, participants spoke favorably of their neighborly relations, but that in the diaries, they spoke of mistrust toward neighbors and revealed neighborhood involvement in vigilante action, such as the killing of a would-be kidnapper. Reasoning that public disclosure about strained relations or illegal activities could be awkward or risky for the research participants, Meth judges the diaries to be more accurate than the focus groups for capturing how neighborly relations could exacerbate fear and violence. In other cases, such as Pollack's (2003) study, discussed in Chapter 4, it is focus groups that are deemed more accurate.

Media researcher Jenny Kitzinger (1994) began to question whether interview data should be considered to report 'reality' at all. Further, she wondered why private statements were so often taken as baseline truths to which to compare what's said in groups. Building on these questions, conversation analyst Sue Wilkinson (1998) maintained that realist and constructionist researchers, working with both focus groups and individual data, too often subscribe to an **individual essentialism**, in which the individual is considered to be inherently more interesting than their social context. This makes it seem that as though 'an individual's "real" or "underlying" views (conceptualized as the views she would express "in private") represent the "purest" form of data' (p. 120). Such essentialism is taken for granted in the mass of analyses that employ one-on-one interviews and 'subtract out' the interviewer's role, says Wilkinson. However, the lively, messy, unpredictable dynamics of focus group talk drive home how inherently social talk is.

Wilkinson and Kitzinger both propose that focus groups be analyzed as Petri dishes in which the interactional work of negotiating identities and ongoingly producing social inequalities is done. Happily, our previous section's strategies for analyzing members' and social scientists' categories can be used to do just that. Moreover, they say, focus groups can be used to establish how their members construct knowledge. This might be done by exploring the content of talk, *in identifying members' vocabularies and central concepts*; for example, in their uses of rice to represent culture (Murakami, 2001) or in the vocabulary used to talk of the vagina (Braun, 2000; see also Braun and Wilkinson, 2005). But, keep in mind that sticking to content while ignoring interactive processes is not the CA way. Strategies for looking at how groups interact and thereby shape the knowledge that they are producing are what we'll look to now.

A strategy that Hydén and Bülow (2003) devised in response to Wilkinson's argument is *to ask whether and how the set of participants in a focus group orient to being in a group*. This is analogous to Karl Marx's (1847/2008) famous distinction between a 'class in itself,' a group of people who happen to be in the same social class, and a 'class for itself,' a group of people defining themselves as a collective with common interests. To figure this out, you can first pay attention to pronouns, noticing whether when participants speak in terms of 'I,' or 'we,' and whether 'we' aligns them with others co-present in the focus group room. This ties in, say

Hydén and Bülow, to the question of whether participants actively **establish** – and re-establish – **a common communicative ground** (p. 311), in relation either to the interview topic and tasks or to some shared characteristic.

To try out this strategy, we can use Textbox 8.8's transcript of a focus group of 1st year Biology students at a Canadian university. (Although it's not up to snuff with the CA transcription requirements, we've noticed that these requirements are somewhat relaxed in focus group-related articles, perhaps in order to achieve greater transparency for a broader readership.) In it, the moderator's use of 'us' (line 1) intimates that the participants could understand themselves to have a common communicative ground of being co-present. His reference to 'your best class last semester,' proposes that being students could also constitute a common ground. When participant F says 'I don't know if we're allowed to mention profs' names' (lines 4–5), she characterizes the participants as having the common ground of a shared orientation to the task of answering appropriately.

Textbox 8.8: I think many of us had him

MO = moderator

F = a female student

MO: I'd like us to first begin by thinking about last semester and I'd
like to ask you about what was your best class last semester? What
made it the best?
F: I'll start. My favorite class last semester was Chemistry. I don't know
if we're allowed to mention profs' names.
MO: It doesn't really matter, whatever feels comfortable.
F: We had Dr. xxx, or at least I had him. I think many of us had him
maybe. I just really... It really changed my view on Chemistry after
that class. The first test was really difficult, but I think a lot of us, we
realize how we need to change of studying strategies. It was
interesting the course itself and I think I remember even towards the
end, he told us so much about just water itself. We had a newfound
understanding and interpretation for water, like how important it is. I
think it was a really great course.

Source: by permission of L. Donaldson

As F elaborates on her favorite class (lines 7–14), she quickly repairs her opening 'We had Dr. xxx' (line 7) in a way that distinguishes between two collectives: the 'us' co-present in the room (line 7), and the particular 'we' who had studied with Dr. xxx (line 7). Her repair is accountable as both an orientation to carrying out the task appropriately, and to those co-present. Meanwhile, her statement about a 'newfound understanding and interpretation for water' (lines 12–13) is one that would resonate more with students of the sciences than with others. Therefore, it implicitly proposes that being in the Sciences is a common ground. In just four turns, co-presence, the interview task, being students, being Science students, and having studied with Dr. xxx have all been nominated as reasons that the participants could orient to one another as a collective. As this group's talk progresses, overlapping yeahs and head nods, as well as contributions that link to earlier ones (e.g., 'I actually had the same experience') will do what Hydén and Bülow call **adding to the common ground**, and therefore producing the group's shared knowledge. However, as Hydén and Bülow (2003) illustrate, that's not always the case. Focus group participants may also refrain from creating a common ground, remaining atomized and responding serially to the moderator.

For an example of how the common ground is built up, we turn to Bente Halkier's (2010) analysis of how focus groups of Danish women speak about cooking norms. A thematic analysis of their talk might conclude that this group's consensus was that deep fat frying of food is bad, though the food can be delicious. A conversation analysis would instead ask how this common ground was established in interaction. Halkier demonstrates that deep fat frying becomes a conversational resource for mending the fences between a pair of group members, Birgit and Dorte. Their dispute becomes apparent via a pair of disaffiliative extreme case formulations about fish fingers early in the transcript in Textbox 8.9, when Birgit says 'my kids love them,' and Dorte says 'nobody likes fish fingers.'

The group members' orientation to saving face can be understood as a reason that deep fat frying, as one of many possible characteristics of fish fingers, comes into conversational play. The members manage to affiliatively concur that deep fat frying has its flaws, with Birgit conceding, 'Yes, all right, I can only admit that.' As Halkier discusses, Karen then holds out a conversational olive branch by speaking of her deep-fried cheese as a delicacy. Birgit re-enters the fold by praising this dish alongside others. Further, in a face-saving act, Birgit also mentions her own homemade preserves, which Halkier frames as a resource for Birgit to claim that her cooking fits into the 'good' category. That Dorte now agrees with Birgit can be read as another face-saving act, patching over the earlier disagreement. The group's common ground about deep fat frying is thus produced in relation to members' moves of affiliation and disaffiliation.

Textbox 8.9: Nobody likes fish fingers

Sonja:	When I was a child, when we had fish it was these frozen fish fingers...
Karen [interrupts]:	Yes, THAT is disgusting [Sonja: He, he...] ... that is bad cooking.
Dorte:	Yes, it is.
Sonja:	That is simply YUKKY.
Birgit:	Yes, my kids love them...
Dorte [interrupts]:	No, nobody likes fish fingers.
Birgit:	Yes, I like them.
Karen:	It's the same with that breaded fish you can buy, it's only breading.
Birgit:	No, that depends on which ones you buy ... some of it is okay to buy...
Karen [interrupts]:	I will rather buy it without breading, and then ... [pause]
Birgit [interrupts]:	...where there is a lot of fish ... [pause] [Karen: do it myself] but that is [Sonja: You don't know what's in there] obvious...
Karen:	No.
Sonja:	It looks like such stuff.
Karen:	Yep.
Sonja:	Oh yes, that's bad cooking too. To me bad cooking is doing it with deep-frying.
Birgit:	Yes, all right I can only admit that [Karen: Yes] to you ... we don't use that either.
Karen:	I also think...
Sonja [interrupts]:	But then again, it's that fat.
Karen:	I actually used it, I used it to deep-fry those camembert cheeses for dessert, but I have begun to make that in the oven ... that's actually the only deep-fry...
Dorte:	It's a long time since you have made that dessert for us.
Karen:	Yes, he he.
Birgit:	It's actually quite a while since I've had it, you know with a little bit of homemade blackberry preserve...
Dorte:	Yes.

Source: Halkier, 2010: 79

Textbox 8.10: A Summary of Strategies for Studying Focus Groups through a CA Lens

- Identify members' vocabularies and central concepts.
- Ask whether and how the set of focus group participants orient to being in a group.

CHAPTER SUMMARY

Conversation analysts' strategies for being reflexive can largely be understood as applying concepts discussed in earlier chapters. In keeping with the stringent empiricism discussed in Chapter 5, their strategies continue to rely on only visible or audible evidence, eschewing narrative analysts' introspections about their emotions or inner selves. In keeping with their attunement to how institutions are talked into being (Chapter 7), conversation analysts interpret the interview as an example of institutional talk-in-interaction. Their strategies show how members' orientations to the goals of reflecting on the past, collecting data neutrally in the present, and conducting analysis in the future, influence how members orient to turn-taking, questioning, and answering. All this, in turn, has profound effects on the data collected and knowledge subsequently produced. The interview, furthermore, can reflexively be studied for how social categories are formulated, negotiated, and referenced, using the strategies of Chapter 6. Finally, we turn a critical CA lens to the special case of the group interview, interrogating individual essentialism and using strategies that question reflexively how individuals can constitute themselves as groups, and negotiate a common communicative ground – or be understood in essentialist terms by researchers.

Part III

Analyzing Discourse

What happens when you put three sociologists in a room and ask them to define **discourse** and **discourse analysis**? We put this to the test in a conversation with our graduate student colleague in our initial musings about this part of the book. We found Amber's definition to focus on where discourse is to be found, e.g. in talk, documents, and media, and on what meanings it holds. Katherine defined discourse as what can be said or thought, i.e., she focused on what discourse does. Rawan, our graduate student colleague, viewed discourse as ideas with boundaries around them, these boundaries being either solid or permeable. Her analytical interest was in how these sets of ideas change.

When the definition of discourse, and the focus of discourse analysis, is compared within and across other social scientific disciplines, we see that we were not alone in our diversity. However, from deeper discussion, the three of us did manage to arrive at a common definition. In it, **discourse** is a web of meanings, ideas, interactions and practices that are expressed or represented in **texts** (spoken and written language, gesture, and visual imagery), within institutional and everyday settings. To Eggins and Slade, language is to be studied 'as it is used to enact social life' (1997: 32). Said differently, we accomplish social life, we are part of and construct our social life, our relationships with our selves, others and institutions, through language. We also agreed upon a general definition of **discourse analysis** (DA) as the study of these texts of social life. Given this book's focus, we orient toward DA strategies applicable to talk data that range from interviews to fieldwork recordings to government hearings, while noting that many of these strategies are readily applicable to non-talk texts, such as newspaper articles, autobiographies, and academic works.

Let us provide an example of discourse and discourse analysis and some more general contextualization of the value of discourse analysis before we proceed further. **Hegemonic masculinity**, a term associated with the work of R.W. Connell (e.g., Connell, 1987) is an example of a discourse. As a pattern of practice, of actions performed, role expectations, and identities (Connell and Messerschmidt, 2005), hegemonic masculinity ascribes power and privilege to men's conformity to heteronormativity and specific attitudes and behaviors (e.g. rationality, leadership) that contribute to their dominance over women. Analyses of the discourse

of hegemonic masculinity could have as their starting point the strong silent man of the Marlboro cigarette ads or statistics on the glass ceiling in contemporary corporations, or something more relevant to our focus on talk: parents telling boys not to cry.

Why consider discourse analysis as an analytic strategy if you have talk data? If you're interested in unpacking a web of socially constructed meanings and considering their implications, this strategy is for you. Across disciplines, there is a general consensus that discourse analysis helps us understand how social interaction is involved in how discourses are constructed, how they change, and what their effects are, as realized foremost through language. For example, hegemonic masculinity has been used to understand boys' acts of bullying in the classroom and violence and homophobia in sports (Connell and Messerschmidt, 2005). Discourse analysis lets us ask how language creates a social situation and how the situation, in turn, prescribes meaning to the language used (Gee, 1999) - or, more simply, how discourse shapes social relations and vice versa (Ainsworth and Hardy, 2004). Key is that individuals are not perceived as passive vessels into which discourses are poured (Holstein and Gubrium, 1995) or as leading lives determined by discourse. Individuals do have agency but it is agency shaped by their experience of multiple discourses.

Indeed, the draw of DA for many is its emphasis on linking language to power. In DA, language is not understood as value neutral or without consequence but rather plays a key role in the social construction of everyday life. Or, in other words, language can be read as constituting reality with significant effects. In some ways, this is like CA. However, the two diverge with regard to a discourse analyst's assumption that language is imbued with relations of power-knowledge. Where CA begins with curiosity about how shared intersubjectivity (and thus social order) are possible, DA begins with concern about the social order's inequalities. Conversation analysts see rigor in sticking as close to their talk data as possible, while many discourse analysts see virtue in drawing in evidence of inequalities that may lie beyond.

One final note on why you might want to use DA to approach your talk data. The critical tenor of discourse analysis appeals to those who desire to link language to material effects or to unpack the social construction of phenomena in order to bring about social change, to imagine what society *can* and *ought to be* by uniting theory and practice (Hammersley, 1997: 238). For example, Brown and colleagues (2010) propose that understanding how educational discourse in early childhood settings is characterized by classism, sexism and racism can be used to argue for transformation of common classroom practices.

This part of the book is organized as follows: We begin with a pair of chapters that focus on two of the main strands of DA and strategies for applying them to talk data. The first is that of French philosopher Michel Foucault, who sees texts as manifestations of knowledge and power relations that govern social reality. A second strand of analysis, called Critical Discourse Analysis (CDA), emphasizes to a greater extent how talk operates in producing political and cultural change by revealing the politics of micro aspects of language that may, at first glance, appear apolitical. But, not all discourse analysts use Foucault or CDA, or any of the other specialized forms of discourse analysis: many speak of themselves more generically as 'doing discourse analysis' without any more specific allegiances. Our review of such work has found these researchers to share certain central concepts and understandings, regarding how discourse is related to society, identity, power, ideology, and time. Thus, the third chapter in this part discusses a 'garden-variety' discourse analysis.

NINE

Foucauldian Discourse Analysis

One of a student's more interesting moments in a social science academic program is her or his first encounter with influential French philosopher Michel Foucault, whose earliest book was published in 1961. In our home discipline of sociology alone, there are those who have no use for his work, those who tolerate his insights, those who use certain concepts, and those who follow his work avidly. If you feel unsure of his significance, or anxious about the groans and keen faces that greet mentions of his name in courses, at least in our experiences, we hope that our exploration of Foucauldian insights and their application to talk data will be of help. However, before proceeding, we should note that ours is but one reading of Foucault, a scholar whose complex body of work continues to attract debate.

INTRODUCING FOUCAULT

In a series of lectures given at the Pontifical Catholic University of Rio de Janeiro in 1973, Foucault (1973/1994) observed that earlier academics had been defining discourse narrowly. Rather than analyzing the logic of syllogisms, the rules of syntax and poetic meter, or other linguistic facts or laws, he set his sights more broadly. In these lectures, he defined discourse as including statements and systems of statements that are power-laden, persuasive, employed strategically, and part of social practices, interactions, behaviors, and ways of being. Foucault's definition would vary over the course of his career, in relation to the specific project with which he was engaged. For example, in *The Archaeology of Knowledge* (1972), Mills (2004) explains that Foucault spoke of:

- Discourse as a whole, comprised of the totality of all meaningful and consequential statements.
- Discourse as a specific group of interconnected texts, in which case one can ask how their relations are structured. Hegemonic masculinity would be an example of a discourse, understood in this way.
- Discourse as including both texts and the rules and structures that account for their production. In a classroom, the content of what is said (the text) is linked to the turn-taking system by which students and teachers say it (the rules and structures).

Foucault's work had three broad phases, moving from what he called archaeology to genealogy, and then to the unfinished project of technologies of the self. We define and discuss these in order, and begin by showing how the project of archaeology set forth an ontology and epistemology that carries throughout Foucault's scholarship.

Ontology, Epistemology, and Rigor in Post-structuralist Research

Foucault's projects of **archaeology** offered readings of the history of ideas that ran counter to standard narratives of progress. He carried these projects out by looking at the relationship between **connaissance**, a formal body of knowledge and reasoning, and **savoir**, the discursive conditions that constituted it (see Scheurich and McKenzie, 2008). For example, in *History of Madness*, Foucault (1961/2006) is interested in how psychiatry came to be *the* knowledge on madness in the eighteenth century. Psychiatry had depicted its history as an advance over earlier ideas about 'nervous diseases,' or even earlier ideas about madness as an intervention of the cosmos: psychiatrists told a smooth and coherent story of their discipline's progress. Foucault argues otherwise. He contends that psychiatry's emergence was enmeshed in a network of discursive relations among the criminal justice system, the economy, and health care. What had begun as a 'great confinement' of vagabonds, criminals, and beggars who did not meet the moral expectations of the Enlightenment, was converted to a workhouse system – and those who could not conform to its expectations came to be understood as 'mad' (Philo, 2012). Psychiatry and asylums were the solutions. Thus, what appears to have been progress in treating mental illness, Foucault realizes, is contingent upon a mix of contradictory, questionable, and sometimes illogical discourses that serve bourgeois morality. What appears to be an elite body of knowledge that follows higher standards of rigor than common knowledge is thus thoroughly enmeshed in everyday life.

As Scheurich and McKenzie (2008) explain, all this is pertinent to understanding Foucault's epistemology and ontology. The central ideas introduced in *The Archaeology of Knowledge* (1972) were ones that Foucault continued to weave

through his later work. His key proposition was that the figure of a knower who is perceived to observe reality in a rational way has, in fact, emerged through an altogether irrational history. Foucault felt the same about himself as a knower. That is, he did not regard himself as having written an improved history of psychiatry so much as a fiction (Tamboukou, 1999) – a point that speaks to his view of epistemology (the knower) and ontology (what can be known) alike. The knower may seem to know a reality, but it is already and always a construction. Scheurich and McKenzie (2008: 858) nicely summarize Foucault's sense of what can be known and how we know:

> To Foucault, modernity constructed man, the subject, the agent running the world. It was modernity that fashioned the whole of human life as constructed around and for man, the central subject, the central agentic actor. It was modernity that wrote the history of the progressive rational rise of the human sciences guided by and for man, the central subject.

Discourse analysis is thus a strategy for understanding how we come to construct as coherent something that is contingent, messy, and haphazard (Sjölander, 2011).

In essence, Foucault was a social constructionist of a **post-structuralist** variety. He was skeptical of claims about underlying structures or order, and of claims that there is an overarching trajectory to human history, such as the Enlightenment narrative of progress; he rejected the idea of any universal, foundational truth. Instead, he interrogated how knowledges and the appearance of coherence and order are anchored in discursive constructs, constituted by or materialized through not just shared understandings but also social processes and power relations (Breheny and Stephens, 2007) – a point we expand upon below.

Scheurich and McKenzie (2008: 859) sum up their injunctions about rigor in Foucauldian analysis by saying 'don't cherry pick' – you can emphasize certain concepts in your analysis, but you cannot throw away Foucault's broader ontological and epistemological framework. Kendall and Wickham (1999) address a number of common errors of new practitioners of Foucault's methods. Don't get caught up, they say, in the idea that the present 'makes sense' even if histories of the past cover up its haphazard irrationalities. Be alert for contingencies that apparent knowledges hinge upon, and be suspicious of claims about causes. Constantly recall that we are all complicit in the social construction of what we think is real – to argue that we have a standpoint from which to have definitive knowledge is dubious.

This last point, though, is one that feminists have especially contested. Many feminists are drawn to Foucault because his approach gives a way to disrupt the essentialism of dichotomous constructs upon which the gender order rest, i.e., male/female, masculine/feminine, homosexual/heterosexual desire (e.g., Butler, 1990). Moreover, feminists appreciate how Foucault tips over the pedestal of the rational, detached Enlightenment knower, whom they would add is specifically male.

However, to Nancy Hartsock (1990), a sticking point for feminism is that Foucault appears to reject the possibility of an emancipatory truth, and a feminist standpoint from which to know, to critique, to resist, and to effect change. Hold that thought. We will return to it more fully in the next section, once we have introduced other concepts of Foucault's scholarship.

Textbox 9.1: A Summary of How to Approach Discourse as a Foucauldian

- Retain a consistent ontological and epistemological framework.
- Avoid narratives of progress in which the present is more rational than the past.
- Avoid claims about causes.
- If you want to claim a definitive standpoint from which to put forth critique or propose change, consider adopting a feminist standpoint that allies Foucault with embodied knowledge.
- Keep the question about how talk reflects discourse, as opposed to individuals' meanings.

UNPACKING POWER, KNOWLEDGE, AND THE SUBJECT

Foucault's (1978) *History of Sexuality (Volume 1)* is an excellent example of how he analyzes discourse and how several of his key theoretical insights interconnect. In it, Foucault analyzes Western discourse about sexuality from the seventeenth to the twentieth century and challenges the 'repressive hypothesis,' that being the dominant discourse that Western sexuality is a repressive one. This discourse makes reference, for example, to talk of sex being censored and prudishness characterizing social relationships, such as those between parents and children or teachers and students. Foucault posits that this hypothesis did not suffice.

He counters it by arguing that extensive knowledge on sex was being produced, and that this can be understood in terms of what he calls **power–knowledge** relations; the hyphen refers to how power and knowledge can be understood to be co-constituted. Analyzing political and economic discourses on sex, Foucault demonstrates that various procedures are used to produce the 'truth' of sex, one of these being confession – of sin, of crime, of love – in public or private, to priests, justice officials, family members, educators, and so forth. By the eighteenth century, there was 'a great archive of the pleasures of sex' (1978: 63). Foucault also uncovers several discursive shifts about sexuality, such that by the nineteenth century, knowledge on sex had its own four discernable 'privileged' objects of knowledge: the hysterical woman, the masturbating child, the Malthusian couple (a married heterosexual couple); and the perverse adult (Foucault, 1978: 104–5). Foucault additionally observes that, in the twentieth century, mechanisms of

repression began to loosen. For instance, the morally regulative discourses around homosexuality that emerged in the nineteenth century came to be disturbed by other reverse discourses, such as those demanding that same-sex relations be understood as legitimate expressions of intimacy.

The History of Sexuality exemplifies Foucault's **genealogical** approach, in which discourse is studied over time in order to reveal power–knowledge frameworks and the complex processes involved in their construction. Describing the 'procedures, practices, apparatuses and institutions involved in the production of discourses and knowledges, and their power effects' (1978: 276) is the objective of his genealogies. In following historical, discursive traces, a genealogy seeks to understand the present, and to offer a 'history of the present.' Echoing some of what archaeology is, some people wonder whether Foucault's genealogy is altogether different. We follow Scheurich and McKenzie's (2008) conclusion that the ontology and epistemology of the two are alike, but take Carabine's (2001) point that genealogical projects are more concerned with power. Further, we observe that Foucault's starting point is different in the genealogies: they begin not with a connaissance, but with an awareness of multiple, sometimes competing discourses.

Foucault understood **power** differently than other key theorists and this understanding is central to how power operates in his methods of discourse analysis. Karl Marx, for example, saw power as class-based, as an economic elite's infringement upon ordinary persons' rights whereas Max Weber perceived power as the ability to exert control over people despite their objections. Both of these theorists saw power as *possessed* by people, a class, or an institution, and being used to oppress. For Foucault, power is *relational*, and, thus, in his works, he often speaks of **power relations** to underscore this. In *The History of Sexuality*, he writes of power as:

- An ever-transformative force that could constrain and change a situation but that could equally create or produce it.
- Able to reaffirm other power relations in a system.
- Able to be isolated from other power relations.

Although power is fluid and ubiquitous, one might say 'you know it when you see it.' That is, power becomes apparent when it is exercised (Townley, 1993: 520). Summing this up, in Foucault's words, power is 'not an institution, and not a structure; neither is it a certain strength we are endowed with; it is the name that one attributes to a complex strategical situation in a particular society' (1978: 93).

Language is but one instance of power relations. Foucault studied discourses (which involve language) as bodies of knowledge and asked what power relations underpin them. He dissolved the idea that knowledge may lead to power, but instead saw the two as interdependent: 'There cannot be particular types of subject of knowledge, orders of truth, or domains of knowledge except on the basis of political conditions that are the very ground on which the subject, the

domains of knowledge and the relations with truth are formed' (Foucault, 1973: 15, cited in Townley, 1993). Discourses, embedded as they are with power–knowledge relations, are productive, shaping the very knowledge individuals are exposed to and act upon. Importantly, in Foucault's (1978) analysis, a particular discourse doesn't inherently belong to a particular side of a conflict. A discourse also isn't a jigsaw puzzle of pieces designed solely to fit together. Instead, a discourse or its elements can be used in multiple and even contradictory strategies, in what Foucault called **tactical polyvalence**: instead of jigsaw puzzle pieces, think Lego®.

Let's now look more closely about what it is about knowledges that Foucault sought to understand, namely, to analyze the origins of objects and subjects in knowledge. According to Foucault, **objects**, something to be studied and known, are not exterior to discourse but constituted by discourse. Said differently, power–knowledge relations create objects (see Pascale, 2008b; Townley, 1993). For example, take *The History of Sexuality*'s 'hysterical woman,' a woman diagnosed as disordered for failing to conform to expectations about nuclear family relations. She thus has become an object of knowledge constituted by the discursive history of sexuality. Foucault (1973/1994) reasoned that an object must be constituted by discourse in order for it to be spoken about. His interest was in showing how social practices create new forms of knowledge and therefore new objects.

Purvis and Hunt (1993) additionally remind us that Foucault himself said that a central objective of his scholarship was to understand how, over time, humans are made into **subjects** of discourses, a process that he called **subjectification.** A woman diagnosed as hysterical or a woman who knows this diagnosis to be culturally available can construct a subject position for herself that conforms to this discourse. The discourse, thus, is constituting as well as limiting the woman's ways of being and of perceiving her self. Foucault was not focused on the individual, her feelings, or her interpretations, so much as in how discourses insert people into subject positions (Mills, 2004). He did not start by taking for granted that 'the hysterical woman' existed, any more than Simone de Beauvoir (1949), writing, 'One is not born, but rather becomes a woman' (p. 267), had taken for granted that 'woman' existed. Rather, he was interested in discursively analyzing how this subject position came into being.

How Foucault understood the interrelationships between power and subjects within discourse is perhaps most clear when we consider his argument that discourses **discipline**: they socialize people to conform to rules of behavior, and punish them if necessary. In *Discipline and Punish: The Birth of the Prison* (1977), for example, Foucault explains the eighteenth century prison design of the **Panopticon**, in which a central watchtower would be surrounded by cells. The design would enable officers' surveillance of all prisoners but would not permit prisoners to directly observe the officers in return. Nonetheless, prisoners' awareness that they could be under the surveillance of officers at any moment

prompted them to engage in self-surveillance: to self-discipline or self-police their behavior, to behave as model prisoners to avoid further punishment. In essence, Foucault argued that the ubiquitous gaze of the Panopticon produced prisoners as self-regulating moral subjects. In the case of the prison, we see how the self is constantly evaluated in relation to a discourse that specifies what performance of subjectivity is normative and culturally available: the model prisoner. Foucault's great attention to the subject in *Discipline and Punish* underscores the interrelations of power, knowledge, and the subject. If discourses are constituted by and constitutive of power–knowledge relations, individuals are positioned and bodies are disciplined; individuals must take up available subject positions in order to make sense of discourses.

Another theme central in *Discipline and Punish* was that bodies mattered, a theme that Bauman (1983) says had largely been overlooked by earlier social theorists, who saw individuals as disembodied carriers of thoughts and beliefs. In Foucault's *Discipline and Punish* the Panopticon gazes on prisoners, the errant are punished, and model prison behavior is enacted, whereas in his *Madness and Civilization,* vagabond bodies are reformed to be economically productive or separated out and labeled 'mad.' Power, whether economic, political, or moral, is thus said to be 'written on' the body.

Recall the question of Nancy Hartsock's, which we had raised in the ontology section, of whether Foucault would allow for a feminist standpoint from which to know and argue for change? In McLaren's (2002) reading, Foucault's criticism of the Enlightenment knower does leave room in which to posit an embodied knower compatible with feminism. This is because of Foucault's (1978) emphasis on how subjectivity is embodied, i.e., on how he understood the body to be the 'condition of subjectivity' (McLaren, 2002: 83), rather than separable from it. We can know through our bodies, our bodies are acted upon, and it is with our bodies that we act.

Foucault's final, unfinished work on the **technologies of the self** (Martin et al., 1988) tends to be cited by those who interpret Foucault to be compatible with feminist and other emancipatory projects. Earlier works of his had looked at specific historical practices, such as *The History of Sexuality*'s confession, by which individuals performed 'operations' on their selves, on their attitudes and conduct, to achieve that which they desired: greater wellbeing. In the 'Technologies of the self' essay, Foucault (1988) considers a variety of ancient Greek and early Christian practices, from meditating on the worst that could happen, to renouncing temptations, to interpreting dreams. In so doing, he showed how individuals could come to understand themselves as subjects, and express their agency. Some readers of this work on technologies of the self regard it as opening a door to resistance and the formulation of counter-discourses (e.g., McNay, 1994), and thus to counter worries that Foucault's scholarship is applicable to predominantly docile and conformist bodies, gives little weight to individual agency (Smith, 1993), sees little scope for change, and is gloomy and nihilistic.

DOING FOUCAULDIAN DA

In this section, we outline how from a Foucauldian perspective, the analysis of talk data can be for several strategic purposes. We caution readers, however, that our emphasis on isolating strategies is somewhat misleading. As our summary of Foucault's central contributions attests, most of his insights are interconnected. For example, it's difficult to understand how subjectivities can be constituted in discourse without first understanding the relations between power, knowledge, and discourse. Thus, we separate the strategies here only to present them as straightforwardly as possible.

In Foucauldian discourse analysis, talk data can be used to engage in **deconstruction**, the process of unearthing discourses in relation to power, knowledge, and subjects. Before we turn to these, we wish to mention the caveat Bastalich (2009) has raised about whether it's even legitimate to interrogate the history of *practices* through data collected from *individuals*. Foucauldian researchers who use individually based talk data would, however, say that they are not interested in individual meanings but rather about how talk reflects discourses. This answer can evoke further criticisms of DA in general, such as Hammersley's (2003), for presuming that discourse works from the top down to determine what people take to be objective reality, and for failing to take what people say about their experience of social reality as a valuable source of data. If you're of this mind at the end of this chapter, then you might prefer to use NA.

Strategies for Analyzing Power, Knowledge, and the Subject

One common analytic strategy that we see is to *deconstruct the power–knowledge relations embedded in a discourse and its potential effects*. An insightful example is offered by Green and Sonn (2005). They explored how White Australians discussed their 1990s involvement with Reconciliation, a government-endorsed effort to address the discrimination experienced by Indigenous Australians. A 'cultural connection' discourse seemed to characterize White Reconcilers' talk of their desire to feel connected to Indigenous cultures, values and ways of life. But Green and Sonn argue that this discourse is filtered through a prism of whiteness that uncritically romanticizes Indigenous cultures. Further, respondents who spoke of aims to connect to Indigenous cultures were not interested in social justice but instead wanted Indigenous peoples to share their knowledge so as to correct White Reconcilers' attitudes and behaviors. The talk of White Australians, according to Green and Sonn, therefore reflects appropriation of Indigenous knowledge and subsequent perpetuation of White–Indigenous power relations.

As we assume that language and social action are organized by discourses, another analytic strategy for talk data can be to explore *how discourses constrain or*

enable what it is possible to say in social interaction (including the interview) while assuming that this is not fixed (McHoul and Grace, 1995). The interest here is not so much in *what* one says but 'what constitutes the domain of the sayable from within which one is able to speak' (Pascale, 2008b: 348). For instance, Comber and Nixon (2009) analyzed the ways Australian teachers talk about their profession. In interviews, teachers discussed the importance of relationships with students and of responding to corporate discourses that emphasize accountability, managerialism, and human capital in education. Altogether absent in the interviews were discussions of pedagogy. Comber and Nixon convincingly argue that what teachers left unsaid illustrates that corporate-managerial discourses and practices constrain and induce teachers' conformity to them, which in turn contributes to these discourses' (re)production.

A third analytic strategy is *to expose how a seemingly coherent discourse is ruptured, haphazard, or tactically polyvalent.* Cox and Pringle (2012), for instance, show how the emergence in New Zealand of women's football in the 1970s did not follow a smooth arc of progress. Discontinuity was involved: the women had tried to form a league in 1921 to no avail. Contradictions were involved, as when the Chairman of the women's footballers' league stated in 1975 that:

> I'm not a person for women's lib because I believe women should retain their femininity. They can do this in football, but not in rugby. I think women should retain their femininity, but they should have the same basic rights as men. Nothing should be for men only. My daughter plays football. I don't see why she should go to ballet classes just because she's a girl. (2012: 224)

As Cox and Pringle discuss, among the contradictions here are that the Chairman supported women's rights – so long as they were for women whom he thought were essentially feminine, and that he inexplicably differentiated football from rugby. Finally, contingencies were involved: Cox and Pringle show how the acceptance of women's football depended upon its being framed as a 'family sport,' one that heterosexual women could play in support of their men's football enthusiasm.

Stef Jansen (2000: 393) analyzes how protestors in Yugoslavia used a discourse of being 'victims, underdogs, and rebels' in a tactically polyvalent fashion in relation to two opposing ideas of citizenship: democratic and ethnic essentialist. In 1996–97, protestors against an electoral fraud perpetrated by the regime of Slobodan Milošević used this discourse to characterize themselves as deserving of democratic citizenship. In 1999, when the Milošević regime attacked ethnic Albanians within Yugoslavia's Kosovo region, and NATO retaliated by bombing the Yugoslavian capital, Beograd, the discourse of being 'victims, underdogs, and rebels' was again to surface in a spirit of defiant gallows humor. For instance, says Jansen, who was doing fieldwork in Beograd, people sometimes referred to the city as 'Bombay' (p. 398). The 'victims, underdogs, and rebels' discourse had circulated to become an

element of a larger anti-NATO discourse that was effectively pro-Milošević – and, hence, that propounded a definition of citizenship on an ethnic essentialist basis. The tactical use to which this discursive element was put had thus reversed.

Another analytic strategy is *to deconstruct discourses in talk data and to reveal how they create subjects and/or objects that have implications*, especially for those who experience the discourses as real (Breheny and Stephens, 2007). For instance, Burrell et al. (2010) interviewed women who had experienced early menopause due to surgery, asking about their subsequent decision about whether to use menopausal hormone therapy (MHT). In analyzing their data, Burrell et al. asked: Whose knowledge is privileged or obscured? Which discourses are dominant or subordinate? How is power operating and/or exercised? And how were menopause and MHT being constructed? (2010: 531). They found that several women in their study explained their decisions to use MHT through distinctly medicalized discourse, e.g., their health and wellbeing depended on medication. For example,

> My doctor said because of my age and the reason I went into menopause that I should think of it almost like insulin, that I need it. And I thought well that short period of [distress] between I sort of started and when it sort of kicked in, yeah I go along with that. (2010: 535)

For Burrell et al., the women's complicity with this discourse illustrates the Foucauldian notion that powerful institutions produce discourses about subjects that are then reproduced by these very subjects. Indeed, say Brown et al. (2010), discourses have power if they become part of individuals' everyday perceptions and narratives of self.

Talk data can also be analyzed by the fifth strategy, of *looking at how discourses discipline*. The example we have given of how Foucault studied discipline in the prison environment may have made the concept seem more extreme than ordinary. Propen and Schuster (2008) provide an analysis of how discipline is effected through the technology of 'the victim statement'– a statement that a victim of a crime, such as the daughter of someone who has been murdered, gives in some American courts before a judge hands down a decision about a perpetrator's sentence. Interviews with victim advocates show that this technology disciplines the victims, in that they are given model statements, and told that it's 'okay to cry, and it's okay to be emotional, but you don't want to yell. You don't want to talk in half sentences' (p. 318). But, this technology also disciplines the judges, whom victim advocates characterize as conflicted. Judges are concerned about acknowledging the victims and providing them the experience of catharsis, and yet also about handing down a sentence compliant with penal law and phrased in a way that preserves the appearance of the bench's fairness. This analysis reminds us that discipline is not a one-way street.

Textbox 9.2: Pepping yourself up

Interviewer:	What do you mean by 'pepping yourself up'?
Helena:	Feeling a bit more fancy than ordinarily. I put on a bit more delicate clothes, more delicate underwear, do my hair in a slightly different way, put a little bit more make-up on.
Interviewer:	But why is it necessary to change underwear? Nobody sees it.
Helena:	Nobody sees it, that's right. But you can feel it, sense it.
Interviewer:	How do you feel after changing?
Helena:	You perhaps identify more with the type that the lingerie indicates you are [. . .] It's a mood.

Source: Jantzen et al., 2006: 195

Finally, we can analyze talk for insights into how discourses speak to embodied subjectivities, as Jantzen and colleagues (2006) do in their study of how women talk about their lingerie purchases. What is written on the body is a sexualized image, a certain weight and shape that represents normative ideas of femininity. Women talk about this in terms that seesaw between the subject position of being controlled, and that of being in control. In rejecting 'grandma's gigantic underwear' (p. 184) or 'brothel-like' (p. 185) lingerie, they are exerting agency, but the parameters of their agency and of what can be purchased are in the control of others. Further, Jantzen et al.'s study exemplifies the analytic strategy of using talk data to discern technologies of the self. In Textbox 9.2, the way that women speak of putting on lingerie also shows them to be performing operations on their selves, their mood, and their potential for happiness.

Textbox 9.3: A Summary of Strategies for Doing Foucauldian DA

- Track the emergence of discourse(s).
- Focus on the construction of objects and subjects in discourse(s).
- Explore the power–knowledge relations that constitute discourse and are constituted by discourse.
- Assess how discourses constrain or enable some talk and not others.
- Consider which knowledge is privileged and which is not.
- Deconstruct the embodied subjectivities in discourse.
- Reveal technologies of the self.

CHAPTER SUMMARY

The work of Michel Foucault is often used by scholars to engage in discourse analysis of talk with the primary focus being on how the talk of people reflects and (re-)produces discourses and/or is constrained by discourses. To some, this use of Foucault's work would be surprising since Foucault himself did not study talk data. And to the uninitiated and perhaps somewhat cautious researcher, reading a work that adopts a Foucauldian approach is one thing – and attempting to adopt the approach is quite another. Thus, in this chapter, we have described Foucault's influence on the post-structural paradigm and cautioned the analyst about the importance of being aware of Foucault's epistemological and ontological assumptions, such as one does not discover 'truth' with a capital T through discourse analysis. The meaning-oriented individual, who motivates so much of NA, is, in Foucault's eyes, a discursive construct. Instead, to Foucault, the nexus of power, knowledge, and the subject is a useful starting point for strategies considering the relationships between people, society, and discourse.

TEN

Critical Discourse Analysis

Emerging in the mid-twentieth century, Critical Discourse Analysis (CDA) is another major strand of discourse analysis popular in the social sciences. Its major purpose is explicitly political: to critique and change material conditions in society, with the starting point of a social problem, injustice, or inequality, such as racism in education, sexism in politics, or coercion at the border. CDA scholars are not so concerned with formulating a unified analytic strategy as with adapting several tools to their purpose. Thus, their general consensus is that CDA is not a paradigm or school of thought. It is an uncentered movement or intellectual field of scholars with a shared concern, to inquire into power and social inequality and their **semiotic** (language, gesture, and visual imagery) dimensions (Fairclough and Wodak, 1997; van Dijk, 2008; Wodak, 1999). The emphasis on the uncenteredness of this movement is deliberate; some CDA scholars resist the idea of CDA becoming conventional or institutionalized for fear that it would lose its criticality (Billig, 2002).

Critical Discourse Analysis is found throughout social science disciplines, but has its roots in the critical linguistic traditions established by Norman Fairclough, Ruth Wodak and Teun van Dijk. Linguists generally study discourse as social interaction that takes **linguistic** form – speech and writing, or talk and text – and researchers study the structures of language (morphology), how sentences are constructed within language (syntax), the sounds or signs of how language is spoken (phonetics), and the meanings of language ascribed through relationships, for example, between words and symbols (semantics). What CDA scholars contributed was a greater emphasis on the action of language but with attention to social and political thought (Breeze, 2011) and especially its political implications or emancipatory potential. Overall, in CDA, the analytical emphasis is on language in the creation, framing, and understanding of social interactions and problems (Fairclough, 1992; Wodak, 1996) and is motivated by a passionate aspiration to

put analysis to the ends of social justice. In an oft-cited early text, *Discourse and Social Change* (1992), Fairclough introduced CDA's capability to conceptualize and analyze discourse in three ways:

- As text: linguistic characteristics and format. For example, one can analyze vocabulary such as word choice and metaphor; grammar; cohesion; and text structure such as turn-taking.
- As practice: a thing created, disseminated, and consumed. For example, one can analyze the circulation of linguistic objects; representation; and above-the-sentence dynamics like coherence and intertextuality.
- As social practice: ideological and hegemonic impact. For example, one can analyze the ordering, aligning, and changing of discourse for strategic reasons of power, oppression and resistance.

UNDERSTANDING THE PRINCIPLES OF CDA

In research with talk data, there are a few CDA tenets that are especially useful to keep in mind (see Textbox 10.1). First, CDA assumes the discursiveness of power relations (Tenet 2). Similar to what we have seen in Foucault's conception, power is not reduced to a focus on the individual or people doing or saying things but is defined relationally (Fairclough, 1992). Social inequalities are understood to originate in and to be legitimized through language (Fairclough, 1992; Wodak, 1996). Thus, as van Dijk (2008: 85) explains, CDA 'primarily studies the way social power abuse, dominance and inequality are enacted, reproduced and resisted by text and talk in the social and political context.' What we can see here is the unabashed politics of CDA, which is markedly different from Foucault's tendency to describe without prescribing. We also see that the idea of resistance is central; no one reading CDA would come away wondering whether it was nihilistic. So, CDA shares with Foucauldian DA the principle that 'power relations are discursive' but inflects them very differently.

Textbox 10.1: Tenets of CDA

The **main tenets of CDA** according to Fairclough and Wodak (1997: 271–80) are:

1 CDA addresses social problems.
2 Power relations are discursive.
3 Discourse constitutes society and culture.
4 Discourse does ideological work.
5 Discourse is historical.
6 The link between text and society is mediated.
7 Discourse analysis is interpretative and explanatory.
8 Discourse is a form of social action.

Second, we see that CDA researchers more consistently position themselves and their research participants as agents of change (Tenets 1 and 3). Again, we see the importance of political imagination and will in CDA because, ideally, CDA will produce findings that can be used to create social change. The relationship between discourse and society (and/or culture) in CDA is such that equal attention is given to structure and agency. Here, CDA adapts Anthony Giddens's (1984) **structuration theory**, which says social systems are produced and reproduced in social interaction with people playing a central role; CDA researchers replace 'social systems' with 'discourses' (Blommaert and Bulcaen, 2000). CDA also shares with Foucauldian discourse analysis the idea that, as bodies of knowledge, discourses are socially constructed, never fully cohesive, and permeable. CDA has been commended for recognizing that individual actors are at play in discursive strategies and can use them to create opportunities for resistance.

Third, in CDA, discourses are understood to have ideological aspects that have become taken for granted (Teo, 2000) (Tenet 4). When used in CDA, **ideology** is a term gleaned from the work of Karl Marx, who perceived the ideas of those who hold power, i.e. the bourgeoisie, to be the ruling ideas, those that organize political, economic systems. To say that these ruling ideas are ideological is to say that they shape the proletariat's (or everyday working class citizens') **false consciousness**, a mistaken perception of their interests and class identity. This false consciousness, in turn, perpetuates the ruling class' domination. Wodak (1996) explains that in CDA the concern becomes how discourses reflect, produce, or reproduce ideology. The key, from the perspective of CDA, is to understand how discourse is underpinned by ideology and that discourse does ideological work. Once this understanding is gleaned, the researcher as a public intellectual is in an optimal position to argue for change.

Fairclough (2001a) deliberately roots his interest in the ideological work of discourse in the theorizing of Antonio Gramsci (1971). This Marxist scholar argued that **hegemony** explains the power of ruling classes, a power that depends not so much upon coercion as on the creation of consent to 'common sense' assumptions. (Note that we discuss more finely Marxism, ideology and discourse again in the following chapter.) Importantly, CDA scholars such as Wodak (1996) do not claim that all discourses are ideological, e.g. that they only produce people's mistaken belief systems. As van Dijk (2006: 129) explains: 'People do many other things with words at the same time.'

Ontology and Epistemology in a Critical Paradigm

In the tenets discussed above, we have seen CDA to adopt the post-structural understandings that what can be known is relative, that discourses are socially constructed and ever-changing, and that discourse is specifically constituted by

power–knowledge relations. But in assigning researchers the role of social critics, CDA's ontological and epistemological grounding can also seem to be contradictory and to part ways with Foucault, who – as we have seen – resisted the epistemology that there was a position from which he, or any knower, could make claims about what ought to be.

In its ideas about criticism and change, as well as those about ideology, CDA is drawing from **critical theory**, which is associated with a group of twentieth century neo-Marxist theorists, including Max Horkheimer, Theodor Adorno, Herbert Marcuse, and Jürgen Habermas, collectively referred to as the Frankfurt School. Critical theory takes up Marx's scholarship, which argued that what we know and how we can know it are grounded in the real material conditions in which we live, and contributes insights about how cultural, psychodynamic, and social processes enter into this. The Frankfurt School's ontology, like Marx's, was one of critical realism: there is a concrete world in which practices related to ownership of the means of production have material consequences for people. The Frankfurt School subscribed to an epistemology that saw as possible and necessary a standpoint from which to assert knowledge, criticize, and prescribe directions for culture and society. As Max Horkheimer argued, critical theory can serve 'to liberate human beings from the circumstances that enslave them' (1982: 244).

How coherent can CDA be if it fuses the activist standpoint and insights of a (realist) critical social theory paradigm with the insights of a (constructionist) post-structuralist one? This is a question that particularly troubles Hammersley (1997). And we can see how those who hold to an orthodox reading of either theory would be horrified. Hammersley proposes that CDA researchers should become committed post-structuralists, dispense with the notion that their politics flow from a standpoint of a definitive knower, and instead call their politics a matter of personal choice. This would mean CDA researchers no longer being able to claim that their conclusions point the definitive way to emancipation.

But, we find CDA scholars to be generally less concerned about this than Hammersley would wish. In the spirit of pluralism within the broad movement that is CDA, Fairclough (2001b), for example, accepts that CDA could also be put forth from a conservative stance. We add that a person committed to the general goal of CDA, to bring about change, could be quite taken with the bridging of two paradigms. CDA seems to work quite happily with the idea that there is a reality that is partially socially constructed and partially materially constituted, and that discourses thus have both social and material bases and consequences, such as social inequality. We perceive this in Tenet 7 of CDA as well (see Textbox 10.1), in that the movement purports to do work that is both interpretive – speaking to the social constructedness of reality – and explanatory – speaking to its materiality.

Rigor in CDA

Recall that in CDA, the foremost concern is about social problems and change. Scholars' ideas about rigor sidestep questions about error reduction and the status of the 'evidence' that discourse analysis creates. For CDA, to effect change researchers should *be convincing about the trustworthiness of their claims*. For example, Wood and Kroger (2000) maintain that linguists employing discourse analysis are more convincing about the trustworthiness of their claims if they document those claims in a diligent and orderly fashion. The reader can then assess the soundness of the claims according to the plausibility and coherence of the findings. In nursing research, Stevenson (2004) draws on the work of Potter (1996) to argue that researchers can assess the trustworthiness of their findings by focusing on **deviant cases**, which are perceived to justify or support the discovery of patterns of phenomena, and by checking with participants as to whether the analysis supports their understandings.

In the model that Fairclough (2001b) puts forth for analysis, to start with a social problem means to seek to produce knowledge with emancipatory potential. Rigor includes asking whether the social order 'in a sense "needs" the problem' (p. 33). Answering involves *reflecting on the relation of discourse to other dimensions of the social order that are networked with it, and that it represents*, including means of production, social identities, and values. (For those of us who find it easiest to think about cultural matters, this means we'll have to think about economics too.) If the problem is 'needed,' then recommendations for how to bring about social change will require you to begin to radically re-envision the social order. Rigor here means thinking big.

Some scholars have a concern with how CDA does not have a very clear position on truth and validity. Hammersley (1997), whom we saw to point out CDA's ontological and epistemological contradiction, criticizes the strategies used by CDA researchers and their claim that their research is to be evaluated by its political implications. He finds this lacking. He argues that since CDA analysts question the truth of claims made within the discourses that they study, these researchers need to do a better job equally questioning their own claims and acknowledging the ideological influences on these too. From this, we recommend that researchers *apply a **reflexivity** specifically focused on ideological, political, and ethical stances*. (In Chapter 12, we'll expand on the concept of reflexivity, which can have many other foci.) Indeed, we note that CDA scholars respond to these tensions around validity by maintaining that their analysis yields interpretations, which are best thought of as plausible and more or less accurate, rather than as definitive truth claims (Wodak, 1999). Some CDA scholars also would say that the 'critical' in 'Critical Discourse Analysis' includes acknowledging one's values and beliefs in shaping the research and that interpretations are always inherently incomplete.

Breeze (2011) voices another concern, that when CDA practitioners draw conclusions about what people take from what they read, see, and hear, they often fail to mention that their research subjects may take things differently, or to discuss

what evidence they have one way or another. Conversation analysts would agree with Breeze. They caution that CDA is prone to importing as context what research subjects themselves may not treat as relevant (e.g. Schegloff, 1999; Widdicombe, 1995), i.e., they fail to heed Schegloff's dictum of relevance and procedural consequentiality (see Chapter 5). In response, CDA practitioners consider conversation analysts to naively refuse to lift their eyes from their transcripts – to fail to think big. While CDA practitioners are not about to follow Schegloff's dictum, they could do as Breeze suggests when analyzing texts such as political speeches, television news, advertising images, and policy documents, i.e., *attend where possible to how these texts are received* by their listeners, viewers, and users. For example, analysis of readers' comments on a political speech that is posted online can inform analysis of the speech itself. This is a matter given much thought in communication and literary studies, where it is addressed by reception (Hall, 1980) or reader-response theory respectively (Radway, 1984).

Textbox 10.2: A Summary of How to Approach Discourse through CDA

- Strive for a trustworthy and persuasive presentation of findings.
- Connect discourse to other dimensions of the social order.
- Be reflexive about your ideological, political, and ethical stances.
- Keep in mind that texts may be interpreted in multiple ways by their audiences.

DOING CDA

As we've mentioned, CDA originated in linguistics and has spanned out to other disciplines. Scheuer (2003: 143) summarizes the research strategies within CDA as ranging

> from grammatical and micro-sociological analyses to studies of wider social contexts on a macro-sociological level, often with reference to global political movements, ideologies, and market tendencies, and often with an overt political agenda.

At the micro end of this range, we find some linguists' work that focuses on the finer details of talk and that shares with CA an interest in the mechanisms of sequential organization (Mills, 2004). Although the terms introduced throughout the CA chapter are all basic in such CDA, the CDA practitioners' strategies differ in that they reject the criteria of relevance and procedural consequentiality, define context as they see fit, and speak freely of power and ideology. At the more macro, abstract, or philosophical end of the range (Ainsworth and Hardy, 2004), we find other linguists, along with CDA practitioners from disciplines such as sociology or health studies (e.g., Funk, 2013; Gazso, 2007; Johansson et al., 2010). These researchers analyze the content of talk for its themes and situate these themes in

broader contexts. While the strategies we outline below are sometimes illustrated with micro-level work and sometimes with macro-level work, keep in mind that, as CDA is eclectic, you can mix and match.

CDA Strategies

The first analytic strategy we introduce is that of using talk data to understand how discourses shape, and are shaped by, social interactions or institutional processes and practices. In one of the studies she discusses in *Disorders of Discourse*, Ruth Wodak (1996) takes up Foucault's argument that discourses permit some actions and prohibits others, and uses it in analyzing the doctor–patient interaction. Wodak considers discourses in this, and other, institutional interactions to be bounded by rules that are both manifest or latent, that make some communications possible and others not. For example, in the conventional medical clinic, given its socio-historical context, doctors ask questions of a patient in order to diagnose an illness; the patient does not ask questions of the doctor. Wodak further acknowledges Foucault's insight that even if some rules and conventions change so that discourses become less constraining, the discourses are no less imbued with power. So, if a doctor creates the space wherein patients can ask questions in return, this may result in patients raising their concerns more freely but to a limit – when doctors re-assert their power in these relationships.

To illuminate this, in Textbox 10.3 we show an except from Wodak's that comes from a doctor–patient dialog in an out-patient ward of a Viennese hospital. In the transcription convention used, lines are bracketed together when two people speak at the same time, while parentheses (..........) refer to inaudible talk.

Textbox 10.3: If you don't ask

141	P:	It's, well - it's - what's it called Mulox or something.
142	[DR:	Maalox yes
	[P:	The Maalox – it was prescribed – but I never
143	P:	got it. This is just an example (........) for starters
144	[DR:	mhm
	[P:	of that. (........) By now – by now I know that
145	[DR:	Right.
	[P:	if you don't ask (...................)
146	DR:	So when did you have the shortness of breath – please tell me?

Source: Lalouschek et al., 1990: 38, trans. Markus Gerke

In her analysis of this conversation in *Disorders of Discourse*, Wodak (1996) points out how, after the patient has introduced his concern about not receiving the Maalox, the doctor agrees with his rationalization (lines 144–145) that this did not happen because the patient had failed to ask for it. The doctor even seems to praise the patient with 'That's right' (line 145), and then effects a brisk change of topic (line 146). What Wodak finds most interesting here is how the doctor uses such mechanisms to maintain the discourse of medical authority, even in a space in which patient–doctor dialog is comparatively open.

In another study illustrating this strategy, Teresa Carbó (1992) begins with the puzzle of why Mexican parliamentary debaters of 1920 to 1960 routinely interrupted one another, and why rules of order that specified that interrupters should be subjected to strict sanctions, such as being prohibited from further speech during a session, went unenforced. We can read her study as asking why a text (the rules of order) and its reception (parliamentarians' behavior) differed. Among Carbó's answers is one based in Mexican political history. The Institutional Revolutionary Party had been in power in Mexico throughout the period in question, and any legislation it proposed was bound to pass. In Carbó's interpretation, the parliamentarians were using interruptions – and even inviting them with provocative remarks that demanded an immediate response (i.e., they were first-pair parts of adjacency pairs) – in order to perform the appearance of being engaged in genuine debate. Because the parliamentarians had internalized a discourse specifying that normative democratic debate should be spirited and polemical, transgressing the written rules of order was, paradoxically, a way in which they cooperated and conformed.

The use of the analytic strategy of focusing on the relationships between social interactions and institutions may involve more deliberately *building the bridge between micro interactions and macro structures,* such as organizations, institutions including the economy, or the greater social structure of a given society. Van Dijk (2001: 354) observes that, from the perspective of CDA: 'a racist speech in parliament is a discourse at the microlevel of social interaction in the specific situation of a debate, but at the same time may enact or be a constituent part of legislation or the reproduction of racism at the macrolevel.' Take for instance Shiao-Yun Chiang's (2010) unpacking of the rhetorical strategies by which CNN anchor Lou Dobbs publicly debated with Janet Murguia, president of a Hispanic civil rights organization in the USA, about her accusations that he had expressed racism toward undocumented migrants. In one passage from the debate, Dobbs says to Murguia, 'You would not even be involved in this debate on illegal immigration unless the preponderance of those illegal aliens [being discussed] were Hispanic. And you know that is a fact' (p. 289). Chiang points out how, here, Dobbs positions himself the objective possessor of 'a fact' and Murguia as being self-interested and subjective. Elsewhere in the debate, Dobbs trumps Murguia's statements by calling them contrary to free speech and the US Constitution. Chiang maintains that to claim to a wide viewership that hate speech amounts to freedom of speech contributes at the macro level to the legitimation of racism.

Sometimes the researcher who pursues a micro–macro bridging strategy emphasizes whether and how individual agency is constrained by structure, or is used to contest it. Johansson et al. (2010) studied how occupational therapists and municipal bureaucrats in Sweden talked about home modification services, such as adding handrails to bathrooms. Such services facilitate aging people's continuing residence in their homes instead of long-term care facilities. Johansson et al. found the therapists spoke of feeling pressured to act toward clients according to a bureaucratic discourse that emphasized rules and regulations. They also found that an economic discourse of cost effectiveness could enter into the therapists' interactions with clients, as this therapist indicated:

> Yes, you also think of the patients and their needs. But at the same time, you try to keep some kind of cost awareness. So you suggest what is possible and that's also motivated pricewise. (p. 571).

However, among the occupational therapists, ideology was not all that entered in their interactions with clients. Johansson et al. found some of them to interact according to a human rights discourse and encourage their clients to exercise autonomy and self-determination:

> I try to find out what they want themselves, of course, and explain that they have the option of making their own additions, and that it's like up to them if they want this, 'yes'. I tell them often that, 'You have the right to say, 'no', so that they know that. (p. 575)

Thus, Johansson et al. encouraged other researchers to consider how moral motivations could be a source of agentic resistance against the role of economic ideology in the allocation of welfare services.

Deconstruction is a key analytical strategy of CDA, as it has been for Foucault. Researchers aim to *deconstruct how power and/or ideology are implicated in the constitution of discourses and are an effect of discourses*. Within this vein, CDA can reveal how discourses are oppressive, power is legitimized, ideology is perpetuated, and inequalities are constructed or maintained. CDA, for example, can be used to uncover hidden or implied meanings of language, as illustrated in Mele and Bello's (2007) excellent study of exchanges between drivers and security personnel at highway checkpoints in Nigeria. These checkpoints had been institutionalized in response to dominant, interactional dynamics – discourses – of smuggling, drug pushing, and armed robbery. Security personnel solicited and legitimized drivers' bribing of them by making drivers feel guilty for the hardships of tropical weather and unpaid salaries that they were experiencing. Mele and Bello employ CDA to uncover how the security personnel went about 'kola collection' (p. 443), a phrase meaning 'nut collection,' but used to refer to the collection of bribes. As the following exchange between security personnel (SP) and a driver (D) suggests, this was not the only veiled expression in use:

SP: Alhaji, gari yayi zafi. {Sir, the town is hot}

D: To yaya za a yi? {So, what can be done?}

SP: A suba mana ruwa. {Pour us some water} (p. 443, authors' translation)

Mele and Bello explain that the word 'heat' figuratively means 'broke' or 'financially troubled,' while the word 'water' figuratively means 'bribe.' Key to their interpretation that checkpoint discourse is imbued with power is that these words had meanings on both literal and figurative planes. If security personnel came under suspicion of wrongdoing, they could legitimize their exchanges by claiming that they were simply asking for water because they were hot. 'Kola collection' thus encapsulates how power relations filter through the discursive experience of highway checkpoints, although these had been intended to make highways safer.

We can also *explore talk data with an emphasis on discourse and social change*. For instance, Fairclough (2009) reconsiders the work of MacDonald (1994) who interviewed people in England who were officially unemployed and receiving income support benefits, whilst engaging in 'under-the-table' work for employers whom they would find in pubs. Fairclough argues that their experiences of unemployment result from processes of globalization (i.e., of international finance and trade, mobilizations of workers, and flows of information through new technologies) in which discursive representations play a part. However, unemployed people could also reshape the discourse of globalization by re-appropriating its key terms, putting them to uses counter to their original meaning. For example, Fairclough observes that in the following excerpt, one such person gives voice to the neoliberal economic discourse of globalization when he refers to 'flexibility,' a notion key to free trade and global market competition, and uses it to justify laboring while on income support:

> He [the 'hirer and firer'] just shows his face in 'The Rose Tree' or 'The Gate' and people jump and ask him for work. When I was working there I've seen him just drive off in his van around the pubs and he'll come back with another twenty men to work, an hour later. No one asks any questions.
>
> [...] It's a matter of us being cheaper. It's definitely easier than having a lot of lads taken on permanently. It would cost them more to put them on the books or pay them off. It's just the flexibility. You're just there for when the jobs come up, and he (the 'hirer and firer') will come and get you when you're needed. You need to be on the dole to be able to do that. Otherwise you'd be sitting there for half the year with no work and no money at all. (MacDonald, 1994: 515, cited in Fairclough, 2009: 336)

Fairclough concludes that people who are unemployed can thus reshape global capitalism in ways that may fall outside official government discourses on globalization.

Another strategy for looking at the relation of discourse to change focuses on *the* **recontextualization** *of discourse,* i.e., on how arguments, strategies, practices, and discourses are moved from one context to another (Bernstein, 1990;

Fairclough, 2009; Wodak, 1999). In such moves, these entities are transformed or re-appropriated because they are disarticulated in one context and rearticulated in another, where they produce different meanings and consequences. (This idea bears relation to that of Foucault's tactical polyvalence of discourse.) It is because these moves include dissemination of information, which any change involves, that Fairclough (2009) sees recontextualization as central to social change.

Asimakou and Oswick (2010) illustrate how recontextualization can be taken up through the use of talk data in their study of how a UK-based multinational oil company's research and development (R&D) laboratories were transformed into an 'innovation park' of independent consultancies. They interviewed 41 R&D professionals to understand how they perceived the recontextualization of a commercial discourse associated with business and the 'bottom line' into the laboratory space. Asimakou and Oswick discovered the R&D professionals to experience the recontextualization in several ways, including: as a shift in focus from research needs to the needs of the oil company as their customer; as a reconstitution of workplace practices, such as by introducing teams to ensure that the laboratories were efficient; and as a reformulation of research identities into managerial ones. As one scientist put it:

> at the early stage [of a project] they want you to present Net Present Values for 5–6–7 years, and that is very hard for the programme, and that puts off many colleagues, who say 'hang on, I am a mechanical engineer, or a I am a chemist, or whatever, I am a lab-technician, or . . ., I have a pretty good knowledge of the job I am supposed to do, but I am not very strong in finance'. (p. 287)

Asimakou and Oswick stress that because the R&D professionals perceived this recontextualization to gradually trickle in, there was no marked crisis point around which they could mobilize.

In addition to exemplifying how recontextualization is linked to change, Asimakou and Oswick's (2010) study helpfully shows how CDA can be put to the use of understanding *how a discourse can shape identities.* Ainsworth and Hardy (2004) explain that, in CDA, it's equally important *to observe how identity categories and classifications are socially constructed in the first place.* They discuss the implications of turning people into social problems, giving the example of the emergence of the category of 'elderly workers,' who are constructed as inflexible when they're in the workplace yet as a drain on society when they're unemployed. An example using talk data is Murdocca's (2003) analysis of how Canadian newspapers took up the story of a woman named Colette Matshimoseka, who had been hospitalized with a serious illness after returning to Canada. Drawing on van Dijk's (1988) insight that ideological work is done when media reports package quotations, reflecting subjective opinions, alongside fact, Murdocca shows how quotations calling Matshimoseka 'Ebola woman' and 'Congo woman' (p. 26) narrowed her identity to a diseased, debased, and racialized one. Further, Murdocca discusses how an immigration minister's statements that Matshimoseka had brought a 'new fear'

(p. 26) across the border effectively assigned to Canada the category of an undefiled national space, thereby justifying the tightening of border controls, and erasing a history in which European settlers had carried infectious diseases to Aboriginal populations.

Textbox 10.4: A Summary of Strategies for Doing CDA

- Explore how discourses shape social interactions and institutions.
- Problematize the bridge between micro interactions and macro structures.
- Explore how power constitutes discourse and is an outcome of discourse.
- Consider what power is legitimized, and what ideological work discourse does.
- Inquire into the role of discourse in social change.
- Assess how discourses shift and change over time or in different contexts.
- Examine the relation between discourse and identities/identity categories.

CHAPTER SUMMARY

Critical Discourse Analysis is a movement, possessing core principles but embracing a variety of ideas about power, some stemming from Foucault's scholarship and others drawing upon Marxism and critical theory. The very idea of CDA as a movement might be disturbing to some who desire to name one theory or one theorist as they pinpoint the origins of an approach. But for others, the appeal of CDA is the sheer innovation by which one can analyze talk data as but one kind of discourse and with intentions that are unabashedly political and responsive to social injustices. CDA holds that, in a colloquial sense, discourse does 'stuff.' It constructs ideas, actions, and practices and with ideological implications. Individuals 'do' things too, but they are not the focus, for their doings are shaped by discourse. In sum – from looking at material practice and how interactions are shaped by discourse, to the hidden and other meanings of words and power behind them and how a discourse moves and evolves – there are several strategies for doing CDA.

ELEVEN

Garden-variety Discourse Analysis

Recall that what we term 'garden-variety' is discourse analysis that is not wed to any particular theorist or movement. The term captures the many studies we came across wherein researchers speaking of using 'discourse analysis' or 'critical discourse analysis' (in deliberate lower-case), blend together several theoretical and methodological insights in eclectic ways, and sometimes acknowledge that Foucauldian or CDA insights number among them. But in this practice of DA, scholars don't always have to name names or their approach in order to move forward. Here we synthesize what we saw to be the ideas, assumptions, and strategies that they generally share.

UNDERSTANDING THE DISCOURSE–SOCIETY DIALECTIC

The tenet that discourse and society are related is central to discourse analysis writ large, and not limited to Foucauldian discourse analysis or CDA. Discourse is perceived as both constructed by society and shaping what society is. Mills (2004: 10) incorporates this dialectic into her very definition of discourse as: 'groupings of utterances or sentences, statements which are enacted within a social context, which are determined by that social context and which contribute to the way that social context continues its existence.' Garden-variety DA shares with CDA the understanding that there are two distinct levels of interaction – that of the macro order of society, which includes such institutions as the economy, family, and media, and that of the micro level of interaction – and prioritizes the relation between the two. Researchers adopting a garden-variety approach will analyze talk data for *how discourses shape social interactions and institutions and vice versa.*

This is identical to a CDA strategy we introduced earlier. However, here, we are interested in how the use of this strategy from a garden-variety approach does not have to refer to Fairclough, Wodak, van Dijk, or other CDA scholars.

Funk's (2013) study of how the meaning of family roles and responsibilities for chronically or terminally ill patients are shaped by home health discourse is a good example of this strategy. Funk interviewed managers, administrators, and other decision-makers in health care agencies in British Columbia, Canada. In these decision-makers' discourse, 'home first' caregiving by families was taken for granted as a desired model of care. But they also reflected on how this approach might not meet the family members' expectations of how much support the agencies would provide; there was a degree of difference between the discourse and public expectations. Funk also convincingly argues the possibility of negative implications of home health discourses, such as when care at home becomes constituted as normative and imperative and thereby can lead to the denial of choice to individuals and families.

Here's another everyday example with the potential to be formulated into a project oriented to this strategy. As a member of a parents' group volunteering at her daughter's licensed day care facility, Amber agreed to engage in fundraising for new playground equipment, only to find discourses shaping social interaction. At a monthly meeting, the group had discussed new kinds of equipment that their children might enjoy, such as teeter-totters, slides, climbing structures, tricycles, and hopscotch patterns on the asphalt. A week later, as Amber was chatting with the day care Director, the following exchange (roughly paraphrased) took place.

Textbox 11.1: The *Ontario Day Nurseries Act*

Director: There has been a lot of talk that some parents want to purchase new slides and climbing structures with the money we fundraise.

Amber: We did talk about slides and climbing structures among other things.

Director: Well, our day care staff, who are ECEs [licensed early childhood educators], are concerned about the safety risks of this kind of playground equipment. There's been a lot of research that shows the risks are greater than the reward.

Amber: Oh, okay. I understand. But we did have other ideas too.

Director: How do you feel about me and another Director visiting the parents' group to explain the research on playground equipment? We could also remind parents that we need to conform to the *Ontario Day Nurseries Act* and cannot just purchase anything.

Amber: That does sound like a good idea.

This example illustrates how the social interactions of fundraising parents, and of children at play, are shaped by macro-level governmental and institutional discourses about childhood, early childhood development, law, and risk. At the micro level these are expressed by the Director's invoking a credentialed occupational category (the 'ECE'), the *Ontario Day Nurseries Act*, and the knowledge established by 'the research,' as justifications that Amber, thinking to herself, 'Oh my goodness, my daughter could get seriously hurt!' willingly accepted. Further, this example illustrates how Amber suspended her academic identity, through which she possesses skills for evaluating playground equipment research, in favor of an identity as mother. Both of these involve subjectivity, a point we now turn to in detail.

UNRAVELING IDENTITIES AND SUBJECTIVITIES

Garden-variety discourse analysts can use Foucault- and CDA-informed strategies to focus on subject positions and identities, but also offer strategies influenced by a different view of why social scientists should care about these. To explain, we'll start off by comparing how the various strategies we've looked at thus far in this book approach a tangled clump of concepts: the self, identity, subject position, and **subjectivity**.

In NA, we'd seen self to come to the fore, along with questions of meanings and interpretations, such as of how we can make sense of our selves to ourselves, and understand our selves to be continuous at the same time as we know that we have the potential to change. In CA, we saw researchers to be indifferent to such questions about inner states and self-understandings. Instead, they questioned how social order is talked into being, including through use of identity categories that proved malleable, fluid, and amenable to various ends (e.g., the category of 'bad woman' could be used to warrant a judgment of 'bad neighbor' in Textbox 6.1). Although Sacks (1995: 40) had spoken of categories as rich in inferences, what those inferences tended to be, how they were connected, and what interests they might serve fell outside CA's purview. It is DA's forte to ask how great webs of discourse and power relations are implicated in bringing subject positions into being (Foucault's way of putting it) or socially constructing identities (CDAs).

However, some garden-variety DA shares the NA interest in interpreting individuals' searches for the meanings and understandings of identity categories. Foucauldian discourse analysts would rarely set aside their concern that projects of self-understanding, including various technologies of the self, are enmeshed in the modern ideal of the 'rational knower'– the very ideal that Foucault's work casts in doubt. But garden-variety discourse analysts generally don't trouble themselves all that much about ontology or epistemology. Some of them might call Foucault's reading too deterministic; some might agree with Clarke (2008: 511), who suggests that Foucault's work lacks 'any sense of

emotion, passion or motivation in the construction of self.' Capitalized Critical Discourse Analysts might wonder how far an interpretive approach to the inner experience of identity can take us down the road to change, and whether visible actions that express agency aren't more important. But, the garden-variety discourse analysts would likely say that understanding individual dilemmas is a necessary first step.

Garden-variety discourse analysis can understand **identity** sociologically as how we see ourselves and how others see us, as developed in interaction (Jaworski and Coupland, 2006). Or, as per literary theorist Donald Hall (2004), identity can be understood as traits and beliefs that provide one with a personality and way of being. Relevant facets of identity can include mother, florist, or mystic and include meanings and expectations associated with them. Identity, from a post-structural discourse analytic perspective, however, is constituted by and realized through discourses, and thus identity, too, is fluid and malleable. As we shift into post-structuralism, we shift from viewing an individual as having an identity of X to the discursive construction of identity X.

Subjectivity is a term connected to identity and sometimes used interchangeably with it, which can be confusing to say the least. Subjectivity refers to a person's perceptions and interpretations – or their self-consciousness as Donald Hall (2004) writes – about their identity, in interaction with others and in making judgments about their social world. For example, you may be reading this book because various discourses have thrust you into the subject position of 'academic' or shaped what 'an academic' identity is. Your subjectivity, however, is comprised of your attitudes, perceptions, feelings, and self-understandings pertaining to what an academic is or should be. To be sure, garden-variety discourse analysts ask how subjectivities are shaped by and made possible by discourses, but Foucault's sense of subjects being disciplined to internalize and strive to reproduce what's 'normal' is not always built into their approach.

In the garden-variety approach, talk data can be analyzed for *how discourses represent and/or shape social identities*. The language that respondents use in an interview can be understood as organized by available, already present and explicit discourses that contain and perpetuate available identities. Hvas and Gannik (2008) interviewed women experiencing menopause to understand which available discourses they drew upon in deciding whether to manage menopause with medication and/or hormone therapy. One of their assumptions in undertaking this research was that when women choose one discourse over another, they are positioning themselves as a subject in this discourse (p. 178). They discovered that women drew on a plurality of discourses including the 'biomedical discourse,' the 'alternative discourse,' and the 'feminist/critical discourse'. In adopting a 'biomedical discourse,' for example, women believed menopause to be a biological fact and therefore took up the identity of patient in need of guidance and medication from gynecologists in order to control their bodies.

Discourses can also be deconstructed *to discern how they reflect or (re-)produce identities and subjectivities that can be contradictory.* Analyzing interviews with young francophone women from Quebec, Canada who participated in team sports, Ravel and Rail (2006) sought to discover how the women positioned themselves in culturally available discourses about gender, sexuality, and embodied identities. According to these women, one culturally available discourse for lesbian sportswomen rested on discursive constructions of them as 'butches.' A butch, in their view, has a specific identity and is involved in particular kinds of social interactions. She is '"(a little) fat", "vulgar", "pays little attention to her appearance", "walks like a cowboy" and "has a mullet"'(p. 402). Ravel and Rail discovered that, contrary to this discourse, many sportswomen (re)presented themselves as *gaie*, a Quebecois positioning they chose because it means 'female homosexual.' The participants also shared an understanding that *gaie* means fun, joyfulness, and belonging.

Exploring the unsaid or implicit discourses that underlie how people produce their understandings of their social worlds can also be a strategic goal of analysis. This often entails deconstructing talk 'on the surface' (or at face value) for the discursive constructions underlying it. Pascale (2008a) analyzed common-sense knowledge about race expressed in interviews with a diverse group of Californians. One respondent said that he thought of race as 'ethnic background [...] the culture from which the individual has emerged' but also identified himself as 'Caucasian' and 'coming from essentially White northern European stock' (p. 731). This understanding, Pascale explains, intermingles a newer cultural account of race with an older biological one. Most respondents spoke of race as color, as nationality, as culture, or a matter of blood. As Pascale says,

> Common sense secures the social, historical, political, and economic spaces that give race its materiality by producing race as a matter that requires no thought – which leads people to believe they simply *see* race. (p. 733)

The problem is that underlying these understandings are historical politics of racism that few respondents are aware of or understand to oppress others.

Textbox 11.2: A Summary of Strategies for Unraveling Identities and Subjectivities

- Explore how discourses shape social interactions and institutions, and vice versa.
- Ask how discourses represent and/or shape social identities and subjectivities, keeping an eye out for contradictions.
- Study the unsaid or implicit discourses underlying understandings of social worlds.

ANALYZING POWER AND DISCOURSE

As in both Foucauldian discourse analysis and CDA, power in garden-variety discourse analysis is conceptualized as multi-faceted and ubiquitous. Garden-variety discourse analysts continue to perceive the language used in interaction to express power relations and have political effects beyond the immediate conversation and situation in which it occurs. Garden-variety discourse analysts acknowledge that some individuals and institutions may appear to hold and practice power, but they continue to emphasize that this appearance is constituted by and constitutive of discourses.

A popular strategy is therefore to explore *how some discourses are privileged and not others*. This is often a strategy used in research that explores how discourses connect to social policies or institutions. Sunderland and colleagues (2009) contrasted Australian policy discourse about persons with disabilities to transcripts from focus groups of persons who had survived strokes or experienced traumatic brain injuries. They discovered that Australian policy discourse presented disability in largely negative terms such as vulnerability, neediness, and inferiority. Generally missing from this discourse are the possibilities of happiness, fulfillment, and aspiration voiced by persons with disabilities, such as in this focus group participant's statement about his upcoming graduation:

> yeah last semester was really hard but I'm gonna go out on a high because I'm really putting a lot of effort into it and I really want to do it really good and that's for my own sense of excitement [...] and I just see that after that life will be great because I've done what I wanted to do all my life already. So it's cream on the, icing on the cake. (2009: 709)

Sunderland et al. refer to the discourse of joy as a missing or **silent discourse** in existing policy texts. They explain that by silencing joyful discourses about disability and exposing the public solely to negativity, persons with disabilities become further marginalized and socially excluded, justifying the extension of only minimal rights to them. Just like CDA researchers, those who employ garden-variety DA do not shy away from considering the political significance of their work.

Analysis following this strategy can be motivated by the insights and critical commentary of those affected by a discourse and the subject positions that it supports. Brown, Souto-Manning and Laman (2010) explored how Accelerated Reading, a mandatory program adopted for elementary schools in the southeastern USA, discursively constructed students' interpretations of what a 'good reader' was. This program required students to progress through color-coded reading levels, in which they were to pass tests about a narrow selection of books in order to earn points. Students criticized books that represented the speech and lifestyles of racialized people as though they were 'colored White folk' (p. 520), the rote memorization required to pass the tests on lower-level 'baby books' (p. 523), and

the awarding of more points to students passing the tests on higher-level books. The following exchange between Mariana (Souto-Manning) and a student named Michael illustrates his awareness that, as an English-language learner, he would be unable to match the successes of another student named Levi:

> Michael: But these books I read ... they are dumb books. They're less than a point. Levi's books are ten points. He's dark blue. No I think he's black now. He's black. He reads one book and I have to read zillions. He's a way better reader than me.
>
> Mariana: Not really.
>
> Michael: Yeah ... I think it's because he already understands what's happening and I have to learn about what's happening, learn letters, learn everything. I will never be as good as Levi. (2010: 522)

Brown et al. conclude that a White, middle-class discursive construction of a good reader as a competitive individualist, well versed in White culture, was being privileged by the Accelerated Reading program.

Using Ideology in Garden-Variety DA

> There is nothing either good or bad, but thinking makes it so.
>
> William Shakespeare, Hamlet

How discourse is related to ideology is an important question for discourse analysts, and one that they answer differently depending on what they take ideology to mean. As discussed in Chapter 10, in sociology and other social science disciplines, **ideology** is a term most closely tied to the work of Marx, who understood ideology to support power relations that privilege one class and not others and those unprivileged were unaware of this inequality because of their false consciousness.

But, surprise! What we didn't mention in the CDA chapter is that Marx also used **ideology** in a second sense, referring to how it appeared in religious, legal, political, aesthetic, and other active debates about class interests – thus contradicting the altogether negative definition of ideology as an illusion that one class imposes upon unknowing others (see Hall, 1996; Williams, 1983). Cultural theorist Stuart Hall (1996) explains that this looser, value-neutral sense of ideology has come to prevail. He defines it as

> *all* organized forms of social thinking [encompassing] the practical as well as the theoretical knowledges which enable people to 'figure out' society, and within whose categories and discourse we 'live out' and 'experience' our objective positioning in social relations. (1996: 26)

Van Dijk similarly offers a definition of ideology in this second sense as 'political or social systems of ideas, values or prescriptions of groups or other collectivities' (1998: 3).

In the first Marxist sense of ideology, to speak of a 'dominant ideology' would be redundant, whereas in the second sense of ideology used by both Marx and Hall, it works. In the first Marxist sense, ideology is all about class. In the second, ideology can pertain to other social categories, i.e. the ideology of heteronormativity pertains to categories of sexuality. Because both senses can be used in discourse analysis, *if you use 'ideology,' you should aim to be precise about what you mean by it.* Do you think of ideology as an oppressive class-related illusion of which we're generally unaware? Choose the first and be prepared to explain how you and perhaps also the people whose talk you are analyzing have been capable of lifting the veil of illusion. Do you think ideologies could be dominant or non-dominant, class-related or related to other social groupings, and possible to consciously and agentically contest? Choose the second. Do you think Foucault was right in saying that we can't tell a false way of thinking from a true one, and that what might seem to be oppositional positions are embedded in the same power–knowledge relations as the dominant ones (see Hall, 1992)? If so, don't use 'ideology' at all.

Whatever their definition, discourse analysts tend to differentiate discourse from ideology but to also see the two as intimately connected. How might this work? To Stuart Hall, people formulate their intentions as shaped by ideology, meaning that ideology predates individual social interactions. People therefore 'speak through' the ideologies active in their society. To Purvis and Hunt (1993), the relation between ideology and discourse is one of implication. They understand discourses to organize lived experiences of social relations and all thought, understandings, and social experiences, while ideologies are those specific forms of discourse that represent the interests of social categories, and are themselves constructed through discourse. The strategy emerging from this is *to analyze discourses for their ideological implications,* that is, for whether and how they rest on, perpetuate or illuminate ideologies. (We include the 'whether' question here because it depends on your definition of ideology: recall Wodak's (1996) comment that not all discourse does the ideological work of reproducing a mistaken belief system.)

Rebecca Jennings's (2004) analysis of the Hall Carpenter Oral History Archive, a collection of transcripts of interviews with lesbians, conducted in Britain between 1945 and 1970, is an excellent example of garden-variety discourse analysis that combines several of the concepts we have been discussing. Studying the transcripts, Jennings observed that the topic of lesbian home lives and domesticity was not much asked about by interviewers and not much told about by the respondents. Jennings attributed the interviewers' discursive practice of not asking to the liberal feminist ideology of their day, which did not celebrate women's domesticity

so much as their work outside the home, such as the respondents' police or Royal Air Force careers. She explained the respondents' not telling in terms of the limited housing options available for single women in the post-war, which meant that many continued to live in their parents' homes or found temporary housing such as bedsits. Because an exclusionary discourse had positioned domesticity as the domain of wives and mothers, Jennings concluded that, 'lesbian interviewees had no discourse of lesbian domesticity on which to draw in discussing their home lives. As a result, they largely erased their experiences of home from the lesbian narratives' (p. 442). Implicit in Jennings's analysis is that feminist ideology and discourses about domesticity had both changed since the interview participants' day, providing her with a standpoint from which to perceive a silenced discourse in the first place.

Participants' life experiences, expressed through their discourse, can also provide a vantage point from which to perceive ideology. We draw an example from Amber's (Gazso, 2009) research with low-income parents in Western Canadian provinces about their experience of provincial social assistance regulations, including the expectation that they must seek paid employment or participate in work and education training programs (welfare-to-work) in order to remain eligible for monthly benefits. When asked about her workforce experience, Rebecca, an Aboriginal woman who holds a BA, did not speak about welfare regulations alone, but also implied that the ideology of racism, which is premised on white superiority, was affecting her access to jobs (see Textbox 11.3).

Textbox 11.3: You're not going to get there

Rebecca: [...] I used to do anything that would come along ... like even waitressing, or dishwashing or stuff like that. Anything that would come along I would do because it was a job right? And now you try and find them and they say you're overqualified or sorry, you know, there's someone else.

Interviewer: What do you think that's all about?

Rebecca: I think they're [self-]prejudiced. I know it ... It was easy for them to give me work ... worked as a dishwasher or a waitress or something. But try and get something a little bit higher. *Uh uh,* you're not going to go there. The color of my skin matters. No matter what people say. It matters. And, it's a very, very prejudiced [place] ... I face it, I face it everyday so I guess it's all my life. But I've learned how to handle it without having to get angry. I just know it's just, um, people just don't understand. They just don't understand the culture ... And when they don't understand they get scared.

Source: Gazso, 2009: 155

Textbox 11.4: A Summary of Strategies for Analyzing Power and Ideology

- Analyze how some discourses are privileged and others not – and whose discourses they are.
- If you use the term 'ideology,' be sure of what you mean by it.
- Analyze the ideological implications of discourse(s).
- Ask whose or which knowledge is obscured or silenced in the talk.

WORKING WITH TIME

Time has proven central to the understanding of narratives, and – through the use of the next-turn proof strategy – to the rigor of conversation analysis. In discourse analysis of the garden-variety, time is also central in that all discourse is understood to be historically contextualized and constituted. In some research, the objective may be to trace the evolution of a discourse. In garden-variety discourse analysis, the researcher may also aim to deconstruct when and how a discourse emerged or to document shifts in discourse. This is a project that, on the surface, is similar to Foucault's genealogy, but the researcher may disagree with Foucault's view that all histories are fictions.

Deconstructing and historically situating a keyword in discourses over time, one with connotations and effects rippling far beyond its simple definition, can be an analytical strategy. Fraser and Gordon (1994), for example, conduct a genealogical analysis of the welfare-related meanings in the USA of the word 'dependency' from the pre-industrial period to 1990s post-industrial society. This analysis covers many domains, from economics (e.g., the Depression era's New Deal), to medical and psychological disciplines, to policy responses to poverty, such as the English Poor Law and the US Aid to Families with Dependent Children, and mingles talk data such as political campaign speeches and welfare recipients' commentary with written texts. In the industrial era, for example, they observe how dependency on social assistance shifted from being seen as evidence of state support in times of need to being understood as evidence of bad character. Indeed, their key analytical insight is to unpack when stigma became attached to perceptions of poor people as dependent on welfare. It is here that Fraser and Gordon's approach diverges from that of Foucault's, in that they feel free to criticize the present construction of dependency.

Another strategy might be to *locate a discourse's emergence within other discourse(s).* For example, Brenner (2009) took on the novel project of locating 'women's rights' rhetoric in the foreign-policy discourse of the Bush Administration between 2001 and 2004. In her analysis of speeches, Brenner discovered what she terms 'dialogical frames' of women's rights that are not mutually exclusive. For example, the 'us vs. them' frame centers around depictions of women's rights as being violated

in parts of the world other than the US, e.g. Sudan, Iraq. The US is presented as the protector and empowerer of personal freedoms and moral authority. In 2001 remarks, Bush explains that the invasion of Afghanistan was not just about ending the power of the Taliban but about ending the brutalization of Afghan women too (p. 21). Brenner (2009) concludes not by arguing that Bush's claims were disingenuous but by highlighting how feminist concerns entered into foreign-policy discussions at a period of time that seemed devoted to the War on Terror and, thus, how change appears possible when new discourses emerge alongside apparently dominant ones.

Textbox 11.5: A Summary of Strategies for Analyzing Time

- Locate a keyword in discourse over time.
- Study a discourse's emergence within another discourse.

CHAPTER SUMMARY

This chapter has reviewed an approach to discourse analysis that we call 'garden variety.' Readers may be heartened to know that we too agree that garden-variety discourse analysis may not be a necessarily appealing name for their analysis. We use this term to denote a theoretically understated discourse analysis that has an ordinary 'feel' to it, one in which the concept of discourse is taken for granted rather than announced with fanfares about Foucault, CDA, or anything else. Researchers of this kind share a focus on discourse and its relationships with individuals and society and are free to take this up in eclectic ways, particularly in how they formulate and use concepts such as 'identity and subjectivity,' 'power,' and 'ideology.' For instance, in CDA ideology is often formulated with reference to Karl Marx but in garden-variety DA we see the influence of cultural theorist Stuart Hall. The challenge of garden variety's eclecticism is to not trip yourself up.

TWELVE

The Interview in Discourse Analysis

Like other talk in the preceding chapters, discourse analysts understand the interview to **instantiate** discourses, meaning that discourses are articulated through or presented in the interview, talk that is understood to be socially constituted. Thus, in contrast to realist NA, in which tests of accuracy can be applied to respondents' talk, in DA, truth is not at issue. DA researchers share this assumption, but recall that they come at it from different paradigms. Critical theorists would argue that talk is constituted by discourse, but is also both shaped by and grounded in material relations. In a Marxist sense, talk may then reflect the false consciousness of people who do not perceive how discourses shape their material relations. For example, interviewing mothers on social assistance, Amber has met several mothers who find fault with case workers and with people who abuse the social assistance system, but who never criticize the system itself. Meanwhile, post-structuralists like Foucault remind us that discourse, as related during an interview, is always connected with or governed by power–knowledge relations.

Our focus in this chapter is on the place and use of reflexivity in discourse analysis, given its assumptions about talk data. DA perspectives on reflexivity about the interview contain noteworthy points of comparison and contrast to the NA perspectives of Chapter 4 and the CA perspectives of Chapter 8. In NA, reflexivity about the interviewer's role and methods matters because the meanings voiced in the interview are understood to be jointly produced by interviewers and respondents. Especially because NA is a largely humanist enterprise in which individuals and their searches for meanings matter, interviewers' selves, their biographies, consciousnesses, standpoints, emotions, and embodiments, are all prime tools for interrogating how this joint production happens. By contrast, in DA, as in CA, we see less attention to an introspective reflexivity on the interviewer/researcher's

part. The main exception is that CDA researchers are expected to implicitly or explicitly reveal how their politics inform their research, especially in the analysis phase. Discourse analysts distinguish themselves from conversation analysts by insisting that the context of the interview extends beyond the specifics of its talk, into the macro level of discourses and structural inequalities. In DA, reflexivity involves observing whether and how these macro-level phenomena infuse the interview, and are involved in its knowledge production. The individual matters only as a carrier of discourse.

In our reading of discourse analytic works, we see researchers reflecting about the interview and the talk data produced in three ways: 1) the ubiquity of power in and around the interview encounter; 2) the way that discourses are used in interviewers' and researchers' performances of identities; and 3) how discourses are used to position one's self. In the following discussion, we write about power, performativity, and positioning separately. It is fair to say that they are not mutually exclusive, so much as divided here in an attempt to present analytic strategies as simply as possible. In this chapter, we also discuss the relationship between the interview and DA in a general matter unless the distinction between analytic approaches – Foucauldian, Critical Discourse, and garden-variety – matters.

BEING REFLEXIVE ABOUT POWER IN DA

The Power of Discourse

Because dominant discourses powerfully enable and constrain what can be said and thought, it is valuable to reflexively *contemplate what respondents leave unsaid in an interview – and what forces might make it unsayable or unthinkable*. For example, interviewing dieticians and nutritionists about how they understood cultural differences in their clients' diets, Marjorie DeVault (1995) found direct talk of race to be conspicuously absent. DeVault gives the example of how an African–American dietician, Janetta Thompson, speaks of her career choice (see Textbox 12.1).

In this excerpt, says DeVault, Thompson speaks obliquely of racialized neighborhoods and locales, and of 'people like me.' Her hesitations here serve as indicators of the difficulties in articulating race-related experiences to a white person whom she has scarcely met. But race is also implicitly present in Janetta's talk of informal supports and economic opportunities in her community. DeVault further discerns the relevance of race to Thompson's and other racialized nutritionists' narratives as they speak of ceilings to their career advancement or about the error of lumping groups of clients together without sensitivity to their food preferences. For DeVault, talk is shaped by racial–ethnic dimensions of social organization, or as we interpret, discourses of race, whether or not race is explicitly spoken about.

Textbox 12.1: Sort of like an inner-city kind of thing

Then I, um

(pause)

a woman at the school said she knew someone who worked in a community
center.

And I got really excited about that, because I wanted to work- in a,

sort of like an inner-city kind of thing.

That's where I'm from, [Eastern City],

and I wanted to work with people who were like me, in a sense.

So I went on an interview at the [Westside] clinic, in [the city].

And- it was nice, you know,

everyone knew each other there, and knew their patients.

And

I was just so excited, and

The woman,

she happened to be in the WIC program.

And I- had never heard of WIC before, I had never,

you know, but anyway –

But I was just so excited!

Source: DeVault, 1995: 617–18

In other work, DeVault (1990) uses the label **linguistic incongruence** to encompass respondents' silences as well as talk that hesitates, stumbles, and is fragmented or self-contradictory, all of which she sees as marking how dominant discourses hamstring respondents as they try to articulate alternatives. McKenzie-Mohr and Lafrance (2011) apply this concept in observing how participants addressed them in interviews about fraught topics. For example, McKenzie-Mohr found that women who had been raped struggled to articulate how the dominant 'don't blame the victim' discourse paradoxically governed them as victims, having no agency and no capacity to have avoided being raped. In speaking with her, the participants would preface their statements with comments 'This might sound weird' and ended with 'Do you know what I mean?' (p. 61), thereby indicating their awareness that the dominant discourse was failing them.

Melissa Hyams (2004), however, turns our attention to alternative interpretations of respondents' silences. The example in Textbox 12.2, from focus groups that she conducted with young Latina women about their gender identities, demonstrates deliberate silence on the part of Sorcha.

Textbox 12.2: I don't have any feelings about who I am

Melissa: What else can you tell us about the feelings you have about who you are?

Sorcha: I don't have any feelings about who I am. I don't know.

Melissa: [To the group] Is there anything you wanted to say or include or talk about or make sure that I don't forget to include that hasn't been talked about?

Sabrina: Venessa wants to know if it's dangerous to put –

Venessa: She's trying to put me wrong about a stupid tampon and how it feels and everything and I don't really care. I don't want to use one, period.

Regina: Me neither.

Sabrina: I've heard other people say it feels OK and it doesn't bug.

Melissa: We could talk about tampons if that's what you want.

Source: Hyams, 2004: 110

Hyams proposes that the participants' silence around 'feelings about who you are' could indicate that the participants are oppressed, unable to find a voice with which to speak of the conflict between discourses in which an adult subjectivity is independent but a woman's subjectivity is selfless. In other words, this silence could be akin to those that DeVault (1995) and McKenzie-Mohr and Lafrance (2011) discussed. However, Hyams also reflexively speculates her faulty expectation that 'young Latina women's experiential knowledge' existed prior to the focus groups, ready for her to scoop it up – an expectation that Hyams concludes to be in tension with the Foucauldian understanding that experiential knowledge is not 'real' so much as constituted, alongside subjectivities, through power relations in the group setting. Hyams's final possibility is that the participants are resisting the obligation to 'confess' their feelings. This possibility connects to a larger discourse of confession that we introduce next.

The Power of the Research Process

'Western man has become a confessing animal,' (1978: 59), writes Michel Foucault in the *History of Sexuality (Volume 1),* referring to how uses of the disciplinary technology of confession have burgeoned since being instituted for religious purposes in the Middle Ages. Nowadays,

> [o]ne confesses in public and in private, to one's parents, one's educators, one's doctor, to those one loves; one admits to oneself, in pleasure and in pain, things it would be impossible to tell to anyone else, the things people write books about. (1978: 59)

With the last entry on his list, Foucault implicates the research process. The process comes under further scrutiny in David Silverman's (1993) conception of **the interview society**, which characterizes the post-World War II interviewing Zeitgeist. Atkinson and Silverman (1997) connect the dots between the social scientific research interview and the explosion of mass media, in which exhibitionist interviews on tabloid talk shows have persuasively normalized self-revelation and reified the 'authentic' self. Even the high school reunion can be understood in such terms, says Vinitzky-Seroussi (2000), in an article that would explain why one of us spent her reunion swilling down vodka coolers.

The interview and the research process can thus be understood as sites of confessional knowledge production, of coercions that govern the subject. Therefore, respondents' silences are not always struggles to speak in some forbidden tongue, but can instead permit them to resist the research process. In Foucault's (1978) framing of this, 'silence and secrecy are a shelter for power, anchoring its prohibitions; but they also loosen its holds and provide for relatively obscure areas of tolerance' (p. 101). The resultant analytic strategy is *to examine the interview or broader research process for its disciplinary power, or for resistance to it.*

L. Mun Wong (1998) offers a cautionary tale about an interview gone wrong, which we can read as resistance. While he was conducting fieldwork with women welfare recipients in New Jersey, a talkative woman named Dorcy actively pursued the possibility of being interviewed by him. After a few weeks of her cheerful, giggly overtures, Wong decided to go ahead. But the interview fell flat. He writes:

> Even after my transcription, her answers seem brief. Dorcy was very inarticulate. Her silences and 'I don't knows' punctuated every question. My probing questions were deafening, and at some points, my questioning began to seem longer than her narrative. She was giving me monosyllabic answers and was speaking in such a soft tone that I could hardly make out a word she said. She refused to elaborate her stories and discuss her life. (1998: 191)

Afterward, Wong concluded that, 'I over-anticipated and swallowed the women's receptiveness to the research' (p. 192). Against his intentions, the interview had been a coercive encounter for Dorcy, whom he surmised to have participated in order to receive the $20 respondents' stipend. In resisting his questions, Dorcy was refusing to 'embody the role of the social repository – a receptacle of information for me to retrieve' (p. 192).

Jinjun Wang (2006) uses CDA to examine how the interview method contains latent acts of power. Owing to the plethora of definitions of power, it's important to note that he chooses to define it in Weberian terms (see Chapter 10) as 'the ability to control and constrain others; as the capacity to achieve one's aim;

as the freedom to achieve one's goals and as the competence to impose one's will on others' (p. 531). Wang contends that because questions are expected to have answers, a person who withholds an answer is running against the grain of conversation and must provide an account for having done so. The basic convention of the interview method thus empowers interviewers to extract knowledge. This analysis uses exactly the notion of question–answer adjacency pairs that we had seen conversation analysts introduce in Chapter 5. Yet, Wang's conception of question-asking as consistently an exercise of power is antithetic to CA principles, not only because it homogenizes what questions do but also because conversation analysts are skeptical about the notion of power. Although Wang would not win conversation analysts over to his quantitative technique of testing for disparities in the rate of different speakers' question-asking, it is a strategy that one could easily apply.

In taking up how discourse analysts have studied anorexic subjects, Paula Saukko (2000) questions the tendency of discourse analysts to conduct analyses that are themselves disciplinary, incessantly representing the anorexic as 'the too-good middle-class girl' (p. 313), the dupe of discourses that tell her she is flawed and that silence other possible subject positions. Saukko proposes that using the Foucauldian concept of 'technologies of the self' would better acknowledge that anorexic women understand themselves to possess agency and to be making choices. Saukko's analysis of how she and other anorexic subjects speak of themselves shows the tactical polyvalence of this 'good girl' figure, who can be used equally to criticize middle-class ideals and to demean women as whiners. Her study is also one of the rare discourse analyses in which the analyst shows how her own experiences can be used reflexively alongside others, in a form of writing that she calls 'quilting.'

The Micro–Macro Dynamics of Power

So far, we have talked about how to reflexively examine how respondents' talk reflects their struggles against the power of discourses, as well as how the research process (as represented by the person of the interviewer) is a powerful act of knowledge extraction. Now, we examine the interaction of respondents and interviewers as individuals possessing agency and exerting power, at the same time as they are always instantiating macro-level discourses.

We can analyze instances when exertions of power by researchers or participants, discursively constituted, affect the outcome of the interview. Bay-Cheng and colleagues (2006) convincingly describe how moderators in group settings can regulate talk according to dominant discourses. Their illustrations come from a program designed to empower young adolescent girls to break away from traditional gender norms. Bay-Cheng et al. found that although the program succeeded in changing girls' conformity with these norms, it nonetheless regulated the participants.

Group moderators stopped, ignored, or shaped the girls' talk according to two discourses, which Bay-Cheng et al. named the Pollyanna Imperative – referencing a 1913 girls' book with a relentlessly sunny protagonist – and Normative Feminisms (p. 83). The following example illustrates how mentors stopped girls' talk by invoking the Pollyanna Imperative to be 'nice' in all situations:

> As two girls argued one day, one said to the other, 'I never wrote you: I don't even like you!' A mentor intervened and stopped this talk by saying, 'That's not how we talk to our friends.' In a similar situation, another mentor said to a girl, 'You can't say that, it isn't nice.' (p. 84)

Mentors could also convey that there was only one correct, feminist response or behavior – normative feminism – in their shaping of girls' talk: e.g. 'Instead of looking at your body as something to look pretty, look at it for its function' (p. 85). Bay-Cheng et al. conclude that even though the program was intended to free girls from traditional gender socialization, in interaction they were disciplined through discourses that were ironically conformist.

Elizabeth Hoffmann (2007) reminds us that, although respondents may lack interviewers' academic privilege, they are empowered to regulate their interviewers' experiences because they possess the data that the interviewer seeks. (In so saying, she is more sanguine about the interview than the interview society's proponents would allow.) She provides the example of an interview with an older coal miner wherein she used language that fell outside of the miner's experience. When Hoffmann referred to a 'chairperson,' she writes, 'He took exception to this word. "Chairperson? ChairPERSON?!" he bellowed with, possibly mock, rage. "Never! ChairMAN! Chairman." Contrite, I apologized. "Good point. He's a man: I'll say chairman"' (p. 335). In Hoffman's reflection, this exchange, illustrates how she was obligated to speak to some participants in ways befitting the ideological framework – or discursive constitution – of their workplaces.

Another example of a power flow between respondent and interview comes from Katherine's dissertation research on US university students' Holocaust knowledge. In one of these interviews, Miles, a participant who had been raised as Catholic, spoke of his relationship to the Holocaust with reference to the views of 'some of my friends,' and then 'one of my friends' and later 'my friend' (Bischoping, 2005: 149). As the talk progressed, Miles eventually revealed that this friend was his male partner – this in the early 1990s, when homophobia ran rampant at Katherine and Miles's campus (Bischoping, 2005). It turned out that the Holocaust mattered to Miles both because gay men had been persecuted in it, and because of how profoundly it continued to affect his Jewish partner. From Miles's side, the interview can be read as a series of interactive tests of whether Katherine would use her power to reproduce a dominant homophobic discourse. Had she failed these tests, it seems likely that he would not have been so forthcoming. Miles was demonstrating the power of data possession of which Hoffmann (2007) writes.

Textbox 12.3: A Summary of Strategies for Being Reflexive about Power

- Contemplate respondents' silences, and identify discourses making some words or ideas unsayable or unthinkable.
- Examine the interview or research process for its disciplinary power over respondents, and for their resistance.
- Analyze how discursively constituted exertions of power by interviewers or respondents affect interview outcomes.

BEING REFLEXIVE ABOUT PERFORMATIVITY AND PERFORMANCE

As we saw in our earlier chapters in this section, identities and subjectivities can be central interests in discourse analysis. Here we refine these foci still more by linking them to concepts of performance and performativity, as they pertain to interview interaction. We do so by looking to scholars who undertake either Foucauldian inspired analysis or a more garden-variety discourse approach.

Performative, **performance**, and **performativity** are terms that form something of a bridge between CA to DA. Linguists' **speech act theory** (Austin, 1962; Searle, 1975) studies how people use declarations to perform actions, calling objects or situations into being. A classic example is that of the vow of marriage. Saying 'I do' is **performative**, making one into a husband or wife, and producing this identity for others' eyes. Many constructionists have taken up the idea that identities can be produced through talk or other interaction. Harold Garfinkel (1967) and Erving Goffman (1976), figures who will be familiar from the CA part of this book, took a lead in theorizing that gender is a routine accomplishment embedded in, and omnirelevant to, everyday interaction. West and Zimmerman's work (1987) drew on these influences in their elegant proposal that no one *has* a gender. Instead, we engage in '**doing gender**' in our everyday interactions, in **performances** that are facilitated by how others perceive us. The art of doing gender involves agentically managing our interactions so that they are seen as gender-appropriate according to socially constructed standards for men and women, and so that our identities as either women or men are unremarkable.

Enter Judith Butler. In *Gender Trouble* (1990), a notable contribution to discourse analysis and queer theory alike, she draws on the inspiration of Foucault and other post-structuralists in considering related questions. Butler agrees with West and Zimmerman that gender is not an interior essence waiting to be discovered or disclosed. But, she departs from them in boldly seeking to dissolve the binaries of male/female, masculine/feminine, and even a binary of sex (as biological)/gender (as socially achieved). In saying that 'gender is always a doing' (1990: 25), Butler acknowledges that doing gender involves putting on performances visible to others as normatively gendered. But her conception stresses that through

acts of doing gender, we discursively constitute gender identities and subjectivities: they are not causes of performances, so much as effects. (Foucault [1978] had said the same of sex.) Thus, where West and Zimmerman imagine subjects who go about agentically producing their identities through performances, Butler concentrates on how gender identities are anticipated and produced, made possible by discourses in their cultural contexts, whether in alignment with heteronormative gender relations or subverting them.

In her later *Bodies that Matter*, Butler (1993) uses the example of a North American doctor's reaction to the birth of a child to illustrate that acts of gendering occur repetitiously, conditioned through and constituted by discourses. Proclaiming 'it's a girl' immediately brings 'girlhood' and complementary discourses of femininity to bear on the infant's subject position, subjectivity, and her prospective performance. **Performativity**, in Butler's conception, refers to how discourses interconnect with subject positions, subjectivities, and performances. As Chris Brickell (2003: 167–8) observes, we should therefore *be cautious about how we employ the term performativity in discourse analysis*. If we wish to be reflexive about people's actual performances of gender or other identities in the interview, our interest is in what 'doings' occur there and how these are socially situated and constituted, thereby involving discourses. But, if we wish to be reflexive about performativity, Brickell says that our interest would be in how our methods let us see how discourses *invoke* and regulate subject positions of gender or otherwise.

If we work with these understandings, an analytic strategy is to be *reflexive about our own performance as researchers and respondents' performance of identities in the interview.* Daniel Conway (2008) offers considerable insight in this regard. Drawing on the work of Riessman (2003), he maintains that interviews are goal-driven performances of the roles of interviewer and respondent, who perform desired selves according to objectives such as answering the questions or developing rapport. Conway discusses how performances variously shaped his interviews with white South African men who had refused to serve in the apartheid military. Conway reads one respondent's expression of derogatory views of women and the African National Congress as the respondent's performance of a 'bonding ploy' (p. 350) occasioned by shared whiteness and gender. Conway also divulges how he altered his own performance of masculinity so as to encourage a reticent respondent, whom he understood to be gay, to talk about sexuality:

> I was more expressive with my hands, tried to be more chatty and laugh more at what the interviewee said [...] performing a masculine self that could be perceived as more *camp* and perhaps more liable to create rapport with a gay male interviewee. (2008: 351)

In these examples, what Conway characterizes as agentic performances of research identities intermeshed with discursively available performativities of whiteness and masculinity.

We note that because Conway is silent about his own sexuality in this article, his tactic opens up the question of whether he duplicitously performed a self that was not truly his own – a question that itself hinges on the notion of sexuality as an essence one has, rather than as something one does. Further, Conway's very reflexivity about this makes it difficult to question his ethics. Reading Conway's study prompted our graduate student colleague, Selom Chapman-Nyaho, to reflexively examine how he performed race in his interviews. His thoughts on this are shown in Textbox 12.4.

Looking at this essay with West and Zimmerman's lens of agentic performance, we can see that Selom is like Conway in speaking of his doings of researcher, race, and other identities. Throughout, he performs in bonding ways that appear sympathetic to participants, whether by expressing sarcasm, casual irreverence, or familiarity with their experiences; even when he disagrees with respondents, he does so invitingly. He gets the data he thinks of as there, inside the respondents, waiting to be expressed. He 'almost loses' it in the face of racist assertions, but refrains, doing his researcher identity in ways that feel 'conflicted or fake' in relation to doing black identity; to do the identity of a black researcher, at this juncture, becomes impossible.

The essay looks rather different when we read it with Butler's eye to performativity, to what discourses and subjectivities – such as 'middle-class blackness' – people are producing and reproducing. From this reading, we can understand Selom's reflections as speaking to which norms he sees he is to follow to constitute himself as black in particular settings; the coercion to produce a particular blackness in some places, but not others, reveals the performativity of race. As well, reading Selom's reflections with more attention to discourse and less to agency, we see that not only the participants and principal consultant's statements, but also Selom's not 'losing it,' reproduce a color-blind and racist discourse, a white subjectivity that can complacently discriminate, and a black subjectivity as the conflicted fake. A reflexive examination shows the research process to reproduce knowledge aligned with racial discourses and power relations.

As we observed earlier in this chapter, reflexivity may not always involve the researcher reflecting about themselves and their relation to the data collection and analysis. It's also possible to reflexively *investigate how data collection methods make performances of identities possible*. An interesting example that we read in this way is Jennifer Ingrey's (2012) Foucauldian-infused study of how secondary school students in Canada understood gender binaries and of whether their experience in school structures, such as bathrooms, regulated and disciplined their gendered subjectivities.

Using data consisting of students' drawings of bathrooms as well as interviews, Ingrey (2012) found that students' perceptions of school bathrooms could echo Butler's arguments about a gender binary powerfully ordering social life. Some students drew pictures of bathrooms that reiterated this binary, and, when interviewed about their drawings, held to it. Leo, for example, could see only two genders as

Textbox 12.4: Performing Race in Interviews

The missing subtext has an effect on how I read the Conway study. If I knew that he were gay I'd feel more comfortable reading about his change in performance. But his study has made me think more about how I definitely perform certain roles when I conduct interviews and focus groups. And thinking about it that way is far more interesting than insider/outsider pondering about the different groups I encounter.

When I was interviewing black police officers for my Master's thesis, I quite consciously adopted a blackness that both assumed an understanding of the passive racism one might expect in the workplace and a sympathetic familiarity for the kinds of complaints black people will occasionally make (to insiders) about the apocryphal 'black community'. I assumed a very middle-class blackness.

When I've done fieldwork among youth for a project bringing them into policing environments, I perform a bumbling irreverence that masks my authority. A colleague of mine, in contrast, tends to draw on her youth worker and social work experience to come across as helpful. The differences between our focus groups are too complex for easy conclusions, especially without considering gender and probably race. But, the differences in our day-to-day relationships with the students are revealing: I get told which rap artists to listen to, which teachers they hate, and how much pot they smoke and she gets asked for advice about school and personal problems.

When I interviewed police officers as part of the assessment of this youth program, I made a point of displaying a subtle sarcasm about aspects of the program. This was productive because as soon as the officers got a whiff of the idea that I wasn't totally on board with the 'higher-ups' overwhelmingly positive embrace of what they were doing for at-risk kids, their criticisms came easily. I'm actually looking forward to finding a place to write about a cop I cruelly dubbed 'little big man' because the change in his demeanor was so dramatic partway through our interview.

Overall, I think I perform in ways that make respondents feel comfortable and as though either they're teaching me something or I understand and relate to their analyses. But this doesn't mean I always agree. In fact, I've found it often better to tell people when I disagree but to do it in a way that invites them to work harder to convince me they're right. The only time I've ever felt conflicted or fake was when I conducted a focus group for a consulting firm on diversity with a group of white teachers for a school board I'm not allowed to name. I had to sign a non-disclosure agreement. They were so incredibly racist and it was awful. I almost lost it when one explained how she didn't even see me as black and that I'm pleasant and clearly educated and have a beautiful smile. (I'm guessing this is as opposed to all the miserably angry unqualified minorities the school board was hiring, since this is what they were all complaining about right before.) If I had kids, I think that would be the moment when I'd enroll them in the Africentric school. Afterwards I felt even shittier when I reported to the principal consultant and she told me she knew I'd be good for that focus group because she figured white people would feel comfortable being racist around me. I wonder if she'd endorse me if I listed that as a skill on my LinkedIn profile – white people feel comfortable being racist around me?

Source: by permission of Selom Chapman-Nyaho

possible, regardless of others' beliefs. But the interviews also showed other students' perceptions of gender were not as fixed as their drawing had suggested. For example, Raj's drawing represented women with an hourglass figure decorated with flowers, while men were represented by a muscular figure on horseback. Although Raj conflated sex and gender in this drawing, in the interview he expressed some openness to the idea of having a transgender bathroom space. The interview method created a possibility for Leo, however, to discuss how he could see only two genders as possible, regardless of others' beliefs. For him, gender was unavoidably a binary.

Textbox 12.5: A Summary of Strategies for Being Reflexive about Performativity/Performance

- Be careful about whether you are analyzing performativity or performance – and in what sense – in your use of discourse analysis.
- Be reflexive about respondents' and one's own performance of identities in the interview.
- See whether and how methods create possibilities for respondents' performances of identities.

BEING REFLEXIVE ABOUT POSITIONING

We have discussed how people interact according to available discourses and in Chapter 10 drew upon Foucault, in particular, to show that people take up subject positions relative to discourses. Now we discuss how to be reflexive about **discursive positioning**, i.e., about the act of constructing one's experiences according to one's personal positions in social settings and while informed by the discourses available in their social context (Adjei, 2013).[1]

In an interview, positioning can vary according to the topic and setting as well as the relations between the researcher and participants. Although this may sound similar to the concept of **positionality** we had considered in Chapter 4's discussion of standpoint theory, the concepts are distinct. Whereas in standpoint theory we are the sum of biographies that we create in relation to others, in DA's use of positioning, our biographies are, furthermore, constructed and acted upon in relation to discourses. A person can have a standpoint as a Muslim in post-9/11 USA and have to position themselves in relation to discourses of Orientalism and the War on Terror, an act that necessarily involves performativity and power–knowledge relations. In the remainder of this section, we explore analytic strategies for studying positioning in interviews.

[1] Discursive positioning is sometimes associated with discursive psychology (see Chapter 8).

Reflexivity may involve the analytical strategy of discovering how respondents speak through discourses that are elsewhere constituted and then positioning their selves in relation to these discourses in the interview. Currie and colleagues (2007), for example, interviewed Canadian girls aged 11 to 16 about feminism, in order to understand how girls speak of dominant discourses about feminism and femininity, and then position themselves vis-à-vis these discourses. They found their respondents could be quite critical of the conventional femininity of popular girls. For instance, a respondent named Pete disassociated herself from available discursive categories. She disparaged girls who would 'build their life around boys' (p. 387) – a belief that would seem to coincide with a feminist subjectivity. However, Pete's views of feminism were mixed. Currie et al. use the excerpt below to show how Pete positioned herself as feminist when speaking of how feminism achieved equality between women and men, but distanced herself from what she called an 'outrageous' feminism:

Pete:	Like, there is: 'Yeah, I want to be equal to the men, get paid the same wage for doing the same job.' And there is 'I'm going to go out and be a firefighter just for the sake of having women in the force.'
Shauna [I'er]:	You don't agree with that?
Pete:	Just the outrageous stuff. Or, yeah just some things that aren't don't make sense. Don't click with me. (p. 387)

Currie et al. (2007) were curious about how the girls navigated what would appear – at least to social scientists – to be contradictions in their positionings. In resolving these contradictions, the girls frequently fell back to accounts of personal authenticity and being themselves, so that 'yourself' emerged as a significant identity category in the interview. They also see the young girls' positioning as reflective of their participation in youth sub-cultures and wider Western cultural discourses about women and femininity.

In focus group research, respondents may shift their discursive positionings in relation to both the moderator and other participants. For instance, in his analysis of how children in an East London primary school talk about television, David Buckingham (1991) discusses how his being an adult and a friend of their teacher would give children an impetus to produce knowing criticisms of advertisements or shows that, as one child said, could 'put hate in their [children's] hearts' (p. 230). Elsewhere in the interviews, however, peers took their turns to influence others' positionings relative to discourses of femininity and masculinity. For example, when a boy named Vinh voiced his preference for *She-Ra: Princess of Power*, a female-centered cartoon, 'Because she always goes "I am *She-Ra*!" and she holds up her magic power' (p. 242), he effectively aligned himself with a feminine subject position. Another boy immediately added 'And then her legs look really sexy! [Whistles]' (p. 242), disciplining Vinh and restoring the group's hegemonically masculine positioning.

Buckingham mentions that the school setting in which the focus groups occurred also signaled to the children that they should position themselves in ways that would please adults.

This observation leads into the strategy of *understanding positioning as governed by the norms/rules of the interview context*. Compared to the one above, this strategy emphasizes to a greater extent that discourses are power-laden and that which can be spoken is governed, and thus is especially useful in the qualitative study of institutional settings rife with rules, policies, and procedures.

Coupland and colleagues (2008) offer an exemplar of such a study, using a discursive psychology approach. Coupland et al. were interested in how talk about emotions was governed by the implicit norms and occupational performance expectations in a UK further education college. They found managers to downgrade the experience and performance of emotions, in utterances such as, 'I'm not the kind of person who gets angry. It's not an emotion that I really have a great deal of experience with,' whereas teachers upgraded the relevance of emotions, in statements such as, 'after the initial shouting and screaming and stamping my feet I've just got on and prepared a load of work' (p. 335). Coupland et al. conclude that emotional behavior is justified by teachers or managers on the basis of whether or not it seems 'reasonable' – a notion that they define differently according to the different discourses governing the two groups' management of emotion at work.

Textbox 12.6: A Summary of Strategies for Being Reflexive about Positioning

- Discover how respondents speak through discourses that are elsewhere constituted and then position their selves in relation to them.
- Understand positioning as governed by the norms/rules of the interview context.

CHAPTER SUMMARY

In this chapter, we have taken a concentrated focus on the interview and how to reflect about it as researchers engaged in discourse analysis. We have seen that, in particular, reflexivity for DA researchers can concern how discourses and power relations extraneous to the interview are (re-)constituted within it and impact upon the knowledge thereby produced. This is quite different than the CA researcher's strenuous belief that social context is created in the interview, not to mention the NA researcher's absorption with how the self serves as a research instrument. Specifically, we have identified strategies that discourse analysts of any stripe can employ to be reflexive about power embedded in or surrounding the interview, the performance and performativities associated with their own and their respondents' identities, and finally their respondents' acts of positioning.

THIRTEEN

Conclusion

NOW THAT YOU'VE READ THIS BOOK

You might feel hopeful. The conceptual vocabulary we've introduced might have you thinking about methods at a more complex, abstract level than you have before. Identifying an ontology and epistemology that suits you and your research question might have helped you rule certain strategies in or out of consideration. You might have read a case study that parallels your own and inspires you. You might feel temperamentally drawn to strategies that suit your appreciation of nuance, your passion for the big picture, your irritation with inconsistencies, or your playful eclecticism. You might have found a strategy whose politics speak to you. For any of these reasons, you might feel excited about taking up your data and resolved about how to conduct your analysis and think through its main issues.

Or, you might feel overwhelmed or confused. Where you once felt you had one strategy, e.g., to code your data for its themes, you might now feel you have too many options. In that case, you might find it helpful to know that we read many works that used only one strategy to great effect. Since we began this book, we've written papers for other projects in which we compare two strategies or use a bricolage of the three or four that best suit our topic. If you have too many good choices, brainstorm about the ones that resonate with you most and then, through a process of elimination and reflection, you can confidently come to a good place. In order to model this, in an upcoming section of this chapter, we'll return to the scenarios with which this book opened, and show you how we would approach them. But first, a summary of what you've learned.

WHAT YOU'VE LEARNED ABOUT TALK

Why talk data? Why these strategies? In Chapter 1, we briefly sketched the three overarching strategies and mentioned that they attended to what was distinctive about talk data in different ways and to different degrees. We now return to our list of the distinctive set of features that talk data offer, and highlight their relevance for narrative, conversation, and discourse analysts.

1. Speakers talk in ways that are socially available to them.

Discourse analysts can take this up in deconstructing how discourses are embedded with, represent, and reproduce power–knowledge relations that have the scope to free, to govern, or to coerce. Some discourse analysts are interested in how, rather than coercing, hegemony may operate by making the ideas of the ruling class appear commonsensical. Still others attend to silences or stumbling speech and ask whose – or which – knowledge is being suppressed.

Narrative analysts have some overlapping concerns. For example, they may consider how collective memories, official histories, extended metaphors, speakers' standpoints, and notions of a 'good' story all shape how experience is known, passed down, or expressed through talk. For some, this shaping is interesting in its own right. But, for other narrative analysts fascinated with how individuals interpret their lived realities, the limits to what language can express and the social patternings of talk may be seen as impediments to accessing experience.

Only conversation analysts are generally sanguine about what's socially available. They can study how, by using mechanisms such as the next-turn proof strategy or maxims for making sense of categories, members sustain the illusion of a shared intersubjectivity, and thus, the social order. Because so much of the work of institutions is accomplished through talk, many conversation analysts are curious about how institutionally specific mechanics of talk, such as its stages or turn-taking rules, are consequentially distinct from those found in ordinary conversation.

2. Talk is uttered by individuals who have agency (or seem to).

Narrative analysis often embraces the individual and often make him the unit of analysis. In so doing, narrative analysts may study fine-grained clues such as an individual's use of imagery to access meanings that he cannot state directly. They may explore how individuals use narratives to make sense of the journeys of their selves. They may examine life course narratives to understand how individuals negotiate the tension between socio-historic context and their agency, or link their lives to others'.

Discourse analysts take a range of views on the individual and her agency. Some are hopeful about how talk can resist ideology, and aim to contribute as public intellectuals in ways that permit others to exert their agency, whether as individuals

or in groups. Some observe how individuals position themselves vis-à-vis discourses. Some are interested in contrasting the identities that discourses construct to individuals' experiences. Others, however, would caution that our subjectivities, our thoughts about ourselves as agents, and this very point about individuals and agency, are discursively constructed in the first place.

Conversation analysts criticize analyses that prioritize the individual over the social. They construe speakers as members, that is, as part of a collective that shares a set of competences and holds one another morally accountable for following unspoken rules of sense-making. Even during acts that other analysts might see as agentic, such as committing acts of 'interactional vandalism' (Duneier and Molotch, 1999), conversation analysts emphasize the unspoken rules to which people nonetheless orient.

3. Talk emerges in the moment.

However structured talk may be, it also has its unpredictable, indeterminate side. Discourse analysts can study this at a grand scale, showing how discourses don't evolve, so much as they change in contradictory and contingent ways. They also can show how small fragments of a discourse can be put to new ends in new contexts. In some DA studies, talk simply represents a discourse; in others, talk is a form of action in which a discourse is inevitably either reproduced or altered.

Conversation analysts would hold that talk-in-interaction is always action. But they would take issue with how discourse analysts speak of talk and discourse in a way that claims to know its context. Instead, conversation analysts foreground how context emerges as members go about their talk, for example, as they fluidly create categories and negotiate their predicates. That this occurs in the interview, too, causes conversation analysts to be skeptical about research that summarizes 'what respondents said' without observing how it had been jointly produced through respondents and interviewers' interaction.

Narrative analysts are also exquisitely aware of how narration and stories emerge through the interplay of audiences with narrators. Many would say that we don't have stories or memories, so much as we reconstruct them time and again; as our gaze toward the future changes, we look back on the past differently. This sets up hurdles for realists who want to use narrative as a source of 'the facts' about the past, rather than to follow a moving target. However, the emergent quality of talk can inspire more constructionist researchers. They might study how bearing witness to histories from below can contribute to social movements, how becoming able to formulate a narrative about trauma can have therapeutic outcomes, or how a speaker can use active/passive voice or repetitions to persuasive effect.

4. Talk is ephemeral, vanishing with the moment in which it occurs.

Conversation analysts cherish the ephemeral moment of talk. By listening and relistening to the microseconds of recorded talk-in-interaction, they gain a

profound appreciation of the complex sense-making efforts that members make in real time. The delicate repair mechanisms that members use to correct what they have misstated or misheard (to put it crudely) are examples.

Some NA strategies originating in literary analysis are equally applicable to ephemeral talk and to the permanence of written narrative. For example, we can study the imagery of both. But, in NA there is also a sense that the ephemerality of spoken narratives is conducive to their being emergent. For example, that everyday talk is a kind of transient performance can mean that it's often subject to more forgiving criteria for fidelity than what's put in writing. Talk's ephemerality also means that narratives too dangerous to be committed to the page, pertaining to events whose material evidence has been obliterated, may be passed on in private whispers. But, is talk truly ephemeral? By contradicting official histories, even whispers leave traces in the social.

Discourse analysts in general would stress that all talk is enduring in its political effects. Further, many discourse analysts are indifferent to the distinction between spoken and written texts; several of the studies whose talk findings we focused on also examined other texts, e.g., policy documents, or newspaper reports. The issue of talk's ephemerality thus can fall away.

5. Talk is embodied, although the social sciences struggle for means of capturing more than words.

The diversity of approaches to talk's embodiment can be seen in the variety of transcription styles represented in this book. For some analytic strategies, paraphrased talk is just as useful as a quotation. But paraphrasing would be anathema in CA and some of the more micro-level CDA work, where the standard is to use Jefferson's or similar transcription methods that are attuned to the pitches, overlaps, micro-pauses and other details of talk. Some CA articles that we read included transcribed gestures or were even accompanied by photographs that showed the direction of members' gazes during talk-in-interaction. This is in keeping with CA's commitment to the empirical, and to its aim of having a transcription method that captures the interactiveness of talk.

Narrative analysts approach embodiment in widely varied ways. Some fine-grained analyses are supported by ways of presenting transcripts that highlight the inherent poetry of speech. Adopting strategies influenced by feminism, anthropology, and cultural geography, some narrative analysts explore how embodied emotions, and emplacement inform understandings of talk data. Others look at how the engagingness of a story is a joint performance of the teller and the listener. Such kinds of reflexivity are in keeping with NA's general interest in individuals' subjective experiences.

While some discourse analysts make little reference to talk's embodiment, how they do is in keeping with their belief that talk is infused with power. They may contemplate how bodies perform the roles of interviewer and respondent, for instance,

by asking whether respondents who fall silent do so because they feel coerced by the interviewer or resistant toward the confessional mode of the interview. In DA, bodies and their performances are inevitably enmeshed in discourses.

6. In particular, in the embodied medium of talk, speakers' bodies can act as signifiers.

Following from the preceding point, we note that in discourse analysis, people can be interviewers or respondents only by performing as such. Discourse analysts can study the doings of interviewer and respondent and ask how wider discourses constitute these subject positions. Being reflexive about talk data from interviews requires attention to performances and performativity. Generalizing from this, discourse analysts can also inquire into how other taken-for-granted social categories such as class or race are signified by their performance, and therefore produced.

In narrative analysis, standpoint theory is sometimes used to discuss speakers' identities as fluid, hybrid, and socially constructed. However, at other times, the use of standpoint theory carries the risk of essentializing social categories. Conversation analysts are especially wary of research that starts from social scientists' sense of what social categories are relevant in talk, and then proceeds to deduce how different groups speak differently. Conversation analysts prefer to observe what categories members themselves treat as relevant, or to take a social scientific category and ask when and how members orient to it.

REMEMBER THOSE SCENARIOS?

We return now to the scenarios we listed at the introduction of this book. We respond to them here with our thoughts about how one could take what has been learned from reading this book to develop the most reasonable strategies of analysis. These are our initial brainstormings and are not meant to be exhaustive.

1. As a graduate student, you've conducted 45 interviews. You have over 1000 pages of near verbatim transcripts of the interviews to analyze. You panic when you look at these pages. You panic more when your supervisor tells you that simply 'coding your data for themes' will not help you at your defense or at the job talks you hope will follow.

Our first thought as we consider this scenario is that unless you've used CA transcription format, you're going to have to re-do everything. So CA would not be our first choice.

Second, it seems to us that this is a case where your topic really matters, your initial guiding research question, and who you talked to. Ask yourself, 'Were you interested in talking to everyday, lay people and finding out about their meanings, interpretations, and lived experiences?' If so, then NA tools could be very helpful, especially the fine-grained strategies that would let you probe for more than themes.

But, if you're more interested in deconstructing how your talk data reproduces taken-for-granted assumptions about something, then DA might be your friend. It could also be the reasonable choice if you interviewed experts, professionals, or institutional actors about a topic rich in political implications.

2. As a researcher, you've encountered numerous challenges in recruiting the 30 participants you've planned for your study. Between timelines and funding troubles, you've had to wrap up your data collection with only 12 interviews completed. You now have talk data, but not enough for the kinds of analytic strategies you're used to. You don't know what to do.

How about writing a reflexive piece? This might be an opportunity for you to take up strategies we discussed in the interviewing chapters for NA, CA, and DA, in order to reflexively examine how you've played a role in this small body of talk and the knowledge produced by it.

3. As a professor, you're responsible for mentoring students to their successful completion of their degrees. You have a meeting with a promising student who has obtained ethics approval for videotaping marital counseling sessions. When you ask him, 'What method of analysis are you planning to use?', he says, 'I don't know what you mean.'

Marital counseling invites considerable storytelling, and one might first think of narrative analysis strategies for that reason. But this could be a red herring. The fact that this talk is constitutive of an institution, orienting to its goals and protocols, makes us think that your student's data (stories and all) could be more amenable to CA strategies for analyzing institutional talk-in-interaction. DA approaches also come to mind. For example, these data might be used to examine how discourses about marriage create and discipline identities such as 'the adulterer' or 'the good wife.'

4. One of your doctoral students intends to do research on understanding the experience of surviving cancer. When you meet to discuss her research proposal, she explains that she thought using a Foucauldian approach would give her work cachet.

We often meet students who think that because they're at our institution they should 'do Foucault.' We don't recommend choosing an approach on the basis of its local popularity. Our immediate thought as we read this scenario is that NA strategies are tailor-made for projects focused on 'experience.' For example, surviving cancer could be studied as a transition in the life course, or as leading to disjunctures or epiphanies in narratives of selves.

A Foucauldian approach might work, for example, if you were interested in how the subjectivity of 'cancer survivor' is constituted by medical and other discourses. Be warned that such a strategy might create an ethical conflict for you, as it would require you to treat what your respondents passionately speak of as real to them as a social construct.

5. You've never been completely satisfied with how you've been analyzing data. You do the same things you always do and, frankly, you're bored. You wonder how you might spice things up.

Why not take pride in your expertise and your intimate familiarity with one way of working by first writing the analysis from the perspective with which you're most comfortable? Then try an analytic strategy from a different perspective, whether it be from NA, CA, or DA. By comparing the outcomes of the two, you have the capacity to make quite an interesting methods – rather than empirical – contribution. Several of the most helpful works that we read in the course of writing this book did just this.

WHY YOU SHOULD CLOSE THIS BOOK

We have reached the end of our time with you. Considering our list of 'to dos' first laid out in Chapter 1, we can now tick off that for each narrative, conversation, and discourse analysis, we have:

- Explained what it is good for, especially the kinds of research questions, settings, or forms of talk data it is suited to.
- Explored its intellectual history, naming founding thinkers and key works.
- Acknowledged its interdisciplinary use.
- Introduced its social theoretical underpinnings and its approaches to ontology and epistemology.
- Discussed standards for rigorous analysis.
- Introduced and discussed key concepts and analytic foci.
- Acknowledged key debates or sticking points you should be aware of, and flagged concepts or terms that tend to be used confusingly in the literature.
- Compared and contrasted it to the overarching analytic strategies and noted points where they discuss the same thing.

In synthesizing the literature, curating analysis strategies, and mapping out debates for narrative, conversation, and discourse analysis, we have met our overarching goal: we have provided you with tools to use to be confident and crafty in completing the analysis for your particular project. Now it is up to you to use them. And we are excited to see the results.

References

Abdelbaki, R., Bischoping, K. and Gazso, A. (2014) 'Faithful, transparent, or treacherous? The sociology of the translator', paper presented at the 31st Annual Qualitative Analysis Conference, June, London, Canada.

Adjei, S.B. (2013) 'Discourse analysis: Examining language use in context', *The Qualitative Report*, 18(50): 1–10.

Aguinaldo, J.P. (2012) 'Qualitative analysis in gay men's health research: Comparing thematic, critical discourse, and conversation analysis', *Journal of Homosexuality*, 59(6): 765–87.

Ahmed, A. (2013) 'Structural narrative analysis: Understanding experiences of lifestyle migration through two plot typologies', *Qualitative Inquiry*, 19(30): 232–42.

Ainsworth, S. and Hardy, C. (2004) 'Critical discourse analysis and identity: Why bother?', *Critical Discourse Studies*, 1(2): 225–59.

Alagoa, E.J. (2001) 'The dialogue between academic and community history in Nigeria', in L. White, S.F. Miescher and D.W. Cohen (eds), *African Words, African Voices: Critical Practices in Oral History*. Bloomington: Indiana University Press. pp. 91–102.

Albright, D. (1994) 'Literary and psychological models of the self', in U. Neisser and R. Fivush (eds), *The Remembering Self: Construction and Accuracy in the Self-narrative*. New York, NY: Cambridge University Press. pp. 19–40.

Alcoff, L. (1988) 'Cultural feminism versus post-structuralism: The identity crisis in feminist theory', *Signs*, 13(3): 405–36.

Anderson, J. and Jones, K. (2009) 'The difference that place makes to methodology: Uncovering the "lived space" of young people's spatial practices', *Children's Geographies*, 7(3): 291–303.

Angrosino, M.V. (1992) 'Metaphors of stigma: How deinstitutionalized mentally retarded adults see themselves', *Journal of Contemporary Ethnography*, 21(2): 171–99.

Anspach, R. (1988) 'Notes on the sociology of medical discourse: The language of case presentation', *Journal of Health and Social Behavior*, 29(4): 357–75.

Anzaldúa, G. (1987) *Borderlands/La Frontera: The New Mestiza*. San Francisco, CA: Aunt Lute.

Arat, Z.F.K. (2003) 'Where to look for the truth: Memory and interpretation in assessing the impact of Turkish women's education', *Women's Studies International Forum*, 26(1): 57–68.

Arias, A. (ed.) (2001) *The Rigoberta Menchú Controversy*. Minneapolis: University of Minnesota Press.

Arminen, I. (1996) 'On the moral and interactional relevance of self-repairs for life stories of members of Alcoholics Anonymous', *Text*, 16(4): 449–80.

Arminen, I. (2000) 'On the context sensitivity of institutional interaction', *Discourse & Society*, 11(4): 435–48.

Asimakou, T. and Oswick, C. (2010) 'The recontextualization of commercialization: The shifting discourse of an R&D unit', *International Journal of Sociology and Social Policy*, 30(5–6): 280–91.

Assmann, J. (2008) 'Communicative and cultural memory', in A. Erll and A. Nünning (eds in collaboration with S.B. Young), *Cultural Memory Studies: An International and Interdisciplinary Handbook*. Berlin, DE: De Gruyter. pp. 109–18.

Atkinson, J.M. and Heritage, J. (1984) *Structures of Social Action: Studies in Conversation Analysis*. Cambridge, UK: Cambridge University Press.

Atkinson, P. (1990) *The Ethnographic Imagination: Textual Construction of Reality*. New York, NY: Routledge.

Atkinson, P. and Silverman, D. (1997) 'Kundera's immortality: The interview society and the invention of the self', *Qualitative Inquiry*, 3: 304–25.

Attwood, B. (2008) 'In the age of testimony: The stolen generations narrative, "distance" and public history', *Public Culture*, 20(1): 75–95.

Austin, J.L. (1962) *How to Do Things with Words*. Oxford, UK: Clarendon Press.

Bailey, N., Housley, W. and Belcher, P. (2006) 'Navigation, interaction and bridge work', *The Sociological Review*, 54(2): 342–61.

Baker, C. (2004) 'Membership categorization and interview accounts', in D. Silverman (ed.), *Qualitative Research: Theory, Method and Practice*, 2nd edn. London, UK: Sage. pp. 162–76.

Bakhtin, M. (1935/1981) *The Dialogic Imagination: Four Essays*. (M. Holquist, ed., C. Emerson and M. Holquist, trans.). Austin, TX: University of Texas Press.

Banasiak, K. (2014) 'Dancing the East in the West: Orientalism, feminism, and belly dance', *Critical Race and Whiteness Studies*, 10(1). Available at: http://www.acrawsa.org.au/files/ejournalfiles/215Banasiak201414.pdf, accessed 1 October 2014.

Barker, L. (2010) 'Using poetry to capture the Aboriginal voice in oral history transcripts', in F. Peters-Little, A. Curthoys and J. Docker (eds), *From Passionate Histories: Myth, Memory and Indigenous Australia*. Canberra, AU: ANU E Press and Aboriginal History Inc. pp. 185–202.

Bastalich, W. (2009) 'Reading Foucault: Genealogy and social science research methodology and ethics', *Sociological Research Online*, 14(2).

Bauer, E. and Thompson, P. (2004) '"She's always the person with a very global vision": The gender dynamics of migration, narrative interpretation and the case of Jamaican transnational families', *Gender & History*, 16(2): 334–75.

Bauer, P.J. (2007) *Remembering the Times of our Lives: Memory in Infancy and Beyond*. London, UK: Lawrence Erlbaum.

Bauman, Z. (1983) 'Industrialism, consumerism and power', *Theory, Culture & Society*, 1(3): 32–43.

Bavelas, J.B., Coates, L. and Johnson, T. (2000) 'Listeners as co-narrators', *Journal of Personality and Social Psychology*, 79(6): 941–52.

Bay-Cheng, L., Lewis, A.E., Stewart, A.J. and Malley, J.E. (2006) 'Disciplining "girl talk": The paradox of empowerment in a feminist mentorship program', *Journal of Human Behaviour in the Social Environment*, 13(2): 73–92.

BBC Radio 1 (2013) 'Mila Kunis talks to Chris Stark off [*sic*] the Scott Mills show on Radio 1', 4 March. Available at: http://www.youtube.com/watch?v=z4Ezruu1oeQ, accessed 1 July 2014.

Beck, C.S. and Ragan, S.L. (1992) 'Negotiating interpersonal and medical talk: Frame shifts in the gynaecologic exam', *Journal of Language and Social Psychology*, 11(1–2): 47–61.

BenEzer, G. (1999) 'Trauma signals in life stories', in K.L. Rogers, S. Leydesdorff, and G. Dawson (eds), *Trauma and Life Stories: International Perspectives*. London, UK: Routledge. pp. 29–44.

Berger, P.L. and Luckmann, T. (1966) *The Social Construction of Reality: A Treatise in the Sociology of Knowledge*. Garden City, NY: Anchor.

Berger, R.J. (2008) 'Agency, structure, and the transition to disability: A case study with implications for life history research', *The Sociological Quarterly*, 49(2): 309–33.

Bernstein, B. (1990) *The Structuring of Pedagogic Discourse*. London, UK: Routledge.

Besnier, N. (1990) 'Language and affect', *Annual Review of Anthropology*, 19: 419–451.

Besnier, N. (1995) 'The politics of emotion in Nukulaelae gossip', in J.A. Russell, J.-M. Fernández-Dols, A.S.R. Manstead and J.C. Wellenkamp (eds), *Everyday Conceptions of Emotion: An Introduction to the Psychology, Anthropology, and Linguistics of Emotion*, NATO Advanced Study Institutes, D-81. Dordrecht, NL: Kluwer. pp. 221–40.

Bhabha, H.K. (1994) *The Location of Culture*. New York, NY: Routledge.

Billig, M. (1999) 'Whose terms? Whose ordinariness? Rhetoric and ideology in conversation analysis', *Discourse & Society*, 10(4): 543–82.

Billig, M. (2002) 'Critical discourse analysis and the rhetoric of critique' in G. Weiss and R. Wodak (eds), *Critical Discourse Analysis: Theory and Interdisciplinarity*. London, UK: Palgrave Macmillan. pp. 35–46.

Bischoping, K. (2005) 'Quote, unquote: From transcript to text in ethnographic research', in D. Pawluch, W. Shaffir and C. Miall (eds), *Doing Ethnography: Studying Everyday Life*. Toronto, Canada: Canadian Scholars' Press. pp. 141–54.

Bischoping, K. (2014) 'Identity and mutability in family stories about the Third Reich', in I. Maček (ed.), *Engaging Violence: Trauma, Memory and Representation*. Hove, UK: Routledge. pp. 56–73.

Bischoping, K. and Dykema, J. (1999) 'Toward a social psychological programme for improving focus group methods of developing questionnaires', *Journal of Official Statistics*, 15(4): 495–516.

Bischoping, K. and Quinlan, E. (2013) 'Health and safety issues in precarious cultural work', *E-Journal of International and Comparative Labour Studies*, 2(2): 97–115.

Blommaert, J. (2001) 'Investigating narrative inequality: African asylum seekers' stories in Belgium', *Discourse & Society*, 12(4): 413–49.

Blommaert, J. (2008) 'Bernstein and poetics revisited: Voice, globalization and education', *Discourse & Society*, 19(4): 425–51.

Blommaert, J. and Bulcaen, C. (2000) 'Critical discourse analysis', *Annual Review of Anthropology*, 29: 447–66.

Bogen, D. (1992) 'The organization of talk', *Qualitative Sociology*, 15(3): 273–94.

Boje, D.M. (1991) 'The storytelling organization: A study of story performance in an office-supply firm', *Administrative Science Quarterly*, 36: 106–26.

Booth, S. and Perkins, L. (1999) 'The use of conversation analysis to guide individualized advice to carers and evaluate change in aphasia: A case study', *Aphasiology*, 13(4/5): 283–303.

Booth, T. and Booth, W. (1996) 'Sounds of silence: Narrative research with inarticulate subjects', *Disability & Society*, 11(1): 55–69.

Bordo, S. (1986) 'The Cartesian masculinization of thought', *Signs*, 11(3): 439–56.

Borland, K. (1991) '"That's not what I said": Interpretative conflict in oral narrative research', in S.B. Gluck and D. Patai (eds), *Women's Words: The Feminist Practice of Oral History*. New York, NY: Routledge. pp. 63–75.

Bourdieu, P. (1999) 'Understanding', in P. Bourdieu (ed.), *The Weight of the World: Social Suffering in Contemporary Society*. Cambridge, UK: Polity Press. pp. 607–26.

Braun, V. (2000) 'Heterosexism in focus group research: Collusion and challenge', *Feminism & Psychology*, 10(1): 133–40.

Braun, V. and Wilkinson, S. (2005) 'Vagina equals woman? On genitals and gendered identity', *Women's Studies International Forum*, 28: 509–22.

Breeze, R. (2011) 'Critical discourse analysis and its critics', *Pragmatics*, 21(4): 493–525.

Breheny, M. and Stephens, C. (2007) 'Irreconcilable differences: Health professionals' constructions of adolescence and motherhood', *Social Science & Medicine*, 64(1): 112–34.

Brenner, A. (2009) 'Speaking of "respect for women": Gender and politics in U.S. foreign policy discourse, 2001–2004', *Journal of International Women's Studies*, 10(3): 18–32.

Brettell, C.B. (1991) 'Introduction: Fieldwork, text, and audience', in C. Brettell (ed.), *When They Read What We Write: The Politics of Ethnography*. Westport, CT: Bergin & Garvey. pp. 1–24.

Brettell, C. (2002) 'Gendered lives: Transitions and turning points in personal, family, and historical time', *Current Anthropology*, 43(Suppl): S45–S61.

Brickell, C. (2003) 'Performativity or performance? Clarifications in the sociology of gender', *New Zealand Sociology*, 18(2): 158–78.

Brockmeier, J. (2010) 'After the archive: Remapping memory', *Culture & Psychology*, 16(1): 5–35.

Brown, S., Souto-Manning, M. and Laman, T.T. (2010) 'Seeing the strange in the familiar: Unpacking racialized practices in early childhood settings', *Race Ethnicity and Education*, 13(4): 513–32.

Browning, L.D. (1992) 'Lists and stories as organizational communication', *Communication Theory*, 2(4): 281–302.

Buckingham, D. (1991) 'What are words worth? Interpreting children's talk about television', *Cultural Studies*, 5(2): 228–45.

Burnell, K.J., Coleman, P.G. and Hunt, N. (2010) 'Coping with traumatic memories: Second World War veterans' experiences of social support in relation to the narrative coherence of war memories', *Ageing and Society*, 30(1): 57–78.

Burrell, B., Valledor, V., Crowe, M. and Whitehead, L. (2010) 'Negotiating competing discourses: The decision to take menopausal hormone therapy following surgical menopause', *Women & Health*, 50(6): 527–43.

Busselle, R. and Bilandzic, H. (2008) 'Fictionality and perceived realism in experiencing stories: A model of narrative comprehension and engagement', *Communication Theory*, 18(2): 255–80.

Butler, J.P. (1990) *Gender Trouble: Feminism and the Subversion of Identity*. New York, NY: Routledge.

Butler, J. (1993) *Bodies that Matter: On the Discursive Limits of 'Sex'*. New York, NY: Routledge.

Carabine, J. (2001) 'Unmarried motherhood 1830–1990: A genealogical analysis', in M. Wetherell, S. Taylor and S.J. Yates (eds), *Discourse as Data: A Guide for Analysis*. London, UK: Sage. pp. 267–307.

Carbó, T. (1992) 'Towards an interpretation of interruptions in Mexican parliamentary discourse (1920–1960)', *Discourse & Society*, 3(1): 25–45.

Centre for Imaginative Ethnography (n.d.) *Welcome to CIE*. Available at: http://imaginativeethnography.org/, accessed 5 December 2014.

Chandler, M. (2000) 'Surviving time: The persistence of identity in this culture and that', *Culture & Psychology*, 6(2): 209–31.

Chandler, M.J., Lalonde, C.E., Sokol, B.W., Hallett, D. and Marcia, J.E. (2003) 'Personal persistence, identity development, and suicide: A study of Native and non-Native North American adolescents', *Monographs of the Society for Research in Child Development*, 68(2): i–138.

Chanfrault-Duchet, M.-F. (1991) 'Narrative structures, social models and symbolic representation in the life story', in S.B. Gluck and D. Patai (eds), *Women's Words: The Feminist Practice of Oral History*. New York, NY: Routledge. pp. 72–92.

Chiang, S.-Y. (2010) '"Well, I'm a lot of things, but I'm sure not a bigot": Positive self-presentation in confrontational discourse on racism', *Discourse & Society*, 21(3): 273–94.

Cho, H., Shen, L. and Wilson, K. (2012) 'Perceived realism: Dimensions and roles in narrative persuasion', *Communications Research*, 20(10): 1–24.

Choi, S. (2011) 'Communicating trauma: Female survivors' witnessing the No Gun Ri killings', *Qualitative Inquiry*, 17(1): 23–34.

Chomsky, N. (1965) *Aspects of the Theory of Syntax*. Cambridge, MA: The MIT Press.

Clark, R.P. (2006) *Writing Tools: 50 Essential Strategies for Every Writer.* New York, NY: Little, Brown and Company.

Clarke, S. (2008) 'Culture and identity', in T. Bennett and J. Frow (eds), *The Sage Handbook of Cultural Analysis*. London, UK: Sage. pp. 510–29.

Clemente, I. (2009) 'Progressivity and participation: Children's management of parental assistance in paediatric chronic pain encounters', *Sociology of Health & Illness*, 31(6): 872–88.

Clifford, J. (1986) 'Introduction: Partial truths', in J. Clifford and G.E. Marcus (eds), *Writing Culture: The Poetics and Politics of Ethnography*. Berkeley: University of California Press. pp. 1–26.

Clifford, J. and Marcus, G.E. (1986) *Writing Culture: The Poetics and Politics of Ethnography*. Berkeley, CA: University of California Press.

Collins, H. (2010) *Tacit and Explicit Knowledge*. Chicago, IL: University of Chicago Press.

Collins, P.H. (1989) 'The social construction of Black Feminist Thought', *Journal of Women in Culture and Society*, 14(4): 745–73.

Comber, B. and Nixon, H. (2009) 'Teachers' work and pedagogy in an era of accountability', *Discourse: Studies in the Cultural Politics of Education*, 30(3): 333–45.

Connell, R.W. (1987) *Gender and Power: Society, the Person and Sexual Politics*. Stanford, CA: Stanford University Press.

Connell, R.W. and Messerschmidt, J.W. (2005) 'Hegemonic masculinity: Rethinking the concept', *Gender and Society*, 19(6): 829–59.

Conway, D. (2008) 'Masculinities and narrating the past: Experiences of researching white men who refused to serve in the apartheid army', *Qualitative Research*, 8(3): 346–54.

Coupland, C., Brown, A.D., Daniels, K. and Humphreys, M. (2008) 'Saying it with feeling: Analysing speakable emotions', *Human Relations*, 61(3): 327–53.

Coupland, J. and Jaworski, A. (2003) 'Transgression and intimacy in recreational talk narratives', *Research in Language and Social Interaction*, 36(1): 85–106.

Cox, B. and Pringle, R. (2012) 'Gaining a foothold in football: A genealogical analysis of the emergence of the female footballer in New Zealand', *International Review for the Sociology of Sport*, 47(2): 217–34.

Craig, A.P. (1997) 'Postmodern pluralism and our selves', *Theory & Psychology*, 7(4): 505–27.

Curaming, R.A. and Aljunied, S.M.K. (2013) 'On the fluidity and stability of personal memory: Jibin Arula and the Jabidah massacre in the Philippines', in K.S. Loh, E. Koh and S. Dobbs (eds), *Oral History in Southeast Asia: Memories and Fragments*. New York, NY: Palgrave Macmillan. pp. 83–100.

Currie, D.H., Kelly, D.M. and Pomerantz, S. (2007) 'Listening to girls: Discursive positioning and the construction of self', *International Journal of Qualitative Studies in Education*, 20(4): 377–400.

de Beauvoir, S. (1949) *The Second Sex*. New York, NY: Random House.

de Certeau, M. (1984) *The Practice of Everyday Life* (S. Rendall, trans.). Berkeley: University of California Press.

De Craemer, W. (1983) 'A cross-cultural perspective on personhood', *The Milbank Memorial Fund Quarterly*, 61(1):19–34.

DeGloma, T. (2010) 'Awakenings: Autobiography, memory, and the social logic of personal discovery', *Sociological Forum*, 25(3): 519–40.

Denzin, N.K. (1989a) *The Research Act: A Theoretical Introduction to Sociological Methods*, 3rd edn. Englewood Cliffs, NJ: Prentice-Hall.

Denzin, N.K. (1989b) *Interpretive Biography.* London, UK: Sage.

DeVault, M. (1990) 'Talking and listening from women's standpoint: Feminist strategies for interviewing and analysis', *Social Problems*, 37(1): 96–116.

DeVault, M. (1995) 'Ethnicity and expertise: Racial-ethnic knowledge in sociological research', *Gender and Society*, 9(5): 612–31.

Dewilde, C. (2003) 'A life-course perspective on social exclusion and poverty', *The British Journal of Sociology*, 54(1): 109–28.

Duneier, M. and Molotch, H. (1999) 'Talking city trouble: Interactional vandalism, social inequality, and the "urban interaction" problem', *American Journal of Sociology*, 104(5): 1263–95.

Eades, D. (1982) 'You gotta know how to talk...: Information seeking in South-East Queensland Aboriginal society', *Australian Journal of Linguistics*, 2: 61–82.

Ebert, T.L. (1986) 'The crisis of representation in cultural studies: Reading postmodern texts', *American Quarterly*, 38(5): 894–902.

Edwards, D. and Potter, J. (1992) *Discursive Psychology.* London, UK: Sage.

Eggins, S. and Slade, D. (1997) *Analyzing Casual Conversation*. London, UK: Cassell.

Eglin, P. and Hester, S. (2003) *The Montreal Massacre: A Story of Membership Categorization Analysis*. Waterloo, Canada: Wilfrid Laurier University Press.

Ehrlich, S. (2002) 'Legal institutions, nonspeaking recipiency and participants' orientations', *Discourse & Society*, 13(6): 731–47.

Ehrlich, S. and Romaniuk, T. (2014) 'Discourse analysis', in R.J. Podesva and D. Sharma (eds), *Research Methods in Linguistics*. New York, NY: Cambridge University Press. pp. 460–93.

Elder, G.H. (1974) *Children of the Great Depression: Social Change in Life Experience*. Chicago, IL: University of Chicago Press.

Elder, G.H. (1978) 'Family history and the life course', in T.K. Hareven (ed.), *Transitions: The Family and Life Course in Historical Perspective*. New York, NY: Academic Press. pp. 17–64.

Elder, G.H. (1994) 'Time, human agency, and social change: Perspectives on the life course', *Social Psychology Quarterly*, 57(1): 4–15.

Erjavec, K. and Volčič, Z. (2010) '"Target", "cancer" and "warrior": Exploring painful metaphors of self-presentation used by girls born of war rape', *Discourse & Society*, 21(5): 524–43.

Erll, A. (2011) 'Locating family in cultural memory studies', *Journal of Comparative Family Studies*, 42(3): 303–19.

Errante, A. (2000) 'But sometimes you're not part of the story: Oral histories and ways of remembering and telling', *Educational Researcher*, 29: 16–27.

Etter-Lewis, G. (1993) *My Soul is my Own: Oral Narratives of African American Women in the Professions*. New York, NY: Routledge.

Ezzy, D. (1998) 'Theorizing narrative identity: Symbolic interactionism and hermeneutics', *The Sociological Quarterly*, 39(2): 239–52.

Ezzy, D. (2000) 'Illness narratives: Time, hope and HIV', *Social Science & Medicine*, 50(5): 605–17.

Fairclough, N. (1992) *Discourse and Social Change*. Cambridge, UK: Polity.

Fairclough, N. (2001a) 'The discourse of new labour: Critical discourse analysis', in M. Wetherell, S. Taylor and S.J. Yates (eds), *Discourse as Data: A Guide for Analysis*. London, UK: Sage. pp. 229–65.

Fairclough, N. (2001b) 'Critical discourse analysis', in A. McHoul and M. Rapley (eds), *How to Analyse Talk in Institutional Settings: A Casebook of Methods*. London, UK: Continuum. pp. 25–38.

Fairclough, N. (2009) 'Language and globalization', *Semiotica*, 173(1/4): 317–42.

Fairclough, N. and Wodak, R. (1997) 'Critical discourse analysis', in T.A. van Dijk (ed.), *Discourse Studies: A Multidisciplinary Introduction, Vol. 2, Discourse as Social Interaction*. London, UK: Sage. pp. 258–284.

Farnsworth, J. and Boon, B. (2010) 'Analysing group dynamics within the focus group', *Qualitative Research*, 10(5): 605–24.

Ferguson, A.A. (1991) 'Managing without managers: Crisis and resolution in a collective bakery', in M. Burawoy, A. Burton, A.A. Ferguson, K.J. Fox, J. Gamson, N. Gartrell, L. Hurst, C. Kurzman, L. Salzinger, J. Schiffman and S. Ui, *Ethnography Unbound: Power and Resistance in the Modern Metropolis*. Berkeley: University of California Press. pp. 108–32.

Few, A.L. (2007) 'Integrating Black consciousness and critical race feminism into family studies research', *Journal of Family Issues*, 28(4): 452–73.

Figes, O. (2008) 'Private life in Stalin's Russia: Family narratives, memory and oral history', *History Workshop Journal*, 65: 117–37.

Finnegan, R. (2006) 'Family myths, memories and interviewing', in R. Perks and A. Thomson (eds), *The Oral History Reader*, 2nd edn. London, UK: Routledge. pp. 177–83.

Fishman, P.M. (1978) 'Interaction: The work women do', *Social Problems*, 25(4): 397–406.

Ford, C. and Stickle, T. (2012) 'Securing recipiency in workplace meetings: Multimodal practices', *Discourse Studies*, 14(1): 11–30.

Forrester, M. and Reason, D. (2006) 'Competency and participation in acquiring a mastery of language: A reconsideration of the idea of membership', *The Sociological Review*, 54(3): 446–66.

Förster, R. (2013) 'Micro-sociology on the rise: The changing sociological field in the 1960s and the case of conversation analysis', *The American Sociologist*, 44: 198–216.

Foucault, M. (1961/2006) *History of Madness* (J. Khalfa, trans.). New York, NY: Routledge.

Foucault, M. (1972) *The Archaeology of Knowledge* (A.M. Sheridan Smith, trans.). New York, NY: Pantheon.

Foucault, M. (1973/1994) 'Truth and juridical form, lectures at the Pontifical Catholic University of Rio de Janeiro', in J.D. Faubion (ed.), *Essential Works of Foucault, 1954–1984, Vol. 3, Power*. New York, NY: The New Press. pp. 1–89.

Foucault, M. (1977) *Discipline and Punish: The Birth of the Prison*. New York, NY: Pantheon.

Foucault, M. (1978) *The History of Sexuality. Vol. 1: An Introduction* (R. Hurley, trans.). New York, NY: Vintage Books.

Foucault, M. (1988) 'Technologies of the self', in L.H. Martin, H. Gutman and P.H. Hutton (eds), *Technologies of the Self: A Seminar with Michel Foucault*. Amherst, MA: University of Massachusetts Press. pp. 16–49.

Frank, G. (1979) 'Finding the common denominator: A phenomenological critique of life history method', *Ethos*, 7(1): 68–94.

Fraser, N. and Gordon, L. (1994) 'A genealogy of dependency: Tracing a keyword of the U.S. welfare state', *Signs*, 19(2): 309–36.

Freud, S. (1900/1999) *The Interpretation of Dreams* (R. Robertson, intro.; J. Crick, trans.). Oxford, UK: Oxford University Press.

Freund, A. (2014) '"Confessing animals": Toward a longue durée history of the oral history interview', *Oral History Review*, 41(1): 1–26.

Frisch, M. (1990) *A Shared Authority: Essays on the Craft and Meaning of Oral and Public History*. New York, NY: SUNY Press.

Frith, H. and Kitzinger, C. (1998) '"Emotion work" as a participant resource: A feminist analysis of young women's talk-in-interaction', *Sociology*, 32(2): 299–320.

Frost, N. (2009) '"Do you know what I mean?": The use of a pluralistic narrative analysis approach in the interpretation of an interview', *Qualitative Research*, 9(1): 9–29.

Funk, L.M. (2013) 'Home healthcare and family responsibility: A critical discourse analysis of talk and text', *Healthcare Policy*, 9(Special Issue): 86–97.

Garcia, A.C. and Jacobs, J.B. (1999) 'The eyes of the beholder: Understanding the turn-taking system in quasi-synchronous computer-mediated communication', *Research on Language and Social Interaction*, 32(4): 337–67.

Garcia, A.C. and Parmer, P.A. (1999) 'Misplaced mistrust: The collaborative construction of doubt in 911 emergency calls', *Symbolic Interaction*, 22(4): 297–324.

Garfinkel, H. (1967) *Studies in Ethnomethodology*. New York, NY: Prentice-Hall.

Gazso, A. (2007) 'Balancing expectations for employability and family responsibilities while on social assistance: Low income mothers' experiences in three Canadian provinces', *Family Relations*, 56(5): 454–66.

Gazso, A. (2009) 'Reinvigorating the debate: Questioning the assumptions about and models of the "family" in social assistance policy', *Women's Studies International Forum*, 32(2): 150–62.

Gazso, A. and McDaniel, S. (2015) 'Families by choice and the management of low income through social supports', *Journal of Family Issues*, 36(3): 371–395.
Gee, J.P. (1991) 'A linguistic approach to narrative', *Journal of Narrative and Life History*, 1(1): 15–39.
Gee, J.P. (1999) *Introduction to Discourse Analysis: Theory and Method*. New York, NY: Routledge.
Georgakopoulou, A. (2007) *Small Stories, Interaction and Identities*. Amsterdam, NL: John Benjamins.
Gheith, J.M. (2007) '"I never talked": Enforced silence, non-narrative memory, and the Gulag', *Mortality*, 12(2): 159–75.
Ghorashi, H. (2008) 'Giving silence a chance: The importance of life stories for research on refugees', *Journal of Refugee Studies*, 21(1): 117–32.
Gibbs, R.W. Jr. (2008) 'Metaphor and thought: The state of the art', in R.W. Gibbs Jr. (ed.), *The Cambridge Handbook of Metaphor and Thought*. New York, NY: Cambridge University Press. pp. 3–13.
Gibson, D.R. (2008) 'How the outside gets in: Modeling conversational permeation', *Annual Review of Sociology*, 34: 359–84.
Giddens, A. (1984) *The Constitution of Society: Outline of the Theory of Structuration*. Berkeley, CA: University of California Press.
Giddens, A. (1991) *Modernity and Self-Identity: Self and Society in the Late Modern Age*. Cambridge, UK: Polity Press.
Giles-Vernick, T. (2001) 'Lives, histories, and sites of recollection', in L. White, S. Miescher and D.W. Cohen (eds), *African Words, African Voices: Critical Practices in Oral History*. Indianapolis: Indiana University Press. pp. 194–213.
Gill, V.T., Pomerantz, A. and Denvir, P. (2010) 'Pre-emptive resistance: Patients' participation in diagnostic sense-making activities', *Sociology of Health & Illness*, 32(1): 1–20.
Goffman, E. (1967) *Interaction Ritual: Essays on Face-to-face Behavior*. New York, NY: Anchor Books.
Goffman, E. (1976) 'Gender display', *Studies in the Anthropology of Visual Communication*, 3: 69–77.
Goffman, E. (1981) *Forms of Talk*. Philadelphia: University of Pennsylvania Press.
Goffman, E. (1983) 'The interaction order', *American Sociological Review*, 48(1): 1–17.
Goldberg, J.A. (1990) 'Interrupting the discourse on interruptions: An analysis in terms of relationally neutral, power- and rapport-oriented acts', *Journal of Pragmatics*, 14(6): 883–903.
Goodey, J. (2000) 'Biographical lessons for criminology', *Theoretical Criminology*, 4(4): 473–98.
Goodwin, M.H. (2002) 'Building power asymmetries in girls' interaction', *Discourse & Society*, 13(6): 715–30.
Gramsci, A. (1971) *Selections from the Prison Notebooks* (Q. Hoare and G. Nowell Smith, eds and trans.). New York, NY: International Publishers.

Greatbatch, D. and Dingwall, R. (1999) 'The marginalization of domestic violence in divorce mediation', *International Journal of Law, Policy and the Family*, 13: 174–90.

Green, M.J. and Sonn, C.C. (2005) 'Examining discourses of whiteness and the potential for reconciliation', *Journal of Communication & Applied Social Psychology*, 15: 478–92.

Guba, E.G. and Lincoln, Y.S. (1994) 'Competing paradigms in qualitative research', in N.K. Denzin and Y.S. Lincoln (eds), *Handbook of Qualitative Research*. Thousand Oaks, CA: Sage. pp. 105–17.

Halai, N. (2007) 'Making use of bilingual interview data: Some experiences from the field', *The Qualitative Report*, 12(3): 344–55.

Halbwachs, M. (1950) *La Mémoire Collective*. Paris: Les Presses universitaires de France.

Halkier, B. (2010) 'Focus groups as social enactments: Integrating interaction and content in the analysis of focus group data', *Qualitative Research*, 10(1): 71–89.

Hall, D.E. (2004) *Subjectivity*. Routledge, NY: New York.

Hall, S. (1980) 'Encoding/decoding', in S. Hall, D. Hobson, A. Lowe and P. Willis (eds), *Culture, Media, Language: Working Papers in Cultural Studies, 1972–79*. London, UK: Hutchinson. pp. 128–38.

Hall, S. (1992) 'The West and the rest: Discourse and power', in B. Gieben and S. Hall (eds), *Formations of Modernity*. Cambridge, UK: Polity Press. pp. 185–227.

Hall, S. (1996) 'The problem of ideology: Marxism without guarantees', in D. Morley and K.-H. Chen (eds), *Stuart Hall: Critical Dialogues in Cultural Studies*. London, UK: Routledge. pp. 24–25.

Hammersley, M. (1997) 'On the foundations of critical discourse analysis', *Language & Communication*, 17(3): 237–48.

Hammersley, M. (2003) 'Conversation analysis and discourse analysis: Methods or paradigms?', *Discourse & Society*, 14(6): 51–81.

Harding, S. (1986) *The Science Question in Feminism*. Ithaca, NY: Cornell University Press.

Hardt, M. and Negri A. (2000) *Empire*. Cambridge, MA: Harvard University Press.

Harris, D.A. and Parisi, D. (2007) 'Adapting life history calendars for qualitative research on welfare transitions', *Field Methods*, 19(1): 40–58.

Hartsock, N. (1983/2003) 'The feminist standpoint: Developing the ground for a specifically feminist historical materialism', in C.R. McCann and S.K. Kim (eds), *Feminist Theory Reader: Local and Global Perspectives*. New York, NY: Routledge. pp. 292–317.

Hartsock, N. (1990) 'Foucault on power: A theory for women?', in L. Nicholson (ed.), *Feminism/Postmodernism*. New York, NY: Routledge. pp. 157–75.

Hekman, S. (1997) 'Truth and method: Feminist standpoint revisited', *Signs*, 22(2): 341–65.

Henley, N.M., Miller, M. and Beazley, J.A. (1995) 'Syntax, semantics, and sexual violence: Agency and the passive voice', *Journal of Language and Social Psychology*, 14(1–2): 60–84.

Henry, R. (1999) 'Measles, Hmong, and metaphor: Culture change and illness management under conditions of immigration', *Medical Anthropology Quarterly*, 13(1): 32–50.

Heritage, J. (1984) 'A change-of-state token and aspects of its sequential placement', in J.M. Atkinson and J. Heritage (eds), *Structures of Social Action*. Cambridge, UK: Cambridge University Press. pp. 299–345.

Heritage, J. (1991) 'Intention, meaning and strategy: Observations on constraints on interaction analysis', *Research on Language and Social Interaction*, 24: 311–32.

Heritage, J. (1998) 'Garfinkel', in R. Stones (ed.), *Key Sociological Thinkers*. New York, NY: New York University Press. pp. 175–88.

Heritage, J. and Clayman, S. (2010) *Talk in Action: Interactions, Identities, and Institutions*. Oxford, UK: John Wiley & Sons.

Herzog, H. (2005) 'On home turf: Interview location and its social meaning', *Qualitative Sociology*, 28(1): 25–47.

Hochschild, A.R. (1983) *The Managed Heart: Commercialization of Human Feelings*. Berkeley: University of California Press.

Hoffmann, E. (2007) 'Open-ended interviews, power, and emotional labor', *Journal of Contemporary Ethnography*, 36(3): 318–46.

Hollander, J.A. (2004) 'The social contexts of focus groups', *Journal of Contemporary Ethnography*, 33(5): 602–37.

Hollway, W. and Jefferson, T. (1997) 'Eliciting narratives through the in-depth interview', *Qualitative Inquiry*, 3(1): 53–70.

Hollway, W. and Jefferson, T. (2000) *Doing Qualitative Research Differently: Free Association, Narrative and the Interview Method*. London, UK: Sage.

Holstein, J.A. and Gubrium, J.F. (1995) *The Active Interview*. Thousand Oaks, CA: Sage Publications.

Horkheimer, M. (1982) *Critical Theory*. New York, NY: Seabury Press.

Horwitz, R.P. (1993) 'Just stories of ethnographic authority', in C.B. Brettell (ed.), *When They Read What We Write: The Politics of Ethnography*. Westport, CT: Bergin & Garvey. pp.131–43.

Housley, W. and Fitzgerald, R. (2002) 'The reconsidered model of membership categorization analysis', *Qualitative Research*, 2(1): 59–83.

Housley, W. and Fitzgerald, R. (2009) 'Membership categorization, culture and norms in action', *Discourse & Society*, 20(3): 345–62.

Howell, M.C. (2001) *From Reliable Sources: An Introduction to Historical Methods*. Ithaca, NY: Cornell University Press.

Huntington, S.P. (1993) 'The clash of civilizations?', *Foreign Affairs* (Summer): 22–49.

Hutchby, I. (1996) 'Power in discourse: The case of arguments on a British talk radio show', *Discourse & Society*, 7(4): 481–97.

Hutchby, I. (2005) 'Children's talk and social competence', *Children & Society*, 19: 66–73.

Hutchby, I. and Wooffitt, R. (2008) *Conversation Analysis*. Cambridge, UK: Polity Press.

Hvas, L. and Gannik, D.E. (2008) 'Discourses on menopause – Part II: How do women talk about menopause?', *Health: An Interdisciplinary Journal for the Social Study of Health, Illness, and Medicine*, 12(2): 177–92.

Hyams, M. (2004) 'Hearing girls' silences: Thoughts on the politics and practices of a feminist method of group discussion', *Gender, Place & Culture: A Journal of Feminist Geography*, 11(1): 105–19.

Hydén, L.-C. and Bülow, P.H. (2003) 'Who's talking: Drawing conclusions from focus groups–some methodological considerations,' *International Journal of Social Research Methodology*, 6(4): 305–21.

Ingrey, J.C. (2012) 'The public school washroom as analytic space for troubling gender: Investigating the spatiality of gender through students' self-knowledge', *Gender & Education*, 24(7): 799–817.

Intemann, K. (2010) '25 years of feminist empiricism and standpoint theory: Where are we now?', *Hypatia*, 25(4): 778–96.

Jansen, S. (2000) 'Victims, underdogs and rebels: Discursive practices of resistance in Serbian protest', *Critique of Anthropology*, 20(4): 393–419.

Jantzen, C., Østergaard, P. and Vieira, C.M.S. (2006) 'Becoming a "woman to the backbone": Lingerie consumption and the experience of feminine identity', *Journal of Consumer Culture*, 6(2): 177–202.

Järvinen, M. (2001) 'Accounting for trouble: Identity negotiations in qualitative interviews with alcoholics', *Symbolic Interaction*, 24(3): 263–84.

Jaworski, A. and Coupland, N. (eds) (2006) *The Discourse Reader*, 2nd edn. New York, NY: Routledge.

Jayyusi, L. (1984) *Categorization and the Moral Order*. London, UK: Routledge & Kegan Paul.

Jefferson, G. (1978) 'Sequential aspects of storytelling in conversation', in J. Schenkein (ed.), *Studies in the Organization of Conversational Interaction*. New York, NY: Academic Press. pp. 219–48.

Jefferson, G. (1980) 'On "trouble-premonitory" response to inquiry', *Sociological Inquiry*, 50(3/4): 153–85.

Jefferson, G. (1990) 'List construction as a task and interactional resource', in G. Psathas (ed.), *Interaction Competence*. Lanham, MD: University Press of America. pp. 63–92.

Jefferson, G. (2004) 'Glossary of transcript symbols with an introduction', in G.H. Lerner (ed.), *Conversation Analysis: Studies from the First Generation*. Philadelphia, PA: John Benjamins. pp. 13–31.

Jennings, K. (2003) *Re-Thinking History*. London, UK: Routledge.

Jennings, R. (2004) 'Lesbian voices: The Hall Carpenter Oral History Archive and post-war British lesbian history', *Sexualities*, 7(4): 430–45.

Johansson, K., Lilja, M., Park, M. and Josephsson, S. (2010) 'Balancing the good – a critical discourse analysis of home modification services', *Sociology of Health & Illness*, 32(4): 563–82.

Johnson, M. (2005) 'Honest acts and dangerous supplements: Indigenous oral history and historical practice in settler societies', *Postcolonial Studies*, 8(3): 261–76.

Jones, R. and Thornborrow, J. (2004) 'Floors, talk and the organization of classroom activities', *Language in Society*, 33: 399–423.

Kagee, A. (2004) 'Present concerns of survivors of human rights violations in South Africa', *Social Science and Medicine*, 59(3): 625–35.

Kaufmann, J. (2010) 'Trans-representation', *Qualitative Inquiry*, 16(2): 104–15.

Keating, E. (1993) 'Correction/repair as a resource for co-construction of group competence', *Pragmatics*, 3(4): 411–23.

Kendall, G. and Wickham, G. (1999) *Using Foucault's Methods*. Thousand Oaks, CA: Sage.

Kendall, M. and Murray, S.A. (2005) 'Tales of the unexpected: Patients' poetic accounts of the journey to a diagnosis of lung cancer: A prospective serial qualitative interview study', *Qualitative Inquiry*, 11(5): 733–51.

Kennedy, E.L. (1998) 'Telling tales: Oral history and the construction of pre-Stonewall lesbian history', in R. Perks and A. Thomson (eds), *The Oral History Reader*. New York, NY: Routledge. pp. 344–55.

Kennedy, R. (2006) 'Stolen Generations testimony: Trauma, historiography, and the question of "truth"' in R. Perks and A. Thomson (eds), *The Oral History Reader*, 2nd edn. London, UK: Routledge. pp. 506–20.

Kidron, C.A. (2012) 'Silent legacies of trauma: A comparative study of Cambodian Canadian and Israeli Holocaust trauma descendant memory work', in N. Argenti and K. Schramm (eds), *Remembering Violence: Anthropological Perspectives on Intergenerational Transmission*. New York, NY: Berghahn Books. pp. 191–228.

Kimura, M. (2008) 'Narrative as a site of subject construction: The "Comfort Women" debate', *Feminist Theory*, 9(1): 5–24.

King, A. (2013) 'Recognising adulthood? Young adults' accomplishments of their age identities', *Sociology*, 47(1): 109–25.

Kitzinger, C. (2000) 'Doing feminist conversation analysis', *Feminism & Psychology*, 10(2): 163–93.

Kitzinger, C. and Frith, H. (1999) 'Just say no? The use of conversation analysis in developing a feminist perspective on sexual refusal', *Discourse & Society*, 10(3): 293–316.

Kitzinger, J. (1994) 'The methodology of focus groups: The importance of interaction between research participants', *Sociology of Health & Illness*, 16(1): 103–21.

Knudsen, J.C. (1990) 'Cognitive models in life histories', *Anthropological Quarterly*, 63(3): 122–33.

Koole, T. (2004) 'Affiliation and detachment in interviewer answer receipts', in H. van den Berg and M. Wetherell (eds), *Analyzing Race Talk: Multidisciplinary Perspectives on the Research Interview*. West Nyack, NY: Cambridge University Press. pp. 178–99.

Kraft, R.N. (2004) 'Emotional memory in survivors of the Holocaust: A qualitative study of oral testimony', in D. Reisberg and P. Hertel (eds), *Memory and Emotions*. New York, NY: Oxford University Press. pp. 347–89.

Kratz, C.A. (2001) 'Conversations and lives', in L. White, S. Miescher and D. William Cohen (eds), *African Words, African Voices: Critical Practices in Oral History*. Indianapolis, IN: Indiana University Press. pp. 127–61.

Kübler-Ross, E. (1969) *On Death and Dying*. New York, NY: MacMillan.

Labov, W. (1972) *Language in the Inner City*. Philadelphia: University of Pennsylvania Press.

Labov, W. (1997) 'Some further steps in narrative analysis', *Journal of Narrative and Life History*, 7(1–4): 395–415.

Labov, W. and Waletzky, J. (1967) 'Narrative analysis', in J. Helm (ed.), *Essays on the Verbal and Visual Arts*. Seattle: University of Washington Press. pp. 12–44.

Lakoff, G. and Johnson, M. (2003) *Metaphors We Live By*. Chicago, IL: University of Chicago Press.

Lalouschek, J., Menz, F. and Wodak, R. (1990) *Alltag in der Ambulanz: Gespräche zwischen Ärzten, Schwestern und Patienten*. Tübingen, DE: Gunter Narr Verlag.

Land, V. and Kitzinger, C. (2005) 'Speaking as a lesbian: Correcting the heterosexist presumption', *Research on Language and Social Interaction*, 38(4): 371–416.

Lanham, R. (2003) *Analyzing Prose*, 2nd edn. New York, NY: Continuum.

Lapum, J., Angus, J.E., Peter, E. and Watt-Watson, J. (2010) 'Patients' narrative accounts of open-heart surgery and recovery: Authorial voice of technology', *Social Science & Medicine*, 70: 754–62.

Laub, D. and Felman, S. (1992) *Testimony: Crises of Witnessing in Literature, Psychoanalysis, and History*. New York, NY: Routledge.

Lefebvre, H. (1974/1991) *The Production of Space* (D. Nicholson-Smith, trans.). Oxford, UK: Blackwell.

Leudar, I., Sharrock, W., Truckle, S., Colombino, T., Hayes, J. and Booth, K. (2008) 'Conversation of emotions: On turning play into psychoanalytic psychotherapy', in A. Peräyklä, C. Antaki, S. Vehviläinen and I. Leudar (eds), *Conversation Analysis and Psychotherapy*. Cambridge, UK: Cambridge University Press. pp. 152–72.

Levin, M. (2014) 'The Bathroom Formula: A corpus-based study of a speech act in American and British English', *Journal of Pragmatics*, 64: 1–16.

Levinson, S.C. (1983) *Pragmatics*. London, UK: Cambridge University Press.

Linde, C. (1993) *Life Stories: The Creation of Coherence*. Cary, NC: Oxford University Press.

Loh, K.S. (2013) '"You have picked a wrong candidate": Latent fragments and reasonable narratives of the British military withdrawal from Singapore,' in K.S. Loh, E. Koh and S. Dobbs (eds), *Oral History in Southeast Asia: Memories and Fragments*. New York, NY: Palgrave Macmillan. pp. 43–59.

Luff, D. (1999) 'Dialogue across the divides: Moments of rapport and power in feminist research with anti-feminist women', *Sociology*, 33(4): 687–703.

Luken, P.C. and Vaughan, S. (1999) 'Life history and the critique of American sociological practice', *Sociological Inquiry*, 69(3): 404–25.

Lutz, C.A. (1988) *Unnatural Emotions: Everyday Sentiments on a Micronesian Atoll and their Challenge to Western Theory*. Chicago, IL: University of Chicago Press.

MacAulay, S.P. (2004) 'Diaspora by degree: Narrative and performance in interviews of expatriates from Wanganui, New Zealand', *Journal of American Folklore*, 117(465): 262–87.

MacDonald, R. (1994) 'Fiddly jobs, undeclared working and the something for nothing society', *Work, Employment and Society*, 8(4): 507–30.

Maheux-Pelletier, G. and Golato, A. (2008) 'Repair in membership categorization in French', *Language in Society*, 37: 689–712.

Maiter, S., Simich, L., Jacobson, N. and Wise, J. (2008) 'An ethic for community-based participatory action research', *Action Research*, 6(3): 305–25.

Malinowski, B. (1923) 'The problem of meaning in primitive languages', supplement to C.K. Ogden and I.A. Richards, *The Meaning of Meaning*. London, UK: Routledge and Kegan Paul. pp. 146–52.

Mandell, N. and Whittington-Walsh, F. (2004) 'Building bridges across sectors: A resource to help create community and academic research partnerships', CERIS Working Paper No. 33. Toronto, ON: Joint Centre of Excellence for Research on Immigration and Settlement – Toronto. Available at: http://www.ceris.metropolis.net/wp-content/uploads/pdf/research_publication/working_papers/wp33.pdf, accessed 31 October 2014.

Marcus, G.E. and Fischer, M.M.J. (1986) *Anthropology as Cultural Critique: An Experimental Moment in the Human Sciences*. Chicago, IL: University of Chicago Press.

Markus, H.R. and Kitayama, S. (1991) 'Culture and the self: Implications for cognition, emotion, and motivation', *Psychological Review*, 98(2): 224–53.

Marley, B. (1973) 'I shot the sheriff' [Recorded by The Wailers]. On *Burnin'* [Vinyl record]. Kingston, JA: Island. (April 1973)

Martin, L.H., Gutman, H. and Hutton, P.H. (1988) 'Introduction', in L.H. Martin, H. Gutman and P.H. Hutton (eds), *Technologies of the Self: A Seminar with Michel Foucault*. Amherst, MA: University of Massachusetts Press. pp. 1–8.

Marx, K. (1847/2008) *The Poverty of Philosophy* (H. Quelch, trans.). New York, NY: Cosimo Classics.

Mason, J. (2008) 'Tangible affinities and the real life fascination of kinship', *Sociology*, 42(1): 29–45.

Mauthner, N.S. and Doucet, A. (2003) 'Reflexive accounts and accounts of reflexivity in qualitative data analysis', *Sociology*, 37(3): 413–31.

Maynard, D.W. (1997) 'The News Delivery Sequence: Bad news and good news in conversational interaction', *Research on Language and Social Interaction*, 30(2): 93–130.

Maynard, D.W. and Clayman, S.E. (1991) 'The diversity of ethnomethodology', *Annual Review of Sociology*, 17: 385–418.

Mazeland, H. and ten Have, P. (1996) 'Essential tensions in (semi-)open research interviews', in I. Maso and F. Wester (eds), *The Deliberative Dialogue: Qualitative Perspectives on the Interview*. Brussels, BE: VUB University Press. pp. 87–113.

McAdams, D.P. (2006) *The Redemptive Self: Stories Americans Live By*. New York, NY: Oxford University Press.

McDaniel, S. and Bernard, P. (2011) 'Life course as a policy lens: Challenges and opportunities', *Canadian Public Policy*, 37(1): 1–13.

McGranahan, C. (2010) 'Narrative dispossession: Tibet and the gendered logics of historical possibility', *Comparative Studies in Society and History*, 52(4): 768–97.

McHoul, A. (1978) 'The organization of turns at formal talk in the classroom', *Language in Society*, 7: 183–213.

McHoul, A. and Grace, W. (1995) *A Foucault Primer: Discourse, Power and the Subject*. New York, NY: Routledge.

McHugh, S. (2012) 'The affective power of sound: Oral history on radio', *Oral History Review*, 39(2): 187–206.

McKenzie-Mohr, S. and Lafrance, M.N. (2011) 'Telling stories without the words: "Tightrope talk" in women's accounts of coming to live well after rape or depression', *Feminism & Psychology*, 21(1): 49–73.

McLaren, M.A. (2002) *Feminism, Foucault, and Embodied Subjectivity*. Albany, NY: State University of New York Press.

McNay, L. (1994) *Foucault: A Critical Introduction*. Cambridge, UK: Polity Press.

McVee, M. (2005) 'Re-visiting the black Jesus: Re-emplotting a narrative through multiple retellings', *Narrative Inquiry*, 15(1): 161–95.

Mead, G.H. (1934) *Mind, Self, and Society: From the Standpoint of a Social Behaviorist*. Chicago, IL: University of Chicago Press.

Mele, M.L. and Bello, B.M. (2007) 'Coaxing and coercion in roadblock encounters on Nigerian highways', *Discourse & Society*, 18(4): 437–52.

Menchú, R. (1984) *I, Rigoberta Menchú: An Indian woman in Guatemala* (E. Burgos-Debray, ed.; A. Wright, trans.). London, UK: Verso.

Meth, P. (2004) 'Using diaries to understand women's responses to crime and violence', *Environment & Urbanization*, 16(2): 153–64.

Miller, J.F. (1996) '"I have a frog in my stomach": Mythology and truth in life history', in G. Etter-Lewis and M. Foster (eds), *Unrelated Kin: Race and Gender in Women's Personal Narratives*. New York, NY: Routledge. pp. 103–19.

Mills, S. (2004) *Discourse*. New York, NY: Routledge.

Minkler, M., Vásquez, V.B., Tajik, M. and Petersen, D. (2008) 'Promoting environmental justice through community-based participatory research: The role of community and partnership capacity', *Health Education & Behavior*, 35(1): 119–37.

Mishler, E.G. (1991) *Research Interviewing: Context and Narrative*. Cambridge, MA: Harvard University Press.

Moerman, M. (1988) *Talking Culture: Ethnography and Conversation Analysis*. Philadelphia, PA: University of Pennsylvania Press.

Mondada, L. (2013) 'Contesting and negotiating epistemic authority in social interaction: Descriptions and questions in guided visits', *Discourse Studies,* 15(5): 597–626.

Morgan, D. (1996) 'Focus groups', *Annual Review of Sociology,* 22: 129–52.

Mukherjee, S. (2010) *Surviving Bhopal: Dancing Bodies, Written Texts, and Oral Testimonials of Women in the Wake of an Industrial Disaster.* New York, NY: Palgrave Macmillan.

Murakami, K. (2001) 'Talk about rice: A discursive approach to studying culture', *Forum Qualitative Sozialforschung/Forum: Qualitative Social Research,* 2(3): Art. 13.

Murdocca, C. (2003) 'When Ebola came to Canada: Race and the making of the respectable body', *Atlantis,* 27(2): 24–31.

Nakane, I. (2011) 'The role of silence in interpreted police interviews', *Journal of Pragmatics,* 43: 2317–30.

Narayan, K. (1993) 'How native is a "native" anthropologist?', *American Anthropologist,* 95(3): 671–86.

Neisser, U. (1994) 'Self-narratives: True and false', in U. Neisser and R. Fivush (eds), *The Remembering Self: Construction and Accuracy in the Self-narrative.* New York, NY: Cambridge University Press. pp. 1–18.

Neisser, U. and Libby, L. (2000) 'Remembering life experiences', in E. Tulving and F.I.M. Craik (eds), *The Oxford Handbook of Memory.* New York, NY: Oxford University Press. pp. 315–32.

Nevile, M. (2004) 'Integrity in the airline cockpit: Embodying claims about progress for the conduct of an approach briefing', *Research on Language and Social Interaction,* 37(4): 447–80.

Norrick, N. (1991) 'On the organization of corrective exchanges in conversation', *Journal of Pragmatics,* 16: 59–83.

Norrick, N. (2005) 'The dark side of tellability', *Narrative Inquiry,* 15(2): 323–43.

O'Connell, D., Kowal, S. and Kaltenbacher, E. (1990) 'Turn-taking: A critical analysis of the research tradition', *Journal of Psycholinguistic Research,* 19(6): 345–73.

O'Connell Davidson, J. and Layder, D. (1994) *Methods, Sex and Madness.* London, UK: Routledge.

Ochs, E. and Capps, L. (1996) 'Narrating the self', *Annual Review of Anthropology,* 25: 19–43.

Okamoto, D.G. and Smith-Lovin, L. (2001) 'Changing the subject: Gender, status, and the dynamics of topic change', *American Sociological Review,* 66(6): 852–73.

Ong, W.J. (2012) *Orality and Literacy: The Technologizing of the Word.* New York, NY: Routledge.

Oriola, T. and Haggerty, K.D. (2012) 'The ambivalent insider/outsider status of academic "homecomers": Observations on identity and field research in the Nigerian Delta', *Sociology,* 46(3): 540–8.

Owens, J. (2007) 'Liberating voices through narrative methods: The case for an interpretive research approach', *Disability & Society,* 22(3): 299–313.

Pascale, C.M. (2008a) 'Talking about race: Shifting the analytical paradigm', *Qualitative Inquiry*, 14(5): 723–41.

Pascale, C.M. (2008b) 'Common sense and the collaborative production of class', *Cultural Sociology*, 2(3): 345–467.

Passerini, L. (1979) 'Work ideology and consensus under Italian fascism', *History Workshop*, 8(1): 82–108.

Peräyklä, A. and Vehviläinen, S. (2003) 'Conversation analysis and the professional stocks of interactional knowledge', *Discourse & Society*, 14(6): 727–50.

Philo, C. (2012) '"A great space of murmurings": Madness, romance and geography', *Progress in Human Geography*, 37(2): 167–94.

Phoenix, C., Smith, B. and Sparkes, A. (2010) 'Narrative analysis in aging studies: A typology for consideration', *Journal of Aging Studies*, 24(1): 1–11.

Polkinghorne, D.E. (2007) 'Validity issues in narrative research', *Qualitative Inquiry*, 13(4): 471–86.

Pollack, S. (2003) 'Focus-group methodology in research with incarcerated women: Race, power, and collective experience', *Affilia*, 18(4): 461–72.

Polonoff, D. (1987) 'Self-deception', *Social Research*, 54(1): 45–53.

Pomerantz, A. (1986) 'Extreme case formulations: A way of legitimizing claims', *Human Studies*, 9: 219–29.

Pope, A. (1711) *An Essay on Criticism*. London: W. Lewis.

Portelli, A. (1981/1991) 'The death of Luigi Trastulli: Memory and the event', in A. Portelli, *The Death of Luigi Trastulli and Other Stories: Form and Meaning in Oral History*. Albany, NY: SUNY Press. pp. 1–26.

Potter, J. (1996) 'Discourse analysis and constructionist approaches: Theoretical background', in J.T. Richardson (ed.), *Handbook of Qualitative Research Methods for Psychology and the Social Sciences*. Leicester, UK: BPS Books. pp. 125–140.

Potter, J. (2002) 'Two kinds of natural', *Discourse Studies*, 4(4): 539–42.

Potter, J. and Hepburn, A. (2005) 'Qualitative interviews in psychology: Problems and possibilities', *Qualitative Research in Psychology*, 2: 1–27.

Propen, A. and Schuster, M.L. (2008) 'Making academic work advocacy work: Technologies of power in the public arena', *Journal of Business and Technical Communication*, 22(3): 299–329.

Purvis, T. and Hunt, A. (1993) 'Discourse, ideology, discourse, ideology, discourse, ideology ...' , *The British Journal of Sociology*, 44(3): 473–99.

Rabinow, P. (1986) 'Representations are social facts: Modernity and post-modernity in anthropology', in J. Clifford and G.E. Marcus (eds), *Writing Culture: The Poetics and Politics of Ethnography*. Berkeley: University of California Press. pp. 234–61.

Radway, J. (1984) *Reading the Romance: Women, Patriarchy, and Popular Literature*. Chapel Hill, NC: University of North Carolina Press.

Raj, D.S. (2000) 'Ignorance, forgetting, and family nostalgia: Partition, the nation state and refugees in Delhi', *Social Analysis*, 44(2): 30–55.

Rapley, T.J. (2001) 'The art(fullness) of open-ended interviewing: Some considerations on analysing interviews', *Qualitative Research*, 1(3): 302–23.

Ravel, B. and Rail, G. (2006) 'The lightness of being "gaie"', *International Review for the Sociology of Sport*, 4(1/2): 395–412.

Raymond, G. (2003) 'Grammar and social organization: Yes/no interrogatives and the structure of responding', *American Sociological Review*, 68(6): 939–67.

Reason, P. and Bradbury, H. (2006) 'Introduction: Inquiry and participation in search of a world worthy of human aspiration', in P. Reason and H. Bradbury (eds), *Handbook of Action Research*, concise paperback edn. London, UK: Sage. pp. 1–14.

Richardson, L. (1992) 'The consequences of poetic representation', in C. Ellis and M. Flaherty (eds), *Investigating Subjectivity: Research on Lived Experience*. London, UK: Sage. pp. 125–40.

Ricoeur, P. (1984) *Time and Narrative* (Vol. 1). Chicago, IL: Chicago University Press.

Ridgeway, C.L. (1997) 'Interaction and the conservation of gender inequality: Considering employment', *American Sociological Review*, 62(2): 218–35.

Riessman, C.K. (2003) 'Analysis of personal narratives', in J. Holstein and J.F. Gubrium (eds), *Inside Interviewing: New Lenses, New Concerns*. Thousand Oaks, CA: Sage.

Riessman, C.K. (2005) 'Narrative analysis', in N. Kelly, C. Horrocks, K. Milnes, B. Roberts and D. Robinson (eds), *Narrative, Memory, & Everyday Life*. Huddersfield, UK: University of Huddersfield Press. pp. 1–7.

Rogan, A.I. and de Kock, D.M. (2005) 'Chronicles from the classroom: Making sense of the methodology and methods of narrative analysis', *Qualitative Inquiry*, 11(4): 628–49.

Rosaldo, M.Z. (1984) 'Toward an anthropology of self and feeling', in R.A. Shweder and R.A. LeVine (eds), *Culture Theory: Essays on Mind, Self, and Emotion*. Cambridge, UK: Cambridge University Press. pp. 137–57.

Rosaldo, R. (1989) *Culture and Truth: The Remaking of Social Analysis*. Boston, MA: Beacon Press.

Rosenthal, G. (1993) 'Reconstruction of life stories. Principles of selection in generating stories for narrative biographical interviews', *The Narrative Study of Lives*, 1: 59–91.

Rosenthal, G. (2003) 'The healing effects of storytelling: On the conditions of curative storytelling in the context of research and counseling', *Qualitative Inquiry*, 9(6): 915–33.

Ross, M. and Buehler, R. (1994) 'Creative remembering', in U. Neisser and R. Fivush (eds), *The Remembering Self: Construction and Accuracy in the Self-narrative*. Cambridge, UK: Cambridge University Press. pp. 205–35.

Roulston, K. (2001) 'Data analysis and "theorizing as ideology"', *Qualitative Research*, 1(3): 279–302.

Roulston, K.J., Baker, C.D. and Liljestrom, A. (2001) 'Analyzing the researcher's work in generating data: The case of complaints', *Qualitative Inquiry*, 7(6): 745–72.

Ryan, L. (2002) '"I'm going to England": Women's narratives of leaving Ireland in the 1930s', *Oral History*, 30(1): 42–53.

Sacks, H. (1972) 'An initial investigation of the usability of conversational data for doing sociology', in D. Sudnow (ed.), *Studies in Social Interaction*. New York, NY: Free Press. pp. 31–74.

Sacks, H. (1995) *Lectures on Conversation*, Volumes 1 & 2 (G. Jefferson, ed.; E.A. Schegloff, intro.). New York, NY: Wiley-Blackwell.

Sacks, H., Schegloff, E. and Jefferson, G. (1974) 'A simplest systematics for the organization of turn-taking in conversation', *Language*, 50(4): 696–735.

Said, E. (1978) *Orientalism*. New York, NY: Pantheon.

Said, E. (1989) 'Representing the colonized: Anthropology's interlocutors', *Critical Inquiry*, 15(2): 205–25.

Sands, R.G. and Krumer-Nevo, M. (2006) 'Interview shocks and shockwaves', *Qualitative Inquiry*, 12(5): 950–71.

Sangster, J. (1994) 'Telling our stories: Feminist debates and the use of oral history', *Women's History Review*, 3(1): 5–28.

Saukko, P. (2000) 'Between voice and discourse: Quilting interviews on anorexia', *Qualitative Inquiry*, 6(3): 299–317.

Schacter, D.L. (2001) *The Seven Sins of Memory: How the Mind Forgets and Remembers*. New York, NY: Houghton Mifflin.

Schegloff, E.A. (1982) 'Discourse as an interactional achievement: Some uses of 'uh huh' and other things that come between sentences', in D. Tannen (ed.), *Georgetown University Roundtable on Languages and Linguistics (1981) Analyzing Discourse: Text and Talk*. Washington, DC: Georgetown University Press. pp. 71–93.

Schegloff, E.A. (1988/89) 'From interview to confrontation: Observations of the Bush/Rather encounter', *Research on Language and Social Interaction*, 22: 215–40.

Schegloff, E.A. (1991) 'Reflections on talk and social structure', in D. Boden and D. Zimmerman (eds), *Talk and Social Structure*. Cambridge, UK: Cambridge University Press. pp. 44–70.

Schegloff, E.A. (1995) 'Introduction', in H. Sacks, *Lectures on Conversation*, Volumes 1 & 2 (G. Jefferson, ed.). New York, NY: Wiley-Blackwell. pp. ix–lxii.

Schegloff, E.A. (1997) 'Whose text? Whose context?', *Discourse & Society*, 8(2): 165–87.

Schegloff, E. (1998) 'Reply to Wetherell', *Discourse & Society*, 9(3): 413–16.

Schegloff, E.A. (1999) 'Naivete vs sophistication or discipline vs self-indulgence: A rejoinder to Billig', *Discourse & Society*, 10(4): 577–82.

Schegloff, E.A. (2000) 'Overlapping talk and the organization of turn-taking for conversation', *Language in Society*, 29: 1–63.

Schegloff, E.A. (2006) 'Interaction: The infrastructure for social institutions, the natural ecological niche for language, and the arena in which culture is enacted', in N.J. Enfield and S.C. Levinson (eds), *Roots of Human Sociality: Culture, Cognition and Interaction*. Oxford, UK: Berg. pp. 70–96.

Schegloff, E. (2007) *Sequence Organization in Interaction: A Primer in Conversation Analysis*, Vol. 1. Cambridge, UK: Cambridge University Press.

Schegloff, E.A. and Sacks, H. (1973) 'Opening up closings', *Semiotica*, 8(4): 289–327.

Schegloff, E.A., Jefferson, G. and Sacks, H. (1977) 'The preference for self-correction in the organization of repair in conversation', *Language*, 53(2): 361–82.

Scheuer, J. (2003) 'Habitus as the principle for social practice: A proposal for critical discourse analysis', *Language in Society*, 32: 143–75.

Scheurich, J.J. (1995) 'A postmodernist critique of research interviewing', *International Journal of Qualitative Studies in Education*, 8(3): 239–52.

Scheurich, J.J. and McKenzie, K.B. (2008) 'Foucault's methodologies: Archaeology and genealogy', in N.K. Denzin and Y.S. Lincoln (eds), *Sage Handbook of Qualitative Research*, 3rd edn. Thousand Oaks, CA: Sage. pp. 841–68.

Schütz, A. (1945/1970) 'The homecomer' in *Alfred Schutz on Phenomenology and Social Relations* (H.R. Wagner, ed.). Chicago, IL: University of Chicago Press. pp. 294–313.

Schütz, A. (1962) *Collected Papers, Vol. I: The Problem of Social Reality* (M. Natanson and H.L van Breda, eds). Dordrecht, NL: Martinus Nijhoff.

Schütz, A. (1964) *Collected Papers, Vol. II: Studies in Social Theory* (A. Brodersen, ed.). Dordrecht, NL: Martinus Nijhoff.

Schwalbe, M. (1995) 'The responsibilities of sociological poets', *Qualitative Sociology*, 18(4): 393–413.

Searle, J.R. (1975) 'A taxonomy of illocutionary acts', in K. Günderson (ed.), *Language, Mind, and Knowledge*, Minneapolis Studies in the Philosophy of Science, Vol. 7. Minneapolis, MN: University of Minneapolis Press. pp. 344–69.

Sherman, T. (2010) 'Proselyting in first-contact situations as an instructed action', *Sociologický časopis/Czech Sociological Review*, 46(6): 977–1009.

Sidnell, J. (2005) *Talk and Practical Epistemology: The Social Life of Knowledge in a Caribbean Community*. Amsterdam, NL: John Benjamins.

Sidnell, J. (2009) *Conversation Analysis: Comparative Perspectives*. Cambridge, UK: Cambridge University Press.

Silverman, D. (1993) *Interpreting Qualitative Data: Methods for Analyzing Talk, Text and Interaction*. London, UK: Sage.

Simmel, G. (1908/1950) 'The stranger', in *The Sociology of Georg Simmel* (K. Wolff, ed. and trans.). New York, NY: Free Press. pp. 402–8.

Sin, C.H. (2003) 'Interviewing in "place": The socio-spatial construction of interview data', *Area*, 35(3): 305–12.

Sinding, C. and Aronson, J. (2003) 'Exposing failures, unsettling accommodations: Tensions in interview practice', *Qualitative Research*, 3(1): 95–117.

Sjölander, A.E. (2011) 'Introduction: Comparing critical discourse analysis and discourse theory', in A.E. Sjölander and J.G. Payne (eds), *Tracking Discourses: Politics, Identity and Social Change*. Lund, SE: Nordic Academic Press. pp. 13–48.

Smith, D. (1974) 'Theorizing as ideology', in R. Turner (ed.), *Ethnomethodology*. Harmondsworth, UK: Penguin. pp. 41–4.

Smith, D. (1987) *The Everyday World as Problematic: A Feminist Sociology*. Boston, MA: Northeastern University Press.

Smith, D. (1993) *Texts, Facts and Femininity: Exploring the Relations of Ruling*. New York, NY: Routledge.

Smith, J., Hollway, W. and Mishler, E. (2005) 'Commentaries on Potter and Hepburn, "Qualitative interviews in psychology: Problems and possibilities"', *Qualitative Research in Psychology*, 2(4): 309–25.

Soni-Sinha, U. (2008) 'Dynamics of the "field": Multiple standpoints, narrative and shifting positionality in multisited research', *Qualitative Research*, 8(4): 515–37.

Sools, A. (2012) 'Narrative health research: Exploring big and small stories as analytical tools', *Health*, 17(1): 93–110.

Speer, S.A. (1999) 'Feminism and conversation analysis: An oxymoron?', *Feminism & Psychology*, 9(4): 471–8.

Speer, S.A. (2002a) '"Natural" and "contrived" data: A sustainable distinction?', *Discourse Studies*, 4(4): 511–25.

Speer, S.A. (2002b) 'Transcending the "natural"/"contrived" distinction: A rejoinder to ten Have, Lynch and Potter', *Discourse Studies*, 4(4): 543–8.

Speer, S.A. (2002c) 'What can conversation analysis contribute to feminist methodology? Putting reflexivity into practice', *Discourse & Society*, 13(6): 783–803.

Speer, S.A. and Parsons, C. (2006) 'Gatekeeping gender: Some features of the use of hypothetical questions in the psychiatric assessment of transsexual patients', *Discourse & Society*, 17(6): 785–812.

Sprague, J. and Zimmerman, M.K. (1993) 'Standpoints and theory: Reply to Tuana', in P. England (ed.), *Theory on Gender/Feminism on Theory*. New York, NY: Aldine de Gruyter. pp. 290–3.

Stanley, L. (2008) 'Madness to the method? Using a narrative methodology to analyse large-scale complex social phenomena', *Qualitative Research*, 8(3): 435–47.

Stanley, L. (2010) 'To the letter: Thomas and Znaniecki's *The Polish Peasant* and writing a life, sociologically', *Life Writing*, 7(2): 139–51.

Steedman, C. (2000) 'Enforced narratives: Stories of another self', in T. Coslett, C. Lury and P. Summerfield (eds), *Feminism and Autobiography: Texts, Theories, Methods*. London, UK: Routledge. pp. 25–39.

Stevanovic, M. (2013) 'Managing participation in interaction: The case of humming', *Text & Talk*, 33(1): 113–37.

Stevenson, C. (2004) 'Theoretical and methodological approaches in discourse analysis', *Nurse Researcher*, 12(2): 18–29.

still eating oranges (2012) *The Significance of Plot without Conflict*, 12 June. Available at: http://stilleatingoranges.tumblr.com/post/25153960313/the-significance-of-plot-without-conflict, accessed 15 November 2013.

Stivers, T., Enfield, N.J., Brown, P., Englert, C., Hayashi, M., Hoymann, G., Rossano, F., de Ruiter, J.P., Yoon, K.-E. and Levinson, S. (2009) 'Universals and cultural variation in turn-taking in conversation', *Proceedings of the National Academy of Sciences of the United States of America*, 106(26): 10587–92.

Stokoe, E.H. (2003) 'Mothers, single women and sluts: Gender, morality and membership categorization in neighbour disputes', *Feminism & Psychology*, 13(3): 317–44.

Stoler, A.L. and Strassler, K. (2006) 'Castings for the colonial: Memory work in "New Order" Java', *Comparative Studies in Society and History*, 42(1): 4–48.

Stoll, D. (1998) *Rigoberta Menchú and the Story of all Poor Guatemalans*. Boulder, CO: Westview Press.

Suchman, L. and Jordan, B. (1990) 'Interactional troubles in face-to-face survey interviews', *Journal of the American Statistical Association*, 85(409): 232–41.

Summerfield, D. (1999) 'A critique of seven assumptions behind psychological trauma programmes in war-affected areas', *Social Science & Medicine*, 48(10): 1449–62.

Sunderland, N., Catalano, T. and Kendall, E. (2009) 'Missing discourses: Concepts of joy and happiness in disability', *Disability & Society*, 24(6): 703–14.

Tamboukou, M. (1999) 'Writing genealogies: An exploration of Foucault's strategies for doing research', *Discourse: Studies in the Cultural Politics of Education*, 20(2): 201–17.

Tanaka, H. (2000) 'Turn projection in Japanese talk-in-interaction', *Research on Language and Social Interaction*, 33(1): 1–38.

Tannen, D. (1987) 'Repetition in conversation: Toward a poetics of talk', *Language*, 63(3): 574–605.

Tannen, D. (1998) '"Oh talking voice that is so sweet": The poetic nature of conversation', *Social Research*, 65(3): 631–51.

Tannen, D. (2007) *Talking Voices: Repetition, Dialogue, and Imagery in Conversational Discourse*, 2nd edn. Cambridge, UK: Cambridge University Press.

Taylor, J. (2011) 'Intimate insider: Negotiating the ethics of friendship when doing insider research', *Qualitative Research*, 11(1): 3–22.

Tedlock, D. (1991) 'Learning to listen: Oral history as poetry', in R.J. Grele (ed.), *Envelopes of Sound: The Art of Oral History*, 2nd edn. New York, NY: Praeger. pp. 106–25.

Teo, P. (2000) 'Racism in the news: A Critical Discourse Analysis of news reporting in two Australian newspapers', *Discourse & Society*, 11(1): 7–49.

The New York Times (2013) *Toronto Mayor Rob Ford Admits to Buying Illegal Drugs*, 13 November. Available at: www.youtube.com/watch?v=IOYXm0U0jBo, accessed 10 August 2015.

Thomas, W.I. and Thomas, D.S. (1928) *The Child in America: Behavior Problems and Programs*. New York, NY: Knopf.

Thomas, W.I. and Znaniecki, F. (1918–1920) *The Polish Peasant in Europe and America: Monograph of an Immigrant Group*. Boston, MA: The Gorham Press.

Thomson, A. (1994) *Anzac Memories: Living with the Legend*. Melbourne, AU: Oxford University Press.

Thomson, A., Frisch, M. and Hamilton, P. (1994) 'The memory and history debates: Some international perspectives', *Oral History*, 22(2): 33–43.

Tilly, C. (2006) *Why?* Princeton, NJ: Princeton University Press.

Timor, U. and Landau, R. (1998) 'Discourse characteristics in the sociolect of repentant criminals', *Discourse & Society*, 9(3): 363–86.

Toronto Star (2013) *Rob Ford: David Letterman Devotes Top 10 List to Mayor; Stewart, Colbert, Leno Leap in Again*, November 15. Available at: www.thestar.com/entertainment/television/2013/11/15/david_letterman_the_top_10_things_going_through_rob_fords_mind_during_the_eightsecond_pause.html, accessed 1 July 2014.

Townley, B. (1993) 'Foucault, power/knowledge, and its relevance for human resource management', *Academy of Management Review*, 18(3): 518–45.

Trouillot, M.-R. (1995) *Silencing the Past: Power and the Production of History*. Boston, MA: Beacon Press.

Tuana, N. (1993) 'With many voices: Feminism and theoretical pluralism', in P. England (ed.), *Theory on Gender/Feminism on Theory*. New York, NY: Aldine de Gruyter. pp. 281–9.

Turnbull, A. (2000) 'Collaboration and censorship in the oral history interview', *International Journal of Social Research Methodology*, 3(1): 15–34.

Uehara, E.S. (2007) '"Disturbing phenomenology" in the pain and engagement narratives of Cambodian American survivors of the Killing Fields', *Culture, Medicine and Psychiatry*, 31(3): 329–58.

Ulichny, P. (1997) 'The mismanagement of understandings in cross-cultural interactions', *Journal of Pragmatics*, 27: 233–46.

Van De Mieroop, D. and Clifton, J. (2012) 'The interactional negotiation of group membership and ethnicity: The case of an interview with a former slave', *Discourse & Society*, 23(2): 163–83.

van der Merwe, C.N. and Gobodo-Madikizela, P. (2008) *Narrating our Healing: Perspectives on Working Through Trauma*. Newcastle, UK: Cambridge Scholars Publishing.

van der Walt, C., Franchi, V. and Stevens, G. (2003) 'The South African Truth and Reconciliation Commission: "Race", historical compromise and transitional democracy', *International Journal of Intercultural Relations*, 27(2): 251–67.

van Dijk, T.A. (1988) *News as Discourse*. Hillsdale, NJ: Lawrence Erlbaum Associates.

van Dijk, T.A. (1998) *Ideology: A Multidisciplinary Approach*. London, UK: Sage.

van Dijk, T.A. (2001) 'Critical discourse analysis', in D. Schiffrin, D. Tannen and H.E. Hamilton (eds), *Handbook of Discourse Analysis*. Oxford, UK: Blackwell. pp. 352–71.

van Dijk, T.A. (2006) 'Ideology and discourse analysis', *Journal of Political Ideologies*, 11(2): 115–40.

van Dijk, T.A. (2008) *Discourse & Power*. New York, NY: Palgrave MacMillan.

Vansina, J. (1985) *Oral Tradition as History*. Madison, WI: The University of Wisconsin Press.

Vinitzky-Seroussi, V. (2000) '"My God, what am I gonna say?": Class reunions as social control', *Qualitative Sociology*, 23(1): 57–75.

Wang, J. (2006) 'Questions and the exercise of power', *Discourse & Society*, 17(4): 529–48.

Warren, C.A.B., Barnes-Brus, T., Burgess, H. and Wiebold-Lippisch, L. with Hackney, J., Harkness, G., Kennedy, V., Dingwall, R., Rosenblatt, P.C., Ryen, A. and Shuy, R. (2003) 'After the interview', *Qualitative Sociology*, 26(1): 93–110.

Waskul, D., Vannini, P. and Wiesen, D. (2007) 'Women and their clitoris: Personal discovery, signification, and use', *Symbolic Interaction*, 30(2): 151–74.

Weatherall, A. (2002) 'Towards understanding gender and talk-in-interaction', *Discourse & Society*, 13(6): 767–81.

Weedon, C. (1999) *Feminism, Theory and the Politics of Difference*. Oxford, UK: Blackwell Publishers.

Welzer, H., Moller, S. and Tschuggnall, K. (2001) *'Opa war kein Nazi': Nationalsozialismus und Holocaust im Familiengedächtnis*. Frankfurt am Main, DE: Fischer.

Werner, A., Isaksen, L.W. and Malterud, K. (2004) '"I am not the kind of woman who complains of everything": Illness stories on self and shame in women with chronic pain', *Social Science and Medicine*, 59(5): 1035–45.

West, C. and Zimmerman, D.H. (1987) 'Doing gender', *Gender & Society*, 1(2): 125–51.

West, D. (2013) 'What's in a sign? Narrative inquiry and Deaf storytellers'. In S. Trahar (ed.), *Contextualising Narrative Inquiry* (pp. 1–19). London: Routledge.

Wetherell, M. (1998) 'Positioning and interpretative repertoires: Conversation analysis and post-structuralism in dialogue', *Discourse & Society*, 9(3): 387–412.

Whitehead, K.A. (2009) '"Categorizing the categorizer": The management of racial common sense in interaction', *Social Psychology Quarterly*, 72(4): 325–42.

Whitehead, K.A. and Lerner, G.H. (2009) '"When are people white?": On some practical asymmetries of racial reference in conversation', *Discourse & Society*, 20(5): 613–41.

Widdicombe, S. (1995) 'Identity, politics and talk: A case for the mundane and the everyday', in S. Wilkinson and C. Kitzinger (eds), *Feminism and Discourse: Psychological Perspectives*. London, UK: Sage. pp. 106–27.

Widdicombe, S. (1998) 'Identity as an analysts' and a participants' resource', in C. Antaki and S. Widdicombe (eds), *Identities in Talk*. London, UK: Sage. pp. 190–206.

Wiggins, S. and Potter, D. (2008) 'Discursive psychology', in C. Willig and W. Stainton-Rogers (eds), *The Sage Handbook of Qualitative Research in Psychology*. London, UK: Sage. pp. 73–90.

Wilkinson, S. (1998) 'Focus groups in feminist research: Power, interaction, and the co-construction of meaning', *Women's Studies International Forum*, 21(1): 111–25.

Wilkinson, S. (2011) 'Constructing ethnicity statistics in talk-in-interaction: Producing the "White European"', *Discourse & Society*, 22(3): 343–61.

Williams, R. (1983) *Keywords: A Vocabulary of Culture and Society*. New York, NY: Oxford University Press.

Wodak, R. (1996) *Disorders of Discourse*. New York, NY: Longman.

Wodak, R. (1999) 'Critical discourse analysis at the end of the 20th century', *Research on Language and Social Interaction*, 32(1&2): 185–93.

Wong, L.M. (1998) 'The ethics of rapport: Institutional safeguards, resistance, and betrayal', *Qualitative Inquiry*, 4(2): 178–99.

Wood, L.A. and Kroger, R.O. (2000) *Doing Discourse Analysis: Methods for Studying Action in Talk and Text*. Thousand Oaks, CA: Sage.

Woodley, K. (2001) 'Let the data sing: Representing discourse in poetic form', *Oral History*, 32(1): 49–58.

Woodward, I. (2001) 'Domestic objects and the taste epiphany: A resource for consumption methodology', *Journal of Material Culture*, 6(2): 115–36.

Wooffitt, R. and Clark, C. (1998) 'Mobilizing discourse and social identities in knowledge talk', in C. Antaki and S. Widdicombe (eds), *Identities in Talk*. London, UK: Sage. pp. 107–20.

Yúdice, G. (1991) 'Testimonio and postmodernism', *Latin American Perspectives*, 18(3): 15–31.

Zimmerman, D.H. (1984) 'Talk and its occasion: The case of calling the police', in D. Schiffrin (ed.), *Meaning, Form and Use in Context: Linguistic Applications*. Ashington, DC: Georgetown University Press. pp. 210–28.

Zimmerman, D.H. (1998) 'Identity, context and interaction', in C. Antaki and S. Widdicombe (eds), *Identities in Talk*. London, UK: Sage. pp. 87–106.

Zimmerman, D.H. and West, C. (1975) 'Sex roles, interruptions and silences in conversation', in B. Thorne and N. Henley (eds), *Language and Sex: Difference and Dominance*. Rowley, MA: Newbury House. pp. 105–29.

Index

Note: Page numbers followed by the letter 'f' indicate footnotes. Page numbers followed by the letter 't' indicate tables.

abstract, in stories 30
accountable 71, 76, 183
  in two-turn sequences 79, 80, 82
  in institutional talk 101, 104
  in qualitative research interviews 118
  repair 125
acknowledgement tokens 103, 106, 119
action research 49
adding to the common ground 125
adjacency pairs 78–9, 80, 82, 84, 85, 103, 106, 172
affiliation 77
agency 25, 27, 130, 158, 182–3
  in CDA 145
  and embodied subjectivities 141
  and emplacement 53
  language of 33–6
  and linguistic incongruence 169
  and micro-macro bridging 151
  in symbolic interactionism 20
  and technologies of the self 135, 172
aphasia 107
assonance 40
authority
  epistemic 85
  in oral history 12
  shared 43, 62
autobiographical memory 11–12, 18

Bastalich, W. 138
Billig, M. 94, 95
Black feminist standpoint theory 46
breaching experiments 70–1
Butler, J. 94, 133, 174–5

categorization *see* membership categorization analysis (MCA)
chat shows 91–2, 106, 171
Chicago School of Sociology 20
closings 85
coda, in stories 31
cognitivism 116
coherence of stories 23–6, 31, 40, 59–60, 62
collective memory 17–18
Collins, P.H. 46
common communicative ground 124–5
competence
  in CA 67, 72, 86, 90, 183
  in oral history 12
complicating action, in stories 31
composure 57
connaissance 132
consistency bias 12
constructionism 5, 9, 72, *see* constructionism versus realism
  and action research 49
  anchored in realism 16, 20
  plausibility 61
  ontology, epistemology and rigor 15–16
  understanding of memory 16–17
constructionism versus realism 5
  in CA 72, 123
  in DA 146, 167
  in NA 9, 15–6, 17, 24, 27, 29, 43–4, 45–6, 47–8, 61
continuer 113
contrast devices 92
conventional plots 21
conversation, ordinary 98f
conversation analysis (CA) 3, 6, 65–8
    see also membership categorization analysis (MCA)
  challenges to 78, 80, 94
  compared to NA 86
    CA analysis of stories 83–84
    understandings of reflexivity 111–12, 115, 147, 167–8
  compared to DA 67, 94, 108, 130, 148, 167–8
  extended sequences 82–4
    topics 84–5
  focus groups 122–7

conversation analysis (CA) *cont.*
founding insight 69–71
interviews 111–18
and its alternatives 93–6
mechanisms 75–85
ontology and epistemology 72
reflexivity in 111, 114, 115, 116, 118
repair 80–2
rigor 73–4
turn-taking 75–80
conversation analysis paradigm 72–4
corpus 73
correction *see* repair
crisis of representation 44–6
critical discourse analysis (CDA) 130, 143–4
compared to CA 172
compared to Foucauldian DA 145–6
main tenets 144–5
ontology and epistemology 145–6
reflexivity in 147
research strategies 148–54
rigor 147–8
critical theory 146, 154
cross-cultural generalizability
in NA 26, 40, 55
in CA 78, 80
cultural dopes 70
cultural repertoires 25, 26

de Certeau, M. 52
dead social scientists' test 116
debates 91–2, 150
deconstruction 138, 140, 151–2, 159, 164
defended subjects 57–59
Denzin, N.K. 13, 21–2
deviant cases 147
disaffilliative acts 77, 79, 80, 82, 125
diagnostic interviews 100, 107
difference, politics of 46
discipline 111, 136, 137, 140, 158, 172, 173, 176
discourse 5, 129, 155
discourse analysis (DA) 3, 6, 129–30 *see also* critical discourse analysis (CDA); Foucauldian discourse analysis; garden-variety discourse analysis
compared to CA 67, 94, 108, 130, 148, 167–8, 182–5
compared to NA 167, 182–5
interviews 167–180
power 168–74
Discourse and Social Change (Fairclough) 144
discursive positioning 178–80
discourse-society dialectic 155–7
discursive psychology 116, 180

economy, principle of 88
educational settings 60, 106, 139, 156–7, 177, 179, 180

Edwards, D. 116
Elder, G. 20
embodiment 50–4, 62, 63, 104, 111, 167, 184
emergency services 100–1, 105–6
emotional labor 109
emotions 51, 59, 63, 167, 180, 184
empirical 72
emplacement 52–4, 63, 184
emplotment 30–3, 54, 55, 56, 57
English as a Foreign Language 81–2, 114, 115
epiphanies 21–2, 37
epistemic authority 85
epistemic gradient 106
epistemology 5
constructionism anchored in realism 16, 20
in the constructionist paradigm 15
in CA 72
in a critical paradigm 145–6
in post-structuralist research 132–3
in the realist paradigm 10
ethnomethodology 70–1, 94, 111 , 174
evaluation, in stories 31–3
everyday talk *see also* conversation analysis (CA); institutional talk-in-interaction
extended sequences 82–4
mechanisms of 75–85
repair in 80–2
taking turns 75–8
two-turn sequences 78–80
extended sequences in everyday talk 82–4
extreme case formulation 120
Ezzy, D. 23, 24

face 69–70
Fairclough, N. 143, 144, 152
false collusive objectification 57
false consciousness 145
fateful moments 21
feelings 51f
feminist standpoint theory 45–6
fidelity
in oral history 38
of stories 61–2
in translation 38–9
figurative language 36–9
first-pair parts 78–9, 113, 114 *see also* adjacency pairs
focus groups 48, 122–7
footing 81
formulation 106–7, 114, 126
extreme case formulation 120, 125
Foucauldian discourse analysis 130, 131–2
ontology, epistemology and rigor 132–4
post-structuralism 133
power, knowledge and the subject 134–7
strategies 138–41
subjectification in 230
Frankfurt School 146
Frisch, M. 43, 62

garden-variety discourse analysis
  discourse-society dialectic 155–7
  identities and subjectivities 157–9
  ideology 161–4
  power 160–1, 164
  time 164–5
Garfinkel, H. 70–1
genealogy 135, 164
generalizability of CA findings 78
gestures 103
Giddens, A. 21, 145
glosses 73
Goffman, E. 69–70, 81
'good' stories
  coherence 59–60
  fidelity 61–2
  liveability 56–9
  reportability 55–6
Gramsci, A. 145
greetings 84, 105–6
group interviews *see* focus groups
group membership *see* identity; membership categorization analysis (MCA)
Guba, E.G. 5, 10

Halbwachs, M. 17–18
Hall, S. 70, 148, 161–2, 165
Hammersley, M. 146–7
Harding, S. 45
Hartsock, N. 45, 134, 137
hearer's maxim 88
hedges 80
hegemonic masculinity 129–30
hegemony 145
heteroglossic 53
hindsight 12
histories from below 18
humanism 3, 7, 27, 49, 57, 167

I, Rigoberta Menchú: An Indian woman in Guatemala (Menchú) 13–14
identity
  as an accomplishment 120
  as connected to subjectivity 158–9
  definition 120
    in discourse 158–9
  identity categories 169
    as debated in CA 93–5
    in discourse 153–4, 259
    in membership categorization analysis (MCA) 153–5
  identity politics 5, 12
  performance and performativity 174–8
ideology
  economic ideology 151
  false consciousness 145, 161, 167
  Foucault on ideology 162
  in garden-variety DA 161–4
imagery 36–9

indexicality 70
individual essentialism 123
insider/outsider status 44–5
instantiation 167
institutional talk-in-interaction
  basics 97–9
  mechanisms 104–9
  stages 99–102
  turn-taking 102–4
interaction order 69–71, 86
interactional knowledge, stocks of 99
interpretation *see* translation
interruptions 72, 77, 93, 94, 150
intersectionality matrix 46
intersubjectivity 70
intertextuality 40
interview society 171
interview strategies
  based on standpoints 47–9
  linking analysis to representation 49–50
interviews 4, 171–2 *see also* reflexivity
  as confession 170–1
  in CA 111–18
  diagnostic 100
  in DA 167–180
  embodiment 50–4
  media 97–8, 103, 104, 150
  in NA 43–63
  qualitative research interviews 112–18

Jayyusi, L. 90
Jefferson, G. 66, 83–4, 84
joint construction of meaning 43

key phrases 36
kishōtenketsu 55
Kitzinger, C. 94, 95, 109

Labov, W. 30–3, 83
Labov & Waletzky's model of the story 30–3, 83
Lakoff, G. 38
language variants 90
life course
  life course perspective 20
  life course processes 19–22
  and social positioning 33
life histories 20, 22, 23, 25–6, 40, 48, 49
lifeworld 70
Lincoln, Y.S. 5, 10
Linde, C. 25–6, 55
linguistics 143
linguistic incongruence 169
linked lives 22
liveability of stories 56–9

Marx, K. 123, 135, 145, 161–2
mass media
  interviews 97–8, 103, 104, 150
  newspapers 153–4

mass media *cont.*
radio 97–8, 106
television chat shows 91–2, 106, 171
master narratives 56–7
Mead, G.H. 15, 23
meaning, joint construction of 43
mediation 107–8
medical practitioners 35–6, 38, 50, 76, 85, 101–2, 140, 149–50
members 71
membership categorization analysis (MCA)
basics 87–9
strategies 89–92, 118–22
membership categorization devices (MCDs) 88
Menchú, R. 13–14
metaphors 37–8
methodological triangulation 13
micro and macro
in CA 70
in DA
in critical discourse analysis (CDA) 148–51
in garden-variety DA 155–7
in interviewing 172–4
in NA 7, 36, 53–4
Mills, S. 155
mnemonic devices 11
moral performance 90

narrative analysis (NA) 3, 6, 7–8
analysis of emplotment 30–33
analysis of agency 33–6
analysis of imagery and figurative language 36–9
analysis of sound and repetition 40–2
compared to CA 86
CA analysis of stories 83–4
understandings of reflexivity 111–12, 115, 147, 167–8
compared to DA 167, 182–5
interviews in 43–63
life history and life course strategies 19–22
oral history strategies 10–19
strategies focused on the self 23–6
narratives 8, 31 *see also* stories
small stories 84
Neisser, U. 15
news interviews 103, 104, 150
newspapers 153–4
newsworthiness *see* reportability
next-turn proof 74, 81, 164
next-turn repair 81
nominalization and voice 35

objects 136
official history 18
omnirelevance 94–5
ontology 5
in the constructionist paradigm 15
in CA 72
ontology *cont.*
in critical discourse analysis (CDA) 145–6
in post-structuralist research 132–3
in the realist paradigm 10
openings 99, 100, 106, 125
oral history
knowing the past through 10–14
knowing the present through 15–19
oral traditions 11
ordinary conversation 98f
orientation, in stories 30–1
other-initiated repair 81
other-repair 82
outsider status 45
overlaps 66, 75, 77, 103, 125

Passerini, L. 10
Panopticon 136–137
past
and archaeology 134
in garden-variety DA 164–5
and genealogy 135
knowing the past through oral history 10–14
plural pasts and their present day meanings 16–19
performance 174–8
performative 174
performativity 71, 174–8
phatic communion 84
phenomenology 70
place 52
plausibility 61
plural pasts 16–19
poetics 40, 41, 46, 49, 51
poetry 50
politics of difference 46
Polkinghorne, D.E. 15–16, 37
Pollack, S. 48
polyphonic narratives 24
polyphonous writing 49
Portelli, A. 16, 17
positionality 45
positioning *see* discursive positioning
positivism 10
post-structuralism 44 *see also* Foucauldian discourse analysis
Potter, J. 116
power
in critical discourse analysis (CDA) 145, 171–2
in DA 168–74
in Foucauldian DA 135, 137–8
in garden-variety DA 160–1, 164
in NA 46
and poetics 46
power relations 18, 135–6
power-knowledge relations 134
deconstruction of 138

predicates 88
preference 79–80
pre-s 82–3
  pre-closing 85
  preface 83
  pre-invitations 82
  pre-questions 82, 105
principle of economy 88
procedural consequentiality 72, 80, 94, 99, 101, 107, 112, 116, 148
project 73
pronouns, use of 34, 49–50
psychotherapeutic model 25
  of trauma 24

radio 97–8, 106
reader-response theory 148
realism 5, 10–13, 61–2, 72, *see* constructionism versus realism
reception theory 148
recontextualization 152–3
redemptive self 56
reflexivity
  definition 3
    in phenomenology 70
  in CA 111–2
    about interviews vs conversation 112–8
    about what talk of social categories accomplishes 118–22
    and focus groups 122–6
    compared to NA 111–2
    compared to DA 167–8
  in DA 167–8
    about power in the interview 168–73
    about performativity/performance 173–8
    about positioning 70, 147, 167–8, 176, 178–80
    compared to NA and CA 167–8
    in critical discourse analysis (CDA) 147
  in NA about embodiment 50–4
    about notions of a 'good' story 54–73
    about standpoint and representation 44–50
    compared to CA 111–2
    compared to DA 167–8
relevance and procedural consequentiality 72, 80, 94, 99, 101, 107, 112, 116, 148
relevance rules 76f
reminiscence bump 11–12
repair 80–2, 119
repetition 40
reportability of stories 55–6
reported speech 53
representation, crisis of 44–6
resolution 30
rhythm 40
Ricoeur, P. 10, 23
rigor 11–12
  in the constructionist paradigm 15–16
  in conversational analysis (CA) 73–4
rigor *cont.*
  in critical discourse analysis (CDA) 147–8
  in post-structuralist research 133–4
  in the realist paradigm 10–13
rigorous realist analysis 10–13
role transition 20–1
Rosaldo, R. 89

Sacks, H. 65, 71
same-turn repair 81
savoir 132
Schegloff, E. 65–6, 76f, 104
second-pair parts 78–9, 113, 114 *see also* adjacency pairs
self *see also* identity
  as essence or as narrative process 23–6
self-initiated repair 81, 119
self-repair 82
semiotic 143
sequences 30–1, 36, 78 *see also* adjacency pairs; two-turn sequences
  in everyday talk 82–4
  in institutional talk 105–6
shared authority 43, 62
silences 52, 170, 171
silent discourse 160
small stories 84
Smith, D. 45
source domain 37
space 52
spatial order 52
speakers of Foreign Languages 59, 81
speech act theory 71, 174
speech impairment 107
stages of institutional talk 99–102
standardized relational pairs 88, 90
standpoint 45
standpoint theory 45–6
  critique 48–9
statement-prefaced questions 103
stocks of interactional knowledge 99
stories 83–4 *see also* narratives
  definition 8, 30–1
  'good' stories 54–62
    coherence 59–60
    fidelity 61–2
    liveability 56–9
    reportability 55–6
  sounds of 39–42, 51
story world 61
structuration theory 145
subalterns 18
subjectification 136, 137, 140, 230
subjectivity 10, 14, 141
  in CA 70
  in garden-variety DA 158–9
survey research 112
symbolic interactionism 20
symbolic violence 57

tactical polyvalence of discourse 136, 139–140
talk, distinctive features 3–4, 182–5
talk shows 91–2, 106, 171
talk-in-interaction 66 *see also* everyday talk; institutional talk-in-interaction
Tannen, D. 37, 40
target domain 37
teachers 60, 139, 180
technologies of the self 137, 141
television chat shows 91–2, 106, 171
tellability *see* reportability
testimonio 13–14, 46
texts 129
thematic analysis 114–15
Thomas, W.I. 20
topics in conversation analysis (CA) 84–5
transcription 44, 50, 66, 73, 184
transcription symbols 67–8
transition-relevance places 75
translation 38–9, 82
transliteration 38
transparency, in translation 38–9
traumatized speakers 24–5, 31, 52, 56, 57–59, 169
triangulation
  data triangulation 13
  methodological triangulation 13
trustworthiness 12, 147
turn-construction units 75
turning points 21–2
turn-taking
  in everyday talk 75–80
  in institutional talk-in-interaction 102–4
two-turn sequences in everyday talk 78–80 *see also* adjacency pairs

unmotivated looking 73

van Dijk, T.A. 150
Vansina, J. 11
viewer's maxim 88
voice 34–6
voyage-and-return plots 21

Waletzky, J. 30–1, 83
Weber, M. 135
West, C. 93–4, 101
Wh- questions 81
Why that now? 73, 74, 89, 93
Wilkinson, S. 123
Wodak, R. 144–5, 149–50
working memory 11
workplace meetings 103

Zimmerman, D. 93–4, 101
Znaniecki, F. 20

'A pleasantly readable and remarkably helpful guide that offers as much to experienced researchers as it does to novices. It clearly presents the "hows" of narrative, content and discourse analysis while simultaneously dealing so thoughtfully with the "whys" of these approaches.'

Dorothy Pawluch, Director of the Honours Social Psychology Program, McMaster University

'This book is an absolute treat. Its engaging style, its comprehensive content, its clear logic, its brilliant use of examples and above all its enormous value to qualitative researchers of all stripes add up to me wishing it had been available years ago!'

Professor Jo Brewis, University of Leicester School of Management

Talk is one of the main resources available to qualitative researchers. It offers rich, meaningful data that can provide real insights and new perspectives. But once you have the data how do you select an appropriate means of analysis? How do you ensure that the approach you adopt is the best for your project and your data?

This book will help you choose strategies for qualitative analysis that best suit your research. It walks you through key decisions, provides actionable game plans and highlights the advantages and challenges of the main approaches. It is packed full of real examples designed to showcase the different tools you might use to meet your own objectives.

Each section of the book focuses on one popular strategy for analyzing talk-based data:

- Narrative Analysis
- Conversation Analysis
- Discourse Analysis

Taken together these sections will help you to fine-tune the link between your primary research question and your methods; to ensure that your theoretical stance fits with your methods; and to reason through your analysis in a way that will be recognizable to the intellectual communities of narrative, conversation, or discourse analysts.

This book is both a starting point and map for any social scientist looking to strategically and purposefully analyse talk data.

Katherine Bischoping and Amber Gazso are Associate Professors of Sociology at York University, Toronto.

SAGE www.sagepublications.com
Los Angeles • London • New Delhi • Singapore • Washington DC

ISBN 978-1-4462-7249-7

9 781446 272497

FSC